Accounting Theory and Practice

Accounting Theory and Practice

M W E Glautier
B Underdown

Fourth Edition

Pitman

PITMAN PUBLISHING
128 Long Acre, London WC2E 9AN

A Division of Longman Group UK Limited

© M. W. E. Glautier and B. Underdown 1976, 1982, 1991
© Guardjust Ltd and B. Underdown 1991

Fourth edition published in Great Britain 1991
Reprinted 1992

British Library Cataloguing in Publication Data
Glautier, M. W. E. (Michel William Edgard) *1932 –*
 Accounting theory and practice. – 4th. ed.
 1. Accounting
 I. Title II. Underdown, B. (Brian) *1935 –*
 657

ISBN 0-273-03310-7

Typeset by Medcalf Type Ltd, Bicester, Oxon
Printed and bound in Great Britain

Contents

Preface to the Fourth Edition   xvii

Preface to the Third Edition   xix

Acknowledgements   xxii

**Part 1
A theoretical
framework**

1   Scope of accounting   **3**

The emerging role of accounting as a social science   4

Accounting in a changing environment   8

Summary   10

References   10

Questions   11

2   Accounting as an information system   **12**

The boundaries of an information system   13

The output of an information system   14

Accounting information and the allocation of resources   20

Behavioural aspects of decision making   21

A systems approach to accounting   21

Summary   23

Questions   23

3   The role of accounting theory   **24**

The nature of theories   24

Accounting theory   25

Approaches to the development of accounting theory   27

Accounting policy makers   35

Summary   35

References   36

Questions   36

**Part 2
Financial accounting
—the historical cost
approach**

Introduction   39

Section 1   Financial accounting practice

4   Financial accounting concepts   **43**

The nature of financial accounting concepts   44

Financial accounting concepts   45

Summary   59

References   60

Question   60

Problems   60

5   **Financial accounting standards**   **62**

The importance of comparability   62

Reasons for concern about standards   63

Standard setting boards   64

SSAP 2 'Disclosure of Accounting Policies'   65

Standards and the Companies Acts   67

Summary   67

Questions   68

6   **The generation of financial accounting data**   **69**

An outline of the information generation process   69

Source documents   69

The entry of basic data in the source books   73

The development of data-processing systems   77

The application of computer systems   77

Computer systems   81

Summary   82

Question   82

Problems   82

7   **Data processing and double-entry bookkeeping**   **84**

The accounting equation   84

Transactions and the accounting equation   85

Simplifying the recording of transactions   87

The nature of double-entry bookkeeping   88

Double-entry bookkeeping as a 'closed' system   93

Accounts as descriptions of transactions   95

The mathematical implications of double-entry
bookkeeping   96

The trial balance   97

Summary   98

Problems   99

8   **Standardized charts of accounts**   **102**

The development of uniformity in bookkeeping   102

The structure of accounting systems and accounts
classifications   103

The nature of charts of accounts   105

Accounting rules in the EC   106

The National Accounting Plan   107

Standardized financial statements   109

Advantages and disadvantages of national accounting
plans   109

Accounting standards and national accounting plans   112

National accounting plans and developing countries   113

Questions   113

Problems   113

Section 2   Periodic measurement

9   Double-entry bookkeeping and periodic measurement   115

Problems in periodic measurement   115

Identifying the revenues and expenses of the period   116

The meaning of revenue and expense   116

Periodic measurement and the accrual concept   117

The accrual of income   118

The accrual of expenses   119

The results of the accrual adjustments   122

The matching of revenues and expenses   124

Stock adjustments   124

Summary   126

Question   126

Problems   126

10 Losses in asset values and periodic measurement   128

The treatment of losses in asset values   128

Losses in the value of fixed assets   128

The nature of depreciation   129

The accounting concept of depreciation   131

Accounting for depreciation   137

Accounting for the disposal of assets   139

Narrowing accounting differences   140

Losses arising from the default of debtors   142

Summary   145

References   146

Questions   146

Problems   146

11 Preparing a profit and loss account and a balance sheet   **148**

Preparing a profit and loss account   148

The formal presentation of the profit and loss account   154

Preparing a balance sheet   155

The formal presentation of the balance sheet   158

Summary   158

Problems   160

12 Reporting recorded assets and liabilities   **166**

The valuation of assets   167

The valuation of fixed assets   167

The revaluation of fixed assets   168

The valuation of current assets   168

The valuation of other assets   172

The valuation of liabilities   179

The valuation of shareholders' equity   181

Summary   182

References   182

Question   182

Problems   182

Section 3   The application of financial accounting method to corporate enterprises

13 Financial accounting information for corporate enterprises   **187**

The nature of corporate enterprises   188

Financial accounting implications of corporate status   190

The capital structure   191

Gearing and the capital structure   192

Accounting procedures applied to the capital structure   194

Published financial statements   198

Taxation in company accounts   219

Summary   224

Problems   225

14 Funds flow and cash flow statements   **229**

The funds flow statement   230

The cash flow statement   240

Summary   243

Problems   244

15 Interpreting and comparing financial reports   **250**

The nature of ratio analysis   251

The analysis of solvency   252

The analysis of financial performance   259

Ratios as predictors of business failure: empirical studies   263

Summary   266

References   266

Problems   266

16 Financial accounting for groups of companies   **270**

The regulatory framework   270

Definition of a group   271

Preparation of consolidated accounts   272

Problems   282

17 Understanding consolidated financial statements   **287**

Accounting for minority interests   287

Accounting for associated companies   291

Mergers and acquisitions   293

Multinational groups   298

The inflation problem   302

Problems   302

Part 3
Financial reporting —alternative valuation approaches

Introduction   307

18 Capital, value, income   **311**

Capital   311

Capital maintenance   313

Income   315

The objectives of income measurement   316

Summary   318

References   319

Questions   319

19 Accounting and economic concepts of income and value   **320**

Accounting concepts   320

Economic concepts   322

Summary   327

References   327

Questions   327

20 Current purchasing power accounting   **329**

Adjustments for general price level changes   329

An appraisal of CPP accounting   334

Summary   336

References   337

Questions   337

Problems   337

21 Current value accounting   **340**

Replacement cost accounting   341

Realizable value accounting   347

Current cost accounting   350

Appendix   361

Summary   365

References   365

Questions   366

Problems   366

Part 4
Financial reporting —extending the disclosure of information

Introduction   373

References   375

22 Evaluation of current financial reporting practice   **376**

Non-compliance with standards   377

The need for a conceptual framework   378

The development of a conceptual framework   380

Other research findings   386

Implications of research findings   391

Summary   392

References   393

Questions   393

23 Reporting to investors   **394**

Problems in identifying investors' needs   394

Basis for a normative theory of reporting to investors   395

Normative definition of investors' information needs   396

Content of cash flow statements   398

Advantages of publishing company forecasts   399

Disadvantages of publishing company forecasts   401

Cash flow versus profit reporting   404

Segment reporting   405

Other aspects of the disclosure problem   406

The importance of educating users of financial reports   409

Summary   410

References   410

Questions   411

24 Reporting to employees   412

Investor and employee reporting compared   412

Financial reporting to employees   413

Reporting for collective bargaining   415

A normative theory of pay bargaining information   416

Summary   419

References   420

Questions   420

25 Social responsibility accounting   421

The nature of corporate social responsibility   422

The objectives of users of social accounting
information   425

The scope of corporate social responsibility   426

Corporate social reporting in the UK   427

The greening of accounting   429

Summary   430

References   430

Questions   431

**Part 5
Planning and control**

Introduction   435

Section 1 A framework for planning and control

26 The meaning of planning and control   439

The processes of management   439

Information and decision making   446

Extended meanings of 'control'   448

Summary   449

Reference   450

Questions   450

27 The cost accounting framework   451

Objectives of cost analysis   451

The elements of cost   452

The problem of overhead costs   453

Costing systems   463

Summary   468

Questions 468
Problems 469

Section 2 Planning

28 Long-range planning 471
Setting long-range objectives and goals 471
The position audit 473
The formulation of strategy 474
The preparation and implementation of the plan 476
The continuous review and updating of the plan 476
The importance of the long-range profit goal 477
Financial planning 480
Summary 481
Questions 481

29 Planning capital expenditure 483
Capital investment decisions 483
Types of capital investment decisions 483
The analysis of capital investment proposals 484
The relevant cash flows 485
Methods of appraising capital investments 485
Investment appraisal and inflation 495
Summary 497
Questions 498
Problems 498

30 Budgetary planning 500
The nature of budgetary planning 500
The need for flexibility 500
The organization of budgeting 501
Steps in budgeting 501
Forecasting sales 503
An illustration of the budgeting process 504
Evaluating the budget proposals 516
Budgetary control 517
Summary 517
Questions 518
Problems 518

31 Cost–volume–profit analysis 521
Applications of cost–volume–profit (c–v–p) analysis 521
Cost analysis and profit planning 522

Break-even analysis   523
Calculating the break-even point   524
The profit–volume chart   527
Profit planning through change   530
The sales mix   533
Cost–volume–profit analysis: some limitations   535
Summary   536
Questions   537
Problems   537

32 Variable costing   **539**
The case for variable costing for stock valuation   539
The variable costing controversy   545
The need for a definition of assets   546
Summary   547
Reference   547
Questions   547
Problems   547

33 Pricing   **549**
The nature of the pricing problem   549
The nature of pricing theories   550
Pricing theory in economics   550
Cost-based pricing theories   552
Cost-based pricing and budgeted costs   553
Target pricing and target costs   560
Summary   560
Questions   560
Problems   561

34 Short-run tactical decisions   **563**
The nature of relevant costs   563
The importance of the contribution margin   564
Opportunity costs   567
Dropping a product line   568
Selling or further processing   569
Operate or lease   569
Make or buy   570
Decision making in the face of limiting factors   571
Linear programming and decision making   573

Summary 577
Questions 578
Problems 578

Section 3 Control

35 Organizing for control 581
The integration of planning and control 581
Responsibility accounting 582
Summary 595
Questions 596
Problems 596

36 Standard costs and variance analysis 598
Standard costs and budgeted costs 598
Applications of standard costing 599
Setting cost standards 599
Setting standard costs for direct material and direct labour 600
Variance analysis for direct costs 601
Setting standards for overhead costs 603
Flexible budgeting 606
Variance analysis for overhead costs 608
Sales variance analysis and the control of revenue 610
Responsibility for variances 613
The investigation of variances 614
Summary 615
Questions 615
Problems 616

37 The control of managed costs 618
The nature of managed costs 618
The control of managed costs 619
The control of administrative costs 620
The control of research and development costs 621
The control of marketing costs 621
Summary 625
Questions 626

38 Behavioural aspects of performance evaluation 627
Managerial style and organization culture 627
The objectives of performance evaluation 628
Leadership styles and the problem of control 628

The effects of budgets on people   630
Budget information and performance evaluation   633
The need for several measures of performance   634
The importance of participation   634
Management by objectives   635
Organization theory   636
Agency theory   638
Summary   639
References   640
Questions   640
Problem   640

Index   643

Preface to the Fourth Edition

Significant developments have taken place since the publication of the Third Edition, making it necessary to update this book in the following areas:

1   In Part 1, the discussion of the theoretical framework of accounting now recognizes the important contribution that has been made by Agency Theory throughout the field of financial and management accounting.

2   In Part 2, the advent of the Unified Common Market in 1992 has made it necessary to introduce a new chapter on Standardized Charts of Accounts that are in use in several member countries. The chapters on the generation of financial accounting data and the interpretation of accounts have been extended. The chapters on Group Accounts now incorporate the provisions of the Companies Act 1989.

3   In Part 3, the abandonment in 1986 of SSAP 16 'Current Cost Accounting' has been noted in the context of the continuing concern that there should be some adjustment for changing price levels.

4   In Part 4, the chapters on the evaluation of current financial reporting practice and reporting to investors include recently issued conceptual frameworks, and the changes introduced to the standard-setting process following the Dearing Report. The text has been updated to take account of recently issued accounting standards. The chapter on social responsibility accounting has been extended.

5   In Part 5, new developments in the field of cost and management accounting relating to new concepts and the advent of advanced manufacturing techniques are discussed, such as JIT accounting, target costing and target pricing. An extended discussion of costing systems now includes operations costing. The chapter on standard costing has been improved.

In this new edition, we have considerably increased the range and quantity of exercise material. Most chapters now include both questions and problems. A Solutions Manual that provides suggested answers is available.

Preface to the Third Edition

The tradition in accounting education has been to focus the teaching of accounting almost entirely upon procedures for processing financial data. The treatment of accounting as a skill, rather than as a body of knowledge, is based on the belief that 'accounting is what accountants do'. Whilst this assertion undoubtedly holds good as a statement of what accountants do, such a view of accounting has serious shortcomings as regards the educational qualities of accounting courses and the education of accountants. First, by restricting the nature and scope of accounting to an exposure of its procedures, it fails to provide an adequate understanding of these procedures in relation to the problems facing accountants. Second, it impedes the recognition of economic and social changes which bear directly on these problems. These changes have made many accounting practices redundant, and have called for a re-structuring of the accounting process. Third, it supports a conviction widespread among students and practitioners that what they have been taught is in the nature of an everlasting truth, or a collection of everlasting truths. Hence, it has hindered the development of accounting.

The most damaging factor as regards the teaching of accounting has been the absence of a theoretical framework to serve as a standard of reference for examining the validity of the assumptions held by accountants. As a result, accounting courses have sometimes tended to be virtually devoid of rigorous analysis, which is characterized by the uncritical acceptance of the assumptions reflected in accounting procedures. It is not surprising, therefore, that teachers of other subjects tend to regard accounting as being qualitatively inferior in the potential which it offers for the development of the mind and person.

This textbook is committed to a different view of accounting education in a number of important respects. First, as its title Accounting Theory and Practice implies, it attempts to provide a theoretical framework for the understanding of the nature of the accounting problem and an appreciation of the purpose of various accounting practices. This approach permits accounting practices to be exposed to critical analysis by means of which their usefulness and relevance may be assessed and their shortcomings exposed. Hence, it provides the teacher and the student with a means of overcoming the most serious criticism made about accounting education. Second, the nature and the scope of accounting is extended beyond accounting procedures by conceiving the essential function of accounting as facilitating socio-economic activities and decisions. Accordingly, we give a global and rounded view of accounting in which the emphasis is appropriately placed on the role of accounting as being the provision of information for decision making. We examine both traditional and new problems, and bring to our analysis developments in other subject areas which are important to accounting. In so doing, we provide for the interdisciplinary nature of accounting and hope to end its isolation as an esoteric collection of procedures. From this viewpoint, we believe that the traditional emphasis placed in first-year texts on the importance of financial accounting is misplaced.

We have emphasized the importance of the scientific method for the development of accounting. In terms of its ultimate objectives, accounting is as scientific as any other discipline. In terms of its ability to develop and apply empirically verified theories, it is far from being a mature science, but it is striving in this direction. We try to reflect this trend in this textbook.

Finally, we believe that accounting is a very important social science. We hope that our readers will develop insights into the social role of accounting at an early stage, and it is for this reason that we decided to adopt a global, rather than a narrow view of the accounting process.

We have interpreted the broad objectives of accounting as being to provide information for the following purposes:

1. Decision-making regarding the use of limited resources, including the identification of crucial decision areas, and the determination of objectives and goals.
2. Effectively directing and controlling human and material resources.
3. Maintaining and reporting on the custodianship of resources.
4. Facilitating social functions and controls.

The textbook is divided into five parts, as follows:

Part 1 A Theoretical Framework
Part 2 Financial Accounting—The Historical Cost Approach
Part 3 Financial Reporting—Alternative Valuation Approaches
Part 4 Financial Reporting—Extending the Disclosure of Information
Part 5 Planning and Control

In Part 1 we discuss the nature and the importance of theory covering every aspect of accounting knowledge and incorporating this knowledge into a unified whole, the purpose of which is the provision of information for decision making.

Part 2 examines the traditional nature of accounting information based on the historical cost approach which illustrates the way of thinking underlying financial accounting practices and looks at the development of financial accounting practice in the context of accounting conventions and standards.

Part 3 examines the problems of financial reporting in terms of alternative valuation methods to those employed in conventional financial accounting, which are based on historical cost.

Part 4 evaluates current financial reporting practices in terms of extending the disclosure of information to investors and employees as well as corporate social reporting.

Part 5 focuses on the role of information for management decision making and examines the needs of management relevant for planning and control.

We would emphasize that although this textbook is divided into five parts, each addressed to a special aspect of accounting, they are nevertheless linked by the provision of a theoretical framework which brings them together and establishes their purposes in the provision of information for decision making.

We believe that this book will be suitable for the following uses:

1   University and Polytechnic first- and second-year degree courses in Accounting;
2   First-year MBA courses in Business Schools;
3   Professional examinations;
4   Practising accountants who wish to acquire a broader viewpoint of the accounting process.

Acknowledgements

We wish to place on record our gratitude to colleagues and friends for the advice and help which they have given us in the course of writing this text. We owe a particular debt to Professor W. Rotch and Charles Clark, who have both been closely associated with every aspect of the book and who have helped us unstintingly, as well as Professor T. A. Lee, Professor R. H. Parker, Professor A. Hopwood, C. P. Rickwood, G. J. Harris, Dr H. C. Dekker, E. C. Johnson, C. Burke, O. A. Bello and P. J. Taylor.

For help with the second edition, thanks are due to R. W. Wallis, M. H. C. Lunt, A. J. Naughton, M. Sherer, A. Southworth and A. Chandiok.

For help with the third edition, thanks are due to F. S. Hall, M. A. Nardone, R. A. Coates, M. Skenfield, R. W. Wallis, Dr A. Goodacre and P. Hughes.

For help with the fourth edition, thanks are due to C. J. Jones and J. Maltby of the University of Sheffield, and Professor J.-C. Scheid of the Conservatoire Nationale des Arts et Métiers, Paris.

We have been privileged as authors to have had so much support from our publishers, Pitman Publishing Ltd, and this book is indeed the outcome of a close partnership between authors and publishers. We wish to thank all those members of the Pitman staff who have worked with us, particularly Navin Sullivan, Martin Marix Evans, James Shepherd, and Eric Dalton. James Shepherd deserves special mention for his patience, tact and above all for all the hard work which he put into the first edition of this book and thanks are due to Eric Dalton for his generous assistance and enthusiasm in planning the second and third.

We are deeply indebted to Simon Lake for his assistance in planning the fourth edition.

Dr Ken Watkins of Sheffield University was one of the original instigators of this book, and we owe much to his friendship.

Part 1

A theoretical framework

Chapter 1
Scope of accounting

Accounting is in an age of rapid transition; its environment has undergone vast changes in the last two decades and an accelerating rate of change is in prospect for the future. Much of what is accepted as accounting today would not have been recognized as such fifty years ago, and one may safely predict that in fifty years' time the subject will bear little resemblance to what it is today.

Changing social attitudes combine with developments in information technology, quantitative methods and the behavioural sciences to affect radically the environment in which accounting operates today, thereby creating the need to re-evaluate the objectives of accounting in a wide perspective. Accounting is moving away from its traditional procedural base, encompassing record keeping and such related work as the preparation of budgets and final accounts, towards a role which emphasizes its social importance.

The changing environment has not only extended the boundaries of accounting but has created a problem in defining the scope of the subject. There is a need for a definition which is broad enough to delineate its boundaries, while at the same time being sufficiently precise as a statement of its essential nature. It is interesting to contrast definitions which were accepted a little time ago with more recent statements. According to a definition made in 1953, 'The central purpose of accounting is to make possible the periodic matching of costs (efforts) and revenues (accomplishments). This concept is the nucleus of accounting theory, and a benchmark that affords a fixed point of reference for accounting discussions' (Littleton, 1953).

The Committee on Terminology of the American Institute of Certified Public Accountants formulated the following definition in 1961: 'Accounting is the art of recording, classifying and summarizing in a significant manner and in terms of money, transactions and events which are, in part at least, of a financial character, and interpreting the result thereof' (AICPA, 1961).

A more recent definition is less restrictive and interprets accounting as the provision of 'information about the financial position, performance and changes in financial position of an enterprise that is useful to a wide range of potential users in making economic decisions' (IASC, 1989). This definition comes closer to our own interpretation of the scope of accounting, and the manner in which we should like to treat its subject matter, but we would add the rider that accounting is moving rapidly now towards a consideration of social welfare objectives. Accordingly, the purpose of accounting may be redefined as 'to provide information which is potentially useful for making economic decisions and which, if provided, will enhance social welfare' (AAA, 1975).

According to this latter viewpoint, the scope of accounting should not be restricted to the private use of information, which has the limited perspective of being concerned with the impact of information on the welfare of individuals as such. The social welfare viewpoint is concerned both with the direct impact of information on individual welfare and with the indirect effects arising, for example, from a change in the allocation of resources.

The actions of individuals have what are known as 'externality effects' which affect the welfare of other members of society. Hence, the social value of information resides in knowledge of these 'externality effects'. The significance of such information may be seen in the context of the various groups having vested interests in business organizations, for example shareholders, managers and employees. It is evident that the supply of information to one group may give them an unfair advantage over the other groups in the decisions they subsequently make, resulting in changes in the allocation of social benefits. The social welfare viewpoint states that in considering the information accountants ought to be supplying and the groups to whom such information should be provided, judgements ought to be made on the basis of the extent to which improvements in the welfare of one group outweigh the sacrifices in welfare borne by other groups.

One aspect of the social welfare theory of accounting is reflected in the development of social responsibility accounting. In the past, the interests of shareholders, investors, creditors and managers have exerted a dominating influence on the development of accounting practices. The social welfare theory of accounting requires that the interests of employees, trade unions and consumers ought to be taken into account, and that the traditional imbalance existing in the supply of information should be corrected. Social responsibility accounting draws attention to the gulf existing between the sectarian interests represented in conventional business accounting and its focus on profit, and the need to see the entire social role of business organization in the context of all those affected by its activities.

The emerging role of accounting as a social science

The social sciences study man as a member of society; they share a concern about social processes, and the results and consequences of social relationships. In this respect, the usefulness of accounting as a social science depends on the benefits which it may bring to society, rather than on the advantages which it may confer upon its individual members. We would say, therefore, that although an individual businessman may benefit from the availability of accounting information, what is much more important is that society as a whole should benefit from the fact that its individual members use accounting information for the solution of business problems.

The history of accounting reflects the evolutionary pattern of social developments and, in this respect, illustrates how much accounting is a product of its environment and at the same time a force for changing it. There is, therefore, an evolutionary pattern which reflects changing socio-economic conditions and the changing purposes to which accounting is applied. From today's perspective, we may distinguish four phases which may be said to correspond with its developing social role.

1   Stewardship accounting has its origins in the function which accounting served from the earliest times in the history of our society of providing the owners of wealth with a means of safeguarding it from embezzlement and in the fact that wealthy men employed 'stewards' to manage their property. These stewards rendered periodical accounts of their stewardship, and this notion still lies at the root of financial reporting today. Essentially, stewardship accounting involves the orderly recording of business transactions, and although accounting records of this type date back to as early as 4500 BC, the keeping of these records, known as 'bookkeeping', remained primitive until fairly recent times. Indeed, the accounting concepts and procedures in use today for the orderly recording of business transactions have their origin in the practices employed by the merchants of the Italian City States during the early part of the Renaissance. The main principles of the Italian Method, as it was then known, were set out by Luca Pacioli in his famous treatise *Summa de Arithmetica, Geometrica, Proportioni et Proportionalita* which was published in Venice in 1494. The Italian Method, which became known subsequently as 'double-entry bookkeeping' was not generally used in Western Europe until the early part of the nineteenth century. Whether or not businessmen kept their accounts in single-entry or double-entry form, stewardship accounting played an important social role during the period of commercial expansion in Western Europe, which followed the Renaissance and characterized that phase known as commercial capitalism. Stewardship accounting is associated, therefore, with the need of businessmen to keep records of their transactions, the manner in which they invested their wealth and the debts owed to them and by them.

2   Financial accounting has a more recent origin, and dates from the development of large-scale businesses which were made possible by the Industrial Revolution. Indeed, the new technology not only destroyed the existing social framework, but altered completely the method by which business was financed. The industrial expansion in the early part of the nineteenth century necessitated access to large amounts of capital. This led to the advent of the joint stock company, which enables the public to provide capital in return for 'shares' in

the assets and the profits of the company. An earlier experience of the joint stock form of trading which had resulted in a frantic boom in company flotations, culminating in the South Sea Bubble of 1720, had instilled public suspicion of this form of trading. Reflecting this mood, Adam Smith himself questioned the ability of the directors of such companies to administer honestly and well any of the most routine and easily checked business matters, for

'. . . being the Managers rather of other people's money than of their own, it cannot well be expected that they should look over it with the same anxious vigilance with which the partners of a private copartnery frequently watch over their own. . . . Negligence and profusion . . . must always prevail, more or less, in the management of the affairs of such a company' (Smith, 1904 edition).

Nevertheless, the Joint Stock Companies Act 1844 permitted the incorporation of such companies by registration without the need to obtain a Royal Charter or a special Act of Parliament. In 1855, however, the Limited Liability Act permitted such companies to limit the liability of their members to the nominal value of their shares. This meant that the liability of shareholders for the debts incurred by the company was limited to the amount which they had agreed to subscribe. In effect, by applying for a £1 share, a shareholder agreed to subscribe £1, and, once he had paid that £1, he was not liable to make any further contribution in the event of the company's insolvency.

The concept of limited liability was a contentious point in the politics of the mid-nineteenth century. The Limited Liability Act 1855 was passed in the teeth of bitter opposition, and one Member of Parliament described the Act as a 'rogues' charter'. Mindful of the potential for abuse which lay within this legislation, and mindful too of the necessity to safeguard the interests of shareholders and investors in these companies, Parliament eventually restated the doctrine of stewardship in a legal form. It made the disclosure of information to shareholders a condition attached to the privilege of joint-stock status and of limited liability. This information was required to be in the form of annual profit and loss accounts and balance sheets. We may say briefly, however, that the former is a statement of the profit or loss made during the year of the report, and the balance sheet indicates the assets held by the firm and the monetary claims against the firm.

Financial accounting is concerned with these two accounting statements as vehicles for the disclosure of information to shareholders in limited companies. The reluctance of company directors to disclose more than the minimum information required by law, and growing public disquiet as to the usefulness of the information contained in financial accounts culminated in the extension of disclosure requirements in the United Kingdom by means of the Companies Acts 1948 to 1989.

Parallel developments have taken place also in the United States, where since the early 1930s there has been a continuous discussion on ways to improve the extent of disclosure of information. The Securities and Exchange Commission has been concerned with the problem of the sufficiency of information disclosed at the time when new issues are sold to the public, and together with the stock exchanges and the accounting profession via the Financial Accounting Standards Board, it has been concerned also with the adequacy of financial information regularly disclosed by companies. For some years, also, the European Community has been trying to move towards a harmonisation of accounting practices both as regards disclosure and the consistency of practices. The Companies Acts 1981 and 1989 which implement the EC Fourth and Seventh Directives respectively are discussed in Chapters 14 and 17.

The legal importance attached to financial accounting statements stems directly from the need of a capitalist society to mobilize savings and direct them into profitable investments. Investors, be they large or small, must be provided with reliable and relevant information in order to be able to make efficient investment decisions. Herein lies one of the most significant social purposes of financial accounting reports. In a changing society, increased recognition that employees have a legitimate right to financial information is evident in the legislation passed or proposed in several European countries.

A more important influence in the demand for the disclosure of financial information to employees stems from the growing strength of the worker participation or codetermination movement. This aspect of accounting will be examined in Part 4.

3 Management accounting is also associated with the advent of industrial capitalism, for the Industrial Revolution of the eighteenth century presented a challenge to the development of accounting as a tool of industrial management. In isolated cases there were some, notably Josiah Wedgwood, who developed costing techniques as guides to management decisions. But the practice of using accounting information as a direct aid to management was not one of the achievements of the industrial revolution: this new role for accounting really belongs to the twentieth century.

Certainly, the genesis of modern management with its emphasis on detailed information for decision making provided a tremendous impetus to the development of management accounting in the early decades of this century, and in so doing considerably extended the boundaries of accounting. Management accounting shifted the focus of accounting from recording and analysing financial transactions to using information for decisions affecting the future. In so doing, it represented the biggest surge forward in seven centuries.

The advent of management accounting demonstrated once more the ability and capacity of accounting to develop and meet changing socio-economic needs. Management accounting has contributed in a most significant way to the success with which modern capitalism has succeeded in expanding the scale of production and raising standards of living.

4 The social welfare viewpoint of accounting is an entirely new phase in accounting development which owes its birth to the social revolution which has been under way in the Western world in the last few years. One aspect is social responsibility accounting which widens the scope of accounting by considering the social effects of business decisions as well as their economic effects. The demand for social responsibility accounting stems from an increasing social awareness of the undesirable by-products of economic activities, and in this connection, one may point to the attention given to environmental problems over the last few years. Increasingly, management is being held responsible not only for the efficient conduct of business as expressed in profitability, but also for what it does about an endless number of social problems. Hence, with changing attitudes, the time-honoured standards by which performance is measured have fallen into disrepute. There is a growing consensus that the concepts of growth and profit as measured in traditional balance sheets and profit and loss accounts are too narrow to reflect what many companies are trying, or are supposed to be trying, to achieve.

Accounting in a changing environment

The process of change has had a dramatic impact on accounting research and practice in recent years. The factors which have affected accounting may be identified as follows:

1 Developments in quantitative methods and in the behavioural sciences have shifted the focus of interest towards decision making. The increased importance of quantitative methods in the management of organizations has meant that the subject of management has become less descriptive and more analytical. Thus, it has become less concerned with describing management as a process and more concerned with the concepts and theoretical models associated with organizations and their decision-making activities. To these developments have been added advances in the behavioural sciences which have increased the level of knowledge existing about the organizational decision-making process.

2 The emphasis on decision making in recent years has brought together disciplines which once were viewed as separate areas of knowledge. Since there are different aspects of decision making—economic, behavioural, sociological and quantitative, accounting has become an inter-disciplinary subject. The accountant has to be knowledgeable over a broad area if he is to be efficient in providing information which is relevant and useful for decision making. The education of the accountant has tended to be traditional and to have a narrow focus on gaining a knowledge of accounting methods. Hence, many accountants were not educated to cope with the

problems of change, and in particular were unable to integrate their own skills with the knowledge relevant to decision making.

3   Traditional accounting areas are being invaded by experts in cognate areas, such as systems analysts, computer programmers and operations research specialists, who bring with them new knowledge and different skills. As a result, the traditional status and role of the accountant is changing.

4   Accounting is not an exact science, although it is a social science. As in the case in other social sciences, accounting concepts do not rest on universal truths or general laws. Accounting concepts are rooted in the value system of the society in which they operate, and are socially determined. Hence, value judgements are applied to the interpretation and significance of economic and social events. The subjective nature of these values implies that there is ample opportunity for controversy as to how events should be measured and for whom such measurements are intended.

5   In particular, the nature of external financial reporting has caused much concern in recent years. The status of the accounting profession has depended to some extent on its monopoly of the auditing and external financial reporting function. Much criticism has been directed at an external financial reporting system that allows management to provide cosmetic improvements to the firm's accounting performance, i.e. the general phenomenon of 'creative accounting' (Griffiths, 1986).

6   The role of business in society has come under greater scrutiny in recent years. Increasingly, business corporations are viewed as accountable to society in general for their actions, in addition to being answerable to shareholders in respect of profitability.

The major consequences which have resulted from the changing environment in which accounting operates may be stated as follows:

1   There has been a dramatic effect on accounting research. Sophisticated statistical techniques are being used increasingly. There has been a movement away from a concern with the processes of accounting to an interest in the analysis of its problems and to theoretical models relevant to these problems. Primarily, accounting is now viewed as influencing human behaviour. At the same time, the influence of economics on the development of accounting practice has increased. For example, it has become highly influential in the area of finance, while the inflation accounting debate has been concerned with issues which are addressed to analysis of the economic events affecting the enterprise. Some of the implications of these developments are considered in Parts 3 and 4.

2   The accountant in management does not exist in isolation. He should be regarded as a member of the management team. We discuss this point further in the next chapter, and suggest that this difficulty may be resolved by adopting a 'systems approach' to accounting.

3   In the United Kingdom, the need to improve accounting practice was recognized formally by the appointment of the Accounting Standards Committee in 1970. More recently, the Dearing Report's (1988) proposals have led to a new administrative structure for accounting standard setting that is designed to improve the quality of accounting standards and to strengthen the enforcement process.

4   Much effort has been directed towards developing a theoretical framework for validating external financial reporting practices in terms of their perceived objectives, and to enable future development to take place in accordance with those objectives. In the United States the Financial Accounting Standards Board, since its inception in 1972, has been engaged in developing a series of statements which have established a conceptual framework for financial reporting. More recently, conceptual frameworks have been issued by the Institute of Chartered Accountants of Scotland, *Making Corporate Reports Valuable* (ICAS, 1988), the International Accounting Standards Committee, *Framework for the Preparation and Presentation of Financial Statements* (IASC, 1989) and the Institute of Chartered Accountants in England and Wales *Guidelines for Financial Reporting Standards*, the Solomons Report (ICAEW, 1989).

5   Finally, the emergence of social responsibility accounting imposes new information objectives for accountants and these will require a new accounting methodology. At present we are able to discuss only the information objectives, though some countries, particularly France, are already legislating for this new accounting development.

Summary

In this chapter, we have examined the development of accounting from its earliest form as a recording activity to its present importance which stems from the objective of providing socio-economic information for decision making.

The history of accounting development reflects the ability to respond to changing social needs. Today, changing social attitudes combine with developments in information technology, quantitative methods and the behavioural sciences to affect radically the environment in which accounting operates. These changes have created a number of problems for the accountant. It is with these problems that this book is concerned.

References

AAA (1975). Report of the Committee on Concepts and Standards for External Financial Reports, *Accounting Review Supplement*, Vol. xlx.

AICPA (1961). *Committee on Terminology, p.9,* American Institute Publishing Co.

Dearing Report (1988). *The Making of Accounting Standards*, Report of the Review Committee.

Griffiths, I. (1986). *Creative Accounting, How to Make Your Profits What You Want Them to Be*, Sidgwick & Jackson.

International Accounting Standards Committee (1989). *Framework for the Preparation and Presentation of Financial Statements*.

Institute of Chartered Accountants of Scotland (1988). *Making Corporate Reports Valuable*.

Littleton, A.C. (1953). *The Structure of Accounting Theory*, AAA Monograph No.5, p.30.

Solomons, D. (1989). *Guidelines for Financial Reporting Standards*, Research Board of the ICAEW.

Smith, A. (1904). *Wealth of Nations*, ed. Cannon, Vol.2, pp.233, 246.

Questions

1   In what ways have the definitions of accounting changed over time?
2   Discuss the concepts of stewardship, financial, management and social responsibility accounting.
3   Examine the main factors which have affected the development of accounting in the last twenty years.

Chapter 2

Accounting as an information system

The term 'system' is commonly used today, and we read much about environmental systems, ecological systems, economic systems and political systems. Indeed, we live in the age of systems. Reduced to its utmost simplicity, a system is a set of elements which operate together in order to attain a goal. The following are examples of systems analysed in this manner:

System	Elements	Basic goal
Social club	Members	Recreation
School	Teachers, students, textbooks, buildings	Education
Police	Men, equipment, communication network, buildings	Crime control

From the foregoing illustrations, we can see that systems vary considerably in their appearance, their attributes, their elements and their basic goals. They have certain characteristics in common, however, for they consist of parts which interact together to achieve one or more objectives. Systems, therefore, do not consist of random sets of elements, but of elements which may be identified as belonging together because of a common goal.

A system may also be seen as consisting of three activities: input, processing of input, and output. Sometimes, one hears references to closed systems and open systems, and these terms refer to the nature of the relationship between these systems and their environment. An open system is one which interacts with its environment, and a closed system is one which does not. We may classify a business organization as an open system which has a dynamic interplay with its environment from which it draws resources and to which it consigns its products and services. An example of a closed system is a chemical reaction in a sealed container. The important distinction between an open and a closed system is that the former is constantly rejuvenated by its environment, whereas the latter tends to run down through loss of energy which is not replaced from the environment.

Accounting is often analysed as a series of activities which are linked and form a progression of steps, beginning with observing, then collecting, recording, analysing and finally communicating information to its users. We may say, therefore, that *accounting information* has a special meaning in that it is data organized for a special purpose, that is, decision making. The task of the accountant is to transform raw data into information. Data itself is simply a collection of facts expressed as symbols and characters which are unable to influence decisions until transformed into information. We see in Part 2 how conventions existing among accountants for the treatment of data gives accounting information a distinctive character.

Accounting is a social science which lends itself easily to analysis as an information system, for it has all the attributes of a system. It has a basic goal, which is to provide information, and it has clear and well-defined elements in the form of people and equipment. Moreover, accounting has the typical activities of systems, consisting of input, processing and output, as shown in Fig. 1.1.

Fig 1.1

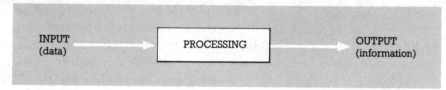

The application of systems analysis to the treatment of accounting facilitates our study of accounting as a social science, and enables us to examine its various activities in terms of the relevance of its output for decision-making purposes.

The boundaries of an information system

An important aspect of accounting as an information system is the definition of its boundaries. A system exists as an independent entity in an environment, and the nature of its relationship with that environment is very important. We have already made reference to the distinction which exists between 'open' and 'closed' systems. We must now turn our attention to a closer examination of the boundaries of a system, by which we mean identifying a system in such a way that we are able to distinguish it from its environment.

In the previous section, we mentioned that the accountant selected raw data relevant to his purpose. The filtering process by which he selects accounting data is provided by the conventions of accounting, which play a deterministic role in defining accounting information. This filtering process may be taken as one boundary between the accounting system and its environment: that point at which raw data becomes input data. The data selected forms the input into the processing system which provides accounting information. This information output is used by groups of decision makers, which are identifiable, and it is evident that a decision-oriented information system should produce information which meets the needs of its users. Clearly, these should be specified in accordance with a theory of users' requirements. We may say, therefore, that the other boundary to an accounting information system is established by the specific information needs of its users. We may model these boundaries as in Fig. 1.2.

Fig. 1.2

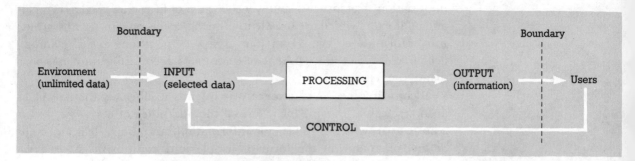

This analysis of accounting as an information system enables us to make some important deductions. First, the goal of the system is to provide information which meets the needs of its users. If we can sufficiently and accurately identify these needs, we can then specify the nature and character of the output of the system. Second, the output requirements should determine the type of data selected as the input for processing into information output. Third, welfare considerations may be taken into account in the selection of data, in accordance with the objective of accounting stated in Chapter 1.

In this connection, the idea of *control* indicated (in Fig. 1.2) shows that users' needs should determine not only the nature of data input but also the extent of the data input which should be determined by a cost-benefit analysis related to these needs and the impact of their decisions on society.

An important application of the concept of an information system's boundaries will be seen in Part 4, where we examine the problems of financial reporting in the context of investors' needs for information which may not be provided by the accountant. If users' needs are ignored, accounting information is deprived of the objectives which otherwise would enable us to validate accounting practices in the area in terms of the theoretical frameworks discussed in Chapter 3.

The output of an information system

The foregoing discussion has served to indicate the importance of the needs of users of accounting information, for such needs determine the objectives of an accounting information system.

There are several groups of people who have vested interests in a business organization—managers, shareholders, employees, customers and creditors. Additionally, the community at large has economic and social interests in the activities of business organizations. This interest is expressed at national level by the concern of government in various aspects of firms' activities, such as their economic well-being, their contribution to welfare, their part in the growth of the national product, to mention but a few obvious examples; and at local level by the concern of local authorities and bodies in the direct socio-economic impact of the activities of local businesses.

It is evident that an examination of the types of decisions made by various users of accounting information may be taken as a basis for stipulating the objectives of an accounting information system, and therefore, for evolving a normative theory of accounting by which to judge the relevance and usefulness of the information produced by accountants. We discuss the nature of theory construction in accounting in Chapter 3, and the problems associated with the formulation of normative theories of accounting in respect of the needs of different user groups in Part 4. In this chapter, we initiate these discussions by stating the general nature of the needs of different groups of information users.

In general terms, users of accounting information should be regarded as decision makers interested in determining the sacrifices which must be made to obtain the benefits which are expected to flow from the decisions to which they commit themselves. Since all the sacrifices and the benefits necessarily materialize in the future, by reason of the nature of the decision-making process, uncertainty plays a critical role in assessing the sacrifices and benefits associated with particular decisions. It will be argued in Part 4 that rational decision makers will seek to maximize long-run returns consistent with the degree of risk which they regard as acceptable.

The information needs of shareholders and investors

Historically, business accounting developed to supply information to those who had invested their wealth in business ventures. As we saw in Chapter 1, financial accounting emerged in the nineteenth century as a result of the need to protect investors in joint stock companies trading under limited liability. It has been evident for a long time that the information needs of investors are not adequately met by published balance sheets and profit and loss accounts. In Part 2 we examine the nature of the information disclosed to shareholders and investors, and in Part 4 we subject traditional financial accounting practice considered in Part 2 to a critical analysis based on the question 'What information should be provided to investors?' To answer this question, we begin our discussion in Part 4 with an inquiry into the objectives of shareholders in business corporations. By stating that they are concerned with the value of their investment and the income they expect to derive from their holding we are able to enquire into the nature of the information which they need in order to make rational decisions.

The information needs of management

Organizations fall into two broad classes: those having profit or business objectives, and those having welfare objectives. In this book, we are concerned mainly with business organizations, but it should be remembered that many accounting methods employed in business organizations are also employed by welfare or non-profit organizations. As regards the management of organizations, little difference exists between the information needs of managers of business organizations and those of the managers of welfare organizations.

The management process may be analysed into three major functions—planning, organizing and controlling the activities of the organization. Planning involves setting objectives for the organization, and devising strategies to attain those objectives. Organizing means establishing the administrative structure for implementing plans. Controlling is the process of observing and measuring actual performance so that it conforms with the planned and required performance. Thus, controlling means identifying deviations from planned performance, and taking such corrective action as may be necessary.

These various management functions have one thing in common: they are all concerned with making decisions, which have their own specific information requirements. Planning decisions, for example, are directed towards realizing broad goals which, in addition to the organization's survival and its profitability, usually include the intention to grow and to capture a large share of the market for its products. Other goals include product leadership, increased productivity and improved industrial relations. There is an element of conflict between various organizational objectives, and it is the function of management to reconcile them through the planning process.

We devote Part 5 of this book to the examination of the accounting information needs of management, and the manner in which these needs are met. The scientific management of organizations has considerably extended the demand for accounting information, and the nature of the accounting problem. As we shall see, the influence of the behavioural sciences and the need for more information generally has created measurement problems.

The information needs of employees

It is a popular view that the interests of employees are in direct conflict with those of the firm, and in particular with those of management. Unless employees are able to share in the profits of business organizations, they are effectively dissociated from their activities if we suppose that the objective of business organizations is to maximize profits and maximize returns to shareholders. This classical concept of the objective of business enterprises is being replaced as a result of the social changes taking place in our society, and there is a broadening view of the social and economic responsibilities of management. It is recognized that employees have a vested interest in the outcome of management decisions of every kind. Improvements in industrial democracy through employee participation in management decisions have important implications for the supply of information to employees. A number of firms are already investigating this question. As regards the settlement of wage disputes, the question of profit sharing between employees, shareholders and management can only be settled properly on the basis of a full disclosure of the relevant facts.

The immense importance of good industrial relations, of harmony between management and employees, is acknowledged already in the literature of management science. It is evident that there must be eventually a symmetry of treatment between shareholders, management and employees in respect of the accounting information which each group requires and receives. We may say, therefore, that the economic and social role of accounting in this particular context has not yet been properly explored. We touch upon these issues in Part 4.

The information needs of governments

To a greater or lesser degree, all Western governments intervene in the activities of business organizations in the process of managing what is known as a 'mixed economy', that is, an economic system consisting of both state-controlled and privately controlled business organizations. Government agencies, such as central statistical services, ministries of commerce, industry, employment, etc., collect information about the various aspects of the activities of business organizations. Much of this information is a direct output of the accounting system, for example, levels of sales activity, profits, investments, stocks, liquidity, dividend levels, proportion of profits absorbed by taxation etc. This information is very important in evolving policies for managing the economy.

Governments, in addition, can compel the disclosure of information which is not otherwise made available to the public, such as future investment plans, expected future profits and so on.

By and large, however, governments expect accounting information to be presented in a uniform manner, so that the rules applying to accounting methods and the preparation of accounting reports for government use are the same as those which govern the nature of accounting information disclosed to investors and shareholders. If governments base policy decisions on accounting information which distorts the true position, it is evident that the ill-effects of such decisions will be widely felt. The failure to adjust for the effect of inflation, for example, not only gives an excessive view of company profits but may lead the government to believe that company profits are running at a sufficiently high level to enable firms to finance investments and to provide an adequate return to shareholders. Accordingly, all parties having an interest in business organizations should be concerned with the quality of the accounting information produced, as well as the relevance of that information to their own needs. It is for this reason that we devote Chapter 4 to a thorough examination of the conventions which govern the nature of financial accounting information.

The information needs of creditors

We define as creditors all those who have provided goods, money or services to business organizations and have accepted a delay in payment or repayment. Creditors may be short-term or long-term lenders. Short-term creditors include suppliers of materials and goods, normally described as trade creditors, credit institutions such as bankers and hire-purchase firms who lend money for interest on a relatively short-term basis, and those who have provided services and are awaiting payment, for example, employees, outside contractors who have made repairs, electricity and gas undertakings who have rendered invoices and have not yet been paid. Long-term creditors are those who have lent money for a long period, usually in the form of secured loans.

The main concern of creditors is whether or not the organization is creditworthy, that is, will it be able to meet its financial obligations? They are interested in the organization's profitability only insofar as it affects its ability to pay its debts. On the other hand, creditors are very concerned with the firm's liquidity, that is, those cash or near-cash resources which may be mobilized to pay them, as well as the willingness of banks and other creditors to await payment. Creditors react quickly to changes of opinion about a firm's credit-worthiness, and if there is any doubt about a firm's ability to pay, they will press for immediate settlement of debts and probably drive into liquidation a firm whose prospects in the medium and longer term are not necessarily bad.

Creditors are interested, therefore, mainly in financial accounting information which affects solvency, liquidity and profitability, that is, with obtaining reports which will describe a firm's financial standing. We consider these aspects of financial reporting in Part 2, and in particular examine the adequacy of criteria applied to the analysis of financial statements, such as solvency, liquidity and profitability ratios.

The information needs of other groups

We have dealt so far with the information needs of four major groups which have vested interests in business organizations, and we have discussed the nature of their information requirements. How far and how adequately their information needs are suitably satisfied depends largely upon the pessure which these groups exert upon the accountant to produce information tailored to their needs. How well they are able to articulate their information needs, how well accountants are able to understand the reasons why the information is needed and how willing and able accountants are to provide that information will be the theme of much of this book. We may say, for example, that the information needs of management are more adequately met than those of employees, shareholders, creditors and also governments. But there are two other groups in society interested in the activities of business organizations, and who are pretty well excluded from receiving information: the local community and customers.

The information needs of the local community

Local communities are very dependent on local industries, not only because they provide employment, but also because they directly affect the entire socio-economic structure of the environment. Firms provide employment, create a demand for local services, cause an expansion in commercial activities, as well as extensions in the provision of welfare services as the economic well-being of the community improves. Large firms, in particular, are able to exert a dominating influence on the local social framework which often is reflected in the corporate personality of the inhabitants. Miners, steelworkers, shipbuilders and workers in the motor industry have styles of living and attitudes forged to some extent by the industries in which they work and the communities in which they live.

Local industries have positive and negative influences on the locality. Pollution, despoliation and congestion are all negative aspects of their activities that constitute external direct and indirect social and economic costs, which are borne by the community.

The local community has an interest in the activities of local industries, and requires much more information on social benefits and costs than the public relations-type information which is presently disclosed. The social audit points to a possible remedy for the lack of objectivity in the information presently disclosed.

The information needs of customers

In recent years, consumer councils and other bodies have restored in some measure the disproportionate balance of power which has appeared in our society between the large and powerful producers of consumer goods and the voiceless masses of our population who, subjected to subliminal advertising, monopoly practices, and suffering from ignorance, have been at the former's mercy. In a few instances, the Monopolies Commission has acted to protect consumers, but its power to intervene is based upon law.

Customers may well have little influence in markets increasingly dominated by large business organizations, and it is difficult to see how, even if more information were made available, the balance might be redressed. Certainly, customers are interested in information indicating the fairness of pricing policies, such as the relative proportion of unit price which consists of costs, profits and taxes, and in the differential costs between one product and another produced by the same firm at a different price. For example, why should one electric shaver cost £10 more than another, and in what ways is this difference value for money? Clearly, there will be many more social changes in our society before questions of this sort will be recognized and adequately answered.

Accounting information and the allocation of resources

The various groups of information users which we have just discussed share a common concern, which is to make decisions about the allocation of scarce resources between competing ends. Students of economics will find such a statement echoes a popular definition of the subject matter of economics. The importance of accounting information is that it makes such an allocation possible in a market economy, where individuals and organizations are largely free to allocate the resources which they control between competing ends. Therefore, the theoretical objective of an accounting information system is to enable information users to make optimal decisions, so as to make the best allocation of available resources within their control. Optimal decision making may be understood only in relation to the objectives of decision makers, so that the various groups of information users whose needs we have just discussed may be said to have very different and occasionally competing decision objectives. Optimal decision making requires that the results of decisions should have a certain quality: that they should be the best possible which can be achieved under given circumstances, and implies a standard against which actual results can be compared.

We are stating, therefore, that the objective of accounting information systems is to enable decision makers to attempt to optimize the allocation of the resources which they control and to assess the actual results of their decisions against the forecast results. A measure of the efficiency of the decision-making process is the extent to which the actual result compares to the optimal result. In this connection, 'efficiency' and 'effectiveness' are used in the literature in a special sense. The term 'efficiency' is usually reserved for the analysis of input–output relationships, so that the 'efficiency' of a factory production process may refer to the degree of technical skill with which inputs of production factors are transformed into finished goods, and to the success with which input factors' values in monetary terms are transformed into outputs also valued in monetary terms. By contrast the term 'effectiveness' is reserved for the analysis of the success with which policy objectives are attained. Thus, we may talk of 'organizational effectiveness' in discussing how well management decisions lead to the attainment of organizational objectives.

Consequently, the 'effectiveness' of an accounting information system is the extent to which it enables its users to make optimal decisions. By examining the different objectives which we assume they have, we are able to judge the 'effectiveness' of accounting information by reference to the relevance of that information to the types of decisions which they wish to make. Management makes decisions about the allocation of men, materials, machines and money in such a way that the firm's objectives may be reached. As we see in Part 5, firms have different objectives, and profit is one of these objectives. Often, it is thought that the size of the firm's profit reflects the 'efficiency' of management in transforming inputs of factors of production into sales of finished goods. It is evident, however, that in our analysis profit figures, though important, should not be confused with 'managerial effectiveness'.

Behavioural aspects of decision making

The central purpose of accounting is to produce information which will influence behaviour. Unless accounting reports have the potential to influence decisions and actions, it is difficult to justify the cost of preparing such reports. Traditionally, accounting reports have been addressed to shareholders and investors. In Part 4, the behavioural aspects of investor decision making are discussed and the role of accounting information in that context will be examined. In particular, the response of the Stock Exchange to the disclosure of accounting information through the reaction of share prices will be seen to be one way in which the influence of accounting reports of investors may be judged. In Part 5, the behavioural aspects of decision making within organizations are examined and the role of management accounting information as an influence in this respect will be discussed.

Since, from a management point of view, the purpose of accounting information is to enable the organization to attain its goals, it must follow that the effectiveness of accounting information is evidenced in the manner in which it affects behaviour. In this sense, unless accounting information produces the desired action, it has served no purpose at all. Research has shown, for example, that even when managers have all the information which they need, they do not always make good decisions. Hence, the human process which leads managers to recognize or fail to recognize the significance of accounting information deserves a better understanding, and accountants need to be aware of the role of accounting information to enable managers to identify their mistakes and to learn from them. Feedback information plays an important part in this process.

A systems approach to accounting

The study of the firm as an organization consisting of several systems, for example, an operating system, a financial system, a personnel system and a marketing system, enables one to see the accounting system as one element of an interacting whole. This manner of seeing the nature of the various elements of an organization is known as the systems approach.

The accounting system is the most important element of an organization's information system, for the following reasons:

1 The accounting information system enables management and external information users to get a picture of the whole organization.
2 The accounting information system links other important information systems such as marketing, personnel, research and development, and production, in that the information produced by these systems can be expressed in financial terms in planning strategy to attain organizational goals.

Moreover, the systems approach permits the integration of accounting into a coherent framework in which its role is concerned with the provision of information for decision making.

This kind of approach allows accounting information to be viewed as affecting all members of society having connections with business organizations, in terms of the welfare theory of accounting mentioned in Chapter 1. Furthermore, the systems approach requires account to be taken of all the sources of information available to an individual. For example, as we see in Part 4, investors receive information from sources other than financial reports. The Stock Exchange is often able to anticipate the information contained in such reports. Therefore, in considering the changes which ought to be made to accounting information disclosed to investors, the systems approach requires the informational content of the other sources of information available to investors to be taken into account.

The systems approach also enables us to integrate modern technological developments into the study of accounting. With the development of the computer, rapid advances have been made in electronic data processing. These advances have affected accounting in a number of ways. First, information systems have been formalized, so that information may be fed directly from the computer to decision makers without the intervention of accountants. Second, computers have made possible the merger of accounting and non-accounting information, leading to the integration of information services and reductions in duplication and hence information costs. Third, there has been greater accuracy of the information provided, resulting directly from the reduction of duplication.

Finally, the systems approach widens the possible applications of information. Thus, one of the developments which has influenced management decision making in recent years is operational research, which is concerned with the study of the behaviour of the various parts or subsystems of an organization in such a way that all its activities may be analysed as a whole. Operational research uses mathematical techniques for solving business problems, and its growing importance is reflected in the increasing use of management decision models which attempt to predict and compare the outcome of alternative strategies. Traditionally, mathematicians have specialized in the expression and solution of complex logical problems, and although the techniques which they evolved had a potential use for decision making in organizations, they were not employed in business situations because of the time lag which existed in the processing of data. The advent of the computer has closed the technological gap, and has greatly contributed to the increased importance of quantitative methods in management. The information required for operational research studies is often not of the type handled by traditional accounting systems. The systems approach, therefore, not only coincides with the manner of studying organizations by operational research scientists, but by encouraging the integration of accounting and non-accounting information it increases the range of applications of the information produced by such systems.

Summary

We began this chapter with an examination of accounting as an information system consisting of three activities—input, processing and output. The systems characteristic of accounting suggests that the systems approach is the ideal way of studying the subject. It is not sufficient, however, to view accounting purely as an operating system, for its relevance and usefulness may only be judged by the degree with which its output meets the needs of the users of accounting information. By identifying the basic goal of an accounting information system as being the provision of information for decision making, we provide a framework by which to judge the effectiveness of that system.

There are many approaches to the study of decision making— economic, behavioural and quantitative—and the interdisciplinary nature of decision theory has the inevitable consequence that accounting has also become an interdisciplinary subject. The systems approach facilitates an interdisciplinary study of accounting because it requires that it be viewed, not in isolation, but as one element in a broad informational context.

Questions

1　Discuss the nature of accounting as an information system.
2　State the groups of persons having vested interests in a business organization and examine the nature of their information needs.
3　Evaluate the role of accounting information in the allocation of resources
4　Explain what is meant by the 'systems approach', and examine the reasons for its application to the study of accounting.

Chapter 3

The role of accounting theory

Underlying the discussion of accounting as an information system is the important question of the field of knowledge to which accounting information refers. This raises issues about the nature and significance of accounting theory and the relationship between accounting theory and accounting practice.

The purpose of this chapter is to consider these various problems with a view to establishing the role of accounting theory.

The nature of theories

Essentially, theories are generalizations which serve to organize otherwise meaningless masses of data, and which thereby establish significant relationships in respect of such data. The construction of theories requires a process of reasoning about the problems implicit in the data under observation, as a means of distinguishing the basic relationships. Thus, theory construction is a process of simplification, which requires assumptions that permit the representation of reality by a generalization that is easily understood. The close association of theory and data, or facts, is fundamental to the notion of good theory, for the reliability of a theory is dependent not only upon the facts to which it refers, but also upon an interpretation of those facts requiring validation and continuous reassessment.

Theories are concerned with explanation. Explanation relates a set of observations to a theoretical construction of reality which fit those observations. If no theoretical scheme that does this reasonably well is available, the desire for explanation leads to the creation of a scheme of ideas which provides a definition of the problem observed as well as an understanding of it in the form of explanation. In both cases, relating observations to existing theory, and constructing theory to fit observations, have the objective of providing explanation of those observations.

A misunderstanding of the relationship that exists between facts and theories gives rise to a great deal of misconception about the role of theories. Thus, the complaint that 'it's all right in theory but not in practice' implies that the person making the complaint must hold the belief that an alternative theory provides a different explanation of the facts in question.

The word 'theory' itself gives rise to misunderstanding, and may mean different things to different people. This arises because explanations are made at different levels. At one extreme, explanations are purely speculative, resulting in speculative theories, for example that 'outer-space probes are affecting the weather'. To the natural scientist, speculative theries are not really theories at all and explanations have to be conclusive before they are given the status of theories. To this end, their assumptions require verification by the test of experience. At another extreme are to be found explanations which are accepted only when they have been verified. Empirical theories are constructed by the process of verifying assumptions, or hypotheses, through the test of experience. This process is known as the 'scientific method', and is illustrated in Fig. 1.3.

Fig. 1.3

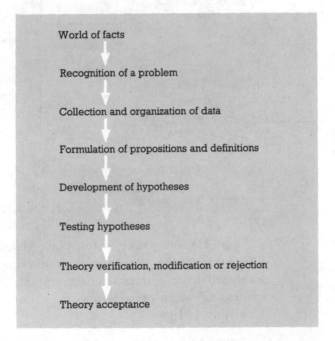

World of facts

Recognition of a problem

Collection and organization of data

Formulation of propositions and definitions

Development of hypotheses

Testing hypotheses

Theory verification, modification or rejection

Theory acceptance

Empirical theories assist in making 'predictions', for while they consist of generalizations which explain the present, future occurrences also replicate the same conditions. It is in providing both explanations and predictions that empirical theories have acquired such importance in making decisions about the future which are based on assumptions derived from experience.

Accounting theory

The word 'theory' is also used at different levels in the literature of accounting. Thus, references to 'accounting theory' may mean purely speculative interpretations or empirical explanations. These references usually do not indicate the level of theory which is implied.

According to Hendriksen,

'Accounting theory may be defined as logical reasoning in the form of a set of broad principles that (1) provide a general frame of reference by which accounting practice can be evaluated, and (2) guide the development of new practices and procedures. Accounting theory may also be used to explain existing practices to obtain a better understanding of them. But the most important goal of accounting theory should be to provide a coherent set of logical principles that form the general frame of reference for the evaluation and development of sound accounting practices.' (Hendriksen, 1982.)

The relationship between accounting theory and accounting practice is indicated in Fig. 1.4, as is the influence of policy makers in relating accounting theory to accounting practice.

Fig. 1.4

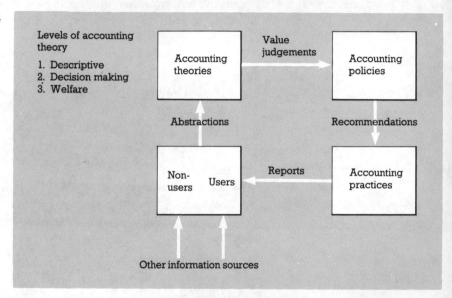

Figure 1.4 shows that the role played by theory in accounting is very different from that played in the natural sciences, where theories are developed from empirical observations. The converse is the case in accounting, since practice may be changed to accommodate theory. According to Ijiri,

'Contrary to the fields of linguistics, meteorology or chemistry, accountants can change their practices relatively easily. Therefore, it becomes an essential problem for accountants to know how accounting practices should be developed in the future. The sanctions by which accounting policies have become implemented are quite essential in understanding the field of accounting, since it is possible to change practices to fit theories!! This is unthinkable for scientists in other fields for whom phenomena are almighty. No matter how beautiful and elegant the theory may be, if it does not fit the empirical phenomena, it is replaced by one which fits better.' (Ijiri, 1971.)

Figure 1.4 also illustrates how the form of accounting information reported to decision makers depends on the practices adopted. These practices are imposed by accounting policy makers who, having knowledge of accounting theories, have the responsibility of responding to the needs of users of accounting information.

It is evident that deficiencies in the four significant areas denoted in

Fig. 1.4, namely, accounting theory, policy making (by the profession and the government), accounting practice, and the use of accounting information, impair the usefulness of an accounting information service. Thus, the failure of policy makers to incorporate research findings in the policies they devise may reduce the potential usefulness of accounting information.

Approaches to the development of accounting theory

Several approaches to the development of accounting theory have emerged in the last two decades. These approaches may be identified as follows:

1 descriptive;
2 decision usefulness:
    (i) empirical;
    (ii) normative
3 welfare.

The descriptive approach

Theories developed using the descriptive approach are essentially concerned with what accountants do. In developing such explanations, descriptive theories rely on a process of inductive reasoning, which consists of making observations and of drawing generalized conclusions from those observations. In effect, the objective of making observations is to look for similarity of instances, and to identify a sufficient number of such instances as will induce the required degree of assurance needed to develop a theory about all the instances which belong to the same class of phenomena.

As applied to the construction of accounting theory, the descriptive approach has emphasized the *practice* of accounting as a basis from which to develop theories. This approach has attempted to relate the practices of accountants to a generalized theory about accounting. In this view, accounting theory is to be discovered by observing the practices of accountants because 'accounting theory is primarily a concentrate distilled from experience . . . it is experience intelligently analysed that produces logical explanation . . . and . . . illuminates the practices from which it springs' (Littleton and Zimmerman, 1962).

The descriptive approach results in descriptive or positive theories of accounting, which explain what accountants do and enable predictions to be made about behaviour, for example, how a particular matter will be treated. Thus, it is possible to predict that the receipt of cash will be entered in the debit side of the cash book.

In effect, the descriptive approach is concerned with observing the functional tasks which accountants have traditionally performed. In 1952, the Institute of Chartered Accountants in England and Wales stated that 'the primary purpose of the annual accounts of a business is to present information to proprietors showing how their funds have been utilized, and the profits derived from such use' (ICAEW, 1952).

Underlying the descriptive approach is the belief that the objective of financial statements is associated with the stewardship concept of the management role, and the need to provide the owners of businesses with information relating to the manner in which their assets have been managed. In this view, company directors occupy a position of responsibility and trust in regard to shareholders, and the discharge of these obligations requires the publication of annual reports to shareholders. With the growth of large corporate enterprises, the weakening of the links between ownership and management created a need for a more elementary notion of stewardship, in which the disclosure of financial information was aimed at protecting shareholders from fraudulent management practices.

In recent years a number of writers have applied agency theory to the relationship between managers and shareholders in companies (Watts and Zimmerman, 1985). Managers are hired by the shareholders of a company to administer the firm's activities, thus establishing an agency relationship. The objectives of managers and shareholders may not be in perfect agreement. For example, the utility maximizing behaviour of managers could be in conflict with shareholder interests. One of the conclusions which is suggested by agency theory is that mutual benefits are perceived by management and shareholders from the disclosure of audited information. Routine financial reporting is a means by which shareholders can monitor the actions of managers.

As we see in Part 2 and Part 4 when discussing the work of the Accounting Standards Committee in relation to the development of accounting standards, it is evident that the descriptive approach to theory construction in accounting plays an influential role in shaping perceptions of the problems of accounting and the manner in which they should be solved. In effect, the Accounting Standards Committee has been concerned with discussing the varied practices used by accountants and reaching a consensus on the most feasible basis on which to reduce the diversity of these practices through the process of standardization.

Figure 1.5 below illustrates the framework within which descriptive accounting theory has developed.

Fig 1.5

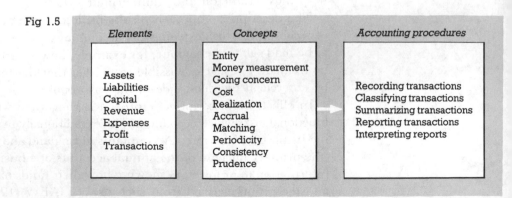

Elements	Concepts	Accounting procedures
Assets Liabilities Capital Revenue Expenses Profit Transactions	Entity Money measurement Going concern Cost Realization Accrual Matching Periodicity Consistency Prudence	Recording transactions Classifying transactions Summarizing transactions Reporting transactions Interpreting reports

Elements and concepts

The establishment of elements and concepts is very important to the development of a theoretical framework. Accounting elements and concepts are used to describe the events that comprise the existence of business of every kind. For this reason accounting is often characterized as 'the language of business'. The elements and concepts listed in Fig. 1.5 provide the essential material of accounting theory.

Assets are things of value which are possessed by a business. In order to be classified as an asset the money measurement concept demands that a thing must have the quality of being measurable in terms of money. The assets of a business comprise not only cash and such property as land, buildings, machinery and merchandise, but also money which is owed by individuals or other enterprises (called debtors) to the business.

Liabilities are the amounts owing by the business. Most firms find it convenient to buy merchandise and services on credit terms rather than to pay cash. This gives rise to liabilities known as trade creditors. Liabilities arise also when a firm borrows money as a means of supplementing the funds invested by the owner. The reason why amounts of money owed to the creditors by a business are known as liabilities is that the business is liable to them for the amounts owed.

Capital is the excess of assets over liabilities and represents the owner's investment in the business. As we will illustrate in Part 2, the assets of a business must always be equal to the liabilities and the owner's capital. This is the result of double-entry bookkeeping, whereby each transaction has a twofold effect.

Revenue is earned by a business when it provides goods and services to customers. Whereas a trading business will derive revenue mainly from the sale of merchandise, a business which renders services, such as a solicitor, will derive revenue as a result of charging for the service. It is not necessary for a business to receive cash before recognizing that revenue has been earned. As we discuss in Chapter 4 the accrual concept recognizes revenue which arises from the sale of goods or services on credit.

Expenses are incurred in earning revenue. Examples of expenses are wages and salaries paid to employees and rent paid to the landlord. If expenses are not paid when they are incurred the amount is recorded as a liability.

Profit results when the total revenue of a business for a certain period, such as a year, exceeds the total of the expenses for that period. As we will see in Part 2, profit accrues to the owner of the business and increases his investment. The increase is reflected in the owner's capital, being a liability due to him.

Transactions are events which require recognition in the accounting records. They originate when changes in basic concepts are recorded. A transaction is financial in nature and is expressed in terms of money.

Accounting concepts

Accounting concepts determine the rules which are applied to accounting procedures. Accounting concepts are continually being adapted to meet the changing demands of business, and at any point in time there may be more than one accepted way of treating a particular class of transaction. A thorough knowledge of these concepts is necessary for a complete understanding of financial statements. Accounting concepts are discussed in Chapter 4.

Accounting procedures

Recording is the process by which financial transactions are systematically placed in accounting records. Recording may be made in the form of pen markings by hand, or it may be accomplished by various mechanical or electronic devices. Transactions are analysed so that they can be *classified* according to a predetermined system. Periodically, this recorded and classified information is summarized in the form of financial statements and reports to the managers of an enterprise and to other interested parties. *Interpreting* basically refers to that utilization of the recorded, classified and summarized data which reveals and emphasizes significant changes, trends and potential developments in the affairs of an enterprise.

Financial statements

Conventional accounting procedures are associated with the periodic production of financial statements. Two such statements are the balance sheet, and the profit and loss account. Their contents are illustrated below. Funds flow and cash flow statements are additional financial statements, which explain the flow of financial resources to and from the enterprise. They are dealt with in Chapter 13.

1   *The balance sheet*, sometimes called the statement of financial position, lists the assets and liabilities of the business at the end of the accounting period. It provides a measure of the capital invested by the owner(s) in the business. Shown below is an illustration of a balance sheet drawn up at 31 December 19X1 for Ivor Camera who operates as a photographer.

   It will be seen that the balance sheet has four main sections —fixed assets, current assets, capital and other liabilities. This classification assists in the financial analysis of the business. Fixed assets are used in the business, and are not intended for resale. They include assets having a long life, such as buildings, plant, machinery and vehicles. Current assets are those which are transformed during the operating cycle into cash, inventories such as materials, supplies, work-in-progress and finished goods, as well as debtors.

Ivor Camera
Balance sheet at 31 December 19X1

Owner's capital:	£	£	Fixed assets	£	£
Capital 1 Jan.	20 000		Buildings	16 000	
Profit for 19X1	10 000		Equipment	7 000	
	30 000				23 000
Drawings	5 000				
		25 000			
Current liabilities:			Current assets		
Creditors		4 000	Stock	1 000	
			Debtors	4 500	
			Cash	500	
					6 000
		29 000			29 000

Cash is always shown as a current asset, as it is available for immediate use by the business.

2 *The profit and loss account* is used to show the calculation of the profit of the business for the accounting period. The account below illustrates the manner in which this calculation is made by the deduction of expenses from the revenues of the period.

Ivor Camera
Profit and loss account for the year ended 31 December 19X1

	£	£
Revenues:		
Fees earned		18 500
Expenses:		
Rent	3 000	
Advertising	1 000	
Heating and lighting	500	
Supplies used	2 000	
Travelling	2 000	
		8 500
Net profit for the year		10 000

It will be seen that the net profit for the year is added to the owner's capital in the balance sheet. Until such time as the owner draws upon that profit, it remains in the business as 'retained profit'. In effect, the net profit increases the invested capital, and drawings reduce it.

Decision usefulness approaches

The expansion of behavioural research into accounting during the 1970s resulted in an interest in decision usefulness theories of accounting. This mood was well captured in the following statement by the American Accounting Association in 1971:

'To state the matter concisely, the principal purpose of accounting reports is to influence action, that is, behaviour. Additionally, it can be hypothesized that the very process of accumulating information, as well as the behaviour of those who do the accounting, will affect the behaviour of others. In short, by its very nature, accounting is a behavioural process.' (AAA, 1971.)

Two types of decision usefulness theories of accounting have resulted from this approach, namely, empirical and normative theories.

Empirical approach

The early 1970s witnessed a substantial increase in empirical research which was designed to make accounting research more rigorous and to improve the reliability of results. Sophisticated statistical techniques became increasingly used for this purpose. Furthermore, the expansion of university courses in accounting increased the number of students with a quantitative background, who could conduct research in this way. The university departments of accounting, desiring to enhance their status within the universities, viewed the possibility of empirical research based on the 'scientific method' as a useful springboard to this end. The implications of the empirical approach to research in accounting were significant in the development of accounting theory. These implications are discussed further in Part 4.

Normative approach

Unlike empirical research, which concentrates on how users of accounting information apply this information in decision making, the normative approach to theory construction is concerned with specifying the manner in which decisions ought to be made as a precondition to considering the information requirement.

The normative approach focuses on the decision models which should be used by decision makers seeking to make rational decisions. This focus is seen as providing insights on the information needs of decision makers, as a basis for developing accounting theory.

The normative approach is used in this text as the basis for examining the information needs of investors and employees. It is the approach in recent attempts to develop conceptual frameworks for financial reporting which were noted in Chapter 1. This approach is discussed in Part 4.

The welfare approach

The welfare approach is an extension of the decision-making approaches, which considers the effects of decision making on social welfare. Basically, decision-making approaches limit the field of interest to the private use of accounting information. If accounting information had a relevance limited to private interests, the decision-making approaches would provide a sufficient analysis of information needs. It is because of the external social effects of decisions made on the basis of accounting information that there is imputed a social-welfare dimension to accounting theory.

The theoretical objective of the welfare approach is the maximization of social welfare, which is defined as the benefits accruing to all members of society from decisions made by individuals about the use of resources under their control. In this respect, a disadvantage of the classical individual decision-making approach which hitherto has been reflected in the debate about accounting policies is that it does not provide a basis for developing accounting policies which would maximize social welfare. Implicit in this view is that accounting should provide information for decision making by individuals, without any consideration of social welfare effects. As May and Sundem (1976) pointed out, such a delineation of *what* accounting policy makers should be concerned with precludes the possibility of making comparisons of alternative policies having different social welfare effects.

The welfare effects associated with the use of financial statements may be discussed from various standpoints.

1   The effects of financial information on the welfare of individual decision makers may be deemed to be one important standpoint. Since investment decisions imply the comparison of alternative investments, external users of financial information require as much consistency and comparability as is practicable between the financial statements of enterprises generally. We discuss this point further in Part 4, but it may be mentioned at this stage that it is the lack of comparability between the financial statements of enterprises which lay at the root of much criticism of the accounting profession in recent years.

2   The effects of financial information on social welfare may also be seen from the standpoint of the distortion arising from the possession of superior knowledge by one segment of a particular group of users, which would have consequential changes in the distribution of wealth within one group. For example, if an investor has access to inside information about an enterprise, and this information is not freely available to other investors, he would be able to make decisions which may improve his welfare at the expense of other investors.

3   The effects of financial information may also be viewed from the standpoint of the allocation of resources in the economy. The importance of accounting information as regards the allocation of scarce resources was discussed earlier in Chapter 2. Financial statements provide investors with data which assist in establishing the market price of company shares. As we see in Part 4, there is research evidence to show that accounting data have an important effect on share prices. Ideally, financial reports should contain data which make it possible for investors to evaluate investment opportunities, if the allocation of resources throughout the economy

is to maximize social welfare in accordance with classical economic theory.

4   The approaches to accounting theory mentioned so far assume that information is a free commodity, and therefore that no costs are incurred in producing information. Clearly, from a social welfare viewpoint, costs are significant in considering the level of information to be made available, given that resources are scarce and could be employed in other activities. The costs of collecting and processing data and distributing information should be taken into account in considering the level of information provided to users. The difficulty which stands in the way of developing this analysis further lies in the problem of defining and measuring the benefits associated with the use of information, for the optimum level of information output ought also to be seen from the perspective of the payoffs associated with costs. As we shall see below, some attempts have been made to define the payoffs which may be associated with information costs.

5   The effects of financial information on welfare may be viewed from the standpoint of the vested interests of groups within an organization. The needs of these groups were discussed in Chapter 2. It is evident that the alteration of accounting policies in favour of one group and away from another will affect the distribution of income and wealth within society. In this respect, the movement towards disclosing information to employees and the concept of social responsibility accounting, which are discussed in Chapters 24 and 25 respectively, are clearly causing such a change.

Staubus (1977) lists potential positive and negative payoffs to various groups which result from producing one particular type of information under general headings, as follows:

Potential positive payoffs from an accounting method

1   Direct payoffs to parties associated with the entity, namely, present and prospective owners, creditors, suppliers, customers, employees and government taxing and regulatory bodies, through:
    (a) improvements in their own decisions, using information supplied by the entity and produced with the accounting method or information system in question, and
    (b) higher direct compensation from the entity due to its more effective management and greater profitability with the aid of the information in question.

2   Payoffs to competitors through more useful information about the reporting entity's activities.

3   Diffused benefits through the better functioning of the economy, such as through the allocation of resources, reduction in variations in the level of economic activity, and the effects of the division of income as between investment and consumption.

Potential negative payoffs from an accounting method

1   Reduction in the profitability of competitors, and in distributions to their constituents, through better decisions by the reporting entity.
2   Reduction in the profitability of the reporting entity through better decisions by its competitors and by its creditors, suppliers, customers and employees who bargain with the entity.
3   Reduction in the profitability of the entity due to the effects upon management decisions of reporting to shareholders and others by means of the accounting method under evaluation.
4   The costs of producing information, such as accounting and auditing costs.
5   The costs of analysing and using accounting information.

Clearly, a major difficulty in developing welfare theories of accounting lies in the complexities involved in any attempt to maximize welfare. Since there are multiple users of financial statements, the costs and the benefits to each user of a particular accounting measure would be impossible to calculate. Arrow's impossibility theorem demonstrates the impossibility facing society of making rules on a collective basis which also satisfy the needs of particular individuals (Arrow, 1963).

Nevertheless, these difficulties should not detract from the significance of the welfare approach to developing accounting theories. While it would be unreasonable to demand those responsible for making accounting policies to construct a system of financial reporting which maximizes social welfare, it should be apparent to them that welfare considerations should be of prime importance in policy making.

Accounting policy makers

There are two main groups which determine accounting policy. First, the government employs the legislative process to ensure that a minimum level of information is disclosed in company reports. It also acts as a spur to prompt the accountancy profession into action, where there is an apparent urgent need. An example of this influence was the establishment of the Sandilands Committee by the Government to consider the problem of accounting under conditions of price level changes. This problem will be discussed in Chapter 20. Another example was the Employment Protection Act, 1975, which places a general duty on the employer to disclose information requested by trade union representatives at all stages of collective bargaining. This problem is discussed in Chapter 24.

Second, the accountancy profession itself acts as a regulatory body and deals with the problems of accounting standards implied in financial reports. The influence of the accountancy profession in making accounting policy is introduced in Chapter 4.

Summary

This chapter has been concerned with an examination of the role of accounting theory in developing knowledge through the construction of theories. The importance of such theory construction for the improvement of accounting practice has also been discussed. The nature of theory was examined in detail in order to establish precisely the significance of theory to knowledge in general, and to accounting in particular. The several approaches to the development of accounting theory were reviewed. Attention was drawn to the successive stages beginning with descriptive theories, and proceeding to normative and to decision-making theories of accounting. The chapter concluded with an introduction to a movement towards welfare-oriented theories of accounting, and a discussion of the role of those responsible for making accounting policies in using the insights produced by research and incorporated in theories of accounting.

References

AAA (1971). Report of the committee on the behavioural science content of the accounting curriculum, *Accounting Review Supplement,* **46**.

Arrow, K.J. (1963). *Social Choice and Individual Values* (2nd edn), Wiley.

Hendriksen, E.S. (1982). *Accounting Theory* (4th edn), Richard D. Irwin.

Ijiri, Y. (1971). Logic and sanctions in accounting, in Sterling, R.R. and Bentz, W.F. (eds), *Accounting in Perspective*, South Western Publishing Co.

ICAEW (1952). *Accounting in Relation to Changes in the Purchasing Power of Money*, Recommendation No. 15, paragraph 1, May.

Littleton, A.C. and Zimmerman, V.K. (1962). *Accounting Theory: Continuity and Change*, Prentice-Hall.

May, R.J. and Sundem, G.L. (1976). Research for accounting policy: an overview, *Accounting Review*, October.

Staubus, G.J. (1977). *Making Accounting Decisions*, pp. 36–7, Scholars Book Co.

Watts, R.L. and Zimmerman, J.L. (1985) *Positive Accounting Theory*, Prentice-Hall.

Questions

1 Examine the nature of theories.
2 Analyse the relationship between accounting theory, accounting policy and accounting practice. To what extent does the quality of accounting policy and accounting practice depend on accounting theory?
3 Distinguish 'elements', 'concepts' and 'accounting procedures'.
4 Define the following terms: assets, liabilities, capital, profit and expenses.
5 What is a balance sheet? What is a profit and loss account? How are these two statements related?
6 Contrast the descriptive and normative approaches to theory construction.
7 Explain how the welfare approach to accounting theory differs from other approaches.

Part 2

Financial accounting – the historical cost approach

Introduction

In so far as business firms are concerned, a distinction is normally made between *financial accounting*, which is the activity of recording and analysing the financial results of transactions as a means of arriving at a measure of the firm's success and financial soundness, and *management accounting*, which is the activity of providing information to enable management to make efficient decisions as regards the use and allocation of the firm's resources. In this part, the traditional practices of financial accounting based on historical cost valuations are examined. The approach used is based on a descriptive analysis of the practices of accountants, and leads to a descriptive theory of financial accounting. Therefore, we are concerned with *what* accountants do and the conventions and standards by which their activities are regulated.

As we pointed out in Chapter 3, financial reports produced on the basis of financial records may be analysed also in terms of the relevance of the information provided to users for the purposes of decision making. We suggested that such analysis should be conducted in terms of a normative theory. In this part, we restrict ourselves to the discussion of descriptive theories of financial accounting which focuses on accounting practices only, and address the problem of users' needs in Part 4, using normative theories for that purpose.

The purpose here is to examine the nature and the practices of financial accounting which is concerned with the following activities:

1 recording financial transactions:
2 summarizing and presenting financial information in reports.

Financial accounting information is used by various interested parties. Managers require financial information to evaluate the financial results of past decisions, because the evaluation of past performance is an important part of management decision making. Shareholders and investors need financial information which will enable them to predict their income from the firm and the value of their investment, and to judge the risks attached thereto. Hence, shareholders and investors require financial accounting information for the purpose of making decisions about their investment. In addition to shareholders and investors, there are other external users of financial information, notably the Inland Revenue, which requires a firm to submit financial accounts for the purpose of assessing its tax liability, and trade unions and employees who have a vested interest in the financial performance of the company.

The nature and methods of financial accounting are determined to a considerable extent by the concepts which exist among accountants for identifying, evaluating and communicating financial information. This is particularly true of the information which is provided for external users such as shareholders and investors. It is evident that unless accountants obey the same rules as regards selecting, measuring and communicating information to external users, the latter will be at a disadvantage in respect of the reliance which may be attached to the information they receive. The usefulness of accounting concepts lies in the uniformity and comparability of information which is made possible thereby. Accounting concepts secure for external users a greater degree of comparability in the information provided by the same firm over a period of years. Accountants do not attempt, however, to meet the specific information needs of external users, and the information which they provide is dictated by the concepts which they have followed for a very long time, rather than by the information needs of external users.

The users of external reports have no direct control over their content. We may contrast Fig. 2.1, which illustrates the boundaries of the financial accounting system for external users, against the user-oriented model shown on page 14 (Fig. 1.2). In this case, there is no direct control by the user over the final output. Hence, it may be suggested that the information system for external decision-makers is not user-oriented. The output, and therefore also the input, into this system is determined by concepts embodied in accounting tradition and in law.

Fig. 2.1

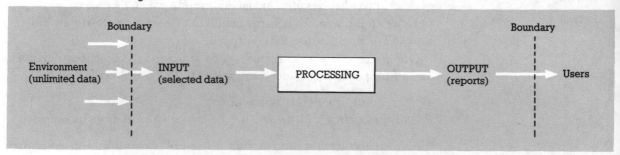

A basic assumption underlying communication is that there is a clear separation between the transmitter and the receiver of information. This is acknowledged also in financial reporting by the distinction drawn between the function of the accountant as the transmitter of information and the external user as the receiver of information. The external user relies upon the accountant to provide him with a significant supply of information for making economic decisions. It is for each user to evaluate and interpret this information when formulating decisions which only he may make. It is not the objective of the accountant as the preparer of financial reports to make such evaluations and draw conclusions for the external user. Consequently, it is not the function of the internal accountant to value a firm for the external user: on the contrary, it is for the investor to establish the value of the firm as an investment and to bear the risk involved in acting on such a valuation. The function of the internal accountant is to assist the external user in valuing the firm by the provision of such information as is necessary for that purpose.

In line with this reasoning, we consider in this part the problems associated with the production of financial accounting information. We examine how data is selected from the environment, and the manner in which it becomes an input into the financial accounting system. We discuss also the manner in which the output of the financial accounting system is formulated as financial reports. We examine in Part 4 the relevance of these reports to the decisions which shareholders and investors wish to make.

We have limited our analysis of financial accounting information to those aspects which we consider important and relevant to the textbook as a whole. In Section 1, we examine financial accounting method to gain an understanding of its nature and of the principles underlying its procedures. In Section 2, we analyse the process of periodic measurement, which is one of its main applications. In Section 3, we select for closer analysis the application of financial accounting procedures to the production of financial statements for corporate enterprises.

One important application of financial accounting method relates to the use of accounting records for the day-to-day control of assets and liabilities. These technical aspects of control are treated as a 'background subject' in this text, so as not to detract from the important theoretical and practical aspects of the accountant's role in providing information for decision-making purposes.

Section 1

Financial Accounting Practice

Chapter 4

Financial accounting concepts

The concepts of financial accounting are particularly significant to the development of accounting theory in two ways. First, they are themselves part of an empirical process for developing rules of financial accounting. In this sense, they may be regarded as belonging to the corpus of accounting theory. Second, they reflect the influence of institutional forces which shape the philosophy of accounting in a given economic and social environment. Thus, the accounting profession in the United Kingdom and in the United States is a powerful influence in shaping the development of accounting within the context of the problems found in those countries.

The concepts of accounting discussed in this chapter may be seen as related to the general problem of developing viable theories of financial accounting. As we shall see, their origin lies in a historical process of development. The ongoing nature of this process is discussed in Chapter 5, where the review of the concepts of financial accounting by the accounting profession is seen to focus on the formulation of standard accounting practices.

We mentioned in the Introduction to this part that the nature of financial accounting information is dictated not by the needs of external users, but rather is determined to a considerable extent by the concepts which exist among accountants for identifying, evaluating and communicating financial information.

In this chapter, we analyse the nature and the effects of accounting concepts on the manner in which accountants generate financial information. The need for these concepts is discussed, as well as the problems which they pose. The chapter concludes with a discussion of the need for financial accounting standards to reduce the diversity of accounting practices which exist under traditional concepts.

In effect, the concepts and standards discussed in this chapter reflect and explain the systems of thought which determine accounting practice, and which form the basis of the descriptive theory of financial accounting to which this part is addressed.

The nature of financial accounting concepts

Accounting concepts define the assumptions on which the financial accounts of a business are prepared. Financial transactions are interpreted in the light of the concepts which govern accounting methods. In effect, the concepts of financial accounting largely determine the interpretations given in financial reports of the events and results which they portray. For example, the concept relating to the recognition of revenue determines the dimension of the profit reported to shareholders and the value of the enterprise as judged from the balance sheet.

If accountants as a group wish to change some of their concepts they are free to do so. Indeed, accounting bodies in Britain and in the United States are engaged in the review of their concepts and practices, and for this purpose, the Financial Accounting Standards Board was established in the United States in 1972 (replacing the Accounting Principles Board). In the United Kingdom the Accounting Standards Committee was established in 1970 with similar objectives and was replaced by the Accounting Standards Board in 1990.

The term 'accounting concepts' serves in another sense to underline the freedom accountants have enjoyed in determining their own rules. There is no tradition of State interference in the United States and United Kingdom, for example, as regards the practice of accounting. Such laws as are to be found are contained in statutes dealing with the activities of corporate bodies, such as the Companies Acts, which specify the nature of the accounting information that must be disclosed to shareholders, and the Income Tax and Corporation Tax Acts, which impose a duty on business firms to submit accounting information for the purpose of assessing the liability to tax. So far, neither Parliament nor the Courts have issued directives to the accounting profession as regards the concepts which they should observe. In France, by contrast, there is a different political tradition, and there is legislation dealing with accounting practices and they are detailed in the *Plan Comptable*, which is an edict issued by the French government detailing the manner in which accounting statements should be prepared.

Fig. 2.2

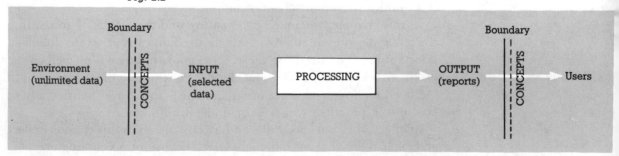

Figure 2.2 illustrates the manner in which financial accounting concepts act as filters in selecting data as input into the processing system and as output of information for users.

Financial accounting concepts

Financial accounting is founded on the following concepts:

1 entity
2 money measurement
3 going-concern
4 cost
5 realization
6 accruals
7 matching
8 periodicity
9 consistency
10 prudence

The entity concept

The practice of distinguishing the affairs of the business from the personal affairs of its owner originated in the early days of double-entry bookkeeping some 400 years ago. Accounting has a history which reaches back to the beginning of civilization, and archaeologists have found accounting records which date as far back as 4000 BC, well before the invention of money. Nevertheless, it was not until the fifteenth century that the separation of the owner's wealth from the wealth invested in a business venture was recognized as necessary. This arose from the use of paid managers or stewards to run a business who were required to render accounts of their stewardship of the funds and assets. Consequently, the 'capital' invested in the business represented not only the initial assets of the business but a measure of its indebtedness to the owner. This principle remains enshrined in modern financial accounting, and the owner is shown as entitled to both the 'capital' which he has invested in the business, and also the profits which have been made during the year. The accounting and legal relationship between the business and its owner is shown on the balance sheet, which states the firm's assets and liabilities and hence indicates its financial position and well-being.

Example

J. Soap recently inherited £30 000 and decides that the moment is opportune for him to realize his life-time ambition and open a hairdressing salon. Accordingly, he makes all the necessary arrangements to begin on 1 April 19X0, under the name 'J. Soap—Ladies Hairdresser', and commits £10 000 of his money to that business. He therefore opens an account at his bank under the name 'J. Soap—Ladies Hairdresser', or he may simply call it the 'No. 2 account'.

As a result, the financial position of the firm on 1 April 19X0, from an accounting point of view will appear as follows:

J. Soap—Ladies Hairdresser
Balance sheet at 1 April 19X0

Capital	£10 000	Bank balance	£10 000

The business is shown as having £10 000 as its asset at that date, and as owing J. Soap £10 000, that is, recognizing its indebtedness to him in respect of the capital he has invested therein.

The accounting effect of the entity concept is to make a clear distinction between J. Soap's private affairs and his business affairs: what he does with his remaining £20 000 is of no concern to the accountant, but what happens to the £10 000 invested in the business is the subject-matter of accounting.

The interesting aspect of the entity concept is that it establishes a fictional distinction between J. Soap and the business which is not recognized in law: he remains legally liable for the debts of the business, and should the business fail, he will have to pay the creditors out of his private funds.

In the case of corporations, there is a legal distinction between the owners, that is, the shareholders and the business, so that the shareholders are not liable for the corporation's debts beyond the capital which they have agreed to invest. The accounting treatment of the relationship between the shareholders and the corporation is no different from that accorded to the sole trader and his business, except of course that the capital of the corporation is divided into a number of shares.

Example

Multiform Toys plc was registered on 1 April 19X0 as a public limited company, the objective being to manufacture a wide range of children's toys. The promoters need £100 000 to launch the company. They offer for sale 100 000 £1 ordinary shares to the public, and agree themselves to subscribe for 25 000 shares.

If we assume that all the shares have been issued and paid for on 1 May 19X0, the balance sheet will be as follows:

Multiform Toys Ltd
Balance sheet at 1 May 19X0

Share capital	£100 000	Bank balance	£100 000

The promoters are now shareholders, together with those members of the public who have subscribed for the shares. The liability of the company to the shareholders amounts to £100 000, and the company has £100 000 cash to pursue its objectives.

The effect of the entity concept in the case of an incorporated business is to recognize the separate identity of the company from that of its shareholders. The shareholders themselves are not liable for the debts of the company, and their liability is limited to thc £100 000 which they have subscribed. We shall discuss the full implications of incorporation from an accounting point of view in Chapter 13.

The money measurement concept

Both trade and accounting existed before the invention of money, which we know began to circulate in the sixth century BC. Its role as a common denominator, by which the value of assets of different kinds could be compared, encouraged the extension of trade. By Roman times, money had become the language of commerce, and accounts were kept in money terms. Hence, there is an accounting tradition which dates back some 2000 years of keeping the records of valuable assets and of transactions in monetary terms. It is not surprising, therefore, that accounting information today reflects the time-hallowed practice of dealing only with matters capable of expression in money.

The money measurement concept sets an absolute limit to the type of information which may be selected and measured by accountants, and hence limits the type of information which accountants may communicate about a business enterprise.

Example

The Solidex Engineering Co Ltd is a long-established company which specializes in the production of a single component used in the manufacture of mining gear. The balance sheet at 31 December 19X0 reveals the following position:

The Solidex Engineering Co Ltd
Balance sheet at 31 December 19X0

	£		£
Share capital	100 000	Land and buildings	30 000
		Equipment	25 000
		Stocks	30 000
		Bank balance	15 000
	100 000		100 000

For some time, it has been known that a competitor has developed a better product, and that the company is likely to lose its market. The managing director is ill, the production manager and the accountant are not on speaking terms and the labour force is resentful about the deterioration in working conditions in the factory. The buildings are dilapidated, but the land itself is valuable. The equipment is old and needs a great deal of maintenance, and as a result, there is a considerable wastage of labour hours because of machinery breakdowns.

It is clear from the foregoing example that the most significant information of interest to shareholders is not what is contained in the balance sheet but the information which is left out of it, which is much more relevant to an understanding of the firm's position. Yet, the accountant is unable to measure and communicate that information to shareholders directly in money terms, although all these facts may explain poor profit figures. The reader of a financial accounting report should not expect, therefore, that all or perhaps even the most important facts about the business will be disclosed, and this is why there is such a premium on 'inside' information in order to make correct assessments of the firm's true position. One of the major problems of accounting today is to find means of solving the measurement problem: how to extend the quality and the coverage of information in a way which is meaningful. The advantage of money terms is that the layman is able to grasp the meaning of facts which are stated in money, and it remains the obvious standard of measurement.

There are further problems associated with the practice of using money as a standard of measurement in accounting. Money does not have a constant value through time, nor does the value of specific assets remain the same in relation to money. Until recently, accountants turned a blind eye to this problem by assuming that the money standard did have a constant value. The rising rates of inflation in the 1960s and 1970s destroyed this fiction.

Financial accounting records serve two distinct and important purposes. First, they provide evidence of the financial dimensions of rights and obligations resulting from legal contracts. For this purpose these records must be kept in the form of unadjusted money measurements. Second, they are used as a basis for providing financial information for shareholders, investors and a variety of users who need such information for decision making. For this purpose, money measurements must reflect the economic reality of business transactions and for this reason must be adjusted for changes in price levels. In this part we discuss the first purpose of financial accounting records, and in Parts 3 and 4 we discuss the second.

The going-concern concept

The valuation of assets used in a business is based on the assumption that the business is a continuing one, not on the verge of cessation. This concept is important: many assets derive their value from their employment in the firm, and should the firm cease to operate the value which could be obtained for these assets on a closing-down sale would be much less probably than their book value.

Example

The Zimbabwe Gold Mining Company Ltd has been mining gold for many years. Its assets consist of a mineshaft half a mile deep which enables the company to reach the gold reef, small-gauge railway tracks and trucks within the mine, lifting gear, conveyor belts, crushing plant and sundry equipment. The balance sheet at 1 April 19X0 shows the following position:

The Zimbabwe Gold Mining Company Ltd
Balance sheet at 1 April 19X0

	£		£
Share capital	500 000	Mineshaft	500 000
Retained profit	300 000	Land and buildings	25 000
		Plant and equipment	200 000
		Tools	15 000
		Gold in transit	50 000
		Bank balance	10 000
	800 000		800 000

The mineshaft was sunk originally with the money raised by the issue of shares, and the other assets were financed out of loans which were repaid out of profits, which were not distributed to shareholders. In terms of the entity convention the total liability of the company to shareholders is, therefore, £800 000—which is the amount they might expect to receive if the company ceased to operate. For the time being, apart from £60 000 in gold or cash, their interest is substantially the mineshaft and the plant and equipment amounting to £700 000. If the gold reef ceased to be economically workable and the mine had to be abandoned, the mineshaft, being purely a hole in the ground, would become valueless, as would much of the plant. Hence, it is unlikely that shareholders would get back even a fraction of their investment.

The going-concern concept indicates the need to relate the value of assets to future profits which they make possible. This concept opens the way for the method favoured by economists of finding the present value of an asset by reference to the discounted value of future returns which are expected to be derived from the use of that asset.

The cost concept

Accountants determine the value of an asset by reference to the cost of acquisition, and not by reference to value of the returns which are expected to be realized. Hence, the 'value in use' of assets which the going-concern concept maintains is the cost of acquisition. To the accountant, the difference between the value in use and the cost of acquisition of an asset is profit:

value in use – cost of acquisition = profit

Example
W.E. Audent & Son is a firm of chartered accountants with a large audit

practice. Its major asset is the staff of audit clerks. The value in use of the staff may be calculated by reference to the hourly rate at which their services are charged out to clients; the cost of securing their services to the firm is represented by their salaries; and the annual profit of the firm is the difference, less, of course, the administrative expenses of running the firm.

In accounting, cost is used as a measure of the financial 'effort' exerted in gaining access to the resources which will be deployed in earning revenues. Since these resources are secured through financial transactions, the financial effort is measured at the time of acquisition, which coincides, of course, with the legal obligation to pay for those resources in money. The cost concept raises the following problems:

1 The historical cost of acquisition of assets is not a dependable guide to their current value because it fails to reflect:
   (a) changes in the general purchasing power of money.
   (b) changes in the specific value of individual assets in relation to money.
2 The historical cost of acquisition of assets used up in the activity of earning profit does not form a dependable basis for calculating profit.

Example

John Smith is a dealer in hides. He obtains his yearly supplies from Canada in the autumn, and sells them in the United Kingdom during the ensuing 12 months. In October 19X0 he bought 2000 hides at an average cost of $20 Canadian, equivalent to, let us say £10, and by September 19X1 had sold them all at an average price of £20, making a profit of £20 000. Meanwhile, the price of Canadian hides has increased by 50 per cent so that to replace stock he has sold during the year he will now have to pay an average of £15 a hide. Hence, the profit of £20 000 is overstated by £10 000 because the hides sold have been valued at £10 instead of £15 each—which is their current value in Canada.

3 The accounting practice of writing off the cost of certain assets as depreciation against revenue means that it is possible to remove the cost of these assets from the accounts altogether. For a long time, for example, it was the practice of banks to reduce the value of land and buildings to £1 and so create secret reserves.
4 Since incurring a cost depends upon a financial transaction, there are assets which create profits for the firm which can never appear as such in the accounts. Often the major asset of a highly successful firm is the knowledge and the skill created as a result of teamwork and good organization. This asset will not appear in the accounts, since the firm has paid nothing for it, except in terms of salaries which have been written off against yearly profits. Allied to this

problem is the failure to make any mention in the balance sheet of the value of the human assets of the firm. Long ago, the economist Alfred Marshall stated that 'the most valuable of all capital is that invested in human beings' (Marshall, 1964), and it is universally recognized that the firm's human assets are its chief source of wealth. Yet, it is only recently that accountants have begun to recognize this fact, and efforts are now being made to find ways in which information on the value of human assets may be most appropriately presented. Other important assets of which no mention is made in financial accounting statements are, for example, the value to the firm of its hold on the market, which may be a very valuable asset if the firm enjoys a monopoly position, and the value of the firm's own information system, which will affect the quality of its decisions.

Many of the most controversial issues in financial accounting theory and practice revolve around the cost concept. External users of financial statements basically wish to have information of the current worth of the firm on the basis of which they may make investment decisions. Accountants argue that there must be an objective basis to the information which they provide, and to them 'objectivity' means being able to verify information from the results of transactions which create legal rights and obligations. The need to report the legal rights and obligations existing in money terms, and the desire to express the values of the assets and liabilities in real terms under changing money values has been at the heart of the debate about inflation accounting.

The realization concept

The realization concept is also closely related to the cost concept, for as the recorded value of an asset to the firm is determined by the transaction which was necessary to acquire it, so any change in its value may only be recognized at the moment the firm realizes or disposes of that asset. The realization concept reflects totally the historical origin of accounting as a method for recording the results of transactions. To an accountant there is no certainty of profit until a sale has been made: hence, increases in value which have not been realized are not recorded as profit.

The realization concept is strongly criticized by economists. They argue that if an asset has increased in value then it is irrelevant that it has not been sold. For economists, it is sufficient that the gain in value could be realized for that gain to be recognized. The realization concept, it is true, may lead to absurd conclusions.

Example

William James and George Lloyd have bought a pair of dilapidated cottages in Gwynedd for £50 000. They spend £20 000 on restoring the cottages, so that their total cost amounts to £70 000. Both cottages are identical and form part of one unit, that is, they are semidetached. The cottages were bought as part of a speculative venture to make profit out of the popularity of Welsh cottages as holiday homes. A businessman from Manchester offers to buy both cottages for £100 000 each, but the partners decide to sell only one of the cottages and to retain the other for sale at a higher price in the future.

From an accounting point of view, the cottage which is sold is recognized as being worth £100 000, and the difference of £65 000 between the accounting cost and the sale price is the realized profit. The second cottage, which could also have been sold for £100 000 to the same man, is recorded as being worth only £35 000— being the costs associated with acquiring and restoring it.

Unrealized gains in value are widely recognized by non-accountants. Bankers, who are perhaps the most cautious of men, are prepared to lend money on unrealized values: businessmen reckon as gains increases in the value of assets even though they are unsold—yet accountants will not do so unless and until a contract of sale has taken place which creates a legal right to receive the agreed value of the asset sold.

As a result of the realization concept, two classes of gains may be distinguished—'holding gains', which are increases in value resulting from holding an asset; and 'trading or operating gains', which are gains realized as a result of selling assets. 'Holding gains' are not recorded, but 'operating gains' are reported. The realization concept means, in effect, that the reported profit of a business is a part only of the total increases in value which accrue to a firm during an accounting period.

The realization concept does not require the accountant to await the receipt of cash before recording a transaction. Indeed, in many cases the delivery of goods and the receipt of cash occur after the legal agreement which determines the timing of the transaction.

Example

On 1 January 19X0, Midlands Motor Engineers receive an order from one of their accredited dealers for five tractor engines each costing £400. The engines are despatched on 10 January, and on 5 February a cheque for £2000 is received in payment.

From a legal point of view, the acceptance of the order on 1 January marks the timing of the sale, and the creation of the contractual obligation to deliver the engines as well as the contractual right to receive payment. Accounting follows the law in this respect, and it is common practice to write to confirm the receipt of an order and its acceptance, so as to leave no doubt as to the legal and accounting position.

On occasions, however, when a contract is for work which cannot be completed for a long period of time, the contract may stipulate when rights to payment arise. This is particularly the case as regards large civil-engineering contracts, shipbuilding contracts and large Government contracts. In these situations, accounting practices once more follow the law, and the timing of the right to receive cash is determined by the contract.

Example

Westlands Civil Engineering Co Ltd is awarded a Government contract for the building of a fifty-mile section of a motorway. The work is required to be completed in three years. Payments are to be made by the Government on the basis of work completed in each three-monthly period. It is agreed that an independent firm of quantity surveyors will certify the cost of work completed in each period, and that these certificates will form the basis for calculating the period payments to the company on the 'percentage-of-completion' method.

In accordance with this contract, the timing of the realizations will depend upon the issue of the certificates by the quantity surveyors.

The accruals concept

The realization concept asserts that gains in value may not be recognized until the occurrence of a transaction is reinforced by the accruals concept, which applies equally to revenues and expenses.

The accruals concept makes the distinction between the receipt of cash and the right to receive cash, and the payment of cash and the legal obligation to pay cash, because in practice there is usually no coincidence in time between cash movements and the legal obligations to which they relate.

Let us examine first the manner in which the accruals concept applies to revenue. Revenue may be defined as the right to receive cash, and accountants are concerned with recording these rights. Cash receipts may occur as follows:

1   concurrently with the sale;
2   before a right to receive arises;
3   after the right to receive has been created;
4   in error.

The accruals concept provides a guideline as to how to treat these cash receipts and the rights related thereto.

Example

Mrs Smith is an old lady who occupies a flat owned by Mereworth Properties Ltd. The rent is payable monthly in advance on the 1st day of each month, and amounts to £250 a month. She is very forgetful, and rarely does a month pass without some complication in the payment of her rent.

On 1 January she sends her cheque for £250 for the rent due for

January. This rent is due and payable to the company, and must be included as revenue for that month. On 10 January Mrs Smith sends another cheque for £250, thinking that she had not paid her rent for January. This is a cash receipt to which the company is not presently entitled, and it must either be returned to Mrs Smith, or kept on her behalf as a payment in advance of her February rent. The company returns her cheque saying that she has already paid her rent for January, and she receives this letter on 20 January. She forgets to pay her rent on 1 February. The accountant is obliged to include the rent due in February in the revenue for that month, even though it is only ultimately paid on 15 March. Until Mrs Smith has paid her rent for February, she will be a debtor of the company for the rent owing.

Similar rules apply to the treatment of expenses incurred by the firm. Expenses may be defined as legal obligations incurred by the firm to pay in money or money's worth for the benefit of goods or services which it has received. Cash payments may occur as follows:

1 at the time of purchase;
2 before they are due for payment;
3 after due date for payment;
4 in error.

The accruals concept requires the company to treat as expenses only those sums which are due and payable. If a payment is made in advance, it must not be treated as an expense, and the recipient is a debtor until his right to receive the cash matures. Cash paid in error is never an expense, and until it is recovered the person to whom it was paid is also a debtor. Where an expense had been incurred, however, and no payment has been made, the expense must be recorded, and the person to whom the payment should have been made is shown as a creditor.

We will see in Chapter 8 the importance of the accruals concept as regards record-keeping and the presentation of financial accounting statements.

The matching concept

One of the important purposes of financial accounting is to calculate profit resulting from transactions. This means identifying the gains resulting from transactions and setting off against those gains the expenses which are related to those transactions. The realization concept identifies the timing of gains, and the accrual concept enables the accountant properly to record revenues and expenses; neither, however, helps the accountant to calculate profit. The matching concept links revenues with their relevant expenses.

Example
On 1 April Cash and Carry Ltd purchase for resale 2000 tins of beans

at a cost of 5p a tin. The selling price is 8p a tin. During the month of April 1000 tins are sold. What is the profit for the month which is attributable to this line of goods?

We know that the expenses are 2000 × 5p = £100, and that the revenues are 1000 × 8p = £80. On the face of it, therefore, Cash and Carry Ltd have made a loss of £100 less £80, that is, £20. This conclusion is nonsense, because we are setting off against the sale proceeds of 1000 tins the cost of acquiring 2000 tins.

In accordance with the matching concept, the accountant establishes the profit for the month of April by calculating the cost of purchasing 1000 tins of beans and setting this expense against the revenue realized from the sale of these tins:

Sales revenue	1 000 tins @ 8p = £80
Cost of sales	1 000 tins @ 5p = £50
Profit	£30

The 1000 tins remaining unsold remain in the accounting records as assets, and when they are eventually sold the profit from sales will be calculated by deducting the cost of acquisition from the sales revenue realized.

The matching of revenues and expenses is sometimes a most difficult problem in accounting, because many types of expense are not easily identifiable with revenues.

Example

Bloxwich Pharmaceutical Co Ltd manufactures and sells pharmaceutical products. Its major activity is the manufacture of antibiotics, which accounts for 80 per cent of its sales revenue. The remaining 20 per cent of its sales is derived from beauty creams. Its expenses for the year 19X0 are as follows:

Manufacturing costs of antibiotics	£500 000
Manufacturing costs of beauty creams	20 000
Administrative costs	100 000
Selling and financial costs	50 000
Research and development costs	150 000
Total expenses for the year	£820 000

In the same year, the total revenue from sales of both antibiotics and beauty creams amounts to £1 000 000. Calculate the profit on the antibiotics side of the business.

We can begin to answer this problem as follows:

Sales revenue from antibiotics (80% of total)	£800 000
Manufacturing costs of antibiotics	500 000
	300 000
Other expenses	?
Profit on antibiotics	?

Clearly, we need more information in order to allocate the administrative, selling and financial costs between antibiotics and beauty creams. It is unlikely that an exact allocation could be made, and in the end, an estimate would be made.

The research and development costs of new antibiotics and beauty creams are a more difficult problem. Strictly speaking, we should not set these costs against the revenues of the year, since the benefit will not occur in this year. Much of it, however, may not lead to new products. Therefore, if we ignore this expenditure, the company's reported profit will be inflated and unrealistic.

From the foregoing example, it is seen that the exact matching of revenues and expenses is often impossible. Nevertheless, the computation of periodic profit requires that expenses be allocated, where necessary, in order that the financial results may be stated in a consistent manner.

The concept of periodicity

The custom of making periodic reports to the owner of a business dates from the time when wealthy men employed servants to manage and oversee their affairs. Periodic accounting has its origin in the idea of control, and company law sees the role of financial reports as being essentially the communication of information from the managers of the business, that is the directors, to the owners of the business, that is the shareholders. However much we may disagree with this view of the relationship of directors and shareholders as being unrealistic, we must accept that there is an element of shareholder control over directors which stems from the legal duty laid on the latter to issue reports on their stewardship of the firm's assets.

The concept of periodicity is now established by law as regards certain types of reports such as balance sheets and profit and loss accounts. The Companies Act requires yearly reports to shareholders, and the Income Tax Acts require accounts for all businesses to be submitted annually. However, there is nothing to prevent companies from providing information at more frequent intervals to investors, if they so wish.

Annual reports have grown out of custom, and many would question the wisdom of selecting an arbitrary period of twelve months as a basis for reporting upon the activities of a business. The idea of annual reports is deeply entrenched, and even the government runs its business on a yearly basis and budgets for one year, although many of its activities are continuing ones which cannot be seen correctly in the perspective of twelve months. This is also true for all large companies, and many smaller businesses.

Example

Universal Chemicals Ltd manufactures a wide range of chemical products and has factories throughout the country. Owing to unusually difficult labour relations, rising raw material costs and stiffening competition, its reported profit for the year ended 31 December 19X0 has decreased by 10 per cent over the previous year. Its borrowings, however, have increased by 20 per cent owing to an enlarged capital investment programme which is designed to add substantially to profit in about five years' time.

Clearly, in this case the reader of the report for the year 19X0 should consider the report in context, and look to the long-term trend of profits and to the better financial position which is expected in the future.

The concept of periodicity as expressed in yearly accounting fails to make the important distinction between the long-term trend and the short-term position. Hence, it limits the usefulness of the information communicated to shareholders and investors.

The matching and periodicity concepts seek to relate the transactions of one particular year with the expenses attributable to those transactions. From a practical point of view, accountants carry forward expenses until they can be identified with the revenues of a particular year, and carry forward receipts until they can be regarded as the revenue of a particular year in accordance with the realization convention. Since all assets are 'costs' in accounting, the convention of periodicity creates difficulties with regard to the allocation of fixed assets as expenses of particular years. We examine this matter when we discuss depreciation in Chapter 10.

So far we have mentioned the effect of the concept of periodicity on the usefulness of information communicated to external users, and we now comment on its effect on profit measurement. The majority of economists treat accounting profit as the 'income' of a business, and hence as a measure of the income which investors and shareholders derive from their investment in the firm. As a result, they impose the economic criteria appropriate to the measurement of economic income to accounting profit and disapprove of the shortcomings of accounting profit which they see as stemming from accounting concepts for calculating periodic income. Ideally, an accurate measurement of the profit or loss of a business can be made only after the business has ceased operating, sold off all its assets and paid off all its liabilities. The net profit accruing to investors would then be the difference between the sum total of all their receipts, either as dividends or capital repayments, and their initial investment. It is clear, however, that accounting profit is merely the result of completed transactions during a stated period: the concept of periodicity is a statement of this view.

The concept of consistency

The usefulness of financial information lies to a considerable extent in the conclusions which may be drawn from the comparison of the financial statements of one year with those of a preceding year, and the financial reports of one company with those of another company. It is in this way that we may deduce some of the most important information for decision-making, such as an indication that there has been an improvement in profit since last year and that therefore it is worth buying more shares, or the profit of Company A is better than that of Company B and given current share prices one should switch from holding shares in Company B and buy those of Company A.

The comparability of financial statements depends largely upon the choice of accounting methods and the consistency with which they are applied. A change in the basis on which a firm values stocks, for example, may result in a profit figure different from that which would have been computed had the accountant adhered to a consistent basis of valuation. If firms wish to change their method for treating a particular problem, such as the valuation of stocks or the value attached to a particular asset, they may do so, but they should mention the effect on the profit of the change in accounting methods.

Comparing the accounts of different companies is much more difficult, and unfortunately the accounting methods of individual firms are not always the same. There is no uniformity of accounting methods which would provide the consistency of treatment of information necessary for the comparison of the accounts of different companies. Whereas the accounting concept of consistency is generally followed by individual firms, there is no agreement at all that different firms should use the same accounting methods. Hence, the needs of investors for greater comparability of information between companies is frustrated by accounting concepts which insist on consistency, but allow different methods of measurement and treatment which cannot yield comparable results. The Accounting Standards Committee is charged with the task of trying to secure agreement on appropriate accounting methods which will ensure a higher degree of comparability of accounting information, and in this part we examine some of its achievements so far. It is clear that European integration will hasten progress towards uniformity in accounting standards.

The concept of prudence

Prudence reflects the accountant's view of his social role and his responsibilities towards those for whom he provides information. It is seen at work in some of the concepts which we have examined in this chapter, for example, the realization concept which requires the realization of a gain before it may be recognized, and the cost convention which holds that the value of an asset is the cost of acquisition.

There are two principal rules which stem directly from the concept of prudence:

1 the accountant should not anticipate profit and should provide for all possible losses;

2 faced with two or more methods of valuing an asset, the accountant should choose that which leads to the lesser value.

These two rules contravene some accounting concepts, for example, the cost concept, for if the market value of trading stocks has fallen below the cost of acquisition it must be valued at the market value. Equally, the logic which underlies the realization concept as regards gains, that there is no certainty of a gain until there is a sale, does not extend to the treatment of anticipated losses. Thus, accountants provide for losses in value which are sufficiently foreseeable to make them a present reality, on the basis that to ignore such losses might mislead the user of accounting information. One of the clearest explanations of the policy of prudence was made by G.O. May as long ago as 1946, as follows:

'. . . the great majority of ventures fail, and the fact that enterprises nevertheless continue is attributable to the incurable optimism (often dissociated from experience) as well as to the courage of mankind. In my experience, also, losses from unsound accounting have most commonly resulted from the hopes rather than the achievements of management being allowed to influence accounting dispositions. To me, conservatism is still the first virtue of accounting, and I am wholly unable to agree with those who would bar it from the books of accounts and statements prepared therefrom and would relegate it to footnotes.' (May, 1946).

The caution of the accountant may well be a foil for the optimism of businessmen but, although it may be desirable for the accountant to be prudent in the estimates which he makes, the selection of accounting methods for recording and presenting information on the basis that they deliberately understate assets of earning should not be an overriding principle. Investors and shareholders need reliable and useful information: to understate is as bad as to overstate—investment in a business may be discouraged if it appears to be less valuable than it really is. Users of accounting information, as all others who are faced with making decisions, look for guidance to the lowest value, the highest value and the probable value. In restricting accounting information to the statement of the lowest value, the accountant is not fulfilling the social role expected of him as a supplier of comprehensive financial information.

Summary

Accounting concepts serve as guideposts, but tend to emphasize the reliability of information rather than its usefulness. The conflict between reliability and usefulness is controversial. At one extreme, some accountants contend that if a measurement is useful, further justification is unnecessary. At the other extreme, others hold that the reliability of accounting information is the most important criterion, and will ultimately determine the extent to which external users accept accounting statements for making investment decisions. The role of a conceptual framework for financial accounting is to validate external accounting practices in terms of their perceived objectives rather than traditional accounting concepts. These developments are examined in Part 4.

References

Marshall, Alfred (1964). *Principles of Economics*, 8th edn, Macmillan (London).

May, G.O. (1946). *Financial Accounting: A Distillation of Experience*, Macmillan (New York).

Question

Examine the role of so-called concepts in the analysis of accounting transactions and the preparation of financial statements.

Problems

1 Consultat Inc. is a firm of consulting engineers, newly established to advise on a large project taking three years to complete. Their fee for this work is a percentage of the total project costs, payable on completion of the project. In the interim, advances on the final fee are made at six-monthly intervals. The total project costs will not be known until the project is completed. The following advances were received by Consultat Inc. during the three-year period:

year ended 31 December 19X0   £25 000
year ended 31 December 19X1   £30 000
year ended 31 December 19X2   £30 000

When the total costs were computed during the year ended 31 December 19X3, it was found that a further sum of £50 000 was due to Consultat Inc.

Required:
(a) Explain how you would show the payments made to Consultat Inc. during the periods covered by the project. Justify your explanation in terms of the concepts of accounting which you consider apply to this situation.
(b) Would you change your reasoning at all in the light of the following information?

   (i) the advance payments are not contractual but discretionary on the part of the paying company;
   (ii) a clause in the consulting agreement requires Consultat Inc. to undertake— free of charge—extra work to remedy defects appearing within three years of the completion of the project.

Suggest how you would treat these problems by reference to accounting concepts.

2 Bloxwich Engineers Ltd borrows £100 000 at a fixed interest rate of 10 per cent for a period of five years for the purpose of acquiring a stamping press of advanced design. Suggest how you would treat the accounting aspects of the transactions associated with the acquisition and the financing of the stamping press in the following circumstances:

(a) by the end of the third year of use, the stamping press has been depreciated to £70 000, but due to a new design having appeared, its market value is only £30 000. The stamping press, nevertheless, continues to generate the same level of revenue as it did in the first year of use;
(b) during the fourth year, the stamping mill generates only £8000 of revenues, and the Managing Director of Bloxwich Engineers Ltd has written an instruction to the effect that 'since the mill is now making a loss of £2000 when interest is taken into account', it should be sold forthwith. The market value has now fallen to £15 000. The monies realized are to be applied to the acquisition of further plant, and the interest charge remains to be paid during the following and final year of the loan.

Support your discussion of the accounting problems you have identified by reference to the conventions which justify your reasoning.

3   Lewis, Jones and Peers, newly qualified as architects, decide to form a partnership on 1 January 19X0. During their first year of business, a substantial operating loss is realized, amounting to £20 000. They had anticipated such a loss and had provided sufficient funds to cover it when they first formed the partnership. 'After all', said Peers, 'it is well known that the first year of practice for architects always produces a loss, since they are really establishing the business. They do, in fact, earn little money as they build up contacts which will earn future revenues'. 'That's right,' continued Lewis, as he was explaining to the accountant, who has prepared the profit and loss account showing the loss of £20 000, 'you can't show the £20 000 as a loss, when it is the cost of setting up the business. To be consistent with the facts, you have to show the £20 000 as an asset on the balance sheet'. 'Yes, I agree,' concluded Jones, 'that is the most conservative way of looking at the situation. Then, we recognize the creation of an asset we can write off over several years and match against the future revenues which are really the result of this year's efforts.'

How would you deal with the arguments of your clients, if you were the accountant in this situation? Refer the problems you see to such accounting concepts as are applicable to them, and in particular, explain how you would deal with the terms 'consistent' and 'prudence' used by the partners in their discussion with you.

Chapter 5

Financial accounting standards

The financial accounting concepts discussed in Chapter 4 were seen as core elements in the development of a descriptive theory of financial accounting. The review of the concepts of financial accounting which was conducted by the accounting profession in the 1970s, and which has resulted in the publication of a series of Statements of Standard Accounting Practice, is part of the ongoing process of developing accounting practice by seeking consensus among practitioners.

The concepts allow a variety of alternative practices to coexist. As a result, the financial results of different companies cannot be compared and evaluated unless full information is available about the accounting methods which have been used. Not only have the variety of accounting practices permitted by the conventions of financial accounting made it difficult to compare the financial results of different companies, but the application of alternative accounting methods to the preparation of the financial reports of the same company have enabled entirely different results to be reported to shareholders.

The need for the imposition of standards arose because of the lack of uniformity existing as to the manner in which periodic profit was measured and the financial position of the enterprise represented. The purpose of this chapter is to examine the significance of the development of accounting standards for a descriptive theory of financial accounting based on concepts and consensus.

The importance of comparability

The information contained in published financial statements is especially important to external users, such as shareholders and investors, for without such information they would have to take decisions about their investments under a considerable degree of uncertainty. A major problem is that there are no formal channels for communicating to companies the type and nature of the financial information which external users believe they require, and the manner in which such information ought to be presented. Traditionally, Parliament has assumed the responsibility for legislation specifying the type and the minimum level of information which companies should disclose, and the accounting profession has assumed the responsibility for ensuring the proper presentation of such information. In this respect, it is evident that the concepts applied to the presentation of financial information should not permit too much discretion, and that the manner in which financial information is treated in financial statements should conform to carefully considered standards.

The function of accounting standards may best be examined by reference to the basic purpose of financial statements, which may be stated as being concerned with the communication of information affecting the allocation of resources. Ideally, such information should make it possible for investors to evaluate the investment opportunities offered by different firms and to allocate scarce resources to the most efficient. In theory, this process should result in the optimal distribution of resources within the economy, and should maximize their potential benefit to society.

In this analysis of the purpose of financial statements, it is apparent that one of the most important criteria for the presentation of financial information is that which ensures an appropriate standard of comparison betwen different firms. The accounting methods used by different firms for presenting information should allow appropriate comparisons to be made. For example, they should not enable a company to report profits which result simply from a change in accounting methods, rather than from increased efficiency. If companies were free to choose their accounting methods in this way, the consequence might well be that deliberate distortions would be introduced in the pricing of shares on the Stock Exchange, leading eventually to a misallocation of resources in the economy. This would occur because relatively less efficient companies would be able to report fictitious profits, and as a result divert capital to themselves on more favourable terms than those available to the more efficient companies which have adopted rigorous accounting methods.

| **Reasons for concern about standards** | In the United Kingdom, the Institute of Chartered Accountants in England and Wales began to make recommendations about accounting practices as early as 1942. Ultimately, a series of twenty-nine recommendations on accounting practices were issued with the objective of codifying the best practices which ought to be used in particular circumstances. However, there were several disadvantages to this procedure: |

1   The recommendations were not mandatory, and were issued for the guidance of members of the Institute.
2   The recommendations did not result from fundamental research into the objectives of accounting, but merely codified existing practices.
3   The recommendations did not reduce the diversity of accounting methods. For example, Recommendation No. 22, 1960, which was concerned with stock valuation, advocated five different methods of computing the cost of stock. Furthermore, four of these methods could be computed differently for partly and fully finished stocks.

To complicate matters further, Recommendation 22 stated that cost could be defined in three different ways!

In the late 1960s, there was a spate of public criticism of financial reporting methods, which arose from the publicity accorded to aspects of the financial statements of a number of companies. These included Pergamon Press, General Electric Company and Vehicle and General Company. The manner in which these cases jolted the accounting profession may be judged from the example of the General Electric Company.

In 1967, the General Electric Company (GEC) made a takeover bid for Associated Electric Industries (AEI). AEI produced a profit forecast for that year of £10 million, which was based on ten months' actual profit and two months' budgeted profit. The GEC takeover bid was successful, and afterwards GEC reported that, in fact, AEI had made a loss of £4.5 million for that year. According to GEC auditors, £9.5 million of the £14.5 million difference between the two calculations of profit for 1967 was due to difference in judgement about such matters as the amounts written off stock and the provision for estimated losses.

The angry reaction of the press to the disclosure of the amended figures for 1967 centred on the fact that two accounting firms could justifiably produce such widely differing results for the same year. One observer commented that it appeared that accounting was really an art form, and that it seemed that two firms of accountants looking at the same figures were capable of producing profit figures as far apart as a Rubens is from a Rembrandt.

Standard setting boards

The response of the accounting profession to this criticism was to establish the Accounting Standards Committee. This was replaced in 1990 by the Accounting Standards Board.

The prime objective of the Accounting Standards Committee has been to narrow the areas of difference and variety in accounting practice. The procedure used for this purpose is initiated by the issue of an 'Exposure Draft' on a specific topic for discussion by accountants and the public at large. Comments made on the Exposure Draft are taken into consideration when drawing up a formal statement of the accounting method to be applied when dealing with that specific topic. This formal statement is known as a Statement of Standard Accounting Practice (SSAP). Once the Statement of Standard Accounting Practice has been adopted by the accounting profession, any material departure from the standard used in presenting a financial report is to be disclosed in that report.

To date, the following Statements of Standard Accounting Practice have been issued:

Statements of Standard Accounting Practice Issued
SSAP 1   'Accounting for the Results of Associated Companies'
SSAP 2   'Disclosure of Accounting Policies'

SSAP 3   'Earnings per Share'
SSAP 4   'The Accounting Treatment of Government Grants'
SSAP 5   'Accounting for Value Added Tax'
SSAP 6   'Extraordinary Items and Prior Year Adjustments'
SSAP 8   'The treatment of Taxation Under the Imputation System in the Accounts of Companies'
SSAP 9   'Stocks and Long-Term Contracts'
SSAP 10 'Statements of Source and Application of Funds'
SSAP 12 'Accounting for Depreciation'
SSAP 13 'Accounting for Research and Development'
SSAP 14 'Group Accounts'
SSAP 15 'Accounting for Deferred Taxation'
SSAP 16 'Current Cost Accounting' (*abandoned in 1988*)
SSAP 17 'Accounting for Post Balance Sheet Events'
SSAP 18 'Accounting for Contingencies'
SSAP 19 'Accounting for Investment Properties'
SSAP 20 'Foreign Currency Translation'
SSAP 21 'Accounting for Leases and Hire-purchase Contracts'
SSAP 22 'Accounting for Goodwill'
SSAP 23 'Accounting for Acquisitions and Mergers'
SSAP 24 'Accounting for Pension Costs'
SSAP 25 'Segmental Reporting'

The list of topics on which Statements of Standard Accounting Practice have been issued shows that the work of the Accounting Standards Committee has profoundly affected the development of accounting theory and methods. The discussion of individual Statements of Standard Accounting Practice will be referred to in later chapters, where the topics covered by these documents themselves are analysed.

The earlier discussion in this chapter of the relationship between accounting concepts and accounting methods implies matters of accounting policy. For this reason SSAP2, which deals with the disclosure of accounting policies, is highly significant to the central issues to which this chapter is directed and its provisions are examined in detail in the following section.

SSAP2 'Disclosure of Accounting Policies'

SSAP2 is addressed to the relationship between accounting concepts, accounting methods and accounting policies. The relationship is illustrated in Fig. 2.3, where it is seen that accounting concepts provide the foundations to both accounting methods and policies. These are defined by SSAP2 as follows:

- *Fundamental accounting concepts* are broad general assumptions which underlie the periodic financial accounts of business enterprises.
- *Accounting bases* are the methods which have been developed for expressing or applying fundamental accounting concepts to financial transactions and items. By their nature, accounting bases are more

Fig. 2.3

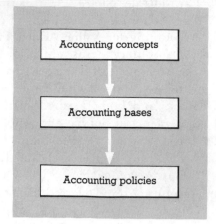

diverse and numerous than fundamental concepts, since they have evolved in response to the variety and complexity of types of business and business transactions and, for this reason, there may justifiably exist more than one recognized accounting basis for dealing with particular items.

- *Accounting policies* are the specific accounting bases judged by business enterprises to be most appropriate to their circumstances and adopted by them for the purpose of preparing their financial accounts.

SSAP2 states that there are four fundamental accounting concepts which should be regarded as established standard concepts. They are as follows:

- *The going-concern concept*, which implies that the enterprise will continue in operational existence for the foreseeable future. This means, in particular, that the profit and loss account and balance sheet assume no intention or necessity to liquidate or reduce significantly the scale of operation.
- *The accruals concept*, which requires that revenue and costs are accrued, matched with one another so far as their relationship can be established or justifiably assumed, and dealt with in the profit and loss account of the period to which they relate, provided, generally, that where the accruals concept is consistent with the prudence concept (see below), the latter prevails. The accruals concept implies that the profit and loss account reflects changes in the amount of net assets that arise out of the transactions of the relevant period, other than distributions or subscriptions of capital. Revenue and profits dealt with in the profit and loss account are matched with associated costs by including in the same account the costs incurred in earning them, so far as these are material and identifiable.
- *The consistency concept*, which requires that there should be consistency of accounting treatment of like items within each accounting period and from one period to the next.
- *The concept of prudence*, which requires that revenue and profits are not anticipated, but recognized by inclusion in the profit and loss

account only when realized in the form either of cash or of assets (usually legally enforceable debts), the ultimate cash realization of which can be assessed with reasonable certainty; provision be made for all known liabilities (expenses and losses) whether the amount of these is known with certainty or is a best estimate in the light of the information available.

SSAP2 is concerned with ensuring that accounting bases are disclosed in financial reports, whenever significant items are shown which have their significance in value judgements, estimated outcome of future events or uncompleted transactions, rather than ascertained amounts. In the words of SSAP2,

'In circumstances where more than one accounting basis is acceptable in principle, the accounting policy followed can significantly affect a company's reported results and financial position, and the view presented can be properly appreciated only if the principal policies followed are also described. For this reason, adequate disclosure of the accounting policies should be regarded as essential to the fair presentation of financial accounts.'

Standards and the Companies Act

In Chapter 12 we examine the legal requirements which apply to the financial reporting procedures of companies and the manner in which financial accounting information must be disclosed in the profit and loss accounts and balance sheets. Two aspects of these requirements are directly related to the accounting concepts and standards considered in this chapter.

First, the four fundamental accounting concepts of SSAP2 have become enshrined in law by the Companies Act 1981. Final accounts prepared within the terms of this act must follow these concepts. Second, since 1948 all final accounts prepared for the purpose of compliance with the Companies Acts have been required to give a 'true and fair view', an obligation described as 'overriding'. This means that if the final accounts are to contain the information which is sufficient in quantity and quality to satisfy the reasonable expectations of users then they should be prepared in accordance with the concepts and standards formulated by the accountancy profession.

Summary

The concepts of financial accounting and the Statements of Standard Accounting Practice issued by the Accounting Standards Committee represent a theory of accounting which has evolved by descriptions of the practices of accountants.

The concepts of accounting have resulted in the evolution of a variety of practices. Consequently, the lack of uniformity has made it difficult for users of financial reports to compare the results of different companies. The need for comparability has been judged to be one of the most important criteria for the presentation of financial reports. The reasons for concern about the quality of accounting information based on concepts were discussed, and were seen to relate to the different results which could be drawn from the same set of data.

The purpose of this chapter was to examine the work of the Accounting

Standards Committee, and its importance. While this work has been very carefully undertaken, and has resulted in the reduction of variety of accounting practices, the final judgement may be seen to rest in the absence of a financial reporting theory which reflects clearly established objectives of accounting.

Questions

1   Discuss the purpose underlying the issue of UK accounting standards.
2   Identify the four 'fundamental accounting concepts' mentioned in SSAP2 and compare them with the corresponding concepts discussed in Chapter 4.
3   Explain the meaning of an 'accounting base'. State why accounting bases are more diverse than fundamental concepts.

Chapter 6

The generation of financial accounting data

In a previous chapter, we examined the nature and the boundaries of the financial accounting system. We noted that the concepts of financial accounting constituted one of the boundaries in so far as they act as a filtering process for the data which is fed into the financial accounting system. We concluded that these concepts played a crucial role in determining the nature of financial accounting information.

This chapter examines the processes involved in the generation of financial accounting data prior to its transformation into accounting information.

An outline of the information generation process

The output of financial accounting information is the result of a process involving the following stages:

1   the preparation of source documents;
2   the entry of basic data into source records;
3   the posting of data from the source records into the ledger, which is a permanent record of data.

The production of financial accounting information in the form of reports is illustrated in Fig. 2.4.

Although the principles underlying the financial accounting system remain unchanged, its processes have and are continually undergoing modification and improvement. In particular, technological change has dramatically affected these processes. The advent of the computer has considerably speeded up and streamlined the data recording process, and indeed, as we shall see, has permitted the integration of several stages of this process into a single operation.

In this chapter we are concerned with an analysis of the traditional data recording practices relating to source documents and source books, and examine the impact of the computer on these practices. We will examine the process of preparing financial reports in subsequent chapters.

Source documents

As we explained in Chapter 4, financial accounting data originates in transactions. Source documents capture the details of these accounting events. They also have a very important functional purpose as regards the activities of an enterprise.

Fig. 2.4

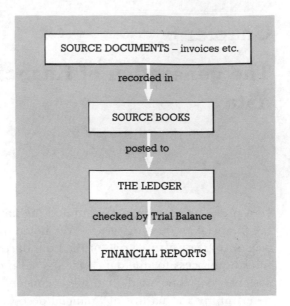

Data flows are generated by a business and classified according to their sources.

1 Financial accounting data flows are generated from activities conducted between the firm and external groups such as customers and suppliers of materials, goods, services and finance.
2 Data flows generated internally constitute a substantial volume of the total information flows.

These flows are generated and channelled through a Management Information System (MIS) the function of which is to meet the needs of management for the purposes of planning and control. Since the firm is an open system, it is clear that the initial impetus for any activity stems from some agent in the firm's environment. The relationship between external and internal data flows and the documentation involved in facilitating these flows are illustrated in Fig. 2.5. This shows the focal role played by accounting data in relation to the firm's basic operations as well as the nature of the source documents involved in the generation of financial accounting data.

Source documents related to sales

The function of the sales department is to encourage the sales of the firm's products. Once a salesman has concluded a sale with a customer, he completes a sales order form. The original is sent to the customer as an acknowledgement of the order, and in the case of a credit sale, one copy of the sales order form goes to the credit control department for approval. If the goods are in stock, the credit control department will pass the authenticated sales order form to the stock control department so that the release and despatch of the goods may be effected. An advice note is sent to the customer when the goods are despatched

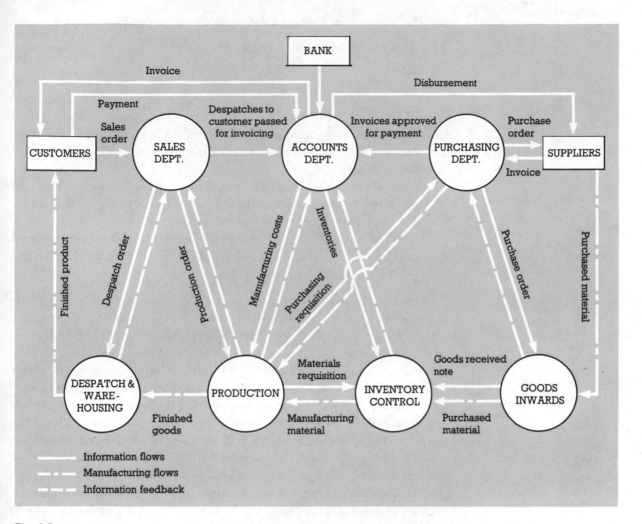

Fig. 2.5

advising the date of despatch and mode of delivery. The goods are normally accompanied by a delivery note stating the description of the goods and the quantity involved though not the price. The customer acknowledges receipt of the goods by signing the delivery note.

When the goods have been released by the stock control department for despatch, a further copy of the sales order stating the date of despatch is sent to the sales invoice section of the accounts department, so that the sales invoice may be prepared. The sales invoice states the nature, quantity and price of the goods ordered and the amount due to the firm by the customer. Customers are normally required to pay within one or more months, depending on the agreed credit terms. Often, however, customers are required to pay on receipt of the invoice, though some firms issue statements each month showing the number of invoices sent to the customer during the month and the total sum due in respect of the month's orders.

The copy sales invoice is the source document which provides the data which will be recorded in the financial accounting system.

The sales order form is used, therefore, for the following purposes:

1 As a record and confirmation of a sale. One copy of the sales order form will be kept by the sales department.
2 As a means of initiating a procedure for checking the credit-worthiness of a customer prior to proceeding with the completion of the order.
3 As a document authorizing the release of the goods from stock. One copy of the sales order will be retained by the stock control department.
4 As a means of checking and despatching the right goods to the right customer by the despatch department. One copy of the sales order is kept by this department for this purpose.
5 As a means of preparing the sales invoice which will state the amount due from the customer. One copy of the sales order will be retained by the accounts department.

Where goods are not kept in stock but are manufactured to order, the receipt of an order puts the production process in motion. We examine the cost accounting process in Part 5, but for the purposes of this chapter, we may note that a copy of the production order will be sent to the production manager and one copy to the accounts department, which is responsible for collecting all the costs associated with the manufacture of the goods ordered. Figure 2.5 shows that the materials required may be obtained either from existing stocks or by purchase. Where the required materials are held in stock, the issue of a materials requisition form to the stock control department will procure the release of these materials. One copy of the materials requisition form will be retained by the stock control department and one copy will be sent to the accounts department for costing purposes. Where the required materials have to be purchased, the production department issues a purchase requisition form to the purchasing department.

Source documents related to purchases

The purchasing department obtains the raw materials, equipment and supplies needed by the firm. Each request is made on a requisition form stating the nature and the quantity required, which is signed by an authorised person. The purchasing department selects a suitable supplier and sends him a purchase order form setting out the description, quantity and required delivery date of the goods, together with instructions as regards dispatch and invoicing. The purchase order will refer to the quoted price of the goods according to the supplier's catalogue or other statements of the supply price, although quoted prices in advertisements are not binding on suppliers. In effect, the purchase order form is an offer to purchase and when accepted by the supplier constitutes a legal contract between buyer and seller. Copies of the purchase order are distributed to the several departments concerned, namely the receiving department which needs to know the details and the date of receipt of the goods, the stock control department to advise of the pending arrival of goods and to serve as a check on the receiving department, the accounts department for checking that the price quoted compares with the price list, and the ordering department, to confirm that the order has been placed.

Source documents related to the receipt of goods

Upon delivery of the goods, the receiving department verifies that the goods delivered compare in every detail to the copy purchase order. When they agree, a goods received note is prepared which details the description of the goods received, their quantity, quality and condition. A copy of the goods received note is sent to the department concerned with the audit of the receipt of goods, which is usually the purchasing department. A copy is also sent to the accounts department and the department responsible for the order. The stock control department is notified also because it is responsible for the storage, distribution and control of stocks. The stock control department maintains records of stocks, and ensures that adequate stock levels are maintained.

In due course, the supplier sends an invoice stating the description, quantity and price of the goods ordered, the date of acceptance of the order, which is usually shown as the date of dispatch of the goods, and the amount now owing. The invoice is checked by the accounts department against the goods received note, and if there are no queries then the invoice is cleared for payment in due course. Normally, invoices are paid monthly. This permits the workflow in the accounting department to be efficiently organized and allows the payment procedure to be properly supervised.

The entry of basic data in the source books

The accounting record of the events described in the source documents begins with the issue or receipt of invoices. Although legal obligations are created with the acceptance of an order, either by the firm or its suppliers, for practical reasons, these obligations are not recorded until they are formally stated. Should there be any dispute, however, about the existence of an order, the appropriate source document provides evidence of that order.

The practice of keeping daily records of accounting events in a diary or roughbook dates from the early history of accounting. The practice of keeping a daily journal was recommended by Paciolo in 1494 for the purpose of enabling the businessman to check daily the records kept by his clerk. Once agreed, they could be entered into the ledger. It became a golden rule in accounting that no entry should appear in the ledger which has not first been entered in the journal.

At first, the journal was used to record all commercial transactions. They were entered chronologically and showed the details of these transactions as well as the ledger account to which the entry was ultimately posted, as shown in the table below.

Date	Journal description	Folio	Dr. £	Cr. £
5 Jan.	Goods Dr. 　　To A. Smith Being 100 shirts bought for resale	L5 L7	100	100
5 Jan.	B. Jones Dr. 　　To Cash Being wages due to the week ending 5th January	L10	5	5

The data entered in the journal consisted of:

1   the date of the transaction;
2   the name of the purchaser or the asset purchased;
3   the name of the seller or the asset sold;
4   the sum involved;
5   a short narrative describing the transaction.

Periodically, the entries in the journal were transferred to the main record, described as the ledger, by a procedure known as posting. The folio references in the journal indicated the pages in the ledger to which the postings were made.

As trade expanded and the number of transactions increased, it became the practice to group the entries to be made in the journal into the following classes:

1   purchases of trading goods on credit;
2   sales of trading goods on credit;
3   cash receipts and payments;
4   all other transactions.

This classification enabled entries of like nature to be kept together, and facilitated the operation of entering data into the source books. It led to the division of the journal into four parts, which were renamed as follows:

1   the purchases day book, in which were entered credit purchases;
2   the sales day book, in which were recorded credit sales;
3   the cash book, in which were recorded all cash transactions;
4   the journal proper, in which were recorded transactions which could not be recorded in the other source books. The journal proper has been retained as a book of original entry for such transactions.

The day books

Since the bulk of source documents relate to the purchase or sale of goods, the function of the purchases and sales day books is to allow such data to be collected and posted to the ledger. An example of a purchases day book is given below:

Purchases day book

Date	Name	Invoice No.	Folio	£
1 June	S. Smith	101	L15	50
2	W. Wright and Co.	113	L20	35
2	J. James	148	L10	140
3	T. Tennant	184	L16	20
3	Transferred to purchases account		L50	245

The posting of the purchases day book to the ledger is effected by crediting the account of each supplier with the value of the goods supplied and transferring the total value of all purchases in the period to the purchases account. The details entered in the day books are obtained from the invoices, which are filed and kept for at least six years when they may be destroyed.

The sales day book is written up in the same manner as the purchases day book, except that the source document is a copy of the invoice sent to the customer.

The cash book

Only cash transactions are entered in the cash book, the purpose of which is to record all receipts and payments of cash. As we will see, the cash book has a dual role, being a journal and a ledger account.

As the practice grew of using cheques for the settlement of business debts, so the cash book came to reflect this practice, and to record all payments out of and into the firm's bank account.

Unlike the day books, the cash book records receipts and payments side by side, so that flows in and out are seen together and their impact on the balance may be readily seen. At the end of the accounting period, the cash book is reconciled with the bank statement by means of a bank reconciliation statement which explains any difference between the balance recorded in the cash book and that recorded by the bank. This difference is due to the time lag between the posting of a cheque to a creditor and its clearing through the bank, delays in clearing cheques paid in, bank charges and direct payments into and out of the banks.

Where transactions take place in cash as well as by cheques, and cash discounts are given and allowed, the cash book is given extra columns, and becomes known as a 'three-column cash book'. The transfer of cash in and out of the bank account is recorded as well as the receipts and payments by cheques, as follows:

Cash book

Date	Details	Folio	Discounts all'd £	Cash £	Bank £	Date	Details	Folio	Discounts rec'd £	Cash £	Bank £
1 Jan.	Balance	J1		50	800	1 Jan.	B. Brown	L3	7		103
1	Sales	L15		60		1	Purchases	L14		20	
1	W. White	L9	5		95	1	Cash				20
1	Bank			20							

The explanation of some of these entries is as follows:

1 Jan. B. Brown—this represents the payment of an account owing to Brown amounting to £110 which was settled by the payment of £103, the balance being in the form of a discount which was received.

1 Jan. W. White—this represents the receipt of a cheque for £95 in settlement of an amount owing of £100, a discount of £5 being allowed.

1 Jan. Bank—this represents a cash cheque drawn on the bank for £20. The corresponding payment of cash by the bank is shown on the other side of the cash book.

For security reasons, few firms like to keep large sums in cash about their premises and cash takings are banked daily. Moreover, it is sound practice to use cheques for the settlement of debts, so that there is generally no need to keep cash on hand beyond relatively small sums. All firms, therefore, tend to have a petty cash box to meet any immediate need for cash, for example, enabling a secretary or porter to take a taxi to deliver a document, or to buy a small article which is urgently required.

The cashier is usually entrusted with the petty cash box and any payments must be claimed by means of a petty cash voucher signed by an authorized person, who is usually a head of department. The cashier is given a petty cash float which may be, say, £50 and pays out petty cash only against petty cash vouchers, which he retains. As the petty cash float decreases, so petty cash vouchers of an equivalent value accumulate in the petty cashbox. In due course, the vouchers are checked or audited and the petty cash paid out is refunded to the cashier, thereby restoring the petty cash float to its original sum.

Division of the ledger

A firm large enough to divide its journal into day books and cash books will probably also need to divide its ledger. The sales ledger (or debtors ledger) contains all the personal accounts of the firm's customers. The purchases ledger (or creditors ledger) contains all the personal accounts of the firm's suppliers. The nominal ledgers (also general ledger or private ledger) contains the rest of the firm's accounts. The main reason for dividing the ledger is that it allows several people to be engaged in the recording process and permits sectionalization of the work around these groups of accounts.

The development of data-processing systems

Although the system of source documents remains today much as we have described, the system for processing the data they contain has been improved dramatically by developments in computer technology. These developments have reduced the size of computers available and they enable most businesses, no matter how small, to take advantage of advanced technology. Indeed, the distinction between mini- and micro-computers has become increasingly blurred as technology has developed. New chips, such as the intel 32-bit 30386, have vastly increased the speed and processing power of micro-computers. A typical IBM AT or clone now runs at something like 10 times the speed of earlier PCs. Internal hard disks with a capacity equivalent to that of 1000 floppy disks are now available and micros are ideal for use as file servers at the centre of a network of other micros and peripheral devices such as printers. This allows more than one person at a time to access and modify the company's data, thus allowing, for example, one person to process sales at the same time as someone else processes purchases or receipts. Furthermore, it is possible to buy a 386 based machine with 2 + megabytes of *Random Access Memory* (processing space) and a storage capacity of 100 megabytes (enough for quite a large business) for less than £3000, while the minimum configuration suitable for a business, including a printer, would cost somewhat less than £1500. At the same time as hardware has developed, so has software. These 'off the peg' packages of programmes have become more 'user-friendly' in approach, except that as they develop and become capable of performing more functions they tend to become more complex.

The application of computer systems

Computer systems can be seen as falling into two main areas for our purposes: special accounting packages and more general packages which may have accounting implications.

Accounting applications
1   stock recording and control;
2   sales ledger;
3   purchase ledger;
4   nominal ledger;
5   payroll;
6   job costing;
7   invoicing.

It makes sense for these applications to be integrated because every sale will eventually be reflected in the sales ledger and nominal ledger and there are many other interrelationships as illustrated below.

Integrated accounting packages should not be seen as mere straightforward replacements for similar manual systems. The careful design of coding systems allows a considerable amount of useful information to be produced, almost without cost, as a by-product of the recording system. This might include information such as the amount of sales generated by individual sales representatives, or the amount of sales in a particular region as an aid to marketing decisions. The way the coding system is designed is of particular importance and is derived from an analysis of the information needs of the business.

More general applications

1   Planning and control through the use of spreadsheets. This might include budgeting, financial modelling etc. It is common for data to be exported from the accounting system described above into a spreadsheet for further manipulation.
2   Word processing. This will allow for more effective communication with customers, suppliers and other business contacts. Mail merge facilities allow for 'personalized' mailshots. It is also possible to link a word processing package with other applications such as spreadsheets or accounting packages to produce letters and reports including up-to-date financial information as either numbers or graphs.
3   Databases. These allow for more effective recording of business contacts which can be used, for example, as a way of identifying specific 'targets' for promotions etc.
4   Communications. This is an area which is expanding rapidly and where the computer is, yet again, demonstrating its usefulness. For example, it is possible to use the computer to send data to another computer or a fax machine at times when that machine would otherwise be inactive, or to take advantage of cheaper rates for phone calls (e.g. the middle of the night).

Electronic data storage and retrieval

Earlier in this chapter we considered the role of source documents for capturing details of accounting events. In a manually operated system, each stage in processing data is both a source of potential error and involves a labour cost. For example, the manually operated ledger system of a wholesale warehouse on the receipt of an order could involve:

1   noting the order in a sales order daybook;
2   writing a sales order form;
3   typing a despatch note;
4   calculating an invoice value involving quantity, price discounts and VAT;
5   typing the invoice;
6   posting the invoice to the sales ledger;
7   typing monthly statements;
8   analysing the age structure of the customer's account balances in order to ascertain how long they have remained unpaid;

9 updating stock records for the goods dispatched;
10 typing purchase orders to replenish stock.

Computers may be programmed to make decisions automatically and the implications of this characteristic for data processing are featured in the following example.

Example

Figure 2.6 illustrates the facilities available in an integrated computer system for processing a sales order. The sales order is fed into the computer, which then accesses information from the debtor's ledger and up-to-date information from stock records.

First, the computer provides information on the outstanding customer's balance and shows whether the customer is credit-worthy. Credit limits are established in advance for each customer. The computer adds the value of the order to the balance outstanding on the customer's account in the sales ledger, and compares the total with the credit limit. If the credit limit has not been reached, the order is cleared for further processing. If the credit limit has been reached, the operative will need to confirm that the order will or will not be processed. This procedure allows the company to exercise a meaningful credit control check and to avoid processing any orders for customers with an excessive debt.

Second, the computer provides details of the stock available and allows the firm to identify immediately which items can be despatched. For these items, the computer's despatch/invoice program would automatically produce a despatch note (to send to the warehouse) and an invoice (to send to the customer).

Third, the invoice is automatically posted to the customer's account in the sales ledger and, via the sales daybook, to the sales account in the nominal ledger.

Fourth, the computer adjusts the stock records in respect of the order and calculates a new balance. It compares the new balance with the balance in stock which is required for each particular item. A 'reorder point' will have been determined for each item of stock. If the stock level falls below the reorder point, then the computer produces a purchase requisition in order to replenish the stock to the designated level.

Fifth, at the month end, statements of account are produced automatically showing how much customers owe the firm at a given date and an analysis of the age structure of debtors. Also, the system will automatically produce letters to customers detailing the amount and age of their debt and requesting payment. The text of these letters can be modified in order to create the impression that they are not just computer output. This type of facility has proved extremely valuable in speeding up payments by customers.

This example illustrates how an integrated computer system reduces drastically the number of manual operations performed.

Fig. 2.6

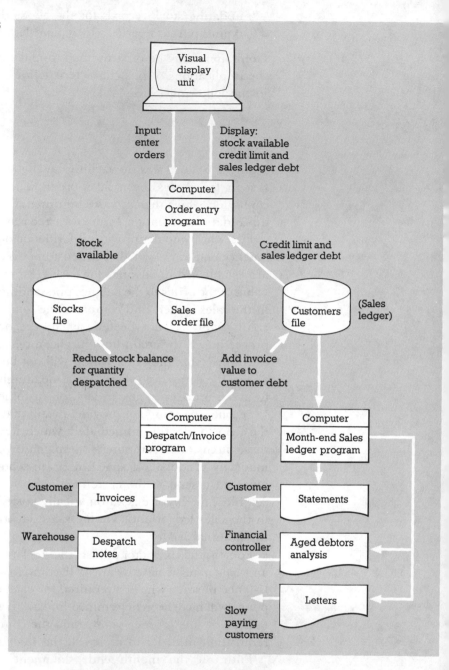

Furthermore, the level of information provision is improved in terms of speed and accuracy and the cost of data processing is greatly reduced.

Ways of reducing manual data input

Many enterprises are looking at ways of reducing the input of manual data even further. Typical of these developments are the point-of-sale terminals in shops using bar codes and light pens which identify the items sold. This information is fed directly into the computer and updates the stock level. Stock monitoring and control procedures are thereby improved. Fewer items of more lines can be kept on the shop floor, thereby enabling retailers to make more effective use of the available space.

Data transfer systems

There are two main types of system for the transfer of data collected by the terminals. Online or real time systems are permanently connected directly to the central computer and produce virtually instantaneous updating of the computer's records. The type of system is used by building societies and banks for their own customers. The other system is batch transfer where data is collected by a small computer, is grouped together, and then sent down the line to the main computer. Such a system might be used by a bank for customers of other banks. Also, it is being used increasingly as a way for sales representatives to process orders. The sales representative will enter details into a portable computer and will then send the data to the company's main computer for processing, either by reporting in to a location with a company computer terminal or by sending the data down a public telephone line. Great care must be taken over security for systems which can be accessed through public telephone lines.

The type of transfer system selected will depend on circumstances. A real time system will generally be more expensive than a batch system but it will update records more quickly and may well be more secure.

Computer systems

The type of computer system a firm requires may be considered from the overall model illustrated in Fig. 2.7.

Fig. 2.7

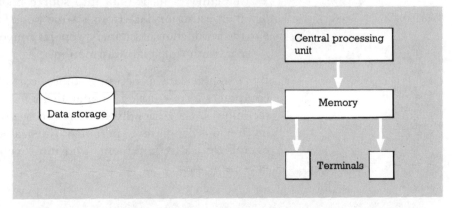

Data storage incorporates all the data storage files, e.g. sales and purchase ledgers and stock records. The firm has to decide the number of records it requires to maintain in order to determine the size of storage to be supported by the computer system. Storage devices can be floppy disks (for use in microcomputers), hard disks (used in all categories of computers) or tapes and cartridges (used mainly for keeping security copies of data held on disk storage).

Terminal is the name given to an input–output device which is at the end of a communication line. They can be printers or visual display units (VDUs). The number of terminals will be determined by:

1   the volume of input and output data required;
2   the number of different locations which require access to the enterprise's records to be displayed on either VDUs or printed reports (statements, invoices etc.).

The *computer memory* will determine:

1   The size of computer programs that can be used. For example, some very sophisticated modelling packages require a large computer memory for their operation.
2   Whether more than one program can be run at the same time. Where it can, this is often referred to as a multi-user system. This allows one person to have access to the sales ledger, say, on one VDU while another person has access to the stock records on another VDU.

The *central processing unit* (CPU) is the device that accesses data storage and executes instructions. The capability of the CPU used will determine:

1   the number of terminals it will support;
2   the size of the data storage that can be attached;
3   whether a multi-user system can be operated.

Summary

The generation of financial accounting information is a process involving the following stages:

1   the generation of data through the preparation of source documents;
2   the entry of basic data into source books;
3   the posting of data from source books into the ledger;
4   the production of financial reports converting financial information data into financial information.

By making data processing more cost-effective, developments in computers have enabled smaller firms to take advantage of computer techniques. User-friendly systems can be operated by people who have no previous computer experience. Integrated computer systems reduce overall clerical requirements and improve the accuracy and speed of processing data.

Question

What do you understand by a 'source document'? Give three examples of source documents, and explain their importance to the accounting process.

Problems

1   Name the books of original entry to be used for recording the following transactions, and state the accounts to be debited and credited:

Transaction (a)   Purchase of equipment on credit.
Transaction (b)   Payment of cash to a creditor.

Transaction (c)   Bank charges paid.
Transaction (d)   Receipt of cash from a customer.
Transaction (e)   Sale to a customer on credit.
Transaction (f)   Goods returned by a customer.

2   Prepare journal entries for the following transactions and indicate the journal in which they would normally appear:

1 April   Received invoice for £400 being equipment purchased from Equipment Supplies Ltd.

2 April   Received invoice for £700 for goods supplied by Jones Ltd.

4 April   Received cheque for £50 from J. Brown for goods supplied. Sent cheque to S. Supplier for £250 in payment of purchases effected in March.

5 April   Received an invoice from Standfast Supplies Ltd for goods supplied £800.

6 April   Invoiced J. Shepherd for goods sold £98.

7 April   Received a cheque for £70 from W. Smith in settlement of his account for goods sold.

8 April   Received Rates Statement showing rates due £500.

9 April   Banked weekly cash takings of £700.

3   Show the following entries as they would appear in a three-column cash book:

1 May   Credit balance at bank £700, cash in hand £5.
         Cash drawn from bank for the till £30.
         Cheque sent to Brown for £67 in settlement of amount due of £70, discount being received for prompt payment.

2 May   Received cheque from Jones for £45 in payment of invoiced amount of £47, less cash discount.

3 May   Cash sales for the day £190.

4 May   Banked cash sales of previous day £190.

5 May   Sent cheque to Blewett £100 being instalment due on loan repayment.

6 May   Took £10 out of till for taxi fares.

Chapter 7

Data processing and double-entry bookkeeping

We saw in the preceding chapter that financial accounting data has its source in original records of financial transactions. We noted two very important aspects of data generation. First, when reporting to external users, accounting information is presented usually in a form which is concerned with the monetary aspect of a firm's activities. It ignores data which deals with the type and quantities of resources which the firm utilizes, the nature and the quantity of its products, and the quality and usefulness of those products to society. Equally, traditional accounting is not concerned with the activities of the firm as a social unit consisting of people whose livelihood and happiness depend on its financial success as well as the manner in which their working lives are organized. Nor, indeed, does accounting concern itself with the role and importance of a particular firm as regards society as a whole. Second, we noted that accounting conventions play a determining role as regards the nature and the quality of the data which is processed.

The purpose of this chapter is to examine the structure which has evolved for handling financial accounting data.

The accounting equation

Financial accounting is based on a simple notion known as the accounting equation. The accounting equation depicts the equality which exists between the resources owned by the enterprise and the claims against the enterprise in relation to those resources.

One side of the accounting equation expresses, in monetary terms, the resources held by the enterprise. These resources are known as 'assets'. The acquisition of assets by the enterprise will have been financed by funds provided either by the owner(s) or from borrowings. The funds provided by the owner(s) constitute the 'capital' of the enterprise. The funds borrowed constitute liabilities and are known as such. Therefore, the other side of the accounting equation describes how the acquisition of assets has been financed and the claims which exist against the business as a result.

The accounting equation may be stated as follows:

capital + liabilities = assets

The concept underlying the accounting equation is that the enterprise itself is a vehicle through which assets are held and utilized, and that claims exist against those assets to their full monetary value. Given that liabilities arising from borrowings are stated as legal debts of determined monetary sums, the owners of the enterprise are entitled to the balance of the assets after liabilities have been settled. Accordingly, the accounting equation may be used to express capital as follows:

capital = assets − liabilities

It follows from our discussion in Chapter 4 that the balance sheet is founded on the accounting equation, for it is a list of the assets held by the enterprise against which is set a list of the claims existing against the enterprise. Both lists are equal in total.

Transactions and the accounting equation

Given that the balance sheet indicates the financial position of an enterprise at a given point in time, successive transactions would maintain the accounting equation on which the balance sheet rests, though its dimensions and its constituent elements would vary. It is possible to record the effects of successive transactions on the balance sheet equation.

Transaction 1

Returning to the example cited earlier (see page 45), where J. Soap invested £10 000 on 1 April 19X0 in a ladies hairdressing business, on 1 April 19X0 the opening transaction would be shown as follows:

Balance sheet 1

	£		£
Capital	10 000	Assets: Bank balance	10 000

The manner in which the subsequent transactions affect the balance sheet through the accounting equation may be seen from the following examples:

Transaction 2

J. Soap paid the monthly rent for the business amounting to £500. This is an expense of the month. Its effect on the balance sheet is to reduce cash by £500, and at the same time reduce the capital by the same amount. The balance sheet after this transaction would appear as:

Balance sheet 2

	£		£
Capital	9 500	Assets: Bank balance	9 500

Transaction 3

J. Soap purchased equipment for £2000 from Hairdressers' Supplies Ltd on credit. As a result, a new asset appears on the balance sheet as the equipment, and a liability of £2000 appears in respect of the amount owing. The balance sheet now appears as follows:

Balance sheet 3

	£		£
Capital	9 500	Assets: Equipment	2 000
Liability:			
Creditor	2 000	Bank balance	9 500
	11 500		11 500

It will be noted that, although the balance sheet totals increase by £2000, there is no change in the capital of the business. Instead, the balance sheet shows that the equipment purchased has been financed by a liability of exactly that amount.

Transaction 4

J. Soap paid salaries amounting to £200 in cash for part-time assistance. This is an expense of the month, and its effect on the balance sheet is to reduce cash by £200 and the capital by the same amount. The balance sheet now appears as follows:

Balance sheet 4

	£		£
Capital	9 300	Assets: Equipment	2 000
Liability:			
Creditor	2 000	Bank balance	9 300
	11 300		11 300

Transaction 5

J. Soap's revenue from clients for April amounted to £1500, of which £400 was received in cash. Clients who had accounts with him were charged a total of £1100, and at the end a sum of £100 remained outstanding in respect of these credit accounts. The effect of these transactions is to increase the capital by £1500 and to increase cash at bank by £1400. The amount outstanding of £100 requires a new asset account to be opened—Debtors—in the sum of £100. The balance sheet now appears as follows:

Balance sheet 5

	£		£
Capital	10 800	Assets: Equipment	2 000
Liability:		Debtor	100
Creditor	2 000	Bank balance	10 700
	12 800		12 800

Transaction 6

J. Soap withdraws cash in the sum of £400 for his own use. The effect of this withdrawal is to reduce capital by £400 and cash by the same amount. The withdrawal of cash from the business is the reverse of the first transaction in which J. Soap invested in the business. Consequently, the capital account is reduced by the amount of the withdrawal. The balance sheet now stands as follows:

Balance sheet 6

	£		£
Capital	10 400	Asses: Equipment	2 000
Liability:		Debtor	100
Creditor	2 000	Bank balance	10 300
	12 400		12 400

Simplifying the recording of transactions

The process of drawing up a new balance sheet after each transaction would be extremely cumbersome in practice, given the large number of transactions which an enterprise may conduct daily. The problems are threefold. First, how to calculate the effects of successive transactions in terms of the profit they have generated? Such a calculation would explain why there occurred an increase in the capital from an original amount of £10 000 to £10 800, prior to the withdrawal made by J. Soap. Second, how to reflect the investment of the owner, J. Soap, in a convenient manner? Such a calculation would involve summarizing the effects of transactions on the capital account as it stands at the end of the accounting period. Third, how to devise a system of recording transactions which avoids the necessity of drawing up successive balance sheets?

The first problem is resolved by summarizing all transactions associated with the profit-earning process during the period in a statement known as the profit and loss account. Unlike the balance sheet, which states the financial position of the enterprise at different points in time, the profit and loss account seeks to establish the success or failure of the enterprise as the result of transactions over a period of time. The preparation of the profit and loss account involves identifying the revenues of the period, and the expenses which may properly be charged against those revenues. In the example of J. Soap above, the successive balance sheets for the month of April, which resulted in the increase in the capital account from £10 000 to £10 800 by balance sheet 5, may be summarized by a profit and loss account for April 19X0 as follows:

J. Soap—Ladies Hairdresser
Profit and loss account for April 19X0

	£	£
Revenue		1 500
Expenses:		
Rent	500	
Salaries	200	700
Net profit for April		800

The second problem, namely portraying the investment of the owner of the business at the close of the accounting period, involves using both the profit and loss account of the period and the balance sheet at the close of the period. In this respect, the profit and loss account and the balance sheet complement each other. The profit and loss account summarizes the operating results between successive balance sheets, and these results are reflected in the capital shown on the closing balance sheet. The factors which have affected the value of the owner's capital at the date of the closing balance sheet may be summarized in a detailed statement of the capital account. As regards the example of J. Soap given above, the analysis of the capital account would be shown on the closing balance sheet as follows:

J. Soap – Ladies Hairdresser
Capital account as at 30 April 19X0

	£	£
Balance, 1 April 19X0		10 000
Net profit for April	800	
less: Drawings	400	400
Balance, 30 April 19X0		10 400

The third problem, that of devising a system of recording transactions which avoids drawing up successive balance sheets, was resolved several centuries ago by the invention of the system of double-entry bookkeeping.

The nature of double-entry bookkeeping

The collection and recording of data is known as bookkeeping. The practice of recording financial data in 'books' dates from a very long time ago. These books were usually 'bound books'—bound so as to prevent the possibility of fraud by either the insertion or the removal of pages. Nowadays, mechanical and electronic data processing have frequently removed the bookkeeper as a person concerned with entering the results of financial transactions into the books. Instead, large firms have computerized the keeping of the books, and smaller firms use electronic accounting machines which make use of 'cards' which form parts of a 'bank' of cards.

The double-entry system of bookkeeping, however, remains the basis for record keeping regardless of whether or not a firm employs advanced data-processing techniques, mechanical or manual methods. It is, therefore, the logical method for recording financial information, and as such the basis of financial accounting practice.

The term 'double-entry' adds a special meaning to the process of bookkeeping. It is a method of recording financial data as transactions involving flows of money or money value between different accounts. It involves a network of integrated accounts, in which an account is designated for each accounting item. The entries recorded on the successive balance sheets of J. Soap for April 19X0 would appear in a double-entry bookkeeping system.

Transaction 1

The initial investment of £10 000 cash by J. Soap in the ladies hairdressing business is shown as a flow of money from the capital account to the cash book, as follows:

Capital account	Cash book
——————— £10 000 ———————►	

Business transactions are represented in double-entry bookkeeping as flows of money or money value between the various accounts concerned, but clearly any one transaction involves only one flow, as shown above. In order to identify the direction of any one flow, all accounts are divided into two parts. A flow out of the account is recorded on the right-hand side, and a flow into an account is recorded on the left-hand side. Hence, the transaction shown above would appear as follows:

Capital account	Cash book
——————— £10 000 ———————►	

Flows out could conveniently be described by a minus sign, but the accounting convention which dates from the Italian origins of bookkeeping utilizes the term *Credit* (Cr.), which means 'to give'. Likewise, flows in could be described by a positive sign, but the accounting appellation is *Debit* (Dr.), which means 'to owe'. Hence, this additional information may be inserted in the accounts to identify the direction of the flow, and replacing the arrow which we have used up to now.

Capital account		Cash book	
	Cr.	Dr.	
	£10 000	£10 000	

There are now only two additional items of information which are required to identify the transaction flow, namely the point of origin and the point of destination. These, too, are made easy in bookkeeping by the simple expedient of describing in the credited account where the flow has gone, and by inserting in the debited account the source of the flow.

Capital account		Cash book	
	Cr. Cash £10 000	Dr. Capital £10 000	

In practice, accountants know very well that the left-hand side of an account is the debit side, and vice versa for the right-hand side, so that they do not head up the accounts with Dr. or Cr. In the old days, they used to add the word *By* on the narration of credit entries, and *To* on the narration of debit entries—but this too is unnecessary, and most accountants have abandoned the practice. The reader will occasionally find entries recorded as follows:

Capital account

	By cash	£10 000

Cash book

To capital	£10 000	

We will not, however, use these superfluous terms. Lastly, the date of the transaction must be recorded, and it is done as follows:

Capital account

	19X0 1 April	Cash £10 000

Cash book

19X0 1 April	Capital	£10 000	

To simplify the exposition of the double-entry bookkeeping system in the examples which follow, the dates will be omitted.

In the manner in which transactions are recorded under this method, the reader will have been quick to notice an important feature—the flow has remained constant in value as it has moved from the credited account to the debited account. As a result, double-entry bookkeeping possesses a mathematical foundation which has its logic in the simple proposition that as regards any one transaction the credit must be equal to the debit. At any time, therefore, the arithmetical precision of the bookkeeping process may be checked by adding up all the debit entries and all the credit entries. If the total debit entries do not equal, that is balance with the credit entries, there has been an error in the recording process. As we see on page 98, the trial balance is the means whereby accountants check for arithmetical errors in recording transactions. If the trial balance shows a difference as little as 1p between the total debits and the total credits, the error must be found. This is because accountants know that the result of a great many cumulative errors may boil down to a difference of only 1p.

Double-entry bookkeeping is a logical and precise system for recording financial transactions as flows of money or money value. It is easy to operate, and simple to adapt to modern computer methods by using positive and negative electric charges to signal whether an account should be debited or credited.

Transaction 2

The payment of rent £500 by J. Soap is interpreted as a flow of money from the cash book to the rent account. It reduces cash by £500 and appears as an increase in the balance shown in the rent account by £500. The rent account is an 'expense' account which will be transferred later for the purposes of calculating the net profit for April. The entries will appear as follows:

Cash book			Rent account		
		£			£
	Rent	500	Cash		500

Transaction 3

The purchase of equipment on credit for £2000 by J. Soap from Hairdressers' Supplies Ltd does not yet involve the payment of cash, but requires the debt owing to Hairdressers' Supplies Ltd to be shown. This is effected by crediting the account of Hairdressers' Supplies Ltd with £2000. The entries would be as follows:

Hairdressers' Supplies Ltd account

		£
	Equipment	2 000

Equipment account

	£
Hairdressers' Supplies Ltd	2 000

Transaction 4

The payment of £200 as wages is another example of an expense account. Note that in the case of such accounts, the persons receiving payment are not named on the accounts themselves. Separate records would be kept in the form of a wages book, rent book, etc. The entries would be as follows:

Cash book

	£
Wages	200

Wages account

	£
Cash	200

Transaction 5

The treatment of the revenue generated from the sale of hairdressing services involves two problems. First, the cash sales involving the receipt of cash amounting to £400 are entered directly as follows:

Sales account

	£
Cash	400

Cash book

	£
Sales	400

The treatment of credit customers is rather more complex. First, the individuals concerned are shown in the debtors' ledger. The total amount of credit sales during the month of £1100 appears in a summary account known as the debtors' account. The entries are as follows:

Sales account

	£
Debtors	1 100

Debtors' account

	£
Sales	1 100

The payments made by debtors during the month totalled £1000, leaving an amount outstanding of £100 at the end of April and shown as follows:

Debtors' account

	£		£
Sales	1 100	Cash	1 000
		Balance	100
	1 100		1 100

Cash book

	£
Debtors	1 000

In effect, these various entries would appear as follows:

Sales account

	£
Cash	400
Debtors	1 100

Cash book

	£
Sales	400
Debtors	1 000

Debtors' account

	£		£
Sales	1 100	Cash	1 100
		Balance	100
	1 100		1 100

Transaction 6

J. Soap withdrew £400 for his personal use. This transaction, which reduces his capital account by £400, could be entered directly as follows:

Capital account				Cash book	
	£		£		£
Cash	400	Balance	10 000	Capital	400

The effect of this transaction would be to reduce the capital account by £400 to £9600. This reduction could be shown as follows:

Capital account				
		£		£
Cash		400	Balance	
Balance		9 600	B/d	10 000
		10 000		10 000

In order to minimize entries in the capital account in respect of regular withdrawals by the owner of a business, the normal practice is to show them in a separate drawings account. At the end of the accounting period, the drawings account is transferred to the capital account, so that only one entry is made in respect of drawings. Using the drawings account, the withdrawal of £400 would be shown as follows:

Drawings account			Cash book	
	£			£
Cash	400		Drawings	400

Double-entry bookkeeping as a 'closed' system

We noted in Part 1 that the term 'system' is commonly used to mean any unit which may be identified as an independent whole, having its own objectives and its own internal functions. An 'open' system is one whose behaviour is affected by external factors. The British economy, for example, is an 'open system' because it is affected by its trading relationships with the rest of the world. A 'closed' system is one in which all the functions are internalized in the system, and are not affected by outside factors. Double-entry bookkeeping has the characteristics of a closed system in that all the transactions recorded take place within the accounts system. By this we mean that all flows resulting from transactions are depicted as having their origin in an account which is found in the system, and they have their destination in another account in the system. It is impossible for a flow to originate from an account outside the accounts system. Likewise, it is impossible for a flow of money or of money value to go to an account outside the accounts system.

Example

Let us go back to the example given above. J. Soap opens up a business under the name of 'J. Soap—Ladies Haidresser'. He invests £10 000 in cash into the business. The effect of the entity convention is that J. Soap opens and keeps separate books for the business of J. Soap—Ladies Hairdresser, which is regarded as a separate entity from J. Soap himself. Double-entry bookkeeping gives expression to the entity convention since all the accounts of J. Soap—Ladies Hairdresser relate only to the financial transactions of that business. J. Soap himself is an external party as far as the business is concerned.

The question is—how can we depict the flow of £10 000 from J. Soap into the business? Now, we have said that no flow may originate from outside the accounts system. Hence, we must have an account within the accounts system whence it has originated. That account is the account of J. Soap himself in his capacity as owner of the business, which we described above as the capital account. The source of the flow of £10 000 is therefore found in the capital account, and its destination is the cash account.

Capital account

		19X0	£
		1 April	10 000

Cash book

19X0	£		
1 April	10 000		

Let us suppose for a moment that on 2 April J. Soap decides that he has put too much money in the business and wishes to take out £3000. In the accounts system, the transaction could be shown as follows:

Capital account

19X0		£	19X0		£
2 April	Cash	3 000	1 April	Cash	10 000

Cash book

19X0		£	19X0		£
1 April	Capital	10 000	2 April	Capital	3 000

The significance of these entries reflects the fact that accounting is not concerned with the destination of the actual sums of money, but simply with portraying the full transaction as a *record* of the flow of money. Successive entries are made in accounts which have been opened, and where a transaction involves a new account then that account is opened. Likewise, if an account is no longer needed, it is closed.

The implications of these statements as far as bookkeeping being a closed system of accounts are:

1   The bookkeeping system of any firm is infinitely elastic in size. As many accounts are opened as are necessary to record in full the transactions which have taken place. It is not surprising, therefore, that large businesses have many thousands of accounts.

2   All the accounting flows of money or of money value take place between the various accounts found in the system. The accounts system, therefore, consists of a set of 'interlocking accounts'.

3   The accounts themselves represent 'realities'—whether they are persons or assets involved in transactions.

4   Firms are continually involved in transactions: this activity is mirrored in the constant flow of money and of money value in the accounts system.

5   Since all the flows have both their source and their destination in the accounts to be found in the system, the total debits and the total credits remain equal at all times. If this is not so, there are one or more errors.

Accounts as descriptions of transactions

We have already noted that the accounts system is used to describe the direction of a flow of money or of money value, as well as the timing of the flow. Business transactions affect a firm in different ways: some are concerned with the acquisition of assets to be used in earning profits, others concern the supply of capital to the firm, either by the owner or by lenders, others relate to goods purchased or sold to persons so that the exchange of goods expressed as money value creates rights or liabilities in money terms, and others yet relate to revenues and costs.

If a firm is to make any sense of the large number of accounts kept, some grouping is necessary, so that accounts of the same business nature are kept together. The integration of accounts into groupings enables the accountant to extract the information which he needs with much greater ease. For example, to find out how much is owed to persons by the business, the accountant has merely to go to the accounts of the creditors. This term means that such persons have been the source of a flow of money, or of money value to the firm, and have not been repaid. Likewise, the debtors' accounts are referred to to find out how much is owing to the business by those people who have received money or money value and have not settled their accounts.

Transactions frequently involve two or more different classes of accounts.

Example

J. Soap supplies hairdressing services to Mrs B. Brown and her two unmarried daughters, to the value of £20 on 1 April 19X0. In the acounts of J. Soap, the transaction will be shown as a flow of money value (goods) from the sales account, which is a nominal account to Mrs B. Brown's account, which is a personal account.

Sales account

		19X0	£
		1 April Mrs B. Brown	20

Mrs B. Brown account

19X0	£		
1 April Sales	20		

Since Mrs Brown has received services from J. Soap she is a debtor to the amount of £20. At the end of the month, J. Soap will send her a statement showing that £20 is due for payment. Mrs B. Brown sends her cheque for £20, which will be banked on 1 May. This is shown as another transaction, the settlement of a debt, as follows:

Mrs B. Brown account

19X0	£	19X0	£
1 April Sales	20	1 May Cash	20

Cash book

19X0	£		
1 May Mrs B. Brown	20		

Thus, this transaction is one between a personal account and a real account. At this point, we may make two interesting observations:

1 A 'credit' transaction is a flow of money value to or from a personal account, and involves the creation of a debt towards the business, or a liability against the business. Hence, the use of the terms debtor and creditor respectively to denote the nature of such legal rights and obligations.

2 The payment of any liability involves another accounting transaction which records the flow of money from or to the appropriate personal account to or from the cash book. In this connection, the cash book records all the money flows through the firm's bank account.

The mathematical implications of double-entry bookkeeping

We have already noted that the arithmetical accuracy of the entries made in the accounts may be verified by means of a trial balance which involves comparing the total debits with the total credits.

During any accounting period, there may have been several entries in an account, so that several debits and several credits may be shown. A simple calculation may be made to calculate the net balance, for the purpose of the trial balance itself, and to ascertain the net state of the account.

Example

In the foregoing example several cash transactions took place during the month of April, as follows:

Cash book

	£		£
Capital	10 000	Rent	500
Sales	400	Wages	200
Debtors	1 000	Drawings	400

If we wish to ascertain the balance on the cash book, the procedure for so doing is simply to add up both sides of the account and to calculate the difference. This difference is the balance.

Cash book

	£		£
Capital	10 000	Rent	500
Sales	400	Wages	200
Debtors	1 000	Drawings	400
		Balance	10 300
	11 400		11 400

This balance represents the excess of the debits over the credits and it indicates that the bank balance is £10 300 in hand. In order to show this fact in the account after it has been balanced, the balance is brought down as a debit balance.

Cash book

	£		£
Capital	10 000	Rent	500
Sales	400	Wages	200
Debtors	1 000	Drawings	400
		Balance c/d	10 300
	11 400		11 400
Balance b/d	10 300		

Balancing the accounts is the first stage in preparing the trial balance. Some accounts will have debit balances and others will have credit balances. When we compare the total balances, they should be equal.

The trial balance

The trial balance is a list of balances extracted from all the accounts arranged in such a way that the debit balances are listed on one side and the credit balances on the other side.

Example

The following trial balance was extracted on 30 April 19X0 from the books of J. Soap—Ladies Hairdresser:

Trial balance as on 30 April 19X0

	Debit balances £	Credit balances £
Capital account on 1 April 19X0		10 000
Drawings	400	
Cash	10 300	
Rent	500	
Wages	200	
Equipment	2 000	
Sales		1 500
Debtors	100	
Creditors		2 000
	13 500	13 500

The trial balance not only serves to act as a check on the arithmetical accuracy of the bookkeeping process, but is a summary of the balances of all the accounts, which, as we shall see in the next chapter, serves as a working paper in the course of preparing financial statements. We note that in the process of summarizing information for the purpose of the trial balance, the personal accounts of the debtors and the creditors have been totalled.

The trial balance will not reveal the following types of errors:

1 Errors of omission, where a transaction has been completely overlooked.
2 Errors of principle, where an amount is correctly recorded but is placed in the wrong class of account—for example, where the purchase of equipment is shown under purchases rather than under equipment.
3 Errors of commission, where an amount is correctly recorded in the correct class of account, but is entered in the wrong account—for example, where a sale of £50 to Mr B. Brown is entered in Mrs B. Brown's account.
4 Errors of original entry, where the transaction is recorded in the wrong amount—for example, where a sale to Mrs B. Brown of goods to the value of £20 is recorded as £2 in the sales journal.
5 Errors in recording the direction of the flow, although the correct account is recorded—for example, instead of being shown as a debit to the cash book and a credit to Mrs B. Brown's account it is shown the other way round.
6 Compensating errors which cancel each other out will not be revealed. Thus, an error in adding up the trade debtors which is cancelled out by a similar error in adding up the trade creditors will not be revealed.

Summary

The evolution of double-entry bookkeeping has provided accountants with a method of processing data in a systematic manner, and with a means of checking the accuracy of accounting records which was built into its processes by virtue of the interlocking nature of the accounts system. At the end of an accounting period, it is axiomatic that the total debit entries must be equal to the total credit entries and vice versa.

With the advent of the computer the usefulness of the double-entry method as a check on the accuracy of record keeping has largely disappeared. Nevertheless, double-entry bookkeeping remains the basis for recording financial transactions as flows of money, or of money value from one account to another, whether or not the accounts system is computerized.

Far more significant, however, as regards the usefulness of the data recorded in the double-entry system are the effects of accounting conventions, which require in particular that the values recorded should be determined by transactions.

Problems

1 Show the effects of the following transactions on the accounting equation. For this purpose, enter these transactions in columns as under:

Col. 1 Capital	+	Col. 2 Liabilities	=	Col. 3 Assets
....		....		....
....		....		....

Transaction (a) J. Johnson opens a garage by investing £20 000 in cash in the business
Transaction (b) he borrows £5000 from the bank
Transaction (c) he purchases petrol for £1000 and pays in cash
Transaction (d) he buys equipment to the value of £10 000 and agrees to pay that amount within four weeks
Transaction (e) he purchases second-hand cars from Middleton Motors and pays £15 000, being the agreed amount
Transaction (f) customers pay £2000 for services rendered
Transaction (g) wages paid amount to £1000.

2 Show the accounting effects of the following transactions by reference to the balance sheet and the profit and loss account. (Example: cash sale £200 would add £200 to revenue on the profit and loss account and £200 to the asset cash on the balance sheet.)

Transaction	Accounting effects	
	Balance sheet	P & L a/c
Cash sales £400	....	....
Cash purchases £75	....	....
Received from trade debtor £35	....	....
Equipment purchased on credit terms £345	....	....
Invoice received for repairs to machinery £67	....	....
Wages paid £78	....	....
Payment of rent due last month £90	....	....
Equipment sold as scrap £20 (book value £10)	....	....
Loan received £600	....	....
Bank interest charged £49	....	....

3 Bill Cashing sets up practice as an architect, investing £10 000 of his own money into the business and effecting a transfer of that sum from his personal account to his

business account at the Midland Bank Ltd. The transfer is effected on 1 January 19X0, the date on which he formally commenced. The following transactions took place in the following month:

Event

1	1 January	Paid office rent for January £200.
2	1 January	Purchased office equipment on account from Equipit Ltd £1000.
3	1 January	Purchased office supplies on account from W. Brown for £150.
4	3 January	Hired a junior out of school.
5	4 January	Surveyed a property for A. Bond and sent out an invoice of £50.
6	7 January	Decided to transfer his own car to the business at a value of £2000.
7	10 January	Bought petrol for £10, paid by cheque.
8	11 January	Took a client to lunch at a cost of £20, and was asked to prepare plans for a new factory for which work he estimated he would earn £1200.
9	17 January	Conducted another property survey for A. Bond and invoiced him for £60.
10	20 January	Took another prospective client to lunch at a cost of £30, and found that he would not be able to undertake work for that client.
11	30 January	Paid the office junior his monthly wage of £70.
12	30 January	Sent a cheque to Equipit Ltd for £1000.
13	30 January	Sent a cheque to W. Brown for office supplies £150.
14	30 January	Banked a cheque received from A. Bond for £50.

Required:

Enter these transactions in Bill Cashing's accounting records, and test the arithmetical accuracy of your work by preparing a trial balance when you have completed the entries needed to be made.

4 As at 31 December 19X0, the accountant of AB Ltd extracted a trial balance from the firm's accounting records and, there being a difference, inserted a balancing figure in a suspense account.

Later, it was found that:

(a) a payment of £150 for stationery in the cash book had been posted in the ledger as £50;

(b) a total of £637 in the sales day book had been carried forward as £673;

(c) an amount of £60 paid to S. Jones on 2 January 19X1 had been included in the purchase ledger balances shown in the trial balance;

(d) goods which cost £75 had been returned to R. Brown and, while a correct entry had been made in the purchases returns book, £175 had been posted to the credit of R. Brown's account in the sales ledger;

(e) at the beginning and end of the accounting period stocks were valued at £1250 and £2250 respectively. In error, the latter figure had been shown in the trial balance;

(f) discounts allowed amounting to £325 had been credited to the appropriate nominal ledger account;

(g) £256, being the amount of discounts received, had been debited to the nominal ledger as £265;

(h) cash at bank was shown in the trial balance as £350. In fact this was the balance shown by the bank statement which on 31 December 19X0 was £20 in excess of the bank balance correctly recorded in the cash book.

After rectification of the above discrepancies the books balanced.

Required:

Show journal entries necessary to correct the above errors and set out the suspense account as it would finally appear in the books.

5 (a) Harold Davies is the proprietor of a small building firm. He does not understand the term 'balance sheet' and asks you to explain to him whether the following items should be on his balance sheet. Indicate the nature of the items (e.g. current asset, long-term liability, not applicable etc.) and give the reason for your answer.

    (i) stock of sand and cement;

    (ii) air compressor purchased for cash;

    (iii) air compressor hired for three weeks;

    (iv) wages paid to labourer;

    (v) lorry used for transporting materials;

    (vi) diesel fuel in lorry fuel tank;

    (vii) washing machine bought for Mrs Davies;

    (viii) bank overdraft;

    (ix) petty cash in hand;

    (x) £2000 owing to an uncle who says Harold need not pay until five years have elapsed.

(b) Explain what effect the following transactions will have on a balance sheet to which they relate:

    (i) Shareholders invest a further £20 000 in the company.

    (ii) The company buys raw material for cash £1200.

    (iii) The company buys raw material on credit £4000.

    (iv) The company pays £5000 to its creditors.

    (v) The wages payable are paid £2000.

Chapter 8

Standardized charts of accounts

The process of securing greater uniformity in accounting practice in the United Kingdom under the auspices of the Accounting Standards Committee has limited itself to the issue of successive accounting standards dealing with particular issues.

Accountants and business firms remain free to devise suitable data processing systems in which ledger accounts are not required to be kept in a standardized manner.

The application of computers to the process of bookkeeping and the preparation of financial reports requires the use of Charts of Accounts, based on accounts classifications containing accounts having numerical codes. Accounting software automatically processes transactions once they are entered manually into the computer.

Charts of Accounts predate the appearance of accounting software. Several EC countries, for example France, have accounting laws that require firms nation-wide to keep their books in a uniform manner through the use of the Official Chart of Accounts.

The purpose of this chapter is to review the development of standardized accounting systems using Charts of Accounts, and to consider the implications of such systems for the further development of accounting in the Unified Common Market.

The development of uniformity in bookkeeping

Accounting developments in recent years have had their main origins in three different sources:

1 the development of accounting standards, which as we saw in Chapter 5, have the purpose of reviewing the application of accounting principles to particular problems with the intention of creating greater uniformity of accounting practices. In the United Kingdom, and in the USA, the Accounting Standards Board (ASB) and the Financial Accounting Standards Board (FASB) respectively are responsible for issuing a series of standards to be applied by professional accountants. This development also manifested itself internationally through the International Accounting Standards Committee (IASC), that likewise proceeded to issue a series of accounting standards of a similar nature. In effect, the development

of accounting standards is perceived as an activity reflecting closely the accounting traditions of the English-speaking world.

2   the development of computer applications to the process of recording and analysing accounting data. Software companies and professional accounting firms gave business enterprises a new accounting technology that enabled the rapid processing of data and production of accounting statements for management and for financial reporting purposes. This has become a world-wide technology, which together with the appearance of international and indeed multinational professional accounting firms is giving an international character to accounting practice.

3   the appearance of the Unified Common Market grouping the economic, business and political interests of European member countries. An earlier wish of member nations to achieve greater uniformity of accounting practice among countries having quite different accounting traditions and structure led in the first instance to the Fourth and Seventh EC Directives. The Fourth Directive was concerned with creating a degree of uniformity in financial reporting by companies within the EC, and in particular the content and format of balance sheets, profit and loss statements, funds statements and notes to the accounts. The Fourth Directive also restated four cardinal accounting principles to be:

(a) going concern
(b) accruals
(c) consistency
(d) prudence.

The 'true and fair view' principle used in the United Kingdom was adopted by the Fourth Directive as the standard to which financial reports for external users should conform.

However, the Fourth Directive did not deal with the principal differences that were found among member countries. These related to the prevalence of accounting traditions in Continental Europe different from those found in the United Kingdom. In France and in other Latin countries, governments rather than the professional bodies are responsible for accounting rules, decreed as laws. A most important aspect of accounting law is the Uniform Chart of Accounts, that requires every business to have the same accounting system.

The structure of accounting systems and accounts classifications

The basic classification of accounts, that provides the framework for bookkeeping worldwide, reflects four major categories of transactions classified by nature:

1   Financing transactions, that include the capital account, long-term loans, and current liabilities, that represent the financial structure of the business.

2   Investment transactions, that include fixed and current asset accounts and represent the economic structure of the business in the form of the assets used in its operations.

3   Revenue transactions, that include all those accounts recording income flows to the business during the accounting period.

4   Expense transactions, that include all those accounts recording expenses incurred in earning revenues of the accounting period or which relate to the accounting period.

The first analysis of accounting data originating from primary records in the form of invoices etc. involves a judgement as to which of these four classes of accounts are affected by individual transactions. Once that judgement is made, the bookkeeping entries are made and are recorded permanently in the ledger. Figure 2.8 shows the basic accounting model.

Fig. 2.8

**The Basic Accounting Model –
AN INTERNATIONAL INTERPRETATION**

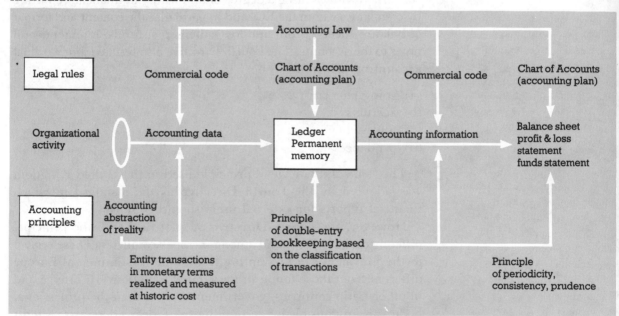

The ledger consists of four different data zones. Access to the data lodged in the financing and investment classes of accounts permits the balance sheet to be extracted: the data lodged in the revenue and expenses accounts allows the preparation of a profit and loss statement and, consequently the measurement of periodic profit. Figure 2.9 shows the correspondence between the basic classification of accounts and the balance sheet and profit and loss statement.

Sub-categories of accounts are opened within these four basic classes of accounts, thereby permitting a more detailed analysis of transactions. For example, investment transactions are formally defined as asset

Fig. 2.9

The Permanent Memory—Basic Model

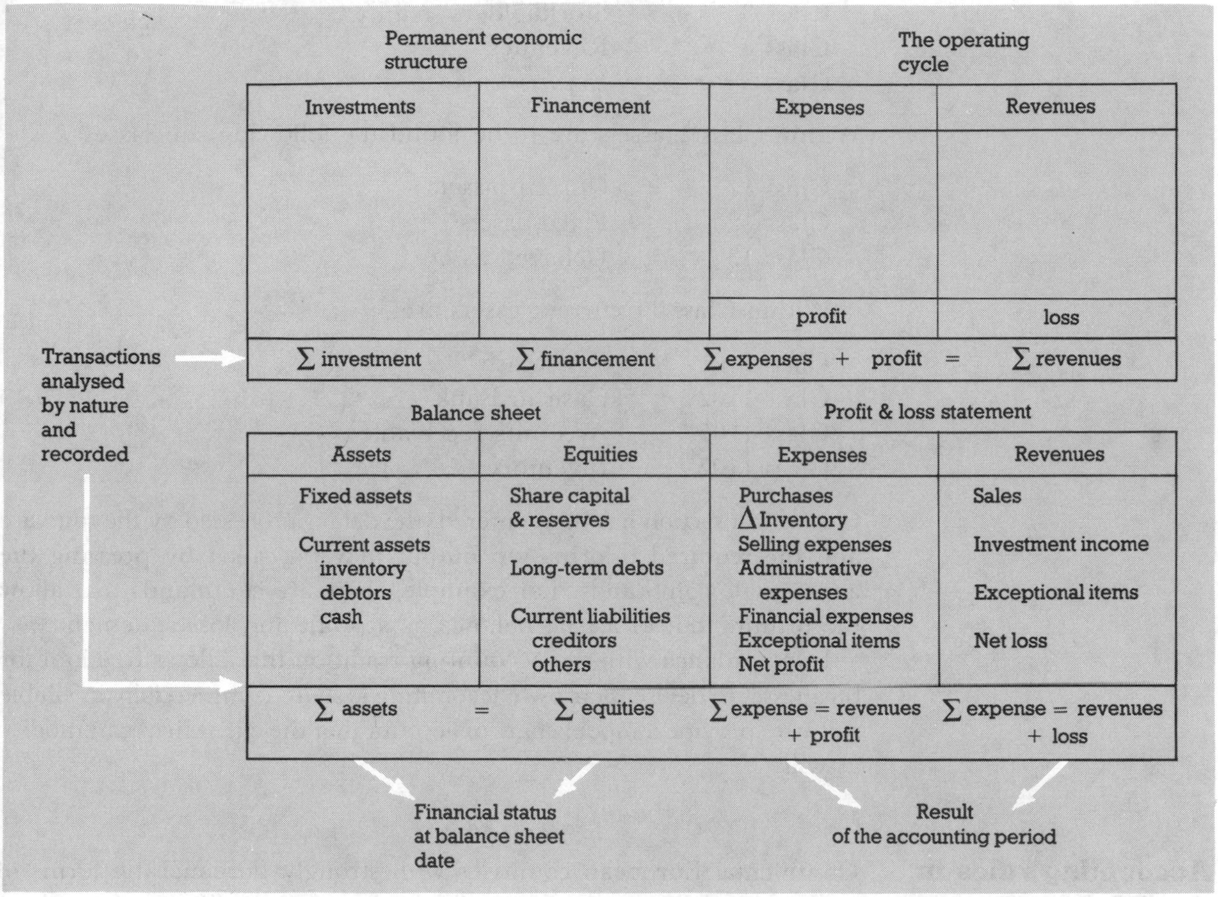

Permanent economic structure		The operating cycle	
Investments	Financement	Expenses	Revenues
		profit	loss
$\sum$ investment	$\sum$ financement	$\sum$ expenses + profit =	$\sum$ revenues

Transactions analysed by nature and recorded →

Balance sheet		Profit & loss statement	
Assets	Equities	Expenses	Revenues
Fixed assets	Share capital & reserves	Purchases Δ Inventory	Sales
Current assets inventory debtors cash	Long-term debts	Selling expenses Administrative expenses	Investment income Exceptional items
	Current liabilities creditors others	Financial expenses Exceptional items Net profit	Net loss
$\sum$ assets =	$\sum$ equities	$\sum$ expense = revenues + profit	$\sum$ expense = revenues + loss

Financial status at balance sheet date

Result of the accounting period

accounts, and within this broad category are found subclasses of accounts, for example fixed and current asset accounts. These subclasses are also defined by their nature, thereby facilitating a more extensive analysis of the asset-earning structure. Within these subclasses themselves are to be found further categories again defined by nature.

The nature of charts of accounts

A chart of account may be defined as a systematic method of bookkeeping in accordance with a predetermined plan for recording transactions, that consists of a limited number of accounts grouped in broad categories analysed by nature and further subdivided into lower level subcategories.

A characteristic feature of charts of accounts is the use of the decimal system of numbering for the orderly referencing of subcategories of accounts.

Generally, the four major categories of accounts mentioned earlier are extended to provide a better fit with the broad classifications used for balance sheets and profit and loss statements.

For example, a software widely sold in the USA has the following broad classification and numbering:

Class 1	Assets
Class 2	Liabilities
Class 3	Stockholders' equity
Class 4	Revenues
Class 5	Expenses

Within Class 1 assets are to be found the following subclasses:

Class 11	Current assets
Class 12	Fixed assets
Class 13	Deferred assets

Within Class 11 current assets are:

Class 1101	Petty cash
Class 1102	Cash in Bank
Class 1105	Accounts receivable
Class 1107	Inventory

Once a transaction has been entered, the data is processed by the software and the required information output may be called by pressing the appropriate commands. For example, there are commands that allow the printing out of a trial balance or a profit and loss statement.

In accordance with the accounting tradition that allows freedom for businesses to devise their own accounting system, commercially available software provide a model chart of account that the client firm can modify at will.

Accounting rules in the EC

Continental European countries with strongly bureaucratic forms of government have accounting traditions that are very different from those found in the United Kingdom. The differences that are found may be summarized as follows:

1 Accounting is made subject to Government legislation. The accounting profession has no delegated authority to make accounting regulation.
2 The practice of accounting is made subject to the Commercial Code, and the tax laws.
3 There is less emphasis on accounting principles, but great significance is attached to orderly bookkeeping and uniformity of accounting practice.
4 In France and several other Latin countries, Government delegates authority from reviewing the practices of accounting to a permanent Government Accounting Commission.
5 The actual practice of bookkeeping and the presentation of financial statements in the form of balance sheet, profit and loss statements and funds statements must be in the prescribed form. Consequently, all firms maintain standardized bookkeeping systems and produce uniform sets of financial statements.

6 Macro-economic considerations outweigh private sector interests with regard to the need for information relevant to decision-making. The Central Bank, the Central Statistical Services and other Government agencies have ready access to economic data relevant to the management of the Government. This data is made routinely available as business data is easily aggregated from uniform accounting statements produced by private sector business enterprises.

The National Accounting Plan

France provides the clearest example of the concept of the national Accounting Plan (*Plan Comptable Révisé* 1982). All business firms registered in France are required to keep their accounting system in accordance with the detailed provisions of the National Accounting Plan. In effect, the *Plan Comptable Révisé* is a detailed guide to bookkeeping that lists accounts authorized for use in accordance with a decimalized referencing system. Recording a transaction involves ascertaining which account numbers should be used for the purpose. The *Plan Comptable Révisé* is widely available in the form of a handy folder for reference purposes.

In its generally used form, the *Plan Comptable Révisé* groups accounts into 7 basic categories analysed by nature, as follows:

1 Capital accounts
2 Fixed asset accounts
3 Stock and work-in-progress accounts
4 Personal accounts
5 Financial accounts
6 Expense accounts
7 Revenue accounts

Table 2.1 illustrates the outline framework of the *Plan Comptable Révisé* as far down as accounts bearing two digits. Within these categories, further numerical breakdowns going as far as 5 digits are to be found. This produces quite exact classification of accounting transactions in such detail as would not be found in English accounting practice. For example, in Class 6 Expense accounts are to be found the following:

60 Purchases
    601   Purchases for stocks—Raw materials and supplies
        6011   Materials A
        6012   Materials B
        6017   Supplies A, B, C.
    602   Purchases for stocks – Other supplies
        6021   Consumable materials
            60211   Material C
            60212   Material D
        6022   Consumable supplies
            60221   Combustibles
            60222   Cleaning materials
            60223   Factory and workshop supplies

Table 2.1 Revised Accounting Plan 1982 (France)

Class 1 Capital accounts (capital, loans and similar creditors)	Class 2 Fixed asset accounts	Class 3 Stock and work-in-progress accounts	Class 4 Personal accounts	Class 5 Financial accounts	Class 6 Expense accounts	Class 7 Revenue accounts
10 Capital and reserves	20 Intangible assets	30	40 Suppliers and related accounts	50 Trade investments	60 Purchases	70 Sales of goods and services
11 Profit or loss brought forward	21 Tangible assets	31 Raw materials	41 Trade debtors and related accounts	51 Banks, financial and similar institutions	61 External services	71 Stock variation
12 Profit or loss for the financial year	22 Fixed assets under concession	32 Other consumables	42 Employees and related accounts	52	62 Other external services	72 Work for own purposes and capitalized
13 Investment grants	23 Fixed assets in course of construction	33 Work in progress (goods)	43 Social Security and other public agencies	53 Cash in hand	63 Taxes, direct and indirect	73 Net income recognized on long-term contracts
14 Provisions created for tax purposes	24	34 Work-in-progress (services)	44 The Government and other public bodies	54 Imprest accounts and credits	64 Personal costs	74 Operating subsidies
15 Provisions for liabilities and charges	25	35 Finished goods	45 Group companies and proprietors accounts	55	65 Other operating charges	75 Other operating income
16 Loans and similar creditors	26 Participating interests and debts relating thereto	36	46 Sundry debtors and creditors	56	66 Financial costs	76 Financial income
17 Debts related to participating interests	27 Other financial assets	37 Goods for resale	47 Suspense accounts	57	67 Extraordinary charges	77 Extraordinary income
18 Branch and inter-company accounts	28 Provisions for depreciation of fixed assets	38	48 Prepayments and accruals	58 Internal transfers	68 Depreciation, amortization, transfers to provisions	78 Depreciation and provisions written back
19	29 Provisions for loss in value of fixed assets	39 Provisions for loss in value of stocks and work-in-progress	49 Provisions for loss in value on personal accounts	59 Provisions for loss in value on financial accounts	69 Profit sharing by employees, taxes on profits and similar items	79 Charges transferred

Adapted from Nobes, C. and Parker, R. (eds.) (1981) *Comparative International Accounting*, Richard D. Irwin, Homewood, Illinois, and reprinted with the permission of the authors.

<pre>
            60224   Shop supplies
            60225   Office supplies
            60226   Motor vehicles fuel
            60227   Other transport supplies
            60228   Small tools
      6026 Packaging
            60261   Irrecoverable packaging
            60265   Recoverable non-identifiable packaging
            60267   Miscellaneous packaging.
</pre>

In addition to setting out a highly formalized and rigidly defined bookkeeping system, the *Plan Comptable Révisé* contains further guidance with regard to recording transactions in certain accounts.

Standardized financial statements

The notion of the standardized national accounting plan extends to standardized financial statements in the form of the balance sheet, and profit and loss statement, and funds statement. Notes to the accounts are required in accordance with the Commercial Law.

As regards the two statements drawn directly from the accounting system, namely, the balance sheet and the profit and loss statement, the *Plan Comptable Révisé* requires them to be prepared in the legally required form. Moreover, it stated the precise reference numbers of the accounts that are to be aggregated for financial statement presentation. The format of presentation is also legally prescribed.

The Fourth Directive went some way in requiring member countries to amend their company law in order to standardize the content and presentation of corporate financial statements. Current United Kingdom legislation brings this country in line with other EC members in respect of content and format of corporate financial statement presentation. These may be in the vertical or in the horizontal form. Tables 2.2 and 2.3 below provide examples of permitted presentations.

Accordingly, it may be seen that the movement for the standardization of accounting systems is developing under the influence of those EC countries that have adopted formalized charts of accounts.

Advantages and disadvantages of national accounting plans

Advocates of national accounting plans are mainly to be found among Governments concerned with having macro-economic information emanating in a standardized and readily usable form from the corporate sector of the economy.

Tradition in the United Kingdom has been to leave the choice of accounting systems to professional accountants, who are free to devise client-oriented accounting systems. Hence, the first problem relates to the orientation of national accounting plans towards statistically relevant information for government use, as opposed to financially relevant information for use by management and investors. In France, for example, accounting tax forms have to be filled up in accordance with the *Plan Comptable Général* 1982.

Table 2.2 United Kingdom standardized balance sheet for companies (Companies Act, 1985)

PUBLISHED ACCOUNTS: FORMAT FOR MODIFIED BALANCE SHEET

	£	£
A. Called up share capital not paid		X
B. Fixed assets		
I Intangible assets	X	
II Tangible assets	X	
III Investments	X̲	
		X
C. Current assets		
I Stocks	X	
II Debtors	X	
III Investments	X	
IV Cash at bank and in hand	X̲	
	X	
D. Accruals and deferred income	X̲	
	X	
E. Creditors: Amounts becoming due and payable within one year	(X)	
F. Net current assets (liabilities)		X̲
G. Total assets less current liabilities		X
H. Creditors: Amounts becoming due and payable after more than one year	X	
I. Provisions for liabilities and charges	X	
J. Accruals and deferred income	X̲	
		(X)
		£X̲̲
K. Capital and reserves		X
I Called up share capital		X
II Share premium account		X
III Revaluation reserve		X
IV Other reserves		X
V Profit and loss account		X̲
		£X̲̲

As shown in the case of France, accounting plans can be offered in modified forms to suit the sectorial character of particular groups of businesses, for example, banks, insurance, cooperatives etc. With respect to the generality of business enterprises operating in the industrial, commerical or service sector, it could be argued that the wide-ranging

Table 2.3 United Kingdom standardized profit and loss statement for companies (Companies Act, 1985)

PUBLISHED ACCOUNTS: FORMAT FOR PROFIT AND LOSS STATEMENT

	Format 1: Operational Format	£	£
1	Turnover		X
2	Cost of sales		(X)
3	Gross profit (or loss)		X
4	Distribution costs	X	
5	Administrative expenses	X	
			(X)
			X
6	Other operating income		X
			X
7	Income from shares in group companies	X	
8	Income from shares in related companies	X	
9	Income from other fixed asset investments	X	
10	Other interest receivable and similar income	X	
			X
			X
11	Amounts written off investments	X	
12	Interest payable and similar charges	X	
			(X)
	Profit on ordinary activities		X
13	Tax on profit (or loss) on ordinary activities		(X)
14	Profit (or loss) on ordinary activities after taxation		X
15	Extraordinary income	X	
16	Extraordinary charges	(X)	
17	Extraordinary profit (or loss)	X	
18	Tax on extraordinary profit (or loss)	(X)	
			X
			X
19	Other taxes not shown under the above items		(X)
20	Profit (or loss) for the financial year		£X

	£
Profit (or loss) for the financial year	X
Dividends paid and proposed	(X)
Transfers to (from) reserves	(X)
Retained profit (or loss) for the financial year	£X

numbers of stipulated accounts found in a national accounting plan is sufficiently varied to meet the needs of most businesses.

It is noteworthy that the large international accounting firms have developed their own standard accounting procedures for installing accounting systems in client companies. The obvious advantages of uniformity in this sense, even for professional accounting firms are as follows:

1   Staff training costs can be reduced as new staff can be trained on

standard procedural manuals that provide a reference base for dealing with most recording problems.

2   The use of standard procedure manuals guarantees minimum quality standards in accounting systems performance.

3   Specialization of labour permits high quality staff to concentrate on difficult problems, and less experienced staff to work on routine standardized procedures.

4   Monthly and year-end financial statements can be routinely prepared through computer programs that process data flowing from standardized accounting systems.

In this connection, it is interesting to note that in France, the national accounting plan has facilitated the subcontracting of monthly and year-end financial statement preparation to specialist accounting firms providing such a service to a host of small and medium-sized businesses. Data stored in the firm's computer is sent through modem transmission to the specialized agency, and financial statements are produced and returned within 48 hours.

5   In the case of large international accounting firms, 'high tech' accounting practice developed in the advanced countries, such as the USA and the UK, can easily be transferred to other countries.

Some of the disadvantages of national accounting plans relate to the rigidity that exists in highly formalized systems, and the high costs involved in modifications to the national plan. Certainly, this was the experience of French companies compelled to change over from the *Plan Comptable* 1957 to the *Plan Comptable Révisé* 1982.

A further and important disadvantage of the national accounting plan relates to the lack of flexibility relative to new environmental factors that affect business methods, and particularly those recognized by new accounting standards. In this connection, accounting changes that require new accounting treatment would involve new legislation. Such would be the case for capital lease accounting, inflation accounting etc.

Accounting standards and national accounting plans

Although national accounting plans are relatively rigid and inflexible with regard to new accounting developments, they are not incompatible with accounting standards themselves. As noted earlier, the accounting standards movement in the United Kingdom has been concerned with increasing the uniformity of accounting practices that are permitted under existing accounting principles.

Accounting practices that relate to measurement, valuation and cost allocation affect data inputs into the accounting system. Therefore, many current accounting standards can be made to operate under national accounting plans. In this regard, several EC countries that have national accounting plans are members of the International Accounting Standards Committee, and are able to adopt International Accounting Standards, if they do not violate the principles underlying their own national accounting plans.

National accounting plans and developing countries

Developing countries face acute shortage of skilled personnel in almost all areas of business activity. National accounting plans offer such countries a way of overcoming this problem with respect to the shortage of skilled accounting personnel.

National accounting plans can be made to meet the needs of economies at different levels of development and of sophistication of business methods. Thus, several former French colonies in Africa have adopted national accounting plans that are modified forms of the French national accounting plan.

Questions

1   What do you understand to be *uniformity* in accounting?

2   What are the three main trends that in recent years have fostered uniformity in accounting practice?

3   Assess the significance of the Fourth Directive to increasing uniformity of accounting practice in the EC.

4   Define the basic accounting classification and explain its importance.

5   What do you understand by a chart of accounts?

6   Compare a chart of accounts and a national accounting plan.

7   What are standardized financial statements?

8   Discuss the advantages and disadvantages of national accounting plans and charts of accounts.

Problems

1   John Sparks, a newly qualified accountant, is offered employment by Highfields & Partners, a firm of professional accountants with a large farming clientele. The existing partners have agreed with him that, subject to satisfactory performance over a period of three years, he would be offered partner status on terms to be negotiated.

    Highfields & Partners had retained traditional bookkeeping methods, and the only equipment found in the office were electronic typewriters and calculating machines, considered as representing a considerable advance on the 'old-fashioned way'. A Journal, Cash and Ledger in book form were kept for each client, and entered monthly from vouchers.

    None of the existing employees and current partners has experience of computers, and none knows of the advantages that computers offer for financial accounting.

    Required:
    Imagine yourself as John Sparks and write a memorandum to the partners outlining the improvements and economies that could be realized through computerized and standardized bookkeeping.

2   Devise a classification of accounts that could be utilized in creating a chart of accounts for small business enterprises.

Section 2
Periodic Measurement

Chapter 9

Double-entry bookkeeping and periodic measurement

In Chapter 7, we examined the double-entry method as a means of recording financial transactions as flows of money or of money value. We said that firms are continually involved in transactions, and that this activity is mirrored in the double-entry bookkeeping process by the constant flow through the accounts system of the money or money values involved in those transactions.

The accounts system is merely a repository of financial data about transactions. To be meaningful, this data must be extracted from the accounts system and organized in such a way that it is useful to those who need information for decision making. The concept of periodicity which we mentioned in Chapter 4 represents the view that, although the activities of a firm continue through time so that the decisions taken at one point in time cannot be separated from their effects whenever they materialize, those activities should nevertheless be regularly assessed. In other words, the financial health of a business should be tested at periodic intervals. The concept of periodicity poses problems in adapting the data recorded in the accounts system so that it will correctly reflect the result of the transactions concluded in the selected period, and the financial health of the firm at the end of that period. The two accounting statements employed for this purpose are the profit and loss account for the year, and the balance sheet as at the end of the year.

The purpose of this chapter is to examine the preliminary stages in the preparation of these statements.

Problems in periodic measurement

The reader will recall that when we discussed the concept of periodicity in Chapter 4, we noted that not only should the transactions of a period be identified, but also that the expenses attributable to those transactions should be matched with the revenues derived from them in accordance with the matching concept.

The first major problem, therefore, in adapting the information recorded in the accounts system has a twofold aspect, i.e. to identify:

1   the revenues attributable to transactions during the year;
2   the expenses related to those revenues.

The second major problem concerns adjustments which must be made in order to arrive at a measure of the surplus or deficit of revenues over expenses. These adjustments involve an element of judgement, for example, how much to provide for depreciation and bad debts, and what adjustments to make in respect of expected losses. Such adjustments are made because the end product is a statement of the profit or loss made in the accounting period. We consider these problems in the next chapter.

The idea of periodic measurement which underlies financial reporting presents complex problems which we analyse in Part 3.

Identifying the revenues and expenses of the period

The data recorded in the accounts system provides the basis for identifying the revenues and expenses of an accounting period. First, we need to extract from the accounts system the data recorded in respect of all the transactions concluded in the period. We saw in Chapter 7 that the summary of all the transactions is obtainable by means of a trial balance drawn up on the last day of the accounting period.

Example

The following trial balance was extracted from the books of John Smith on 31 December 19X0, being the end of the first year of trading.

	£ Dr.	£ Cr.
Capital		25 000
Motor vehicles	10 000	
Furniture and fittings	2 500	
Purchases	31 000	
Bank balance	6 000	
Sales		70 000
Debtors	18 000	
Creditors		3 500
Rent	4 500	
Salaries	22 800	
Insurances	400	
Motor expenses	2 000	
Light and heat	1 000	
General expenses	300	
	98 500	98 500

The meaning of revenue and expense

The trial balance does not distinguish between flows of profit and flows of capital, neither does it make a distinction between expenditure incurred to earn revenue and expenditure on the acquisition of assets. The first problem is to identify the revenues of the year, and this is a matter of definition. By revenue we mean the flows of funds, that is money or rights to money, which have resulted from the trading activities of the business, as distinct from funds (capital) invested by the owner or loans made by creditors and others. In this case, the only revenue item shown on the trial balance is from sales amounting to £70 000. The second problem is to identify the expenses. We define expenses as the costs of running the business during the accounting period. In contrast, capital expenses are the costs incurred in acquiring fixed assets or adding to the profit-earning structure of the firm. The calculation of periodic profit is by means of a formula which deducts expenses from revenues:

periodic profit = revenues – expenses

Looking at the trial balance, the expenses of the year, as defined, are as follows:

	£
Purchases	31 000
Rent	4 500
Salaries	22 800
Insurances	400
Motor expenses	2 000
Light and heat	1 000
General expenses	300

An alternative definition of expenses, is that adopted by accountants, who treat as expenses all those costs the benefit of which has been exhausted during the year. Looking at the expenses which we have identified in the trial balance, it is clear that the benefit derived by the firm from expenditure on these items is limited to the accounting period. The only exception is the goods purchased which have not been sold by the end of the year, and we discuss this problem in Chapter 11.

We have completed, therefore, the first stage in periodic measurement by identifying the revenue and expenses attibutable to the 'profit-earning' transactions of the firm during the year, which we may list as follows:

	£		£
Purchases	31 000	Sales	70 000
Rent	4 500		
Salaries	22 800		
Insurance	400		
Motor expenses	2 000		
Light and heat	1 000		
General expenses	300		

Periodic measurement and the accruals concept

The next task of the accountant is to ensure that the revenues and expenses are attributable to the accounting period. It is the normal practice to record in the expense accounts those amounts actually paid during the period. As a result, at the end of the period, these accounts may be understated or overstated. Likewise, it is possible that there may be some outstanding revenue due to the business, other than sales revenue, which must be brought into the year's profit.

The governing principle which affects these adjustments is the accruals concept discussed in Chapter 4. The accruals concept, it will be recalled, makes a distinction between the receipt of cash and the right to receive cash, and the payment of cash and the legal obligation to pay cash. As there is often no coincidence in time between the creation of legal rights and obligations and the transfer of cash, it follows that the accountant must scrutinize the revenue and expenses accounts to make sure that amounts due and payable are accrued. Similarly, payments made in advance must be excluded and carried forward to the next accounting period. The adjustments are effected in the accounts themselves.

The accrual of income

At the end of an accounting period, the total sales revenue will have been recorded in the accounts system, and the amounts unpaid by customers in respect of these sales will have been included under sundry debtors. The outstanding income which may not already have been recorded is limited, therefore, to income other than sales, such as rent receivable, commissions receivable etc. The accountant must adjust his end-of-year figures so as to include all the income to which the business is legally entitled, even though it has not been received.

Example

On 1 December 19X0, John Smith had sublet a portion of his premises, which had never been utilized, for a monthly rent of £60 payable in advance on the first of each month. By 31 December 19X0, the date on which the trial balance was extracted, the rent receivable had not yet been received. To accrue the rent receivable, the accountant must enter the amount accrued in the rent receivable account as follows:

Rent receivable account

	19X0	£
	31 Dec. Accrued	60

This amount is taken to the profit and loss account as profit for the year 19X0, and at the same time is brought down as a debt due to the business by being shown as a *debit balance*.

Rent receivable account

19X0	£	19X0	£
13 Dec. Profit & loss account	60	31 Dec. Accrued c/d	60
	60		60
19X1			
1 Jan. Accrued b/d	60		

Students are often puzzled that rent receivable should be a credit. The reason is that the rent receivable account is used to denote the source of a flow of funds so that there is a flow out from the rent receivable account into the cash account. Let us assume that on 1 January 19X1, the rent outstanding is paid. The entries would be as follows:

Rent receivable account

19X1	£	19X1	£
1 Jan. Accrued b/d	60	1 Jan. Cash	60

Cash book

19X1	£	
1 Jan. Rent receivable	60	

In adjusting the receipts for the year so that they will correctly show the income of the year, the accountant accrues income not yet received, as we have seen above, but also carries forward to the following year any receipts of the current year which are the income of the following year.

If, however, there had been an omission of income from the accounts of the preceding year, and this income is received in the current year, it would be impossible to go back and adjust the accounts of the previous year. Those accounts will have been closed at the end of that accounting period. The accountant will include last year's income in the current year's account, and indicate that it was an omission from last year, or explain how this income arose. Adjustments of this nature often arise out of the settlement of legal disputes or compensation claims.

The accrual of expenses

The accrual of expenses occurs much more frequently than the accrual of income, for it is the nature of things that firms delay the payment of expenses. As a result, nominal accounts such as rent, insurance, wages, light and heat etc. have to be adjusted to show the total payments due and payable in respect of the accounting year. Occasionally, however, firms are obliged to pay in advance for services, so that there is a possibility that a portion of the payment relates to the next accounting period. Accordingly, the accrual of expenses involves two types of adjustments:

1 an accrual in respect of expenses of the year which have not yet been paid;
2 an exclusion from the recorded expenses of that part which relates to the next year.

Example

Let us return to the trial balance extracted from John Smith's books. We are informed that:

1 The yearly rent is £6000 payable quarterly. The rent of £1500 payable on 1 December had not been paid.
2 Insurance premiums paid amounting to £400 included a payment of £50 in respect of a new policy taken out on 31 December 19X0.

It is clear, therefore, that the legal obligation in respect of the rent is understated in the rent account by £1500. Equally, the insurance premiums applicable to the year ended 31 December 19X0 amount to £350 and not £400. It is necessary to adjust these accounts as follows:

1   to increase the rent chargeable as an expense by £1500;
2   to decrease the insurance chargeable as an expense by £50.

Underpayment of rent

Let us assume that the rent payments were made on due date as follows:

Rent account

19X0		£	
1 Feb.	Cash	1500	
1 May	Cash	1500	
1 Aug.	Cash	1500	

The amount which should be charged against the income for the year ended 31 December 19X0 is £6000. The rent unpaid at the 31 December 19X0 may be accrued as follows:

Rent account

19X0		£	
1 Feb.	Cash	1500	
1 May	Cash	1500	
1 Aug.	Cash	1500	
31 Dec.	Accrued	1500	

Having made this adjustment, the rent account for the year ended 31 December 19X0 may be closed by transferring the rent of £6000 to the profit and loss account for the year ended 31 December 19X0. The rent unpaid is, of course, a liability of the firm on the 31 December 19X0, and is shown by bringing down the amount accrued as a credit balance on the rent account. The adjusted rent account will appear as follows:

Rent account

19X0		£	19X0		£
1 Feb.	Cash	1500	31 Dec. Profit & loss a/c		6000
1 May	Cash	1500			
1 Aug.	Cash	1500			
31 Dec.	Accrued c/d	1500			
		6000			6000
			19X1		
			1 Jan. Accrued b/d		1500

We note the rent outstanding at 31 December 19X0 is £1500, and we have brought this amount down to show:

1 that there is a credit balance outstanding at 31 December 19X0;
2 that on 1 January 19X1 there is an outstanding liability in respect of the previous year, so that the firm will have to pay £7500 during the year ended 31 December 19X1.

The trial balance on 31 December 19X0 may now be adjusted as follows:

	£	£
Rent	6000	
Rent accrued		1500

If the firm pays the rent outstanding on 2 January 19X1, and thereafter pays the rent on due date, the rent account for the year 19X1 will appear as follows:

Rent account

19X1		£	19X1		£
2 Jan.	Cash	1500	1 Jan. Accrued b/d		1500
1 Feb.	Cash	1500	31 Dec. Profit & loss a/c		6000
1 May	Cash	1500			
1 Aug.	Cash	1500			
1 Dec.	Cash	1500			
		7500			7500

Prepayment of insurance

Let us assume that the insurance premiums were paid in advance as follows:

1 January 19X0	£350
31 December 19X0	50
	£400

These transactions will be shown in the insurance account as under:

Insurance account

19X0		£	
1 Jan.	Cash	350	
31 Dec.	Cash	50	

The premium paid on 31 December 19X0 is the prepayment of an expense for the year ending 31 December 19X1. Hence, it cannot be shown as an expense for the year ended 31 December 19X0. Thus the purpose of the adjustment is:

1 to measure the expense applicable to the year ended 31 December 19X0, and to transfer this amount to the profit and loss account for that year;
2 to carry forward the premium paid in advance to the following year.

The adjusted account will appear as follows:

Insurance account

19X0			£	19X0		£
1 Jan.	Cash		350	31 Dec. Profit & loss a/c		350
31 Dec.	Cash		50	31 Dec. Prepaid c/d		50
			400			400
19X1						
1 Jan.	Prepaid b/d		50			

We may note that the insurance prepaid at 31 December 19X0 is brought down as a debit balance on 1 January 19X1, and as a result:

1. there is a debit balance in favour of the firm on 31 December 19X0;
2. the firm will not have to pay the premium of £50 in the subsequent year, if the yearly premium is only due and payable on 1 January each year.

The trial balance on 31 December 19X0 may now be adjusted as follows:

	£	£
Insurance	350	
Insurance prepaid	50	

Assuming that the firm pays the insurance premium in the following year on due date, the insurance account for that year will be as follows:

Insurance account

19X1		£	19X1	£
1 Jan.	Prepaid b/d	50	31 Dec. Profit & loss a/c	400
1 Jan.	Cash	350		
		400		400

The reader will observe how easily the accounts system permits the adjustments made in respect of the accruals of revenue and expenses to be reconciled with the subsequent receipts and payment of cash. Although we have interfered with the recording process in order to adjust the accounts so as to reflect the true picture at the end of the accounting period, the double-entry system continues to record the accounting flows and is not itself affected by the adjustments which have been made.

The results of the accrual adjustments

The reader will recall that the trial balance is merely a working paper which the accountant uses to extract the information which he requires from the accounts system, and to check its accuracy. We may alter the original details shown on the first trial balance to reflect the adjustments which we have so far made.

Example

The adjusted trial balance for John Smith's business as at 31 December 19X0 may be set out as follows:

	£ Dr.	£ Cr.
Capital		25 000
Motor vehicles	10 000	
Furniture and fittings	2 500	
Purchases	31 000	
Bank balance	6 060	
Sales		70 000
Debtors	18 000	
Creditors		3 500
Rent	6 000	
Rent accrued		1 500
Insurance	350	
Insurance prepaid	50	
Salaries	22 800	
Motor expenses	2 000	
Light and heat	1 000	
General expenses	300	
Rent receivable		60
	100 060	100 060

The effect of these adjustments on the revenues and expenses for the year ended 31 December 19X0 may be summarized as follows:

	£		£
Purchases	31 000	Sales	70 000
Rent	6 000	Rent receivable	60
Salaries	22 800		
Insurance	350		
Motor expenses	2 000		
Light and heat	1 000		
General expenses	300		

It will be noted also that the adjustments have given rise to the following balances on the accounts:

	£ Dr.	£ Cr.
Rent accrued		1500
Insurance prepaid	50	

As these balances represent sums owing by the business and debts due to the business, they will be shown, as we shall see in Chapter 11, as liabilities and assets respectively at the end of the accounting period.

The matching of revenues and expenses

The purpose underlying the accountant's efforts to identify and correctly measure the revenues and expenses of an accounting period is to attempt to match them so as to obtain a measure of the 'financial effort' of earning the revenues of that period. The accountant's concern is always with financial efficiency which he equates with profit. The matching of expenses and revenues is far more complicated than appears at first sight. So far, we have assumed that by correctly measuring the revenues and expenses attributable to the accounting year they have been correctly matched. In other words, we have made the assumption that the expenses of the accounting period are the expenses related to the revenues of that period. The realization concept permits the accountant to recognize only financial results in the form of sales revenues. It is well known, of course, that there is a time-lag between buying or manufacturing goods for sale and selling them. At the end of an accounting period, therefore, there will always be goods awaiting sale and raw materials unused. The expenses attributable to unsold goods and unused materials, usually described as stocks, must be excluded from the expenses of the period and carried forward to the next accounting period, when the goods will have been sold and the materials used. The importance of stock adjustments to the correct measurement of periodic profit is crucial.

Stock adjustments

By definition, the closing stock at the end of an accounting period is the residue of the purchases of that period which remains unsold or unused.

Example

John Smith's purchases account includes all goods purchased during the year ended 31 December 19X0. At the end of the year, the stock of materials unused is quantified, and its cost price is valued at £3000. The accounting problems relating to this stock are as follows:

1   Since the business has to pay for all goods purchased, it would be illogical to reduce the purchases account by the amount of stock at the end of the year. Hence, the purchases account must not be adjusted and the total purchases must be charged as expenses.
2   By charging all purchases against sales, however, the profit for the year would be overstated by £3000. Means must be found, therefore, to take the closing stock out of the profit calculation. This is effected by opening stock account on 31 December 19X0 and posting the stock to it.

Stock account

19X0	£	
31 Dec.	3000	

As soon as an account is opened for the purpose of recording a flow of value it is necessary to describe the source of the flow and its destination. We know that the purchases account is not the source of the flow of stocks to the stock account, because we have deliberately refused to adjust the purchases account. We know also that, but for the need to measure profits, we would not value stocks at the end of the year. Hence, by a fiction, the accountant states that the stock adjustment comes from the profit and loss account which is employed to measure profit. The full accounting entries are, therefore, as follows:

Profit and loss account for the year ended 31 December 19X0

		19X0	£
		31 Dec. Stock	3000

Stock account

19X0	£	
31 Dec. Profit & loss a/c	3000	

The effect of these entries is to solve the problem of profit measurement, because the *credit* flow from the profit and loss account is taken into the calculation of profit, as follows:

	£		£
Purchases	31 000	Sales	70 000
		Closing stocks	3 000

The stock account is an interesting account because it exists only to measure profit and since that is done on the last day of the accounting year, the stock account only exists for one day. In fact, the closing stock on the last day of the year is the opening stock on the first day of the next accounting year. Hence, on the first day of the next accounting period, the stock must be posted to the profit and loss account of the next period, as follows:

Profit and loss account for the year ended 31 December 19X1

19X1	£	
1 Jan. Stock	3000	

Stock account

19X0	£	19X1	£
31 Dec. Profit & loss a/c	3000	1 Jan. Profit & loss a/c	3000

The reader will now observe that the stock account has served its purpose and may be closed. This is done by drawing a double line beneath the entries.

Stock account

19X0	£	19X1	£
31 Dec. Profit & loss a/c	3000	1 Jan. Profit & loss a/c	3000

In practice, the account will not reverse the stock into the profit and loss account of the year 19X1, until 31 December 19X1 when he prepares that account. As a result, the trial balance for the year ended 31 December 19X1 will include a debit balance in respect of the stock account in the amount of £3000. As the trial balance is always extracted before the stock adjustment is made, the opening stock always appears on the trial balance but the closing stock is never shown.

Summary

In this section of Part 2, we consider the procedural problems involved in periodic measurement. This chapter deals with the problems of adapting the financial accounting data lodged in the data-processing system to the objective of measuring periodic profit.

The first stages in the measurement of periodic profit are:

1   the identification of the revenues attributable to transactions concluded in the accounting period;
2   the identification of the expenses related to those revenues.

The accruals concept requires the inclusion of amounts receivable and payable, as well as amounts received and paid, in the measurement of revenues and expenses. We examined the accounting procedures involved in accruing revenue and expenses.

The objective of periodic measurement is the matching of revenues and expenses to establish accounting profit. The exclusion of stocks unsold at the end of the accounting period is a further problem in periodic measurement considered in this chapter.

Question

State the concepts which apply to the manner in which periodic revenues and expenses are identified and related. Illustrate your answer.

Problems

1   If goods which cost £10 000 were in stock on 1 January, goods purchased during the year amounted to £40 000 and goods costing £15 000 were in stock at 31 December, state the cost of the goods which were sold during the year.

2   From the following information construct the combined Rent and Rates Account for the year ended 30 June 19X9 showing the figures that would appear for rent and rates in the profit and loss account and the figures that would appear in the balance sheet as at 30 June 19X9.

The property of the business was rented at £1600 per annum payable quarterly in arrears on the usual quarter days. The rates were £600 per annum payable half yearly in advance on 1 October and 1 April in each year. The rent was one quarter in arrears on 30 June 19X8 and the rates for the half year to 30 September 19X8 had not been paid.

The following transactions took place during the year to 30 June 19X9:

19X8
July 2   Cash—One quarter's rent to 24 June 19X8
July 2   Cash—Half year's rates to 30 September 19X8
Oct. 10   Cash—Half year's rates to 31 March 19X9
Oct. 10   Cash—One quarter's rent to 29 September 19X8

19X9

Jan. 4   Cash—One quarter's rent to 25 December 19X8
April 6   Cash—Half year's rates to 30 September 19X9
April 6   Cash—One quarter's rent to 25 March 19X9

3   Star Enterprises Ltd is a company formed to manage the affairs of a successful
    pop group. All the group's revenue and expenses are recorded in the company's
    books. The group's recording contract with IME Records stipulates a payment
    of advance royalties of £50 000 on the recording of a record. Actual royalties are
    50p per record. Any sales in excess of 100 000 copies will result in additional royalties
    being paid. If sales are less than 100 000 then any excess advance is recouped from
    future payments.

    During the year ended 31 March 19X8 the company received the following
    royalties:

	£	£
Advance Record 1		50 000
Advance Record 2	50 000	
less: Shortfall on Record 1	17 000	33 000
Additional royalties		
Record 2		44 000
Advance Record 3		50 000

Record 3 was recorded and released shortly before the year end. No sales figures
are yet available.

The company has also incurred advance expenditure of £35 000 on promoting
a tour the group will undertake during April 19X8.

Required:

(a) State the accounting principles which are used in revenue and expense recognition.
(b) Write a report to the management of the company advising on the treatment of
    royalties and advance expenditure, and showing how these items will be treated
    in the accounts to 31 March 19X8.

(Problem supplied by A.J. Naughton, Leeds Polytechnic)

Chapter 10

Losses in asset values and periodic measurement

In the previous chapter, we discussed the various adjustments to the data in the double-entry book-keeping system, so that this data might correctly reflect the income and expenses appropriate to the activities conducted during the accounting period in question. The accrual of revenues and expenses involved, as we saw, the exclusion of payments and receipts for other periods.

In this chapter, we discuss adjustments which are made in respect of losses in asset values. The first which we will examine concerns the depreciation of fixed assets. The second is the loss in the value of debtors caused by the recognition that a portion of the debtor balances will not be paid and must be recognized as bad debts, and that a further portion may ultimately prove to be bad so that a provision for doubtful debts must also be made.

The treatment of losses in asset values

The concept of prudence requires that losses should be recognized as soon as they become evident, so as to ensure that profit and capital values are not overstated in financial reports. Losses in asset values appear under a variety of guises. Losses of cash and stock by theft, embezzlement or accidental damage are written off immediately against income, insurance recoveries being treated as a separate matter. Losses to fixed assets due to accidental damage, theft or other causes are also written off against income, as are losses arising on the sale of fixed assets which result from a difference between the sale price and the book value of the assets sold. Most fixed assets also diminish in value as their usefulness is exhausted over a period of years. Finally, losses in asset values also result from the exercise of judgement, as in the case of bad debts when accountants have to decide whether a recorded value does exist at all. In this connection, a discretion exists as regards the valuation of assets such as goodwill and organization costs, usually described as 'fictitious assets', in that intangible asset values are frequently written off purely as an act of judgement.

Losses in the value of fixed assets

Losses in the value of fixed assets arising through sale, accidental loss or theft present no difficulties from an accounting viewpoint, for such losses are written off immediately against income. By contrast, the diminution in value described as depreciation has been the subject of much controversy. As an accounting concept, depreciation is of a complex nature and now occupies an important role in three different areas of the subject. First, it is related to the problem of cost allocation, both as regards the matching of revenues and expenses in the process of profit measurement, and as regards product costing in management accounting. Second, it is related to the concept of capital maintenance in income theory. Third, it is central to decision making as regards the life and the replacement of fixed assets. The notion of depreciation has varied and multiplied in such a way that its analysis is not an easy matter. In this chapter, we take a limited view of depreciation, and concern ourselves solely with its financial accounting implications.

The nature of depreciation

The term 'depreciation' is susceptible to four different meanings:

1   a fall in price
2   physical deterioration
3   a fall in value
4   an allocation of fixed-asset costs.

Depreciation as a fall in price

A fall in the price of an asset is one aspect of depreciation, but it is not a reliable guide to a valid accounting concept of depreciation. A fall in price may occur independently or any decrease in the usefulness of an asset, for example, the immediate fall in price occurring on the purchase of a new asset.

Depreciation as physical deterioration

Depreciation in this sense means impaired utility arising directly through deterioration or indirectly through obsolescence. It is implied in much of the discussion of this concept of depreciation that an asset is 'used up', so that the 'use' of an asset is the extent to which it has been used up. It is evident that these ideas are represented in the rates of depreciation which are attached to depreciable assets. It should be noted, however, that an asset is not necessarily 'used up' through use, because adequate maintenance may prevent deterioration in some cases. Thus, if irrigation ditches are well maintained, they will not deteriorate through use.

The concept of depreciation as deferred maintenance has not been properly investigated, although it is a concept of depreciation which may be more relevant than conventional concepts as regards certain types of assets.

Depreciation as a fall in value

There are problems associated with the use of the term 'value' and the relationship of depreciation to the concept of value. Value may mean 'cost value' 'exchange value', 'use value' (utility) or 'esteem value'.

Clearly, 'cost value' is not affected by events occurring after acquisition, so that it is not meaningful to relate depreciation to a fall in cost value. 'Exchange value' changes only twice in the experience of the owner of an asset—at the point of purchase and at the point of sale. In this sense, depreciation may mean only a fall in price between two points, and we have already discussed this concept of depreciation. Depreciation as a decrease in utility is also already covered by the concept of physical deterioration, while the notion of the esteem value of an asset is entirely subjective and not amenable to an objective concept of measurement.

If one attempts to relate the notion of depreciation to economic income, however, one would have the basis of an accounting concept of particular usefulness for decision making. The economic value of an asset is regarded as the discounted value of expected future cash flows associated with that asset in a particular use. Hence, depreciation may be conceptualized and measured as the progressive decrease in the net cash flows yielded by the asset as its economic utility declines through time, for whatever reason. Normally, of course, its income-earning capacity falls due to increasing inefficiency arising from physical deterioration. As regards certain classes of assets, for example computers, falls in economic value have occurred more rapidly from obsolescence.

Depreciation as cost allocation

The orthodox view of accountants is that depreciation represents that part of the cost of a fixed asset which is not recoverable when the asset is finally put out of use. Provision for this loss of capital is an integral cost of conducting the business during the effective commercial life of the asset and is not dependent upon the amount of profit earned.

The practice of treating depreciation as an allocation of historical cost is based on two assumptions:

1 that the expected benefit to be derived from an asset is proportional to an estimate usage rate;
2 that it is possible to measure that benefit.

Hence, the current practice is part of the procedure of matching periodic revenues with the cost of earning those revenues. The essential difference between fixed assets and current operating expenses is that the former are regarded as costs which yield benefits over a period of years, and hence must be allocated as expenses against the revenues of those years, whereas the latter yield all their benefits in the current year, so that they may be treated as the expenses of that year and matched against the revenues which they have created.

The practice of treating depreciation as an allocation of costs presents a number of serious theoretical problems. The known objective facts about an asset are few, and adequate records are not usually kept of the various incidents in the life in use of an asset apart from its purchase price. Repair and maintenance cost, for example, are charged separately, as are running costs. Other unresolved problems concern the selection of appropriate bases for allocating the cost of depreciable assets, for example, should depreciation be calculated by reference to units of actual use rather than time use? Finally, should the residual value of an asset be regarded as a windfall gain or should it be set off against the replacement cost of the asset rather than used as a point of reference for calculating the proportion of the cost of fixed assets which should be allocated as depreciation?

The accounting concept of depreciation

According to the AICPA, depreciation accounting is 'a system of accounting which aims to distribute the cost . . . of tangible capital assets, less salvage (if any), over the estimated useful life of the unit . . . in a systematic and rational manner. It is a process of allocation, not of valuation.' (AICPA, 1953.)

From the foregoing definition, two important points may be made:

1   Depreciation accounting is not concerned with any attempt to measure the value of an asset at any point of time. One is trying to measure the value of the benefit the asset has provided during a given accounting period, and that benefit is valued as a portion of the cost of the asset. Hence, the balance-sheet value of depreciable assets is that portion of the original cost which has not yet been allocated as a periodic expense in the process of profit measurement. It does not purport to represent the current value of those assets.
2   Depreciation accounting does not itself provide funds for the replacement of depreciable assets, but the charging of depreciation ensures the maintenance intact of the original money capital of the entity. Indeed, a provision for depreciation is not identified with cash or any specific asset or assets.

Factors in the measurement of depreciation

Four factors are important in the process of measuring depreciation from an accounting viewpoint, as follows:

1   identifying the cost of the asset;
2   ascertaining its useful life;
3   determining the expected residual value;
4   selecting an appropriate method of depreciation which must be systematic and rational.

Identifying the cost of the asset

Depreciation is calculated on historical cost values, which include acquisition costs and all incidental costs involved in bringing an asset into use. In the case of buildings, for example, cost includes any commissions, survey, legal and other charges involved in the purchase, together with the costs incurred in preparing and modifying buildings for a particular use. In the case of plant and machinery, all freight, insurance and installation costs should be capitalized.

Problems occur where a firm manufactures assets, for example, an engineering firm may construct a foundry. In such cases, the cost of labour, materials etc. associated with the activity of construction should be segregated from those associated with the normal trading activities, and capitalized. There are costing problems involved in ascertaining such costs. Moreover, improvements effected to existing assets should be capitalized. The distinction between a repair and an improvement is not always easy to establish. In some circumstances, the intention may be to repair but the cheaper solution is a replacement. An old boiler, for example, may be replaced more cheaply than repaired. The cost of repairs is chargeable as a current expense: the cost of replacement should be capitalized.

Ascertaining the useful life of an asset

The useful life of an asset is defined as that period during which it is expected to be useful in the profit earning operations of the firm. In most cases, the useful life is determined by two factors:

1 the rate of deterioration;
2 obsolescence.

The rate of deterioration is a function of the type of use to which the asset is put, and the extent of that use. A lorry used by civil engineering contractors may have a shorter life expectancy than a lorry employed by cartage contractors, for the former may operate in rough terrain, whereas the latter is used on roads. It is not unusual to find that the estimated useful life of a lorry in the first case may be two years or less, whereas the estimated life in the second may well be four years. Moreover, an asset used intensively will have a shorter life than one used for shorter periods. In this respect, assets are built to certain specifications which determine to some extent their durability in use. The useful life is determined on the basis of past experience, which is a good indicator of the probable life of a particular asset.

It should be pointed out, however, that the estimated useful life of an asset is also a question of policy and may be determined accordingly. Thus, a car-hire firm may decide to renew its fleet each year, and in this case the useful life of its fleet of cars is one year for the purpose of calculating depreciation.

The problem of taking obsolescence into account in assessing the useful life of an asset is altogether more complex, for obsolescence occurs with the appearance of an asset incorporating the result of technological developments. In respect of certain assets, such as cars, each year may see the introduction of an improved model, so that owners of fleets of cars may decide that obsolescence, or assumed obsolescence, is a more important factor in the useful life of cars than depreciation. Relying on new models or improved versions each year, a firm may decide to renew its fleet each year. However, it is hard to distinguish the extent to which such decisions are influenced by the need to have the latest product or to avoid excessive repair bills stemming from large mileages. It would seem, therefore, that obsolescence is one factor which affects the useful life of fixed assets and accelerates their progress towards the scrapheap. Accordingly, the estimated useful life of an asset is determined by that length of time for which, as a matter of policy, it is wished to employ an asset. That length of time will be a function of a number of factors, but the most important will be the increasing cost of employing that asset due to higher yearly maintenance cost and possible declining revenues.

From a theoretical point of view, there is a point at which the net cash inflows associated with an asset are equal to the costs of operating that asset. Those costs may be expressed as the opportunity costs represented by revenues forgone as a result of using that asset rather than replacing it, or the opportunity costs represented by alternative returns, which may be derived from cash outlays committed to repairs and maintenance. These two measures of opportunity cost are not necessarily equivalent. In terms of this analysis, the length of useful life of an asset would be determined as in Fig. 2.10.

Fig. 2.10

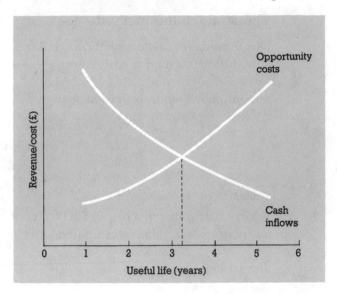

Determining the expected residual value

The residual value of an asset is estimated at the time of acquisition so that the net cost may be allocated to the accounting periods during which the asset is usefully employed. The residual value is the expected realizable value of the asset at the end of its useful life. Hence, the residual value will depend on the manner and on the length of time that the asset is to be used. Where, for example, it is intended to use an asset until it is completely worn out or obsolete, its residual value will be negligible. Where, as in the case of the replacement of fleets of cars, the length of useful life is shortened to one year, the residual value will be higher.

Where it is intended to extract the maximum use from an asset, the residual value should be nominal: where it is intended to replace the asset when it still has some useful life, its residual value should be estimated on a conservative basis so as to minimize the effect of variations in the price of second-hand assets. The cost allocated against the revenues of the accounting periods involved are calculated as follows:

Cost of acquisition (say)	£2000
Residual value (say)	200
Cost to be allocated as depreciation	1800

Selecting the method of depreciation

There are several methods of depreciation but the more common are the straight-line method and the decreasing-balance method.

The matching convention requires that 'the choice of the method of allocating the cost of a long-term asset over its effective working life should depend upon the pattern of expected benefits obtainable in each period from its use' (Barton, 1984).

The straight-line method

The formula for calculating the annual depreciation provision under the straight-line method is as follows:

annual depreciation provision

$$= \frac{\text{acquisition cost} - \text{estimated residual value}}{\text{expected useful life in years}}$$

Example

A lorry is acquired at a cost of £3000. Its estimated useful life is 3 years, and its residual value is estimated at £600.

$$\text{annual depreciation provision} = \frac{£3000 - £600}{3 \text{ years}}$$

$$= \underline{£800 \text{ per annum}}$$

The straight-line method allocates the net cost equally to each year of the useful life of an asset. It is particularly applicable to assets such as patents and leases where time is the key factor in the effluxion of the benefits to be derived from the use of an asset. Although it is in general use for other fixed assets, it suffers from the following disadvantages:

1 it does not reflect that the greatest loss in the market value occurs in the first year of use;
2 it does not reflect the unevenness of the loss in the market value over several years;

3 it does not reflect the diminishing losses in value which occur in later years, as the asset approaches the end of its useful life.

For these reasons, the straight-line method of depreciation does not provide an accurate measure of the cost of the service potential allocated to the respective accounting periods during which an asset is employed.

The decreasing-balance method

To calculate the annual depreciation provision under this method, a fixed percentage is applied to the balance of the net costs not yet allocated as an expense at the end of the previous accounting period. The balance of unallocated costs decreases each year, and, theoretically, the balance of the unallocated costs at the end of the estimated useful life should equal the estimated residual value. The formula used to calculate the fixed percentage to be applied to the allocation of net costs as depreciation is as follows:

$$r = 1 - n\sqrt{\frac{s}{c}}$$

where *n* = the expected useful life in years
  s = the residual value (this value must be significant or the depreciation rate will be nearly one)
  c = the acquisition cost
  r = the rate of depreciation to be applied.

Example

Calculate the rate of depreciation to be applied to a lorry acquired at a cost of £3000, having an expected useful life of three years and an estimated residual value of £600.

$$r = 1 - \sqrt[3]{\frac{£600}{£3000}}$$

$$= 0.4152 \text{ or } 41.52\%$$

The depreciation calculation for each of the three years would be as follows:

		£
	Cost	3000
Year 1	Depreciation at 41.52% of £3000	1246
	Unallocated costs end of year 1	1754
Year 2	Depreciation at 41.52% of £1754	728
	Unallocated costs end of year 2	1026
Year 3	Depreciation at 41.52% of £1026	426
	Residual value at end of year 3	600

In practice, the annual percentage rate of depreciation is not calculated so precisely. A rate is selected which approximates to the estimated useful life, for example an estimated useful life of three years would imply a 33 ⅓ per cent rate of depreciation. The advantage of the decreasing-balance method is that it approximates reality in respect of certain assets, for example motor vehicles, where the depreciation calculated in the first year is greatest, thereby reflecting the greater loss in market value at this stage of a vehicle's life.

Depreciation and total asset costs

The total costs associated with the benefits derived from fixed assets consist of depreciation and the costs of repairs and maintenance. It follows, therefore, that the proper application of the matching convention to the allocation of total asset costs requires that depreciation and repairs and maintenance be considered jointly as regards selection of an appropriate method for allocating total asset costs to the accounting periods benefiting from their use. The depreciation calculated under the two methods which have been examined may be compared in Figs 2.11 and 2.12.

The cost of repairs and maintenance may be assumed to increase through time, as the asset deteriorates through use. This is reflected in real life by the expectancy that the first year in use should be relatively trouble free. The pattern of repair and maintenance cost is illustrated as in Fig. 2.13.

The total annual assets costs under the straight-line and decreasing-balance methods of depreciation may be compared as in Figs 2.14 and 2.15.

From the foregoing illustrations, it may be seen that the decreasing-balance method provides a better allocation of total asset costs over the useful life of an asset than the straight-line method.

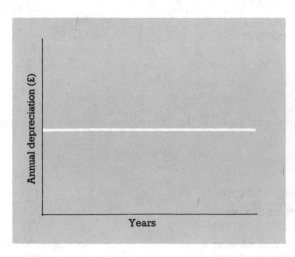

Fig. 2.11

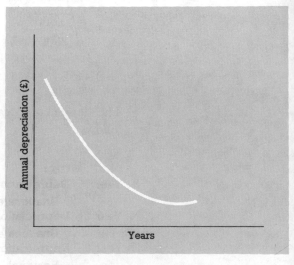

Fig. 2.12

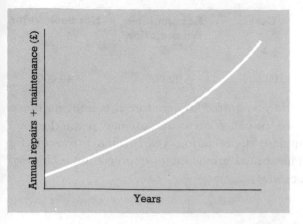

Fig. 2.13

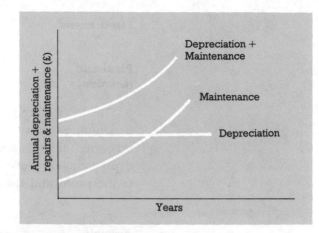

Fig. 2.14

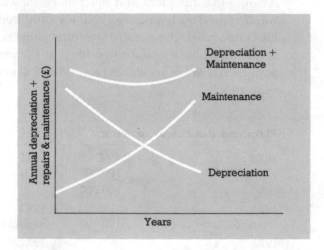

Fig. 2.15

Accounting for depreciation

There are several methods for providing for depreciation. Legislation requires that the following information in respect of fixed assets be shown on the balance sheet:

1 the cost or valuation, as the case may be;
2 the aggregate amount provided or written off since the date of acquisition or valuation, as the case may be, for depreciation or diminution in value.

The net book value of fixed assets is the difference between *1* and *2* above.

Example

The historical cost of plant and machinery is £100 000. Accumulated depreciation to date is £60 000 and the net book value is, therefore, £40 000. This information is disclosed as follows:

Fixed assets	Cost	Accumulated depreciation	Net book value
	£	£	£
Plant and machinery	100 000	60 000	40 000

The accounting procedure required to generate this information is to debit the acquisition cost, or valuation as the case may be, in the asset account, and to accumulate depreciation yearly in a provision for depreciation account. The annual provision for depreciation is charged to the profit and loss account.

Example

Assume that the plant and machinery shown in the previous example was acquired on 1 January 19X0 for £100 000, that its estimated useful life is five years, the expected residual value is nil, and that depreciation is calculated on a straight-line basis at the rate of £20 000 a year. The appropriate accounts would record the following data by the end of the year 19X2.

Plant and machinery account

19X0	£	19X0	£
1 Jan. Cash	100 000	31 Dec. Balance c/d	100 000
	100 000		100 000
19X1		19X1	
1 Jan. Balance b/d	100 000	31 Dec. Balance c/d	100 000
19X2		19X2	
1 Jan. Balance b/d	100 000	31 Dec. Balance c/d	100 000
19X3			
1 Jan. Balance b/d	100 000		

Provision for depreciation account

19X0	£	10X0	£
31 Dec. Balance c/d	20 000	31 Dec. Profit & loss a/c	20 000
	20 000		20 000
19X1		19X1	
		1 Jan. Balance b/d	20 000
31 Dec. Balance c/d	40 000	31 Dec. Profit & loss a/c	20 000
	40 000		40 000
19X2		19X2	
		1 Jan. Balance b/d	40 000
31 Dec. Balance c/d	60 000	31 Dec. Profit & loss a/c	20 000
	60 000		60 000
		19X3	
		1 Jan. Balance b/d	60 000

Profit and loss account for the year ended 31 Dec. 19X0

	£
Provision for depreciation	20 000

Profit and loss account for the year ended 31 Dec. 19X1

	£
Provision for depreciation	20 000

Profit and loss account for the year ended 31 Dec. 19X2

	£
Provision for depreciation	20 000

Accounting for the disposal of assets

The cost of the benefits derived from the use of assets cannot be ascertained until the assets have completed their useful life and have been sold or otherwise disposed of. In the meantime, the annual provision for depreciation is merely an estimate of that actual cost. The practice is to make an adjustment to the profit for the year of sale in respect of any difference between the book value and the realized value of the asset. It is not the practice, therefore, to attempt to reopen previous years to make a correction for the actual depreciation suffered.

The method is to open an asset realization account, and to reverse the existing entries in the asset and the provision for depreciation accounts in respect of the asset sold or disposed of, recording directly in the asset realization account the sale price, if any, obtained.

Example

On 31 December 19X3, plant and machinery acquired at a cost of £100 000 in 19X0 was sold for £30 000. The accumulated depreciation to date was £60 000. The accounting procedure for dealing with this event is as follows:

Plant and machinery account

19X3	£	19X3	£
1 Jan. Balance b/d	100 000	31 Dec. Asset realization	100 000
	100 000		100 000

Provision for depreciation account

19X3	£	19X3	£
31 Dec. Asset realization	60 000	1 Jan. Balance b/d	60 000
	60 000		60 000

Cash book

19X3	£
31 Dec. Asset realization	30 000

Asset realization account

19X3	£	19X3	£
31 Dec. Plant & machinery	100 000	31 Dec. Cash	30 000
		31 Dec. Provision for depreciation	60 000
		31 Dec. Profit & loss a/c	10 000
	100 000		100 000

Profit and loss account for the year ended 31 December 19X3

	£		
Loss on sale of plant and machinery	10 000		

Narrowing accounting differences

In Chapter 5 we discussed the problems created in the financial reporting process by the existence of a variety of practices permitted by the concepts of accounting. These problems appear in the lack of comparability between the financial reports of different companies, and in the consequent inability of users of financial reports to make informed judgements about different enterprises. The Accounting Standards Committee was established with the purpose of narrowing the areas of difference and variety.

Depreciation is one area where substantial differences exist between the range of accounting methods permitted by the concepts of accounting. In common with other controversial topics in accounting, many of the differences have their origins in the means adopted for allocating costs. As it is impossible to devise cost allocation methods which are entirely objective, accountants resort to methods which are more or less arbitrary. For example, the straight-line method of depreciation assumes that asset costs should be allocated to successive periods in uniform amounts, whereas the decreasing-balance method of depreciation assumes that rate of allocation should be constant through time. The assumptions underlying these alternative methods are defensible in the context of the circumstances which they also assume. In effect, 'for each situation in which allocation is contemplated, there is a variety of possible allocation methods, each of which could be defended. The allocation problem arises because there is no conclusive way to choose one method in preference to all others, except arbitrarily.' (Thomas, 1974.)

Although there is no solution to the problems posed by the existence of competing methods of allocating fixed asset costs through depreciation to successive accounting periods, users of financial reports may be assisted in evaluating the financial results reported, and making the adjustments necessary when comparing different companies. It was for this reason that the Accounting Standards Committee issued SSAP 12 'Accounting for Depreciation'.

The 1970s witnessed an increasing tendency for companies to account for the effects of inflation upon fixed assets which led to wide variations in the treatment of depreciation. The statement is essentially a restatement of basic principles.

Depreciation is defined in SSAP 12 as the 'measure of the wearing out, consumption or other reduction in the useful economic life of a fixed asset, whether arising from use, effluxion of time or obsolescence through technology or market changes'. Depreciation should represent a fair allocation of the asset's value over the useful life of the asset. To determine a fair allocation requires consideration of the cost or valuation of the asset, its nature and expected useful life and its estimated residual value. Cost less residual value should then be allocated over the periods which benefit from the asset's use throughout its expected useful life.

The statement requires that provision for depreciation of fixed assets having a finite useful life be made by allocating the cost or revalued amount less estimated residual values of the assets as fairly as possible to the periods expected to benefit from their use. On a revision of the estimated useful life of an asset, the undepreciated cost should be charged over the revised remaining useful life. Where the method of depreciation is changed, which is permissible only where the new method will give a fairer presentation of the results and financial position, the undepreciated cost should be written off over the remaining useful life on the new basis, commencing with the period in which the change is made, and the effect, if material, disclosed in the year of change. Where assets are revalued, depreciation should be based on the revalued amount and current estimate of remaining useful life with the effect, if material, disclosed in the year of change.

The following should be disclosed in the financial statements for each major class of depreciable asset:

1   the depreciation methods used;
2   the useful lives or the depreciation rates used;
3   total depreciation allocated for the period;
4   the gross amount of depreciable assets and the related accumulated depreciation.

No specific method of depreciation is laid down in the statement, this being the responsibility of the management of the business, i.e. to select a method most appropriate to the asset in question. Freehold land need not normally be depreciated but buildings with a limited life should be. This latter requirement was a major innovation. Prior to SSAP 12, it was common practice for depreciation not to be provided for buildings on the ground that market values tended to exceed net book values shown on the balance sheet. SSAP 12 takes the view that because buildings have a limited life, they should be depreciated using the same criteria applied to other fixed assets. This requirement provoked strong objection from property investment companies. SSAP 19 'Accounting for Investment Properties' (1981) allows companies not to provide for depreciation in respect of investment properties. An investment property is defined as an interest in land and or buildings, where construction work and development are completed and which is held for its investment potential.

Losses arising from the default of debtors

The necessity to give credit to customers results in the investment of substantial funds in what are in effect short-term loans. There are three important financial aspects as regards debtors which are of interest to both management and investors. First, there is the problem of working capital management in respect of the balance of claims in favour of and against the firm, and its implications in respect of liquidity and solvency. Second, there is the problem of the overall level of debtors in relation to other assets, and the need for the firm to have sufficient funds to invest in the maintenance and expansion of its profit-earning structure. This has implications for present and future profitability. Third, there is the risk associated with the recovery of amounts due from debtors. This is a problem of credit control and the prevention of losses due to default by debtors.

The valuation of amounts due from debtors at the end of an accounting period presents no difficulty as regards determining debtor balances in an objective manner. Provided that accounting records have been kept properly, the objectivity of the valuation of debtors is founded in the law of contract and is a claim enforceable at law against debtors. The recoverability of debts, however, is a question to which the accountant must address himself, since the concept of prudence requires that losses should be recognized when they arise. The recoverability of debts for financial reporting purposes is a question of law in some cases and of judgement in others. Thus, where a debtor has been declared bankrupt the recoverability of the debt is subject to the law of bankruptcy, and where no dividend is likely, the loss must be recognized and the amount written off as bad. When, however, a debtor cannot be traced or is unable to pay owing to personal circumstances and the sum involved does not warrant legal action, then the decision to recognize the loss is a matter of judgement. By and large, accountants examine the debtors ledger at the end of the financial year and identify those debts likely to be bad debts by reference to the delay in payment and the attempts made to secure payment. Debts considered irrecoverable are written off by debiting the profit and loss account and if they should be recovered subsequently then the debt is restored in the debtors ledger.

Failure to deal adequately with the problem of defaulting debtors will distort the measurement of profit and asset values in the following respects:

1   The measurement of profit for an accounting period will be overstated to the extent that any credit sales taken into profit have created debts which are not recoverable.

2   The measurement of profit for the subsequent accounting period will be understated to the extent that debts created in the previous

accounting period are recognized belatedly as bad and written off against the profit of the subsequent accounting year.

3   The balance sheet statement of the value of debtors includes debts which, though legally enforceable, are irrecoverable. It is not possible, for example, to recover debts from bankrupt persons, or persons who cannot be traced.

Accordingly:

1   bad debts should be recognized as soon as they arise;
2   the risk of further possible losses should be anticipated in accordance with the concept of prudence.

Accounting practice is to deal separately with the problem of debts which are recognized as bad, and to anticipate further losses in the future. In effect, three types of debts are distinguished:

1   good debts;
2   bad debts;
3   doubtful debts.

The treatment of bad debts

Careful supervision of debtors' accounts will minimize bad debts. The enforcement of time limits for settlement of accounts helps in the prevention of a buildup of arrears and in identifying doubtful debts. Once a debt is recognized as bad, it should be written off immediately, so that the list of debtor accounts represents only good debts, that is, those expected to be paid in full.

Example

H. Smith Ltd, a firm of building contractors, had been regular customers of Hervey Building Supplies Ltd and enjoyed a credit limit of £1000. On 1 January 19X0 the balance on its account in the books of Hervey was £900, and purchases in January 19X0 totalled £150. H. Smith informed Hervey on 5 February of its inability to pay its account. Hervey stopped further credit to H. Smith until the position was clarified. Shortly thereafter, it was discovered that H. Smith was insolvent, and that it was unlikely that any of the debt of £1050 would be paid. On 1 March, it was decided to treat the debt as a bad debt.

The accounting entries in the books of Hervey would be as follows:

H. Smith Ltd account

19X0	£	19X0	£
1 Jan. Balance	900	1 March Bad debt	1050
31 Jan. Sales	150		
	1050		1050

Bad debts account

19X0	
1 March H. Smith Ltd	1050

At the end of the accounting period, the total on the bad debts account is debited to the profit and loss account.

Example

Assume that the only bad debt suffered by Hervey Building Supplies Ltd was in respect of H. Smith Ltd in the sum of £1050, as above. The bad debts account for the year ended 31 December 19X0 would be closed as follows:

Bad debts account

19X0	£	19X0	£
1 March H. Smith Ltd	1050	31 Dec. Profit & loss a/c	1050
	1050		1050

Profit and loss account for the year ended 31 Dec. 19X0

19X0	£	
Bad debts	1050	

The treatment of doubtful debts

The question of doubtful debts, as distinct from bad debts, is examined only at the end of each accounting period. A final scrutiny of the debtors account will eliminate all those accounts considered to be bad and the necessary transfers will be made to the bad debts account. Of the remaining debtors, some may ultimately prove to be bad but there may be reasonable grounds for hoping that all remaining debtors will settle their accounts. The concept of prudence requires that the risk should be discounted of further debts proving to be bad. The normal practice is to create a provision for doubtful debts out of the current year's profit, without seeking to identify particular debts as being doubtful of recovery. There are several methods of estimating doubtful debts. The most common method is to allow past experience to establish the percentage of debtors which prove to be bad, and to calculate the provision for doubtful debts by applying this percentage to the debtors outstanding at the end of the accounting period. A more accurate method is to classify debtor balances in terms of their age, and to apply to the several groups of debts the loss rates established by experience.

Example

The sales ledger balances existing in the books of the Bumpa Trading Company at the end of the financial year are as follows:

Duration of debts	Amount	Loss rate %	Provision
	£		£
Less than 1 month	10 000	1	100
1–2 months	3 000	3	90
2–3 months	1 000	5	50
3–4 months	500	10	50
Over 4 months	100	20	20
	14 600		310

One of the advantages of this method of creating a provision for doubtful debts is that it enables management to understand the relationship between the slow collection of debts and the financial losses caused by defaulting debtors.

The accounting entries would be as follows:

Profit and loss account for the year ended 31 December 19X0

	£	
Provision for doubtful debts	310	

Provision for doubtful debts account

	19X0	£
	Profit & loss y.e. 31 Dec.	310

The provision for doubtful debts is not identified with any individual debtors. It is carried forward as an estimated liability, and may be shown on the balance sheet as follows:

Balance sheet as at 31 December 19X0

. . . . . .		£	£
Debtors		14 600	
less: Provision for doubtful debts		310	
			14 290

In this manner, the objective of presenting a realistic valuation of trade debts is achieved.

Summary

This chapter examined two important items in the measurement of periodic profit, namely, depreciation and financial losses resulting from bad debts. Both are concerned with the manner in which losses in asset values should be recognized. Depreciation is a difficult problem from a theoretical viewpoint, and its treatment in accounting as an allocation of historical costs is a limited view of this problem. Nevertheless, such treatment is compatible with the matching concept for the allocation of asset costs to the revenues derived from their use. Not all assets are depreciable, and depreciation should take into account all the relevant costs of acquisition as well as the useful life of assets.

Two methods of depreciation were examined, and their implications discussed. The adjustments required on the sale or disposal of assets were also examined.

Losses caused by defaulting debtors were analysed and their impact on the measurement of periodic profit was discussed. Accounting adopts a two-stage approach to this problem, namely the recognition of losses actually incurred by declaring certain debts as *bad*, and the provision against the risk of loss through creating provisions for doubtful debts.

References

AICPA (1953). Accounting Research Bulletin No. 43.

Barton, A.D. (1984). *The Anatomy of Accounting,* University of Queensland Press.

Thomas, A.L. (1974). The allocation problem: Part 2, *Studies in Accounting Research,* p. 2, AAA.

Questions

1 Analyse the main factors which should be considered when selecting a policy for depreciating fixed assets.
2 Explain the main provisions of SSAP 12.

Problems

1 Lodgemoor Company acquired a machine on 1 July 19X1 for £48 000 and immediately spent a further £2000 on its installation. The machine was estimated to have a useful life of eight years and a scrap value of £4000 at the end of this time.
Required:
Compute the depreciation provision for the year ended 30 June 19X2 if the company chooses to use:
(a) The straight-line method
(b) The decreasing-balance method

2 Beale Company purchased a machine on 1 January 19X1, at an invoice price of £142 600. Transportation charges amounted to £2000, and £3400 was spent to install the machine. Costs of removing an old machine to make room for the new one amounted to £1200, and £200 was received for the scrap value of the old machine.
Required:
(a) State the amounts of depreciation which would be provided on the machine for the first year on a straight-line basis and on a decreasing-balance basis, assuming an estimated life of eight years and no salvage value expected at the end of that time.
(b) Compute the depreciation provision for the year ended 31 December 19X3, assuming a revised total life expectancy for the machine of 12 years; assume that depreciation has been recorded through December 31 19X2 on a straight-line basis.

3 From the following information relating to the fixed assets of a business prepare the following accounts as they should appear in the ledger:
(a) plant and machinery;
(b) motor vehicles;
(c) plant and machinery provision for depreciation;
(d) motor vehicles provision for depreciation;
(e) asset realization.
   The plant and machinery was acquired on 1 January 19X5, at a cost of £7500, and the motor vehicles were acquired on 1 July 19X7, at a cost of £3500.
   It has been the practice of the business to depreciate assets using the straight-

line method and they estimate the life of the plant to be ten years and that of the motor vehicles to be five years.

The accounts of the business are made up to 31 December in each year and it is usual to calculate depreciation for a full year on the assets in the possession of the business at balance sheet date.

During the year to 31 December 19X9, a new machine costing £1000 was acquired and a machine bought on 1 January 19X5 for £500 was sold for £325; and a car costing £750 on 1 July 19X7 was sold for £400.

4   The year-end balance on the debtors' account amounted to £100 000. Net sales for the year totalled £1 200 000. Explain how you would deal with the following information.
   (a)   An analysis of the sales ledger indicates that irrecoverable debts amount to £11 400.
   (b)   Past trends suggest that 5 per cent of debts eventually should be provided as doubtful.
   (c)   The existing provision for doubtful debts is £3000.

5   A business maintains in its ledger a combined bad debts and provision for doubtful debts account. The provision was created in the accounts for the year ended 31 March 19X1 by calculating an amount equal to 5 per cent of the £10 000 outstanding debts at that date. During the year ended 31 March 19X2 bad debts of £250 were incurred and at the balance sheet date the outstanding debts amounted to £12 500. It was decided to maintain the provision for doubtful debts at 5 per cent of the outstanding debts. During the year to 31 March 19X3, bad debts of £270 were incurred and the debts outstanding at balance sheet date amounted to £10 000. It was decided to adjust the doubtful debts provision to an amount equal to 4 per cent of the debts outstanding at 31 March 19X3.

Required:
   (a)   Record the above in the ledger of the business.
   (b)   Show the entries that would appear in the profit and loss account for each of the years to 31 March 19X1, 19X2 and 19X3 and on each of the three balance sheets made up to those dates.

Chapter 11

Preparing a profit and loss account and a balance sheet

In Chapter 10, we examined the role of the trial balance as a working paper which enables the accountant not only to check the arithmetical accuracy of the entries recorded during an accounting period, but which also serves as a basis for considering adjustments to be made for the purpose of measuring periodic profit. The extraction of a trial balance at the close of the accounting period is the first step, therefore, in the preparation of a profit and loss account and a balance sheet.

We examined in Chapter 9 how the trial balance is adjusted in respect of the accrual into the accounting period of revenues and expenses, and we analysed in Chapter 10 the nature of the losses in asset values which have to be taken into consideration in the measurement of periodic profit.

The purpose of this chapter is to summarize the various adjustments which must be made to the trial balance, and the manner in which these adjustments are incorporated into the process of preparing a profit and loss account and a balance sheet.

Preparing a profit and loss account

The preparation of a profit and loss account is a two-stage exercise. The first stage is an informal one and consists of using the trial balance as a worksheet for accumulating all the data which incorporate the various adjustments we referred to earlier. When the adjusted trial balance has been certified and confirmed, the adjustments are formally entered in the appropriate accounts, and the profit and loss account is formally included in the accounts system. It is important to remember that the profit and loss account is an account to which the revenue and expense accounts for the accounting period are transferred as summarized totals, and which exists solely for the purpose of measuring the accounting profit for that period. As we see in Part 4, the profit and loss account is essential to the process of financial reporting, and many problems in this respect arise from the fact that the profit and loss account is an integral element in financial accounting, and is subject to its conventions.

The following example illustrates the nature of the profit and loss account.

Example

Let us return to the trial balance given on page 116, which listed the balances extracted from the books of John Smith on 31 December 19X0, at the end of the first year of trading:

	£ Dr.	£ Cr.
Capital		25 000
Motor vehicles	10 000	
Furniture and fittings	2 500	
Purchases	31 000	
Bank balance	6 000	
Sales		70 000
Debtors	18 000	
Creditors		3 500
Rent	4 500	
Salaries	22 800	
Insurances	400	
Motor expenses	2 000	
Light and heat	1 000	
General expenses	300	
	98 500	98 500

We noted in Chapter 9 that the following adjustments were required:

1 Rent unpaid at the end of the year was £1500.
2 Insurance paid in advance amounted to £50.
3 Rent receivable, but not recorded in the account, amounted to £60.
4 Closing stocks at 31 December 19X0 were valued at £3000.

We are now given the following additional information:

1 Depreciation is to be provided on the undermentioned assets and calculated on the reducing-balance method. Their estimated residual values are shown in brackets.

| Motor vehicles | 20% | (£1000) |
| Furniture and fittings | 10% | (£250) |

2 Bad debts to be written off amount to £180, and a provision for doubtful debts is to be made of £178.

Adjusting for accruals

We saw also that the adjustments for accruals and prepayments resulted in the following revisions of balances in the trail balance:

	Original balance	Adjustment	New balance
	£	£	£
1 Rent	4500	1500	6000
2 Insurance	400	50	350
3 Insurance prepaid	—	50	50
4 Rent receivable	—	60	60

We explained in Chapter 4 that items 1, 2 and 3 represented adjustments to the revenues and expenses of the year and affected the profit and loss account. The following resulting balances of the accounts affect the balance sheet and we shall see later in this chapter how they are incorporated in that statement:

	£ Dr.	£ Cr.
Rent accrued		1500
Insurance prepaid	50	

The corrected total revenues and expenses may now be listed on a worksheet used in the preparation of the profit and loss account:

Draft profit and loss account for the year ended 31 December 19X0

	£		£
Purchases	31 000	Sales	70 000
Rent	6 000	Rent receivable	60
Salaries	22 800		
Insurance	350		
Motor expenses	2 000		
Light and heat	1 000		
General expenses	300		

Adjusting for stocks

We noted in Chapter 9 that periodic measurement involved valuing the stocks of goods unsold at the end of the accounting period. The closing stock is valued, as we saw in Chapter 4, in accordance with the cost concept, and represents the residue of the purchases of the year which have not been sold at the year end, and which will be sold in the next accounting period. Opening stocks are shown, therefore as a *debit balance* in the trial balance, whereas closing stocks do not appear, since they are valued after the close of the accounting period. It is for this reason that the appropriate entries must be made in the stock account to make possible the measurement of periodic profit. In the example in question, there is no opening stock because it is the first year of trading.

We saw in Chapter 6 that the adjustment for closing stock had a twofold effect. First, it is effected by means of a credit to the profit and loss account and a debit to the stock account. Second, it results in a debit balance in the stock account which must be incorporated in the balance sheet.

The closing stock is entered on the draft profit and loss account as follows:

Draft profit and loss account for the year ended 31 December 19X0

	£		£
Purchases	31 000	Sales	70 000
Rent	6 000	Rent receivable	60
Salaries	22 800	Closing stock	
Insurance	350	31 December 19X0	3 000
Motor expenses	2 000		
Light and heat	1 000		
General expenses	300		

Adjusting for the loss in asset values

We mentioned in Chapter 10 the most important losses in asset values which the accountant has to recognize in the measurement of periodic profit. We do not propose to deal in this text with the variety of gains and losses in asset values which may occur, since we are concerned only with the process of periodic measurement and with the most significant losses in asset values which enter into that process.

In the example, we are required to deal with depreciation, bad and doubtful debts.

Calculation of depreciation

It is the usual practice to detail in the profit and loss account the component elements of the provision for depreciation, and as we shall see later fixed assets are also described in their categories on the balance sheet. The provision for depreciation in respect of the different fixed assets may be reconciled, therefore, with the yearly provision for depreciation shown on the balance sheet.

		£	£
1	**Motor vehicles**		
	Cost	10 000	
	Estimated residual value	1 000	
	Net cost for depreciation purposes	9 000	
	Depreciation for the year 19X0 at 20%	1 800	1 800
	Residual balance for depreciation in following years	7 200	
2	**Furniture and fittings**		
	Cost	2 500	
	Estimated residual value	250	
	Net cost for depreciation purposes	2 250	
	Depreciation for the year 19X0 at 10%	225	225
	Residual balance for depreciation in following years	2 025	
	Total depreciation for the year		2 025

Calculation of the provision for doubtful debts

Duration of debt	Balance £	Loss rate, %	Provision £
Less than 1 month	15 960	½	80
1–2 months	1 800	5	90
2–3 months	40	10	4
over 3 months	20	25	4
	17 820		178

These adjustments may be included in the draft profit and loss account as shown below:

Draft profit and loss account for the year ended 31 December 19X0

	£		£
Purchases	31 000	Sales	70 000
Rent	6 000	Rent receivable	60
Salaries	22 800	Closing stock at	
Insurance	350	31 December 19X0	3 000
Motor expenses	2 000		
Light and heat	1 000		
General expenses	300		
Depreciation			
Motor vehicles	1 800		
Furniture and fittings	225		
	2 025		
Bad debts	180		
Provision for doubtful debts	178		

Calculating the periodic profit

The details shown on the draft profit and loss account above are sufficient to permit the calculation of the profit for the year ended 31 December 19X0. The profit and loss account is set out, however, so as to enable significant information to be immediately apparent. In this respect, a distinction is made between *gross* profit and *net* profit, the former being the profit resulting after the deduction from the gross sales revenue of expenses directly connected with the production or purchase of the goods sold, while the latter reflects the deduction of overhead expenses from gross profit. Although the net profit is the most important result, dividing the profit and loss account into two parts highlights the burden of overhead expenses, as well as focusing attention on important aspects of business activity.

Calculating gross profit

In the case of a trading business—as is the case in the example quoted— the gross profit from trading may be shown as follows:

	£		£
Purchases	31 000	Sales	70 000
less: Closing stock at			
31 December 19X0	3 000		
Cost of sales	28 000		
Gross trading profit	42 000		
	70 000		70 000

This arrangement shows the following points:

1   Although purchases amounted to £31 000, the cost of goods actually sold amounted to only £28 000. Hence, the gross trading profit expressed as a percentage of sales is:

$$\frac{42\ 000}{70\ 000} \times 100 = 60\%$$

This percentage is often referred to as the gross profit ratio. Expressed as a percentage of cost sales, the gross trading profit is:

$$\frac{42\ 000}{28\ 000} \times 100 = 150\%$$

2 The level of trading activity may also be judged from the average length of time stock is held. The rate of stock turnover may be calculated as follows:

$$\frac{\text{cost of sales}}{\text{average stock}}$$

The average stock is obtained by the arithmetic mean of the opening and closing stock. In the example under consideration, the rate of stock turnover for the year was as follows:

$$\frac{28\ 000}{3\ 000} = 9.3 \text{ times}$$

so that stock was held for approximately 39 days (365 days ÷ 9.3), or replaced approximately 9.3 times in the year.

The segregation of the gross trading profit in the process of calculating periodic profit provides useful ratios for the analysis of trading performance, and for indicating areas of trading where efficiency might be improved.

It is the practice for firms to identify the nature of gross profit. Thus manufacturing firms show manufacturing gross profit, contracting firms show contracting gross profit and so on.

The problems of deciding which expenses to include in the calculation of the gross profit lies in defining direct as distinct from indirect operating expenses. Direct expenses, such as purchases, freight and other expenses associated with the acquisition of goods for resale, for example, are included in the calculation of gross profit.

Calculating the net profit

The calculation of the net profit is affected by charging against the gross profit the indirect expenses accumulated in the trial balance, and other expenses such as depreciation, bad debts and provisions for the year ended 31 December 19X0 may be calculated as shown:

Net profit for year ended 31 December 19X0

	£		£
Rent	6 000	Gross trading profit	42 000
Salaries	22 800	Rent receivable	60
Insurance	350		
Motor expenses	2 000		
Light and heat	1 000		
General expenses	300		
Depreciation			
Motor vehicles	1 800		
Furniture and fittings	225		
	2 025		
Bad debts	180		
Provision for doubtful debts	178		
	34 833		
Net profit	7 227		
	42 060		42 060

Miscellaneous income, such as interest, rents and dividends, which form a minor element in the business profit, are usually shown in the calculation of the net profit rather than in the calculation of the gross profit.

The segregation of the net profit calculation also affords a clearer view of significant ratios. The net profit is itself the most significant performance result, and its dimensions may be assessed not only in relation to the gross trading profit, but also to gross revenue. The net profit as a percentage of sales indicates the level of activity required to produce £1 of net profit, and may be calculated as follows:

$$\frac{\text{net profit before interest and tax}}{\text{sales}}$$

Thus, whereas the percentage of gross profit to sales was 60 per cent, the percentage of net profit to sales was only 13 per cent, indicating thereby not only the relative burden of direct and indirect expenses but also the relative efficiency of the business.

The formal presentation of the profit and loss account

Although the profit and loss account is part of the accounts system, and may be shown in an account form, its formal presentation has been influenced by its use as a financial reporting statement. This influence has encouraged the further classification of indirect expenses into selling, administration and financial expenses, and the presentation of the profit and loss account in a vertical form as follows:

John Smith Esq. trading as general dealer
Profit and loss account for the year ended 31 December 19X0

	£	£	£
Sales			70 000
Cost of sales			
Purchases		31 000	
Less: Closing stock		3 000	
			28 000
Gross trading			42 000
Other income			
Rent			60
Total profit			42 060
Selling and distribution expenses			
Salesmen's salaries	12 000		
Motor expenses	2 000		
Depreciation—motor vehicles	1 800	15 800	
Administrative expenses			
Rent	6 000		
Office salaries	10 800		
Insurance	350		
Light and heat	1 000		
General expenses	300		
Depreciation—furniture and fittings	225		
		18 675	
Financial expenses			
Bad debts	180		
Provision for doubtful debts	178	358	
Total overhead expenses			34 833
Net profit			7 227

Preparing a balance sheet

The preparation of the balance sheet is a two-stage process, and, in this sense, it follows the same pattern as the preparation of the profit and loss account, that is, an informal stage based on a work-sheet, and a formal stage represented by the balance sheet presented as a financial report. There are, however, a number of important differences between a profit and loss account and a balance sheet. First, from a procedural point of view, the profit and loss account is part of the accounts system and, as we explained earlier, it is itself an account. By contrast, the balance sheet is not an account, but a list showing the balances of the accounts which remain following the preparation of the profit and loss account. Second, the profit and loss account is the effective instrument of periodic measurement in accounting, whereas the balance sheet does not do other than state residual balances. Third, residual debit balances are shown on the balance sheet as *assets,* but there are problems stemming from this description which we discuss in Chapter 12. Fourth, by attaching accounting measurements to debit and credit balances described as assets and liabilities respectively, the balance sheet is often interpreted as indicating the net worth of the business. This is a misconception, and in the case of corporations has led to much controversy. We explore these problems further in Part 3.

Collecting and classifying balances

The preparation of the balance sheet need not await the entry of all the adjustments into the individual accounts following the preparation of the profit and loss account. It may be prepared in draft form from the trial balance and the finalized draft of the profit and loss account.

Debit balances are either assets, losses or expenses. The preparation of the profit and loss account involves the removal from the trial balance of all expenses in respect of the year, so that any debit balances remaining are treated as assets. These assets, as defined, are classified as follows:

1   Long-term assets representing an enduring benefit to the enterprise. Long-term assets, described as fixed assets, for example plant and machinery, are subject to depreciation. Other long-term assets, such as land and intangible assets, may or may not be subject to depreciation or other changes in their book value. We examine these problems in Chapter 12.

2   Short-term assets, described as current assets, include the following:

   (a)   closing stocks at the end of the accounting period;
   (b)   trade debtors;
   (c)   prepayments on expense accounts, for example, insurance paid in advance;
   (d)   bank balance and cash.

The measurement of closing stocks presents particular problems, which we discuss in Chapter 12. We have already examined the accounting problems relating to trade debtors which arise from the writing-off of bad debts and the making of provisions for doubtful debts. We shall deal presently with the verification of bank balances and overdrafts.

By contrast, credit balances are either liabilities, revenues or investments in the firm in the form of capital and long-term loans. The removal of periodic revenues from the trial balance means that the remaining credit balances are either liabilities or investments. The provision for depreciation is one of a number of exceptions to this rule. These exceptions, as in the case of prepayments shown as debit balances, arise from accounting procedures. Credit balances are collected and classified as follows:

1   capital account, representing the owner's original investment in the firm and accumulated profits less drawings;
2   long-term borrowings;
3   short-term liabilities, described as current liabilities, which include such credit balances as sundry creditors, accrued expenses, payments received in advance, provisions for taxation and bank overdrafts.

Verifying balances

Accounts are usually subjected to yearly audits, that is, they are checked by a firm of professional accountants. The purpose of the audit is not only to check the accuracy of the records, but also to ensure that the statements contained in those records are correct. Thus, the physical existence of assets in the assets' accounts is verified, as are the existence of liabilities in various creditors' accounts. In the case of corporations, audits are obligatory and auditors are appointed by shareholders. In this connection, they are required to report that both the profit and loss account and the balance sheet reflect a true and fair view of the information they are legally required to convey.

Bank reconciliation statement

It is unlikely that on any specific day the bank balance shown in the cash book will correspond with the statement of the balance at the bank account issued by the bank. This is due not only to the normal delays occurring in the process of clearing cheques, but also to delays in lodging and presenting cheques for payment. Moreover, payments and receipts may be effected directly through the bank. For example, dividends and interest receivable may be paid directly into the bank account, and routine payments may be effected by standing orders and direct debit procedures. The bank also charges commission, fees and interest directly to the account, and the bank statement is used to convey these details to the client.

The bank reconciliation statement reconciles the balance at the bank as per the bank statement with the bank balance as per the cash book, whenever a bank statement is received.

When preparing a balance sheet, the bank balance as shown in the cash book must be supported by a bank statement stating the balance on the last day of the accounting period, and the bank reconciliation statement explains any differences which have not been already adjusted in the cash book. Thus, any charges such as bank commission and interest will be entered in the cash book and will be shown as expenses in the profit and loss account. In effect, therefore, the bank reconciliation statement explains the nature of the unadjusted differences between the cash book and the bank statement.

Example

The bank balance according to the cash book was £6060 on 31 December 19X0. The bank statement balance was £6560. The difference is explained as follows:

1   cheques received from debtors on 31 December 19X0 which were not banked until 2 January 19X1 amounted to £250;
2   cheques sent to creditors on 31 December 19X0 and not presented for payment until after 1 January 19X1 amounted to £750.

Bank reconciliation statement as on 31 December 19X0

	£
Balance at bank as per bank statement	6560
add: Cheques received but not credited	250
	6810
less: Cheques issued but not presented	750
Balance at bank per cash book	6060

The formal presentation of the balance sheet

In the case of corporations, legislation provides rules for the presentation of both the profit and loss account and the balance sheet. As we see in Chapter 13, these rules apply to published financial reports. The rules reflect the practices of the accounting profession, and are designed not only to secure sufficient disclosure but also to permit salient features to be quickly recognized. It is usual, therefore, to classify assets and liabilities in groupings as we mentioned earlier, and to rank them according to liquidity. Thus, asset groupings are shown from the most fixed to the most liquid, and liabilities from the long-term to the most current.

The importance of the balance sheet, together with the profit and loss account for the purpose of financial reporting and investment decision making, has focused attention on the arrangement of particular groupings to assist the interpretation and the analysis of results. We deal with this analysis in Chapter 15, but we may mention at this stage that the relationship between long-term finance and long-term investment needs of the firm (long-term capital as defined in finance) and short-term finance and short-term financial needs (working capital) is important to financial analysts. Other areas of interest are the return on capital employed which is the ratio of net profit to equity capital (owner's investment in the firm), liquidity and solvency.

The vertical form of presentation of the balance sheet is illustrated on page 159.

Summary

This chapter has been concerned with the accounting procedures for preparing and presenting the two main financial reports, namely, the profit and loss account and the balance sheet.

The extraction of the trial balance at the close of the accounting period marks the first stage in the preparation of these reports. Earlier chapters have examined the adjustments required for the purposes of periodic measurement. These include accruals, depreciation and adjustments in respect of bad and doubtful debts. All these adjustments are effected informally on working sheets, and once they have been verified and confirmed, the final accounts are drawn up.

John Smith Esq Balance sheet at 31 December 19X0

Fixed assets	Cost £	Depreciation to date £	Net £	£	£
Motor vehicles	10 000	1 800	8 200		
Furniture and fittings	2 500	225	2 275		
	12 500	2 025	10 475	10 475	
Current assets					
Stocks at cost			3 000		
Debtors		17 820			
less: Provision for					
doubtful debts		178	17 642		
Accruals and					
prepayments			50		
Bank balance			6 060		
			26 752		
Current liabilities					
Creditors		3 500			
Accruals		1 500	5 000		
Net working capital				21 752	
					32 227
Capital employed					
Capital account				25 000	
Net profit for the year				7 227	
					32 227

The importance of the profit and loss account lies not only in the fact that it is the main vehicle of periodic measurement and provides the measurement of periodic profit, but also in that it is part of the accounts system. The objective purpose underlying the preparation of the profit and loss account is the measurement of net profit, which is used as a basis for measuring business efficiency. The distinction between gross profit and net profit facilitates the analysis of the financial results, as does the classification of expenses under various categories.

By contrast, the balance sheet is a list of residual balances following the preparation of the profit and loss account. It forms no part of the accounts system. The balance sheet is used in conjunction with the profit and loss account in the analysis of the financial performance of the business, and the treatment and classification of assets and liabilities are important to this analysis. Consequently, particular attention is paid to the manner in which important financial aspects of the business are highlighted in the presentation of the balance sheet.

Problems

1   Jack Daw has prepared the following balance sheet as at 30 June 19X8:

	£			£	£
Capital account			Plant at cost	8 000	
Balance, 1 July 19X7	10 000		Less: Depreciation	2 000	6 000
Profit for the year	2 050		Vehicles at cost	3 000	
	12 050		Less: Depreciation	1 000	
					2 000
Creditors and					
provisions	5 000		Stock		7 000
Bank overdraft	1 000		Debtors	3 200	
			Less: Provision for		
			doubtful debts	200	3 000
			Cash	—	50
	18 050				18 050

Daw asks you to audit his accounts and in the course of your examination you find the following:
(a) A dividend of £100 has been paid direct to the bank and no entry has been made in the books.
(b) A debt of £100 is irrecoverable and you agree with Daw that the provision for doubtful debts should be fixed at 10 per cent of the remaining debtors.
(c) A purchase of plant, costing £500, has been charged to repairs. It was agreed that this should be depreciated by 10 per cent on cost.
(d) The stock on 30 June 19X8 was overvalued by £250.
(e) On counting the petty cash you find there is only £10 in the box. It seems likely that the balance has been stolen by an employee.
Required:
(a) A statement showing the necessary adjustments to the profit for the year to 30 June 19X8.
(b) The amended balance sheet as at 30 June 19X8.

2   The balances in the books of account for John Reeve at 31 March 19X7 are given below:

Sales	50 000
Purchases	30 000
Stock, 1 April 19X6	35 000
Administration expenses	5 000
Selling expenses	5 000
Trade creditors	27 000
Bank overdraft	32 000
Trade debtors	55 000
Debentures	50 000
Plant and machinery, at cost	80 000
Plant and machinery, depreciation provision, 1 April 19X6	30 000
Fixtures and equipment, at cost	40 000
Fixtures and equipment, depreciation provision, 1 April 19X6	10 000
Capital account, 1 April 19X6	51 000

You are also given the following information:
(a) On 31 March 19X7, the stock was valued at £40 000.
(b) Depreciation of plant and machinery and fixtures and fittings is to be calculated at the rate of 20 per cent of cost.

Required:

Using the vertical form of presentation, prepare the profit and loss account for the year ended 31 March 19X7 and a balance sheet as at that date.

3   The following trial balance was extracted from the books of T. Bone as at 31 December 19X6.

	£	£
Capital account		20 500
Purchases	46 500	
Sales		60 900
Repairs	848	
Motor car (cost)	950	
Car expenses	318	
Freehold land and buildings	10 000	
Bank balance	540	
Furniture and fittings (cost)	1 460	
Wages and salaries	8 606	
Discounts allowed	1 061	
Discounts received		814
Drawings	2 400	
Rates and insurances	248	
Bad debts	359	
Provision for bad debts, 1 Jan. 19X6		140
Trade debtors	5 213	
Trade creditors		4 035
General expenses	1 586	
Stock, 1 Jan. 19X6	6 300	
	86 389	86 389

The following matters are to be taken into account:
(a) Stock at 31 December 19X6 was £8800.
(b) Wages and salaries outstanding at 31 December 19X6 were £318.
(c) Rates and insurances paid in advance at 31 December 19X6 amounted to £45.
(d) During the year, Bone took goods ex-stock valued at £200 for his own use. No entry has been made in the books in this respect.
(e) Depreciation is to be provided at the rate of 20 per cent on the motor and at 10 per cent on furniture and fittings.
(f) The provision for bad debts is to be reduced to £100.

Required:

Prepare a profit and loss account for the year ended 31 December 19X6, and a balance sheet as at that date.

4   Matt Spode is a china wholesaler. A trial balance extracted from his books on 31 December 19X9 revealed the following balances:

	£	£
Capital account		112 000
Purchases	92 400	
Sales		157 240
Premises at cost	64 000	
Motor vehicles at cost	30 000	
Accumulated depreciation of motors		8 200
Fixtures & fittings at cost	6 500	
Accumulated depreciation – fixtures & fittings		1 100
Motor expenses	7 300	
Rates	2 300	
Balance at bank	4 200	
c/frwd	206 700	278 540

		£	£
	b/frwd	206 700	278 540
Wages and salaries		42 000	
Drawings		9 600	
Insurance		2 000	
Trade debtors		18 000	
Provision for doubtful debts			560
Trade creditors			15 000
Sundry expenses		16 200	
Long-term loan			20 000
Stock at 1.1.19X9		19 250	
Cash in hand		350	
		314 100	314 100

The following information was available at 31 December 19X9:

(a) Stock at 31 December was £22 400.

(b) There were wages and salaries of £1200 owing.

(c) There was a payment of £1200 on September 30th to cover 12 months insurance.

(d) On reviewing debtors, it was discovered that a debt of £800 would not be recovered and that a further £1200 was doubtful.

(e) Depreciation is 25 per cent reducing balance on motors and 10 per cent straight line on fixtures and fittings.

(f) Loan interest at 10 per cent has not been allowed for.

Required:

Prepare a profit and loss account and balance sheet for Matt Spode to cover the period in question.

5   The following trial balance was drawn up from the books of A. Merchant at 31 December 19X7:

	£	£
Capital account: A. Merchant		
Capital account at 1 January 19X7:		90 000
Introduced by A. Merchant during year		1 500
Drawings during the year	8 000	
Gross profit for the year		27 000
Stock, 31 December 19X7	23 600	
Selling and distribution expenses	4 500	
Motor vehicles at cost	20 000	
Freehold premises at cost	30 000	
Provision for depreciation of motor vehicles at 31 December 19X6		4 000
Debtors and Creditors	52 000	31 100
Bank balance	8 750	
Rates and insurances	6 000	
Office salaries	3 000	
Office expenses	1 250	
Doubtful debts provision		2 500
Bad debts written off	500	
Discounts	1 500	3 000
	159 100	159 100

Required:

Prepare a profit and loss account for the year ending 31 December 19X7, and a balance sheet as at that date taking into account the following:

(a) Provision is to be made for depreciation of motor vehicles for the year at the rate of 20 per cent per annum on the cost of the vehicles.

(b) The doubtful debts provision is to be adjusted to an amount equal to 5 per cent of the outstanding debtors.

(c) The rates are £4000 per annum and have been paid to 31 March 19X8.

6   Jackson owns a retail shop. From the few records he keeps the following information is available for the beginning and end of 19X4:

	1 January £	31 December £
Cash in shop till	350	250
Bank overdraft	800	300
Stock	2600	3300
Owed by customers	4500	5100
Owed to suppliers	1450	1900
Loan from wife	4000	2500

Notes:

(a) Jackson tells you that during 19X4 he took from the till, before making the weekly bankings:
   (i) £200 a week for his personal expenses, and
   (ii) £80 a week for his assistant's wages.

(b) Returned cheques show that all payments out of the bank account were to suppliers except:
   (i) a payment of £250 to an insurance company, being £150 for the insurance of the shop's contents and £100 for the insurance of Jackson's own house, and
   (ii) a payment of £600 for furniture for Jackson's own house.

(c) During the year Jackson had paid business expenses of £3100 through his private bank account.

(d) Although no record of it is kept, Jackson owned the shop purchased on 1 January 19X0 for £40 000 and shop fittings and fixtures purchased on the same date for £6000. It is agreed that fair rates of depreciation are 5 per cent per annum on cost for the shop and 10 per cent per annum on cost for the fittings and fixtures.

Required:

(a) Calculate Jackson's profit for 19X4.

(b) Compile a statement of the financial position of this business on 31 December 19X4.

7   A businessman has no double-entry records of his transactions but has a cash book from which the following summary for the year ended 31 December 19X5, has been prepared:

	£
Bank overdraft, 31 December 19X4	7 500
Receipts from trade debtors	90 000
Further capital introduced	30 000
Loan from X on 31 March on which interest is payable at the rate of 5 per cent a year	20 000
Payments to trade creditors	35 000
General expenses	9 000
Wages	12 000
Drawings	22 000

(continued overleaf)

Summary of cash book (contd.)

On 3 December 19X4, the business had

trade debtors for	70 000
trade creditors for	50 000
stocks valued at	30 000
sundry fixed assets which had cost	60 000
provision for depreciation	10 000

On 31 December 19X5 there were

trade debtors for	85 000
trade creditors for	65 000
stocks valued at	27 000
sundry fixed assets which had cost	68 000

Draft a profit and loss account for the year ended 31 December 19X5, and a balance sheet as at that date, providing for 5 per cent depreciation of the fixed assets on a straight line basis.

8   From the following information relating to Snailsby a village shopkeeper who keeps no proper books of account, prepare accounts for the year ended 30 June 19X6.

Summary of banking account

	£		£
Opening balance	2 600	Payments for goods	
Shop takings paid in	98 740	bought for stock	57 180
Sale of motor van, 1 Jan		Payments of business	
19X6	3 600	expenses	6 720
		Private items	5 400
		Purchase of new motor van,	
		1 Jan. 19X6	8 500
		Closing balance	27 140
	104 940		104 940

	30.6.19X5	30.6.19X6
	£	£
Stock in trade	24 000	29 000
Amount owing for goods sold	800	1 250
Amount owing for goods bought	7 640	18 400
Amount owing for business expenses	1 320	730
Furniture, fixtures and fitting	6 000	6 000
Motor van	4 500	8 500
Cash in hand	800	350

Of shop takings of £6000 which were not banked, £1500 were used to pay various business expenses.

Estimated annual depreciation on written-down values: furniture, fixtures and fittings, 5 per cent; motor van, 20 per cent.

The cost of the van sold during the year was £5625.

9   On 30 June 19X9 the bank column of John Smith's cash book showed a debit balance of £12 600. On examination of the cash book and bank statement the following was revealed:

(a)   Cheques amounting to £935 which were issued to creditors and entered in the cash book before 30 June were not presented for payment until after that date.

(b) Cheques amounting to £230 had been recorded in the cash book as having been paid into the bank on 30 June, but were entered on the bank statement on 1 July.

(c) A cheque for £70 had been dishonoured prior to 30 June, but no record of this fact appeared in the cash book.

(d) A dividend of £340 paid direct to the bank had not been recorded in the cash book.

(e) Bank interest and charges of £60 had been charged in the bank statement but not entered in the cash book.

(f) No entry had been made in the cash book for a trade subscription of £15 paid by banker's order in January 19X9.

Required:

(a) To make appropriate adjustments in the cash book bringing down the correct balance.

(b) To prepare a statement reconciling the adjusted balance in the cash book with the balance shown in the bank statement for 30 June 19X9 which was a credit balance of £13 500.

Chapter 12

Reporting recorded assets and liabilities

In this chapter we examine further the logic and the methodology which underlie the traditional manner in which assets and liabilities are recorded and depicted on the balance sheet. First, we discuss the conventional historical cost valuation of assets and the implications of this method of valuation for balance sheet purposes. Second, we discuss the adjustments to historical cost values which are made at the stage of preparing the balance sheet. Third, we review the implications of the variety of different results obtained from traditional accounting practices. In this chapter, therefore, the concern is with historical cost valuation. The discussion of current cost accounting is deferred to Part 3.

The financial accounting concepts we examined in Chapter 4 may be said to have their origin in the concept of stewardship accounting. A number of these concepts have a determining influence on valuation for financial reporting purposes, and reflect the stewardship concept of financial reporting as regards the manner in which boards of directors should communicate information to shareholders about the way in which their funds have been handled. For example, when a transaction occurs, it is said that both parties to the transaction are agreed as to the exchange value of the asset involved: that value may be verified at that point, that is, it is an objective measure of value for accounting purposes. It follows, therefore, that the cost of acquiring assets has traditionally been thought to provide the best method of valuing assets for financial reporting purposes on the assumption that the objective of financial reporting is to explain to shareholders how their funds have been utilized.

Since the stewardship concept of financial reporting has its roots also in the prevention of frauds, it is interesting to note that one of the major arguments in favour of historical cost valuation is the prevention of fraud. Accountants feel that to depart from this basis of valuation would open the way to fraudulent practices since other measures of value are essentially in the nature of opinions and judgement.

Note that the concept of prudence leads to a modification of the cost concept in certain cases, and to reporting to shareholders the lowest likely value. If the net realizable value of stocks, for example, is lower than its historical cost value, the concept of prudence requires that the net realizable value be adopted.

The concept of consistency requires that once a basis of valuation has been adopted, it should not be changed except for valid reasons.

Finally, it should be noted that company law stipulates the manner in which values should be reported. In the United Kingdom, the law reflects the concepts of accounting, and in this respect we may say that in developing legal rules for financial reporting, the law has followed its tradition of codifying concepts existing among practitioners.

The valuation of assets

The key to an understanding of the manner in which the accountant approaches the problem of valuation is to be found in the classification of assets. Fixed assets are long-term assets whose usefulness in the operations of the firm is likely to extend beyond one accounting period. They are not intended for resale, so that their value depends upon the expected future cash flows they are intended to generate. By contrast, current assets are those intended to be exhausted in the profit-earning operations of the next accounting period, and this includes their availability for meeting current liabilities.

There are three general rules for valuing fixed assets:

1   The enterprise should be considered as a going concern, unless the facts indicate the contrary. Thus the valuation of fixed assets should reflect the continued expectation of their usefulness to the enterprise. For this reason, their realizable value is inappropriate, and their historical cost is regarded as the most objective measure of value. Historical cost includes the original purchase price and, in addition, all other costs incurred in rendering the asset ready for use.
2   Changes in the market value of fixed assets are traditionally ignored in the valuation process.
3   Depreciation in value attributable to wear and tear should always be recognized.

The valuation of fixed assets

The valuation of land

Land is valued at cost despite rises or falls in market value. Cost includes broker's commission, surveying and legal fees and insurance charges. In addition, draining, levelling and landscaping costs and other improvements such as fencing, sewerage and water mains should be included, though it is quite common in the case of farm accounts for these improvements to be shown separately because of the different tax allowances which they occasionally enjoy. Land is not generally regarded as susceptible to depreciation.

The valuation of buildings

Buildings are valued on a historical cost basis—whether they have been acquired or constructed. Construction costs include such incidental expenses as architect's fees, inspection fees and insurance costs applicable to a construction project. Where an existing building is purchased, the costs of rendering the building suitable for its intended purpose should be added to the purchase price in arriving at its historical cost value.

The valuation process for building differs from that of land in two ways:

1 A cost of maintenance is involved in the repairs which have to be made from time to time in the upkeep of the building. Such maintenance expenses are charged as they are incurred to the profit and loss account. Additions and improvements to the building, which are distinguished from repairs, must be capitalized and added to the value of the building.
2 Buildings depreciate with age. The accounts value should be shown at cost less the accumulated depreciation to date.

The valuation of plant and machinery and other fixed assets

Plant and machinery, furniture and fittings, motor vehicles, tools and sundry equipment are usually valued at historical cost with proper allowance for depreciation. Cost includes purchase price, freight charges, insurance in transit and all installation costs. As we saw in Chapter 10, the purpose of depreciation in accounting is to allocate the cost of fixed assets to the several years of their useful life to the firm.

The revaluation of fixed assets

During the 1960s the practice of historical cost accounting for fixed assets was modified in an attempt to deal with the problems created by changing prices. Increasingly, companies adopted the practice of revaluing fixed assets, and reporting the revalued figures in the balance sheet.

The practice of revaluing assets was recognized by legislation in the United Kingdom in 1948, when the Companies Act of that year stipulated that fixed assets should be shown at cost, or, if it stands in the company's books at a valuation, the amount of the valuation. No guidance was given, however, by the Act as to when a valuation should be made, except in the case of property where a 'substantial difference' between cost and market value should be indicated in the balance sheet. Surveys carried out by the Institute of Chartered Accountants and by the Sandilands Committee, established by the British government to consider the problem of inflation accounting, revealed that many companies were departing from the historical cost principle in their financial reports, though revaluations of property were much more common than revaluations of other fixed assets, while most companies were retaining the historical cost method of calculating depreciation. The Sandilands Report (1975) concluded that

'The piecemeal way in which revaluations have been carried out has created considerable confusion and difficulty. Few companies have revalued all their assets, few revalue their assets on a regular annual basis, and few disclose the exact basis of the revaluation. The result is that present-day balance sheets in this country consist of a mixture of entries at historical cost and valuations prepared on different bases.'

The valuation of current assets

Current assets consist of cash and other assets, such as debtors and stocks, which are expected to be converted into cash or to be used in the operations of the enterprise within one year. The most complex problems lie in the valuation of the three different types of stocks—raw materials, work-in-progress and finished goods. The production process may be viewed as adding value to successive categories of stocks, that is, from raw material to finished goods. Stock values, therefore, affect the profit and loss account as well as the balance sheet. Since they are an important constituent of the expenses chargeable against sales revenue, they occupy a key position in the determination of periodic profit.

Stocks

Stocks are valued at the lower of cost and net realizable value. SSAP 9 'Stocks and Long-Term Contracts' requires that the cost of stocks 'should comprise that expenditure which has been incurred in the normal course of business in bringing the product or service to its present location and condition'. Acquisition costs reflected in stock values should be added to the costs of purchasing, of packaging and of transport. Where applicable, trade discounts should be deducted from the purchase price. There are, however, many different methods for determining the cost value of stocks, and these methods produce valuations which differ markedly from each other. A simple example serves to illustrate how three different valuation methods lead to divergent values.

Example

A firm has an opening stock of 100 items valued at £1.00 each. During the accounting period, 100 units were purchased for £1.20 each and a further 100 units were purchased for £1.30 each. There remained 100 units in stock at the end of the accounting period, that is, after 200 units had been sold for £300.

The firm is considering the effects of the undermentioned three methods of stock valuation:

1   first in, first out (FIFO);
2   last in, first out (LIFO);
3   weighted average cost.

The effects of these alternative methods may be seen from the tabulation of stock data below:

	Unit	Unit cost (£)	Value (£)
Opening stock	100	1.00	100
First purchase	100	1.20	120
Second purchase	100	1.30	130

1   The FIFO method assumes that the oldest items in stock are used first, so that the items in stock are assumed to be the remnants of more recent purchases. The result of the application of FIFO to the given data is that the cost of goods sold during the year is taken to be £220, and the value of the closing stock is £130.

Advocates of the FIFO method argue that its underlying assumption is in accordance with conventional practice that goods purchased first are sold first, and that this method eliminates the opportunities for management to manipulate profit and stock values by selecting out of the existing stock the values which serve their purposes best. Under conditions of rising prices, FIFO requires that the stock of the earliest date and prices be deemed sold first, with the effect that the profit and loss account reflects a higher level of profit than would have been the case if current replacement costs had been used. Closing stock values are shown at the more recent acquisition prices and approximate current replacement costs.

2   The LIFO method assumes that the most recently purchased stocks are used first, so that the items remaining in stock at the end of the year are assumed to be the remnants of earlier purchases. Under this method, the cost of goods sold during the year is taken to be £250, and the value of the closing stock is £100. The LIFO method has the opposite effect, therefore, to that of FIFO on the measurement of profit and the valuation of closing stock.

Though LIFO approximates the replacement cost basis of valuation as regards the input of resources to the profit earning process, it does not necessarily correspond with replacement cost valuation. LIFO reflects the latest cost price of the specific commodity, which may or may not be the actual replacement cost. In the case of seasonal buying, for example, the cost of the last purchase may not be equivalent to the current replacement cost. As a result, LIFO eliminates only an indeterminate part of the effects of specific price changes. Indeed, when sales exceed purchases, that is, when stocks are being depleted, the gap between replacement cost and LIFO may become very great. A classic example of this situation arose in the United States during the Korean War, which resulted in stock reduction on such a scale that Congressional approval was given for next-in-first-out stock valuation as a relief for taxpayers who were on the LIFO basis! A further disadvantage of the LIFO method of stock valuation is that it leads to distortions in balance sheet valuations.

3   The weighted average cost method requires the calculation of the unit cost of closing stock by means of a formula which divides the total cost of all stock available for sale during the accounting period by the physical units of stock available for sale.

The weighted average cost of the 300 units available for sale may be calculated as follows:

$$\frac{\text{total cost of annual stock}}{\text{total annual units of stock}} = \frac{£350}{300} = £1.167 \text{ per unit}$$

Hence, the cost of goods sold during the year is £233, while the value of the closing stock is £117. The weighted average cost method is a compromise, therefore, between the extreme points established by FIFO and LIFO respectively.

Example

The effects of different methods of stock valuation on the calculation of profit may be seen in the example given below. For simplicity, it is assumed that the business is considering a change in the method of valuation which gave an opening stock value of £100.

	FIFO	LIFO	Weighted average
	£	£	£
Purchases	250	250	250
add: Opening stock	100	100	100
	350	350	350
less: Closing stock	130	100	117
Cost of goods sold	220	250	233
Sales	300	300	300
Net profit	80	50	67

This simple example shows that the closing stock may be valued at £130, £100 or £117, depending on the assumptions made about the flow of costs. Three different profit figures result from using different stock valuation methods, namely £80, £50 and £67. It should be remembered that the closing stock for one year becomes the opening stock of the following year. Therefore, in the long term, there will be no difference in the calculation of the net profit of the business. It is in the short term that different stock valuation methods give different results. This fact emphasizes the significance of any changes in the stock valuation method used. Although the Companies Act 1985 allows the use of LIFO, SSAP 9 states that the LIFO method does not usually bear a reasonable relationship to actual cost, and so at present LIFO is not usually appropriate as a method of stock valuation.

Long-term contracts

Construction contracts, such as those for dams, roads, ships and industrial plants may take years to complete. At the end of a given accounting period, a contracting company has to determine the extent to which a profit or loss should be recognized as arising only on the completion of the contract. Profit realization rests on a factual basis. On completion date, all revenues and costs are known, and the profit earned on the contract may be determined readily. If the contract covers several accounting periods, this method of accounting for profit will result in wide profit fluctuations over these periods. SSAP 9 'Stocks and Long-Term Contracts' states that 'where the business carries out long-term contracts and it is considered that their outcomes can be assessed with reasonable certainty before their conclusion, the attributable profit should be calculated on a prudent basis and included in the accounts for the period under review'. Attributable profit may be calculated as follows:

$$\text{accrued profit} = [\text{total contract price} - (\text{costs to date} + \text{estimated costs of completion})] \times \frac{\text{work certified to date}}{\text{total contract price}}$$

It is the normal practice in long-term contracts to have stages certified as completed for the purpose of determining progress payments. The issue of a work-completed certificate justifies the calculation of the profit or loss to be taken at that point. No profit should be recognized until it may be predicted with reasonable certainty. As soon as it becomes evident that a loss on completion is likely, the entire loss and not merely the accrued proportion must be recognized immediately.

Example

S. Nicholl, contractor, had undertaken to extend a factory building for I. McClure at a contract price of £100 000, estimating the work will take 18 months to complete. At the financial year end he estimated that costs to date were £30 000 and that a further £50 000 would be involved in completing the project. The value of work certified was £25 000. J. Nicholl would estimate attributable profit as follows:

	£	£
Contract price		100 000
Costs to financial year end	30 000	
Estimated costs to complete	50 000	
		80 000
Estimated total profit		20 000

$$\text{attributable profit} = \frac{\text{work certified to date}}{\text{total contract price}} \times \text{estimated total profit}$$

$$= \frac{\pounds25\ 000}{\pounds100\ 000} \times \pounds20\ 000 = \pounds5000$$

Debtors

The problems associated with the valuation of debtors were discussed in Chapter 10.

The valuation of other assets

Investments

In financial accounting, investments are defined as shares and other legal rights acquired by a firm through the investment of its funds. Investments may be long term or short term, depending upon the intention of the firm at the time of acquisition. Where investments are intended to be held for a period of more than one year, they are in the nature of fixed assets: where they are held for a shorter period, they are in the nature of current assets. Shares in subsidiary and associated companies are usually not held for resale, and hence would be classified as being of the nature of fixed assets. Short-dated government stocks, for example, may provide a convenient vehicle for the investment of excess funds not immediately needed. Such short-term holdings would be classified as current assets in the balance sheet. It is the practice, however, to show investments separately in the balance sheet and not to include them under the heading of 'fixed assets'.

Investments are recorded at their cost of acquisition, and while substantial decreases in value may be written off against current profit, appreciations in value are not recognized until realized.

Legislation in the United Kingdom requires that a note be appended to the balance sheet in respect of both long- and short-term investments, where there is a difference between the book value and the market value. In the case of long-term investment, there is the further requirement of distinguishing investments which are quoted on the Stock Exchange from unquoted investments as follows:

	£	£
Investments		
Quoted securities (market value £57 000)	80 000	
Unquoted securities (director's valuation £7000)	15 000	
		95 000
Current assets		
Marketable securities (market value £25 000)	20 000	
		20 000

Intangible assets

Intangible assets do not have any physical features, rather they represent legal rights and relationships beneficial to their owner. The most important single characteristic of intangible assets is the high degree of uncertainty regarding the value of the future benefits to be received. The most common examples are:

1   patents, copyrights, and trade marks;
2   research and development costs;
3   goodwill.

Patents

A patent is a legal right to exploit a new invention, and is obtained following the registration of its specification with the Department of Trade. Patents are recorded at cost and are amortized (written off) over their effective life, usually on a straight-line basis. A similar treatment is applied to other such exclusive rights which are granted by government authority, for example, copyrights and trade marks.

Research and development costs

SSAP 13 defines research and development under three main headings:

(a) pure research: experimental or theoretical work undertaken primarily to acquire new scientific knowledge or technical knowledge for its own sake;

(b) applied research: original or critical investigation undertaken in order to gain new scientific or technical knowledge and directed towards a specific practical aim or objective;

(c) development: use of scientific or technical knowledge in order to produce new or substantially improved materials, devices, products or services, to install new processes or systems prior to the commencement of commercial production or commercial applications, or to improving substantially those already produced or installed.

As regards expenditure falling within these first two categories, which may be regarded as part of a continuing operation required to maintain a company's business and its competitive position, this should be written off against revenue in the year in which expenditure is incurred. This excludes the cost of fixed assets acquired or constructed for research and development activities over a period of time which should be capitalized and written off over the useful life of the assets. Expenditure on development should be written off in the year of expenditure except in the following circumstances, where it may be deferred to future periods:

1. there is a clearly defined project;
2. the related expenditure is separately identifiable;
3. the outcome of such a project has been assessed with reasonable certainty as to its technical feasibility, and its ultimate commercial viability;
4. if further development costs are to be incurred on the same project, the aggregate of such costs, together with related production, selling and administration costs are reasonably expected to be more than covered by related future revenues; and
5. adequate resources exist, or are reasonably expected to be available, to enable the project to be completed and to provide any consequential increases in working capital.

In the circumstances defined above, development expenditure may be deferred to subsequent years, and shown on the balance sheet as an asset to the extent that its recovery can be regarded as reasonably assured. Deferred development expenditure should be reviewed at the end of each accounting period, and when the circumstances which have justified the deferral of the expenditure no longer apply then the expenditure to the extent considered irrecoverable should be written off immediately.

It is interesting to compare SSAP 13 with the US standard FASB Statement No. 2, which prescribes that all expenditure on research and development should be written off in the year incurred rather than capitalized as intangible assets. The American approach is inconsistent with the accruals and matching concepts, and therefore cannot be justified in accordance with descriptive accounting theory. However, the standard has greatly simplified accounting practice in this area and has eliminated the manipulation of research and development expenditure for the purpose of adjusting reported profit.

Goodwill

Goodwill may be described as the sum of those intangible attributes of a business which contribute to its success, such as a favourable location, a good reputation, the ability and skill of its employees and management, and its long-standing relationships with creditors, suppliers and customers. The valuation of goodwill is a controversial topic in accounting because of its vague nature and the difficulty of arriving at a valuation which is verifiable. Hence, in view of its lack of accounting objectivity, it is generally excluded from the balance sheet. Goodwill only enters the accounting system in connection with a valuation ascribed to it in the acquisition price of a business. In such a case, that portion of the purchase price which exceeds the total value of the assets less the liabilities taken over, represents the amount paid for goodwill. At this point, therefore, there is no objective measure of the value of goodwill.

There are two viewpoints regarding the manner in which goodwill should be treated in financial reports. One viewpoint is that goodwill should be eliminated from the balance sheet by being deducted from the shareholders' equity by an adjustment to the reserves, as soon as goodwill arises by the acquisition of any business. According to this view, goodwill is a payment made by shareholders for the expected future earnings of the business acquired. Hence, the goodwill is associated directly with the interests of the shareholders in the company.

The other viewpoint is that goodwill should be shown as an asset, and be treated as other fixed assets. Therefore, goodwill should be capitalized and written off over a period of years. This treatment is commonly found in the United States. Proponents of this view argue that an expense has been incurred in acquiring the benefit of future earnings. As the benefit associated with goodwill is exploited, and the enhanced earnings actually materialize, they should be matched with the costs associated with the goodwill which gave rise to them. If costs are not matched in this way, there is an overstatement of profit.

SSAP 22 'Accounting for Goodwill' (1984) requires that purchased goodwill should normally be eliminated from the accounts by immediate write-off against reserves. However, the standard also allows a company to carry goodwill as an asset and to amortize (depreciate) it through the profit and loss account over its useful economic life.

Following a two-year review by the ASC of the practical and theoretical issues that arise in accounting for goodwill, ED 47 (1990) proposed that companies will no longer be allowed to write off goodwill to reserves at the time they acquire it. Instead, goodwill acquired as part of a business will have to be shown on the balance sheet and reduced by an annual charge to the profit and loss account calculated to write it off completely over its economic life, or written down if it suffers a permanent diminution of value. The maximum write-off period proposed is 20 years although, if exceptional circumstances justify it, a longer period of up to 40 years may be used. These exceptional circumstances should be disclosed and explained. Internally generated goodwill will continue to be excluded from the balance sheet.

Brands

There has been considerable controversy in the UK recently regarding accounting for brands. This originated from the decision of several large companies to attribute values to their brand names and include the values in their balance sheets. The objectives of these companies were to add strength to their balance sheets, improve their share prices, diminish their vulnerability to takeover and increase their borrowing power. Certainly, the balance sheets of these companies were transformed by their decision on brands. Two major issues relate to these decisions. First, there is no generally accepted method of objectively valuing brands. The uncertainties surrounding the calculations of brands cast doubts on their usefulness to users. Second, as it was stated in the Introduction to this part, it is not the objective of the balance sheet to place a value on a company.

In their report to the ICAEW's Research Board, Barwise *et al.* (1989) concluded that the issue of brand accounting is 'inseparable from the accounting treatment of goodwill'. The Accounting Standards Committee adopted the same view in a technical release (TR 780) which was published in 1990:

The ASC's analysis leads it to conclude that whatever definition is adopted the term 'brand' describes what is generally regarded for accounting purposes as goodwill. It is concluded that for such purposes brands are subsumed within goodwill and this should be accounted for in accordance with the requirements for accounting for goodwill.

Leases

A lease is a contract which grants the right to operate or use property for a specified period of time. The lessor retains the ownership of the asset, but conveys to the lessee the right of use in consideration of the payment of a specified rent.

The traditional approach to accounting for leases has been to record the transactions in their legal form. Thus, the lessee merely debits the rent due and payable to the profit and loss account. Since the lessee has no ownership right, no asset is shown on the balance sheet. The lessor, on the other hand, remains the owner of the asset leased, which he records as an asset on his balance sheet. At the same time, the rent receivable is recorded as revenue in his profit and loss account. Seen from a business viewpoint, the lessee acquires the use of an asset without needing to buy it. Therefore, he avoids the necessity of raising finance for its acquisition. Had the lessee acquired the asset, and borrowed money to that end, both the assets and the debt would have been recorded on the balance sheet. For this reason, leasing is frequently referred to as 'off-balance-sheet financing'. The leasing of assets is a practice which is increasing. The traditional treatment of leases in accounting may be misleading to users of financial statements wishing to assess a company's state of affairs.

SSAP 21 'Accounting for Leases and Hire Purchase Contracts' prescribes an alternative treatment, which seeks to reflect the economic nature of a leasing transaction by bringing leases on to balance sheets.

The standard's principal requirement is for lessees to capitalize finance leases, i.e. those which transfer substantially all the risks and rewards of ownership of a leased asset to the lessee. A capitalized asset is then depreciated over its useful life. A corresponding liability for future lease payments is recorded at the net present value of the future payments. The interest rate applied to find net present value is the rate 'implicit in the lease'. Part of each lease payment is treated as being payment of interest on the outstanding liability: the balance is debited against the liability. Therefore, instead of charging the full amount of lease payments against profits, the lessee charges depreciation and interest. In any one year, the sum of these two charges may exceed or fall short of the lease payment but over the period of the life of the asset the total of depreciation and interest will equal total lease payments.

In the lessor's accounts, the lease transaction is treated as though it were an outright sale. He records a deferred receivable which is the counterpart of the lessee's liability.

Example

A lessee enters into a lease for an item of plant. The following details apply:

Fair value of asset	£100 000
Residual value of asset	nil after 5 years
Lease terms	£25 000 for 5 years commencing 1.1.19X0

The implicit rate of return which equates five payments of £25 000 annually in advance of the purchase price of £100 000 is approximately 12.5 per cent. The lessee's profit and loss account will reflect both the finance charge and depreciation on the asset as follows:

Profit and loss accounts

Year	Average amount outstanding	Charge to interest at 12.5%	Depreciation, 20% straight line	Total
	£	£	£	£
19X0	75 000	9 375	20 000	29 375
19X1	59 375	7 422	20 000	27 422
19X2	41 797	5 225	20 000	25 225
19X3	22 022	2 978	20 000	22 978
19X4			20 000	20 000
		25 000	100 000	125 000

The balance sheets would record the net book value of the asset and the obligations show the outstanding principal of the loan together with the accrued interest for the year. The amount of principal outstanding is apportioned to show the amount falling due within one year and that which falls due after more than one year of the balance sheet date.

Balance sheets

Year	19X0	19X1	19X2	19X3	19X4
Cost	100 000	100 000	100 000	100 000	100 000
Depreciation	20 000	40 000	60 000	80 000	100 000
	80 000	60 000	40 000	20 000	—
Current liabilities					
Obligations under finance lease	15 625	17 578	19 775	22 022	—
Accrued interest	9 375	7 422	5 225	2 978	—
	25 000	25 000	25 000	25 000	—
Deferred liabilities					
Obligations under finance lease	59 375	41 797	22 022	—	—
	84 375	66 797	47 022	25 000	—

In our example we have used the actuarial approach for capitalizing the finance lease. SSAP 21 states that the rule-of-78/sum-of-digits method may normally be regarded as an acceptable method. The calculations using the rule of 78 are shown below.

Year	Rental (£)	Interest charge (£)
19X0	25 000 × 4/10	10 000
19X1	25 000 × 3/10	7 500
19X2	25 000 × 2/10	5 000
19X3	25 000 × 1/10	2 500
19X4	—	—
		25 000

The valuation of liabilities

Liabilities may be defined as existing financial obligations which the firm intends to meet at some time in the future. Such obligations arise from legal or managerial considerations and impose restrictions on the use of assets by the firm for its own purposes.

To be recognized, a liability must satisfy the following tests:

1 the liability must exist at the present time;
2 it must involve expenditure in the future;
3 it must be ascertained with reasonable accuracy;
4 it must be quantifiable;
5 its maturity date must be known at least approximately (Barton, 1984).

The capital invested by the owner or shareholders in an enterprise is not regarded as a liability in accounting. We deal with the accounting treatment of the owner's or shareholders' equity presently, but we should mention at this stage that shareholders have a right at law to the payment of a dividend once it has been declared. As a result, unclaimed dividends are shown as current liabilities. It is the practice to show proposed dividends as current liabilities also, since such proposed dividends are usually final dividends for the year which must be approved at the annual general meeting before which the accounts for the year must be laid.

The valuation problem

The valuation of liabilities is part of the process of measuring both capital and profit, and is important to such problems as capital maintenance and the ascertainment of a firm's financial position. Hence, 'the requirements for an accurate measure of the financial position and financial structure should determine the basis for liability valuation. Their valuation should be consistent with the valuation of assets and expenses' (Barton, 1984). The need for consistency arises from the objectives of liability valuation, which are similar to those of asset valuation. Probably the most important of these objectives is the desire to record expenses and financial losses in the process of measuring profit. However, the valuation of liabilities should also assist investors and creditors in understanding the financial position of the firm.

In accordance with the manner of valuing assets in economics, liabilities may be valued at their discounted net values; in accordance with accounting concepts, they may be recorded at their historic value, that is, the valuation attached to the contractual basis by which they were created.

Example

A firm acquired a piece of land for £20 000 on 1 January 19X0, £10 000 being payable immediately and £10 000 on 1 January 19X1. No interest is payable on the outstanding balance. The two different valuations of the outstanding liability at 1 January 19X0 are as follows:

1 Discounted net value of £10 000 assuming that the current rate of interest is 10 per cent:

$$£10\ 000 \times \frac{100\%}{100\% + 10\%}$$

i.e. £10 000 × 0.9091 = £9091.

2 Historical value of £10 000 by reference to the contract to pay £10 000 on 1 January 19X1 is, of course, £10 000.

There is no gap between the two methods of valuation as regards liabilities which are payable immediately, and it is only as the maturity date of liabilities lengthens that the gap appears. While accounting conventions dictate that the valuation of liabilities should be based on the sum which is payable, it is accounting practice to make a distinction between current and long-term liabilities. As regards current liabilities, there is little difference between the discounted net value and the contractual value of liabilities. In this connection, current liabilities are defined as those which will mature during the course of the accounting period. The gap between the two methods of valuation is significant as regards long-term liabilities. Long-term liabilities are valued on the basis of their historical value, that is, by reference to the contract from which they originated, and hence, during periods of inflation or where the interest payable is less than the current market rate of interest, the accounting valuation will certainly be overstated by comparison with the discounted net value. Here again, a true perspective on this problem may be obtained by reference to the separate role of the accountant and the investor which we stated in the introduction to this part. The accountant records the liability as the sum which will be payable: it is for the investor to value the real cost of that future burden.

Contingent liabilities

SSAP 18 'Accounting for Contingencies' defines a contingency as a condition which exists at the balance sheet date, the outcome of which will be confirmed only by the occurrence or non-occurrence of one or more uncertain future events. It is not intended that uncertainties connected with accounting estimates fall within the scope of this standard, for example the amount of bad debts. Contingencies to which the standard refers are the existence of unresolved legal cases or insurance claims at the balance sheet date.

Where the amount of a loss can be estimated with reasonable certainty, such a loss should be accrued on the balance sheet itself. Where the amount of the loss is uncertain, the nature of the contingency should be disclosed in the notes to the accounts.

Deferred liabilities

The two major types of deferred liabilities are:

1 deferred performance liabilities;
2 deferred tax liabilities.

Deferred performance liabilities exist under a number of forms, the most common being prepayments which cannot be taken into the profit of the current year and are carried forward to the following year. We examined the adjustments required to deal with prepayments in Chapter 9. Other deferred performance liabilities are created under contracts of sale which provide for after-sale services. Thus, sales of many consumer appliances include labour-free servicing of appliances under guarantee. While the realization concept requires the accrual of revenue in the year of sale, provision should be made for the deferred performance liability in the form of an estimate of the after-sale servicing costs. This may be obtained by reference to past experience and expressed as a percentage of total sales for the purpose of calculating the amount to be shown as a liability.

Deferred tax liabilities arise from the fact that tax is assessed in relation to 'taxable profit' and not to 'accounting profit'. Hence, while the taxation authorities use the information contained in the annual accounts for the purposes of computing the taxable profit, the tax payable in respect of that profit is not finally assessed until the subsequent year or years. For this reason, a provision is made for the tax likely to be payable and will show it as a deferred tax liability.

The valuation of shareholders' equity

A consideration of the valuation of shareholders' equity is beyond the scope of this book and properly belongs to the theory of finance. Nevertheless, the shareholders' equity is a significant section of the balance sheet for two reasons:

1 it completes the accounting equation as follows:

assets – liabilities = shareholders' equity

2 it links the balance sheet and the profit and loss account, since retained profits form part of shareholders' equity.

The accounting valuation of the shareholders' equity is made up of a number of items:

1 the cash received from shareholders in respect of the shares issued to them;
2 the premiums, if any, paid by shareholders over and above the nominal value of issued shares;
3 the accumulated capital and revenue reserves from past profits;
4 undistributed retained profit carried forward for distribution in a subsequent year, in the form of dividend equalization accounts or otherwise.

The accounting valuation of the shareholders' equity has virtually no significance in relation to the market value of the equity, which is determined, in the case of public companies, by reference to the share price quoted on the Stock Exchange. The economic valuation of the shareholders' equity may be derived from the present value of discounted future net cash flows expected to be earned by the firm.

As regards the valuation of the shareholders' equity, the accountant is concerned only with recording the historical values associated with its several constituent elements in accordance with accounting conventions. He leaves the problem of valuation to the investor.

Summary

It is necessary to understand the logic and methodology which underlie the recorded values of assets and liabilities in order to appreciate the nature of financial accounting information. A number of concepts surround the problem of valuation of assets and liabilities shown on profit and loss accounts and balance sheets.

This chapter examines the accounting approach to the valuation of fixed and current assets, and considers the effects of inflation in modifying the historical cost concept for fixed asset valuation. The chapter also illustrates the effects of traditional accounting practices in creating variety in the accounting treatment of different items. The valuation of liabilities is also discussed, although it presents a less difficult problem from an accounting viewpoint. Nevertheless, accounting makes virtually no contribution to the valuation of the shareholders' equity, although this is a central problem for shareholders and investors.

References

Barton, A. D. (1984). *The Anatomy of Accounting,* 3rd edn, University of Queensland Press.

Barwise, P., Higson, C., Likierman, A. and Marsh, P. (1989). *Accounting for Brands,* ICAEW and London Business School.

The Sandilands Report (1975). *Report of the Inflation Accounting Committee,* p. 100, HMSO Cmd 6225.

Question

Examine the problems of accounting for research and development expenditure, and explain the requirements of SSAP 13.

Problems

1   You are the Chief Accountant of a retailing company which operates from a number of departmental stores throughout the country. You are approached early in 19X2 by a member of your staff who is preparing the annual accounts for the Barnsley store for the year ended 31 December 19X1. He seeks your advice on the following matters:
    (a) how to treat the goodwill arising on the acquisition of a local bakery during 19X1. The Barnsley store acquired the bakery for the purpose of securing its own supply of bread. The cost was £85 000 including goodwill of £20 000;
    (b) whether to depreciate the cost of the freehold of the furniture department's warehouse which was purchased during the year. The cost was £44 000 split between land £10 000 and buildings £34 000. Legal fees of £800 were incurred;
    (c) how to value two items of stock about which he is unsure. These are:
      (i) a large stock of over-ordered Christmas cards costing £780
      (ii) a stock of skateboards purchased in 19X0 for £1000;
    (d) whether to treat an advertising campaign as an expense in 19X1 or to carry it forward to 19X2. The campaign costing £1700 involved a series of

advertisements in the *Barnsley Sun* newspaper in December 19X1 informing readers of the January sale. The sale was not as popular as it has been in recent years.

Required:
Draft a memorandum to your staff setting out the accounting principles to be followed in each of the above cases and give advice on the most appropriate treatment in the circumstances given.

(Problem supplied by A. J. Naughton, Leeds Polytechnic)

2 The summarized balance sheet of Demiwood Ltd for 31 December 19X8 is shown below.

	£	£
Share Capital		250 000
Revenue Reserves		95 000
		345 000
10% Debentures		86 000
		431 000
Fixed Assets (all tangible)		295 000
Current Assets	221 000	
Current Liabilities	(85 000)	
Net current assets		136 000
		431 000

On 1.1.19X9 Demiwood Ltd bought out the McMaltby Company which was a private company with a summarized balance sheet at 31.12.19X9 as follows:

	£	£
Capital		62 000
Represented by:		
Tangible fixed assets		
Freehold Premises		25 000
Plant		20 000
		45 000
Current Assets	32 000	
Current Liabilities	(15 000)	
Net current assets		17 000
		62 000

An independent valuer estimated that McMaltby's premises were worth £60 000 and its plant was worth £25 000 at replacement cost. It was also estimated that stock was undervalued by £5000 but that debtors were overvalued by £3000.

The agreed price for McMaltby was £120 000 which was made up of cash from a new loan of £100 000 and £20 000 in liquid assets that Demiwood already owned. The McMaltby Company ceased to exist on 1.1.19X9 and all its assets and business activities became part of Demiwood Ltd.

Required:
(a) Calculate the goodwill arising on the takeover of the McMaltby Company.
(b) Explain how goodwill would normally be treated in Demiwood's books.
(c) Prepare a summarized balance sheet for Demiwood immediately following the takeover.

3   A fire completely destroyed Arthur's timber yard and all his accounting records, during the night of 31 December 19X6.

From duplicate bank statements and circularization of his debtors and creditors, Arthur was able to ascertain the following figures.

	£
Debtors, 1 January 19X6	5 130
Creditors, 1 January 19X6	1 790
Cash paid to creditors during the year	22 220
Cash received from debtors during the year	30 080
Creditors, 31 December 19X6	1 870
Debtors, 31 December 19X6	6 050

Arthur's trading accounts for the two years ended 31 December 19X5 were as follows:

	Year ended Dec. 19X4	Year ended Dec. 19X5		Year ended Dec. 19X4	Year ended Dec. 19X5
	£	£		£	£
Opening stock	1 235	1 700	Sales	18 850	25 740
Purchases	13 660	17 718			
	14 895	19 418			
less: Closing stock	1 700	1 400			
	13 195	18 018			
Gross profit	5 655	7 722			
	18 850	25 740		18 850	25 740

Assuming that the ratio of gross profit to sales was the same in 19X6 as in previous years, calculate the value of the stocks destroyed by fire. Submit your workings.

4   Viva Ltd does not keep records of stock movements. A physical stocktaking is made at the end of each quarter and priced at cost. This figure is used for compiling quarterly accounts. Draft accounts have been prepared for the year ended 31 March 1980, but have not been completed as the details of the stock count on 31 March 1980 have been mislaid and cannot be found. The company operates on a gross-profit markup of 33⅓ per cent of cost.

You have ascertained the following facts:

(a)   the total of sales invoiced to customers during January, February and March 19X1 was £53 764. This figure includes £4028 relating to goods despatched on or before 31 December 19X0. The total of the goods despatched to customers before 31 March 19X1 but invoiced in the following month was £5512;

(b)   the total of purchase invoices entered in the purchase day book during January, February and March 19X1 was £40 580 and this figure includes £2940 in respect of goods received on or before 31 December 19X0. Invoices relating to goods received in March 19X1 but which were not entered in the purchase day book until April 19X1 totalled £3880;

(c)   the value of the stock at cost on 31 December 19X0 was £42 640;

(d)   in the stock sheets at that date:
   (i)   the total of one page was over-cast by £85
   (ii)   120 items, the cost of which was £2 each, had been priced at 40p each
   (iii)   the total of the stock in one section, which was £5260, had been included in the summary as £5620

Required:

Show how you would arrive at the figure for the stock at cost as on 31 March 19X1.

(Problem supplied by A. J. Naughton, Leeds Polytechnic)

5　Purchases and sales data for the first three years of a firm's operation were as follows (purchases are listed in order of acquisition):

	19X1	19X2	19X3
	£	£	£
Sales			
	12 000 units @ 50	15 000 units @ 60	18 000 units @ 65
Purchases			
	4 000 units @ 22	5 500 units @ 32	7 000 units @ 40
	6 000 units @ 25	6 000 units @ 34	4 500 units @ 43
	5 000 units @ 30	4 000 units @ 37	5 000 units @ 45

Required:

(a)　Prepare a schedule showing the number of units on hand at the end of each year.

(b)　Compute the year-end stocks for each of the three years using (i) FIFO, (ii) LIFO, (iii) Average Cost

(c)　Calculate the gross profit for each of the three years based on (i) FIFO, (ii) LIFO and (iii) weighted average.

(d)　Which method of stock valuation do you consider the most appropriate? Why?

6　Z Ltd is engaged upon a contract the price of which is £250 000. At 31 December 19X8 the expenditure on the contract is as follows:

Materials issued from store	£42 000
Wages	39 820
Expenses directly chargeable to the contract	12 130
Materials purchased and delivered direct to the site	4 910
Plant in use on site valued at	6 840
Proportion of overhead charges	790

The amount of work completed to date as certified by the architect after 20 per cent retention money was £100 000. Materials in stock at the site were valued at £970 and depreciation is to be charged at 5 per cent. Prepare the contract account showing the proportion of profit you would advise should be taken to the profit and loss account.

7　Builders Ltd commenced work on 1 July 19X7 on a contract the agreed price of which was £250 000. Expenditure incurred during the year to 30 June 19X8 was as follows:

Wages £60 000; Plant £17 500; Materials £42 500; Sundry expenses £4000; and Head Office charges allocated to the contract amounted to £5500. Part of the plant which had cost £1300 was sold for £1500.

Of the contract price £100 000 representing 80 per cent of the work certified had been received by 30 June 19X8 and on that date the value of the plant on the site was deemed to be £4500 and that of the unused materials £1250. Work costing £12 500 had been completed but not certified at 30 June 19X8.

It was decided to estimate what further expenditure would be incurred in completing the contract for the purpose of computing the estimated total profit that would be made on the contract and to take to the credit of the profit and loss account for the year a proper proportion thereof.

The estimate of additional expenditure that would be required, based on the assumption that the contract would be finished in six months' time, was as follows:

(a) Wages to complete £52 800.
(b) Materials in addition to those in stock on 30 June 19X8 would cost £35 000.
(c) Sundry expenses would amount to £1800.
(d) Plant in addition to plant in hand at 30 June 19X8 would cost £6500 and the residual value of plant at 31 December 19X8 would be £3750.
(e) Contingencies would require a further £3500.

Prepare a contract account at 30 June 19X8.

8 Rover Company leases certain heavy equipment from the London Leasing Company under an eight-year lease. The economic life of the equipment is ten years. No residual value will remain at the end of that period. The lease agreement calls for eight annual payments of £100 000 beginning at the inception of the lease. The first payment is to be made on 1 January 19X0. Each payment thereafter falls to be made on the first day of the year. The fair value of the equipment is £1 million. Rover Company depreciates similar assets by the straight-line method.

Required:
Show how the transaction would be recorded in Rover Company's final accounts.

Section 3

The
Application
of Financial
Accounting
Method to
Corporate
Enterprises

Chapter 13

Financial accounting information for corporate enterprises

We mentioned in the introduction to this part (p. 39) that the selection for closer analysis of the application of financial accounting procedures to the generation of finanical information for corporate enterprises was justified on two grounds:

1 The industrial and commercial expansion which has occurred in the Western industrialized countries over the last 100 years has been affected to a considerable extent by the activities organized by companies. Probably the most important factor in this expansion has been the facility afforded by the corporate structure for the mobilization of large supplies of capital lodged in the private sector of the economy. Consequently, the study of corporate activity constitutes an important area of interest to students of accounting and the management sciences generally, many of whom will make their careers as company executives. Applying the criterion of relevance to the selection of teaching material has led us to focus attention on corporate financial accounting as the major application of financial accounting method of interest to students. Therefore we have excluded large areas of conventional material found, for example, in the application of financial accounting method to partnership activities and to such problems as the accounting treatment of royalties and returnable containers.

2 We have devoted Part 4 to the analysis of financial reporting, which is concerned with the supply of financial information to shareholders and investors. Many financial reporting problems stem directly from the application of financial accounting procedures to the generation of the information content of financial reports. Hence, this section serves also as a necessary introduction to Part 4. The efficiency of the corporate sector of the economy depends, in the first instance, upon a sufficient flow of investment funds to that sector, and an efficient allocation of available funds among individual companies. The quality of the investment decision-making process depends to a large extent upon the quality and adequacy of financial information available to investors. Herein lies the social importance of the information content of financial reports.

The purpose of this chapter is to examine the financial accounting implications of incorporation, and the procedures applied to the financial accounting problems peculiar to public as distinct from private companies. We define public companies as those private-sector companies in which the public at large may become shareholders, and private companies as those private-sector companies which have a restricted and selected number of individuals as shareholders.

The nature of corporate enterprises

Companies are created and regulated by law. By a legal fiction, the legal personality of a business enterprise established as a company is different from the legal personality of the various individuals having an interest therein, whether as owners, managers or employees. This means, for example, that although a company has no physical life, it may nevertheless own property, enter into contracts, sue and be sued in a court of law and undertake any activity consistent with the objectives envisaged at the time of its creation. It acts through its employees, whether as managers or subordinates, with whom it enters into contracts of employment.

The proprietors of a company are recognized in law as being those persons owning its capital. The capital is divided into shares or stock, and by acquiring shares, investors become shareholders. As evidence of their legal title to the shares they own, shareholders are issued with share certificates. Shares are transferable property rights, and may be negotiated either privately or through a stock exchange. Stock exchanges have rules for granting permission for the shares of individual companies to be traded on them, or to be 'quoted on the Stock Exchange', which is the term given to such permission.

Companies are usually established by the formal registration of documents with a Public Registrar charged with enforcing statutory provisions in respect of enterprises operating as companies. In the United Kingdom, for example, individuals wishing to incorporate themselves for the purpose of carrying on trade are called promoters, and it is their responsibility to arrange for the process of incorporation. This involves lodging a number of documents with the Registrar of Companies and paying the required fees. The two most important documents are the memorandum of association, which defines the powers and objectives of the companies, and the articles of association which contains the rules for its internal regulation. The name, objectives and the capital clauses are found in the memorandum of association. For our purposes, the capital clause is the most important, for it states the number, classes and nominal value of the shares which the company has power to issue. The authorized capital is stated in the capital clause, and it is the maximum capital which the company may raise. The capital clause may be altered, however, by a formal process.

A company obtains capital by the issue of shares. Investors are invited to apply for shares. They usually have to pay a portion of the purchase price on application and the balance when the shares have been formally allotted to them. The capital clause states the value of each share as a nominal figure. Thus, the authorized capital may be stated to consist of 1 million shares of £1 each, giving the company an authorized capital of £1 million. When a company offers shares for sale, however, it may set a price which is higher than the nominal value, and it need not offer for sale all the shares which it is authorized to sell. That portion of the authorized capital which is sold is called the issued capital.

Once shares have been issued, they become the property of the individual investors who have acquired them, and these investors are free to sell their shares to anyone. The sale price is negotiated between buyer and seller, and the deal may be effected through a Stock Exchange if the shares are quoted shares. The seller transfers his shares formally to the buyer by notice to the company, and the buyer is registered in the register of shareholders as the new shareholder. Shares transferred in this way are known as registered shares. An alternative type of shareholding, which is restricted by law in some countries, is known as a bearer share. A bearer share is more easily transferred than a registered share since the share certificate does not detail the name of the shareholder, and he is not registered in the register of shareholders. Consequently, bearer shares are transferable by hand.

A company receives only the issue price of a share. The legal effect of shareholding is to grant ownership rights in respect of the fraction of capital represented by the share, and a right to receive the appropriate portion of corporate net profit distributed in the form of a dividend. Companies usually retain a portion of net profit for reinvestment, and distribute the balance as dividends. We will consider shortly the accounting consequences of the distinction made between retained profit and distributable profit.

The distinction between ownership and management is one of the most distinctive features of corporate activity. As owners, shareholders may be considered as having ultimate control over the activities of the company through their right to appoint directors. The rights of shareholders to exercise control over the affairs of companies are defined by legislation. Once appointed, directors exercise day-to-day control of the company's affairs, and although they are accountable to shareholders, the diffusion of shares among many shareholders usually places directors in a very strong position *vis-à-vis* shareholders. Although they are treated as stewards of corporate assets on behalf of shareholders, the effective power to make decisions of major importance in respect of those assets lies almost entirely in their hands. We discuss in Part 5 problems of corporate planning and control in terms of managerial responsibility.

Social change is affecting the traditional method of regulating corporate enterprise in a number of ways. First, the recognition of the right of employees to share managerial responsibility is an important feature of the democratization of corporate control. Some European countries have already legislated for two-tier boards of directors, and this feature has been included in the *Societas Europea SE,* the European Company which is formed by registration in the European Commercial Register kept by the Court of the European Communities in Luxembourg. Employee participation in the management of companies is an explicit admission that the interests of employees are as important as those of shareholders. Second, the concept of social responsibility, which we discuss in Part 4, further broadens the classical notion of stewardship as a definition of the function of directors to include a responsibility to all sections of society having an interest in the activities of corporate enterprises. Thus, consumers, as well as the local community, are included in the group of those having a vested interest in the nature of corporate activity.

Financial accounting implications of corporate status

Corporate status, as distinct from the one-man type of business which we examined in Section 2, implies a distinctive treatment of the capital structure and of the allocation of the net profit as between dividends and retained profit.

The normal procedure for dealing with the financial accounting implications of corporate status is to establish a separation of functions between the accountant and the company secretary. The former is usually concerned with the financial accounting procedures directed at recording business transactions: the latter usually maintains the register of shareholders, including such details as the record of shareholders' names and addresses, class and number of shares held, instructions regarding correspondence and payment of dividends. Much of the routine work of the secretary's department in this respect involves recording the transfer of shares and the payment of yearly dividends to shareholders. The specialized nature of share transfer work, as well as its sheer volume in some corporations, often requires a separate department under a share transfer registrar. In such cases, the share transfer registrar is a senior official of the company.

The financial accounting aspects of the share capital with which the accountant is concerned consist of the ledger records associated with shareholders, that is, the share capital account, the dividend account, and those accounts retaining profit in the form of capital or current reserves. We will deal with the nature of these accounts shortly. These accounts are concerned with aggregate figures.

Example

Excel Corporation Limited is a public company having a share capital of one million £1 shares held in different proportions by 20 000 individual shareholders. The detailed records of the individual shareholding are kept by the registrar, and the accountant will keep the following ledger record:

Share capital account

	Sundry shareholders	£1 000 000

The capital structure
The capital structure may consist of both share capital and loan capital, and represents the long-term capital available to the company, as distinct from the short-term capital represented by the credit facilities offered by trade creditors and bank overdrafts. Shareholders are regarded at law as owners. The share capital is at risk, and in the event of business failure shareholders may lose all the capital invested since they rank last as claimants on the residual assets of the corporation. By contrast, loan capital is made available by creditors on a long-term basis. Thus, a company may invite the public to supply loan capital for a period of, say, five years at a rate of interest of, say, 10 per cent. Individuals may offer varying sums, and receive from the company a debenture certificate. Debentures frequently involve the mortgage of specific corporate assets to the body of debenture-holders represented by a trustee for debenture-holders, and in the event of the company defaulting in any way on the conditions of the debenture instrument, the specified assets may be seized and sold on behalf of the debenture-holders. The charge on the corporate assets may be fixed, as we have mentioned, or floating, that is, not be specific as regards any particular assets but applying to all corporate assets. Debenture-holders are guaranteed, therefore, both repayment of loan capital and interest as specified in the conditions of issue. It is the duty of the trustee for the debenture-holders to act before any loss threatens debenture-holders. Very large and financially strong companies may be able to raise long-term loans without mortgaging their assets to lenders. They issue certificates of indebtedness described as unsecured notes, which also carry an obligation to pay interest and to redeem at the end of the stated period. Holders of unsecured notes rank as ordinary creditors in liquidation.

Shares, debentures and unsecured notes may all be quoted on the Stock Exchange and transacted between buyers and sellers. Appropriate registers of debenture-holders and holders of unsecured notes must be kept by the company.

The share capital may consist of different classes of shares, but the two most common classes of shares are preference shares and ordinary shares.

Preference shares give preferential rights as regards dividends, and often as regards the repayment of capital on winding-up. Preference shares may be issued as redeemable preference shares, that is, they may be redeemed and cancelled by the company. Preference shares may also be issued as cumulative preference shares, which means that if the net profit of any particular year is insufficient to pay a dividend to preference shareholders of this class, the right to receive a dividend for that year is carried forward to the following year, and so on, until such time as the accumulated dividend entitlement may be declared and paid out of profits. Preference shareholders are usually entitled to a fixed dividend expressed as a percentage of the nominal value of the share. Thus, a holder of 100 preference shares of £1 each carrying a fixed dividend rate of 8 per cent will be entitled to a total yearly dividend of £8. However, preference shares may also be issued as participating preference shares, meaning that in addition to the fixed-dividend-rate entitlement, they participate in the remainder of the net profit with ordinary shareholders. It is common for conditions to be imposed limiting the participating rights of such shares to allow for a minimum level of dividend for ordinary shareholders. Thus, a participating preference share may carry a right to a fixed dividend of 8 per cent and a right to participate in the remaining net profit after the ordinary shareholders have received their dividend.

Ordinary shares provide the bulk of the share capital. In return for bearing the risk involved in financing corporate activities, ordinary shareholders enjoy the right to the whole of the net profit—either as dividends or, if retained, as the increased value of net corporate assets—subject to the rights of preference shareholders. Some companies obtain the whole of the share capital in the form of ordinary shares. The reason for issuing a variety of shares—preference shares of different classes and ordinary shares—is to tap the funds held by investors with differing investment needs. A young man with money to invest will be looking for growth in the value of his capital and will be attracted to buying ordinary shares in a company having good prospects of expansion. A retired person looking for a safe investment providing a steady income, may wish to hold some preference shares. Institutional buyers, such as pension funds and insurance companies, also have a wish to hold shares of different classes. Deferred shares are a separate class of shares to both preference and ordinary shares, and may be issued in restricted numbers to managers of the company. In such a case, deferred shares carry an entitlement to dividend only after the ordinary shareholders have received a specified dividend rate.

Gearing and the capital structure

The nature of the capital structure has important implications for financial management purposes, and in this respect, the gearing is an important consideration.

The gearing expresses the relationship between the proportion of fixed interest (loan capital) and fixed dividend (preference shares capital) to ordinary shares. A company with a large proportion of fixed interest and fixed dividend bearing capital to ordinary capital is said to be highly geared.

Example

Companies Alpha, Beta and Gamma have the same total capital which is issued as follows:

	Alpha	Beta	Gamma
	£	£	£
Share capital			
8% Preference shares of £1 each	40 000	10 000	—
Ordinary shares of £1 each	20 000	80 000	100 000

Loan capital

7% Debentures of £100 each	40 000	10 000	—
	100 000	100 000	100 000

The gearing of these three companies may be calculated as follows:

1 Alpha (40 000 + 40 000): 20 000 or 4:1;
2 Beta (10 000 + 10 000): 80 000 or 0.25:1;
3 Gamma : 100 000 or ∞.

Alpha is, therefore, the most highly geared company.

The importance of the gearing is that fluctuations in net profit may have disproportionate effects upon the return accruing to ordinary shareholders in the case of a highly geared company, and hence on the pricing of ordinary shares on the Stock Exchange. Directors looking for stability in the price of the company's ordinary shares will be swayed by this consideration when faced with raising further capital. For taxation reasons, the net cost of debenture interest may be lower than the net cost in dividends of further issues of ordinary shares. Similarly, fixed dividend preference shares may also cost less than issuing ordinary shares. The following example shows the effects of fluctuating net profit levels on the return to ordinary shareholders, assuming that the available net profit is wholly distributed.

Example

The consequence of fluctuations in net distributable profit on ordinary shareholders in Alpha Company, Beta Company and Gamma Company geared in the ratios established in the example above may be judged as follows:

	Alpha			Beta		Gamma	
	£	£	£	£	£	£	£
Assuming net profit of £15 000							
Net profit		15 000			15 000		15 000
8% Preference shares	3 200			800		—	
7% Debentures	2 800			700		—	—
		6 000			1 500		
Available for ordinary shares		9 000			13 500		15 000
Maximum dividend for ordinary shareholders	$\frac{9\ 000}{20\ 000}$ = 45%		$\frac{13\ 500}{80\ 000}$ = 16.875%			$\frac{15\ 000}{100\ 000}$ = 15%	

	Alpha			Beta		Gamma	
	£	£	£	£	£	£
Assuming net profit of £10 000						
Net profit		10 000		10 000		10 000
8% Preference shares	3 200			800		—
7% Debentures	2 800			700		—	—
		6 000		1 500		
Available for ordinary shares		4 000		8 500		10 000
Maximum dividend for ordinary shareholders	$\frac{4\ 000}{20\ 000}$	=20%	$\frac{8\ 500}{80\ 000}$	=10.625%	$\frac{10\ 000}{100\ 000}$	=10%

Hence, in a highly geared company such as Alpha, a fall of 33⅓ per cent in net profit has produced a fall of 56 per cent in the maximum dividend payable to ordinary shareholders.

Accounting procedures applied to the capital structure

The share capital

We mentioned earlier that a distinction exists between the authorized capital and the issued capital. The former is the maximum limit in the total value of shares of different classes which a company is permitted to issue under the conditions of its registration; the latter is the nominal value of shares of different classes which have been issued. The reason why companies do not establish the value of the authorized capital greatly in excess of their anticipated requirement lies in the taxes imposed on the value of the authorized capital, which deter promoters from incurring unnecessary expenses.

The financial accounting procedures applied to the treatment of the share capital may be said to have two main objectives:

1 recording the issue of shares and the consideration received in respect of such shares;
2 providing information about the share capital in the balance sheet.

We do not propose to deal with the procedures applied to the redemption of redeemable preference shares, or those applied to the issue of bonus shares, since these procedures are not essential to the thesis of this book. It may be mentioned, however, that bonus shares are commonly issued free of cost to existing shareholders in proportion to their shareholdings by way of distribution of accumulated profits.

Recording the issue of shares

It has become the practice for companies seeking to make an issue of shares to the public to employ the services of merchant bankers not only to act as advisers but also to deal with the details of the issue, such as issuing the prospectus advertising the offer of the shares for sale, recording the applications from investors and the monies received with the applications, the allotment of shares to individual shareholders where an offer has been oversubscribed, and arranging for the shares undersubscribed to be taken up by the underwriters who have acted as insurers in respect of the issue of the shares in return for a commission. The detailed accounting procedures for dealing with the issue of shares need not detain us, for they have become part and parcel of a rather specialized aspect of work.

The central financial problems relating to the issue of shares concern the nature of the shares to be issued, that is, whether to issue preference or ordinary, how many to issue and the price to be attached to such shares. All these are problems in respect of which a company will seek expert advice. The financial accounting procedures which we shall consider reflect merely the outcome of the decisions taken.

We mentioned earlier that shares are described in the memorandum of association as having a nominal value. This practice applies in the United Kingdom, although in the United States, for example, it is the practice for shares not to have a nominal value, and they are issued as 'shares of no par value'. This means that the recorded issue value of the share capital reflects the price determined at the time of issue.

In the United Kingdom, the practice of attaching a nominal value to shares makes it possible for an issue of shares to be made:

1   at par, that is, a share having a nominal value of £1 is issued at a price of £1.
2   at a premium, that is, a share having a nominal value of £1 is issued at a price higher than £1.
3   at a discount, that is, a share having a nominal value of £1 may be issued at a price which is less than £1. In practice, legislation attaches very strict conditions to the issue of shares at a discount.

A number of considerations affect share issues, not the least of which is that the issue should be a financial success. This means that the company should receive a realistic price for the shares offered and that the issue should be wholly subscribed.

The following examples show the accounting procedures applied to the issue of ordinary shares at par and at a premium.

The issue of ordinary shares at par
The Omega Co Ltd has issued 2 million £1 ordinary shares at par. The purchase price has been paid on application and allotment and the company's cash book has been debited with the amount received. The entries in the company's accounts are as follows:

Ordinary share capital account

		Sundry ordinary shareholders	£2 000 000

Sundry ordinary shareholders

Ordinary share capital	£2 000 000	Cash	£2 000 000

Cash book

Sundry ordinary shareholders	£2 000 000		

The detailed list of individual shareholdings does not form part of the financial accounting system, but rather of the register of shareholders. Hence, the sundry ordinary shareholders account does not exist as such: it is represented by the register of shareholders. From a financial accounting viewpoint, only the ordinary share capital account and the cash book are significant.

The issue of ordinary shares at a premium
The Onedin Co Ltd has issued 2 million £1 ordinary shares at a premium of 50 pence that is, at £1.50 a share. The purchase price has been paid on application and allotment and the company's cash book has been debited. The practice in the United Kingdom is to separate the par value of the shares from the share premium. Legislation allows a greater flexibility in the application of the share premium account, for example in redeeming preference shares at a premium.

The accounting entries are as follows:

Ordinary share capital account

		Sundry ordinary shareholders	£2 000 000

Share premium account

		Sundry ordinary shareholders	£1 000 000

Sundry ordinary shareholders

Ordinary share capital	£2 000 000	Cash	£3 000 000
Share premium	1 000 000		
	£3 000 000		£3 000 000

Cash book

Sundry ordinary shareholders	£3 000 000		

As we explained earlier, the sundry ordinary shareholders do not exist as a formal account, but are found in the register of shareholders. Consequently, the only accounts of significance are the ordinary share capital account, the share premium account and the cash book.

In the United States and Canada, the practice for the last 50 years has been to issue shares of no par value. This simplifies the accounting process, for there is no need to have a share premium account and the share capital account shows the amount actually received from the sale of shares. The case against shares of fixed nominal value is that they bear no relation to the real value of the issued shares, and hence the nominal value is virtually meaningless except as a measure of growth.

The procedures outlined above apply equally to the treatment of other classes of shares.

Loan capital

There is very little difference in the accounting treatment of loan and share capital. Registers of debenture-holders and of holders of unsecured notes are kept, and the method of issue is identical to that of shares in so far as the issuing process tends to be conducted on behalf of the company by merchant bankers. Debentures may be issued at par, at a premium or at a discount. Premiums received on the issue of debentures are regarded as capital profits, and are usually transferred to a capital reserve account. Discounts allowed on the issue of debentures are treated as capital losses, and legislation in the United Kingdom requires such discounts to be shown separately on the balance sheet until they are written off.

Example

Hightrust Investment Company offers for sale 10 000 9 per cent debentures in units of £100 at a premium of 5 per cent. The debentures are repayable on 31 December 2002. The accounting entries are as follows:

9% Debentures 2002 account

	Sundry debenture-holders	£100 000

Capital reserve account

	Sundry debenture-holders	£5 000

Cash book

Sundry debenture-holders	£105 000	

As in the case of the issue of shares, details of individual debenture-holders would be found in the register of debenture-holders.

Distributable profits

The important difference between a limited company and a sole trader lies in the manner in which periodic profit is appropriated. In the case of the sole traders, the net profit belongs to the owner and is transferred to the capital account at the end of the accounting period. By contrast, once the net profit of a company has been ascertained, the board of directors have to decide the proportion which should be paid out to shareholders as dividends and the proportion which should be retained. The amount of dividend declared from time to time should be determined by sound financial principles that ensure that the profits calculated as available for distribution have been established in accordance with accepted accounting principles.

In considering the manner in which the net profit should be appropriated, the following factors are important:

1 Adequate provision should be made in respect of corporation tax payable on the net profit for the year. In this connection, under- or overprovisions in respect of previous years have to be taken into account.
2 Adequate provision should be made for anticipated expenditure on the replacement of fixed assets. During periods of inflation, in particular, the cost of replacing fixed assets exceeds amounts provided for depreciation.
3 Adequate provision should be made for capital expenditure which is to be financed out of earnings.
4 Where a company wishes to provide a degree of stability in the level of yearly dividends by means of a dividend equalization account, care should be taken that sufficient reserves are accumulated in that account.
5 The level of retention of profit should also be dictated by working capital requirements, and for this purpose transfer of net profit to a general reserve may be made.

The Companies Act 1980 introduced complex provisions that deal with distributed profits. The Act provided that no company may make a distribution except out of accumulated realized profits less accumulated realized losses. There is one exception to this rule. If a company has revalued a fixed asset, and subsequently calculates depreciation on the higher revalued figure, the depreciation attributable to the excess may be counted as a realized profit.

It is quite common for companies to distribute only about half their after-tax profit to shareholders. Usually an interim dividend is declared during the account period in anticipation of a final dividend, which is declared after the final results for the year have been ascertained.

Published financial statements

The statutory requirements relating to the disclosure of financial information are governed by the Companies Acts 1948, 1967, 1976, 1980 and 1981, as consolidated in the Companies Act 1985, and the Companies

Act 1989. Many of the statutory requirements contained in these Acts have been enlarged as the result of the issue of Statements of Standard Accounting Practice. A company listed on a stock exchange in Great Britain or Ireland must observe certain additional requirements, which are contained in the history agreement included in the Federation of Stock Exchanges book *Admission of Securities Listing*.

Form and content of financial statements

The Companies Acts require every company to maintain adequate accounting records, and to prepare financial statements in respect of each accounting year, known as the accounting reference period. The following documents must be presented to the annual general meeting of shareholders:

1   a profit and loss account,
2   a balance sheet,
3   a directors' report,
4   an auditors' report.

The auditors' report is a formal attestation of the verification of the accounts kept by the company and of the financial reports extracted from these accounts. In effect, the auditors are required to attest the requirement that 'every balance sheet shall give a true and fair view of the state of affairs of the company as at the end of its financial year, and every profit and loss account shall give a true and fair view of the profit or loss of the company for the financial year.' The true-and-fair-view rules requires that the information contained in the financial statements is sufficient in quantity and quality to satisfy the reasonable expectations of users. By and large, these expectations will be determined by generally accepted accounting practices, and this implies that accounting standards will be observed. Consequently, financial statements which deviate from accounting standards without adequate justification or explanation may not be deemed to give a true and fair view in a court of law.

The Companies Act 1981 (CA81) implemented the European Economic Community's Fourth Directive, aimed at harmonizing the accounts of member countries. This directive applies only to the accounts of individual companies; group company accounts are dealt with in the Seventh Directive. However, the Companies Act 1981 requires that group accounts shall be prepared as far as possible to comply with the accounting rules laid down for individual companies. Accounting for groups of companies is considered in Chapters 16 and 17.

The Companies Act 1981 introduced major changes in British company legislation:

1   Precise formats for the profit and loss account and balance sheet are prescribed for the first time in United Kingdom law and they

require disclosure of considerably more detail than was previously the case.

2 Fundamental principles (concepts) for the preparation of published accounts are prescribed. First, the company is to be presumed to be carrying on its business as a going concern. Second, all accounting principles are to be applied consistently from one financial year to the next. Third, the amount of any item is to be determined on a prudent basis and in particular only profit realized at the balance sheet date is to be included in the profit and loss account. Fourth, revenues and expenses are to be accounted for on an accruals basis. Fifth, in determining the aggregate amount to be shown in respect of any item in the accounts the amount of each individual component asset or liability must be determined separately. Sixth, amounts in respect of items representing assets or income may not be set off against amounts in respect of items representing liabilities or expenditure.

The first four of these principles are the fundamental accounting concepts discussed in Chapter 5. If it appears to the directors of a company that there are special reasons for departing from any of these six principles in preparing the company's accounts then the particulars of the departure, the reasons for it and its effects must be given in a note to the accounts.

3 Historical cost and alternative accounting rules are prescribed. These rules do not differ from those generally followed in practice; they merely represent a shift from non-statutory to statutory regulation. They will be detailed later in this chapter. The alternative accounting rules allow assets to be valued at their current cost.

4 A distinction is drawn between the publicity and filing requirements of different companies according to their size. Small and medium-size companies must present a full set of accounts to their shareholders. However, they may file modified reports with the Registrar of Companies. Details of the qualifying conditions and exemptions are considered later in this chapter.

The Companies Act 1989 introduced a requirement to state whether the accounts have been prepared in accordance with applicable accounting standards and give details of, and the reasons for, any material departures. Small and medium-size companies are exempt from this disclosure requirement.

The profit and loss account

The Companies Acts provide two horizontal and two vertical formats for the presentation of the profit and loss account. Essentially, the two formats may be distinguished by the way in which costs are analysed. Format 1 analyses costs by type of operation, while format 2 analyses costs by type of expenditure. The vertical format of these two different types of analyses are now given:

Profit and loss account—format 1

1 Turnover
2 Cost of sales
3 Gross profit or loss
4 Distribution costs
5 Administrative expenses
6 Other operating income
7 Income from shares in group companies
8 Income from shares in related companies
9 Income from other fixed-asset investments
10 Other interest receivable and similar income
11 Amounts written off investments
12 Interest payable and similar charges
13 Tax on profit or loss on ordinary activities
14 Profit or loss on ordinary activities after taxation
15 Extraordinary income
16 Extraordinary charges
17 Extraordinary profit or loss
18 Tax on extraordinary profit or loss
19 Other taxes not shown under the above items
20 Profit or loss for the financial year

Profit and loss account—format 2

1 Turnover
2 Change in stocks of finished goods and in work in progress
3 Own work capitalized
4 Other operating income
5 (a) Raw materials and consumables
  (b) Other external charges
6 Staff costs:
  (a) wages and salaries
  (b) social security costs
  (c) other pension costs
7 (a) Depreciation and other amounts written off tangible and intangible fixed assets
  (b) Exceptional amounts written off current assets
8 Other operating charges
9 Income from shares in group companies
10 Income from shares in related companies
11 Income from other fixed-asset investments
12 Other interest receivable and similar income
13 Amounts written off investments
14 Interest payable and similar charges
15 Tax on profit or loss on ordinary activities
16 Profit or loss on ordinary activities after taxation
17 Extraordinary income
18 Extraordinary charges
19 Extraordinary profit or loss
20 Tax on extraordinary profit or loss
21 Other taxes not shown under the above items
22 Profit or loss for the financial year

The Acts require disclosure of the following items on the face of the profit and loss account although they do not appear in the formats:

1 profit or loss on ordinary activities before taxation,
2 transfers and proposed transfers to and from reserves,
3 the aggregate amount of dividends paid and proposed.

A company must adhere to the format it has chosen in subsequent accounting years, unless in the opinion of the board of directors there are special reasons for a change. Details of any decision to change the format must be given in the note to the accounts.

The profit and loss account must be prepared in the order and under the headings given in the formats. Each item in the format is prefixed by an arabic number, which need not be shown in the published accounts. It is permissible to amalgamate certain items if the amount involved is not material, or if such an amalgamation facilitates the assessment of the company's affairs. It is also possible to adapt the title or to rearrange the position of certain items where the special nature of the company's business requires such alteration.

In addition to the items shown in the formats, and those noted above, the Companies Acts specify certain items of information which must be shown on the face of the profit and loss account or in notes to the accounts. In particular, (1) corresponding amounts for the preceding financial year must be shown for every item in the profit and loss account and the notes thereon—where a corresponding amount would not be comparable with the current-year item, an adjusted corresponding amount must be shown, particulars of the adjustment and the reasons for it being included; (2) the accounting policies followed by a company in determining the amount of profit or loss must be stated.

Turnover

Turnover means any amount derived by the company from the provision of goods and services in the context of its ordinary activities. The term turnover replaces the term sales previously used. It includes all receipts from these activities after deduction of traded discounts, value added tax and any other sales-based tax (e.g. excise duty).

Additionally, there must be disclosed in notes to the accounts the following information relating to the analysis of the turnover:

1 where the company carries on two or more classes of business which differ substantially from each other, the amount of the turnover attributable to each class,
2 where the company has traded in different 'markets' (defined by geographical boundaries), the amount of the turnover attributable to each market must be stated.

Expenditure

In calculating the cost of sales, distribution and administrative expenses (Format 1), the following must be included:

1 Provisions for depreciation or diminution in value of assets. Amounts written off investments must be shown separately.
2 Directors' and employees' emoluments. Additionally, notes to the accounts must show the following information:

In respect of directors, distinguishing between directors' fees and directors' salaries:
(a) Aggregate emoluments, including fees and percentages, expense allowances charged to United Kingdom tax, pension contributions paid in respect of them and benefits in kind;
(b) Aggregate of directors' and past directors' pensions, excluding pensions from schemes maintained by contributions;
(c) Aggregate of compensation paid to directors or past directors for loss of office;
(d) Prior-year adjustments arising from expense allowances being disallowed for tax purposes, or a director retaining emoluments for which he was previously accountable.

In respect of employees:

(a) the average number of employees, calculated by dividing the annual number of employees by the number of weeks in the accounting year. Where format 1 is used, there must be shown in respect of all employees taken into account in determining the relevant annual numbers:

   (i) wages and salaries paid to employees,
   (ii) social security costs (being contributions by the company towards any state social security or pension scheme),
   (iii) other pensions costs (being contributions to company pension schemes and pensions paid).

(b) The average number of employees for each category of employees, such category being defined by the directors having regard to the manner in which the company's activities are organized.

3 Sums payable for the hire of plant and machinery, the sums so payable being shown in the notes to the accounts.
4 Auditors' remuneration, the total payable being shown in the notes to the accounts.
5 Sums paid in respect of any exceptional transactions, being defined as transactions falling outside the ordinary activities of the company.

Other operating income

Other operating income includes income from normal operations which does not fall under any other headings, e.g. royalties and rent received. Income from rents of land and buildings (net of out goings) must be shown separately if this is a substantial part of a company's revenue.

Other investment income

The four formats require income from other fixed-asset investments and other interest receivable and similar income to be shown separately. Income from listed investments must be separately identified in the notes if not in the profit and loss account.

Amounts written off investments

This item is required to be shown on the face of the profit and loss account. Where a fixed-asset investment has diminished in value a provision for the diminution in its value may be made. However, where the reduction in value of any fixed asset (including investments) is expected to be permanent, a provision for the diminution in value must be made. Consequently, no asset may be stated at a net value in excess of its estimated recoverable amount. Where the reasons for any provision for diminution in value no longer apply, the provision must be written back to the extent that it is no longer necessary.

Interest payable and similar charges

There must be shown in the notes to the accounts information relating to the interest charged in respect of the following:

1   Bank loans and overdraft and other loans made to the company which are either repayable otherwise than by instalment and fall due for repayment within five years from the end of the accounting year, or repayable by instalment, the last of which falls due for payment before the end of that period.
2   Loans of any other kind made to the company, i.e. those repayable wholly or in part after more than five years.

Profit or loss on ordinary activities before taxation

As previously stated, this item must be shown on the face of the profit and loss account. The figure reported must represent the balance of all previously mentioned items including exceptional items (see below) that relate to the ordinary activities of the company, but excluding taxation and extraordinary items (see below).

Extraordinary items, exceptional items and prior year adjustments

The required formats for the presentation of the profit and loss account provide headings for extraordinary income, extraordinary charges and tax on extraordinary profit or loss. The Companies Acts do not define extraordinary items. They are interpreted in the light of SSAP 6 'Extraordinary Items and Prior Year Adjustments' as 'those items which derive from events or transactions outside the ordinary activities of the business and which are both material and expected not to recur frequently or regularly. They do not include items which, though exceptional on account of size or incidence, derive from the ordinary activities of the business.' SSAP 6 defines prior-year adjustments as 'those material adjustments applicable to prior years arising from changes in accounting policies and from the correction of fundamental errors'. They do not include the normal recurring correction of fundamental errors and adjustments of accounting estimates made in prior years. It should be noted that the definition of extraordinary items includes and defines 'exceptional items'. Details of extraordinary items will be given in notes to the accounts. Exceptional items must be included in the calculation of profit or loss on ordinary activities before taxation, and details given in a note relating to the profit and loss items in which they are included. Exceptional items include:

1   Abnormal charges for bad debts and write-offs of stocks and work-in-progress and research and development expenditure.
2   Abnormal provisions for losses on long-term contracts.

Where prior-year adjustments, as defined in SSAP 6, have occurred, resulting in any material amount being included in the profit and loss account, separate disclosure of their effect must be shown. The relevant prior-year adjustments are those arising from changes in accounting policies or the correction of some fundamental mistake. Such adjustments may be dealt with through reserves.

Taxation

The requirements of the Companies Acts are twofold. First, the profit and loss account must disclose the net profit or loss on ordinary activities before taxation, and the taxation charge on those activities should be deducted to give the net profit or loss on ordinary activities after taxation. Second, the notes to the accounts must contain the following additional information:

1   the amount of the charge for United Kingdom corporation tax;
2   if that amount would have been greater but for double taxation relief, the amount it would have been but for such relief;
3   the amount of the charge for United Kingdom income tax;

4 the amount of the charge for taxation imposed outside the United Kingdom profits, income and (so far as charged on revenue) capital gains.

These notes must also specify the base on which the charge to United Kingdom corporation tax and income tax in calculated, and given details of any circumstances affecting the liability to corporation tax, income tax and capital gains in the current and succeeding years.

Appropriation of profit

The following items must be disclosed separately:

1 Any amounts set aside for the redemption of share capital or the redemption of loans.
2 Any amount set aside or withdrawn, or that is proposed to be set aside or withdrawn from reserves.
3 The aggregate amount of any dividends paid and proposed.

The balance sheet

The Companies Acts provide two formats for the balance sheet presentations, one vertical the other horizontal. Once a company has chosen which format it intends to adopt, it may not alter that choice without giving an explanation to shareholders in a note to the accounts.

Note from the vertical format shown hereunder that the Acts provide for the classification of broad headings by a letter prefix. Major subdivisions are identified by roman numerals, minor subdivisions by arabic. These prefixes do not have to be shown on the published balance sheet, but are used to set out the manner in which accounting items have to be aggregated on the balance sheet, and the extent to which information has to be disclosed. In this regard, note particularly that any item shown on the format which is preceded by a letter or roman-numeral prefix must be disclosed in a company's published balance.

A company's balance sheet may include any item not otherwise shown on the proposed format, and indeed may show any item in greater detail than is required by the Companies Acts. The following items may not, however, be treated as assets in any company's balance sheet:

1 preliminary expenses;
2 expenses and commissions relating to the issue of shares or debentures;
3 research costs.

With regard to the arrangement of items, it is provided that items preceded by arabic numerals on the format may be amalgamated if they are not material or if the amalgamation facilitates the assessment of the company's state of affairs. In the latter case, the individual items amalgamated must be disclosed by note. Furthermore, these items may be shown in a different order or may have their title adapted where the special nature of the company's business requires such alteration.

Balance sheet—format 1

A Called-up share capital not paid
B Fixed assets
    I Intangible assets
        1 Development costs
        2 Concessions, patents, licences, trade marks and similar rights and assets
        3 Goodwill
        4 Payments on account
    II Tangible assets
        1 Land and buildings
        2 Plant and machinery
        3 Fixtures, fittings, tools and equipment
        4 Payments on account and assets in course of construction
    III Investments
        1 Shares in group companies
        2 Loans to group companies
        3 Shares in related companies
        4 Loans to related companies
        5 Other investments other than loans
        6 Other loans
        7 Own shares
C Current assets
    I Stocks
        1 Raw materials and consumables
        2 Work in progress
        3 Finished goods and goods for resale
        4 Payments on account
    II Debtors
        1 Trade debtors
        2 Amounts owed by group companies
        3 Amounts owed by related companies
        4 Other debtors
        5 Called-up share capital not paid
        6 Prepayments and accrued income
    III Investments
        1 Shares in group companies
        2 Own shares
        3 Other investments
    IV Cash at bank and in hand
D Prepayments and accrued income
E Creditors: amounts falling due within one year
        1 Debenture loans
        2 Bank loans and overdrafts
        3 Payments received on account
        4 Trade creditors
        5 Bills of exchange payable
        6 Amounts owed to group companies
        7 Amounts owed to related companies
        8 Other creditors including taxation and social security
        9 Accruals and deferred income
F Net current assets (liabilities)
G Total assets less current liabilities
H Creditors: amounts falling due after more than one year

1 Debenture loans
2 Bank loans and overdrafts
3 Payments received on account
4 Trade creditors
5 Bills of exchange payable
6 Amounts owed to group companies
7 Amounts owed to related companies
8 Other creditors including taxation and social security
9 Accruals and deferred income

I   Provisions for liabilities and charges
    1 Pensions and similar obligations
    2 Taxation, including deferred taxation
    3 Other provisions

J   Accruals and deferred income

K   Capital and reserves
   I   Called-up share capital
   II   Share premium account
   III   Revaluation reserve
   IV   Other reserves
    1 Capital redemption reserve
    2 Reserve for own shares
    3 Reserves provided for by the articles of association
    4 Other reserves
   V   Profit and loss account

As with the profit and loss account, general disclosure rules for establishing the comparability of accounting numbers are provided. Thus, corresponding amounts for the previous year must be shown for all balance-sheet items, and where, for example, due to a change of accounting policy the numbers are not comparable, adjustments must be made to the previous year to establish comparability. Equally, corresponding amounts must be given, and they must likewise be adjusted if necessary, in respect of every item stated in the notes to the balance sheet (other than amounts relating to the movements on fixed assets, reserves and provisions). Full amounts must be disclosed, and there should be no setoff of items representing assets against items representing liabilities.

As stated previously, the Companies Acts prescribe historical cost and alternative accounting rules. The Acts acknowledge that the historical cost of purchase or production is the primary method of valuing assets. Purchase price is defined to include expenses incidental to acquisition. Production cost is defined to include all costs directly attributable to the production of the asset and may also include a reasonable proportion of indirect costs as well as any interest paid on money borrowed to finance the asset in question. The inclusion of distribution cost is specifically prohibited.

Fixed assets

Subject to any provision for depreciation or diminution in value, fixed assets are to be shown at purchase price or production cost, as the case may be. Fixed assets with limited useful economic life must be depreciated.

A provision for the diminution in value of a fixed-asset investment may be made, and must be made in respect of any fixed asset where the reduction in value is expected to be permanent. The fixed assets so reduced are shown at their reduced amount on the balance sheet, and the provision for reduction in value disclosed in a note to the accounts or shown on the profit and loss account.

While maintaining historic cost valuations as the normal basis for balance sheet purposes, the Companies Acts allow alternative valuation bases provided that the items affected and the basis of valuation is shown in a note to the accounts. This permits companies to revalue assets or to use current cost valuations. The amount of profit or loss arising from the adoption of an alternative accounting valuation must be credited or debited, as the case may be, to the revaluation reserve.

The Companies Acts require the following information to be disclosed in respect of each fixed asset item:

1   the aggregate purchase price, production cost or alternative accounting valuation at the beginning and end of the accounting reference period, showing the effect of acquisitions, disposals or transfers or any revaluation during this period.
2   the cumulative provision for depreciation, or diminution of value as at the beginning and end of the accounting reference period, showing the annual provision arising from the disposal of any asset and any other adjustment to the provision.

Example

The requirements of the Companies Acts would be satisfied by the following presentation:

	Freehold land and buildings	Plant and machinery	Total
	£000	**£000**	**£000**
Cost:			
At 1 January	1000	200	1200
Additions	30	40	70
Disposals	—	(20)	(20)
	1030	220	1250
Accumulated depreciation	**£**	**£**	**£**
At 1 January	200	50	250
Depreciation for the year	20	24	44
Disposals	—	(19)	(19)
At 31 December	220	55	275
Net book values	**£**	**£**	**£**
At 31 December	810	165	975

With regard to *intangible assets*, these must be included on the face of the balance sheet under this main heading, with the following subheadings included either on the face of the balance sheet or in a note: development costs; concessions, patents, licences, trade marks and similar rights and assets; goodwill; and payment on account. The Acts make the following provisions:

1 *Development costs* (but not research costs) may be capitalized, but only in 'special circumstances'. In practice, this treatment must be read in conjunction with SSAP 13 'Accounting for Research and Development', discussed in Chapter 12, which defines the special circumstances that must exist before development costs may be capitalized. Where development costs are capitalized and shown on the balance sheet, the Companies Acts require that notes must be appended disclosing (a) the period over which the costs are being written off and (b) the reason for capitalizing the development costs.

2 *Concessions, patents, licences, trade marks etc.* may be shown on the balance sheet only if they have been acquired by purchase and are not required to be shown under goodwill, or if they were created by the company itself.

3 *Goodwill* may be shown as an asset on the balance sheet only if it was acquired by purchase. In such a case, it must be written off over a period which does not exceed its useful economic life.

Investments

The formats show that investments may be reported either in the category of fixed assets or of current assets. Investments intended to be retained by a company on a continuing basis should be treated as fixed assets, while any other investments should be listed under current assets. When investments are of a long-term nature then they must be classified under the following headings:

1 Shares held in group companies, where the company is a member company in a group of companies.

2 Loans to group companies. Group companies are discussed in Chapter 16.

3 Shares in related companies, where the company is related to another company in which the relationship involves at least 20 per cent shareholding by one company in another.

4 Loans to related companies.

5 Other investments other than loans, for example, shares in companies which are neither group nor related companies.

6 Other loans.

7 Own shares, where—as allowed by the Companies Acts—a company is allowed to purchase its own shares.

The valuation of investments poses particular problems, where there is no stock exchange quotation for shares or debentures. The Companies

Acts do not require unquoted investments to be valued, and the requirements would be satisfied by the conventional historical cost of such investments.

Where investments are listed on a recognized stock exchange, the aggregate market value must be disclosed, where this value differs from the value at which they were stated on the balance sheet.

Current assets

The value to be placed on any current asset is the lower of the purchase price or production cost and the net realizable value. With regard to stocks, the Companies Acts require stocks to be subdivided into the following categories:

1 raw materials and consumables,
2 work in progress,
3 finished goods and goods for resale,
4 payments on account.

Stocks may be valued using any of the recognized valuation methods, namely FIFO (first in first out), LIFO (last in first out), or weighted average cost.

As noted in Chapter 12, SSAP 9 'Stocks and Long-Term Contracts' does not recommend the use of LIFO. Any material difference between the value of the stock shown on the balance sheet and its replacement cost, or, if more appropriate, the most recent purchase price, must be disclosed for each category of stocks.

Debtors must be disclosed as a main heading on the balance sheet and the following items must be disclosed, either on the face of the balance sheet or in the notes thereto: trade debtors, amounts owed by group companies; amounts owed by related companies; other debtors; called-up share capital not paid; prepayments and accrued income. Additionally, the amounts falling due after more than one year must be shown separately for each item.

Creditors

The Companies Acts require creditors to be shown under the following subheadings either on the face of the balance sheet or in the notes thereto: debenture loans, bank loans and overdrafts; payments received on account; trade credits; bills of exchange payable; amounts owed to group companies; other creditors including taxation and social security; and accruals and deferred income. The amounts falling due after more than one year must be shown separately for each item.

Provisions for liabilities and charges

This item must be shown on the face of the balance sheet as a main heading and the following subheadings must be disclosed either on the face of the balance sheet or in the notes thereto: pensions and similar obligations; taxation, including deferred taxation; other provisions. The Companies Acts define provision for liabilities and charges as 'an amount retained as reasonably necessary for the purpose of providing for any liability or loss which is either likely to be incurred, or certain to be incurred, but uncertain as to the amount or as to the date on which it will arise.'

Share capital

The share capital issued and the amount called up must be shown separately. Where the company has issued shares of different classes, the number and aggregate nominal value of each class must be given by name on the balance sheet. Where redeemable shares have been issued, the following information must be given:

1 the earliest and latest dates on which the company has power to redeem the shares;
2 whether those shares must be redeemed in any event, or are liable to be redeemed at the option of the company;
3 whether any premium (and if so, what) is payable on redemption.

Moreover, if there has been an issue of shares during the financial year, the following information must also be given:

1 the reason for the issue;
2 the class of shares issued;
3 in respect of each class of shares issued, the number issued, their aggregate nominal value and the consideration received by the company.

Reserves

The Companies Acts do not give a general definition of a 'reserve' but it is generally accepted that the term 'reserve' does not include the following:

1 a provision for depreciation, renewal or diminution in value of assets;
2 a provision for a known liability;
3 a provision for undue fluctuations in charges for taxation.

Any share premium account and any revaluation reserve must be shown separately under 'reserves', and any other reserve built up by the company must be shown under an appropriate heading. The profit and loss account balance must be shown separately.

In the event that there has been any transfer to or from the reserves shown as separate items during the accounting period, there must be shown by way of note to the balance sheet the following information:

1   the amount of reserves at the beginning of the year;
2   the amounts transferred either in or out, and the source and application of such amounts;
3   the amounts of reserves at the end of the year.

Guarantees and financial commitments

The following information, if not included in the accounts, must be given in the notes:

1   particulars of any charge on the assets of the company to secure the liabilities of any person, indicating where practicable, the amount secured;
2   the estimated amount of future capital expenditure;
3   pension commitments, both provided for and not provided for;
4   particulars of other financial commitments which are not provided for in the accounts but which are relevant to assessing the company's state of affairs.

Contingent liabilities

These were defined in Chapter 12. The following information must be given with respect to any contingent liability:

1   the amount or estimated amount of the liability;
2   its legal nature;
3   whether any valuable security has been provided by the company in connection with that liability, and if so what.

Other disclosure requirements

Among other disclosure requirements to be noted are the following:

1   there must be disclosed in a note to the accounts the accounting policies used by the company in determining the amounts shown as items in these accounts;
2   the basis of translation of any item originally denominated in foreign currencies and translated into sterling must be shown.

Example

Sloan Products plc
Report and accounts for the year ended 31 December 19X6

The following illustration conforms with the requirements of the Companies Acts for the publication of profit and loss accounts and balance sheets except that comparative figures are omitted for the sake of clarity. The illustration does not take account of the supplementary disclosures required by Statements of Standard Accounting Practice, such as earnings per share information nor of the Stock Exchange Listing Agreement. In the illustration the profit and loss account and the balance sheet follow Format 1.

Sloan Products plc
Profit and loss account for the year ended 31 December 19X6

Notes		£000
2	Turnover	22 340
	Cost of sales	(15 782)
	Gross profit	6 558
	Distribution costs	(1 801)
	Administrative expenses	(1 972)
3	Operating profit	2 785
6	Investment income	18
	Interest payable and similar charges	(158)
	Profit on ordinary activities before taxation	2 645
7	Tax on profit on ordinary activities	(808)
	Profit on ordinary activities after taxation	1 837
8	Extraordinary items after taxation	(52)
	Profit for the financial year	1 785
9	Dividends paid and proposed	(900)
	Retained profit for the year	885

Sloan Products plc
Balance sheet at 31 December 19X6

Notes		£000	£000
	Fixed assets		
10	Intangible assets		30
11	Tangible assets		7 828
12	Investments		150
			8 008
	Current assets		
13	Stocks	1 574	
14	Debtors	1 436	
15	Investments	68	
	Cash at bank and in hand	63	
		3 141	
16	**Creditors:** Amounts falling due within one year	(1 840)	
	Net current assets		1 301
	Total assets *less* current liabilities		9 309
17	**Creditors:** amounts falling due after more than one year	360	
18	**Provisions for liabilities and charges**	134	(494)
			8 815
	Capital and reserves		
19	Called-up share capital		6 000
	Share premium account		123
20	Revaluation reserve		104
21	Profit and loss account		2 588
			8 815

Sloan Products plc
Notes to the accounts at 31 December 19X6

1 **Accounting policies**

(a) **Basis of accounting**

The accounts have been prepared under the historical-cost convention, modified by the revaluation of properties.

(b) **Depreciation**

Depreciation is provided on all tangible fixed assets, other than freehold land, at rates calculated to write off the cost or valuation, less estimated residual value, of each asset evenly over its expected useful life, as follows:

Freehold buildings	40 years
Plant and machinery	10 years

(c) **Goodwill**

Goodwill acquired for cash relating to a business purchased by the company is amortized over 5 years. In the opinion of the directors this represents a prudent estimate of the period over which the company will derive a direct economic benefit from the products acquired as part of the business.

(d) **Research and development expenditure**

This is written off in the year in which it is incurred.

(e) **Stocks and work-in-progress**

These are stated at the lower of cost and net realizable value. In general, cost is determined on a first-in, first-out basis and includes transport and handling costs; in the case of manufactured products cost includes all direct expenditure and production overheads based on the normal level of activity. Net realizable value is based on estimated selling price less further costs expected to be incurred to completion and disposal.

(f) **Foreign currencies**

Assets and liabilities in foreign currencies are translated into sterling at the rates of exchange ruling at the balance sheet date.

(g) **Pensions**

Retirement benefits to the present employees of the company are funded by contributions from the company and employees. Payments are made to pension trusts, which are financially separate from the company, in accordance with calculations made periodically by consulting actuaries. The cost of these contributions and of providing pensions to some former employees is charged against the profits of the period.

2 **Turnover**

Turnover represents the invoiced amount of goods and services provided during the year, excluding value added tax. The analysis of turnover and profits is as follows:

	Turnover £000	Profit £000
Class of business		
Domestic appliances	16 004	1 953
Water sports	6 336	692
	22 340	2 645
Geographical analysis		
United Kingdom	7 673	
United States	2 342	
Europe	12 325	
	22 340	

3 **Operating profit**

	£000
Operating profit is stated after charging:	
Depreciation	1 052
Amortization of goodwill	10
Hire of plant and machinery	43
Auditors' remuneration	11
Exceptional bad debt	7

4 **Employee information**

(a) **Number employed**

The average number of employees during the year was as follows:

Office and management	70
Domestic appliances	231
Water sports	68
	369

(b) **Payroll costs**

The aggregate payroll costs were:	£000
Wages and salaries	3 912
Social security costs	455
Other pension costs	188
	4 555

5 **Directors' emoluments**

	£000
Fee	37
Other emoluments	282
Pensions to past directors	16
	335

The chairman received emoluments of £42 000 and the highest-paid director £46 000. The emoluments of the other directors were within the ranges:

£15 001 – £20 000	2
£20 001 – £25 000	4
£30 001 – £35 000	7

6 **Investment income and interest payable**

	£000
Income from listed investments	18
Interest payable on bank loans, overdrafts and loans repayable within five years	17
on other loans	141
	158

7 **Tax on profit on ordinary activities**

	£000
Corporation tax at 35% on taxable profit for the year	756
Deferred taxation	52
	808

8 **Extraordinary items**

	£000
Redundancy and other costs relating to the closure of the Manchester factory	78
less: Tax thereon	26
	52

9 Dividends

		£000
Ordinary dividend:		
interim (paid)	5.0p per share	300
final (proposed)	10.0p per share	600
	15.0p	900

10 Intangible fixed assets

	£000	£000
Goodwill		
Cost		50
Accumulated amortization at 1 January 19X6	10	
Provision for the year to 31 December 19X6	10	20
Net book value at 31 December 19X6		30

11 Tangible assets

Cost or valuation	Freehold Land £000	Buildings £000	Plant and machinery £000	Total £000
Cost:				
At 1 January 19X6	100	1 250	9 250	10 600
Revaluation surplus	104	—	—	104
Additions	32	87	800	919
Disposals	(15)	(100)	(280)	(395)
At 31 December 19X6	221	1 237	9 770	11 228
Depreciation:				
At 1 January 19X6	—	480	2 083	2 563
Provision for year	—	32	1 020	1 052
Disposals	—	(75)	(140)	(215)
At 31 December 19X6	—	437	2 963	3 400
Net book values:				
At 31 December 19X6	221	800	6 807	7 828

Part of the freehold land was revalued on 1 June 19X6 by Wheeler and Wright, chartered surveyors and valuers. It was valued on 'an open-market existing-use basis' and resulted in a revaluation surplus of £104 000. This has been credited to a revaluation reserve in the balance sheet.

12 Investments

	£000
Cost:	
At 1 January 19X6	125
Additions	25
Disposals	—
At 31 December 19X6	150

	£000
Listed investments	140
Unlisted investments	10
	150

	£000
Valuation:	
Listed investment at market value	210

The unlisted investment comprises £10 000 ordinary shares in Vesta plc, representing 15 per cent of the issued share capital of that company. Vesta plc was incorporated in Great Britain which is the principal country of operation. Taxation of £7500 would be payable if the investments were sold at valuation.

	£000
13 **Stocks**	
Raw materials	407
Work-in-progress	283
Finished goods	884
	1 574

Current replacement costs exceed costs of the above items as follows:

	£000
Raw materials	6
Work-in-progress	4
Finished goods	12
	22

	£000
14 **Debtors**	
Trade debtors	1 082
Other debtors	298
Prepayments and accrued income	56
	1 436

15 **Investments**

Short-term deposits	68

	£000
16 **Creditors: amounts falling due within one year**	
Bank loans and overdrafts	42
Trade creditors	286
Taxation and social security	1 105
Accruals	7
Proposed dividends	400
	1 840

	£000
17 **Creditors: amounts falling due after more than one year**	
11% debentures	360

The debentures are secured by a floating charge over the company's assets. They are repayable at the company's option between 2000 and 2007 with a final redemption date of 31 December 2007.

	£000
18 **Provisions for liabilities and charges**	
Pensions and similar obligations	43
Taxation, including deferred taxation	79
Other provisions	12
	134

	£000
19 **Called-up share capital**	
Allotted, issued and fully paid:	
Ordinary shares of £1 each	6 000
Authorized 5m ordinary shares of £1 each	8 000

	£000
20 **Revaluation reserve**	
At 1 January 19X6	—
Revaluation of land	104
Balance at 31 December 19X6	104

21	**Profit and loss account**	**£000**
	At 1 January 19X6	2 111
	Retained for year	477
		2 588

22	**Capital commitments**	**£000**
	Contracted for but not yet provided	72
	Authorized by directors but not yet contracted for	230
		302

23 **Contingent liabilities**

The company is being sued by a German customer for late delivery of goods. The company has denied liability under the contract. The maximum amount which could arise as a liability is £5000.

The directors' report

There is a general requirement that the directors' report should contain a fair review of the development of the business of the company during the year and its position at the end of the year. The directors' report should deal with the following matters in particular:

1 principal activities of the company during the period and any significant changes in those activities;
2 dividend payments recommended;
3 future developments, giving an indication of likely future developments in the business;
4 research and development, giving an indication of activities in this area;
5 significant changes in fixed assets;
6 names of directors who have served at any time during the year;
7 directors' interests in contracts;
8 company's interests in the shares or debentures of the company;
9 post-balance-sheet events, particulars of important events affecting the company which have occurred since the end of the year;
10 political and charitable contributions;
11 a statement of the company's policy on the employment, training and career development of disabled persons;
12 any other matter which is material to the shareholders' appreciation of the company's state of affairs.

Small and medium-sized companies

We noted earlier that the Companies Acts allow small and medium-sized companies to file modified accounts with the Registrar of Companies, although they must still prepare accounts in full form for presentation to their members. A company qualifies to be treated as small or medium-sized for a financial year if, both for that year and the preceding year, it satisfies any two or more of the following conditions:

	Small	**Medium**
Turnover not exceeding	£2m.	£8m.
Balance sheet total not exceeding	£0.975m.	£3.9m.
Employees less than	50	250

The modifications available to small and medium companies are summarized in Fig. 2.16.

Taxation in company accounts

Before April 1973, company profits were liable for corporation tax and any distributions made to shareholders were liable to income tax in the hands of shareholders. Clearly, this system attempted to encourage companies to retain their earnings and increase investment.

The imputation system

The system of corporation tax now adopted in the UK is known as the imputation system. It has two basic objectives: (1) to eliminate the built-in discrimination which applied under the previous scheme against the distribution of profits; (2) to harmonize with systems within the EC.

The rules of the imputation system are as follows:

1 A company pays corporation tax at a single rate on all its profits whether distributed or not.
2 A company distributing profits in the form of dividends is required to make an advance payment of corporation tax (ACT). This rate is limited to the basic rate of income tax, at present 25 per cent, and is deemed to have been borne by ('imputed to') the shareholders.

Fig. 2.16

	Small companies	Medium-sized companies
Directors' report	Not required	Required in full
Profit and loss account	Not required	May commence with 'gross profit' by combining: Items 1, 2, 3 and 6, Format 1 Items 1-5, Format 2
Balance sheet	Only main headings and amounts are required, but aggregate debtors/creditors due after more than one year must be disclosed.	Required in full
Notes to the accounts	Only the following required: 1 accounting policies 2 share capital 3 allotments 4 particulars of debts 5 basis of foreign currency translation	Analysis of turnover and profits not required
Particulars of salaries of directors and higher-paid employees	Not required	Required

Example

A company with taxable profits of £80 000 declares a net dividend of £21 000. The rate of corporation tax is assumed to be 35 per cent.

	£
Profits before tax	80 000
Corporation tax at 35%	28 000
	52 000
Net dividend	21 000
Retained profit	31 000

The advance corporation tax in respect of the dividend of £21 000 is calculated by assuming that the net dividend is a sum paid after advanced corporation tax at the rate of 25/75ths as follows:

	£
Net dividend	21 000
ACT	
£21 000 × 25/75	7 000
Gross amount of cash outflow	28 000

1 Advance corporation tax paid in advance of 'mainstream' corporation tax of £21 000 (£32 000 – £7000).
2 It is imputed to the individual shareholder in the form of tax credit which covers his liability to basic income tax at 25 per cent.

Where a shareholder's marginal rate is higher than 25 per cent, he will pay the difference between the basic and his actual rate.

Two methods of showing corporation tax in the profit and loss account are:

	£	A £	B £
Taxable profit		80 000	80 000
Corporation tax	28 000		28 000
less ACT	7 000		
Mainstream corporation tax		21 000	
		59 000	52 000
Dividends paid net	21 000		21 000
add: ACT	7 000	28 000	
Retained profit		31 000	31 000

Both presentations give the same retained profit, but differ in their treatment of ACT. In method A, ACT is treated as part of the cost of the dividend, whereas method B treats it as part of the tax on the company's profit. SSAP 8 'The Treatment of Taxation Under the Imputation System in the Accounts of Companies' recommends method B:

'The fact that the dividend will carry a tax credit is a matter affecting the receipt rather than the company's method of accounting for the dividend. Accordingly, it is considered appropriate that dividends should be shown in the profit and loss account at the amount paid or payable to the shareholders. . . . It follows that the charge in the profit and loss accounts should embrace the full amount of corporation tax and not merely the mainstream liability.'

The above presentations illustrate a point of principle fundamental to the present system of corporation tax. The payment of dividends and consequently ACT to the Inland Revenue does not affect the total corporation tax paid by the company. It alters the timing of the payment. ACT is payable under a regular quarterly accounting system which ensures that payments of ACT outstanding are settled within three months of dividends being paid. The mainstream corporation tax liability is normally settled nine months after the end of the accounting period.

Computing taxable profit

Financial accounting, which is governed by a 'true and fair' presentation of financial position and the results of operations, does not share in all respects the principles which govern the computation of taxable profits. Differences between 'book' and tax accounting originate from the following:

1   Some items which appear in the profit and loss account are not allowed for tax purposes. These include entertaining expenses of home-country customers and certain types of donations and subscriptions.
2   Dividends received from other companies resident in the UK, which are known as franked investment income, do not incur corporation tax, because the company making this payment will already have paid ACT on this dividend.
3   Timing differences. The first two categories give rise to permanent differences where, because of legislation, particular revenues or expenses are omitted from the computation of taxable profit. A timing difference, on the other hand, arises when an item is includable or deductible from profit for tax purposes in one period, but in profit for general reporting purposes in another. The different treatment of fixed assets creates timing differences because depreciation is not an allowance deduction for tax purposes, capital allowances being granted instead.

Example

A company has accounting profit of £150 000, depreciation of £50 000, entertaining expenses and donations of £10 000, dividend received of £10 000 and capital allowances of £100 000. Taxable profit is calculated as follows:

	£	£
Accounting profit		150 000
add: Depreciation		50 000
add: Entertaining etc.		10 000
		210 000
less: Capital allowances	100 000	
less: Dividend received	10 000	110 000
Taxable profit		100 000

Deferred taxation

The provision for deferred taxation originates from the timing differences which we discussed above. SSAP 15 'Accounting for Deferred Taxation' is intended to bring a greater degree of uniformity to the accounting treatment of taxation where there are differences of timing between accounting and taxation recognition of income or expenditure. According to this statement

'The effect of timing differences on taxation liability in relation to reported profit would be of little significance if taxation was not regarded as relevant to the performance of the business for the period, and the only accepted indication was the profit before taxation. The view is widely held, however, that the profit after taxation is an important indication of performance being the fund of earnings which supports (or perhaps does not support) the distribution of profit by way of dividend. So far as the balance sheet is concerned, the relationship between funds provided by shareholders and other sources of finance may be distorted if provision is made for deferred taxation which can be demonstrated with reasonable probability not to be needed.'

SSAP 15 identifies five categories of timing differences:

1 short-term timing differences from the use of the receipts and payments basis for taxation purposes and the accruals basis in financial statements: these differences normally reverse in the next accounting period;

2 availability of capital allowances in taxation computations which are in excess of the related depreciation charges in financial statements;

3 availability of stock appreciation relief in taxation computations for which there is no equivalent charge in financial statements (note that stock relief is no longer a timing difference for deferred-taxation purposes).

4 revaluation surpluses on fixed assets for which a taxation charge does not arise until the gain is realized on disposal;

5 surpluses on disposals of fixed assets which are subject to rollover relief.

The accounting procedure is to debit the profit and loss account for any year with the tax on accounting profit. The difference between this debit and the corporation tax due for the year is transferred to a deferred taxation account, which must be shown separately in the balance sheet.

Example

A company buys a machine for £50 000 which it intends to use for five years. Using the straight-line depreciation method, £10 000 would be written off each year. However, given the present system of capital allowances (100 per cent of the cost of the equipment) for tax purposes, the entire cost of the machine may be written off in the first year. We assume accounting profit is £200 000. Deferred taxation for the year is calculated as follows:

	£
Accounting profit	200 000
add: Depreciation	10 000
	210 000
less: Capital allowances	50 000
Taxable profit	160 000
Tax on accounting profit (35% of £200 000)	70 000
Tax on taxable profit (35% of £160 000)	56 000
Deferred taxation	14 000

The profit and loss account would be debited with the full amount of tax of £70 000 described as follows:

Corporation tax (including £14 000 credited to deferred taxation account)	£70 000

The deferred taxation account balance of £14 000 would be shown as a separate item in the balance sheet.

Summary of SSAP 15 'Accounting for Deferred Taxation'

The potential amount of deferred tax for all timing differences should be disclosed by way of note, distinguishing between the various principal categories of deferred tax and showing for each category the amount that has been provided within the accounts.

Deferred taxation dealt with in the profit and loss account should be shown separately as a component of the total tax charge or credit in the profit and loss account or by way of note to the financial statements. The profit and loss account or a note thereto should indicate the extent to which the taxation charge for the period has been reduced by accelerated capital allowances and other timing differences.

Deferred taxation account balances should be shown separately in the balance sheet and described as 'deferred taxation'. They should not be shown as part of shareholders' funds.

Summary of SSAP 8 'The Treatment of Taxation Under the Imputation System'

Dividends received must be shown with the related tax credit, the tax then being included in the taxation charge in the profit and loss statement.

Dividends paid or proposed must be shown without the related tax credit or ACT.

ACT on proposed dividends should be included as a current tax liability in the balance sheet, the proposed dividend being shown in current liabilities without the addition of the related ACT. The charge for corporation tax in the profit and loss account should show the total liability and not merely the mainstream liability.

Summary

In this chapter, we have examined the nature of limited companies and the financial accounting implications of incorporation. These implications stem from the manner in which they are capitalized and from the manner in which the net profit is appropriated. We discussed particular financial problems such as gearing.

The accounting procedures relating to the share capital are concerned principally with recording the issue of share capital, and with providing information about the share capital in financial accounting reports. There is little difference between the accounting treatment of share capital and loan capital.

The accounting procedures applicable to periodic profit are concerned with the manner in which the profit is appropriated to various purposes. The size of the dividend is a matter of financial policy which directors have to consider in relation to capital requirements, its effect on the share price and the availability of other sources of finance.

We considered also the procedures relating to the payment of dividends, and in this way maintained the focus of the chapter on the financial accounting problems arising directly from corporate status.

We discussed the extent to which financial information is disclosed to shareholders and noted the limited extent of this disclosure, and indicated that this is an important controversy in accounting which would be discussed in Part 4.

We examined the nature of taxation in company accounts and the importance of accounting standards.

Problems

1 The partnership of Black, White and Grey are considering forming a limited company to obtain the benefits of limited liability. However, they are uncertain as to whether the capital of the company should be in shares or debentures and are also unsure of the method of appropriating profit.

At 31 December 19X0 the capital accounts of the partners were:

Black	£44 000
White	36 000
Grey	48 000

Interest of 10 per cent per annum is allowed on the capital accounts.

Black is the managing partner and receives a salary of £20 000 p.a. White works part-time but does not receive a salary. Grey takes no active part in the business. The balance of profits are shared equally.

The budgeted profit for 19X1 is £260 000 before any appropriation to the partners.

Required:
(a) Advise the partners on the difference between debentures and ordinary shares and suggest the most appropriate capital structure for the new company.
(b) Advise the partners on a suitable method of rewarding themselves when the company is formed. Prepare a profit and loss appropriation account for year

ended 31 December 19X1 on the assumption that the company is formed on 1 January 19X1, and your recommendations are accepted. Assume a corporation tax rate of 35 per cent.

(Problem supplied by A.J. Naughton, Leeds Polytechnic)

2　Scheid and Sons Ltd are considering expanding their operations. Several alternative strategies are being discussed for financing this expansion. The latest balance sheet of the company as at 31 December 19X3 is as follows:

Scheid and Sons Ltd
Balance sheet at 31 December 19X3

	£	£
Fixed assets		
Land and buildings		40 000
Plant and equipment		90 000
		130 000
Current assets		
Stocks	50 000	
Debtors	40 000	
Cash	5 000	
	95 000	
Creditors: amounts falling due after more than one year	25 000	
Net current assets		70 000
Total assets *less* current liabilities		200 000
Creditors: amounts falling due after more than one year:		
12% loan repayable 19X9		90 000
		110 000
Share capital and reserves		£
8% cumulative preference shares of £1 each		30 000
Ordinary shares of £1 each		50 000
Profit and loss account		30 000
		110 000

The board of directors has identified the following possible alternative ways of obtaining the additional £50 000 required during the following year:
(a)　Issue additional ordinary shares
(b)　Issue additional 8 per cent preference shares
(c)　Raise an additional long-term loan at 12 per cent.
Discuss the company's existing capital structure in terms of its gearing, and examine the advantages and disadvantages of each alternative method of financing the expansion plan.

3　The Huby Haulage Company Ltd produced the following trial balance at the end of December 19X8. Using this and the additional information following prepare a profit and loss account, appropriation account and balance sheet for the year ended 31 December 19X8.

(a)　Drivers' claims for £150 relating to overnight expenses had not been taken into account.
(b)　The parts and consumables account included parts valued at 1 January 19X8 at £15 000. A stocktake at 31 December 19X8 revealed that parts valued at £18 000 were held at that date.
(c)　It was estimated that there was a prepayment of £4000 with regard to licences and insurance at the end of 19X8.
(d)　The company depreciates its vehicles at 25 per cent on the straight line basis.
(e)　Tax is estimated at £22 400.

	£	£
£1 ordinary shares fully paid		200 000
Retained profit	-	70 000
10% Debenture		50 000
Sales		365 000
Bank and cash	20 000	
Motor lorries—at cost	360 000	
—accumulated depreciation		110 000
Freehold property	165 000	
Repairs and renewals	22 000	
Drivers' wages	60 000	
Maintenance wages	15 000	
Parts and consumables	70 000	
Licences and insurance	20 000	
Administration salaries	20 000	
Sundry administrative expenses	12 000	
Drivers' overnight expenses	6 000	
Directors' salaries	25 000	
	795 000	795 000

(f)   There is a proposed dividend of £20 000.

(g)   Standard rate tax is 25 per cent.

4   Nether Edge plc, a retailing company, has an authorized share capital of 700 000 ordinary shares of £1 each. The following trial balance was extracted from the books of account as at 31 December 19X2.

	Dr £000	Cr £000
Issued share capital		560
Share premium account		140
Profit and loss account		180
10% Debentures		100
Furniture and fittings at cost	400	
Depreciation to 31 December 19X1		200
Cash balances	112	
Trade creditors		120
Trade debtors	500	
Stock at 1 January 19X2	400	
Hire charges (distribution, vehicles etc.)	680	
Purchases	1 000	
Administrative expenses	300	
Deferred taxation		80
Distribution costs	200	
Accrued expenses		50
Auditors' remuneration	40	
Interim dividend (paid on 1 July 19X2)	14	
Advance corporation tax (paid on interim dividend)	6	
Trade investments at cost (market value £170 000)	140	
Debenture interest (gross)	10	
Dividends received (on 1 December 19X2)		30
Turnover		2 400
Prepaid expenses	58	
	3 860	3 860

You are also given the following information:

(a)   Turnover excludes value added tax.

(b)   Stock at 31 December 19X2 was valued at £600 000.

(c) Depreciation of £80 000 is to be charged on the furniture and fittings for the year to 31 December 19X2.

(d) Administration includes directors' emoluments of £110 000.

(e) The corporation tax payable (based on the profits for the year to 31 December 19X2 at a rate of 35 per cent) is estimated to amount to £100 000. The current standard rate of income tax is 25 per cent.

(f) Redundancy costs of £46 000 (not expected to recur) had accrued on 31 December 19X2, but upon which there will be corporation tax relief of £16 000.

(g) The company proposes to pay a final ordinary dividend of 10 per cent.

Required:

Prepare financial statements for publication, together with relevant notes. (Work to the nearest £1000.)

5   The following data has been extracted from the records of Purple plc at 31 March 19X5:

	£
Turnover	18 108 488
Cost of sales	16 471 616
Distribution costs	864 531
Administrative expenses	1 494 228
Surplus on sale of fixed assets	11 054
Interest receivable	21 721
Losses due to seizure of imported sugar	351 890
Overdraft interest	139 001
Loan interest (loan repayable 31 March 20X5)	162 299
Corporation tax for the year	691
Cost of discontinued activities	30 202
Dividends (interim 0.25p per share)	17 292
Transfer from reserves	1 389 105

You are also given the following information:

(a) Number of ordinary shares in issue during the year: 7 192 380.

(b) Turnover excludes value added tax.

(c) Distribution costs and administrative expenses given above include the following items:

	£
Depreciation	365 928
Directors' emoluments	105 773
Auditors' remuneration	26 020
Hire of plant and machinery	3 084

(d) The taxation charge for the year is made up as follows:

	£
Corporation tax at 35%	—
ACT written off	(7 410)
Adjustment to previous year	8 101
	691

You are required to prepare a profit and loss account for publication; together with any notes required. It should comply with the Companies Acts.

Chapter 14

Funds flow and cash flow statements

The two financial statements discussed so far constitute the traditional format by which information is conveyed about the financial performance and the financial status of the enterprise. The profit and loss account provides details of financial performance resulting in the net profit figure; the balance sheet is an explanation of the financial status of the enterprise in the form of a listing of its assets and liabilities at the close of the accounting period.

Accounting flows may be classified into three distinct types – profit flows, funds flows and cash flows. Therefore, funds flow and cash flow statements are needed to obtain a complete picture of accounting flows in respect of an accounting period.

The funds flow statement provides a reconciliation between the opening and closing balance sheets for a given accounting period through an explanation of the changes which have occurred. This explanation is in the form of an analysis of the sources of additional funds available to the enterprise during the accounting period, as well as an analysis of the manner in which they have been utilized. Consequently, the funds flow statement covers both the funds internally generated and additional external funds obtained by the enterprise during the accounting period. The funds flow statement deals with the changes which have occurred in the size of the business, as well as changes in the structure of assets, liabilities and invested capital. For all enterprises of a stipulated size, SSAP 10 'Statement of Source and Application of Funds' imposes a disclosure of a periodic funds flow statement, in addition to the traditional profit and loss account and balance sheet.

The cash flow statement is more closely associated with the analysis of liquidity in the strict form of cash available to the enterprise during the accounting period. It provides a reconciliation of the opening cash balance with the closing cash balance, showing the cash inflows from all sources and the analysis of all cash outflows. The cash flow statement has a special importance for financial management purposes, since cash is the most vital financial resource. The cash flow statement is a summary of the cash book. Since firms control cash by using their bank account for depositing receipts in the form of cash or cheques, and for making payments, the cash flow statement is essentially addressed to cash at bank. The cash-in-hand situation would be shown as an item in the cash flow statement. Monthly board of directors meetings have on their agenda a review of the liquidity situation in the form of a cash flow statement for the month ended and a forecasted cash flow for the coming month. The cash flow statement has not been made the subject of a disclosure requirement, and remains an internal management document.

The funds flow statement

The financial status of an enterprise changes over time. Its growth will be manifested in the increase of total assets and total liabilities. Clearly, a successful business will be making profits of which a portion will be reinvested in the form of further acquisition of fixed or current assets, or the reduction of debts or current liabilities.

Example 1

The profit and loss account of Gemini Ltd for the year ended 31 December 19X1 showed net profit of £1500. The balance sheets as at 1 January 19X1 and 31 December 19X1 were as follows:

	Balance sheet at	
	1 January 19X1	31 December 19X1
	£	£
Fixed assets	2500	3500
Net current assets	1000	1500
	3500	5000
Capital and reserves	£	£
Called-up share capital	2000	2000
Other reserves	1500	1500
Profit and loss account		1500
	3500	5000

It is evident in this example that the net profit for the year ended 31 December 19X1 has been retained in the business, and has been applied to financing the acquisition of additional fixed assets of £1000 and of additional net current assets of £500.

The statement of source and application of funds for the year ended 31 December 19X1 could be expressed as follows:

Statement of source and application of funds for the year ended 31 December 19X1

Source of funds	£	Application of funds	£
Net profit for the year	1500	Purchase of fixed assets	1000
		Increase in net current assets	500
	1500		1500

In this example, the increased size of the firm in terms of larger assets during the year ended 31 December 19X1 is entirely explained by reference to the retained profit which has financed this expansion.

The growth of an enterprise as a result of profitability only is a rare phenomenon. Successful businesses are able to grow at a faster rate than improving profit allows because they arc able to attract further funds in the form of borrowings and additional capital.

Example 2

The profitability of Gemini Ltd during the year ended 31 December 19X1 has encouraged the directors to seek to expand the business more rapidly than could be financed out of profits. The shareholders were asked to subscribe further capital of £5000 in the ensuing year, and a debenture loan of £5000 was also obtained in that year. The net profit for the year ended 31 December 19X2 amounted to £4000, and the opening and closing balance sheets were as follows:

| | Balance sheet at | |
	1 January 19X2	31 December 19X2
	£	£
Fixed assets	3 500	11 500
Net current assets	1 500	7 500
	5 000	19 000
Less: Creditors: amounts falling due after more than one year		
Debenture loan	—	5 000
	5 000	14 000
Capital and reserves	£	£
Called-up share capital	2 000	7 000
Other reserves	1 500	1 500
Profit and loss account	1 500	5 500
	5 000	14 000

The statement of source and application of funds for the year ended 31 December 19X2 could be shown as follows:

Statement of source and application of funds for the year ended 31 December 19X2

Source	£	Application	£
Net profit for the year	4 000	Purchase of fixed assets	8 000
Additional share capital	5 000	Increase in net current assets	6 000
New debenture loan	5 000		
	14 000		14 000

Consequently, the profit and loss account only partly explains changes in the size of a business between two successive balance sheets. A complete explanation can be given only by taking into account also sources of funds other than those coming from profits.

Moreover, given that a firm has had additional sources of funds available to it during an accounting period, there is interest in having explanations of the manner in which those funds have been applied in its business. Example 2 shows how the statement of source and application of funds explains not only the total additional sources of funds obtained during the accounting period, but also how they have been applied.

Funds may be applied in increasing the asset side of the balance sheet. In the foregoing examples, it has been assumed that the additional sources of funds have been applied to increasing the total assets, and therefore the size of the balance sheet has been increasing.

Funds may also be applied to reducing repayment debts, without there being any increase in assets.

Example 3

During the year ended 31 December 19X3, the continued success of Gemini Ltd was shown in a bumper profit of £10 000. The directors decided to distribute an interim dividend of £5000 from this profit and also to repay the debenture loan of £5000 before maturity. These transactions took place on the 31 December 19X3. The balance sheets at 1 January 19X3 and 31 December 19X3 were as follows:

	1 January 19X3	31 December 19X3
	£	£
Fixed assets	11 500	11 500
Net current assets	7 500	7 500
	19 000	19 000
Less: Creditors: amounts falling due after more than one year		
Debenture loan	5 000	—
	14 000	19 000
Capital and reserves	£	£
Called-up share capital	7 000	7 000
Other reserves	1 500	1 500
Profit and loss account	5 500	10 500
	14 000	19 000

The statement of source and application of funds plays a special role in the supply of information to shareholders and investors, and for this reason it became usual practice for it to be included with the profit and loss account and the balance sheet in annual published company reports.

The nature of funds flows

The purpose of the statement of source and application of funds is to provide the following information:

1 the additional sources of funds which the firm has obtained during the accounting period;

2 how these additional sources of funds have been applied during the accounting period.

The statement of source and application of funds may be compared with the balance sheet, in the sense in which the statement of source and application of funds deals with the changes in the financial structure of a business *over one accounting period,* while the balance sheet is a cumulative statement showing the totality of such changes *over the life of the enterprise* to the date of the balance sheet.

A major difference, however, between the items shown on the balance sheet and those appearing on the statement of source and application of funds lies in the 'funds' concept used by the latter.

The nature of the funds flows depicted in the statement of source and application of funds is associated with the idea of 'funds' expressed as 'liquid funds'. For example, if a firm raises a loan of £1000, the liquid funds resulting from that loan are £1000. Similarly, if an asset is sold for £1000, the liquid funds flowing to the firm amount to £1000. Conversely, if there is a repayment of a loan then the liquid funds applies to the debt reduction amount to £1000.

Sources of liquid funds result, typically, from additional capital, new loans, the sale of fixed assets, the reduction of working capital and, of course, operating profits.

Applications of liquid funds are, typically, the purchase of fixed assets, the repayment of loans, the increase in working capital, the payment of dividends and taxes on profits.

Measuring funds flow

The information required for the preparation of the statement of source and application of funds is obtainable by first comparing the relevant balance sheets for the accounting period to be covered. This comparison will highlight the changes in the balance sheet which are to be explained by the statement of source and application of funds.

Example 4

The following balance sheets relate to Mistrol Ltd:

| | Balance sheet at | | | |
	31 December 19X4		31 December 19X5	
	£	£	£	£
Fixed assets				
Land and buildings	20 000		22 000	
Plant and machinery	15 000		13 000	
		35 000		35 000
Current assets				
Stocks	30 000		25 000	
Debtors	27 000		23 000	
Cash at bank and in hand	5 000		7 000	
	62 000		55 000	

Creditors: amounts falling due within one year:				
Trade creditors	(32 000)		(25 000)	
Taxation	(15 000)		(10 000)	
Net current assets		15 000		20 000
		50 000		55 000

Capital and reserves	£	£	£	£
Called-up share capital		10 000		12 000
Other reserves		30 000		30 000
Profit and loss account		10 000		13 000
		50 000		55 000

Summary of balance sheet changes

	£	£	£ (+)	£ (−)
Fixed assets				
Land and buildings	20 000	22 000	2000	
Plant and machinery at cost *less* depreciation	15 000	13 000		2000
Current assets				
Stocks	30 000	25 000		5000
Debtors	27 000	23 000		4000
Cash at bank and in hand	5 000	7 000	2000	
	62 000	55 000		
Creditors: amounts falling due within one year:				
Trade creditors	(32 000)	(25 000)		7000
Taxation	(15 000)	(10 000)		5000
Net current assets	15 000	20 000		
Total assets	50 000	55 000		
Capital and reserves:				
Called-up share capital	10 000	12 000	2000	
Other reserves	30 000	30 000		
Profit and loss account	10 000	13 000	3000	
	50 000	55 000		

Explanation of balance sheet changes

The changes emerging from a straight comparison of the two balance sheets are not sufficient in themselves for the purpose of measuring funds. Further information is required.

Fixed assets

The changes in these accounts are analysed as follows:

Land and buildings—cost of installing partition: £2000

Plant and machinery—the net decrease of £2000 is explainable in terms of the disposal of old equipment originally costing £2000 and written down to £1000 in the books, the acquisition of new equipment for £3000, and the depreciation for the year of £4000. The old equipment realized

£1200. There was a gain on asset realization of £200 shown in the profit and loss account.

The funds flow relating to fixed assets is:

Application of funds	£	£
Land and buildings	2000	
Plant and machinery	3000	
		5000
Source of funds		
Funds realized from disposals		1200

Note

The gain on asset realization of £200 shown in the profit and loss account is an accounting gain. The funds flow resulting from the disposal is the sale value realized of £1200.

Current assets

In terms of funds flow analysis, the reductions in stocks of £5000 and of trade debtors of £4000 are considered as sources of funds. They result from the partial liquidation of funds that had been invested in stocks and trade debtors. Conversely, increases in these items would be treated as applications of funds.

Changes in cash at bank and in hand may be explained as follows:

- Increases are treated as *applications* of funds.
- Decreases are treated as *sources* of funds.

It may be noted, therefore, the cash balances are treated in the same way as other current assets as regards funds flow analysis. In this example, the increase of £2000 in the cash balance is an *application* of funds during the accounting year ended 31 December 19X5.

Creditors

Increases in creditor balances are treated as *sources* of funds during the year in which they occur, and decreases in these balances are treated as *applications* of funds. In the logic of funds flow analysis, creditors represent sources of finance, and the reimbursement of the credits obtained are applications of funds. Accordingly, the decrease in trade creditors of £7000 is interpreted as an application of funds.

The taxation account is an exception to this practice. The taxation account is credited with the amount provided for taxation in respect of the current financial year and debited with tax payments made. The tax payments themselves may relate to the current financial year and also to preceding financial years. The amount credited to the taxation account, representing an amount due to the Inland Revenue, is not treated as a source of funds as would be the case if the Inland Revenue were treated as a trade creditor. This is because the statement of source and application of funds show net profits *before* taxation as the originating source of funds from operations. It would be double counting, therefore, to show an increase in the balance on the taxation account on the balance sheet as a source of funds. Taxes on profits are regarded as application of funds *only when they are paid*. In the example shown, the change in the taxation account balance is ignored for the purposes of the statement of sources and application of funds.

Capital

Additional injections of capital are sources of funds. In this example, the additional capital subscribed of £2000 is a source of funds.

Reserves

Changes in reserves result merely from book transactions—they do not give rise to funds flows. Reserve accounts, as well as similar book transactions such as provision accounts, are used in connection with the transfer of accounting balances.

Profit and loss account

The profit and loss account balance of £13 000 represents the retained profit as at 31 December 19X5. To ascertain the funds flowing from operations, it is necessary to refer to the profit and loss account itself. The net profit or loss shown in the profit or loss account results from accounting practice in which

(a) book gains and losses on asset disposal will be included in the calculation of the net profit or loss, and
(b) non-cash expenses in the form of provisions will have been debited.
   Some important items, such as provisions for depreciation of fixed assets, for doubtful debts etc., do not create cash outflows. Accordingly, the net profit or loss for the year has to be adjusted and recalculated in terms of funds flows from operations.

Assume that in the example of Mistrol Ltd the profit and loss account for the year ended 31 December 19X5 is as follows:

	£
Turnover	125 000
Cost of sales	75 000
Gross profit	50 000
Other costs and expenses	25 000
	25 000
Gain on asset disposal	200

Profit on ordinary activity	25 200
Tax on ordinary activity	10 000
Profit for the year	15 200
Profit for the year	15 200
Balance b/f	10 000
	25 200
Dividend paid	12 200
Balance c/f	13 200

The provision for depreciation of fixed assets for the year amounted to £4000. The tax actually paid during the year was £15 000, shown as outstanding at 31 December 19X4.

The funds flow from operations is calculated as follows:

	£	£
Profit for the year before tax		25 200
Adjustment for items not involving the movement of funds:		
Depreciation of fixed assets	4000	
Gain on asset disposal	(200)	3 800
Funds generated from operations		29 000

Calculating the funds flow from operations before taxation and dividends allows these latter two items to be shown as application of funds as and when they are paid. Amounts shown on the balance sheet as provisions for taxation and provisions for proposed dividends are ignored when examining the balance sheet for changes susceptible of giving rise to funds flows.

Preparing the statement of source and application of funds

The sources and application of funds calculated above may now be represented in a statement of source and application of funds as follows:

Statement of source and application of funds for the year ended 31 December 19X5

Source	£	Application	£
Funds from operations	29 000	Purchase of fixed assets	5 000
Additional capital	2 000	Taxes paid	15 000
Sale of fixed assets	1 200	Dividend paid	12 200
Decrease in stocks	5 000	Decrease in creditors	7 000
Decrease in debtors	4 000	Increase in cash	2 000
	41 200		41 200

The statement of source and application of funds may be presented in different ways. In the United Kingdom, companies are required to follow SSAP 10 'Statements of Source and Application of Funds' when publishing their financial reports to shareholders.

SSAP 10 'Statements of Source and Application of Funds'

The standard does not define funds, but indicates that the statement of source and application of funds should have as a bottom line the notion of liquid funds. According to SSAP 10,

'a funds statement should show the sources from which funds have flowed into the company and the way in which they have been used. It should show clearly the funds generated or absorbed by the operations of the business and the manner in which any resulting surplus of liquid assets has been applied or any deficit of such assets has been financed, distinguishing the long-term from the short-term. The statement should distinguish the use of funds for the purchase of new fixed assets from the funds used in increasing the working capital of the company.'

SSAP 10 requires the following information to be disclosed:

1   the profit or loss for the period;
2   an adjustment for items charged in the profit and loss account which do not involve the movement of funds, for example, depreciation and other provisions;
3   dividends paid;
4   acquisitions and disposals of fixed assets and other non-current assets;
5   funds raised or expended in increasing or redeeming issued share capital, long-term or medium-term loans;
6   increases or decreases in working capital, subdivided into components;
7   movements in net liquid funds, defined as cash at bank and in hand, as well as cash equivalents (investments held as current assets)— included under this heading are bank overdrafts and other borrowings.

SSAP 10 provides the following model for the statement of source and application of funds.

Statement of source and application of funds for year ended 31 December 19X-

	£	£	£
Sources of funds			
Profit before tax		xxxxx	
Adjustments for items not involving the movement of funds:			
Depreciation		xxxxx	
			xxxx
Total generated from operations			xxxx
Funds from other sources:			
Issue of shares for cash			xxxx
Application of funds			
Dividends paid		(xxxx)	
Tax paid		(xxxx)	
Purchase of fixed assets		(xxxx)	
			(xxxx)

A

Change in working capital

Increase in stocks	xxxx
Increase in debtors	xxxx
(Increase) decrease in creditors, excluding taxation and proposed dividends	xxxx

Movement in net liquid funds
Increase (decrease) in:

Cash balances	xxxx
Short-term investments	xxxx
	xxxx
	A

The model layout proposed by SSAP 10 highlights the following:

1 The net funds flow, taking into account funds from operations and other sources of funds and applications of funds,

2 Increases/decrease in working capital,

3 Movement in net liquid funds.

It is particularly important to note that the layout explains the net funds flow in terms of changes in working capital, and in that context gives a separate emphasis to movements in liquid funds.

Example 5

The statement of source and application of funds for Mistrol Ltd for the year ended 31 December 19X5 shown in Example 4 above resulted in the following presentation:

Statement of source and application of funds for the year ended 31 December 19X5

Source	£	Application	£
Funds from operations	29 000	Purchase of fixed assets	5 000
Additional capital	2 000	Taxes paid	15 000
Sale of fixed assets	1 200	Dividend paid	12 200
Decrease in stocks	5 000	Decrease in creditors	7 000
Decrease in debtors	4 000	Increase in cash	2 000
	41 200		41 200

Redrafting this statement in the form required by SSAP 10 results in the following presentation:

Mistrol Ltd
Statement of source and application of funds for the year ended 31 December 19X5

	£	£
Sources of funds		
Profit before tax		25 200
Adjustments for items not involving the movement of funds:		

Depreciation	4 000	
Gain on asset disposal	(200)	
		3 800
Total generated from operations		29 000
Funds from other sources:		
Issue of shares for cash		2 000
Sale of fixed assets		1 200
Application of funds		
Dividends paid	(12 200)	
Tax paid	(15 000)	
Purchase of fixed assets	(5 000)	
		(32 200)
		—
Change in working capital		
Decrease in stocks	(5 000)	
Decrease in debtors	(4 000)	
Decrease in creditors, excluding		
taxation and proposed dividends	7 000	
Movement in net liquid funds		
Increase in:		
Cash balances	2 000	
Short-term investments	—	
		—

The cash flow statement

The cash flow statement summarizes the flow of cash in and out of the firm over a period of time. In this sense, it is really a summary of the cash account. The cash flow statement is important for a number of reasons. First, by focusing on cash flows, it explains the nature of the financial events which have affected the cash inventory. Thus, if a firm had a balance of £x at the beginning of the accounting period and £y at the end of the accounting period, the cash flow statement will explain the reason for the difference. Second, the cash flow statement is important for financial planning purposes. As we shall see in Part 5, budgeted cash flow statements are a crucial element in the process of budgetary planning, indicating cash surpluses and shortfalls resulting from budget plans. These surpluses and deficiencies are expressed sequentially over the planning period and enable management to deal with the forecasted cash surplus or deficit, the former involving a short-term investment of surplus cash, the latter a short-term borrowing arrangement. Third, the cash flow statement brings into sharp contrast the enterprise's earning capacity with its spending activity. Accounting conventions restrict the profit and loss account to matching periodic revenues with the cost of earning those revenues. The cash flow statement is not restricted in this way: hence, it provides an extended view of the financial inflows and outflows by including both capital and revenue flows. Thus, borrowings and capital injections, as well as proceeds from the realization of assets, are incorporated with the cash generated from sales to give a complete picture of financial inflows: repayments of loans, capital expenditure, dividends and taxation are incorporated with revenue expenses to give a more complete picture of financial outflows.

Our purpose in this chapter is to deal with the historical analysis of cash flows. Planned or budgeted cash flows will be examined in Part 5.

Form and content of the cash flow statement

The objective of a cash flow statement is to reconcile the opening cash with the closing cash at the end of an accounting period. Hence, it begins with the cash at the beginning of the year.

An important distinction between a profit and loss account and a cash flow statement is that the former includes adjustments made in the calculation of periodic profit, whereas the latter excludes such adjustments. The largest item of difference between them is the allocation of fixed-asset costs as depreciation, and it is normal to adjust accounting in this respect to arrive at the cash flow statement of operating revenues. Other differences between the profit and loss account and cash flow statement procedures are reflected in changes in balance sheet items. These would include changes in balances of trade debtors and trade creditors stemming from credit as distinct from cash trading.

The form and content of a cash flow statement, and its purpose may be seen from the following example:

Example 6

The profit and loss account for the year ended 31 December 19X0 showed that Highstreet Stores made a profit of £18 000. Nevertheless, the bank balance had fallen from £10 000 at the beginning of the year to £3000 at 31 December 19X0. Worried by this adverse trend in the cash position in the face of a satisfactory profit, the owner of the business asked his accountant for a full explanation of the reduction in cash.

An analysis of the cash receipts and payments for the year produced the summary of cash movements shown here.

	£	£
Cash receipts		
Receipts from sales and debtors		145 000
Loan raised to extend premises		20 000
		165 000
Cash payments		
Purchases of goods and payments to creditors	109 000	
Wages and salaries	10 000	
Interest and bank charges	1 000	
Extension of premises	30 000	
New fittings	5 000	
Drawings	10 000	
Miscellaneous expenses	7 000	
		172 000
Excess of cash paid over cash receipts during the year		(7 000)

From this information, a cash flow statement for the year was prepared to explain the change in the net cash at the beginning and end of the accounting period. However, in order to produce such a cash flow statement, the analysis of cash receipts and cash payments must be rearranged and classified to show the causes of the cash receipts and the purposes for which cash was paid. It is advisable, therefore, to segregate cash flows associated with current operations from cash flows connected with capital items as shown below.

Cash flow statement for the year ended 31 December 19X0

	£	£	£
Bank balance at 1 January 19X0			10 000
Net cash flows from current operations			
Cash receipts from sales and debtors		145 000	
less:			
Purchases of goods and payments to creditors	109 000		
Wages and salaries	10 000		
Interest and bank charges	1 000		
Miscellaneous expenses	7 000		
		127 000	
		18 000	
less:			
Payments from profits to owner		10 000	
Cash from current operations available for capital purposes		8 000	
Net cash flows on capital items			
Loan incurred		20 000	
		28 000	
less:			
Expenditure on extension to premises	30 000		
Payments in respect of new fittings	5 000		
		35 000	
Excess of cash payments over cash receipts during the year			7 000
Bank balance at 31 December 19X0			3 000

The explanation of the fall in the bank balance from £10 000 to £3000, despite a profit result of £18 000, is to be found in the extent of the capital expenditure during the year. Total capital expenditure amounting to £35 000 was financed to the extent of £20 000 by loan, and £8000 from the cash flow generated by current operations. The difference of £7000 had to be found from cash in the bank.

Cash flows and financial management

The usefulness of cash flow statements extends beyond a simple analysis of receipts and payments. First, as Fig. 2.17 shows, it provides an insight into the critical areas of financial management by identifying two important classes of cash flows, namely operating cash flows and financing

Fig. 2.17

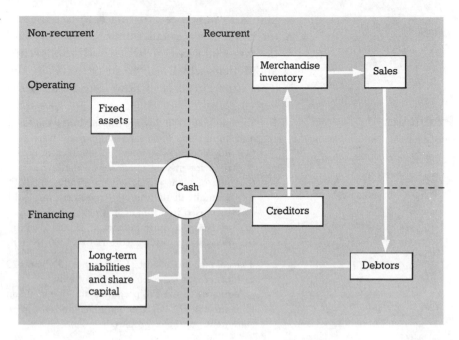

cash flows. This distinction draws attention to the net cash flows from operations and the net financing cash flows. The net operating cash flows classify the capability of the firm to support dividend payments to shareholders. It is these net cash flows which are of critical importance to investors and shareholders, as we see in Part 4. The financing cash flows explain the relationship between the firm and those who finance its operations.

Summary

The profit and loss account and the balance sheet are important because they are used to convey information about the earnings and the financial position of the enterprise. By contrast, cash flow and funds flow statements highlight the financial management aspect. The cash flow statement analyses inflows and outflows with a view to explaining the difference between cash balances at the beginning and close of the accounting period. The funds flow statement details the sources and uses of funds during the accounting period and working capital.

Cash flows and funds flow statements are used to provide supplementary information to that contained in the profit and loss account and balance sheet. Funds flow statements are increasingly used by companies for financial reporting purposes. As we shall see in Part 4, one aspect of the controversy in financial reporting concerns cash flow accounting as an alternative to profit accounting. The argument for cash flow statements in that context is that since a firm's success depends on its ability to maximize its cash flows through time, cash flow statements are more meaningful than conventional profit and loss accounts and balance sheets.

Cash flow and funds flow statements are important for financial planning purposes. In this context, they are associated with budget forecasts. The particular importance of the cash flow budget is to highlight the financial consequence of budget plans and predict the cash surpluses and deficits which will occur periodically through the planning period. This function of cash flow statements is examined in Part 5.

Problems

1 Explain how the following transactions would be reported in a statement of source and application of funds for the year ended 31 December 19X4:
   (a) new capital introduced: £1000 in cash, equipment valued at £2000 previously used for private purposes by the owner of the business;
   (b) sale of plant purchased for £1500 on 30 December 19X0 and depreciated annually at the rate of 10 per cent and sold for £400 on 31 October 19X4;
   (c) increased investment in stocks, during the year of £5400;
   (d) decrease in trade debtors of £3000 over the year;
   (e) decrease in trade creditors of £4000 over the year.

2 The balance sheets as at 31 December 19X5 and 19X6 for James Johnstone, trading as Corner Stores, were as shown below.
   You are required to prepare a statement of source and application of funds for the year ended 31 December 19X6 and also provide a short commentary on the statement you have prepared.

	19X5		19X6	
	£	£	£	£
Fixed assets				
Plant		12 000		14 000
Fixtures		2 000		1 500
Current assets				
Stock	8 000		9 000	
Trade debtors	5 000		7 000	
Cash	3 000		—	
	16 000		16 000	
Creditors: amounts falling due within one year:				
Bank overdraft	(—)		(2 000)	
Trade creditors	(9 000)		(7 000)	
Accruals	(1 000)		(2 000)	
Net current assets		6 000		5 000
Total assets *less* current liabilities		20 000		20 500
Creditors: amounts falling due after more than one year		(8 000)		(10 000)
		12 000		10 500
		£		£
Capital account		12 000		10 500

The following details are also provided:

	£
Plant account: Balance at 31.12.19X5	12 000
Acquisitions 19X6	4 000
	16 000
Depreciation for year	2 000
Balance at 31.12.19X6	14 000

Fixtures account: Depreciation amounting to £500
has been provided for 19X6

		£
Capital account: Balance at 31.12.19X5		12 000
	Capital introduced	1 000
	Net income for 19X6	4 000
		17 000
	Drawings	6 500
	Balance at 31.12.19X6	10 500

3   The balance sheets for Jobin & Co Ltd for the years ended 19X1, 19X2 and 19X3
are as follows:

Jobin & Co Ltd
Balance sheets at 31 December

	19X1 £000	19X2 £000	19X3 £000
Fixed assets			
Plant and equipment	13 200	16 110	16 410
Current assets			
Stocks	2 190	2 280	2 490
Trade debtors	2 040	2 100	2 430
Short-term investments	4 200	1 800	1 290
Cash at bank and in hand	1 920	1 650	2 160
Creditors: amounts falling due within one year			
Short-term loans	(2 340)	(2 580)	(2 550)
Trade creditors	(2 760)	(2 610)	(2 670)
Taxation	(360)	(420)	(530)
	(5 460)	(5 610)	(5 750)
Net current assets	4 890	2 300	2 620
Total assets *less* current liabilities	18 090	18 330	19 030
Capital and reserves			
Called-up share capital	4 500	4 500	4 500
Share premium account	9 000	9 000	9 000
Other reserves	3 280	4 060	4 570
Profit and loss account	1 310	770	960
	18 090	18 330	19 030

Other data	19X1 £000	19X2 £000	19X3 £000
Profit before tax	960	1 020	1 590
Tax on annual profit	360	420	530
Tax paid during the year	300	360	420
Annual depreciation	645	780	900
Dividends declared and paid	360	360	360

In 19X2, equipment was sold at a loss of £210 000. New plant in 19X2 cost
£5 100 000 and in 19X3 cost £1 200 000. Profit transferred to other reserves in
19X2 and 19X3 amounted to £780 and £510 respectively.

Required
Prepare a statement of source and application of funds for 19X2 and 19X3 in
compliance with SSAP 10.

4   Set out below are the condensed balance sheets for Zepf and Co Ltd for 19X1 and
    19X2, and a profit and loss account for the year ended 31 December 19X2.

Comparative balance sheets at 31 December 19X1 and 19X2

	19X1		19X2	
	£000	£000	£000	£000
Fixed assets				
Land and buildings at cost	240		240	
Accumulated depreciation	30		40	
		210		200
Plant and machinery at cost	262		694	
Accumulated depreciation	42		84	
		220		610
Motor vehicles	60		60	
Accumulated depreciation	30		34	
		30		26
		460		836
Current assets				
Stocks	204		234	
Trade debtors	360		432	
Cash at bank and in hand	276		10	
	840		676	
Creditors: amounts falling due within one year:				
Trade creditors	(144)		(192)	
Taxation	(60)		(80)	
Proposed dividend	(16)		(20)	
	(220)		(292)	
Net current assets		620		384
Total assets *less* current liabilities		1080		1220
Creditors: amounts falling due after one year:				
7% debenture loans		140		200
		940		1020
Capital and reserves		£		£
Called-up share capital		600		600
Share premium account		100		100
Other reserves		80		100
Profit and loss account		160		220
		940		1020

Summarized profit and loss account for the year ended 31 December 19X2

	£000	£000
Turnover		1324
Cost of sales		936
Gross profit		388
Distribution costs	98	
Administrative expenses	100	
		198
Profit on ordinary activities		190
Taxation on ordinary activities		80
		110
Loss on the sale of assets		10
Profit for the financial year		100

	£000
Profit for the financial year	100
Ordinary dividend proposed	(20)
Transfer to reserves	(20)
Retained profit for the financial year	60

Plant and machinery recorded at cost of £28 000 and at written-down value of £16 000 was sold for £6000.

Required

Prepare a statement of source and application of funds for the year ended 31 December 19X2 in conformity with SSAP 10.

5   Simpson is a wholesale dealer. After a year's successful trading, his accountant produces a profit and loss account showing net profit of £8000 for the year ended 31 December 19X1. During the same period, however, his balance at the bank fell from £10 000 to £3000.

The balance sheets at 31 December 19X0 and 19X1 are as follows

Balance sheet at 31 December 19X0

	£	£	£
		Accumulated	
Fixed assets	**Cost**	**depreciation**	
Premises	20 000	—	20 000
Equipment	2 000	500	1 500
Vehicles	2 000	700	1 300
	24 000	1 200	22 800

	£	£	
Current assets			
Stock		20 000	
Trade debtors		5 000	
Cash at bank		10 000	
		35 000	
Creditors: amounts falling due within one year;			
Trade creditors		(17 000)	
Net current assets			18 000
Total assets *less* current liabilities			40 800

Capital account	£
Balance as at 1 January 19X0	37 000
Profit for the year 19X0	5 800
	42 800
Drawings	2 000
	40 800

Balance sheet at 31 December 19X1

	£	£	£
		Accumulated	
Fixed assets	**Cost**	**depreciation**	
Premises	20 000	—	20 000
Equipment	2 000	700	1 300
Vehicles	3 000	1 000	2 000
	25 000	1 700	23 300

Current assets	£	£
Stock	24 000	
Trade debtors	4 000	
Cash at bank	3 000	
	31 000	
Creditors: amounts falling due within one year;		
Trade creditors	(10 300)	
Net current assets		20 700
Total assets *less* current liabilities		44 000
Capital account		£
Balance as at 1 January 19X0		40 800
Profit for the year 19X0		8 000
		48 800
Drawings		4 800
		44 000

Required

Prepare a cash flow statement for the year ended 31 December 19X1, and comment on the reason for the decrease in the cash balance.

6   Kashvlow Limited has the following balance sheets for the years ended 31 December 19X0 and 31 December 19X1.

Kashvlow Limited
Balance sheet as at 31 December 19X0

	£	£		£	£ Accumulated depreciation	£
Capital			Fixed assets	Cost		
Ordinary shares		350 000	Buildings	310 000		310 000
Redeemable Preference shares		150 000	Plant	431 000	195 000	236 000
Profit and loss Accounts		210 000	Vehicles	196 000	85 000	111 000
		710 000		937 000	280 000	657 000
Long term liabilities			Investment in associate			120 000
Debentures		50 000	Current assets			
Current liabilities			Stock		100 000	
Taxation	70 000		Debtors		120 000	
Dividend	40 000		Bills receivable		20 000	
Creditors	110 000		Cash in hand		3 000	
Bank overdraft	40 000					
		260 000				243 000
		1 020 000				1 020 000

Kashvlow Limited
Balance sheet as at 31 December 19X1

	£	£		£	£ Accumulated depreciation	£
Capital			**Fixed assets**	Cost		
Ordinary shares		350 000	Buildings	250 000		250 000
Capital Redemption						
Reserve Fund		150 000	Plant	460 000	287 000	173 000
Profit and loss						
Account		139 000	Vehicles	220 000	100 000	120 000
		639 000		930 000	387 000	543 000
Long-term liabilities			Investment in associate			140 000
Debentures		100 000	Loan to associate			40 000
Current liabilities			**Current assets**			
Taxation	80 000		Stock		120 000	
Dividend	60 000		Debtors		170 000	
Creditors	140 000		Bank balance		5 000	
			Cash in hand		1 000	
		280 000				296 000
		1 019 000				1 019 000

Notes:

1 During the year a building was sold for £90 000 and motor vehicles costing £90 000 were sold for £40 000 a book loss of £10 000. New vehicles were bought for £114 000.

2 Depreciation is 20 per cent straight line for plant, and 25 per cent straight line for vehicles.

3 A £15 000 premium on the redemption of preference shares was written off to P & L in the year.

Required:

(a) Reconstruct the company's profit and loss account for 19X1.

(b) Prepare a statement of source and application of funds in the manner suggested by SSAP 10.

Ignore advance corporation tax.

(c) Assess SSAP 10's treatment of dividends and taxes. How would deferred tax be treated if a pure working capital definition of funds were adopted?

Chapter 15

Interpreting and comparing financial reports

Financial reports combine facts and personal judgements, both of which are influenced in the manner of presentation to users by accounting concepts. In attempting to interpret the information disclosed, it is necessary to be aware of the limitations imposed by accounting concepts and methods of valuation which, as we have noted in previous chapters, may seriously distort the basic underlying events of importance to investors.

Ratio analysis is the most widely used technique for interpreting and comparing financial reports. Ratios are useful because they can be used to summarize briefly relationships and results that are significant to an appreciation of critical business indicators of performance, for example, the ratio of net profit to assets employed. Moreover, ratios are particularly useful for the purpose of comparing performance from year to year, and the performance of different companies, given that aggregate figures are always of differing orders of magnitude. However, it must be emphasized that companies differ one from another in many ways and also may change from year to year in terms of strategy. Ratios, on their own, will not be sufficient providers of information about a company. Information of a non-financial nature will generally be required before a meaningful analysis is possible.

The collection of ratios on a systematic basis allows trends to emerge, and throws into relief the significance of changes indicated by the analysis of current events. Since the future is uncertain, the analyst has to rely substantially on past behaviour for predicting future changes. In this respect, the trends indicated by ratios are very useful for making predictions. For example, it is not known which soccer team will win the championship next season. Hence, in making any predictions in this respect, one has to rely on the performance of all the clubs in previous seasons.

The function of ratio analysis, therefore, is to allow comparisons to be made which assist in predicting the future. In this connection, it should be stressed that the fact that Ada Ltd has a ratio of net profit to assets employed of 10 per cent in the year 19X0 is meaningless by itself. To be meaningful, that ratio must be compared with the ratios obtained from the results of previous years, and may be made even more meaningful by comparing it with those of its competitors. In this respect, inter-firm comparisons were facilitated in the United Kingdom when the Centre for Inter-Firm Comparisons Ltd, a non-profit-making organization, was established in 1959 by the British Institute of Management in association with the British Productivity Council. This organisation collects a large amount of management accounting information from its subscribers. Then, maintaining a high level of confidentiality, it computes a whole range of ratios which are reported back to subscribers together with the best, worst and average ratios. By contrast, the external analyst is confined to the information disclosed in published reports, and tends to rely on such other information as he is able to obtain from other sources in assessing the performance and prospects of individual firms.

The nature of ratio analysis

Numerous ratios may be computed from financial reports and from other sources, notably stock exchange share prices. In this chapter, we limit our discussion to a number of important ratios which focus on two critical areas—namely, the ability of the firm to survive and grow, and the efficiency of its financial performance.

From the investor's viewpoint, these particular ratios are related directly to the two central issues, which we postulated in Chapter 1 to be the focal points of a normative theory of financial reporting. We argued that the maintenance and increase of the value of the capital invested was the first consideration, and that the second consideration was the level of income which investors expected to derive from the invested capital. Clearly both these considerations are interrelated and interdependent.

The maintenance of the value of the capital invested depends on the ability of the firm to survive, for shareholders, and particularly ordinary shareholders, bear most of the costs if the company fails. Solvency is the most important criterion of the firm's ability to survive. Solvency is the ability of the firm to meet its debts as they fall due for payment, and it is a matter of both fact and law. If a creditor presses his claim for payment of the amount due, and the firm is unable to pay, its inability so to do is a fact. The firm may have substantial assets which may not be realizable at a fair value if they are sold, especially if that sale is pressurized. Its prospects may not necessarily be bad in terms of its future or even its present ability to generate profits—what is crucial, however, is that it has insufficient liquid resources, that is, cash or near cash, to meet an individual claim, and, moreover, has no further credit facilities available. Solvency becomes a question of law by the formal process in which the creditor seeks the recovery of a debt through a court of law, and upon a direction by the judge that the firm has defaulted upon a payment of a debt ordered by the court, the firm is declared insolvent. The legal procedure for the firm's liquidation by winding-up ensues under a liquidator appointed by the court. Solvency is related, therefore, to the problem of liquidity in relation to the size of current obligations in favour of creditors, and to available credit facilities.

The level of income which investors expect to derive from their investment is related in the first instance to the firm's current financial performance, and in the next instance to its future growth prospects.

The income of shareholders may be seen as consisting of a stream of dividend flows. Over the long term, dividends are related to the level of earnings, that is, realized profit, and this in turn is reflected in the market value of the shares. Ratio analysis enables views to be formulated about the efficiency of current financial performance by relating net profit to such indicators as net assets or share prices, and as far as the investor is concerned by relating dividends to corporate net profit and to share prices. So far as companies with a market quotation are concerned, reported financial performance is a major factor in the determination of share price and hence the wealth of the shareholder. Ratios of financial performance are one way that the market assesses the performance and prospects of a company.

We use the accounts of Ada Ltd which appear below for demonstrating the calculations involved in ratio analysis.

The current stock market price of the ordinary share is £2.

The analysis of solvency

We mentioned earlier that solvency was a question of fact in the first instance. Given the nature of financial reports, it follows that ratio analysis may make only a limited contribution to assessing solvency for the following reasons:

1   The firm's total current liabilities and total current assets at the end of the last accounting period may indicate that its financial stability is precarious, but solvency happens in the present and not in the past. In this respect, a firm may be perfectly solvent on the last day of the accounting period, and may now be insolvent by reason of the sudden withdrawal of a credit facility upon which it relied.

2   The balance sheet does not reveal sources of credit which the firm may tap, nor the willingness of creditors and investors to see the firm through a difficult period.

3   The accounts do not disclose the complete nature of a company. It is important to have a good idea of a company's receipts and payments pattern in interpreting solvency. For example, a supermarket will be able to generate funds from inventories much more quickly than a manufacturing company.

Ada Ltd
Profit and loss account for the year ended 31 December 19X0

	£
Turnover	350 000
Cost of sales	208 000
Gross profit	142 000

Distribution costs	80 000
Administrative expenses	30 000
Interest on long-term loan	4 000
Profit on ordinary activities	28 000
Tax on profit on ordinary activities	14 000
Profit on ordinary activities after taxation	14 000
Preference dividend	2 000
Profit for the financial year	12 000
Ordinary dividend	5 000
Retained profit	7 000

Balance sheet at 31 December 19X0

	£	£
Fixed assets		
Tangible assets at cost less depreciation		130 000
Current assets		
Stock (opening £35 000)	45 000	
Debtors	40 000	
Cash	7 000	
	92 000	
Creditors: amounts falling due within one year:		
Trade creditors	23 000	
Other liabilities	28 000	
	51 000	
Net current assets		41 000
Total assets *less* current liabilities		171 000
Creditors: amounts falling due after more than one year:		
Debenture loans		40 000
		131 000
Capital and reserves		
80 000 £1 ordinary shares		80 000
20 000 10% preference shares		20 000
Profit and loss account		31 000
		131 000

Short-term solvency

Although shareholders risk losing their investment in the event of insolvency, unsecured creditors risk financial losses. In the face of a deteriorating financial situation, long-term creditors, such as debenture-holders, may either attempt to realize their security by selling specific assets mortgaged under the debenture instrument, or they may be willing to hold their hand if a viable rescue operation is mounted. Short-term creditors such as trade creditors are generally not willing to allow credit to a firm which is running into financial difficulties, and action from creditors is usually the precipitating cause of insolvency.

Small firms in difficulties perish quickly: large firms, however, bring losses to many around them, not only to short-term creditors but to financial institutions which have supported capital expenditure programmes and granted credits. Indicators of short-term financial stability are particularly important, therefore, in respect of larger firms whose shares are quoted, for if action is needed to prevent losses early indicators are required to enable such action to be taken. There are two classes of ratios which are useful in this respect:

1   Ratios which relate current assets to current liabilities, and indicate an imbalance between the burden of immediate debts in relation to the firm's ability to meet such debts.
2   Ratios which indicate the rate at which short-term assets are utilized, thereby affording a measure of the elasticity with which they are transformed into cash.

Ratios of current assets to current liabilities

Two ratios in common use are:

1   the current ratio;
2   the acid-test (or quick) ratio.

The current ratio is the ratio of current assets to current liabilities expressed as follows:

$$\frac{\text{current assets}}{\text{current liabilities}}$$

Because Ada Ltd has current assets valued at £90 000 and current liabilities amounting to £51 000 the current ratio is 1.8:1. It will be recalled that the surplus of current assets over current liabilities also measures working capital, that is, the funds conventionally regarded as being available to finance current operations.

A number of problems stem from the use of the current ratio as a predictor of financial stability. First, since current assets include stock and trade debtors as well as cash, an element of subjectivity is introduced into this ratio by methods of valuing stocks and by the assessment of the likelihood of bad debts. Second, an efficient business may be able to reduce stocks and debtor levels without affecting its financial stability, which is secured by a high rate of funds flowing from current operations. Hence, its current ratio may conceivably be relatively low, and it will still be a viable concern. It will be noted also that some businesses, such as cash retailers, will have a rapid stock turnover and few debtors. In such a case we might expect a very low current ratio to represent the norm. By contrast, a firm with a high current ratio represented by high levels of stocks, debtors and cash may be a very inefficient firm, and the current ratio may conceal a poor rate of funds generation, and hence a very unstable situation. For this reason, Glautier (1971) has argued that the current ratio is not a useful indicator of solvency from a theoretical viewpoint. Nevertheless, it should be said that what is a normal current ratio is peculiar to given industries, and financial analysts tend to look for current ratios falling within acceptable limits, for the company's particular sector.

The acid test ratio is particularly easy to misinterpret and this stems partly from the traditional definition of this ratio as follows:

$$\frac{\text{current assets} - \text{stocks}}{\text{current liabilities}}$$

An implication of accepting this definition is that stocks will always be unavailable as providers of short-term funds to meet pressing liabilities. A more flexible definition is required of this ratio which attempts to compare potential sources of short-term funds with potential needs for short-term funds. The traditional definition of the acid test ratio would be entirely inappropriate as a measure of the solvency of a business such as a supermarket chain. It might be entirely appropriate to exclude stock when considering a manufacturing company selling on credit to other commercial concerns, but there will be many other companies where much care will need to be exercised. However, we might argue in general terms, that if a company does not have sufficient assets which will be converted into cash during the normal credit period, then there is likely to be some risk of insolvency. If we assume that Ada Ltd will have to find £51 000 to meet current liabilities out of its short-term resources of debtors and cash, we find that it has only £47 000 to meet those requirements. This is a ratio of 0.92 to 1 and indicates a potential shortfall. But it would be incorrect to place too much emphasis on a single ratio unless we have something against which to compare it.

While the acid test ratio is a stricter indicator of solvency, it suffers from the same disadvantages which affect the current ratio, that is, it ignores the importance of cash flows from current operations and by emphasizing cash and debtors tends to put the less efficient firm in a more favourable light. It should also be emphasized that there is no such thing as universally desirable ratios and, therefore, 'rules of thumb' like 2:1 current ratios and 1:1 acid test ratios might be very misleading.

Ratios of the cash elasticity of current assets (i.e. activity ratios)

Given that current assets normally consist of cash, debtors and stocks, the firm's ability to meet current liabilities depends upon the rate at which cash flows into the firm from current operations. Since sales is the critical event in this respect, the rate at which stocks are sold is clearly crucial. Where a substantial proportion of sales are on credit terms, the rate at which debtors settle their accounts is also crucial. For these reasons, the following ratios are good indicators of the cash elasticity of current assets:

1 average stock turnover;
2 collection period of trade debts.

1   The average stock turnover is calculated by the following formula:

cost of goods sold during the period

average stock held

For Ada Ltd the average stock turnover is as follows:

$$\frac{£208\ 000}{(£35\ 000 + £45\ 000)/2} = 5.2\ \text{times}$$

This ratio means that the average length of time that stocks are held before being sold is 365 days/5.2, that is, 70 days.

The average stock turnover ratio is only a crude measure of the rate at which stocks are sold for the purpose of comparing the cash elasticity of stocks of different enterprises. Different marketing situations face different industries and trades. A butchery will clearly have a much higher stock turnover rate than a firm selling luxury goods. Methods of stock valuation also distort the significance of inter-firm comparisons. It is also important to recognize that average stock as calculated above is only an approximation and that seasonal fluctuations, or increased sales and stockholdings during the year, may seriously distort this figure. A company with major sales at one time of the year such as a fireworks manufacturer could produce wildly differing average stock figures if they are calculated at different times of the year on the above basis.

Nevertheless, the average stock turnover may give a useful indication of trading difficulties facing a particular firm by comparing it with the average stock turnover for previous periods. A fall in the average stock turnover may indicate stiffening competition, adverse marketing circumstances or a degree of obsolescence in the firm's products. At the same time, firms operating in similar markets may be expected to have roughly similar average stock turnover ratios, so that even as a crude ratio of comparability, it may be a useful indicator for investors.

2   An important measure of the cash elasticity of debtor balances may be obtained from the average collection period of trade debtors by using the following formula:

trade debtors × 365

credit sales

If we assume that Ada Ltd sells all its goods on credit we calculate the average collection period as follows:

$$\frac{£40\ 000 \times 365}{£350\ 000} = 42\ \text{days}$$

These calculations show that 42 days is the approximate time required to collect trade debtors outstanding at 31 December 19X0. By applying this ratio, analysts establish if the average collection period for debtors is too slow. A rough rule of thumb which is sometimes used by credit agencies is that the average age of trade debts should not exceed $1\frac{1}{3}$ times the net credit period. If a firm gives 30 days credit for the settlement of debtor accounts, the average collection period should not exceed approximately 40 days. However, information about credit terms is not included in a company's accounts. Again, it must be recognized that the calculation of days sales in debtors is an approximation which assumes more or less consistent sales levels during the year. If a company experienced relatively high sales in the period immediately before the accounting date, this would have the effect of increasing the collection period, since a high current sales level would be compared to a lower average level for the year. Companies will have accurate information available internally through analysis of the sales day book or, more likely, computerized analysis of the average collection period for debtors plus detailed aged debtors lists.

Other factors affecting short-term solvency

In addition to the ratios mentioned above, other factors which should be taken into account when evaluating short-term solvency include:

1   *The size of operating costs.* Neither the profit and loss account nor the balance sheet reveal the cash required to meet current operating costs such as payroll, rent and other expenses. Where a firm has very liquid assets in its balance sheet, and it is faced, for example, with very large payroll obligations, it may be extremely short of cash.
2   *Bank credit.* A firm which has sufficient credit facility at the bank may, as we mentioned earlier, have lower current and acid test ratios.
3   *Seasonal patterns of trade.* Where firms normally expect seasonal patterns of trade, there will be distortions in the solvency ratios arising from seasonal buildup of stocks, trade debtors and cash depletions during the time interval across the peak season as mentioned above. Where such seasonal patterns of trade exist, they must be taken into account when making inter-firm comparisons.

Long-term solvency

We defined solvency as the ability to meet current liabilities as they fall due for payment. The long-term financial stability of the firm may be considered as dependent upon its ability to meet all liabilities, including those not currently payable.

Two ratios which are considered important in this respect are:

1   the shareholders' equity ratio;
2   the interest coverage ratio.

The shareholders' equity ratio

This ratio is considered by many analysts to be equal in importance to the current ratio as an indicator of financial stability. It is computed as follows:

$$\text{shareholders' equity ratio} = \frac{\text{shareholders' equity}}{\text{total assets}} \times 100$$

Substituting figures from Ada's accounts:

$$\frac{111\ 000}{222\ 000} \times 100 = 50\%$$

It is generally felt that the larger the proportion of the shareholders' equity, the stronger is the financial position of the firm. This is related to the notion of 'gearing' which we discussed in Chapter 13. By increasing long-term borrowing, the firm may increase its current assets, thereby creating a more favourable current ratio. At the same time, however, it reduces the shareholders' equity, signalling a possible over-dependence on outside sources for long-term financial needs. This creates a problem associated with high levels of gearing, namely that where net profit tends to fluctuate, a high level of fixed interest payments may greatly impair the ability of the company to make dividend payments and will certainly magnify the variations in earnings attributable to shareholders and hence share prices.

Although no explicit rules of thumb exist regarding desirable shareholders' equity ratios, financial analysts may have a general idea of the appropriate financial structure of a particular company by considering the stability of its profit. The less variable a company's underlying business activities and profits, the more safely it can use long-term debt. The total risk of a company is made up of business risk (i.e. risk inherent in the type of business) and financial risk (i.e. through borrowing) and, therefore, if a company has low business risk it will generally be able to absorb more financial risk.

Interest coverage ratio

The ability of a firm to meet its debt service costs out of current earnings is a rough indicator of its long-term solvency. Long-term loans which are usually in the form of debentures carry interest charges which must be paid regularly. The inability to meet such interest charges places the firm's solvency into jeopardy. The interest cover ratio is calculated as follows:

$$\text{interest coverage ratio} = \frac{\text{profit before interest and tax}}{\text{periodic interest charges}}$$

$$= \frac{\pounds 32\ 000}{\pounds 4000} = 8 \text{ times}$$

Generally speaking, a firm which can cover its debt service costs several times over by its operating profit even in a poor year would be regarded as a satisfactory risk by long-term creditors. The level of safety required would, however, depend on the company's level of business (inherent) risk.

The analysis of financial performance

There are two aspects of a company's financial performance of interest to investors. First, its financial performance may be assessed by reference to its ability to generate profit. Ratios of financial efficiency in this respect focus on the relationship between profit and sales and profit and assets employed. Second, its financial performance may be assessed in terms of the value of its shares to investors. In this sense, ratios of financial performance focus on earnings per share, dividend yield and price–earnings ratios.

The analysis of earning power

The overall measure of earnings performance for purposes of comparison is the return on capital employed. This ratio is made up of several components, two of the most important of which are the asset–turnover ratio and the return-on-sales ratio.

The return on capital employed

There are several ways of expressing this ratio, and care must be taken in making inter-firm comparisons that the basis used is the same. The return on capital employed may be expressed as follows:

$$\text{return on net assets} = \frac{\text{operating profit (before interest and tax)}}{\text{total assets less current liabilities}}$$

$$\text{return on shareholders' equity} = \frac{\text{profit (after interest and tax)}}{\text{shareholders' equity}}$$

In these ratios interest is added back to profit so as to make comparisons between firms with different gearing more comparable.

Return on net assets indicates the efficiency with which management used the resources to earn profit. For Ada Ltd it is computed as follows:

$$\frac{£32\ 000}{£171\ 000} \times 100 = 18.7\%$$

Return on shareholders' equity measures the return which accrues to the shareholders after interest payments to creditors and taxes are deducted. It does not measure the efficiency with which available resources were used, but rather the residual return to the owners on their investment in the business. For Ada Ltd the return on shareholders' equity is calculated as follows:

$$\frac{£12\ 000}{£111\ 000} \times 100 = 10.8\%$$

When comparing the ratios of different companies it is necessary to adjust the data for any differences in accounting policies. However, it will be difficult for an outsider to assess the effects of such differences. Also, the inherent weaknesses of the historic cost accounting system might be especially significant when considering these ratios because the true value of corporate assets may be difficult to assess.

The factors which affect the return on capital employed may be broken down into the following ratios:

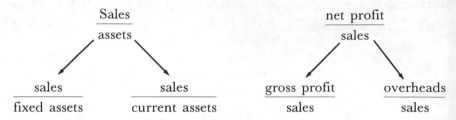

These ratios may be further subdivided, for example, by a closer analysis of the components of current assets, that is, stocks and debtors, and the elements of direct and overhead expenses.

The ratio of return on capital employed (ROCE) is generally expressed as follows:

$$\text{ROCE} = \frac{\text{sales}}{\text{capital employed}} \times \frac{\text{net profit}}{\text{sales}} \times 100$$

Asset/turnover ratios

The first component of the formula for calculating the ROCE is an asset utilization ratio. It is intended to reflect the intensity with which assets are employed. Thus, if the firm has a low ratio of sales to assets, it is implied that some substantial underutilization of assets is occurring, or alternatively that assets are not being efficiently employed. This ratio focuses, therefore, on the use of assets made by management. Because it is a measure of past managerial efficiency in this respect, it is thought to provide a reasonable basis for forecasting management's future efficiency. It is considered to be a prime determinant of the level of future profit flows.

The following ratios may be used and the data for their calculation is derived from the accounts of Ada Ltd.

$$\text{total assets turnover} = \frac{\text{turnover}}{\text{total assets}} = \frac{£350\ 000}{£222\ 000} = 1.6 \text{ times}$$

$$\text{fixed assets turnover} = \frac{\text{turnover}}{\text{fixed assets}} = \frac{£35\ 000}{£13\ 000} = 2.7 \text{ times}$$

$$\text{working capital turnover} = \frac{\text{turnover}}{\text{net current assets}} = \frac{£350\ 000}{£41\ 000} = 8.5 \text{ times}$$

The ratio of net profit on sales

This is the second component of the formula for calculating the ROCE. It seeks to assess the profitability of sales, that is, the efficiency of sales as a critical event in generating profit.

The ratio of net profit on sales varies widely from industry to industry, so that it should be used solely for comparing similar companies in the same industry, or in assessing the performance of the same company over a period of time. Some companies may operate in an industry characterized by low profit margins and high levels of turnover, for example, the manufacture and distribution of foodstuffs. It is also possible that a company might make a strategy decision to move up or down market.

In considering the relevance of ratios of performance, conventional accounting measurements introduce limitations. Current value accounting removes at least two basic difficulties. First, the effect of the timing differences in the acquisition of assets, which results in the aggregation of assets of differing money value being removed, and similar values are added together. Second, the use of historical cost measurements results in arbitrary allocations, e.g. LIFO and FIFO allocations of stocks to the cost of sales. Replacement cost accounting increases the usefulness of ratio analysis by providing uniformity in cost allocations, since all costs are allocated at their replacement price.

For Ada Ltd the ratio is calculated as follows:

$$\frac{£32\ 000}{£350\ 000} \times 100 = 9.1\%$$

The analysis of investment decisions

In buying the shares of a particular company, the investor is seeking to make the best allocation of his investment funds. Although the earnings efficiency of that company is very important to him, it has to be related to its shares. For this reason, several ratios are used by investors to appraise the performance of companies in terms of share prices and yields.

Earnings per share

SSAP 3 requires that all companies listed on a recognized stock exchange show in their published accounts the earnings per share (EPS) for the accounting period and for the previous period. EPS is defined as the profit in pence attributable to each equity share after deducting preference dividend but before taking into account extraordinary items, divided by the number of equity shares in issue. The EPS for Ada Ltd is calculated as follows:

$$EPS = \frac{£12\ 000}{80\ 000} = 15 \text{ pence per share}$$

EPS is an important ratio for two reasons. First, the trend in EPS is a useful indicator to investors in the company of the profitable use of their money. Second, EPS is related by investment analysts to the market price of the shares to derive the price earnings ratio. (See below.) For these reasons, it is important that EPS should be calculated and disclosed on a comparable basis from year to year and between one company and another.

Various complexities arise in the calculation of EPS. One of the complexities originates from the imputation system of taxation which will, in certain circumstances, impose a tax charge on companies which varies according to dividends paid. In these circumstances, intercompany and interperiod comparisons based on the net basis (as calculated above) could be misleading where different earnings figures resulted from the same level of pre-tax profits as a result of dividends paid. SSAP 3 requires that where there is a material difference between EPS calculated on the net basis and on a basis which assumes net distribution of dividends (the nil basis), the EPS calculated on the nil distribution basis should also be shown on the face of the profit and loss account.

Price/earnings ratio

This ratio indicates the number of years it would take to recover the share price out of the current earnings of the company. It is calculated by dividing the market price of the ordinary shares of a company by the EPS figure described above. For Ada Ltd the price/earnings ratio is calculated as follows:

$$\text{price/earnings ratio} = \frac{£2}{15 \text{ pence}} = 13.3$$

What this means is that if £2 is paid for these shares, then 13.3 years of current earnings of 15 pence per share are being bought. Because the current market value of a share reflects the expectations of investors concerning the future profits of a company, the ratio is effectively measuring the market's anticipations for future earnings compared to the current performance of the company. Therefore, the price/earnings ratio is an indicator of the confidence that the stock market has in the company. A low price/earnings ratio suggests a lack of confidence in the company's ability to maintain earnings, while a high price/earnings ratio suggests a belief that the company is expected to increase earnings in the future. However, as with all ratios, interpretation must allow for differences between companies. A highly risky company will be expected to generate higher returns than a 'safe' one and this will be reflected by a relatively lower price/earnings ratio.

Dividend yield

The dividend yield focuses closely on the value of the declared dividends to an investor. It is calculated as follows:

$$\text{dividend yield} = \frac{\text{dividend per ordinary share}}{\text{market price per ordinary share}}$$

In the case of Ada Ltd the dividend per ordinary share is:

$$\frac{£5000}{£80\ 000} = 6.25 \text{ pence}$$

The dividend yield is:

$$\frac{6.25 \text{ pence}}{£2} = 3.1\%$$

The dividend yield shows the return currently earned in the form of dividends from an investment in shares. Future returns will be affected by changes in the rate of dividend and movement in the share price.

Dividend cover ratio (or payout ratio)

The ability of a company to continue to pay current dividend levels in the future may be forecast by the dividend cover ratio, which may be calculated as follows:

$$\text{dividend cover} = \frac{\text{net profit after taxation and preference dividend}}{\text{ordinary dividend}}$$

The dividend cover ratio indicates the proportion of earnings retained by the company and the level of risk in future years, should earnings decline, for the company to be able to maintain the same dividend payments. Interpretation of dividend ratios is difficult because some investors will prefer low payout (dividend) companies and others high payout companies. Other things being equal, a lower payout leads to greater growth in the value of the company which can then be realized by investors in the form of capital gains through the sale of shares. It is not at all clear whether high or low payout policies will have any effect on share prices and returns, but it is likely that investors will prefer companies to adopt a consistent policy.

Ratios as predictors of business failure: empirical studies

Empirical studies have been undertaken to determine the extent to which financial ratios may be used to predict business failure. The ability to predict company failure is particularly important from both the private investor's viewpoint and the social viewpoint, as it is an obvious indication of resource misallocation. An early warning signal of probable failure would enable both management and investors to take preventive measures.

In a study using more powerful statistical techniques than used by his predecessors, Beaver (1966) found that financial ratios proved to be useful in the prediction of failure in that such failure could be predicted at least five years before the event. He concluded that ratios could be used to distinguish correctly firms which would fail from those which would not, with much more success than would be possible by random prediction. One of his significant conclusions was that the most effective predictor of failure was the ratio of both short-term and long-term cash flow to total debt. The next best ratio was the ratio of net profit to total assets. One of Beaver's most surprising findings was that the current ratio was among the worst predictors of failure. Turnover ratios were found to be at the bottom of the list of effective predictors. Generally, Beaver found that 'mixed ratios', which had profit or cash flows compared to assets or liabilities, outperformed short-term solvency ratios which had been believed traditionally to be the best predictors of failure.

In a later study, Beaver (1968) suggested that business failure tends to be determined by permanent factors. He argued that if the basic financial position of a company was sound and profit prospects were good, it would recover from a temporary shortage of liquid assets, but that if the long-term prospects in these areas were not good, business failure could not be prevented by a good liquid position.

Altman (1968, 1983) extended Beaver's univariate (single-variable) analysis to allow for multiple predictors of business failure. He used a multiple discriminant analysis for the purpose of developing a linear function of a number of explanatory variables to predict failure. Altman used 22 financial ratios based on data obtained one year before failure, and selected five financial ratios for the purposes of establishing his final discriminant function. These five financial ratios were:

1   working capital/total assets as an indicator of liquidity;
2   retained earnings/total assets as an indicator of the age of the firm and its cumulative profitability;
3   earnings before interest and tax/total assets as an indicator of profitability;
4   market value of the equity/book value of debt as an indicator of financial structure;
5   sales/total assets as an indicator of capital turnover.

Altman's five-variable model correctly identified 95 per cent of the total sample of companies tested for bankruptcy. This percentage rate of success in predicting failure fell to 72 per cent when the data used was obtained two years prior to failure. As earlier data was used in testing the model, so its predictive ability became more unreliable.

Taffler and Tisshaw (1977, 1983) applied Altman's multiple discriminant analysis to companies in the United Kingdom. They tested the predictive value of 80 different ratios in a variety of combinations. The best results were found when four ratios were combined in accordance with weighting which reflected their significance to the analysis of business failure.

The ratios used by Taffler and Tisshaw and the weightings which they were given were as follows:

1   Profit before tax/current liabilities (53 per cent), which 'is a profitability measure indicating the ability of an enterprise to cover its current liabilities through its earning power. If it has a low or negative value, its downside risk is clearly greater than that for the average company.'
2   Current assets/total liabilities (13 per cent), which 'is related to the conventional current ratio, and is a measure of the working capital position of the firm. The greater the ratio, the sounder the enterprise.'
3   Current liabilities/total assets (18 per cent), 'which measures the company's current liabilities position and is a financial leverage ratio. The greater its magnitude, the more serious the problems the company has to face in financing the cost of its debt and the acquisition of new debt.'
4   Immediate assets—current liabilities/operating costs—depreciation (16 per cent), which 'calculates the time for which the company can finance its continuing operations from its immediate assets, if all other sources of short-time finance are cut off, and is a ratio relatively new to the accounting literature . . . and is akin to the acid test.'

All these empirical studies present evidence to support the conclusion that firms which avoided failure had stronger ratios in areas of significant analysis than firms which failed. The measures used by Altman and Taffler and Tisshaw are expressed by a number known as a 'Z scores'. Scores such as these are now available through on-time data services such as 'Datastream'.

Argenti (1977, 1984) has drawn attention to three limitations of financial ratio analysis which restrict the usefulness of financial ratios for predicting business failure, in the following terms:

1   While ratios may show that there is something wrong and while a sequence of them over time may show that it is getting worse, it is doubtful whether one could predict collapse on the evidence of these ratios alone. The ability of ratios alone to predict corporate collapse has not been conclusively proved.
2   Their value has been eroded by inflation. Figures that appear to show an improvement may conceal a deterioration in real terms.
3   Managers start 'creative accounting' when they know things are wrong, thus hiding the telltale symptoms. Creative accounting involves making the company's results look better than they are, for example, by cutting expenditure on routine maintenance. This phenomenon explains why so many people do not appreciate the serious difficulties of suspect companies until the day on which insolvency is announced.

Summary

Ratio analysis provides the most commonly used indicators to assess and compare the financial performance of companies, both over time and as between different companies. However, unless ratios are collected in a systematic and uniform manner, comparisons may be very misleading. For this reason, they are most useful when collected and developed by such organizations as the Centre for Inter-firm Comparisons.

It is very important that external users of financial reports should understand the limitations of ratios based on conventional accounting measurements, otherwise, their analyses will not be sound nor their interpretations valid. The conclusion which may be drawn from our examination of ratio analysis is that its general usefulness and relevance to investors would be enhanced by increasing the uniformity of financial reporting practices and adopting current value accounting.

Considerable interest exists in the possibility of using financial ratios as predictors of business failure. Several studies have been conducted that show that there exist ratios and combinations of ratios which are significant in this regard. Nevertheless, caution is required in accepting the conclusions suggested by financial ratios as regards business failure.

References

Altman, E. I. (1968). Financial ratios, discriminant analysis and the prediction of corporate bankruptcy, *Journal of Finance*.

Altman, E. I. (1983). *Corporate Financial Distress,* Wiley.

Argenti, J. (1977). *Corporate Collapse: the Causes and Symptoms,* Nelson.

Argenti, J. (1984). *Predicting Corporate Failure,* Institute of Chartered Accountants in England and Wales.

Beaver, W. H. (1966). Financial ratios as predictors of failure, *Journal of Accounting Research,* No. 4.

Beaver, W. H. (1968). Alternative accounting measures as predictors of failure, *The Accounting Review,* January.

Glautier, M. W. E. (1971). Towards a reformulation of the theory of working capital, *Journal of Business Finance,* Spring.

Taffler, R. J. and Tisshaw, H. (1977). Going, going, gone—four factors which predict, *Accountancy,* March.

Taffler, R. J. (1983). The assessment of company solvency and performance using a statistical model—a comparative UK-based study, *Accounting and Business Research,* Autumn.

Problems

1 The following information relates to the operations of the East Lancashire Trading Company for the three year period ended 31 December 19X3:

Profit and loss accounts

	19X3	19X2	19X1
	£	£	£
Net sales	1 000 000	900 000	800 000
Cost of goods sold	600 000	550 000	545 000
Gross profit	400 000	350 000	255 000

Selling and administrative expenses	300 000	275 000	220 000
Net profit before tax	100 000	75 000	35 000
Tax at 50%	50 000	37 500	22 500
Net profit after tax	50 000	37 500	12 500
Dividends	30 000	25 000	10 000
Net increase in retained earnings	20 000	12 500	2 500

Balance sheets

	19X3	19X2	19X1
	£	£	£
Assets			
Land and buildings	500 000	450 000	425 000
Plant and equipment (net)	450 000	500 000	410 000
Stocks (at cost)	635 000	600 000	520 000
Debtors	425 000	410 000	440 000
Bank balance	40 000	55 000	63 000
	2 050 000	2 015 000	1 858 000
Shareholders' equity and liabilities	£	£	£
Ordinary share capital £1 shares			
fully paid	600 000	600 000	600 000
Share premium account	125 000	125 000	125 000
Retained earnings	532 000	512 000	500 000
12% debentures 19X9	200 000	200 000	200 000
Creditors	496 000	493 000	390 000
Accrued expenses	15 000	17 000	9 000
Taxation	52 000	43 000	24 000
Provision for dividends	30 000	25 000	10 000
	2 050 000	2 015 000	1 858 000

Required:

From the foregoing information, calculate the following ratios for the years 19X2 and 19X3 (assume that all sales are on a credit basis and the year is 360 days):

(a) The current ratio
(b) The acid-test ratio
(c) The average stock turnover
(d) The average collection period for debtors
(e) The shareholders' equity ratio
(f) The return on capital employed
(g) The earnings per share.

Evaluate the liquidity position of the company at the end of 19X3 as compared with 19X2.

2 Evaluate the usefulness of financial ratio analysis in assessing the financial state of an enterprise. Use the case below to illustrate your answer.

Case

A summary of the results of Sandygate Enterprises Limited for the last three years is as follows:

	Year ended 31 December		
	19X4	19X5	19X6
	£	£	£
Sales	480 000	560 000	690 000
Profits before tax	63 000	70 000	74 000
Tax	23 000	25 000	28 000
Profits after tax	40 000	45 000	46 000
Dividends	30 000	30 000	36 000
Retained profit for year	10 000	15 000	10 000
	£	£	£
Share capital (600 000 £0.25 shares)	150 000	150 000	150 000
Retained profit	85 000	100 000	110 000
Shareholders' funds	235 000	250 000	260 000
10% debentures	65 000	150 000	150 000
Capital employed	300 000	400 000	410 000
Market price per share at 31 December	£1	£1.50	£1.25
Debt interest	£6 500	£15 000	£15 000

3 Jack and Jill each carry on business as wholesalers of the same product. Their respective accounts for the year ended 31 December 19X6 are as follows:

Profit and loss accounts

	Jack		Jill	
	£	£	£	£
Sales		144 000		140 000
Cost of Sales:				
Opening stocks	28 000		3 200	
Purchases	124 000		121 600	
	152 000		124 800	
Closing stocks	32 000	120 000	4 800	120 000
Gross profit		24 000		20 000
Selling expenses	7 200		2 800	
Admin expenses	8 160	15 360	9 500	12 300
Net profit		£8 640		£7 700

Balance sheets at 31 December 19X6

	Jack	Jill
Freehold property	£20 000	£14 000
Fixtures fittings	21 750	13 840
Motor vehicles	12 000	6 000
	53 750	33 840
Stocks	32 000	4 800
Debtors	28 800	11 200
Bank	8 950	11 360
	£123 500	£61 200
Capital	£108 000	£30 800
Creditors	15 500	30 400
	£123 500	£61 200

Notes

(a) All sales are on credit.

(b) The amounts of debtors and creditors have not changed significantly over the year.

(c) All fixed assets are at written-down value.

Compare the profitability and financial position of the two businesses by:

(a) calculating suitable ratios for each business;

(b) commenting on the significance of the results of your calculations.

Chapter 16

Financial accounting for groups of companies

Corporate growth has manifested itself in several ways. By the process of horizontal integration, firms engaged in the production or sale of comparable goods have combined to create monopoly or semi-monopoly situations. Similarly, the process of vertical integration has been important in the historical process by which the giant corporation has emerged. Vertical integration is the combination of firms having a supplier–customer relationship. Finally, the conglomerate is a group of companies having diversified activities, which has been brought under centralized control. The process of corporate growth has continued unabated for several decades. Today, the multinational corporation has emerged, with activities straddling many nations, creating thereby special managerial and accounting problems. Through these processes groups of companies have emerged as a major feature of modern industrial and commercial organization.

There are many reasons why this external expansion by the process of 'acquiring' or 'merging with' another company is preferred to investing in internal expansion. External expansion provides a growing company with immediate access to productive capacity, distribution networks and suppliers, thereby avoiding startup delays which could be lengthy and costly. Also, by acquiring an existing company, the growing company obtains an existing experience of its problems, profitability and other factors relevant to the new management, indicating the success factors and the pitfalls associated with a new business venture. Similarly, the easiest way of entering a competitive market may be by acquiring an existing company, thereby avoiding the risks and problems which a new entrant to that market would face.

This chapter is concerned with setting out the framework within which the accounting problems of 'groups' of companies may be discussed. These revolve around two principal issues:

1   How should a group be defined?
2   How should consolidated accounts be prepared?

The regulatory framework

United Kingdom law and practice is defined in the Companies Act and SSAP 14 'Group Accounts'. In addition, SSAP 1 'Accounting for Associated Companies' (revised 1982) deals with companies which are closely related to a group, but do not fall within it for the purpose of consolidation. The EC Seventh Directive on Consolidated Accounts was implemented by the Companies Act 1989.

Definition of a group

If two separate companies operate independently of each other, they will maintain separate accounting records and prepare separate financial statements. However, if one company controls the other, a group is said to exist which consists of the controlling or parent company and the controlled or subsidiary company. Both companies will retain their separate legal identity and operations and separate accounting records. Equally, they will remain responsible in law for all their actions and liable to tax on their own profits. However, the objective of preparing financial statements in the form of balance sheets and profit and loss accounts assumes an additional dimension. If the shareholders of the parent company are to be fully informed of its activities, they will need to be informed about the substance of the controlling interest it has in the subsidiary company. This information need is met by the preparation of consolidated accounts for the group, in the form of a consolidated balance sheet, and a consolidated profit and loss account, created by aggregating the separate balance sheets and profit and loss accounts of the parent and subsidiary companies.

The initial problem to be resolved is now to determine when an obligation to produce consolidated accounts exists. United Kingdom law and practice, as reflected in the Companies Acts and SSAP 14, is based on the legal control concept. According to the Companies Act 1989 an undertaking is a parent undertaking in relation to another undertaking, a subsidiary, if:

(a) it holds a majority of the voting rights in the undertaking, or
(b) it is a member of the undertaking and has the right to appoint or remove a majority of its board of directors, or
(c) it has the right to exercise dominant influence over the undertaking:

    (i) by virtue of provisions contained in the undertaking's memorandum or articles, or
    (ii) by virtue of a control contract, or

(d) it is a member of the undertaking and controls alone, pursuant to an agreement with other shareholders or members, a majority of the voting rights in the undertaking.

The main change introduced by the Act is that the definition of a subsidiary is based on a company's ability to exercise control over another, rather than on the ownership of a majority of a particular class of shares. Accordingly, a group is said to exist whenever legal entities which are independent of each other are brought under central management, regardless of the situation of the equity ownership. In addition to implementing the EC Seventh Directive this change to the definition of a subsidiary should curb the use of off-balance sheet finance vehicles used, for example, to reduce the apparent level of group borrowing through special purpose vehicles controlled by the parent company but structured to fall outside the pre-1989 Companies Act definition. Some companies which are not subsidiaries under the present definition will require to be consolidated when the Act comes into effect. Vehicles other than companies, including certain partnerships and joint ventures, can also come within the consolidation requirement.

Finally, as far as definitions are concerned, it is appropriate at this stage to note the existence of the concept of an associated company. The concept was formalized by SSAP 1 (issued January 1971; revised April 1982) to deal with the situation where a company holds an investment in another, the policies of which are subject to significant influence by the investing company, although the parent–subsidiary relationship does not exist. Prior to the 1989 Companies Act this type of investment was referred to as a 'related company' in previous Acts. The 1989 Companies Act introduced the term 'participatory interests' which has a similar but wider definition in that the new term can include interests in undertakings which are not companies. A 'participatory interest' is defined as 'an interest held by an undertaking in the shares of another undertaking which it holds on a long-term basis for the purpose of securing a contribution to its activities by the exercise of control or influence arising from or related to that interest. A holding of 20 per cent or more of the shares of an undertaking shall be presumed to be a participatory interest unless the contrary is shown'.

An associated company is not part of the group and its accounts are, therefore, not consolidated with those of other group companies. Instead, the concept of equity accounting is applied, the principles of which are dealt with in Chapter 17.

Preparation of consolidated accounts

The purpose of preparing consolidated accounts is to present the financial results and position of the companies in the group as though they were a single enterprise. Generally, all companies within a group adopt the same accounting year. When the final accounts of all the separate companies in the group have been prepared, the process of preparing group accounts is begun. To put it very simply, consolidated accounts are prepared by aggregating all the individual balance sheets and profit and loss accounts. The balance sheet and profit and loss account of the parent company are used as the basis for compiling the group balance sheet and profit and loss account. Thus, the shareholders of the parent company receive a group balance sheet and group profit and loss account which are expansions of those of the parent company, resulting from adding to the parent company's accounts those of its subsidiaries.

The objective of consolidation is to present the accounts of the group as if it were a single business. This objective requires that all internal group transactions are eliminated and that only the transactions external to the group are recorded in the consolidated accounts. Examples of internal transactions requiring elimination on consolidation include:

1. Intercompany income and expenditure, such as sales, purchases, rents, royalties, interest or dividends.
2. Intercompany profits and losses included in the assets of the group. Typically, this will affect closing stocks resulting from intercompany purchases and comprising the selling company's profit margin on sales. Accordingly, this profit margin must be excluded from the valuation of closing stock and a corresponding adjustment made to net profit. This is discussed further below.
3. Intercompany debts and claims, whether short-term trading accounts or long-term advances.
4. The investment in the subsidiary recorded in the books of the parent company is cancelled with the issued share capital of the subsidiary.

In a simple situation, the above elimination followed by aggregation of the remaining balances is all that is required to produce a consolidated balance sheet and profit and loss account. However, two further adjustment areas should be recognized and will frequently be encountered.

First, if the parent company owns less than 100 per cent of the total issued capital of the subsidiary, a minority interest is said to exist in that subsidiary. These non-group shareholders have an interest in the profits and net assets of the subsidiary which must be reflected in the consolidation process. United Kingdom practice effects the consolidation on a control rather than an ownership basis and then separately recognizes any minority interest. Thus, even if less than 100 per cent of the issued capital of the subsidiary is owned by the parent company, the whole of the assets, liabilities and profit and loss account items of the subsidiary are aggregated with those of the holding company, and the minority interest is then shown separately in the consolidated financial statements. As far as the balance sheet is concerned, it is necessary to compute the non-group shareholders' interest in the net assets (share capital and reserves) of the subsidiary at the balance sheet date. For profit and loss account purposes, the minority shareholders' interest in the post-tax profits for the year of the subsidiary is calculated and deducted in the consolidated profit and loss account.

Reference was made above to the fact that intercompany profits reflected in the assets of the group must be eliminated on consolidation, with an effect on the net profit of the group. The question arises as to how the adjustment to profit should be effected. While a number of possible methods may be encountered (some of which are discussed in Chapter 17), the general approach adopted in this book for illustration purposes is to treat all intercompany profit adjustments as being adjustments to the reserves of the group as a whole without any effect on the reserves of profits of any individual group company. Thus minority interests in subsidiaries are, through this approach, unaffected by the intercompany profit eliminated.

The second additional adjustment area will arise where the parent company purchased shares in an existing, operating subsidiary and paid a price for the shares which differed from their par (or nominal) value. This difference would arise because the parent company perceived that the accumulated profits (or losses) of the subsidiary at acquisition rendered the shares worth more than (less than) their par value. Such profits or losses existing at the date the parent company purchased its interest in the subsidiary are known as preacquisition profits (losses) and are capitalized as part of the consolidation process, i.e. they are removed from the group's reserves figures and, together with the par value of the shares purchased, are compared with the cost of the investment to the parent company.

If the cost of the investment exceeds the total of share capital plus preacquisition reserves purchased, then goodwill arises on consolidation. Should the cost of the investment be less than the total of share capital plus preacquisition reserves purchased, then negative goodwill arises. The current UK accounting practice applicable to goodwill and negative goodwill is discussed in Chapter 17.

There now follows a comprehensive example, together with worked solution, on the preparation of consolidated financial statements. Further practice questions are included at the end of the chapter.

Example

P plc is the parent company of S plc, the only subsidiary in the P Group. The following are their respective balance sheets and profit and loss accounts as at 31 December 19X0.

The following additional information is available:

1 P plc holds two-thirds of the issued share capital of S plc.
2 P plc has an issued capital of £50 000 shares of £10 each.
3 P plc also holds 10 000 shares in N plc acquired at £10 each. This holding represents 2 per cent of the equity of N plc.
4 P plc has made an interest-free loan of £50 000 to S plc, which is repayable in five years.
5 P plc is owed £60 000 by S plc in respect of sales made to the latter by the former. P plc has no outstanding debts towards S plc at the year end.
6 P plc's closing stock comprised £30 000 purchased from S plc. S plc's profit margin on sales is 10 per cent. The opening stocks did not include any stocks acquired from S plc.
7 S plc's closing stock comprised £20 000 purchased from P plc. P plc's profit margin on sales is 20 per cent. The opening stock also included £20 000 purchased from P plc before it became the parent company of S plc.
8 Intercompany trading transactions were as follows:
   P plc purchases from S plc amounted to £200 000 during the year.
   S plc purchases from P plc amounted to £100 000 during the year.

9 P plc leased a building to S plc at an annual rent of £80 000.

10 S plc has paid a dividend of £30 000, being the dividend declared out of the previous year's profits.

11 P plc purchased its interest in S plc on 1 January 19X0.

Balance sheets at 31 December 19X0

	P plc £	P plc £	P plc £	S plc £	S plc £	S plc £
Fixed assets						
Tangible assets		210 000		180 000		
Investments						
Shares in S plc at cost		210 000		—		
Other shares		100 000		—		
Loan to S plc		50 000				
		570 000			180 000	
Current assets						
Stocks	220 000			80 000		
Debtors						
Trade debtors	420 000			260 000		
Owed by S plc	60 000			—		
Cash	130 000			80 000		
	830 000			420 000		
Creditors: amounts falling due within one year:						
Trade creditors	(480 000)			(79 000)		
Owed to P plc	—			(60 000)		
Net current assets		350 000			281 000	
Total assets *less* current liabilities			920 000			461 000
Creditors: amounts falling due after one year:						
Debenture loan		(100 000)			—	
Owed to P plc		—			(50 000)	
			820 000			411 000
Capital and reserves						
Called-up share capital			500 000			300 000
Retained profits brought forward for 19X0			270 000			90 000
Profit and loss account			50 000			21 000
			820 000			411 000

Profit and loss account for the year ended 31 December 19X0

	P plc £	S plc £
Turnover	2 320 000	1 000 000
Cost of sales	1 070 000	500 000
Gross profit	1 250 000	500 000
Expenses	1 250 000	450 000
	0	50 000
Other operating income:		
Rent from S plc	80 000	—
	80 000	50 000
Income from shares in group companies—		
dividend S plc	20 000	—
Profit on ordinary activities	100 000	50 000
Tax on ordinary activities	50 000	29 000
Profit for the year after tax	50 000	21 000

Explanatory notes: consolidated balance sheet as at 31 December 19X0

1. Cancellation of intercompany debts and claims

The rule requiring the cancellation of intercompany debts and claims is applied as follows:

(a) The cancellation of the loan of £50 000 by P plc to S plc. Therefore, it is eliminated from total group assets and total group liabilities, the net effect on the consolidated balance sheet being zero.

(b) The cancellation of the balance of £50 000 owed by S plc to P plc arising from intercompany sales. Therefore, it is eliminated from total group trade debtors and total group trade creditors, the net effect on the consolidated balance sheet being zero.

2. Cancellation of the parent company's investment in the subsidiary company and the cancellation of the subsidiary company's capital and reserves

The rule requiring the cancellation of the parent company's investment in the subsidiary company and the subsidiary company's capital and preacquisition reserves is applied as follows:

(c) The cancellation from total group assets of the shares acquired by P plc in S plc at their cost of £210 000.

The cancellation from total group capital and reserves of the called-up share capital and preacquisition reserves of S plc amounting to £390 000.

Consolidated balance sheet as at 31 December 19X0—worksheet

	P plc	S plc	P+S plc	Cancellation of intercompany debts and claims	Cancellation of parent company's investments in subsidiary and subsidiary's capital and reserves	Cancellation of inter-company profit/losses	Consolidated balance sheet
Fixed assets	£000	£000	£000	£000	£000	£000	£000
Tangible assets	210	180	390				390
Investments							
Shares in S plc	210	—	210		$-210^{(c)}$		—
Other shares	100	—	100				100
Loan to S plc	50		50	$-50^{(a)}$			—
	570	180	750	-50	-210	—	490
Current assets	£	£	£	£		£	£
Stocks	220	80	300			$-7^{(e)}$	293
Debtors							
Trade debtors	420	260	680				680
Owed by S plc	60	—	60	-60			—
Cash	130	80	210				210
	830	420	1 250	$-60^{(b)}$		$-7^{(e)}$	1 183
Creditors: amounts falling due within one year							
Trade creditors	(480)	(79)	(559)				(559)
Owed to P plc		(60)	(60)	$-(60)$			—
	(480)	(139)	(619)	$-(60)^{(b)}$			(559)
Net current assets	350	281	631	$-{}^{(b)}$	—	$-7^{(e)}$	(624)
Total assets *less* current liabilities	£000	£000	£000	£000	£000	£000	£000
	920	461	1 381	$-50^{(a)}$	$-210^{(c)}$	$-7^{(e)}$	1 114
Creditors: amounts falling due after one year:							
Debenture loan	(100)	—	(100)				(100)
Owed to P plc		(50)	(50)	(-50)			—
	820	411	1 231	$-{}^{(a)}$	$-210^{(c)}$	$-7^{(e)}$	1 014
Capital and reserves:	£000	£000	£000		£000	£000	£000
Called-up share capital	500	300	800		$-300^{(c)}$		500
Retained profits brought forward	270	90	360		$-90^{(c)}$		270
Difference on consolidation (nondistributable reserve)					$50^{(c)}$	$+20^{(f)}$	70
Consolidated profit and loss account (19X0)	50	21	71			$-34^{(g)}$	37
Minority interests					$130^{(d)}$	$+7^{(b)}$	137
	820	411	1 231		-210	-7	1 014

(a), (b), (c) etc. refer to the accompanying explanatory notes.

Consolidated profit and loss account for year ended 31 December 19X0—worksheet

	P plc	S plc	P+S plc	Cancellation of intercompany income and expenses	Cancellation of profit on intercompany closing stock	Cancellation of inter-company distributions	Consolidated profit and loss a/c
	£000	£000	£000	£000	£000	£000	£000
Turnover	2 320	1 000	3 320	−300[i]			3 020
Cost of sales	(1 070)	(500)	(1 570)	+300[i]	(−7)[k]		(1 277)
Gross profit	1 250	500	1 750	—	(−7)[k]		1 743
Expenses	(1 250)	(450)	(1 700)	+80[j]			(1 620)
Operating profit	0	50	50	+80	(−7)		123
Other operating income:							
Rent from S plc	80	—	80	−80[j]			—
Total operating profit	80	50	130	—	(−7)		123
Income from shares in group companies:							
Dividend S plc	20	—	20			(20)[l]	—
Profit on ordinary activities	100	50	150	—	(−7)	(20)	123
Tax on ordinary activities	(50)	(29)	(79)				(79)
Profit for year after tax	50	21	71	—	(−7)[k]	(20)[l]	44
Minority interest in S plc's profit after tax for the year (⅓×21)							(7)[m]
Consolidated profit for the year							37

The substitution in the consolidated capital and reserves of a sum representing the difference between the value of the group's interest in the net worth of the subsidiary as against the cost at which this interest was acquired by the parent company. It is calculated as shown on p. 296.

The negative goodwill is added to reserves on the consolidated balance sheet. (For the effect of the dividend paid by S plc on this figure, see (f).)

	£
S plc: Called-up share capital	300 000
Reserves	90 000
	390 000

	£
P plc: Two-thirds interest therein	260 000
Less: Cost of acquisition	210 000
Difference on consolidation ('negative goodwill')	50 000

(d) Where the subsidiary company is not wholly owned, the interest of minority shareholders has to be recognized on consolidation. It is shown as an external liability of the group, and is calculated as follows:

		£
S plc Called-up share capital		300 000
Preacquisition reserves		90 000
		390 000
		£
Share of minority interests ⅓ thereof		130 000

This is subject to further adjustment for 19X0 profits—see (h) below.

3. Cancellation of intercompany profit/losses

The rule requiring the cancellation of intercompany profits/losses is applied as follows:

(e) The closing stocks held by P plc and S plc resulting from intercompany transactions contain an intercompany profit element which has to be eliminated from the valuation of closing stocks calculated as follows:

	£	£
P plc closing stocks purchased from S plc	30 000	
Intercompany profits thereon being S plc's gross profit margin of 10 per cent		3 000
	£	
S plc closing stock purchased from P plc	20 000	
Intercompany profits thereon, being P plc's gross profit margin of 20 per cent		4 000
Intercompany profit included in closing stocks		7 000

(f) The dividend of £30 000 paid by S plc was in respect of the previous year's profits, i.e. a year before S plc became a subsidiary of P plc. The £20 000 of the dividend received by P plc is a dividend received out of preacquisition profits and as such must be capitalized on consolidation.

In the books of P plc this £20 000 should have been credited to the investment account not to profit, since it represents a return to P plc of part of the cost of its investment in S plc. Since this has not been done in the books of P plc, the adjustment must be effected on consolidation.

In the light of this, the negative goodwill arising on consolidation per note (c) above requires adjustment as follows:

Two-thirds interest in the capital and pre-acquisition reserves of S plc (⅔ × £390 000)		£260 000
Cost of investment	£210 000	
less: Preacquisition dividend	(20 000)	190 000
Difference on consolidation (negative goodwill)		£70 000

(g) The group's consolidated profits for 19X0 have to be calculated, and since no dividends were paid, the sum calculated will be shown on the balance sheet as at 31 December 19X0 as the profit and loss account balance for the year. It is calculated as shown below.

	£	£
Total profits of P plc and S plc as shown		71 000
less: Cancellation of intercompany profits on consolidation:		
Cancellation effected in respect of P plc:		
Dividends received from S plc	20 000	
Cancellation of profit element on closing stock held by S plc and sold by P plc (note (e))	4 000	
Cancellation effected in respect of S plc:		
Cancellation of profit element on closing stocks held by P plc and sold by S plc (note (e))	3 000	27 000
less: Share of minority interests in S plc's profit—⅓		44 000
of £21 000		7 000
		37 000

In accordance with the approach outlined earlier in this chapter, the minority interest in the 19X0 profits of S plc is unaffected by the intercompany profit elimination.

(h) It remains to show total amounts relating to minority interest, i.e.

	£
Share of S plc's profits, calculated as above	7 000
Share of capital and preacquisition reserves (note (d))	130 000
	137 000

Explanatory notes: consolidated profit and loss account for the year to 31 December 19X0

1. Cancellation of intercompany income and expenses

The rule requiring the cancellation of intercompany incomes and expenses is applied as follows:

(i) Intercompany sales and purchases are cancelled, as follows:

	£
P plc sales to S plc	100 000
S plc sales to P plc	200 000
—	300 000

	£
P plc purchases from S plc	200 000
S plc purchases from P plc	100 000
—	300 000

It will be noted that these are, at this stage, self-cancelling adjustments as regards the consolidated gross profit.

(*j*) Other intercompany income and expenses are cancelled, as follows:

	£
S plc rent paid to P plc	80 000

	£
P plc rent income received from P plc	80 000

It will be noted that these are likewise self-cancelling adjustments as regards consolidated operating profits.

2. Cancellation of intercompany profits on closing stocks resulting from intercompany transactions

The rule requiring the cancellation of intercompany profits on closing stocks resulting from intercompany transactions is applied as follows:

(*k*) The intercompany profits on closing stocks amounting to £7000, as calculated above (see (*g*)) have to be eliminated from the consolidated profits. This is most conveniently effected by increasing cost of sales by £7000, the amount of the profit to be eliminated.

3. Cancellation of intercompany distributions

The rule requiring the cancellation of intercompany distributions is applied as follows:

(*l*) The cancellation of intercompany distributions from group profits on consolidation means that the dividends received by P plc from S plc must be eliminated from the consolidated profits. Accordingly, the dividends amounting to £20 000 are eliminated from group revenues. Note (*f*) above pointed out that this is a preacquisition dividend, capitalized on consolidation.

4. Minority interest

The outside shareholders' interest in the subsidiary's net profit after tax for the year is calculated and deducted in the consolidated profit and loss account: ⅓ × £21 000 = £7000.

Problems

1 Set out below are the balance sheets for Macro plc and Micro plc as at 31 December 19X8.

Balance sheets as at 31 December 19X8

	Macro plc			Micro plc		
	£000	£000	£000	£000	£000	£000
Fixed assets						
Tangible assets		5 121			1 230	
Investments						
Shares in						
Micro plc		962			—	
		6 083			1 230	
Current assets						
Stocks	1 244			514		
Debtors						
Trade debtors	2 048			390		
Owed by						
Micro plc	57			—		
Cash at bank	960			46		
	4 309			950		
Creditors: amounts falling due within one year						
Trade creditors	(2 825)			(634)		
Owed to P plc	—			(40)		
Taxation	(315)			(60)		
Net current assets		1 169			216	
Total assets *less* current liabilities			7 252			1 446
Creditors: amounts falling due after one year:						
Debenture loan			(750)			—
			6 502			1 446

	£000	£000
Capital and reserves		
Called-up share capital	1 800	600
Reserves brought forward	4 050	702
Profit and loss account—19X8	652	144
	6 502	1 446

Macro plc bought its holding of 400 000 ordinary shares in Micro plc when the latter's reserves stood at £312 000.

During the year ended 31 December 19X8, Macro plc regularly sold products to Micro plc at a selling price of cost plus 33⅓ per cent. At 31 December 19X8, Micro plc's closing stock included £208 000 purchased from Macro plc.

The difference between the Micro plc's current account of £57 000 shown under debtors on Macro plc's balance sheet and Macro plc's current account of £40 000 shown under creditors on Micro plc's balance sheet is due to the fact that a cheque of £17 000 mailed by Micro plc on 31 December 19X8 was not received by Macro plc until 5 January 19X9.

Required:

Prepare a consolidated balance sheet for the Macro Group as at 31 December 19X8.

2   P plc is the parent company of S plc, the only subsidiary in the P Group. The following are their respective balance sheets and profit and loss accounts as at 31 December 19X0:

Balance sheets at 31 December 19X0

	P plc			S plc		
	£000	£000	£000	£000	£000	£000
Fixed assets						
Tangible assets		40 000			20 000	
Investments						
Shares in S plc		12 000			—	
Other shares		3 000			—	
		55 000			20 000	
Current assets						
Stocks	7 100			6 600		
Debtors						
Trade debtors	8 000			4 000		
Owed by S plc	3 500			—		
Cash	3 400			2 400		
	22 000			13 000		
Creditors: amounts falling due within one year:						
Trade creditors	(12 000)			(10 250)		
Owed to P plc	—			(3 500)		
Net current assets		10 000			(750)	
Total assets less current liabilities			65 000			19 250
Creditors: amounts falling due after one year:						
Debenture loan		(23 000)				
		42 000				19 250
		£000				£000
Capital and reserves						
Called-up share capital		30 000				15 000
Reserves brought forward		10 000				4 000
Profit and loss account for 19X0		2 000				250
		42 000				19 250

Profit and loss accounts for the year ended 31 December 19X0

	P plc £000	S plc £000
Turnover	300 800	150 500
Cost of sales	116 900	59 400
Gross profit	183 900	91 100
Expenses	180 400	88 600
Operating income	3 500	2 500

Income from shares in group companies:		
Dividend S plc	500	—
Profit on ordinary activities	4 000	2 500
Tax on ordinary activities	2 000	1 500
Profit for the year after tax	2 000	1 000
Dividend	—	750
	2 000	250

The following additional information is also available:

1   P plc holds two-thirds of the issued share capital of S plc, comprising 1 000 000 shares of £10 acquired at £12 each.

2   P plc also holds 200 000 shares of £10 in N plc acquired for £3 000 000 representing 10 per cent of the called-up capital N plc.

3   P plc is owed £3 500 000 by S plc in respect of sales made to the latter by the former. P plc has no outstanding debts towards S plc at the year end, and does not purchase stock from S plc.

4   S plc's closing stock included £5 000 000 purchased from P plc. P plc's profit margin on sales is 20 per cent. S plc's opening stock did not include any stock purchased from P plc. Total sales from P to S during the year were £15 000 000.

5   P plc purchased its shares in S plc on 1 January 19X0.

6   The dividend received by P plc from S plc is a distribution in respect of the year 19X0 profits of S plc.

Required:
Prepare consolidated accounts for the group.

3   The balance sheets of Expanding plc and its two subsidiaries Growing plc and Declining plc as at 31 December 19X0 were as follows:

Balance sheets at 31 December 19X0

	Expanding plc	Growing plc	Declining plc
	£000	£000	£000
Fixed assets			
Tangible assets	525	210	60
Investments			
100 000 shares Growing plc	140	—	—
40 000 shares Declining plc	32	—	—
	697	210	60
Current assets			
Stocks	63	83	28
Debtors			
Trade debtors	60	36	15
Growing plc	24	—	—
Declining plc	16	9	—
Cash at bank	10	7	2
Creditors: amounts falling due within one year:			
Trade creditors	(120)	(68)	(46)
Expanding plc	—	(22)	(16)
Growing plc	—	—	(8)
Net current assets	53	45	(25)
Total assets *less* current liabilities	750	255	35

	£000	£000	£000
Capital and reserves			
Called-up share capital (£1 shares)	400	150	50
Reserves brought forward	200	45	—
Profit and loss account for 19X0	150	60	(15)
	750	255	35

The following additional information is available:

1 At 31 December 19X0, goods transferred at cost £2000 were in transit between Expanding plc and Growing plc. A cheque for £1000 was in transit between Declining plc and Growing plc.

2 The closing stock of Expanding plc included goods supplied by Growing plc at an invoiced value of £3600. Growing plc had priced these goods at cost plus 20 per cent, the standard group markup.

3 Expanding plc purchased all its investments in its subsidiaries on 1 January 19X0.

Required
Prepare a consolidated balance sheet for the Expanding Group as at 31 December 19X0.

4 The balance sheets of Pip plc and its two subsidiaries Squeak plc and Wilfred plc as at 31 March 19X1 were as follows:

Balance sheets at 31 March 19X1

	Pip plc	Squeak plc	Wilfred plc
	£000	£000	£000
Fixed assets			
Tangible assets	315	120	77
Investments			
80 000 shares in Squeak plc	110	—	—
50 000 shares in Wilfred plc	45	—	—
Debentures in Squeak plc	5	—	—
	475	120	77
Current assets	250	70	41
Creditors: amounts falling due within one year:			
Trade creditors	(100)	(20)	(30)
Proposed dividends			
Ordinary	(50)	(10)	—
Preference	—	(1)	—
Net current assets	100	39	11
Total assets less current liabilities	575	159	88
Creditors: amounts falling due after more than one year:			
Debenture loan	—	(20)	—
	575	139	88

	£000	£000	£000
Capital and reserves			
Called-up share capital			
Ordinary shares of £1	500	100	80
10% Preference share	—	10	—
General reserves	—	10	—
Profit and loss account	75	19	8
	575	139	88

The profit and loss accounts for the year ended 31 March 19X0 were as follows:

	Pip plc £000	Squeak plc £000	Wilfred plc £000
Balance at 31.3.X0	50	10	(2.4)
Dividend received from			
Squeak plc	2	—	—
Net profit for year	73	32.5	10.4
	125	42.5	8
Transfer to general reserves	—	(10)	—
Dividends paid, ordinary shares		(2.5)	
Proposed dividends			
Ordinary shares	(50)	(10)	—
Preferred shares	—	(1)	—
Balance at 31.3.X1	75	19	8

The following additional information is given:

1 The parent company purchased all its shares in its subsidiaries on 1 April 19X0.
2 There is no intragroup trading.
3 The parent company has recorded only dividend income received from its subsidiaries.

Required
Prepare a consolidated balance sheet for the year ended 31 March 19X1.

Chapter 17

Understanding consolidated financial statements

Accounting for groups of companies is an important area of financial accounting by reason of the tendency of companies to grow by forming or acquiring subsidiary companies. Financial reporting for groups of companies by means of consolidated year-end accounting reports is complicated by a number of problems, which fall into two classes. First, there are technical problems of dealing with the complexity of data to be treated when preparing consolidated accounts. These problems have been explained in outline form in the previous chapter. Second, there are problems of understanding the nature of the consolidation process as it affects the meaning of the information which they contain. This chapter deals with the following topics which are central to understanding consolidated financial statements:

1 minority interests present in subsidiaries that are less than 100 per cent owned;
2 the accounting treatment of associated companies;
3 mergers and acquisitions;
4 goodwill on consolidation;
5 horizontal, vertical and conglomerate groups;
6 multinational groups.

The purpose of this chapter is to provide an introductory overview of the theory and practice of accounting for these complexities.

Accounting for minority interests

In this section, we discuss the problems of accounting for minority interests in consolidated accounts, where a parent–subsidiary relationship exists requiring the full consolidation of the balance sheets and profit and loss accounts of companies so defined.

The assets, liabilities, revenues and expenses of the subsidiary must be consolidated in full with those of the parent company. The procedure for consolidation requires the elimination of intercompany transactions. The minority interests are represented as a separate item on the consolidated balance sheet and the consolidated profit and loss account.

The problems relating to the recognition of minority interests in consolidated financial statements will be considered under the following headings:

1 the nature of the minority interest;
2 calculations required to quantify the minority interest;
3 the treatment of the elimination of extra group profits as far as the minority interest is concerned.

The nature of the minority interest

The question to be addressed here is: what is the nature of the minority interest, as reflected on a consolidated balance sheet? Two principal views exist. One view (the parent company concept) recognizes the parent company as being dominant in its relationship with the minority interest. The minority interest as depicted on the consolidated balance sheet is viewed as a liability of the group rather than a co-owner of the group. One result of this is that no attempt is made under this concept to attribute any goodwill relating to the holding company's acquisition of the subsidiary to the minority interest.

Example 1

H plc purchased 90 per cent of the issued capital of S plc for £90 000 when the net assets of S plc (at fair value) amounted to £80 000.

On consolidation, goodwill of £18 000 arises (i.e. £90 000 – 90 per cent of £80 000). Under the parent company concept, no attempt is made to attribute goodwill to the other 10 per cent of the capital held by the minority interest. (Any goodwill which was so attributed could be quantified as

$$\frac{£18\ 000}{9} = £2000$$

This could be added to goodwill and to minority interest on consolidation.)

SSAP 14 states that the minority interest on a consolidated balance sheet should not be classified as part of shareholders' funds, thus indicating that UK standard practice adopts a parent company approach to the minority interest.

The alternative view is expressed in the entity concept which treats the parent company and the minority as partners or co-owners in the subsidiary. Under this concept, the minority interest is classified as part of shareholders' funds, and in quantifying the amount of that interest, parent company and minority would both be treated alike. Thus, referring back to Example 1, goodwill would be treated as being £20 000 (not £18 000) with £2000 of that goodwill being added to the minority interest as shown on the consolidated balance sheet.

The calculation of minority interests

The objective of calculating minority interests on consolidation can be summarized as follows:

- for balance sheet purposes: to show the interest of the nongroup shareholders in the net assets of the group as at the relevant balance sheet date;
- for profit and loss account purposes: to show the nongroup shareholders' interest in the profit after tax for the year of the subsidiary.

As far as the calculations are concerned, care is needed whenever there is more than one class of capital in the subsidiary, especially if the minority interest differs between the classes.

Example 2

Extracts from the financial statements of S plc for the year to 31 March 19X5 show the following.

Balance sheet		Profit and loss account	
Called-up capital:			
£1 ordinary shares	£500 000	Profit after tax	£65 000
£1 8% preference shares	50 000	Preference dividend:	
	550 000	Paid	(20 000)
		Proposed	(20 000)
Reserves:			
Retained profits	160 000	Ordinary dividend:	
	£710 000	Proposed	(15 000)
Net assets	£710 000	Retained for the year	£10 000

It is known that H plc owns 80 per cent of the issued ordinary capital of S plc and 50 per cent of the issued 8 per cent preference shares.

The calculation of the relevant minority interest figures is as follows:

Profit and loss account

		Minority interest
Profit after tax	£65 000	
less: Preference dividends	(40 000) × 50%	£20 000
Equity profits	£25 000 × 20%	£5 000
Total minority interest for the consolidated profit and loss account		£25 000

Balance sheet

	Minority interest
Called-up share capital:	
Ordinary: £500 000 × 20%	£100 000
Preference: £50 000 × 50%	25 000
Reserves (all preference dividends have been paid or proposed—so consider equity interest only)	
£160 000 × 20%	32 000
Minority interest for the consolidated balance sheet	£157 000

Intragroup profit elimination

As mentioned in Chapter 16, a number of differing views exist as to how adjustments to eliminate unrealized intragroup profits should be effected on consolidation. In some circumstances, the minority interest in the subsidiary may be affected by the choice of elimination method.

One view (as adopted for illustrative purposes in this book) is that the elimination of unrealized intragroup profits is purely a 'consolidation' adjustment and is therefore dealt with in total group profits or reserves, without allocating the adjustment to any specific company. On this view, where a subsidiary sells to a parent company and the goods remain in stock, the calculation of any minority interest in that subsidiary is unaffected by the profit elimination.

A second approach is to allocate the profit adjustment to the accounts of the group company which sold the stock in question. Here, if S plc sells to P plc and the stock remains in the parent company's balance sheet, any profit recorded by S plc on the transaction could be removed from its profit figure. Consequently, the calculation of any minority interest in S plc will be based on the adjusted (reduced) profit figure.

A third approach would, as in method one, treat any adjustment as a group adjustment but limit the adjustment to an amount equal to the parent company's percentage interest in the profits of the selling subsidiary.

Example 3

H plc has owned 80 per cent of the issued capital of S plc since the incorporation of that company. During the year to 31 December 19X5, S plc sold goods to H plc at a profit of £10 000, these goods were unsold by H plc at 31 December. The retained profits per the accounts of the two companies at 31 December 19X5 were H plc £100 000, S plc £50 000. The issued capital of S plc was £60 000 in £1 ordinary shares. The stocks in the balance sheets of the separate companies were H plc £250 000; S plc £170 000.

The three methods outlined above give the following results:

	Method one	Method two	Method three
Profit adjustment	£	£	£
Group reserves	10 000		
S plc reserves		10 000	
Group reserves (80% × 10 000)			8 000
Consolidated reserves	£	£	£
H plc	100 000	100 000	100 000
S plc (80% of £50 000)	40 000		40 000
Profit adjustment	(10 000)	(80% × 10 000)	(8 000)
S plc (80% × 50 000 − 10 000)	£130 000	32 000	£132 000
		132 000	
Minority interest for balance sheet	£	£	£
Subsidiary's capital	60 000	60 000	60 000
Subsidiary's reserves	50 000		50 000
(50 000 − 10 000)		40 000	
	110 000	100 000	110 000
Minority interest (20%)	£22 000	£20 000	£22 000
Consolidated stocks	£	£	£
H plc	250 000	250 000	250 000
S plc	170 000	170 000	170 000
	420 000	420 000	420 000
less: adjustment	(10 000)	(10 000)	(8 000)
	410 000	410 000	412 000

All these methods will be found in practice (together with others not covered here). It should be appreciated that no one method is viewed as being correct and often the amounts involved are immaterial in relation to the group's results and net assets.

Accounting for associated companies

The definition of an associated company was dealt with in Chapter 16. Here it is necessary to consider in detail the accounting treatment required by SSAP 1 in the group accounts.

It will be recalled that an associated company is essentially one over which the investing company exercises a participating interest, but not control. The associate is not consolidated in the group accounts, but instead is dealt with under the equity method of accounting for investments.

This method sets out to state the investment in the associate on the consolidated balance sheet, not at cost but at a figure approximating to the value of the equity interest in the associated. Also, because of the existence of participating interest, the profit and loss account includes the investing company's share of profits of the associated, not just divided income.

Table 2.4 summarizes and compares the equity accounting method with the consolidation method, and Example 4 then shows the SSAP 1 balance sheet presentation of an investment in an associated company.

Table 2.4 Summary and comparison of equity, accounting and consolidation

	Consolidation	Equity accounting
Profit and loss account	The dividend from the subsidiary is eliminated.	The dividend from the associate is eliminated.
	The profit and loss account captions of the subsidiary are aggregated with those of the parent company.	The consolidated profit and loss account includes as a separate item the group's share of the profits and tax of the associate.
	A separate minority interest is calculated and disclosed.	No separate minority interest adjustment is necessary.
Balance sheet	The separate assets and liabilities of the subsidiary are aggregate with those of the parent company.	The investment account is retained, but stated at its equity value (per SSAP 1) i.e.
	The investment account and other internal items are cancelled.	Share of net assets of the associate (less goodwill)　　　　　x Share of the associate's goodwill　　x premium/discount on acquisition　　x x 　　　　　　　　　x

Example 4

Octopus plc acquired a block of shares in Guppy plc for £100 000 on 1 January 19X0, giving it 25 per cent of the called-up capital. At that date the called-up capital and reserves of Guppy plc amounted to £360 000. In the balance sheet of Octopus plc, these shares would be shown at their historic cost of £100 000. On consolidation, Guppy plc would be defined as an associated company. Guppy plc's capital and reserves amount to £600 000 at 31 December 19X0, the net profit for the year being £240 000. Applying the equity method, the interest of the Octopus Group in Guppy plc will be shown as follows:

Consolidated balance sheet 31 December 19X0

	£
Fixed assets	
Investments:	
Shares in related company:	
25% of net assets (25% × £600 000)	150 000
Premium on acquisition (£100 000 − 25% × £360 000)	10 000
	160 000

The premium on acquisition above is, of course, purchased goodwill, the treatment of which is described below:

Mergers and acquisitions

Groups of companies may be formed in two ways. First, a parent company may form a subsidiary company. This is often the case of 100-per-cent-owned subsidiary companies. Second, a company may purchase shares in another company, that company becoming a subsidiary through a business combination.

Business combinations are a frequent topic of discussion in the financial press. They may result from discussions between two companies on the benefits which would flow from a merger of their business. On the other hand, negotiations between two companies may involve the acquisition of one company by the other. This is frequently the case of the big company acquiring a small successful company. They may also result from aggressive expansionist policies of a company seeking to take over another company. In this case, the takeover will take the form of an acquisition of its shares by bidding up a price which will induce shareholders to sell them to the bidding company.

Current practice recognizes these differing situations by employing two different methods of recording business combinations in consolidated accounts:

1   the purchase method (for acquisitions);
2   the pooling of interest method (for mergers).

The purchase method

Under this, the consolidated balance sheet includes the assets and liabilities of the subsidiary at their cost to the group rather than at the values at which they are shown in the subsidiary's balance sheet.

The purchase method requires first the acquisition cost of the subsidiary to be established as a total by reference to the amount of cash paid and the value of shares exchanged for its shares. The second stage is to allocate the acquisition cost to the particular assets and liabilities of the subsidiary. The EC Seventh Directive gives little by way of guidelines on how this difficult task is to be performed, except to say that the acquisition cost should be allocated as much as possible to all identifiable assets and liabilities. SSAP 14 includes a similar requirement, stating that allocation should be on the basis of the 'fair value' of the assets to the buying company. Any difference between the value of the subsidiary's net assets and the purchase consideration represents goodwill—positive or negative (see below).

The pooling method

Here, the business combination is treated as a merger which forms a new business as the result of the pooling of the assets and liabilities of two previously separate and independent businesses. The merger of two companies does not necessarily imply that one company disappears by liquidation. Frequently, mergers are implemented by the formation of a holding company to which the shares of the merging companies are transferred in exchange for shares in the holding company.

If the merging companies remain in business, but operate in the context of a group, then year-end consolidated accounts will have to be prepared. Accounting for mergers recognizes the ongoing nature of the business by the pooling of the interests of the two companies. The assets and liabilities of both companies are therefore simply added together at the value at which they appear in the separate balance sheets, without 'fair value' adjustments arising.

The difference in the accounting treatment of acquisitions and mergers is highlighted by the fact that the former generally leads to the creation of goodwill (which was discussed in Chapter 12), while the latter avoids it completely. Merger accounting was formally recognized in the Companies Act 1981, and the Accounting Standards Committee has issued SSAP 23 'Accounting for Acquisitions and Mergers'. The Companies Act 1989 effectively gives statutory backing to SSAP 23 by requiring that the use of merger accounting must accord with generally accepted accounting practice.

A business combination *may* be treated as a merger rather than as an acquisition in the following circumstances only:

1   if it results from an offer to all equity holders (and all holders of other voting shares), and
2   if the offer is accepted by at least 90 per cent of the equity shareholders (by value and by votes), and
3   if the new parent company did not hold more than 20 per cent of the equity or votes immediately before the merger, and
4   if at least 90 per cent of the fair value of the purchase consideration is in the form of equity shares.

Note that if the above four conditions are satisfied, the business combination *may* be accounted for on a merger basis, but it is not compulsory to do so. However, if the above four conditions are not satisfied, the combination *must* be accounted for as an acquisition.

ED 48, Accounting for Acquisitions and Mergers, which was published in 1990, seeks to introduce a new set of criteria for defining a merger, based on the guiding principle that the combining companies should be substantially equal partners with neither of them being identifiable as the acquirer or acquiree. The detailed conditions to be satisfied are all of the following:

(a) neither party sees itself as acquirer or acquiree;
(b) neither party dominates the management of the combined entity;
(c) the equity shareholders of neither party have, or could have, disposed of a material part of their shareholdings, directly or indirectly, for shares carrying reduced rights in the combined enterprise or any non-equity consideration. (This would prevent transactions involving

vendor placings from qualifying, as well as deals involving straight cash consideration);

(d) no minority interests of more than 10 per cent of the equity remain in any of the enterprises to whom an offer is made;

(e) neither of the combining parties is more than 50 per cent larger than the other, unless special circumstances (which could include voting and share agreements) prevent the larger from dominating the other; and

(f) the share of the equity in the combination allocated to any party to it does not depend on the post-combination performance of the business previously controlled by that party. (This rules out deals involving earn-out clauses.)

As can be seen, these rules are quite different from those presently contained within SSAP 23, which are focused more on the mechanics of the transaction. The proposed rules are extremely restrictive and very few transactions would qualify for merger accounting.

Merger accounting: main principles

The principles of consolidated accounts outlined in Chapter 16 followed acquisition principles. It is now necessary to summarize the main points of merger accounting.

SSAP 23 recommends the following accounting method for mergers. The shares transferred to the holding company as part of a merger should be recorded in the books of the holding company at the nominal value of the shares issued in exchange. No share premium is recognized or necessary on the new shares issued by the holding company. As a consequence of using the nominal value the only difference to be dealt with on consolidation will be the difference between the nominal value of the shares issued as consideration by the holding company and the nominal value of the shares transferred by the shareholders of the new subsidiary company to the holding company. Where the nominal value of the shares issued is less than that of the shares transferred the differences should be treated as a reserve (nondistributable) arising on consolidation. If the nominal value of the shares issued is greater than that of the shares received in exchange, the difference is the extent to which the reserves of the subsidiary have in effect been capitalized consequent on the merger, and this difference should therefore be treated on consolidation primarily as a reduction of the existing reserves; it should be applied first against any unrealized surplus and second against revenue income or realized surpluses. Essentially, this indicates that to the extent that reserves are regarded as capitalized, non-distributable reserves are capitalized before distributable reserves.

Where there is some additional consideration in some form other than equity shares, for example cash or loan stock, the value of such additional consideration should be included by adding it to the nominal value of the shares issued by the holding company, so as to arrive at the total consideration paid for the shares in the merged subsidiary, and this total of the consideration would be debited to the investment in the subsidiary account. By following these procedures the reserves in the consolidated accounts will thus be either:

1 the total of the reserves of the constituent companies increased by any reserve arising on consolidation; or
2 the total of the reserves of the constituent companies reduced by any part of the reserves of subsidiaries which have been in effect capitalized as a result of the merger.

Example 5

In this example the reserves of the constituent companies are increased by a reserve arising on consolidation.

P Ltd has just increased its share capital by issuing 70 000 ordinary shares of £1 each plus a cash payment of £10 000 to gain 90 per cent control of the issued share capital of S Ltd. The separate balance sheets of the two companies immediately after the merger are as follows.

	P Ltd	S Ltd
	£	£
Ordinary shares of £1 each	270 000	100 000
Revaluation reserve		20 000
Revenue reserves	50 000	30 000
	320 000	150 000
	£	£
Fixed and current assets *less* liabilities	240 000	150 000
Investment—shares in S Ltd	80 000	
	320 000	150 000

Note that the cost of the shares in S Ltd is recorded in the books of P Ltd at the nominal value of the shares issued in exchange (£70 000) plus the value of any additional consideration (£10 000 in cash). The 70 000 ordinary shares of £1 each will have been issued at a premium (they must have been to comply with condition (d) above that 90 per cent in *value* of the offer is in equity voting capital) but such premium is not recognized when using the merger- or pooling-of-interest method. In preparing the consolidated balance sheet the investment account in P's books is set against the nominal value of the shares purchased in S Ltd, thus:

		£
Nominal value of shares in S Ltd pooled by P Ltd		90 000
Cost of investment in S Ltd:		
Shares at nominal value	70 000	
Cash	10 000	
		80 000
Capital reserve arising on consolidation		10 000

and the full consolidated balance sheet appears as under:

Consolidated balance sheet after merger

	£
Ordinary shares of £1 each	270 000
Capital reserve arising on consolidation	10 000
Revaluation reserve (90% × 20 000)	18 000
Revenue reserves (50 000 + 90% × 30 000)	77 000
Minority interest (10% × 150 000)	15 000
	390 000
Fixed and current assets *less* liabilities	390 000

The minority interest is calculated in the same manner in a merger as in an acquisition.

Example 6

In this example the nominal value of the shares issued by P Ltd exceeds the nominal value of the shares purchased in S Ltd, and the excess is treated as a capitalization or reserves of the subsidiary. The facts are as in the previous example, but P Ltd issues 110 000 £1 ordinary shares plus cash of £10 000 to gain control of a 90 per cent shareholding in S Ltd. In this case the separate balance sheets of the two companies immediately after the merger are as follows:

	P Ltd	S Ltd
	£	£
Ordinary shares of £1 each	310 000	100 000
Revaluation reserve		20 000
Revenue reserves	50 000	30 000
	360 000	150 000
	£	£
Fixed and current assets *less* liabilities	240 000	150 000
Investment—shares in S Ltd	120 000	
	360 000	150 000

The book value of the shares held by P Ltd in S Ltd is compared with the par value of the shares acquired, thus:

Cost of investment	£120 000
Nominal value acquired (90%)	90 000
Excess	£ 30 000

This excess is to be offset against group reserves, unrealized first, then realized. Thus:

Offset against revaluation reserve (90% × £20 000)	£18 000
Offset against revenue reserves (balance)	12 000
	£30 000

The consolidated balance sheet will be as follows:

Consolidated balance sheet after merger

	£
Ordinary shares of £1 each	310 000
(Capital reserves—nil)	
Revenue reserves (50 000 + 27 000 − 12 000)	65 000
Minority interest	15 000
	390 000
Fixed and current assets *less* liabilities	£390 000

The above examples illustrate that one of the major differences between acquisition and merger accounting lies in the treatment of the reserves of the subsidiary at the date of acquisition. The acquisition (purchase) approach regards these as capitalized at the date of the takeover against the purchase price. The purchase price is based on a realistic assessment of the current values of the shares issued by the parent company. So where the purchase price exceeds the value placed on the proportion of the net assets acquired in the subsidiary, a difference, or figure for goodwill, will arise. The merger or pooling method regards the situation as being one where previously independent companies have merged as voluntary partners and that consolidation should be the mere amalgamation of balance sheets. Taking the valuation of the shares exchanged at face or par value is a mere bookkeeping device to cancel out the shares issued by P Ltd against those of S Ltd on consolidation, with any resulting difference being treated as an increase in reserves (Example 5 above) or as a capitalization of existing reserves (Example 6 above).

Multinational groups

Multinational groups face a number of complex accounting problems, which result from the economic, legal, organizational, managerial and fiscal environment in which they operate. Given that nation states see problems at a national level and set up rules for the conduct of business that reflect national interests, and that multinationals see problems at a global level, it follows that the resolution of conflict is a major preoccupation of multinational groups.

Conflict of accounting principles and procedures

A number of countries have codified accounting systems for business in the form of uniform charts of accounts, to which companies must adhere. In France, for example, the *Plan Comptable Révisé* is a nationalized accounting system setting out classes of accounts, detailing for each class the names of accounts and ascribing to them a number. In accordance with French commercial law, accounts are properly kept only if they accord with the *Plan Comptable Révisé*. A French subsidiary of a US multinational is required to keep its accounts in accordance with the *Plan Comptable Révisé*. At the same time, it must report year-end results for consolidation purposes to the US in the form which fits US practice, which is based upon GAAP (generally accepted accounting principles). This means that the same accounting data must be rehashed again before it is suitable for consolidation. Moreover, French tax law regulates such items as depreciation charges and provisions, and in this way they regulate the extent to which amounts may be charged as expenses. In effect, the accounting profit and the taxable profit correspond closely as a result. When consolidating the accounts of the French subsidiary with the US parent, they must be redrafted to conform with US tax laws. The resolution of these conflicts of accounting and tax rules imposes a heavy burden of work on the French subsidiary.

The International Accounting Standards Board has produced a number of standards to help reduce these problems. It is also the objective of the EC Fourth and Seventh Directives to increase uniformity of accounting principles and methods, but the extent to which harmonization is possible is limited by fundamental differences in the institutions of nations.

The currency problem

The currency problem has two aspects. The financial aspect is the most important and complex one, for it involves the management of corporate resources across different currencies which fluctuate daily on world currency markets. Financial management decisions, the evaluation of investment and of corporate performance, the management of international cash balances and the avoidance of exchange risks are all part of this management problem. Generally, multinationals adopt a base currency as the functional currency for worldwide operations. For US multinationals, this currency is evidently the US dollar. Some non-US multinationals have found it useful also to adopt the US dollar as the functional currency. Some Dutch multinationals have adopted this option and prepare consolidated accounts in US dollars. This means that budgets are set in one base currency, but local activities involve the use of the local currency. It is possible, therefore, for a subsidiary of a US multinational to have a flexible budget as a result simply of currency movements rather than activity variances.

The currency translation problem

Multinational groups experience the currency translation problem in three different ways:

1   Intercompany transactions across currency borders are realized

transactions which are translated at the rate of exchange ruling at transaction date. It was noted in the previous chapter that these transactions are eliminated on consolidation. Therefore, they would be eliminated at the rate of exchange ruling on transaction date. In practice, this requirement means that intercompany transactions have to be recorded separately from external transactions to facilitate consolidation at year end.

2 Intergroup dividends are also realized transactions involving the movement of funds through remittances. They crystallize on the due rate of payment and are translated at the rate of exchange ruling on that date. Again, intergroup dividends are eliminated on consolidation at the rate of exchange ruling on the due date of payment.

The transactions falling under 1 and 2 above do not involve a problem of choice as to which exchange rate to apply. Moreover, they are eliminated on consolidation, and do not influence the overall presentation of group consolidated accounts.

3 The preparation of consolidated accounts involves the consolidation of all remaining assets, liabilities, revenues and expenses in order to show to shareholders the financial status and the net profit of the group as a single unit. It requires the translation of the profit and loss accounts and balance sheets of all companies within a group into one currency, which is the base currency for the group.

  The rate of exchange which should be applied for that purpose has been the subject of much controversy for two reasons:

(a) The assets, liabilities, expenses and revenues to be translated are not the subject of remittances to the parent company. In the case of assets and liabilities, they remain legal rights and obligations expressed in the local currency of the foreign subsidiary. Moreover, non-current items on the foreign subsidiary's balance sheet such as fixed assets, issued capital and reserves are not considered as involving any currency movements in the short term. In the case of current assets and liabilities, they form the substance of the foreign subsidiary's working capital. Given that intercompany items fall to be eliminated on consolidation, the items consolidated also are unlikely to involve currency movements. The expenses and revenue items on the subsidiary's profit and loss account have been transacted across the accounting period, and to translate them with precise accuracy would mean tracking each transaction at a daily exchange rate, thereby imposing an impossible burden of accounting work. Also, they do not involve currency movements.

(b) The purpose of translating the accounts of foreign subsidiaries into the base currency of the group is to place all companies on to a uniform unit of measurement without infringing the historical cost rule of valuation. The problem lies in defining how the historical cost rule should be applied to the assets, liabilities, expenses and revenues of foreign subsidiaries at the close of each accounting period.

Table 2.5 SSAP 20 translation methods

	Temporal	Closing rate/net investment
1 **Uses of method**	Where the foreign currency transaction has a direct effect on the cash flows of the UK company, i.e. (a) 'individual company stage' (e.g. the UK parent company buying/selling overseas or receiving dividends from the overseas subsidiary); (b) 'consolidation stage' of the overseas entity is seen as being merely an extension of the UK company (e.g. overseas subsidiaries which are —selling agencies —group finance companies —group suppliers)	Used at the consolidation stage only, where the overseas entity is seen to be 'semi-independent' of the UK company. It is envisaged that this method would apply to the translation of the accounts of most subsidiaries for consolidation purposes.
2 **Mechanics of method**	Items are translated at the rate ruling when the amount was established in the accounts, *but* items on the balance sheet that at 'current value' are translated at closing rate. Thus: (a) B/S items are 　Fixed assets 　　at cost—acquisition rate 　　at valuation—valuation rate 　Stocks 　　at cost—acquisition rate 　　at NRV—closing rate 　all monetary items—closing rate; (b) P/L items are: 　All except stocks and depreciation—at average rate for the period 　Stocks—as for balance sheet 　Depreciation—as for the related fixed asset	All balance sheet assets and liabilities are translated at closing rate. All profit and loss account items may be translated at *other* closing rates *or* average for the period.
3 **Accounting for the translation gain/loss**	Viewed as a normal risk/benefit of trading overseas and therefore included in the 'profit on ordinary activities' before taxation.	Viewed as a revaluation in sterling of the net investment in an overseas entity and therefore presented as part of the movement for the period of group reserves, profits being unaffected.

The currency translation debate is centred, therefore, on the issue of applying the historical cost principle in the process of consolidating the accounts of foreign subsidiaries, when the items to be translated do not imply any currency movements at balance sheet date.

Although a large number of translation methods have been put forward and used across the years, much of the debate has been resolved by the issue of SSAP 20 'Accounting for Foreign Currency' which sets out two permitted translation methods together with their uses and the accounting treatment of any resulting translation gain or loss. The two methods of translation permitted by the SSAP are known as the temporal method and the closing-rate/net-investment method. Table 2.5 provides a summary of the main points of each method as outlined in SSAP 20.

The inflation problem

Meaningful comparisons of balance sheets and profit and loss accounts from year to year are rendered impossible under inflationary conditions, when the money unit of measurement becomes unstable. This problem had been recognized in the United Kingdom and in many other countries. Some countries, such as the United Kingdom and the United States, have required companies to disclose the effects of inflation in accounts. There is, however, no international standard for dealing with this problem, nor indeed is there a consensus as to how it should be treated. Multinationals are particularly affected because of the variety of inflation rates to which their business is exposed worldwide.

Moreover, although there is no connection in the short term between speculative changes in exchange rates and levels of domestic inflation, some assert that such a connection may be established in the long term. From an accounting viewpoint, financial statements deal with short-term periods of one year, and consequently fluctuations in exchange rates and changes in rates of domestic inflation may both affect the meaning of consolidated accounts involving foreign subsidiaries.

Problems

1   Consider the following draft data relating to the year ended 31 December 19X1 of Royal plc and Butler plc.

Balance sheets	Royal plc £000	Butler plc £000
Fixed assets (net)—tangible	6 500	4 000
Investment in Butler plc—cost	2 000	
Current assets	3 500	3 000
Current liabilities	(4 550)	(2 500)
Debentures (19×9)	(2 000)	(1 500)
	5 450	3 000
Issued ordinary share capital	2 000	1 000
Reserves	3 450	2 000
	5 450	3 000
Profit and loss accounts		
Operating profit before tax	1 100	500
Dividend from Butler plc including tax credit	143	—
Taxation	(433)	(200)
Profit after tax	810	300
Dividends paid	(300)	(200)
	510	100

Royal plc acquired 50 per cent of the ordinary share capital of Butler plc on 1 January 19X1 for £2 000 000 when its reserves were £1 900 000 and sold this holding on 3 January 19X2 for £2 050 000. Goodwill is written off immediately to reserves.

Required:

(a) prepare the 'group' profit and loss account and balance sheet on three bases: when Butler is treated as (i) a subsidiary (ii) an associated company and (iii) an investment.

(b) comment on the validity of these three alternatives.

2 On 3 July 19X6 Expo plc acquired 95 per cent of the issued share capital of Sition Ltd.

The terms of the merger were as follows:

For every 10 shares held in Sition, the shareholder received 8 shares in Expo at an agreed value of £1.90 per share plus £1.50 unsecured 15 per cent loan stock dated 2006.

The draft accounts for the two companies at 31 December 19X6 were as follows:

	Expo plc (£000)	Sition Ltd (£000)
Balance sheet		
Fixed assets	18 650	10 200
Goodwill at cost		1 000
Investments	9 025	
Current assets	3 550	6 650
Current liabilities	(2 850)	(3 200)
	28 375	14 650
Share capital		
£1 ordinary shares	21 600	10 000
Profit and loss	5 350	4 650
15% loan stock	1 425	
	28 375	14 650
Profit and loss account		
Turnover	12 850	8 500
Profit before tax	3 250	1 300
Taxation	590	30
	2 660	1 270
Dividends	1 200	
Retained profits	1 460	1 270

Notes

(i) It is Expo's policy to write off goodwill over 5 years. Sition has not, to date, written off any goodwill and the balance in their accounts relates to a business bought in 19X5.

(ii) At the date of the takeover, the estimated profit of Sition for the year to date was £600 000.

Required

1 Prepare a consolidated balance sheet and profit and loss account in summary form for Expo group, adopting the merger accounting method in line with SSAP 23.

2 Explain the major differences between your statement and the way in which the same information would have been presented using traditional group accounting practices.

3 Assess the relative strengths and weaknesses of merger and group accounting. Explain why merger accounting has only been applied in the UK since 1981.

Part 3

Financial reporting—
alternative valuation approaches

Introduction

We mentioned in Part 1 that the provision of information to meet the needs of users of accounting information should determine the objectives of an accounting information system. Therefore, the criterion by which the effectiveness of an accounting information system should be judged is the usefulness of its information output for the various purposes to which it is applied. Hence, if we could identify the nature of the decision-problems facing the several groups of persons with vested interests in organizations, we could develop normative theories of accounting which would enable us to construct models for communicating information to these groups.

The reader will recall that in Part 1, we identified the following groups as having vested interests in business organizations, namely, management, shareholders and investors, employees, government, creditors, the local community and customers. In Part 2, we examined the methods used in accounting for selecting, processing and presenting information through the medium of three principal statements, that is, the profit and loss account, the balance sheet and the funds flow statement. These statements and their underlying financial accounting procedures interpret all events in monetary terms, in accordance with the basic accounting convention which limits the recognition of events to those which can be expressed in monetary terms.

In effect, the three principal financial accounting statements have meaning in so far as money itself is meaningful in the context in which information is communicated in these statements. For example, the profit and loss account is concerned with establishing the net profit resulting from the transactions of the period under review, and the balance sheet is concerned with representing the financial position of the business as at the date of the balance sheet. It is clear that, whatever is implied by these two statements, much of their meaning depends upon the significance of the money values attached to the various items on which information is given. For example, if an asset is shown at a valuation of £1000 on the balance sheet, does this mean that it could be sold for £1000? Or, does it mean that it originally cost £1000?

In effect, the process of attaching money measurements to accounting events and items is essentially a process of valuation. Valuation enters into accounting measurements in two senses. First, the money standard of measurement is itself unstable through time. One pound today does not have the same value as one pound yesterday, or one pound tomorrow, since the purchasing power of money over goods and services changes. Second, the use of money measurements in accounting implies a choice between one of several different valuation bases. It is possible to represent the original cost of acquisition of an asset by the enterprise as a representation of a past financial effort. Equally, it is possible to represent the value of an asset to the enterprise in terms of the future net benefits it represents.

Accounting for changes in the value of money is a subject which has long occupied the attention of accounting researchers. It was not until 1975, however, and the publication of the Sandilands Report, that the subject received attention from accountants generally. The ensuing lively debate illustrated the problem of producing a consensus regarding the best method of dealing with price level changes. One reason for the controversy which characterized the inflation accounting debate was due to the failure of accountants to reach agreement on the objectives of financial reports.

In Part 1, various approaches to financial reporting practices were discussed. The stewardship concept of financial reporting is identified with historical cost accounting. This concept focuses on safeguarding assets rather than on presenting measurements useful for decision making. Clearly, financial reports should provide some safeguards against the misuse of assets by management, but they should also provide measurements to shareholders indicative of the efficiency with which assets have been employed. The latter type of measurement is relevant for decision making by shareholders and investors.

This part is concerned with the problems of providing measurements relevant for decision making, rather than dealing with the problems implied in stewardship accounting. The analysis of the problems involved in the provision of measurements relevant for decision making requires a prior agreement on the criteria for judging the acceptability of alternative measurements. Conventionally, financial reports have relied on historic cost measurement. It has become apparent, however, that applying the criterion of relevance to users' information needs, historic cost measurements fail to satisfy these needs. The implications of the criterion of relevance are more fully discussed in Part 4.

In this part, we also examine a second criterion which is implied in the selection of appropriate accounting measurements, namely the criterion of feasibility which embraces such aspects of the measurement problem as objectivity, ease of understanding as well as considerations of costs of implementation. It is these issues which are involved in the examination of alternative accounting valuation systems.

Unfortunately, the selection of accounting measurements on the basis of the two criteria of relevance and feasibility does not rely on a simple set of accept/reject decision rules. To some extent each measurement currently available meets both criteria, but meets them at different levels of quality. For example, an accounting method which utilizes a measurement which scores highly for relevance, may not score well for feasibility.

The importance of understanding the interaction and interdependence between valuation and measurement is apparent in such important areas of accounting as income determination and asset valuation. In this sense, the notions of capital and income are largely dependent on valuation concepts.

In this part, six valuation concepts are discussed:

1 *Historical cost*, as we saw in Part 2, is the conventional valuation concept used in accounting. Resources are valued in accordance with their cost of acquisition by the enterprise. The historical cost valuation concept poses many difficulties under price level changes.

2 *Present value* is a concept which relates the value of an asset to the decision to hold it and to derive its utility from using it in the production of income. It is defined as the sum of the future expected net cash flows associated with the use of the asset, discounted to its present value.

3 *Current purchasing power* is basically an adjusted historical cost concept, in which adjustments are made to recorded historical cost values for changes in the purchasing power of money by means of a consumer price index.

4 *Current replacement cost*, in which the value of an asset is determined by the current cost of replacing it, and using the replacement to maintain the same service to the enterprise. It requires current market price data as a basis for preparing financial reports.

5 *Net realizable value* estimates the value of an asset to the enterprise as the amount which would be realized from its sale, after adjusting for selling expenses.

6 *Current cost accounting* is a valuation concept which combines the concept of current replacement cost and net realizable value in determining whether selling (exit) or buying (entry) prices should be used for the purposes of establishing the value of an asset to the business.

This part consists of four chapters, as follows:

Chapter 18, Capital, value, income, deals with the conceptual problems involved in the valuation of the enterprise and the measurement of income.

Chapter 19, Accounting and economic concepts of income and value, considers two different approaches to income measurement and valuation.

Chapter 20, Current purchasing power accounting, examines a proposed method for dealing with the instability of the accounting standard of measurement by indexing its purchasing power as a means of making adjustments for maintaining a constant value.

Chapter 21, Current value accounting, examines proposed methods for dealing with the instability of the accounting standard of measurement in terms of representing asset values at their current value to the enterprise.

Chapter 18

Capital, value, income

We stated in Chapter 2 that the objectives of financial reporting to investors should be found in the decisions which investors have to make about their investment in companies. Hence, we argued, financial reporting should be concerned with the provision of such information as is required for making those decisions. We assumed, also, that investors were principally concerned with the worth of their investments in two senses. First, they are concerned with maintaining and increasing the value of their capital. Second, they are concerned with maintaining and increasing the income which is derived from that capital. Financial reporting ought to be concerned, therefore, with the valuation of shareholders' capital and income. In accordance with the stewardship concept of financial reporting, feedback information is required in order that investors may ascertain the present value of share capital and income. The decision-making concept of financial reporting asserts that financial reports should contain information which is useful in assisting investors to predict future changes in capital and income.

Three concepts are involved in financial reporting—capital, value and income. Together they provide the focus for this part. The purpose of this chapter is to introduce and explain the nature of these three concepts.

Capital

To the economist, the term 'capital' relates to those assets which are used in the production of goods and services. The capital of the firm is represented by the firm's stock of assets, and investment by the firm occurs when the stock is increased. From the point of view of society, the term 'capital' is restricted similarly to those assets which produce goods and services. Capital includes, therefore, physical assets in the form of buildings, plant and machinery, housing, hospitals, schools as well as intangible assets such as technology, human skills (human capital) etc.

In accounting theory, a person's capital is increased by the amount of his periodic income which he has not consumed. Financial accounting procedure effects this transfer by crediting the net profit to the capital account, and if his level of consumption, or drawings, is less than that profit, the capital is increased by the difference. In the case of companies, dividends are analogous to drawings, and retained profit is added to the total of the shareholders' equity. One of the important implications of profit measurement in the case of companies lies in calculating what may be safely distributed as dividends.

Early writers on bookkeeping recommended, as a first step in the record-keeping process, the preparation of an inventory or statement of capital showing all the personal and real property, as well as debts due and owing on the first day of business. Paciolo in 1494 advised the businessman to prepare his inventory in the following way:

'First of all, he must write on a sheet of paper or in a separate book all his worldly belongings, that is, his personal or real property. He should always begin with the things that are more valuable and easier to lose. . . . He must then record all other things in proper order in the Inventory.' (Gene Brown and Johnston, 1963.)

It is evident that at this stage of development, accounting made no distinction between personal capital and business capital. In the course of subsequent developments, however, a distinction emerged between total wealth and wealth committed to business activities. Whereas in Paciolo's time capital was taken to mean the entire amount of what was owned, the capital account became ultimately a device which described and quantified that portion of private wealth invested in a business enterprise.

The development of the entity theory of accounting, as distinct from the proprietory theory, which culminated in the appearance of the joint stock company, gave expression to two important notions. First, as we saw in Part 2, an enterprise could be separated from its owner by a legal fiction and used by him as a vehicle for conducting business. Second, the fictional life granted to the enterprise by accounting practice, and additionally in the case of corporations by law, was to serve limited purposes. The capital account was to remain the umbilical cord linking the enterprise to its owner or owners. In line with this view, the enterprise continued to be regarded as an asset and this view has important implications for the valuation of capital and income.

From the foregoing, it is evident that there are some fundamental differences between economists and accountants in the manner in which the notion of capital is conceptualized. As Littleton (1961) points out, the balance sheet presentation of 'capital' emphasizes its legal rather than its economic aspect, for capital is shown as a liability, whereas in economics, capital refers to assets. The assets held by a business and actively employed by it are usually greater in value than the so-called 'capital'. In the light of modern interests, we may say that the terminology of financial reports in this respect is misleading. However, supposing that the total assets employed by an enterprise were to be redefined as its 'capital', there remain a number of problems:

1   the valuation of business capital;
2   the valuation of investors' financial interests, that is, personal capital;
3   the methods selected for these valuations;
4   the manner in which these valuations are to be communicated.

From our previous discussion of the objectives of financial reporting, we may say that investors are interested primarily in the valuation of their shareholding and this valuation is dependent on the valuation of business capital.

Capital maintenance

We stated earlier in this chapter that investors are concerned with maintaining the value of their capital. The concept of capital maintenance is central to discussions regarding price level adjustments. There is general agreement that profit is a residue available for distribution once provision has been made for maintaining the value of capital intact. Difficulties begin to emerge when discussion turns to the consideration of the meaning of 'capital maintenance'. Several alternative interpretations of this concept have been offered and are illustrated in Fig. 3.1. It will be noted from Fig. 3.1 that five concepts of capital maintenance are listed, as well as six valuation systems. The combinations of capital maintenance concepts and valuation systems indicated in Fig. 3.1 are discussed in this chapter.

Fig. 3.1

Capital maintenance concepts	1 Historical cost	2 Present value	3 Current purchasing power	4 Replacement cost	5 Net realizable value	6 Current cost accounting
A Money amount	Conventional accounting					
B Investment purchasing power		Economic income and value				
C Financial capital			SSAP 7			
D Operating capability				Edwards and Bell		Sandilands SSAP 16
E Disposable wealth					Chambers Sterling	

The money amount concept

According to this concept, the measurement of periodic profit should ensure that the monetary value of the shareholders' equity is maintained intact. In effect, the profit of the period amounts to the increase in monetary terms in the shareholders' equity measured between the beginning and the end of the period. It is this amount which may be distributed to ensure that the money capital is maintained intact. The money amount maintenance concept is reflected in historical cost accounting.

The investment purchasing power concept

This concept defines the assets of the enterprise in terms of their potential earning power, expressed as the present value of all cash flows to be generated in the future. It gives rise to economic income, which may be stated as the change in the earning power of the enterprise in respect of any period plus distributions made to shareholders during such period. This concept of capital maintenance accords with the classical definition of economic income as being the difference between the opening and closing value of shareholders' equity based on such a valuation of assets.

The financial capital concept

The objective of this concept is to maintain the financial capital of an enterprise by constantly updating the historical cost of assets for changes in the value of money. The translation of historical asset cost is effected by a retail price index, and results in the representation of asset values in common units of purchasing power. This concept of capital maintenance purports to show to shareholders that their company kept pace with general inflationary pressures during the accounting period, by measuring profit in such a way as to take into account changes in the price-levels. In effect, it intends to maintain the shareholders' capital in terms of monetary units of constant purchasing power. The use of a retail price index based on the range of goods and services restricts adjustments for changes in the purchasing power of money to those changes which would be experienced by consumers.

The operating capability concept

The financial capital concept of capital maintenance views the capital of the enterprise from the standpoint of the shareholders as owners. Hence, it reflects the proprietorship concept of the enterprise as regards both income and capital, and seeks valuation systems which fit this view. By contrast, the operating capability concept of capital maintenance views the problem of capital maintenance from the perspective of the enterprise itself, thereby reflecting the entity concept of the enterprise.

The operating concept states that the productive (operating) capacity of the enterprise should be maintained as a prime objective in the course of profit measurement. The operating capability concept of capital maintenance asserts that profit is a residue after provision has been made for replacing the resources exhausted in the course of operations. In this view, 'there can be no recognition of profit for a period unless the capital employed in the business at the beginning of the period has been maintained. . . . The starting point will be the various items making up the capital' (Goudeket, 1960). The criteria imposed on profit measurement by the operating concept are reflected by the system of replacement cost accounting, in which assets are valued at their replacement cost to the firm. Replacement cost accounting takes into account changes in the prices of commodities specific to the enterprise, either directly or by using specific price indices to measure changes in the prices of similar commodities.

The disposable wealth concept

Whereas all previous concepts of capital maintenance envisage the enterprise as a going concern, the disposable wealth concept suggests that the maintenance of capital should be viewed from the perspective of the realizable value of the assets of the enterprise. Accordingly, the measurement of periodic profit is required to take into account changes in the realizable value of the net assets attributable to the shareholders' equity. At the beginning of the accounting period, the shareholders' equity, defined as the capital of the enterprise, is valued by reference to the realizable value of assets, after deducting realization expenses. A similar valuation of the net amount which would accrue to shareholders from the realization of assets is made at the end of the accounting period.

The disposable wealth concept of capital maintenance is based on the proprietorship theory of the enterprise. However, it interprets this theory in terms of the 'exit' rather than the 'entry' values of enterprise assets.

Income

The concepts of capital and income are closely related. Irving Fisher (1919) expressed their relationship as follows: 'A stock of wealth existing at a given instant of time is called capital; a flow of benefit from wealth through a given period of time is called income.'

An analogy may be found in the relationship between a tree and its fruit—it is the tree which produces the fruit, and it is the fruit which may be consumed. Destroy the tree, and there will be no more fruit: tend the tree with care and feed its roots and it will yield more fruit in the future.

Once the concept of value is introduced into the relationship between capital and income, however, the exact nature of this relationship becomes clearer. According to Irving Fisher (1969):

'It would seem . . . that income must be derived from capital; and, in a sense, this is true. Income is derived from capital goods, but the value of the income is not derived from the value of the capital goods. On the contrary, the value of the capital is derived from the value of the income. . . . Not until we know how much income an item will probably bring us can we set any valuation on that capital at all. It is true that the wheat crop depends on the land which yields it. But the value of the crop does not depend on the land. On the contrary, the value of the land depends in its crop.'

Economic and accounting theory are both concerned with the relationship between capital and income and in the implications of this relationship. There is agreement between accountants and economists on a number of aspects of the relationship and considerable disagreement as regards the valuation of capital and income. There is agreement, for example, that only income should be available for consumption, and that in arriving at a measure of income, it is necessary to maintain the value of capital intact. Since the ultimate aim of economic activity is the satisfaction of wants, it follows that income is identified as a surplus which is available for consumption. The valuation of income in this analysis is subject to a fairly conservative criterion which Hicks expressed as follows: 'The purpose of income calculations in practical affairs is to give people an indication of the amount which they can consume without impoverishing themselves' (Hicks, 1946).

Income plays a central role in many business and personal decisions, since it is based essentially on the notion of spending capacity. As Hicks pointed out, income should be an operational concept providing guidelines to spending. As applied to business corporations, Hicks's definition of income has been interpreted as the 'amount the corporation can distribute to the owners of the equity in the corporation and be as well off at the end of the year as at the beginning' (Alexander, 1962). It is evident, however, that income is used for other purposes as well. For this reason, we examine the objectives of income measurements before proceeding to the analysis and selection of appropriate concepts.

The objectives of income measurement

Income as a measure of efficiency

Income is used as a measure of efficiency in two senses. First, the overall efficiency of a business is assessed in terms of income generated. Hence, income tends to provide the basic standard by which success is measured. There are clearly problems in focusing upon financial efficiency to the detriment of other concepts of business efficiency—such as its effectiveness as a social unit and its efficiency in developing and using new ideas and processes. Nevertheless, those who support the use of income as a measure of business efficiency argue that in the last analysis all other aspects of efficiency converge on income. Second, shareholders assess the efficiency of their investments by reference to reported income. Hence, the allocation of investment funds, the selection of portfolios and the operations of the financial system depend upon income as a standard by which decisions are taken.

Income as a guide to future investment

As we see in Part 5, the selection of investment projects is made on the basis of estimates of future cash flows. These estimates are self-fulfilling to the extent that risk and uncertainty have been sufficiently discounted in the decision-making process. In a more general way, however, current income acts to influence expectations about the future. This is particularly so as regards investors who have to rely on financial reports and whose willingness to hold and to subscribe for further shares will be affected by reported income.

Income as an indicator of managerial effectiveness

Management is particularly sensitive about the income which is reported to shareholders since its effectiveness both as decision makers and as stewards of resources is judged by reference to reported income. It is in this respect that auditors play a key role in ensuring that the statements placed before shareholders reflect a 'true and fair' view of the financial results. What is 'true and fair' is a contentious problem for accountants. Nevertheless, what is evidently neither true nor fair rarely avoids comment.

Income as a tax base

The tendency of most governments to take a substantial share of corporate income in the form of taxation means that the basis on which corporate tax is assessed is critically important to shareholders and management. Although taxation legislation does not define 'income', it does specify what is taxable and what is deductible in arriving at a measure of taxable income. Much litigation in this area has revolved around the meaning of words, but the taxation authorities accept accounting profit as the base from which to assess taxable profit.

Income as a guide to credit-worthiness

A firm's ability to obtain credit finance depends on its financial status and its current and future income prospects. For this reason, credit institutions and banks require assurances of a firm's ability to repay loans out of future income and look upon current income levels as a guide in this respect.

Income as a guide to socio-economic decisions

A wide range of decisions take into account the levels of corporate income. Thus, price increases tend increasingly to be justified in terms of income levels, and wage-bargaining procedures usually involve appeals by both sides to their effects on corporate income. Government economic policies are guided by levels of corporate income as one of the key social indicators.

Income as a guide to dividend policy

The distinction between capital and income is central to the problem of deciding how much may be distributed to shareholders as dividends. A series of important cases have been concerned with the concept of capital maintenance, and rules have been established for the measurement of distributable income with a view to protecting the interests of creditors. Thus, there is a rule which provides that losses in the value of current assets should be made good, whereas in arriving at the measure of distributable income, there is no need to make good losses in the value of fixed assets.

Nowadays, however, dividend policy is directed towards establishing the proportion of current income which should be retained and the proportion which should be distributed. This is because companies expect to finance their investment needs from retained income.

Income concepts for financial reporting

The application of different accounting valuation concepts to asset valuation and income measurement offers a variety of alternative bases for drawing up financial reports. In this part, we examine the implications of reporting to shareholders on the basis of the six alternative accounting valuation concepts listed in the introduction to this part, namely, historical cost, present value, current purchasing power, replacement cost, net realizable value and current cost.

As stated in the introduction to this part, the evaluation and selection of alternative accounting valuation systems depends on the manner in which they satisfy criteria of acceptability. We noted in particular that the criteria of relevance and feasibility were highly significant in this regard. One problem in evaluating alternative valuation systems for financial reporting purposes is that each alternative satisfies these criteria in different ways. For example, historical cost has a high degree of feasibility but little relevance, whereas present value has a high degree of relevance but little feasibility.

A second problem which will be examined in this part stems from alternative definitions of capital maintenance. Thus, there is some controversy about the manner in which concepts of capital maintenance may be made operational for financial reporting purposes. For example, the debate which followed the Sandilands Report illustrates that the operating capacity concept of capital maintenance does not immediately suggest agreement about the choice of an accounting valuation system which would satisfy the objectives of such a concept.

Summary

The purpose of this chapter was to examine the implications for financial reporting of three concepts—capital, value and income. Two meanings may be attached to the concept of capital. First, capital may be seen as the totality of enterprise assets which give rise to income. Second, capital may be seen as the investment made by shareholders in the equity of the enterprise and from which they expect to derive income in the form of dividends. Investors are concerned not only with the interdependence of the value of their shareholdings and the value of enterprise assets, but also with maintaining the value of that capital. The value of capital and the measurement of income are also interdependent in the sense that income is the difference between the value of capital at two points in time. Therefore, a central issue in the measurement of periodic income is the notion of capital maintenance. Difficulties arise in reporting income due to the different concepts of capital maintenance discussed in this chapter.

Further problems arise in financial reporting from the application of different valuation concepts to asset valuations. The combination of different capital maintenance and asset valuation concepts lies at the heart of much of the controversy in financial reporting. The problem of selecting a financial reporting framework requires the evaluation of alternative accounting valuation systems in terms of criteria of relevance and feasibility.

References

Alexander, S. S. (1962), revised by Solomons, D. 'Income measurement in a dynamic economy', in Baxter, W. T. and Davidson, S. (eds), *Studies in Accounting Theory,* p. 139, Sweet and Maxwell.

Fisher, I. (1919). *Elementary Principles of Economics,* p. 38.

Fisher, I. (1969). 'Income and capital', in Parker, R. H. and Harcourt, G. C. (eds), *Readings in the Concept and Measurement of Income,* p. 40, Cambridge University Press.

Gene Brown, R. and Johnston, K. S. (1963). *Paciolo on Accounting,* p. 27, McGraw-Hill.

Goudeket, A. (1960). An application of replacement value theory, *Journal of Accountancy,* July.

Hicks, J. R. (1946). *Value and Capital,* 2nd edn, p. 172, Oxford University Press.

Littleton, A. C. (1961). *Essays on Accounting,* p. 244, University of Illinois Press.

Questions

1 How do accountants define capital?
2 Compare the accountants' definition of capital with the definition used by economists.
3 Discuss the significance of the concept of 'capital maintenance'.
4 Explain briefly the different concepts of capital maintenance that have been postulated.
5 Identify which of these concepts of capital maintenance would be most appropriate to the following two groups of decision-makers, with brief explanations of your reasons:

(a) corporate shareholders,
(b) management.

6 Explain briefly how accountants measure business income.
7 Review the various purposes for which businesses require income measurements.
8 Explain what you understand as 'value'.
9 'Valuation is a process by which value is established. However, since there are different approaches to valuation, it follows that there are different values'. Comment on this statement.
10 In the light of Question 9, consider the significance of alternative values to the measurement of capital and income.

Chapter 19

Accounting and economic concepts of income and value

Accounting concepts

Accounting concepts of income and value have been influenced mainly by two conventions—the cost and realization convention. These conventions have received much criticism in recent years on the ground that they restrict the usefulness of financial accounting reports for decision-making purposes.

The effects of the cost convention

The basis of valuation in financial accounting is historical cost. This convention clearly conflicts with the going-concern convention of valuation when the value of money itself is changing. In effect, historical-cost income is based on a venture rather than a going-concern view of the firm.

Under the venture concept, each asset purchased is regarded as a separate venture, so that income is determined for each venture. Thus, net income is measured by setting off against revenues the cost of the assets ventured in earning those revenues. The replacement of those assets is treated as a distinct second venture, for which funds should be raised independently.

By contrast, the going-concern concept which is supported by most businessmen and economists holds that the business enterprise should be considered as a unified continuing concern rather than a series of separate individual ventures.

The historical cost method of valuation seriously distorts the measurement of income, when the value of money is changing. This distortion results from the difference between the historical cost and the current cost which, as we shall see later, is a function of the time gap between the acquisition and the utilization of assets committed to earning periodic revenues. For items such as wages and other current expenses, this difference may be very small, but for such assets as stocks and fixed assets there may be a substantial difference between the acquisition cost and the current cost when those assets are charged against revenue under the matching rule. Under conditions of rising prices, the historical cost may bear no resemblance to the current cost of assets, with the result that income is overstated. Conservative asset values on the balance sheet are contrasted by over-optimistic profit measurements in the profit and loss account.

The historical cost method of valuation creates a particular problem in periods of inflation when money units of different values are brought together in the accounting process as though they were money units of the same value. Such arithmetic is quite incorrect, for it involves adding together amounts expressed in different measurement scales. Accordingly, historical cost values are not additive during periods of changing money values.

Example

A firm constructed a building at a cost of £100 000. Ten years later, a similar building was constructed at a cost of £200 000. In accordance with the conventions of historical cost accounting, these two items were added together in the balance sheet to show a total historical cost of £300 000. Clearly, the two buildings are not comparable in the sense that the second building is a building which is either twice as large as the first or more costly to build. In effect, no such conclusions could be drawn. Adding together pounds which represent units of different purchasing power is similar in nature to adding together pints, quarts and gallons without converting them to a common denominator. Consider what would be the effect of such arithmetic on the depreciation provision for the buildings. If we assume that the buildings are in fact identical, an annual rate of depreciation of 5 per cent would provide depreciation at the rate of £5000 for the first building, and £10 000 for the second building. Therefore, it may be concluded that the entire arithmetic underlying the balance sheet representation of asset values would be incorrect under inflation, when asset values purchased at different times are added together in asset totals.

The main advantage which is claimed for historical cost valuation is that it is verifiable. The stewardship approach to financial reporting theory is the major factor which supports this method of valuation. It may be argued, however, that if it is objectivity which the accountant is seeking, he should restrict himself purely to counting cash, since this asset is virtually the only one in respect of which complete objectivity is possible. As soon as the accountant moves away from cash, he is dealing with subjective factors. For example, there are many alternative measures available for valuing stocks, calculating depreciation, allocating overheads and providing for bad debts. Consequently, 'true' objectivity under historical cost valuation is not possible.

The effects of the realization convention

In accordance with the realization convention, the accountant does not recognize changes in value until they have crystallized following a transaction. Until a right enforceable at law comes into existence, gains in book values are ignored for the purpose of income measurement.

It has been suggested that there are two principal reasons which favour the practice of measuring income on realization rather than on accrual. The first is that a sale affords an objective measure of a change in value, and the second is that the sale is generally considered to be the most decisive and significant event in the chain of transactions and conditions making up the stream of business activity.

By focusing on realized gains and ignoring unrealized gains, the realization convention can lead to absurd results.

Example

Two investors each have £1000 to invest. Each invests £1000 in the shares of Texton plc. The shares of Texton plc double in value by the end of the accounting period. On the last day of the accounting period, the first investor sells his shares for £2000 and places this sum in the Homestead Building Society. Hence, one investor has £2000 in the building society and the other holds shares in Texton valued at £2000. They are both equally well-off, yet under the realization convention, the investor who has sold his shares is seen as having realized income of £1000, whereas the investor who has held on to his shares is shown as having no income from this source.

Economic concepts

The process of valuation is central to all aspects of decision making. As we will see in Part 5, capital budgeting decisions require forecasts to be made about the present value of streams of future net cash receipts associated with investment projects. Similarly, investors may also be regarded as exchanging current assets, namely cash or cash equivalents, for a stream of future dividends in the form of cash dividends or increments in the value of their shares.

In this analysis, capital is valued on the basis of discounted future net receipts. Therefore, it is directly relevant to the information needs of shareholders and investors. The value of the firm to the shareholder is computed in such a way as to facilitate the investment decision, which is to seek that investment which will yield the highest value.

In economics, the value of capital is derived from the value of income. The economic concept of income relies on Hicks's definition of income as 'the amount which a man can consume during a period and still remain as well off at the end of the period as he was at the beginning' (Hicks, 1946). This concept of income was adopted by Alexander to define the income of a company as the amount the company can distribute to shareholders and be as well off at the end of the year as it was as the beginning (Alexander, 1962). It is measured by comparing the value of the company at two points in time in terms of the present value of expected future net receipts at each of those two points.

The economic concept of income treats assets of all kinds as representing future receipts expected to flow from them to the firm. The main mesurement problem lies in comparing the capitalized value of the future net receipts expected both at the beginning and at the end of the accounting period, for the difference represents income, that is, what may be consumed under the Hicksian criterion. Hicks himself recognized the problems of measurement involved in his criterion in the following terms:

'At the beginning of the week the individual possesses a stock of consumption goods, and expects a stream of receipts which will enable him to acquire in the future other consumption goods. . . . Call this Prospect I. At the end of the week he knows that one week out of that prospect will have disappeared; the new prospect which he expects to emerge will have a new first week which is the old second week. . . . Call this Prospect II. Now if Prospect I were available on the first Monday, we may assume that the individual would know whether he preferred I to II at that date: similarly, if Prospect I were available on the second Monday he would know if he preferred I to II then. But to enquire whether I on the first Monday is preferred to II on the second Monday is a nonsense question; the choice between them could never be actual at all; the terms of comparison are not in pari materia.' (Hicks, 1946.)

Hicks was making a very crucial point regarding the measurement problem of his criterion, for comparative states of well-offness at Prospect I and Prospect II must be established in order to know how much may be spent. Neither points nor prospects are comparable in reality, for they exist at different times.

The economic concept of income based on Hicks's criterion is an estimate since, in deciding how much may be spent, Prospect II must be estimated from the standpoint of Prospect I. In view of this problem two concepts of economic income have evolved. The first concept is called ex-ante income, and compares Prospect II with Prospect I from the time perspective of Prospect I. The second concept is called ex-post income, and compares Prospect II with Prospect I from the time perspective of Prospect II. Neither concept overcomes the fundamental difficulty which Hicks pointed out, that is, that one cannot compare alternatives which are not available together at the same time in making decisions requiring a concept of income. Despite this difficulty, income ex-ante and income ex-post have become established as central concepts in the theory of economic income.

It is important always to remember that both income ex-ante and income ex-post are based on estimates of future expected net receipts both at Prospect I and Prospect II. The valuation of income is inseparable, therefore, from the valuation of assets, since assets are valued in terms of the present value of the sum of future expected net receipts associated with their use by the firm. The valuation of income and capital in economics is therefore based on predictions.

Estimation of ex-ante income

The nature of ex-ante income may be seen from the following example.

Example

Seeking to maximize the return on its funds, Excel Ltd plans to invest those funds in the purchase of assets, which at 1 January 19X0 are expected to produce the following future net receipts:

Year	Amount
	£
19X0	10 000
19X1	10 000
19X2	10 000
19X3	10 000

This stream of expected future net receipts represents a return on investment of 10 per cent, which may be assumed to be the best return obtainable by Excel Ltd. Accordingly, the present value of those future net receipts discounted at 10 per cent may be calculated as follows:

Year	Expected net receipts at end of year	Present value on 1 January 19X0
	£	£
19X0	10 000	$10\ 000/1.10 = 9\ 091$
19X1	10 000	$10\ 000/(1.10)^2 = 8\ 264$
19X2	10 000	$10\ 000/(1.10)^3 = 7\ 513$
19X3	10 000	$10\ 000/(1.10)^4 = 6\ 831$
Present value of expected future net receipts at 1 January 19X0		31 699

Since the present value of expected future net receipts associated with the purchase of those assets is £31 699, Excel Ltd would be unwilling to pay more than this sum for those assets. Hence, we may say that the economic value of those assets is £31 699 at 1 January 19X0.

The present value of the expected future net receipts on 1 January 19X1 may be calculated as follows:

	£
Cash received at end of year 19X0	10 000
Present value of future new receipts:	
End of year 19X1	9 091
End of year 19X2	8 264
End of year 19X3	7 513
Present value of the assets in terms of actual and future expected net receipts on 1 January 19X1	34 868

The two valuations of the present value of the assets enable us to calculate ex-ante income as follows:

		£
Present value of assets at 1 January 19X1		34 868
	19X0	31 699
Ex-ante income for the year	19X0	3 169

Note that since the income of £3169 represents the expected increase in the value of the assets during the year, given an expected rate of return on investment of 10 per cent, it also represents 10 per cent of the initial value of those assets estimated at £31 699 on 1 January 19X0.

Estimation of ex-post income

In the foregoing example, the income for the year 19X0 has been calculated on the basis that the expected future net receipts at the end of the year 19X0 remained the same as those at the beginning of the year. Under such conditions, ex-ante and ex-post income would be the same.

If, however, the present value of expected future net receipts at the end of the year 19X0 are different from the present value of those expected receipts at the beginning of the year, we may say that the ex-post income is different from the ex-ante income. The ex-ante income refers, therefore, to the estimated income derived from the time perspective of the beginning of the year, and the ex-post income refers to the estimated income derived from the time perspective at the end of the year.

Example

Let it be assumed that the revised estimates of the present value of future net receipts on 1 January 19X1 are as follows (the estimates at 1 January 19X0 are in brackets):

Year	Expected net receipts at end of year as at 1 January 19X1		Present value of expected receipts as at 1 January 19X1		
	£	£	£	£	£
19X0	10 000	(10 000)	10 000		(9 091)
19X1	9 000	(10 000)	8 182	(9 000/(1.10))	(8 264)
19X2	9 000	(10 000)	7 438	(9 000/(1.10)^2)	(7 513)
19X3	9 000	(10 000)	6 762	(9 000/(1.10)^3)	(6 831)
Present value of expected future net receipts on 1 January 19X1			32 382		(31 699)

Ex-post income for the year 19X0, based on the revised estimates established on 1 January 19X1, is as follows:

		£
Estimated present value on 1 January 19X1		32 382
	19X0	31 699
Ex-post income for the year	19X0	683

The ex-post income for the year 19X0 is made up of the following components:

	£
Ex-ante income	3169
Ex-post adjustment	2486
Ex-post income	683

The subjective nature of economic income

The net present value method of valuation presents measurement problems in a number of ways. Accuracy of measurement depends upon the degree of certainty under which the forecasts of expected future cash flows are made. Ideally, the size of the net future cash flows should be estimated with reasonable accuracy as should the time profile of these future cash flows. This is because a sum of money in two years' time is worth more than the sum of money in three years'. We discuss the problems further in Chapter 29 when we examine capital budgeting decisions.

The net present value concept also requires that the discount rate selected for reducing the future cash flows to their present value should reflect accurately the time value of money. If interest rates are going to fluctuate during the time period considered for using the asset, it follows that the present value of the asset will be distorted because the correct discount rate has not been applied.

Because the future cash flows and discount rate cannot be determined with certainty, Edwards and Bell (1961) call economic income 'subject income', and dismiss the concept on the grounds that it cannot be satisfactorily applied on an operational basis. They echo, therefore, Hicks's own dissatisfaction with the concept, which we mentioned earlier in this chapter.

We mentioned in Part 2 that because of uncertainty surrounding the valuation of a firm, it is not the accountant's function to value the firm for the shareholder or investor. On the contrary, it is for the investor to establish the firm's value as an investment and to bear the risk implied in such a valuation. The role of the accountant is to furnish information which is useful for this purpose. The usefulness and relevance of the information provided in financial reports lies in the effectiveness with which it allows the investor to formulate valuations with some degree of accuracy. In the face of uncertainty, accuracy can never be guaranteed, but information about past and current performance may be used as a basis of developing projections and estimates of likely future trends. The adequacy of the accountant's presentation of information for this purpose, the clarity and sufficiency of disclosure are the central problems, therefore, facing the accounting profession in this area. The investor should use the information provided to make his own estimates of future net receipts, and taking into account his assessment of the degree of uncertainty involved in those estimates, he should discount those estimated net receipts by an appropriate discount rate to arrive at his valuation of the firm. This valuation will retain a high degree of subjectivity, for the discount rate will vary from individual to individual depending upon their respective risk preferences. Therefore, the concept of well-offness is really a matter of an individual's personal preferences. For all these reasons, the concept of economic income has little applicability to the problem of financial reporting.

Summary

Conventional accounting concepts of income and value possess a limited usefulness for decision making, because of the limitations inherent in the conventions of historical cost and realization which govern the measurement of accounting income. Under conditions of inflation, conservative asset values on the balance sheet contrast with over-optimistic profit measurement in the profit and loss account. Changes in value are not reported as they occur. Changing money values also undermine the stability of the unit of measurement in accounting.

Under conditions of certainty, economic income provides an ideal concept for financial reporting purposes. The value of the firm's future net receipts may be capitalized, thereby providing the investor with a basis for decision-making.

The presence of uncertainty, which is the general rule, precludes the use of economic income because of its essentially subjective nature. Future cash flows and discount rates cannot be estimated with certainty. For this reason, the accountant does not attempt to value the firm. Instead, financial reports are concerned with past performance, and the investor is required to make his own valuations from the information made available to him.

Despite these practical limitations, the importance of economic concepts of income and value lies in the emphasis they place on value and value changes rather than on historical costs. Moreover, they stress the limitations of accounting conventions such as the realization convention for financial reporting purpose, and emphasize the importance of the concept of capital maintenance to income measurement.

References

Alexander, S. S. (1962). 'Income measurement in a dynamic economy', in Baxter, W. T., and Davidson, S. (eds) *Studies in Accounting Theory,* Sweet and Maxwell.

Edwards, E. O. and Bell, P. W. (1961). *The Theory and Measurement of Business Income,* University of California Press.

Hicks, J. R. (1946). *Value and Capital,* 2nd edn, p. 172, Oxford University Press.

Questions

1. Analyse the effects of the cost convention on the measurement of accounting income.
2. Analyse the effects of the cost convention on accounting valuations.
3. Discuss the modifications that could be made to historic cost accounting that would improve the quality of accounting information for financial reporting purposes.
4. Explain the significance of the realization convention with respect to accounting information. Are accountants justified in their commitment to the realization convention?

5 Explain the essential differences between the accounting and economic approaches to income measurement.

6 Comment briefly on Hicks's definition of income.

7 Comment briefly on Alexander's definition of business income.

8 Explain briefly the relation between income and value in the measurement of economic income.

9 Explain the difference between 'ex-ante' and 'ex-post' income. What are the implications of these two approaches to the measurement of economic income?

10 Comment briefly on the difficulties that could be found in applying economic concepts of income and value to accounting measurements.

Chapter 20

Current purchasing power accounting

Accounting measurements are based on a monetary standard which hitherto has been assumed to be stable. However, experience of recent history has proved this assumption to be unrealistic with the result that the measurement of corporate profit during periods of changing price levels has become a controversial issue.

Price changes may be seen as having general and specific effects. General price changes reflect increases or decreases in the value of the monetary unit. In this case, all individual prices are assumed to change in the same direction, so that the value of a currency in relation to goods and services is different through time. For example, if £15 can only buy today what £10 would have bought on an earlier date, we may say that the price level has increased, the purchasing power of money has fallen and the economy is in a period of inflation.

By contrast, specific price changes occur for several reasons. Changes in consumer tastes, technological improvements, speculation by buyers are all reasons found at the root of specific price changes. Thus, increased demand for houses in the face of a limited supply will force up the price of houses, even if the general price level is constant. It is common, however, for people to hedge against inflation by investing in property and this factor may also influence property prices. Hence, we may say that while specific price changes may occur independently of changes in the general price level, changes in the price level may induce disproportionate changes in the price level of specific goods.

Adjusting for the effects of price changes may take the following forms:

1 general adjustments,
2 specific adjustments based on current costs (see Chapter 21),
3 a combination of (1) and (2) (see Chapter 21).

Adjustments for general price level changes

In 1974, the professional accounting bodies in the United Kingdom recommended that a supplementary statement should be attached to the financial reports of companies showing the conversion of the figures in the financial reports in terms of their current purchasing power (CPP) at the closing day of the accounting period. They recommended that the Retail Price Index (RPI) should be used to effect the conversion of historical cost values into current purchasing power equivalents (SSAP 7, 1974, withdrawn 1978).

CPP adjustments are limited to dealing with changes in the general purchasing power of money which occur during periods of inflation or deflation. Accordingly, the view is taken that the purpose of price level adjustments is to express each item in the financial report in terms of a common monetary unit, that is, in terms of pounds of the same purchasing power. The RPI is assumed to reflect the general movement in price of all goods and services. Thus, the doubling of the RPI from 100 to 200 between two points in time would mean that the purchasing power of money had fallen by half during that time interval.

Historical cost accounting is based essentially on the money amount maintenance concept. Such a concept asserts that all funds available to the firm in excess of the original contribution of funds by shareholders make the firm better off. High levels of inflation experienced in recent years have undermined the validity of this assertion. CPP accounting attempts to deal with this problem by adjusting historical cost measurements for the effects of inflation. As a result, the purchasing power held by the firm is maintained. The profit which results from CPP adjustments may be defined as those gains arising during the accounting period which may be distributed to shareholders, so that the purchasing power of the shareholders' interest in the company is the same at the end of the year as it was at the beginning. However, as we shall see in this chapter, the adjustment of historical cost for the effects of inflation of itself cannot ensure the maintenance of the productive capacity of the assets held by the company. The price level correction alone ignores the fact that capital may be dispersed through changes in individual prices if those relevant to the individual firm rise at a rate slower than the rate of change in the price level. Also, real capital will increase if the relationship is reversed.

Monetary and non-monetary items

For the purpose of CPP accounting it is necessary to distinguish between two classes of items—monetary and non-monetary items.

Monetary items may be defined as those fixed by contract or by their nature and are expressed in pounds regardless of changes in the price level. They include monetary assets such as cash, debtors and loans, and exist as money or as claims to specified sums of money. Holders of monetary assets suffer a loss in the general purchasing power of their assets during periods of inflation. Thus, if one holds money in the form of a bank deposit and the yearly rate of inflation is 25 per cent, the loss in the purchasing power of that money by the end of the period will be 25 per cent.

Monetary items include monetary liabilities such as creditors, bank overdrafts and long-term loans. As the value of money falls during a period of inflation, it follows that the value of such liabilities in current pounds will fall similarly, and this fall represents a purchasing power gain to the debtor. Consequently, those who incur monetary liabilities gain at the expense of creditors during periods of inflation, since they will settle these liabilities with pounds possessing less purchasing power than those they have previously received—directly or indirectly at the time the liabilities were incurred.

Non-monetary items are assets and liabilities such as fixed assets, stocks and shareholders' equity, which are assumed neither to lose nor to gain in value by reason of inflation or deflation. This is because price changes for these items will tend to compensate for changes in the value of money. For example, if stocks on hand at the beginning of the year remain unsold at the end of the year, there will be no purchasing-power loss since one assumes the sale price when they are sold would be adjusted upwards to take account of the fall in the value of money.

If £100 000 was used to purchase land on a date when the RPI stood at 100, and it now stands at 150, the assumption underlying this movement in prices is that £150 000 in today's money have the same purchasing power as £100 000 when the RPI stood at 100. Hence, to report on the purchasing power invested in the land, its acquisition cost should be stated as £150 000. This value does not say anything about the present market value of that particular piece of land. Property values may have increased more or less than the general movement in prices indicated by the RPI. The particular piece of land mentioned in this example may now be worth £300 000 or only £90 000. Hence, the figure of £150 000 represents only the historical cost of acquisition adjusted for the decrease in the general value of the pound.

Nevertheless, the acceptance of the need to adjust accounting measurements for inflation is a recognition of a fundamental proposition in income theory, namely, that provision should be made for maintaining the value of capital intact. Hence, there can be no recognition of income for a period unless it has been established that the purchasing power of the capital employed in a firm is the same at the end of the accounting period as it was in the beginning.

A simple example serves to explain the nature of adjustments which are required to financial reports based on historical cost measurements in order to remove the effects of general price level changes.

Example

Bangored Supplies plc was formed on 1 January 19X0, with a share capital of £75 000 which was fully subscribed in cash on that date. On the same day, equipment was purchased for £45 000, of which £20 000 was paid immediately, the balance of £25 000 being payable 2 years hence. The price level index was 100 on 1 January 19X0.

Goods were purchased in two instalments prior to commencing business as follows:

1st purchase in the sum of £44 000, when the price level index was 110;

2nd purchase in the sum of £45 000, when the price level index was 120.

All sales were made when the price level index was 130, and expenses of £16 000 were also incurred at the same index level. Stocks were valued on the FIFO methods and the closing stock was valued at £29 000. The price level index at 31 December 19X0 was 130.

The profit and loss account and balance sheet in respect of this year, prepared on a historical cost basis, were as follows:

Balance sheet as at 31 December 19X0

	£	£
Fixed assets		45 000
less: Accumulated depreciation		4 500
		40 500
Current assets		
Stock	29 000	
Debtors	19 000	
Bank balance	39 500	
	87 500	
less: Current liabilities	33 500	
Net current assets		54 000
		94 500
Share capital		75 000
Profit and loss account		19 500
		94 500

Profit and loss account for the year ended 31 December 19X0

	£	£
Sales		100 000
Cost of goods sold		60 000
Gross operating income		40 000
Expenses	16 000	
Depreciation (10% of £45 000)	4 500	
		20 500
Net operating profit		19 500

Required:
(a) Calculate the purchasing power gain or loss on the monetary items.
(b) Prepare an inflation adjusted profit and loss account for the year ended 31 December 19X0.
(c) Prepare an inflation adjusted balance sheet as at 31 December 19X0 when the price level index was 130.

(a) Calculation of purchasing power gain or loss on monetary items during the year ended 31 December 19X0

	Unadjusted monetary items	Conversion factor	Adjusted monetary items
	£		£
Net current monetary items on 1 January 19X0 (cash invested)	75 000	130/100	97 500
add: Sales	100 000	130/130	100 000
	175 000		197 500
Less:			
Purchases of equipment	20 000	130/100	26 000
Purchase of goods			
(i) index at 110	44 000	130/110	52 000
(ii) index at 120	45 000	130/120	48 750
Expenses	16 000	130/130	16 000
	125 000		142 750
Net current monetary items on 31 December 19X0	50 000		54 750
Unadjusted net current monetary items on 31 December 19X0			50 000
Purchasing power loss for the year ended 31 December 19X0			4 750

(b) Preparation of inflation-adjusted income statement for the year ended 31 December 19X0

	Unadjusted	Conversion factor	Adjusted
	£		£
Sales	100 000	130/130	100 000
Cost of goods sold			
At index 110	44 000	130/110	52 000
At index 120	16 000	130/120	17 333
Expenses	16 000	130/130	16 000
Depreciation	4 500	130/100	5 850
	80 500		91 183
Net profit	19 500		8 817

(c) Preparation of inflation-adjusted balance sheet as at 31 December 19X0

	Unadjusted	Conversion factor	Adjusted
	£		£
Fixed assets	45 000	130/100	58 500
less: accumulated depreciation	4 500	130/100	5 850
	40 500		52 650
Current assets			
Stock	29 000	130/120	31 417
Debtors	19 000	130/130	19 000
Bank balance	39 500	130/130	39 500
	87 500		89 917
less: Current liabilities	33 500	130/130	33 500
Net current assets	54 000		56 417
Total assets	94 500		109 067
Share capital	75 000	130/100	97 500
Profit and loss account	19 500	—	8 817
Accumulated purchasing power gain			2 750
	94 500		109 067

Calculation of accumulated purchasing power gain
Gain on unpaid balance of purchase price of equipment

Adjusted balance (£25 000 × 130/100)	32 500
Unadjusted balance	25 000
	7 500
less: Loss as computed on monetary items	4 750
Net accumulated purchasing power gain	2 750

An appraisal of CPP accounting

CPP accounting restates historical cost in terms of current purchasing power. It is an attempt to remove the major objection to historical-cost valuations discussed in the previous chapter, namely that the unit of measurement changes when price levels change. The intention is that this objection should be removed by an adjustment which results in units of the 'same purchasing power' being added together in the measurement process.

Common pound accounting can be applied with a high degree of objectivity, required of accounting valuation, as it does not depart in principle from historical-cost-based measurement. Price level adjustments are verifiable by reference to the index used to measure changes in the purchasing power of money, and result in alterations to historical cost measurements which are themselves objective. Therefore, both criteria of objectivity and verifiability are satisfied in CPP accounting.

As we stated earlier, SSAP 7 recommended that companies should continue to publish accounts on a historical cost basis, but that in addition, a supplementary statement should be presented showing the effect of converting conventional accounts into pounds of current purchasing power. The Sandilands Report rules out CPP accounting because it did not like the idea of two sets of accounts, nor the use of different measurement units. According to the Sandilands Report, users of financial reports would be confused.

Another objection to CPP accounting is raised by some authorities who believe that there is no such thing as generalized purchasing power (Gynther, 1974). Organizations and people do not see themselves as holding general purchasing power when they hold money; rather, they see themselves as holding specific purchasing power in respect of those relatively few items which they wish to purchase. Hence, the purchasing power of money should be related to those items on which money is intended to be spent. A unit of measurement which relies for its validity on the purchasing power of money assessed by reference to a set of goods and services will not be equally useful to all individuals and entities.

Moreover, the concept of income on which these adjustments are based is not one which maintains the service potential of capital. A general price index, particularly a consumer's price index, is a weighted average of the price change occurring in a wide variety of goods and services available in the economy. Therefore, adjusting financial data for the effects of inflation is not the same as reporting current values. Price-adjusted data still represents costs, or funds, committed to non-monetary items: these costs are merely translated into the equivalent costs in terms of today's pounds.

General price indices assume that the movements in the price of all goods correspond with each other. However, only by coincidence will a change in the general price index correspond with the change in the price of any particular good or service during the same period. Indeed, there is no reason why they may not move in opposite directions. For example, the price of colour television sets was falling in the 1960s in the UK at a time when the general price index was rising. Hence, if the general price index has increased, many specific price changes will be running at a lower level than the general index, while many others will be running at a higher level, and there may be some specific price decreases. Furthermore, the discrepancies between specific price and general price changes are likely to be even more pronounced when the general price index is based on consumer goods, and the specific price index relates to producer goods, such as those represented by the assets of a typical business enterprise. Thus, a general price index will not be relevant to any business entity which needs to make adjustments to asset valuations in order to maintain the value of its capital in the long term.

Controversy surrounds the treatment of gains and losses arising on monetary items. General price level accounting includes such gains and losses in the periodic income. Hence, a company's pre-tax profit will be dramatically different, according to the nature of its financial structure, before and after these adjustments have been made. Property companies, whose largest balance sheet item is often their liabilities to banks, finance houses and other credit institutions, find their adjusted profit and loss account showing exceptionally good results. But the 'gains' resulting from these adjustments do not increase sums available for distribution as dividends to shareholders, since they are purely accounting adjustments. They could be distributed only by drawing on existing cash resources or by borrowing. Hence, if the net 'gains' on monetary items are regarded as available for distribution, the users of adjusted financial reports could be seriously misled.

Although CPP accounting has serious limitations, many writers have argued the need to adjust accounting income for general inflation. According to Baxter (1984):

'Hitherto we have found little fault with statistical tables (e.g. of national income) in constant prices; we do not decry the indexing of tax allowances; most of us would accept indexed investments as a godsend. Admittedly the retail price index does not reflect precisely the consumption patterns of wealthy shareholders; but the divergence does not seem to be big. No system of inflation accounting will be perfect, and correction of income by a general index seems the least bad of the possibilities.'

Summary

If the value of money is changing, it is clear that the money standard of measurement ceases to be efficient. Financial reports should be adjusted, therefore, for the effects of changes in the value of money for the following reasons:

1 to provide a more accurate basis for assessing the value of a shareholder's investment in a company;
2 to enable more meaningful comparisons to be made between the reported results of successive years;
3 to enable more meaningful inter-company comparisons to be effected.

The unsatisfactory nature of historical cost as a basis for financial reporting is reflected in the fact that companies have been increasingly incorporating partial adjustments for inflation in their reported values. The revaluation of fixed assets by firms in the United Kingdom, and the adoption of LIFO by companies in the United States, are examples of this phenomenon.

CPP accounting allows adjusted historical costs to be matched against current revenues. It computes losses arising through holding monetary items during periods of inflation.

CPP accounting has serious limitations. It may be argued, for example, that in reality generalized purchasing power does not exist; that individuals hold specific purchasing power for the assets they wish to buy. Price level accounting, moreover, does not necessarily maintain the productive capital of the firm: it merely maintains the general purchasing power of the firm. Also, the distribution of monetary 'gains' could seriously affect the firm's liquidity.

References

Baxter, W. T. (1984), *Inflation Accounting,* Philip Allen.

Gynther, R. S. (1974). Why use general purchasing power?, *Accounting and Business Research,* Spring.

SSAP No. 7, Accounting for Changes in the Purchasing Power of Money, London, 1974, withdrawn 1978.

Questions

1. What are the assumptions underlying the money value convention in accounting?
2. Review briefly the possible effects of changes in price levels on accounting data.
3. Contrast 'general' with 'specific' price level changes.
4. State what is meant by current purchasing power accounting.
5. What is the significance of the distinction between monetary and non-monetary items with respect to current purchasing power adjustments.
6. Review the usefulness of indices of the purchasing power of money for the purpose of current purchasing power accounting.
7. Describe how you would convert money measurements recorded at historic cost into their current purchasing power equivalent in calculating periodic profit or loss.
8. Describe how you would convert money measurements accumulated on balance sheets into their current purchasing power equivalent for preparing a year-end balance sheet.
9. Describe how you would dispose of any debit/credit balance resulting from the conversion of historic money cost current purchasing power of:

    (a) an annual profit and loss account
    (b) a closing year balance sheet.

10. Appraise the relevance of current purchasing power accounting.

Problems

1. Vitex plc was created on 1 January 19X0 with a share capital of £150 000, fully paid in cash on that date. The price level index at that date was 100.
    The following transactions were recorded:

    Purchased equipment for £90 000, £40 000 paid when the index was 100, and payment of the balance being deferred for 18 months.

    Purchased goods for £88 000 when the index was 100.
    Purchased goods for £90 000 when the index was 110.

    Sold goods for £200 000 when the index was 120, the cost of sales amounting to £120 000.

    Cash expenses amounted to £32 000, and a depreciation provision of 10 per cent on historic cost of equipment was made at year end.

    Additional information as at 31 December 19X0 was as follows:

Trade debtors	£36 000
Bank balance	£79 000
Creditors	£67 000

    Closing stock was valued at £58 000 on a FIFO basis.
    The index at year end was 120.

    Required:
    (a) Calculate the purchasing power gain or loss on the monetary items.
    (b) Prepare an inflation adjusted profit and loss account for the year ended 31 December 19X0.
    (c) Prepare an inflation adjusted balance sheet as at 31 December 19X0 when the price level index was 130.

2　The directors of Minerva plc are extremely pleased with the progress of the firm. After comparing the 19X2 and 19X6 accounts they find that total assets have increased by more than 30 per cent and in addition the net profits have doubled over the period.

Income statements	19X2 £000	19X6 £000
Sales	1200	2000
Cost of goods sold	880	1350
Gross profit	320	650
Operating expenses (including depreciation)	140	290
Profit before taxation	180	360
less: Taxation	60	120
Profit after taxation	120	240

Balance sheets

	£	£	£	£	£	£
Fixed assets						
Machinery at cost		300			500	
less: Depreciation to date		30	270		214	286
Current assets						
Stocks	140			300		
Debtors	110			140		
Bank	60	310		46	486	
less: creditors: amounts falling due within the year:						
trade creditors	100	210		140	346	
Total assets *less:* current liabilities			480			632
Capital and reserves			£			£
Called-up share capital			300			300
Profit and loss account			180			332
			480			632

You are given the following information:

(a) Over the 5 years the general price level index which was stable in the two years before 19X2 has risen as follows: 19X2 = 100, 19X3 = 120, 19X4 = 125, 19X5 = 135, 19X6 = 150.

　　The price index given each year is the average for that year as well as the index for the end of the year.

(b) 20 per cent of the cost of goods sold in 19X6 were purchased when the price index was at 135, and 80 per cent of the goods purchased when the price index was 150.

(c) The cost of machinery in use, and the depreciation charged, all stated in thousands of pounds each year was as follows:

	19X2	19X3	19X4	19X5	19X6	Total each year
Machinery in use at cost	300					
Additions		80	100	—	20	
Depreciation provisions						
19X2	30					=30
19X3	30	8				=38
19X4	30	8	10			=48
19X5	30	8	10			=48
19X6	30	8	10		2	=50

Required:

Convert the statements for 19X2 and 19X6 so that they will be stated in uniform pounds at the 150 price index. (Compute to the nearest thousand pounds.) Assume that the taxation system has not altered during this period.

3   Enterprises A and B commenced business on 1 January 19X4, when they purchased their respective fixed assets. The balance sheets of A and B at 31 December 19X4 were as follows:

	A £	B £
Fixed assets		
Plant and machinery	4000	2000
less: Depreciation (10%)	400	200
	3600	1800
Building	—	5000
	3600	6800
Current assets		
Stocks	500	400
Debtors	1000	1000
Cash	800	900
	2300	2300
less: Creditors: amounts falling due within a year		
Trade creditors	1000	1200
Net current assets	1300	1100
Total assets less current liabilities	4900	7900
less: creditors: amounts falling due after more than one year		
Long-term loan	—	3000
	4900	4900
Capital reserves	£	£
Issued share capital	4000	4000
Profit and loss account	900	900
	4900	4900

Other information available:

(a) Replacement cost of assets:

	A	B
Plant and machinery	5000	2600

(These refer to the *new* assets not the partly used ones.)

	A	B
Building		7000
Stocks	650	500

(b) The general price index has increased by 20 per cent during the year on a base index of 100 at 1 January 19X4.

(c) Stocks, debtors and creditors accrued evenly throughout the year.

Required:

Using as much information from that above as you consider appropriate answer the question: which enterprise has the better financial performance? Explain and justify your answer.

Chapter 21

Current value accounting

The debate concerning the appropriateness of adjustments for price level changes has highlighted the problems associated with historical cost measures. Neither partial nor general adjustments to historical cost measures deal satisfactorily with the problem of price level changes.

Current value accounting is a radical alternative to the proposals we discussed in Chapter 20. It represents an attempt to combine desirable aspects of economic theory with the conventional accounting method based on historical costs. Current value models use current market prices which are incorporated in the traditional accounting format.

For reporting purposes, concepts of income are required which satisfy the criteria of relevance and feasibility. We noted in Chapter 18 that concepts of income which were relevant were not necessarily feasible and vice versa. Whereas economic income is more relevant to decision making than accounting income, it does not satisfy the criteria of feasibility. By contrast, accounting income fails to satisfy the criteria of relevance, though it does meet the criteria of feasibility.

Current value accounting attempts to bridge the gap between accounting and economic income by providing measurements which are both relevant and feasible. Current values are applied to the measurement of profit and capital for the purpose of financial reporting, thereby providing more relevant information to investors than the information based on historical cost records found in the financial accounting system. Objectivity is maintained in an accounting sense by retaining the realization convention for timing value-changes.

The result is that the financial accounting system recording historical cost data retains its usefulness for establishing the legal rights and obligations created as a result of transactions, whereas the financial reports directed at investors contain information concerning the profit and capital based on the current value of the items appearing in those reports.

Current value accounting takes three forms:

1 Replacement cost accounting—which is based on the current acquisition value of assets, so that in effect, they are valued at their current entry price.

2 Realizable value accounting—which is based on the current realizable value of assets, that is, their current exit price.

3 Current cost accounting—which is concerned with the value to the business of assets. While, in many cases, this value would, in fact, be the replacement cost, in some circumstances it would be the net present value of the future income from the asset or its net realizable value.

Replacement cost accounting

The basic concept underlying replacement cost accounting is that the firm is a going concern, which is continuously replacing its assets. Therefore, the cost of consuming such assets in the profit generation process should be equivalent to the cost of their replacement. Replacement cost accounting differs from current purchasing power accounting in that it is concerned with the manner in which price changes affect the individual firm. It focuses on the specific commodities and assets employed by the firm taking into account changes in the price of such commodities and assets reflected in specific price indices or price indices of groups of similar commodities and assets.

Replacement cost accounting is addressed to the concept of capital maintenance, interpreted as maintaining the operating capacity of the firm, and involves:

1 calculating current operating profit by matching current revenues with the current cost of resources exhausted in earning those revenues;

2 calculating holding gains and losses;

3 presenting the balance sheet in current value terms.

Components of replacement cost profit (RCP)

The treatment of the two components of replacement cost profit (RCP), namely current operating profit and holding gains and losses, is a controversial matter in the literature of accounting.

Current operating profit results from operating activities and is calculated by matching revenues with the current cost of resources exhausted in these activities. Holding gains and losses result from holding rather than operating activities.

According to the method of replacement cost accounting suggested by Edwards and Bell (1961), holding gains and losses should be reported together with current operating profit in the measurement of RCP. In identifying holding gains as they arise, thereby distinguishing these gains from gains occurring on realization, the pattern of profit recognition differs under replacement cost accounting from that associated with conventional accounting profit, as may be seen from the following example:

Example

During the year ended 31 December 19X0, an asset was acquired at a cost of £40. By 31 December 19X0 its replacement cost had risen to £60. It was sold during the year ended 31 December 19X1 for £100, and at the time of sale its replacement cost was £65.

For the purpose of measuring accounting profit, the profit arising from the sale of the asset (assuming no depreciation) would accrue in the year ended 31 December 19X1 and would be calculated as follows:

$$\text{accounting profits} = \text{revenue} - \text{historical cost}$$
$$= \text{£100} - \text{£40}$$
$$= \text{£60}$$

For the purpose of measuring RCP, three distinct gains are recognized which occur as follows:

1 A holding gain in the year ended 31 December 19X0, measured as the difference between the replacement cost at 31 December 19X0 and the acquisition cost during the year, that is, £60 – £40 = £20.
2 A holding gain in the year ended 31 December 19X1, measured as the difference between the replacement cost at 31 December 19X0 and the replacement cost on the date of sale, that is, £65 – £60 = £5.
3 An operating gain resulting directly from the activity of selling, measured as the difference between the realized sale price and the replacement cost at the date of sale, that is, £100 – £65 = £35.

These differing timings of profit recognition may be compared as follows:

Year ended 31 December	19X0	19X1
	£	£
Accounting profit	—	60
Replacement cost profit		
Holding gains	20	5
Current operating gain	—	35

It is clear from this example that the RCP concept provides more detailed information than the accounting profit concept for the purpose of evaluating the results of activities. Moreover, RCP indicates whether the sales proceeds are sufficient to cover the cost of the resources sold, that is, whether the activity of selling itself is efficient. Where the goods sold are manufactured by the firm, current operating profit indicates whether the manufacturing process is profitable, for the input factors of production are valued at their current replacement cost. Hence, from a long-term point of view, it affords a means of evaluating the firm as a going concern.

Profit measurement by historical cost and replacement cost compared

The extent of the differences between these two concepts of profit are revealed by a more comprehensive example.

Example

The financial position of Preifat Ltd, as revealed by the balance sheet as at 31 December 19X0 using historical cost measurements, is as follows:

	£		£
Share capital	1 400	Fixed asset	1 000
		Stock	400
	1 400		1 400

The fixed asset shown on the balance sheet was acquired on 31 December 19X0 and has an estimated life of 5 years, with no scrap value.

Data recorded in respect of the year ended 31 December 19X1 is as follows:

	£
Sales	2 000
Purchases at historical cost	700
Closing stock: at historical cost	200
at replacement cost	250
Cost of goods sold at replacement cost	1 000

It was also estimated that the replacement cost of the fixed asset had risen to £1200 by 31 December 19X1.

On the basis of this information, the accounting profit for the year 19X1 may be computed as follows:

Accounting profit for the year ended 31 December 19X1

	£	£
Sales		2 000
Cost of goods sold:		
Opening stock	400	
Purchases	700	
	1 100	
Closing stock	200	
		900
		1 100
Depreciation (£1 000 ÷ 5)		200
Accounting profit		900

By contrast, the calculation of the components of replacement cost profit gives a more comprehensive analysis of the nature of operating and holding gains, as follows:

Replacement cost profit for the year ended 31 December 19X1

	£	£
Sales		2 000
Cost of goods sold (at replacement cost)		1 000
		1 000
Depreciation (£1200 ÷ 5)		240
(a) **Current operating profit**		760
(b) **Holding gains**		
(i) Realized through use during the year:		
Fixed assets	40	
Stocks	100	
		140
(ii) Unrealized at the end of the year		
Fixed assets	160	
Stocks	50	
		210
Total holding gains		350
Current operating profit plus holding gains		1 100

Note:

1 Depreciation is calculated on the replacement cost of the fixed assets (£1200) rather than on the historical acquisition cost (£1000). By this means, the depreciation provision is more realistic in relation to the current cost of resource utilization.

2 Stocks are charged against sales at their current replacement cost at the time of sale.

3 Holding gains are of two kinds:

(a) Realized holding gains which result from the application of replacement cost values to the input of resources to the profit generation process. In the example, depreciation charged under replacement cost accounting is £40 greater than that charged under historical cost accounting. Similarly, the cost of goods sold under replacement cost is £100 greater than that charged under historical cost accounting. Both amounts represent holding gains realized by reason of the use or the sale of assets.

(b) Unrealized holding gains which result from the increased value of assets held by the firm and remaining unused or unsold at the end of the accounting period. In the example, the unrealized holding gains are calculated as follows:

(i) Fixed assets: unallocated value at the end of the accounting period:

Under replacement cost	£1 200 − 240 = £960
Under historic cost	£1 000 − 200 = 800
Unrealized holding gain	160

(ii) Stock: stock unsold at the end of the accounting period:

Under replacement cost	£250
Under historical cost	200
Unrealized holding gain	50

Historical cost and replacement cost balance sheets compared

The effect of applying historical cost and replacement cost valuations to balance sheets is seen in the following balance sheet drawn from data given in the example.

Balance sheet as at 31 December 19X1
(assuming that all sales and purchases were paid in cash)

	Historical cost	Replacment cost
	£	£
Fixed assets	1 000	1 200
Less: Accumulated depreciation	200	240
	800	960
Current assets		
Stock	200	250
Cash	1 300	1 300
	2 300	2 510
Share capital	1 400	1 400
Retained profit		
Accounting profit	900	
Current operating profit		760
Revaluation reserve		350
	2 300	2 510

Note: Cash balance is calculated as follows:

sales £2000 – purchases £700 = cash £1300

As may be observed, the application of replacement cost values attempts to reflect economic reality by maintaining the value of asset balances in line with changes in the value of money and changes in the specific value of the assets concerned.

The treatment of holding gains

One of the controversial issues in the debate about replacement cost accounting is whether holding gains constitute profit. There is little doubt that current operating profit satisfies the accounting convention relating to realization, and at the same time is directed to the maintenance of capital, which is a basic principle in the measurement of economic income.

From a theoretical viewpoint, there is strong support for the argument that holding gains should not be treated as profit, that is, they should not be regarded as available for distribution. Assuming that the firm is a going concern, the holding gain resulting from the increase in the current replacement cost of specific assets should be retained for the purpose of replacing those assets, for one of the objectives of replacement cost accounting is to ensure the maintenance of capital through the replacement of the values exhausted in earning profit. The distinction between realized and unrealized holding gains, which is important in this respect, may be preserved in the appropriate account, which is the asset revaluation reserve account.

An evaluation of replacement cost accounting

As a method of financial reporting, the objective of replacement cost accounting is to provide a concept of profit which will satisfy the criteria of relevance and feasibility which were discussed earlier.

Replacement cost profit is more relevant to investors than accounting profit for the purpose of decision making. First, it provides for the maintenance of the service potential of capital by charging against revenue the cost of replacing the assets exhausted in earning revenue. Second, an important distinction is made between operating profit and holding gains, thereby allowing investors to appraise the firm as a going concern. Third, it recognizes changes in the value of assets, since they are related to current market prices. For these reasons, investors are provided with information which is more relevant than accounting profit for evaluating the business, and they are placed in a better position to predict the future. By providing more accurate valuations of assets in use, replacement cost accounting is likely to lead to a more efficient allocation of financial resources than that afforded by conventional accounting methods. A further argument in favour of replacement cost accounting lies in the diversity of values found in conventional accounting due to the employment of a variety of valuation methods, such as LIFO, FIFO or average cost. With replacement cost accounting, however, values are uniformly derived from the current replacement cost of specific assets, so that comparisons are much more meaningful.

Criticisms are sometimes advanced against replacement cost accounting on the ground that the measurements involved are subjective. There exist, however, Government Indices which relate to fixed assets of various kinds, which may be employed for the purpose of calculating the replacement cost of specific fixed assets. The Sandilands Committee recommended that the Government Statistical Service should publish as soon as possible a new series of price indices specific to particular industries for capital expenditure on plant and machinery. Such a series of indices should be designed to provide a 'standard reference basis' for making reasonable approximations of current replacement costs. The derivation of replacement costs for stocks could present problems. However, when the various different methods of valuing stocks at the present time are considered, it appears that replacement cost provides a more objective measure.

A major problem arises during periods of rapid technological change. Most authorities argue that since a measure of the profitability of existing operations is required, current replacement costs should be measured in terms of the market prices prevailing for the actual fixed assets which are exhausted in producing profit. Some authorities are opposed to this view, since it seemingly ignores the effect of technological change. They argue that the replacement cost of new-generation assets should be used, because 'the primary interest is in the long-run prospects of the firm, and there seems to be no particular reason why these long-run prospects would be indicated by the prospects of the present mode of production, when becoming obsolete'. Accordingly, if the firm is using a second-generation computer made obsolete by the development of third-generation computers, they argue that the current replacement cost should be based on the current market price of third-generation rather than second-generation computers.

Realizable value accounting

Both historical cost and replacement cost accounting employ entry values, that is, they are based on the acquisition cost of assets. By contrast, realizable value accounting employs exit values, that is, it is based on the realizable price of assets.

The distinction between entry and exit values leads to two different concepts of profit—realized and realizable income. Realized profit arises only upon sale, so that unsold assets are valued at cost. By contrast, realizable profit is based on the current selling price of the assets, thereby indicating the revenue which could be obtained should the assets be sold. As a result, unsold assets are valued not at cost, but at realizable value.

The case for realizable value accounting

The realizable value model is based on the concept of opportunity cost, that is, value is expressed in terms of the benefit lost in holding assets in their present form rather than in the next-best alternative form. For example, as regards closing stocks, the next best alternative to holding stocks is selling them, so that on an opportunity cost basis, the value of closing stocks is what they would realize if sold.

Chambers and Sterling have argued in favour of realizable value accounting. According to Chambers, for example, the most important characteristic of the firm is its capacity to adapt to a changing environment, and in this way, to ensure its survival. The survival of the firm depends, therefore, on its ability to acquire goods and services, which is related to the realizable value of its existing assets. Chambers coined the term 'current cash equivalent' to indicate the realizable value of the firm's currently held assets, that is, the cash represented by those assets and available, if sold, for investing in market alternatives and consequently redeploying its resources (Chambers, 1966; Sterling, 1970).

By contrast, replacement cost accounting reflects a relatively static situation, and does not inform investors about the economic sacrifice made in holding resources in their current form.

Another argument in favour of realizable value accounting is that realizable value profit is an acceptable surrogate for economic income, for it indicates future cash flows which may result from the realization of currently held assets. As argued in Chapter 19, the present value of future cash flows associated with the holding of assets is the most relevant concept of value from the point of view of investors. Backward looking concepts, such as historical cost and replacement cost values, are poor surrogates as predictors of future cash flows.

Finally, a further argument in favour of realizable value lies in its relevance to the needs of creditors for information about the market value of the assets held by a company to which they have extended credit facilities, particularly if the security for loans and other forms of credit is represented by liens or mortgages over such assets.

Components of realizable profit

Realizable profit reflects the periodic change in the value of enterprise capital measured in terms of resale price. It consists of two components:

1   Realized gains resulting from the sale of assets during the accounting period, which are measured as the difference between the actual realized revenue from sale and the realizable value estimated at the beginning of the period.
2   Unrealized gains resulting from changes in the realizable value of assets which have remained unsold at the end of the accounting period.

Example

During the year ended 31 December 19X0 an asset was acquired for £40. At 31 December 19X0, its estimated realizable value was £85, and it was sold during the year ended 31 December 19X1 for £100. The realizable profit for the years ended 31 December 19X0 and 19X1 is as follows:

	19X0	19X1
Realizable profit		
Unrealized gain	£85 − 40 = £45	
Realized gain		£100 − 85 = £15

We noted in our earlier discussion of holding gains arising under replacement cost accounting that such gains could not be treated as part of replacement income. The reason for this view is to be found in the capital maintenance criterion to which replacement cost profit is directed. By contrast, the realizable value concept of profit is directed towards measuring the firm's ability to adapt to a changing environment, and for this purpose profit is required to measure changes in the firm's command over goods and services. This may be measured by reference to both realized gains and unrealized gains which result, as we mentioned earlier, from changes in the realizable value of assets during the year. Hence, under realizable value profit, no distinction is maintained between current operating profit and holding gains. Assets are shown on the balance sheet at their realizable value.

Limitations of exit values

Exit values imply a short-run approach to the analysis of business operations because they entail disposition and liquidation values being shown on the balance sheet. Hence, business operations resulting in realizable profit only indicate that it is worth staying in business in the short run, not that it is worth replacing assets and staying in business in the long term. Realizable value accounting values all assets at exit prices even though many assets are not held for resale.

It has been argued that the crucial test of the usefulness of exit values in financial reports lies in the treatment of highly specific assets, which may have very little value for anyone except the present owner for whom they were constructed. The most extreme example of such assets are mineshafts—which being large holes in the ground have no exit value. Such assets may be presumed to have been worth as much to the firm as their acquisition or construction costs. Otherwise, it is clear that they would not have been acquired or constructed. The question is—what would be the sense of writing such assets down to their current realizable value?

Another limitation of exit values lies in their anticipation of operating profit, before the critical event giving rise to revenue has occurred. It has been argued, for example that

'If profit is to be recognized at a moment of time, we must select that moment. The economist gives a clue in the formulation of entrepreneurship as the function of directing a business, bearing the risks and reaping the rewards of the business. This suggests that profit is earned at the moment of making the most crucial decision or of performing the most difficult task in the cycle of a complete transaction.' (Myers, 1973.)

Where production is the critical event and sale presents no problem, the valuation of profit at net realizable value gives a better indication of managerial performance than does replacement cost. Where selling is the main difficulty, the sale is the critical event which must occur before managerial performance may be correctly evaluated, for without a contract of sale or an active quoted market for the product, the accountant has little evidence of managerial accomplishment. The accountant must assume, in these circumstances, that the product will be sold for at least the break-even price, so that replacement cost is the most suitable measurement of value in these circumstances.

Current cost accounting

Current cost accounting is a modification to historical cost profit to arrive at 'the surplus after allowing for the impact of price changes on the funds needed to continue the existing business and to maintain its operating capability, whether financed by shares or borrowings'.

Current cost accounting utilizes two important theoretical concepts:

1 operating capability,
2 value to the business.

Operating capability

Operating capability is assumed to be represented by net operating assets that include not only physical assets, such as fixed assets and stocks, but also the net monetary working capital.

Value to the business

The concept of 'value to the business' should determine whether exit or entry values should be used in the valuation process. One way of determining 'value to the business' is to reverse the opportunity cost concept, and to define opportunity value as the least costly sacrifice avoided by owning the asset. This approach to the valuation of an asset to the business has been adopted by a number of economists. Bonbright (1937), for example, defined opportunity value in the following terms: 'The value of a property to its owner is identical in amount with the adverse value of the entire loss, direct and indirect, that the owner might expect to suffer if he were deprived of the property.'

In no sense may historical cost be measured as the value of an asset to the business because it is not related to the amount which would have to be paid for the asset, the amount that might be gained from disposing of it or the amount to be gained by holding it. It remains to consider therefore, the other three bases of valuation which were listed in the introduction:

1 the current purchase price (replacement cost) of the asset (CR);
2 the net realizable value of the asset (NRV);
3 the present value of expected future earnings from the asset (PV).

It has been argued (Parker and Harcourt, 1969) that six hypothetical relationships exist between these three values:

	Correct valuation basis
(a) NRV > PV > RC	RC
(b) NRV > RC > PV	RC
(c) PV > RC > NRV	RC
(d) PV > NRV > RC	RC
(e) RC > PV > NRV	PV
(f) RC > NRV > PV	NRV

In (a) and (b) above, NRV is greater than PV. Hence, the firm would be better off selling rather than using the asset. The sale of the asset necessitates its replacement, if the NRV is to be restored. We may say, therefore, that the maximum loss the firm would suffer by being deprived of the asset is RC.

In (c) and (d) above, PV is greater than NRV, so that the firm would be better off using the asset rather than selling it. The firm must replace the asset in order to maintain PV, so that the maximum loss the firm would suffer by being deprived of the asset is again RC.

The general statement which may be made, therefore, in respect of the first four cases (a) to (d) is that, where either NRV or PV, or both, are higher than RC, RC is the appropriate value of the asset to the business. As regards a current asset, such as stocks, RC will be the current purchase price (entry value). In the case of a fixed asset, RC will be the written-down current purchase price (replacement cost), since the value of such an asset will be the cost of replacing it in its existing condition, having regard to wear and tear.

As regards cases (e) and (f), RC does not represent the value of the asset to the business, for if the firm were to be deprived of the asset then the loss incurred would be less than RC. Case (e) is most likely to arise in industries where assets are highly specific, where NRV tends to zero and where RC is greater than PV, so that it would not be worth replacing the asset if it were destroyed, but it is worth using it rather than attempting to dispose of it. The conclusion which may be reached as regards fixed assets is that except in the rare occurrence of case (e) fixed assets which are held for use should be valued at RC if such assets are to represent their value to the business.

Case (f) applies to assets held for resale, that is, where NRV must be greater than PV. If RC should prove to be greater than NRV, such assets would not be replaced. Hence, it implies that they should be valued at NRV or RC, whichever is the lower. This recommendation, despite its superficial resemblance to the lower of cost or market value which we argued to be illogical in Part 2, is not a concession to the convention of conservatism, but represents an attempt to measure the value of assets to the business. If RC exceeds NRV, stocks will not be replaced, so that NRV represents their value to the firm. Conversely, where NRV exceeds RC, stocks are worth replacing, so that their value to the firm is determined by RC.

Application of current cost accounting under SSAP 16 'Current Cost Accounting'

The main features of this method, as expressed under SSAP 16 'Current Cost Accounting' were:

1 Current cost information should be published in addition to historical-cost information as part of the annual financial reports.

2 The current cost accounts should consist of a profit and loss account and a balance sheet with explanatory notes. The appendix at the

end of this chapter illustrates the nature of such documents under current cost accounting.

3 The current cost profit and loss account should show the current cost operating profit or loss. This is derived by making three adjustments to historical cost profit before interest and taxation in respect of depreciation, cost of sales and monetary working capital. The nature of these adjustments are discussed later in this chapter.

4 The current cost profit and loss account should also include a figure attributable to shareholders. This is derived by making a gearing adjustment to the current cost operating profit.

5 Current cost earnings per share based on the current cost profit attributable to shareholders should be disclosed.

6 The current cost balance sheet should include fixed assets and stocks at their value to the business. The balance sheet may be shown in summary form and should include a separate current cost reserve showing the effects of three elements:
   (a) revaluation surpluses or deficits arising from price changes in respect of fixed assets and stocks;
   (b) the monetary working capital adjustment;
   (c) the gearing adjustment.

The depreciation adjustment

The depreciation adjustment reflects the difference between the depreciation calculated on the current cost of fixed assets and the depreciation charged in computing the historical cost profit. The accounting policy adopted for the purpose of calculating the historical cost profit should be followed when calculating the depreciation on the current cost of fixed assets. Hence, once an enterprise has established the current cost of an asset, the determination of the depreciation adjustment is a simple matter. The current cost depreciation charge may be computed by revising the depreciation charge in accordance with the change in the appropriate index level between the year of the purchase of the asset and the current year. This calculation is illustrated below:

Asset Y	Historical cost £	Index factor	Current cost £
Cost in year 1	1 200	$\times \dfrac{200}{150}$	1 600
Depreciation at 10% per annum	720		960
	480		640

Index for Asset Y	
Year	Index
Mid 1	150
End 6	200

Depreciation adjustment

		£
Current cost depreciation per annum	10% of £1 600 =	160
Historical cost depreciation per annum	10% of £1 200 =	120
Depreciation adjustment		40

The adjustment to the current cost reserve

The net increase in the value of Asset Y to be credited to the current cost reserve is arrived at by deducting the net historical cost of Asset Y from its net current cost at the end of year 6, both sums being calculated before taking depreciation into account, as follows:

	Net book value end of year 6 £	+	Depreciation for year 6 £	=	Net book value before depreciation £
Current cost	640	+	160	=	800
Historical cost	480	+	120	=	600
Net credit to the current cost reserve					200

Where the movement in the cost of a major asset is known to have been significantly different from the movement in the relevant index, the current replacement cost of the asset should be obtained from the supplier's price lists or by a valuation performed by external valuers who are experts in the valuation of plant and machinery.

Where an asset has been rendered obsolete in design and technology, reference should be made to its replacement by a modern equivalent asset. The value to the business of the existing asset is then the cost of purchasing that proportion of the modern asset that would give the same output at the same unit cost of production as the existing asset.

The cost of sales adjustment (COSA)

The cost of sales adjustment refers to the difference between the current cost of stocks at the date of sale and the amount charged as the cost of goods sold in computing the historical cost profit. As we will see in Part 5, business enterprises use standard costing systems for the purpose of obtaining timely information about the cost of stocks. These standard costing systems are designed to identify and to reflect, *inter alia*, changes in the current cost of purchased stocks. Where a standard costing system is in use, it is possible to derive an analysis of the variances which are differences between historical and standard costs, and to use this analysis to identify the extent to which current costs differ from standard costs. This information may be used to adjust the standard cost of goods sold to their current costs.

Where standard costing systems are not used, it is possible to average out the changes in the cost of sales. This method involves valuing the opening and closing stocks at the average cost for the year. The cost of sales is established as the purchases of the year, which are already stated at their average price for the year, adjusted by the revised values of the opening and closing stocks.

Example

Historical cost data

	£000
Opening stock	350
add: Purchases	2 300
	2 650
deduct: Closing stock	540
Cost of sales at historical cost	2 110

Index for the cost of stock

At the beginning of the year	100
At the end of the year	120
Average for the year	110

(a) **Revise opening and closing stocks to average cost for the year**

£000

Opening stock $\qquad 350 \times \dfrac{110}{100} = 385$

Closing stock $\qquad 540 \times \dfrac{110}{120} = 495$

(b) **Compute the current cost of sales using the revised amounts for the opening and closing stocks**

	£000
Opening stock	385
add: Purchases	2 300
	2 685
less: Closing stock	495
Cost of sales on current cost basis	2 190

(c) **Calculate the cost of sales adjustment**

	£000
Cost of sales on current cost basis	2 190
less: Cost of sales on historical cost basis	2 110
Cost of sales adjustment	80

The monetary working capital adjustment (MWCA)

The purpose of this adjustment is to apply the concept of current value to monetary assets, to achieve the same effect as do the depreciation and the cost of sales adjustments in respect of fixed assets and stocks.

Monetary working capital consists of trade debtors plus stocks not subjected to the cost of sales adjustment less trade creditors. Provided that it can be shown that it would be misleading to exclude them from monetary working capital, part of the bank balances and bank overdrafts, where applicable, may also be included in monetary working capital.

The objective of the monetary working capital adjustment and the cost of sales adjustments is to take account of the effects of changing prices on the financing requirements necessary to maintain the working capital applied to the day-to-day operations of the business. The relationship between the MWCA made in respect of trade debtors and trade creditors and the COSA is as follows:

1   when sales are made on credit the business has to finance the changes in its input prices until the sales result in a receipt of cash. The part of the MWCA related to trade debtors, in effect, extends the COSA to allow for this; and
2   conversely, when materials and services are purchased from suppliers who offer trade credit, price changes are financed by the supplier during the credit period. To this extent extra funds do not have to be found by the business and this reduces the need for a COSA and in some cases for a MWCA on debtors. The part of the MWCA related to trade creditors reflects this reduction.

SSAP 16 points out that there can be difficulties in practice in identifying, on an objective basis, those monetary assets and liabilities which are part of the net operating assets of the business. Nevertheless, a practical way of doing this has to be accepted if the operating profit is to be identified. Reasonable accuracy and objectivity may usually be achieved by including only trade debtors and trade creditors within monetary working capital, with an extension in the case of financial institutions. However, fluctuations in the volume of stock, debtors and creditors may lead to contrary fluctuations in cash or overdraft. It is necessary to include this element of cash or overdraft within monetary working capital if to do so has a material effect on current cost operating profit. Monetary working capital may also include cash floats required to support the business operations. The treatment adopted should be applied consistently.

Evidently, the method used to compute the monetary working capital adjustment should be compatible with that used to compute the cost of sales adjustment. For example, the sales of finished goods give rise to trade debtors. Hence, all things being equal, changes in the amount of finance required to support the increased level of trade debtors associated with price inflation will tend to be proportional to changes in the cost of goods finished. Consequently, the change in the index of finished goods prices is used to calculate that part of the monetary working capital which relates to supporting trade debtors. Equally, since the purchase of raw materials in the case of a manufacturing company gives rise to trade creditors, the change in the index of raw material prices is used to calculate that part of the monetary working capital which relates to trade creditors.

Example

	End Year 1	**Eng Year 2**
	£	£
Historical cost balance sheets		
Trade debtors	60 000	80 000
Trade creditors	50 000	65 000
Index numbers	**Finished goods**	**Raw materials**
End year 1	100	105
Average year 2	110	114
End year 2	118	120

Trade debtors adjustment

£

Increase in trade debtors £80 000 − £60 000 = 20 000

less:

Index adjustment $£80\,000 \times \dfrac{110}{118} - £60\,000 \times \dfrac{110}{100} =$ 8 576

11 424

Trade creditors adjustment

£

Increase in trade creditors £65 000 − £50 000 = 15 000

less:

Index adjustment $£65\,000 \times \dfrac{114}{120} - £50\,000 \times \dfrac{114}{105} =$ 7 464

7 536

£

Monetary working capital adjustment 3 888

It should be noted that most of the problems associated with the calculation of the monetary working capital adjustment arise from the needs to identify monetary assets and liabilities associated with the net borrowing requirement. This net borrowing requirement affects the gearing adjustment which has to be made under current-cost accounting.

The gearing adjustment

We noted in Chapter 14 that the capital structure of a company has important implications for financial management purposes. In particular, the gearing is important, since it expresses the relationship between fixed interest (loan) capital and fixed dividend (preference) shares on the one hand and ordinary shares on the other. A company that has a large proportion of fixed interest and fixed dividend bearing capital to ordinary capital is said to be highly geared.

The purpose of the gearing adjustment is to allocate equitably the current cost adjustments in order that the full burden should not fall on ordinary shareholders, where they themselves have not financed the entire assets in respect of which the adjustments are made. This adjustment, subject to interest on borrowing, indicates the benefit or cost to shareholders which is realized in the period, measured by the extent to which a proportion of the net operating assets are financed by borrowing. The current cost profit attributable to shareholders is the surplus after making allowance for the impact of price changes on the shareholders' interest in the net operating assets, after provision for the maintenance of lenders' capital in accordance with their repayment rights.

SSAP 16 required a gearing adjustment to be made where a proportion of the assets of the business is financed by borrowing. Net borrowing is defined as the amount by which liabilities (defined in (1) below) exceed assets (defined in (2) below):

1 the aggregate of all liabilities and provisions (including convertible debentures and deferred tax but excluding dividends) other than those included within monetary working capital;
2 the aggregate of all current assets other than those subject to a cost of sales adjustment and those included within monetary working capital.

The gearing adjustment itself results from the application of the gearing ratio to the net adjustments made in converting the historical cost profit to current cost profit. The gearing ratio is found in the relationship between net borrowing (L) and the average ordinary shareholders' interest obtained from the opening and closing balance sheets (S), as follows:

$$\text{Gearing ratio} = \frac{L}{L+S}$$

Example

	Opening balance sheet	Closing balance sheet	Average
Shareholders' interest	£	£	£
Share capital	100	100	100
Reserves (including the current cost reserve)	50	60	55
	150	160	155
Net borrowing	100	110	105
	250	270	260
Current cost adjustments		£	£
Cost of sales			20
Monetary working capital			10
			30
Depreciation			15
Current cost adjustments			45
Gearing adjustment			

$$\text{Gearing ratio} \frac{105}{105+155} = 40.38\%$$

Gearing adjustment			$45 \times 40.38\% = £18$

The gearing adjustment has been the subject of considerable controversy. Everyone would agree that during inflation shareholders benefit from long-term loans, as their repayment is ultimately made in monetary units of smaller purchasing power. It is unclear why the gearing ratio should be applied to the current-cost adjustments rather than to the entire increase in net asset values. SSAP 16 recognized this controversy and stated that:

'There are a number of possible methods for calculating a gearing adjustment. For the reasons set out it is believed that the method defined in the Standard is the most appropriate and, on the grounds of the need for comparability between company accounts, it has been made definitive. This does not prevent those who wish to show in addition the effect of a different method of calculating a gearing adjustment from doing so by way of a note to the accounts. It would help users if those adopting this course explained their reasons for so doing.'

Distributable profit: interpretation and limitations

SSAP 16 considered the relationship between current cost accounting and distribution policy as follows:

'The amounts that can prudently be distributed depend not only on profitability, but also on the availability of funds. This is so with all systems of accounting. When determining distribution policy, consideration must be given to factors not reflected in profit, such as capital expenditure plans, changes in the volume of working capital, the effect on funding requirements of changes in production methods and efficiency, liquidity, and new financing arrangements. The current cost profit attributable to shareholders should not be assumed to measure the amount that can prudently be distributed. Although the impact of price changes on the shareholders' interest in the net operating assets has been allowed for, the other factors still need to be considered. Even if the effect of such factors is neutral, a full distribution of the current cost profit attributable to shareholders may make it necessary to arrange additional finance (equal to the gearing adjustment) to avoid an erosion of the operating capability of the business. However, an increase in the value to the business of the assets may provide increased cover for such financing.'

With regard to interpretation and limitations SSAP 16 stated:

'Current cost accounts allow for the impact of specific price changes on the net operating assets, and thus the operating capability, of the business. The same tools of analysis as those applied to historical cost accounts are generally appropriate. The ratios derived from current cost accounts for such items as gearing, asset cover, dividend cover and return on capital employed will often differ substantially from those revealed in historical cost accounts but should be more realistic indicators when assessing an entity or making comparisons between entities.

'As with historical cost accounting, CCA is not a substitute for forecasting when such matters as a change in the size or nature of the business are under consideration. It assists cash flow forecasts, but does not replace them. It does not measure the effect of changes in the general value of money or translate the figures into currency of purchasing power at a specific date. Because of this it is not a system of accounting for general inflation. Further, it does not show changes in the value of the business as a whole or the market value of the equity.'

The current cost reserve

The current cost balance sheet included a reserve in addition to those included in historical cost accounts. The additional reserve may be referred to as the current cost reserve. The total reserves will include, where appropriate:

1 unrealized revaluation surpluses on fixed assets, stocks and investments; and
2 realized amounts equal to the cumulative net total of the current cost adjustments, that is:
   (a) the depreciation adjustment (and any adjustments on the disposal of fixed assets);
   (b) the two working capital adjustments; and
   (c) the gearing adjustment.

Example of presentation

The appendix reproduces the example of presentation of cost accounts included in SSAP 16.

The progress of SSAP 16 'Current Cost Accounting'

When SSAP 16 was issued, the Accounting Standards Committee announced that it would monitor its progress over a three-year period. A monitoring committee was appointed for this purpose, and over the trial period a number of research projects were also commissioned.

By 1983, it was widely recognized that SSAP 16 had declined in popularity and that many who had originally supported it were now questioning its usefulness. Two main reasons accounted for this changed feeling:

1 from 1980 to 1983, the inflation rate fell constantly, feeding the hope that inflation and its attendant problems would disappear;
2 the Government refused to consider taxing business on a basis consistent with CCA principles. Furthermore, the Government's decision in 1980 to calculate stock relief by reference to the general all stocks' index rather than the specific indices of CCA showed that the Government considered CCA irrelevant for tax purposes.

The monitoring working party took evidence from interested parties and while this revealed considerable dissatisfaction with historical cost accounting, it detected little support for the CCA alternative. Critics of SSAP 16 were especially hostile to the publication of annual reports containing two totally different sets of figures, and the monetary working capital and gearing adjustments received little support. Some argued that SSAP 16 was unsuitable for companies in specialized fields, such as shipping, mining and petroleum. Nevertheless, the monitoring working party recommended that a new standard should be issued that would require financial statements to show the effects of changing prices when these effects were material.

Research into the usefulness of current cost information has concluded that certain types of information are widely used by sophisticated investors. Mixed evidence was found on whether unexpected current cost information leads to changes in share prices, but CCA profit figures appeared to improve the explanation of share prices associated with historical-cost profit. A sense of obligation to investors was advanced as a reason why many companies complied with SSAP 16. The cost of preparing SSAP 16 financial statements was revealed to be relatively inexpensive.

Although this research has been the subject of considerable controversy, advocates of CCA accounting have interpreted it as a justification for continuing the disclosure of CCA information, with limited exemptions where the concept of maintaining operating capability is not applicable (Carsberg and Page, 1984).

In 1984, the publication of ED 35 'Accounting for Changing Prices', contained proposals by the Accounting Standards Committee for an accounting standard to replace SSAP 16. ED 35 did not involve a departure from the concept of 'operating capability', but it did allow simpler methods for calculating the current cost adjustment. In particular, three options were allowed for calculating the gearing adjustment. ED 35 proposed that current cost information be given in the main accounts, either in a note or as part of full current cost accounts, rather than in supplementary cost accounts.

ED 35 provoked generally adverse comment, and the lack of consensus led to its withdrawal in 1985. In June 1985, SSAP 16 was made non-mandatory, and it was finally withdrawn in April 1988. The Presidents of the Professional Accountancy Bodies represented on the Accounting Standards Committee issued a joint statement that 'noting that the subject of accounting for the effects of changing prices is one of great importance, they support the Accounting Standards Committee in its continuing work, and agree that an acceptable accounting standard should be developed.'

Following the withdrawal of SSAP 16, the Accounting Standards Committee issued in 1988 a lengthy document *Accounting for the Effects of Changing Prices: a Handbook*. This handbook is all that remains of the extensive work done on inflation accounting in the United Kingdom over so many years.

Appendix

Example of presentation of current cost accounts

Y Limited and Subsidiaries
Group current cost profit and loss account
for the year ended 31 December 1980

1979			1980
£000			**£000**
18 000	Turnover		20 000
£000			£000
2 420	Profit before interest and taxation on the historical-cost basis		2 900
1 320	*less:* Current cost operating adjustments (note 2)		1 510
1 100	**Current cost operating profit**		1 390
(170)	Gearing adjustment	(166)	
180	Interest payable less receivable	200	
10			34
1 090	Current cost profit before taxation		1 356
610	Taxation		730
480	**Current cost profit attributable to shareholders**		626
400	Dividends		430
80	Retained current cost profit of the year		196
16.0p	Current cost earnings per share		20.9p
5.2%	Operating profit return on the average of the net operating assets		6.0%
£000	**Statement of retained profits/reserves**		**£000**
80	Retained current cost profit of the year		196
1 850	Movements on current cost reserve (Note 4)		2 054
nil	Movements on other reserves		nil
1 930			2 250
14 150	Retained profits/reserves at the beginning of the year		16 080
16 080	Retained profits/reserves at the end of the year		18 330

Where applicable, minority interests and extraordinary items should be presented in a manner consistent with the historical cost accounts.

Example of alternative presentation of current cost profit and loss account

Y Limited and Subsidiaries
Group current-cost profit and loss account
for the year ended 31 December 1980

1979		1980
£000		**£000**
18 000	Turnover	20 000
£000		**£000**
2 420	Profit before interest and taxation on the historical cost basis	2 900
1 320	*less:* Current cost operating adjustments (Note 2)	1 510
1 100	**Current cost operating profit**	1 390
180	Interest payable less receivable	200
920		1 190
610	Taxation	730
310	Current cost profit after interest and taxation	460
170	Gearing adjustment	166
480	**Current cost profit attributable to shareholders**	626
400	Dividends	430
80	Retained current cost profit of the year	196
16.0p	Current cost earnings per share	20.9p
5.2%	Operating profit return on the average of the net operating assets	6.0%

Statement of retained profits/reserves

£000		**£000**
80	Retained current cost profit of the year	196
1 850	Movements on current cost reserve (Note 4)	2 054
nil	Movements on other reserves	nil
1 930		2 250
14 150	Retained profits/reserves at the beginning of the year	16 080
16 080	Retained profits/reserves at the end of the year	18 330

Y Limited and Subsidiaries
Summarized group current cost balance sheet
as at 31 December 1980

1979			1980	
£000	£000		£000	£000
		Assets employed:		
	18 130	Fixed assets (Note 3)		19 530
		Net current assets:		
3 200		Stock	4 000	
700		Monetary working capital	800	
3 900		Total working capital	4 800	
(400)		Proposed dividends	(430)	
(600)		Other current liabilities (net)	(570)	
	2 900			3 800
	21 030			23 330
	£000	**Financed by:**		£000
		Share capital and reserves:		
3 000		Share capital	3 000	
12 350		Current cost reserve (Note 4)	14 404	
3 730		Other reserves and retained profit	3 926	
	19 080			21 330
	1 950	Loan capital		2 000
	21 030			23 330

Y Limited and Subsidiaries
Notes to the current cost accounts for the year ended 31 December 1980

1   **Explanatory notes**
(See paragraph 58 of the Standard and the example in the Guidance Notes)

2   **Adjustments made in deriving cost operating profit**

1979		1980
£000		£000
400	Cost of sales	460
70	Monetary working capital	100
470	**Working capital**	560
850	Depreciation	950
1 320	**Current cost operating adjustments**	1 510

3   **Fixed assets**

	31 December 1980			1979
	Gross	**Depreciation**	**Net**	**Net**
	£000	£000	£000	£000
Land and buildings	3 780	680	3 100	3 070
Plant and machinery	25 780	9 350	16 430	15 060
	29 560	10 030	19 530	18 130

4 Current cost reserve

	£000	£000	£000
Balance at 1 January 1980			12 350
Revaluation surpluses reflecting price changes:			
Land and buildings	200		
Plant and machinery	1 430		
Stocks and work-in-progress	490		
		2 120	
Monetary working capital adjustment		100	
Gearing adjustment		(166)	
			2 054
Balance at 31 December 1980			14 404
of which: realized (*see* (iii) *below*)			2 494
unrealized			11 910
			14 404

(a) Where applicable, surpluses or deficits arising on the following should be shown as movements on reserves:
    (i) the revaluation of investments (other than those included in current assets);
    (ii) the restatement of investments in associated companies; and
    (iii) consolidation differences arising on foreign currency translations.
(b) Where relevant, movements should be shown net of minority interests.
(c) The realized element represents the net cumulative total of the current cost adjustments which have been passed through the profit and loss account, including the gearing adjustment.

5 Financing of net operating assets

The following is the value to the business (normally current replacement cost net of depreciation on fixed assets) of the net operating assets at the balance sheet date, together with the method by which they are financed:

1979 £000		1980 £000
18 130	Fixed assets	19 530
3 900	Working capital	4 800
22 030	**Net operating assets**	24 330
£000		**£000**
19 080	Share capital and reserves	21 330
400	Proposed dividends	430
19 480	**Total shareholders' interest**	21 760
1 950	Loan capital	2 000
600	Other current liabilities	570
2 550	**Net borrowing**	2 570
22 030		24 330

Summary

Current value accounting combines the best characteristics of economic and accounting income, by associating values and changes in values with transactions. Current value accounting takes three forms: replacement cost accounting, realizable value accounting and, current cost accounting.

Replacement cost accounting involves:

1   calculating current operating profit by matching current revenues with the current cost of resources exhausted in earning those revenues;
2   calculating holding gains and losses;
3   presenting the balance sheet in current value terms.

It provides a long-run profit concept, which is associated with existing production processes, thereby maintaining the service potential of capital employed. It provides more useful and more detailed information for decision-making than traditional accounting concepts, while not impairing their 'objectivity'.

Realizable value accounting is a short-run concept of profit, because it implies liquidation values. Hence, it is not a feasible method of accounting for general use.

Current cost accounting utilizes replacement cost and realizable and present values in arriving at the adjustments to be made in converting historical cost profit to current cost profits.

Current cost accounting is concerned with maintaining the operating capability of the capital of the business, defined as comprising both physical and monetary assets, and focuses on finding the value of these assets to the business.

It was a prescribed method in the United Kingdom under SSAP 16 'Current Cost Accounting' published in 1980. The main features of SSAP 16 were examined. They were seen to comprise:

1   a depreciation adjustment applied to fixed assets;
2   a cost of sales adjustment dealing with changes in inventory costs;
3   a monetary working capital adjustment dealing with the impact of inflation on trade debtors, trade creditors, and in certain cases, bank balances and overdrafts;
4   a gearing adjustment dealing with the effects of financing assets by borrowing on the current cost profit attributable to shareholders;
5   a current cost reserve dealing with the effects of these various adjustments.

The decline in the popularity of SSAP 16 was discussed.

References

Bonbright, J. C. (1937). *The Valuation of Property*, p. 71, McGraw-Hill.

Carsberg, B. V. and Page, M. J. (1984). *Current Cost Accounting: the Benefits and the Costs*, Institute of Chartered Accountants in England and Wales.

Chambers, R. J. (1966). *Accounting, Evaluation and Economic Behaviour*, Prentice-Hall.

Edwards, E. O., and Bell, P. W. (1961). *The Theory and Measurement of Business Income*, University of California Press.

Myers, J. H. (1973). 'The critical event and recognition of net profit', in Zeff, S. A. and Keller, T. F. (eds) *Financing Accounting Theory*, McGraw-Hill.

Parker, R. H. and Harcourt, G. C. (1969). *Readings in the Concept and Measurement of Income*, p. 17, Cambridge University Press.

Sterling, R. R. (1970). *Theory and Measurement of Enterprise Income*, University of Kansas Press.

Questions

1 State the objectives of current value accounting, and explain its different forms.

2 Explain the nature and purpose of replacement cost accounting.

3 Explain the significance of the distinction made under replacement cost accounting between current operating profit and losses and holding gains and losses.

4 Comment on the distinction made between realized and unrealized holding gains. How are these gains treated under replacement cost accounting?

5 State the objectives of realizable value accounting.

6 Compare and contrast replacement and realizable value accounting.

7 What do you understand by 'current cost accounting'?

8 State the differences between replacement cost and current cost accounting.

9 Comment briefly on the concept of 'value to the business', used in connection with current cost accounting.

10 Review briefly the adjustments that were required under SSAP 16 'Current Cost Accounting'.

Problems

1 ABC Ltd has traded for several years. Its accounts are kept on a conventional historical cost basis.

Balance sheet

	31.12.X3	31.12.X4		31.12.X3	31.12.X4
	£	£		£	£
Capital	38 100	38 100	Plant	100 800	100 800
Retained profit	8 490	19 260	*less:* Depn.	37 800	44 800
	46 590	57 360		63 000	56 000
Loan	27 000	27 000	Stocks	4 290	7 560
Creditors	3 600	8 600	Debtors	9 000	24 000
			Cash	900	5 400
	77 190	92 960		77 190	92 960

Indices	General	Stock	Plant
	£	£	£
Date capital acquired	50		
Date plant acquired	80		70
Date opening stocks acquired	85.8	110	
1 January 19X4	90	120	100
30 June 19X4	100	130	115
30 September 19X4	105	135	122
31 December 19X4	110	140	130

No purchases or sales of plant took place during the year. No dividends have been paid or proposed. Ignore taxation.

Closing stock was valued at 30 September prices.

Required:
Prepare a balance sheet as at 31 December 19X4 on a CPP basis and on an RC basis.

2   T. A. Lee Ltd carries on business as an electrical appliance wholesaler. The following information prepared on a historical cost basis relates to the year ended 31 January 19X5.

	£	£
Sales		395 810
less: Opening stocks	31 070	
Purchases	243 222	
Closing stocks	(46 088)	228 204
Gross profit		167 606
less: Wages and salaries	65 010	
Selling and administrative expenses	19 668	
Depreciation	20 128	104 806
Net trading profit		62 800

The opening stock was purchased on average on 31 December 19X3, and the closing stock purchased on average on 31 December 19X4. The electrical appliance price index contains the following figures:

31.12.X3	104
31.1.X4	106
31.7.X4	112
31.12.X4	117
31.1.X5	118

The depreciation charge relates to warehouse equipment purchased on the following dates:

	£
30.6.X2	22 800
31.12.X2	36 750
31.3.X3	41 090
Total	100 640

Depreciation is charged at 20 per cent straight line.

The price index for such equipment contains the following figures:

30.6.X2	94
31.12.X2	99
31.3.X3	102
31.1.X4	111
31.7.X4	116
31.1.X5	121

Required:
(a) From the information available restate the trading results utilizing replacement costs.

(b) Discuss the purpose of adjusting the historical cost profit to reflect replacement costs. Briefly discuss the relevance of the replacement cost profit as a guide to dividend policy.

(Problem supplied by A. J. Naughton, Leeds Polytechnic)

3   Keaton Ltd started business 1 January Year 1. Set out below is the balance sheet on a historical cost basis as at 31 December:

		Year 1		Year 2
		£000		£000
Land		110		110
Plant cost	40		40	
depreciation	4	36	8	32
Stocks		90		120
Debtors		30		50
Bank		60		50
		326		362
Creditors		50		80
		276		282
		£		£
Share capital		250		250
Retained earnings		26		32
		276		282

The realizable value of the assets is as follows:

	£	£
Land	150	160
Plant	25	22
Stocks	130	170

The profit and loss account for Year 2 on a historical cost basis is:

	£
Sales	130
Cost of sales	90
	40
Depreciation	4
	36
Dividend	30
Retained earnings	6

Required:
Prepare balance sheets at the end of Years 1 and 2 on the basis of realizable value accounting.

(Problem supplied by A. J. Naughton, Leeds Polytechnic)

4   Barncliffe Ltd prepared summarized historical cost <u>for the year ended</u> 31 December 19X8 as follows:

Profit and loss account

	£	£
Sales		000
Opening stock	40 000	
Purchases	380 000	
	420 000	
Closing stock	50 000	370 000
Gross profit		90 000
Depreciation	5 000	
Expenses	25 000	30 000
Net profit		60 000

Balance sheet

	31 December 19X7	31 December 19X8
Fixed assets	£	£
Buildings at cost	500 000	500 000
less: Aggregate depreciation	105 000	110 000
	395 000	390 000
Current assets		
Stock	40 000	50 000
Trade debtors	20 000	80 000
Cash	40 000	50 000
	100 000	180 000
less: Creditors: Amounts falling due within a year:		
Trade creditors	25 000	40 000
Net current assets	75 000	140 000
Total assets *less* current liabilities	470 000	530 000
less: Creditors: Amounts falling due after more than one year:		
10% debenture loan	100 000	100 000
	370 000	430 000
Capital and reserves	£	£
Issued and paid-up capital	300 000	300 000
Profit and loss account	70 000	130 000
	370 000	430 000

Indices of price levels

	Buildings	Stocks	RPI
At time of raising long-term capital	100	100	100
At time of purchasing building	100	100	100
31 December 19X7	110	110	120
31 December 19X8	60	120	140
Average for 19X8	85	115	130
At time of purchasing opening stocks	110	110	115
At time of purchasing closing stocks	60	118	135

Required:

(a) Prepare (i) CCP balance sheets and profit and loss accounts corresponding to the foregoing historical cost statements.

(ii) CCA balance sheets and profit and loss accounts
corresponding to the foregoing historical cost statements.
(b) Discuss the financial results of Barncliffe Ltd in the light of the alternative
measurements calculated from the CPP and CCA statements you have
prepared.

5   Set out below are the summarized balance sheets of P.I. Ltd for the years 19X2
and 19X1, prepared on a historical cost basis.

	31 March 19X2	31 March 19X1
	£	£
Fixed assets at cost	100 000	100 000
less: Aggregate depreciation	30 000	20 000
	70 000	80 000
Current assets		
Stocks	17 200	14 500
Debtors	28 000	16 000
Cash	4 800	2 000
	50 000	32 500
less: Creditors: Amounts falling due within one year		
Trade creditors	13 000	12 500
Net current assets	37 000	20 000
Total assets *less* Current liabilities	107 000	100 000
less: Creditors: Amounts falling due after more than one year		
Long-term loan	30 000	30 000
	77 000	70 000
Capital and reserves	£	£
Issued and paid up capital	50 000	50 000
Profit and loss account	27 000	20 000
	77 000	70 000

The opening stocks were purchased on 28 February 19X1 and the closing stocks
were purchased on 29 February 19X2.

Required:
Using the following indices where appropriate:
(a) Prepare a schedule of the current cost adjustments to the profit for the year
ended 31 March 19X2, as recommended by SSAP 16.
(b) Prepare a summarized current cost balance sheet as at 31 March 19X2,
including an analysis of the reserves.

Indices	Fixed Assets	Stocks
Date fixed assets purchased	50	—
28.2.19X1	—	145
31.3.19X1	100	145
30.9.19X1	110	170
29.2.19X2	—	186
31.3.19X2	120	190

Note:
(a) It is acceptable to use the stock price index for the calculation of the monetary
working capital adjustment.
(b) The current cost value of the equity capital at 31 March 19X1 was £150 000.

(Problem supplied by A. J. Naughton, Leeds Polytechnic)

Part 4

Financial reporting—
extending the disclosure of information

Introduction

The scope of accounting was defined in Chapter 1 as being 'to provide information which is potentially useful for making economic decisions and which, if provided, will enhance social welfare'. This definition of the scope of accounting was followed by a discussion of the development of accounting theory, where several approaches to accounting theory were discussed. It was seen, in particular, that the current state of accounting knowledge depended substantially on a descriptive approach to accounting theory. This emphasized observations of the practices of accountants as a major source of accounting knowledge. It was for this reason that Part 2 was devoted to an analysis of the knowledge provided by a descriptive approach to accounting theory. Part 3 was seen as necessary in the context of the adjustments considered necessary to historical cost accounting by reason of the instability of the monetary standard of measurement. This instability affects not only the measurement of periodic profit but the valuations which are significant in financial reports.

The problem which must be posed is the relevance of accounting information in the context of the needs of users for decision making. This problem, which was posed in the definition of accounting given in Chapter 1, was only dealt with partly in Part 3. In this part, we return to the implications of the definition of accounting as concerned with information useful for making economic decisions having welfare implications. In this sense, we shall return to the problems instanced in Chapter 3 in the discussion of different approaches to accounting theory. This provides an opportunity for examining the manner in which normative and welfare approaches to theory construction in accounting have a role to play in the development of accounting knowledge.

The provision of information intended for economic decisions has implicit welfare effects. These effects relate not only to the manner in which the welfare of those receiving and using accounting information is susceptible of improvement, but implies some judgemental aspects as regards the balance of influence which different groups can exert on the enterprise in obtaining advantages for themselves.

It is significant that the disclosure of information to external users has been restricted by the influence which management has been able to exert whenever the need for more extensive disclosure to external users has been at issue. The historical reasons why management has a considerable influence within the accounting profession lie in the manner in which the accounting profession developed in the nineteenth century. In effect, the directors of large companies were patrons of the accounting profession, and in many areas of accounting responsibility were able to specify the services which they required, and which became a major source of revenue to accountants. The relationship which developed from this connection has been described as follows:

'Despite the growing need for shareholder protection as reflected in company legislation, accountants would be expected to react slowly and to the minimum extent if such call for more disclosure were not consistent with their patron's wishes. . . . It is manifestly unreasonable to expect individual accountants to make a strong stand for independence when they have not the power to do so. This implication does, in fact, highlight dilemmas facing the profession at the moment. How should it go on supporting disclosure of the information to shareholders or any other parties when it is not in the interests of the patron to do so?' (Tomkins, 1978).

Once it is admitted that the process of social change calls for equity in the disclosure of information to external users, and once the needs of external users are admitted to be important, two important problems appear. First, there is the problem of defining these needs. This problem may be approached in different ways. It is possible simply to conduct empirical research to discover these needs in the statement of what users consider necessary for their purposes. It is also possible to try to understand the decisions with which they are faced and to suggest what information they should require. These two approaches reflect contrasting theories of accounting: the first being descriptive, and the second being normative in character. Second, there is the problem of creating some symmetry of treatment in the manner in which their needs are met. In this problem lie the complex welfare issues suggested in Part 1. This problem involves a breach in the power of management to influence the development of accounting knowledge towards their specific needs. It implies that 'the form and standards of disclosure and the definitions of measurement should be determined by third parties such as the Stock Exchange Commission, the accounting profession, the Courts, and professional investors to meet the requirements of users' (Norby and Stone, 1972). It also implies that the needs of other users such as employees and trade unions should be satisfied.

This part contains four chapters, as follows:

Chapter 22, which considers the implications of research into current practices for future developments in accounting,

Chapter 23, which examines the needs of investors, and suggests the nature of their information needs,

Chapter 24, which discusses the needs of employees for accounting information; and examines the implications of the Employment Protection Act, 1975 in this respect,

Chapter 25, which considers the problem of corporate social responsibility, and the nature of information which is relevant to this area of accounting responsibility.

References

Norby, W.C. and Stone, F.G. (1972). Objectives of financial accounting and reporting from the viewpoint of the financial analyst, *Financial Analysts Journal*, July–August.

Tomkins, C. (1978). *The Development of Accounting*, Discussion paper presented to the Workshop on Accounting in a Changing Social and Political Environment, London.

Chapter 22

Evaluation of current financial reporting practice

Part 2 examined the nature of current financial reporting practice and the efforts which have been made in recent years towards its improvement. We noted that financial reporting practice was made the subject of much criticism during the 1960s on the following grounds:

1 the lack of uniformity in accounting practice made difficult the comparison of the financial reports of different companies;
2 the multiplicity of accounting practices made it possible for management to select alternative presentations of the financial results which allowed earnings to be manipulated and made it possible to conceal economic realities;
3 changes in the value of money added to the difficulty of comparing the financial statements of different companies in a meaningful manner, and added a new dimension to the problem of financial reporting.

The accountancy profession responded to public criticism by establishing the Accounting Standards Committee, charged with the task of producing standards of accounting practice aimed at remedying the problems of financial reporting. However, since accounting is a social science which is rooted in the value system of the society in which it operates, it was to be expected that the programme of the Accounting Standards Committee (ASC) should itself have been the subject of criticism.

A number of attempts have been made to improve the usefulness of accounting standards. In 1978, the ASC published the Watts Report, 'Setting Accounting Standards', which highlighted a number of criticisms of the standard-setting process. An ASC working party went on in 1983 to publish the McKinnon Report which considered ways in which the standard-setting process might be shortened and might be made to involve a greater degree of consultation and explanation.

There was, however, a continuing concern that the standard-setting process needed a thorough revision. In November 1987, the CCAB set up a review committee, named after its chairman, Sir Ron Dearing, to review procedures for developing and enforcing accounting standards in Great Britain and Ireland. The Dearing Report was issued in 1988. It considered the role played by accounting standards and the criticisms levelled against the standard-setting process, and made proposals for radical changes to that process.

The Dearing Committee rejected the idea that accounting standards 'inhibit preparers and auditors of accounts from applying their expert judgement'. It stated firmly that '. . .strong, unambiguous accounting standards covering the main issues that arise in preparing financial statements are needed for the good working of a market economy.' It recognized, however, that the current standard-setting process contained a number of serious weaknesses which had to be addressed. These were:

- The absence of a conceptual framework. This was seen to add to the difficulty of achieving a consistent approach towards accounting standards and hence to lessen the authority commanded by standards.
- The lack of precision of certain accounting standards. Coupled with the number of options permitted by some standards, this allows companies too much flexibility in their choice of accounting treatment.
- The delay in producing accounting standards. The need for all the CCAB bodies to approve standards, and the limited resources available to CCAB were blamed for this.
- The lack of a forum to deal with emerging issues. Where new and unforeseen problems arise, practitioners often solve them on an ad hoc basis, for lack of authoritative guidance.
- Failure to involve non-accountants. Standards continued to be set principally by accountants. In the words of the report, 'The present arrangements have not provided the ideal vehicle for involving preparers, users and others in a way that ensures that accounting standards reflect the needs of preparers and users and hence earn their commitment to them'.

Non-compliance with standards

The report recognized that there is occasionally strong pressure on auditors to accept accounting treatments which are in breach of standards. It expressed the view that it was unreasonable to expect auditors alone to take responsibility for good accounts.

The Dearing Report's conclusion was that there was a need for 'tighter and more timely standards which can earn the support of preparers, auditors and users alike by their quality, but which, in the last analysis, are buttressed by stronger arrangements for securing compliance'. Its recommendations were in line with its analysis of the need for reform.

The Dearing Report recommended the establishment of a new body, the Financial Reporting Council (FRC). This was to oversee two independent entities, the Accounting Standards Board (ASB) and the Review Panel. These recommendations were accepted and implemented, with effect from 1 August 1990. The new bodies then replaced the ASC; their functions included those formerly carried out by the ASC, but also embraced new responsibilities.

The FRC, comprising about 25 members, is intended to give a voice to preparers, users and auditors of accounts. As well as administration and finance of the other bodies, its responsibilities include setting a programme of work for the ASB, guiding it on priorities and advising it on broad matters of policy.

The ASB comprises about 9 members, including a full-time Chairman and technical director. All its members are skilled accountants. It replaces the ASC as the body responsible for issuing accounting standards. An Urgent Issues Task Force (UITF) is an offshoot of the ASB. Its role is to tackle urgent matters not covered by existing standards.

The Review Panel has about 15 members. It is concerned with monitoring the accounts of large companies to note and investigate any departures from accounting standards. In line with the Dearing proposals, the accounts of all plcs and large private companies are required by law to contain a statement that the accounts have been drawn up in accordance with applicable statements of standard accounting practice.

These bodies have powers and responsibilities which exceed those of the ASC. The ASB is able to issue standards on its own authority, whereas the ASC needed to obtain the consent of the CCAB bodies. A new standard requires only a two-thirds majority on the part of the ASB to be approved; in the past, unanimous support was required, which resulted in delays and compromises in drawing up standards. Each standard is to be accompanied by a clear statement of the principles underlying it, the reasons why alternatives were rejected, and the extent to which it is applicable to small companies.

The FRC is pursuing the development of a conceptual framework, using the work done in the USA and by the IASC (as described below). This will initially be on a modest scale only, but additional resources will be made available when the FRC judges it appropriate.

The Review Panel examines accounts, either on its own initiative or in response to outside representations, in cases where departures from standard accounting practice have occurred, and an issue of principle is involved or the accounts do not give a true and fair view. The Review Panel may invite the company's auditors and directors to give evidence.

If it concludes that the accounts need revision in order to give a true and fair view, it will notify the Stock Exchange and any other relevant professional body, and may publish its findings. In the last resort, the Review Panel may bring civil proceedings against a company which will not revise its accounts in order to give a true and fair view.

The need for a conceptual framework

The alterations to the standard-setting process made in response to the Dearing Report address many of the weaknesses perceived by preparers and users of accounts. Arguably, however, the Dearing Committee dealt only with the symptoms of the underlying problem, and not with the problem itself—the absence of a conceptual framework.

The main criticism which may be levelled against the programme adopted by the ASC is that it has failed to establish objectives for financial reports. This results from the failure to develop the accounting standards programme within a framework which would have allowed that programme to proceed in a coherent manner. The Watts Report stated that the ASC was 'frequently criticized for failing to develop an agreed conceptual framework on which a logical series of SSAPs can be based'. The accounting standards programme has to a large extent been prepared within the terms of the four accounting concepts: going concern, prudence, matching and consistency, explicitly recognized in SSAP 2, which stated that it was not the purpose of that standard to establish a theory of accounting, for 'an exhaustive theoretical approach would take an entirely different form and would include, for instance, many more propositions than the four fundamental concepts referred to here'.

However, recognition of only these four concepts has led to contradiction among and between SSAPs. For example, there is an inherent conflict between prudence and matching. Whereas the first draft of ED 14 'Accounting for Research and Development' was based purely on prudence, SSAP 9 'Stocks and Work in Progress', which is discussed in Chapter 32, is based essentially on the matching convention. Therefore, the lack of definition and the absence of a more comprehensive framework than that allowed by consideration of the four concepts explicitly recognized in SSAP 2 has led to contradictions and inconsistencies in the accounting standards programme.

The principal intention of the accounting standards programme has been to secure greater uniformity in the preparation of financial reports in order that there should be more comparability between different companies in this respect. This presupposes that, in their present general format, financial reports provide useful information to external users. The problem lies in the conventions of accounting and the four fundamental concepts proposed by SSAP 2, which do not themselves necessarily offer the best starting point for developing or improving current accounting practice. It may be argued that a more logical method of proceeding would have been to begin with a consideration of the theoretical problems implied in these conventions, to have discussed the implications of research findings, and to have examined the problems of financial reporting in this context.

In Part 1, we took the view that the main objectives of accounting theory should be to provide means for evaluating existing practices, and to provide guidelines for developing new practices. Adopting an information systems approach, we also took the view that as the external users of financial reports have no control over the content of these reports, such reports were not user-oriented. Indeed, the inputs and therefore the outputs of the accounting system are determined by conventions which are embodied in accounting traditions and in law. They are not determined by the needs of external users for making decisions.

The failure to establish a conceptual framework for financial reporting purposes lies precisely in the failure to orient financial reporting practices towards the needs of external users. External users are provided with financial information on a 'take-it-or-leave-it' basis. The information provided is limited in nature, although it could be expanded at little additional cost to the firm. Furthermore, the information is historical in character, and as such may have little relevance to external users concerned with making decisions on the basis of future expectations. Finally, financial reports are issued only periodically, whereas many external users, particularly investors, are making decisions continually.

The development of a conceptual framework

A recent attempt at a conceptual framework was made in 1989 by the International Accounting Standards Committee (IASC)—its *Framework for the Preparation and Presentation of Financial Statements*. The IASC framework is concerned with general-purpose financial statements prepared for users who have to rely on them as their major source of financial information.

Objectives of financial statements

The objective of financial statements is to provide information about the financial position, performance and changes in financial position of an enterprise that is useful to a wide range of potential users in making economic decisions. It is recognized, however, that financial statements do not provide all the information required by users; they portray the financial effects of past events only, and do not necessarily provide non-financial information. Seven potential user groups are identified: investors and their advisers, employees, lenders, suppliers and other trade creditors, customers, governments and their agencies, and the public. Each group has different information needs.

- Investors are concerned with investment risk and return and need information relevant to the decision to buy, retain or sell investments.
- Employees are concerned with their employer's stability and profitability, and with assessing the ability of the enterprise to provide remuneration and retirement benefits.
- Lenders wish to determine whether their loans and the attached interest will be paid when due.
- Suppliers wish to determine whether amounts owing to them will be paid when due.
- Customers are concerned with the continuance of an enterprise.
- Governments require information enabling them to regulate firms' activities, determine taxation policies and compile national statistics.
- The public may be affected by enterprises in different ways. For instance, an enterprise may have a major effect on the local economy. Local residents will want information about the prosperity of the enterprise.

Some, but not all of these information needs are common to all users. The Framework concludes that the provision of information meeting the needs of investors will satisfy most of the needs of other user groups.

The Framework identifies three different information requirements among users of financial statements; these are for information about the financial position of an enterprise, its performance and changes in its financial position. The Framework distinguishes between these three areas:

Financial position: The financial position of an enterprise is affected by its economic resources, its financial structure, liquidity, solvency and ability to adapt to changes in its environment. Information about these factors is relevant in predicting the ability of the enterprise to generate cash and cash equivalents in future.

Performance: Information about performance, and in particular variability of performance, is important for an assessment of the economic resources that an enterprise is likely to control in future.

Changes in financial position: This information enables the user to assess the enterprise's investing, financing and operating activities during its reporting period and hence both its ability to generate cash and its future utilization of cash.

Three financial statements—the balance sheet, profit and loss account and funds flow statement—supply these three different types of information. Notes and supplementary disclosures supply other information needed by users, such as details of resources and obligations not recognized in the balance sheet.

In order to meet their objectives, financial statements are prepared on the basis of two underlying assumptions:

The accrual basis: The effects of events are recognized when they occur, not when cash or cash equivalents are received or paid. Financial statements prepared on this basis are useful because they contain information about past and future events which affect the present financial position of the enterprise.

The going concern basis: The assumption is made that the enterprise neither intends nor needs to curtail or liquidate its operations in the foreseeable future.

It is notable that the IASC recognizes only the above as underlying assumptions. The other two fundamental accounting concepts recognized by SSAP 2—the consistency and prudence concepts—are not given this status. They are discussed elsewhere as part of the qualitative characteristics of financial statements.

Qualitative characteristics

Where alternative measurements or disclosures are available, the Framework identifies four qualitative characteristics which can be used to evaluate the alternatives. These are: understandability, relevance, reliability and comparability.

Understandability

Information should be understandable by users, provided that they have a reasonable knowledge of business and economic activities and accounting, and are prepared to exercise reasonable diligence in studying it.

Relevance

Information is useful in decision-making only if it is relevant. Three factors affect its relevance—its predictive and confirmatory roles, its materiality and its timeliness.

Predictive and confirmatory roles: These are interrelated. Information about the current position or performance provides a basis for prediction. The separate disclosure of abnormal items assists the prediction of likely future results.

Materiality: Information is material if its misstatement or omission could influence the economic decisions of users relying on the financial statements. Materiality depends on the size of the error or item in its context.

Timeliness: Information must be reported without delay if it is to remain relevant to user needs.

Reliability

Useful information must be reliable. Reliability implies four attributes: representational faithfulness, neutrality, prudence and completeness.

Representational faithfulness: If information is to provide a faithful representation of events and transactions, it should account for their substance or economic reality and not merely their legal form.

There are difficulties inherent in reporting economic events, apart from the possible divergence of form and substance. Problems arise both in identifying the events which should be measured and in applying appropriate measurement and disclosure techniques. In some cases, it may be desirable to recognize items while also disclosing the uncertainty attaching to their measurement; in others, uncertainty may be such that they are not recognized.

Neutrality: Information should be presented without bias; it should not be presented or selected with a view to influencing users in a particular direction.

Prudence: Uncertainty attaches to many events and circumstances, such as the collection of debts or the life of plant. Prudence is the exercise of a degree of caution in making the estimates required under conditions of uncertainty. Prudence does not, however, imply the deliberate creation of hidden reserves, overstatement of expenses or liabilities or under-statement of assets or income.

Completeness: Within the bounds of materiality and cost, information should be complete.

Comparability

In order to identify trends, users must be able to compare the financial statements of an enterprise over time in order to identify trends in its performance. They must also be able to make comparison between different enterprises. This implies that enterprises should account for like transactions on a consistent basis. Disclosure of accounting policies and changes in policies are necessary to assist users in making comparisons.

Comparability does not imply uniformity. Accounting policies should be changed if they become inappropriate or if better alternatives are developed.

Balance between benefits and costs

This is a pervasive constraint rather than a qualitative characteristic. The benefits derived from information should exceed the costs of providing it. It is difficult, however, to apply the cost-benefit test in many cases. The determination of costs and benefits is a judgemental exercise. Furthermore, the users enjoying the benefits of information may not be those bearing its costs.

Elements

The Framework identifies five elements which comprise the balance sheet and income statement—assets, liabilities, equity, income and expenses.

Elements of the balance sheet

An asset is a resource controlled by the enterprise as a result of past events and from which future benefits are expected to flow.

A liability is a present obligation of the enterprise arising from past events, the settlement of which is expected to result in an outflow from the enterprise of resources embodying economic benefits.

Equity is the residual interest in the assets of the enterprise after deducting all its liabilities.

For an asset or liability to be recognized, two conditions must be met. An inflow or outflow of economic benefits must be probable and their value or cost must be capable of reliable measurement. Items not meeting both these criteria may still be disclosed in the financial statements by way of note where they are relevant to user needs.

The Framework distinguishes between a present obligation and a future commitment. For instance, the decision by an enterprise to purchase assets in future does not of itself create a present obligation; this will normally arise only when the asset is delivered or the enterprise binds itself to acquire the asset.

Some liabilities, often described as provisions, can be measured only with a substantial degree of estimation. Pension and warranty obligations are examples of such provisions. In some countries, such provisions are not recognized as liabilities because of the degree of estimation involved. The Framework concludes that where a provision represents a present obligation and satisfies the rest of the definition of a liability, it is a liability even if it has to be estimated.

Elements of the income statement

Income is increases in economic benefits during the accounting period in the form of inflows or enhancements of assets or decreases of liabilities that result in increases of equity, other than those relating to contributions by equity participants.

Expenses are decreases in economic benefits during the accounting period in the form of outflows or depletions of assets or incurrences of liabilities that result from decreases in equity, other than those relating to distributions to equity participants.

Income and expenses may be presented in the income statement in different ways in order to enhance the usefulness of the information. For instance, a distinction is often made between items arising in the ordinary course of business and those which are unlikely to recur frequently. It is also usual to distinguish between revenue and gains arising, for instance, on the disposal of non-current assets. Similarly, a distinction may be made between expenses and losses.

Criteria for element recognition

An item is recognized when it is incorporated in the financial statements. It should be recognized when it complies with the definition of an element and satisfies two further criteria:

- It is probable that any future economic benefit associated with the item will flow to or from the asset
- The item has an attribute which can be measured with reliability.

In many cases, the Framework recognizes that the cost or value of an item will be the subject of an estimate. This is acceptable, provided that the estimate is a reasonable one.

Income recognition occurs when an increase in future economic benefits arises, provided that the increase can be measured reliably. Such an increase will relate to an increase in an asset or decrease in a liability. Conversely, an expense is recognized when a decrease in future economic benefits which can be measured reliably, has arisen. Recognition of expenses will occur simultaneously with an increase in liabilities or decrease in assets. An expense will also arise where an expenditure produces no future economic benefits or where such benefits do not qualify or fail to qualify for recognition as assets. It is also possible for an expense to arise without an asset being recognized in cases where a liability arises—for instance a liability under a product warranty.

Revenues and expenses that arise directly or jointly from the same transaction or other events are recognized simultaneously, in accordance with the matching concept.

Measurement bases

The Framework identifies a number of different measurement bases which are used in financial statements. These include:

Historical cost: Assets are recorded at the time of acquisition at the cash or cash equivalent paid for them or at the fair value of the consideration paid for them. Liabilities are recorded at the cash or cash equivalent received when the liability was incurred.

Current cost: Assets are recorded at the amount of cash or cash equivalent that would be payable to acquire the same or a similar asset currently. Liabilities are disclosed at the undiscounted cash or cash equivalent amount payable currently to settle the obligation.

Realizable (settlement) value: Assets are recorded at the amount of cash or cash equivalent currently obtainable by selling the asset in an orderly disposal. Liabilities are recorded at their settlement value, i.e. the undiscounted amounts of cash or cash equivalent expected to be paid to settle the liabilities in the normal course of business.

Present value: Assets are recorded at the discounted present value of the future net cash inflows they are expected to generate in the normal course of business. Liabilities are carried at the present discounted value of the future net cash flows expected to be required to settle the liabilities in the normal course of business.

Historical cost is the most commonly used measurement base; it is generally combined with another measurement base—for instance lower of cost and net realizable value in the case of inventory. The Framework does not recommend a particular measurement base; it is intended to be applicable to a range of measurement methods.

Capital maintenance

The concept of capital maintenance is concerned with the definition of the capital which an enterprise seeks to maintain. It links the concepts of capital and profit by providing the point of reference by which profit is measured; only inflows of assets in excess of those required to maintain capital may be regarded as profit. The Framework identifies two different concepts of capital maintenance:

Financial capital maintenance: Under this concept, profit is earned if the financial (i.e. money) amount of the net assets at the end of the period exceeds that at the beginning. Financial capital can be measured either in nominal money units or units of constant purchasing power.

Physical capital maintenance: Under this concept, profit is earned if the physical productive capacity (or operating capability) of the enterprise (or the resources or funds needed to achieve that capacity) is greater at the end than at the beginning of the period. The current cost basis of measurement is required in order to apply this capital maintenance concept.

The main difference between the two concepts is in their treatment of the effects of price changes. Where the financial capital maintenance concept is applied and capital is defined in terms of nominal monetary units, profit represents the increase in nominal money capital. Increases in the price of assets held over the period, often referred to as holding gains, are conceptually profits, but may not be recognized as such until they are realized on disposal of the assets. If the financial capital maintenance concept is defined in terms of constant purchasing power units, however, profit represents the increase in invested purchasing power over the period. Only that part of the increase in asset prices exceeding the increase in the general level of prices is treated as profit; the remainder of the increase is treated as a capital maintenance adjustment and hence as equity.

The physical capital maintenance concept involves a different approach in that all price changes are regarded as changes in the measurement of the physical productive capacity of the enterprise; hence they are treated as capital maintenance adjustments that are part of equity, not profit.

Other research findings

At the beginning of this chapter we stated that the implications of research findings are important for considering the future development of financial reporting. In this section we examine recent research which has a bearing on this problem.

The efficient market hypothesis

In a perfectly competitive market, it is an axiom of economic theory that the equilibrium price of any commodity or service is established at that point where the available demand is matched with the available supply. The equilibrium price reflects the consensus of those trading in the market about the true worth of a good or service, which is based on all publicly available information. If new information becomes available, it is analysed and interpreted by the market. The market for shares formed by the Stock Exchange appears to have the characteristics of a free and competitive market.

Financial theorists have developed two hypotheses about the way the Stock Exchange operates. The first hypothesis assumes that the market is naive, and the second hypothesis assumes that the market is efficient.

The naive market hypothesis assumes that the market reacts in a naive way to the information contained in financial reports. Thus, it assumes that investors are naive and unable to detect subtleties in financial reporting procedures. Hence, the market as a whole reacts naively to information. As the market is composed substantially of investors who are relatively unsophisticated in the analysis and interpretation of financial reports, it assumes that they determine the behaviour of the market as a whole to information contained in these reports. The difficulty with the naive market hypothesis is that research has shown that financial reports are used thoroughly by a minority of shareholders (Dyckman, Downes and Magee, 1975).

The efficient market hypothesis assumes the following:

1   Investors react to new information in such a way as to cause the price of shares traded on the Stock Exchange to change instantaneously. Therefore, an item of information disclosed in a footnote to the financial report will be impounded in the share price just as surely as it it had been included in the main body of the report.
2   The price of shares traded on the Stock Exchange fully reflects all publicly available information.
3   Abnormal returns cannot be earned by investors, that is, no investor can expect to use published information in such a way as to increase the benefits accruing to him as against those accruing to other investors. Each investor can expect to earn the return on a security commensurate to its risk class.

The assumptions of the efficient market hypothesis have received considerable support from research findings. These findings show that accounting information does have economic significance in that share prices react to new accounting information. Moreover, research indicates that the Stock Exchange reacts almost immediately to the public release of information. Research also shows that sharp price changes occur on the announcement of new information, but no discernible price movements thereafter, since the adjustment made at that time removes the possibility of future abnormal returns to individual investors. This observed behaviour is consistent with the behaviour of an efficient market.

A further condition required of an efficient market is that it should be able to interpret accounting information correctly. A number of research studies have examined the share price reaction to reported earnings reflecting a change in accounting policy. An interesting example of the market's ability to understand changes in accounting policy is illustrated by Sunder's (1975) research into share price reactions to switches in the basis of stock valuation from FIFO to LIFO and from LIFO to FIFO. The expected results on earnings of these changes were discussed in Chapter 12, and it will be recalled that firms switching from FIFO to LIFO will report lower earnings which will coincide with an improvement in economic earnings resulting from a reduced tax bill. Conversely, firms switching from LIFO to FIFO will report higher earnings as a result of that change and will hope that the market will respond positively to this information, thereby compensating for the negative impact of the increased tax bill that would result from the change. While such changes are not permitted in the United Kingdom, they are allowed in the United States and the American research experience of the impact of changes in accounting policy reflected in stock valuation changes is illuminating. In effect, research evidence shows that firms switching from FIFO to LIFO did not encounter any adverse price reactions from the market. On the contrary, average share prices rose by an average of 5 per cent more than would have been expected, taking account of market movements during the year when the change in accounting policy occurred. Sunder's research also indicated no market reaction to switches from LIFO to FIFO. In effect, it appeared that such an attempt to improve share prices was both fruitless and expensive in the context of the increased tax bill resulting from the change.

Indeed, many other studies have shown results similar to those produced by Sunder, and it may be concluded from these studies that the market does not respond to earnings increases that result from cosmetic changes in accounting policies (Beaver, 1981).

Finally, it does appear that there has been no major readjustment of share prices in the United Kingdom since companies began to publish inflation-adjusted accounts in varying forms several years ago (Brayshaw and Miro, 1985). These findings are consistent with the view that the market made its own assessment of the effects of inflation on company profits, and had already made the necessary adjustments for these effects.

The importance of risk

An investor is interested not only in the return which he expects to receive from his investment but also in the risk attached to the investment. This risk may be defined as the probability that he may sustain a financial loss by investing in a particular company. To minimize the risk associated with investing in one company only, the sensible investor will seek to spread his investment over several companies. In effect, the investor will consider the purchase of one particular security in the context of a portfolio of securities.

It is a basic tenet of portfolio theory that rational investors will prefer to hold portfolios of securities which maximize the expected return for a given degree of risk, or which minimize the degree of risk for a given expected rate of return. The individual investor is required to decide for himself the risk he is willing to bear in exchange for the prospect of larger returns, for evidently the larger the returns, the greater the degree of risk usually associated with such returns. In effect, the decision he makes reflects his personal risk preferences. The portfolio of securities an individual will choose will reflect his relative risk preference, and will require predicting the risk associated with the individual securities comprised in the portfolio. It is evident that the analysis of the financial reports of companies should assist individual investors in selecting portfolios of securities.

The development of portfolio theory has been extended beyond the analysis of risk and the selection of securities by means of studies in capital asset prices. Capital asset pricing models seek to explain the manner in which asset prices are determined in relation to the risk attached to the returns involved. While a more extensive review of the significance of portfolio theory is beyond the scope of this text, research in this area shows the significance of risk to the investor, and the manner in which the returns which he expects are associated with risk categories.

The significance of forecasted profits

The objective common to most investors might be defined as the maximization of long-run returns consistent with an acceptable degree of risk. The returns themselves comprise interest and dividend income and capital appreciation in the market value of securities. Given that capital appreciation is closely related to the profit prospects, information useful for forecasting profits would be highly relevant to investors in regard to the broad spectrum of expected returns.

The prediction of profits plays a major role in investment analysis. Foster (1978) quoted an interview survey conducted in 1973 in which 534 investment analysts were asked which factors were considered important in appraising companies. The factor most often cited was— 'an estimate of future profits'. According to Backer (1970), 'security valuation models employed by analysts indicate that future profit is by far the most important determinant of the value of a share of common stock. This explains why a major portion of the security analyst's effort is focused on forecasting company profits.

Investors may attempt to use the series of past reported profits or earnings per share, as a guide to future profitability, and the company's future dividend-paying capability. Several empirical studies have taken as their point of reference the behaviour of accounting profits over time, and used earnings per share information based on historical cost calculations. The conclusions of these studies are that past profit trends are not usually repeated in the future. Although sophisticated statistical techniques were used in these studies, it seems that the process of extrapolating from past profit trends is unlikley to prove useful in forecasting future profitability.

The research conducted by Backer showed that the procedure employed by security analysts for forecasting profits closely parallels that used internally by companies. Initially, this procedure requires a projection of sales. After making a sales forecast, profit margins are examined, and other significant operating ratios are compiled from published profit and loss accounts. These ratios are adjusted for anticipated changes in sales volume, prices and costs, and are then applied to the sales forecasts to obtain profit forecasts.

The significance of non-accounting information

Surveys of the ways in which investors use information and make decisions show that they rely extensively on information sources other than that contained in financial accounting reports (Gibbins and Brennan, 1982).

The preceding sections illustrate that factors concerned with expectations are relatively more important than information contained in financial reports for the purpose of decision-making by investors. The critical factor which affects future earnings is the level of sales. Research by Baker and Haslem (1973) supports this conclusion by ranking the three most significant factors considered by investors when making investment decisions, as follows:

1 The future earnings prospects facing the company.
2 The quality of management.
3 The future economic prospects of the industry in which the company is located.

It follows that financial reports provide only one source of information to investors. The existence of other sources of information may explain why share prices do not necessarily react to the publication of financial reports to the extent that might be expected. Much of the informational content of financial reports is known by the time these reports are published. As one analyst stated, 'much of this data is available in newspapers. For example, the dominant source of General Motors' earnings is passenger cars. General Motors' passenger car production figures are published weekly' (Backer, 1970).

It follows that year-end financial reports are used mainly to confirm information otherwise obtained during the year. Hence, financial reports may provide a useful check on data gathered from non-accounting sources.

It may be argued that the significance of financial reports to external users depends on the degree of their dependence on such reports for information on which to base decisions. Obviously, if financial reports contained the sum total of information available to external users, and there were no other competing and alternative information sources, then the quality of the information contained in financial reports would be of critical importance to efficient decision-making. The availability of competing and alternative sources of information reduces the significance of financial reports.

Hagerman, Keller and Peterson (1973) carried out research into the influence of financial reports on the manner in which investment decisions were made. Under laboratory conditions, investors presented with financial reports based on alternative accounting methods, and having access to no other information, were unable to distinguish between the different accounting interpretations of the same economic event. Under real-life conditions, the possession of information about the events underlying the financial reports enabled investors to adjust the decisions they would have made otherwise, and these adjustments compensated for the effects of differences in accounting policies.

The conclusion of these research studies indicated that, given that investors have alternative sources of information available to them, for example, reports in the financial press and security analyses, which provide a clear understanding of the events underlying financial reports, the search for the best financial reporting procedure is unnecessary. Hopwood (1974) appears to have reached the same conclusion by the process of distinguishing two alternative information contexts. First, in the absence of competing sources of information, or where there are difficulties in using sources of information other than published financial reports—a situation described by Hopwood as a 'monopolistic information context'—the accounting interpretation of events is not subject to validation by alternative information sources and constitutes the major part of the relevant information available. Second, in a 'competitive information context', not only is it possible to validate the accounting interpretation of events, but financial reports become less significant. The availability of many competing or often more timely sources of information enables the investor to gauge more readily the accuracy or the bias of financial reports, and to ignore their conclusions wherever appropriate.

Implications of research findings

The following inferences may be drawn from research conducted in the area of financial reporting.

1 Where there is controversy over which of two alternative measurements should be reported to external users, and no additional costs are involved in reporting both measurements, the solution to the controversy lies in reporting both measurements. Use could be made of footnotes to the financial report for this purpose, and the market may be left to interpret the importance of such additional information.

2 As there is evidence of a direct relationship between the price of a share and its risk, concern for the ordinary investor is ill-founded. The naive invester is a price-taker, and any additional disclosure will be to his advantage. Increased disclosure to the sophisticated investor will improve the predictions which he, the sophisticated investor, is able to make, and thereby reduce the speculative and destabilizing influences associated with the uncertainties of stock market behaviour. As the ordinary investor is likely to be a naive investor, and is a price-taker, he has an interest in share prices behaving in an orderly manner.

The call for simplified financial reports may be naive. It is often suggested that published accounting information should be simplified to the level of the understanding of the average investor. Yet, reflecting the increasing complexities of business organizations, accounting information is becoming more complex (Bird, 1984).

3 Accountants are not the only suppliers of information. Therefore, one of the functions which should be undertaken by the Accounting Standards Committee is to try to minimize the total cost of providing information to investors. This implies that the Accounting Standards Committee should consider the totality of information used by investors in determining the nature of the information content of financial reports.

4 Investors are concerned with assessing risk as well as assessing expected returns. Accordingly, any additional financial information which can be made available will be of benefit.

5 In their present form, financial reports are of limited usefulness to investors. Generally accepted accounting principles act to reduce the potential usefulness of reported financial information. There is a need to produce financial reports which are more relevant to users.

6 Accounting research alone cannot determine the financial reporting process. As we discussed in Chapter 3, research serves merely as an input into the policy-making process. Efficient market research, for example, does not consider the total costs and benefits associated with alternative accounting reporting methods. These imply welfare judgements which have to be made by accounting policy makers (Arnold, 1984).

Summary

The purpose of this chapter has been to evaluate current financial reporting practice, and the problems associated with the content of these reports. It was seen that the reasons which caused dissatisfaction with the status of financial reporting practice require solutions which are able to stand the test of relevance to users' information needs. The failure of the Accounting Standards Committee's programme of reform was argued to lie in the failure to establish a conceptual framework for financial reports. We examined the work of the IASC in this connection.

An important part of the chapter was devoted to examining the usefulness of financial reports in the context of how stock markets react to information contained in these reports. Two hypotheses directed to explanations of behaviour in these markets were discussed. Whereas some investors may be described as naive in their perceptions of information, the presence of sophisticated investors renders the stock market efficient in its interpretation of information in the process of setting share prices. The ability of the stock market to interpret information produced by alternative accounting policies was reviewed.

The chapter contained a discussion of the importance of risk and of information related to future earnings in the context of the information needs of investors. The role of non-accounting information was examined. Implicit in this discussion is the need to improve the extent and the relevance of the accounting information disclosed in financial reports, if the latter are to be useful for decision-making by external users.

References

Accounting Standards Committee, *Setting Accountancy Standards*, 1978.

Arnold, J. (1984). 'Capital market efficiency and financial reporting', in Carsberg, B., and Dev, S. (eds), *External Financial Reporting*, Prentice-Hall.

Backer, M. (1970). *Financial Reporting for Security Investment and Credit Decisions*, NAA.

Baker, H. K. and Haslem, J. A. (1973). Information needs of individual investors, *Journal of Accountancy*, November.

Beaver, W. H. (1981). *Financial Reporting: An Accounting Revolution*, Prentice-Hall.

Bird, P. (1984). 'The Complexities of Simplified Accounts', in Carsberg, V. and Dev, S. (eds), *External Financial Reporting*, Prentice-Hall.

Brayshaw, R. E. and Miro, A. R. O. (1985). The information content of inflation-adjusted financial statements, *Journal of Business Finance and Accounting*, Summer.

Dyckman, T. R., Downes, D. H. and Magee, R. P. (1975). *Efficient Capital Markets and Accounting: A Critical Analysis*, Prentice-Hall.

Foster, G. (1978). *Financial Statement Analysis*, p. 80, Prentice-Hall.

Gibbins, M. and Brennan, P. (1982). 'Behavioral research and financial accounting standards', in Giffin, P. A., *Usefulness to Investors and Creditors of Information Provided by Financial Reporting*, FASB.

Hagerman, R. L., Keller, T. F. and Petersen, R. S. (1973). Accounting research and accounting principles, *Journal of Accountancy*, March.

Hopwood, A. (1974). *Accounting and Human Behaviour*, Accountancy Age Books.

IASC (1989). *Framework for the Preparation of Financial Statements*.

ICAEW (1988). Report of the Dearing Committee.

Sunder, S. (1975). Accounting changes in inventory valuation, *The Accounting Review*, April.

Questions

1 Why has financial reporting attracted criticism in recent years?
2 In what respects do the proposals of the Dearing Committee represent an improvement to the accounting standard-setting process?
3 How do the objectives of financial statements differ from most of traditional accounting practice?
4 What do the findings of efficient market research show?
5 What are the implications of the research findings discussed in this chapter for the development of financial reporting?

Chapter 23

Reporting to investors

The central problem of financial reporting has been stated as resting in the need to define its objectives as a precondition to resolving the difficulties which have arisen in the last two decades. In the previous chapter, it was noted that the failure of the Accounting Standards Committee lies in its failure to define clearly the objectives of its programme of reform and standardization. It was argued, also, that these objectives should be defined in terms of the information needs of users concerned with making decisions. Therefore, the investigation of this problem ought properly to begin with identifying these needs.

The purpose of this chapter is to consider the problems implied in identifying the information needs of investors.

Problems in identifying investors' needs

At a superficial level, the identification of the information needs of users appears deceptively simple. It seems that it would be sufficient to question users of financial reports and to observe the way in which they make decisions as a means of identifying the decision models used and the information requirement of such models. Accordingly, repeated questionnaires and interviews would isolate the information requirements of users of financial reports. Yet such a method has not proved satisfactory, although it appears ideally suited to the research problem implied.

In effect, the reason why the straightforward questionnaire method has not met with success lies in part in the problems discussed in the previous chapter. Evidently, being accustomed to using financial reports containing information specified largely by accounting conventions, users are unable to make a clear distinction between the type of information they are using and the type of information they should be using. For example, if a naive investor is asked for his views on how the information content of these reports might be improved, he may well reply, 'by reporting a bigger and better balance sheet'.

A further difficulty lies in the making of correct observations of the decision models used by investors. Such observations can reveal only the information currently used. Clearly investors will be obliged to use what information is available, even though it may be deficient in some respects.

For these reasons, it is clear that empirical research into the decision models employed by users cannot produce satisfactory conclusions about investors' information needs. It follows that the rejection of empirical research compels the consideration of alternative methods of constructing a theory about the information needs of investors. It is suggested, therefore, that progress could be made by adopting a normative approach to the construction of such a theory which is based on a formulation of the decision models which investors ought to be using when making decisions.

Basis for a normative theory of reporting to investors

A starting point in discussing the case for a normative theory of reporting to investors is to examine the implicitly normative characteristics of the process of reporting to users. In this respect, the Corporate Report (Accounting Standards Committee, 1975) stated that reports should be (1) relevant, (2) understandable, (3) reliable, (4) complete, (5) objective, (6) timely, (7) comparable. These characteristics were clearly set out:

1 'Relevance is the characteristic which embodies the fundamental notion that the corporate reports should seek to satisfy, as far as possible, users' information needs.'

2 'Understandability does not necessarily mean simplicity, or that information must be presented in elementary terms, for that may not be consistent with the proper description of complex economic activities. It does mean that judgement needs to be applied in holding the balance between the need to ensure that all material matters are disclosed and the need to avoid confusing users by the provision of too much detail.'

3 'The information presented should be reliable in that users should be able to assess what degree of confidence may be reposed in it. The credibility of the information in corporate reports is enhanced if it is independently verified, although in certain circumstances it may be useful for an entity to supply information which is not verifiable in this way.'

4 'The information presented should be complete in that it provides users, as far as possible, with a rounded picture of the economic activities of the reporting entity. Since this is likely to be complex, it follows that corporate reports as we define them are likely to be complex rather than simple documents.'

5 'The information presented should be objective or unbiased in that it should meet all proper user needs and neutral in that the perception of the measurer should not be biased towards the interest of any user group. This implies the need for reporting standards which are themselves neutral as between competing interests.'

6 'The information presented should be timely in the sense that the date of its publication should be reasonably soon after the end of the period to which it relates.'

7 'The information should be expressed in terms which enable the user to compare the entity's results over time and with other similar entities.'

The characteristic of relevance is agreed generally to be the most important, for 'relevance is the primary standard and requires that the information must bear upon or be usually associated with actions it is designed to facilitate or results desired to be produced. Known or assumed information needs of potential users are of paramount importance. . . .' (AAA, 1966.)

Another attempt to identify the information needs of investors was made by the Institute of Chartered Accountants of Scotland (ICAS, 1988) in their discussion document 'Making Corporate Reports Valuable'. The ICAS identified what it described as the fundamental information needs of external users:

(i) Information about the entity's objectives and its performance towards achieving them.
(ii) A comparison of an entity's total wealth now with that at its previous reporting date and the reasons for the change.
(iii) Information about the entity's likely future status, performance and resources.
(iv) Details of the entity's present and projected environment.
(v) Information about the ownership and control of the entity and about the background of its management.

The ICAS makes the point that there is considerable overlap between the information needs of investors and those of management. Of the five types of information listed above, (i) to (iv) are needed by internal management as well as by external investors. The ICAS advocates a closer integration of management and financial accounting information. Current financial reporting is normally irrelevant for management decision-making, in that it emphasizes past events and contains little information about future prospects: the ICAS proposes much more extensive disclosure of prospects, in the interests of both investors and managers.

Normative definition of investors' information needs

The problem of defining normatively the information needs of investors may usefully begin by a review of the economics of decision making. In this analysis, it is axiomatic that decision makers are interested in determining the extent of the sacrifices which must be made for the benefits which are expected to follow from the decision. Economic decisions are considered as having three important dimensions, namely the amount involved, the timing, and the uncertainty associated with the amount and the timing of benefits or sacrifices.

Interpreted in terms of the interests of investors, benefits or sacrifices are expressed in terms of the cash flows between themselves and the enterprise. Accordingly, 'investors are concerned with the enterprise's ability to generate cash flows to them and with their own ability to predict compare and evaluate the amount, timing and related uncertainty o these future cash flows' (Trueblood Report, 1973).

It follows that the decisions which investors make require information enabling them to judge the acceptability of cash flows expected to arise from a given investment. The reasoning associated with investors' decision models is that they are assumed to invest in order to be better off as a result than if they had not invested. In effect, this assumes that they are prepared to forgo the benefit of present consumption for the expectation of the higher future consumption made possible by future higher income.

Investors are assumed to invest when the current cost of the investment (and of the consumption forgone) is less than their own valuation of the investment. Conversely, they will disinvest when the current cost of the investment (and the consumption forgone) is greater than their own valuation of the investment. In effect, investors and potential investors are assumed to be constantly comparing the alternative of having cash available for present consumption against the alternative of having cash available in the future for future consumption.

These assumptions may be summarized in an investors' cash flow model and expressed symbolically as follows (AAA, 1969; Revsine, 1973):

$$V_0 = \sum_{i=1}^{n} \frac{D_i \alpha i}{(1+B)^i} + \frac{I_n \alpha n}{(1+B)^n} - I_0$$

where:

V_0 is the net subjective value of the gain or loss to be obtained by an investor for a specific investment at time 0, that is, the investor's estimate of the current value of the investment minus the maximum price he would be willing to pay for the investment. He will increase his investment when V_0 is greater than the market value of his current holdings, he will realize part of his investment when V_0 falls below the market value, and he will maintain his investment at its current level when V_0 equals the market value.

D_i is the dividend per share expected during the period i.

αi is a certainty equivalent factor which adjusts the expected cash flows to a value such that a given investor is indifferent between D_i and a cash flow which is certain to be paid. This factor is determined by each investor's attitude to risk. If he is risk averse, αi will assume a value between 0 and 1. If the investor is a speculator and a risk-taker, αi will be greater than 1.

B is the opportunity rate for a risk-free investment and represents the minimum required return during period i.

I_n is the expected market price at the end of the holding period n.

I_0 is the price of the investment at time 0, when the investment decision is made.

The investor's cash flow model depicted above implies that the investor is concerned primarily with estimating the dividends and the risks associated with an investment. This decision model provides a basis for formulating a normative definition of his information needs, which would include the following (Arnold and Hope, 1975):

1 Forecasts of the cash flows expected by the enterprise in the future.
2 Forecasts of the cash expected for all segments of the enterprise in the future.
3 Statements of actual cash flows with explanations of the differences arising between the forecasted and the actual cash flows. This information would have the purpose of providing evidence of the reliability of forecasts made by the enterprise. Clearly, forecasts of future cash flows will be given more credibility and will be considered more reliable to the extent to which it is shown that deviations between forecasts made in the past and subsequent results are small.
4 Statements of changes in expectations of future cash flows with explanations of such changes.
5 Statement of the dividend policy which the enterprise intends to pursue in the future.
6 Forecasts of the realizable value of assets.

Content of cash flow statements

The foregoing normative definition of the information needs of investors emphasizes the significance of the cash flow statement in developing a normative theory of financial reporting to investors. According to this definition, the objective of the cash flow statement should be both to inform investors of the cash flows which they may expect to receive from the enterprise, and to provide evidence of the reliability of cash flow forecasts made in cash flow statements. It may be argued that a cash flow statement should show for at least each of the last three reporting periods the actual cash flows of the enterprise and the latest forecasted cash flows which were made in respect of these three periods. Moreover, the cash flow statement should also show for at least the next three reporting periods the latest forecasts of the cash flows expected by the enterprise as well as the last previous forecasts made by the enterprise in respect of these three periods. It may be argued that a cash flow statement presented in such a form would satisfy the need for information relating to expected future cash flows in the foreseeable period ahead, as well as evidence of the reliability of the previous forecasts made by the enterprise.

Macdonald, Bird and Climo (1974) have suggested that published cash flow statements should distinguish the following elements:

1 Recurrent cash flows which are associated with transactions expected to recur in the normal course of business at least once in each accounting period. Specifically included are trading flows, taxation outflows associated with other recurrent cash flows, and distributions to investors other than realization of their investment (that is, including dividend and interest payments but excluding repayment of loans and share capital).
2 Non-recurrent cash flows, which are those associated with

transactions expected to occur and possibly recur in the normal course of business, but not regularly in each accounting period. Specifically included are flows which are associated with the realization, acquisition and provision of capital resources; finance provided by investors; and the realization of the investments of investors.

3   Extraordinary cash flows, which are those associated with transactions not expected in the normal course of business. specifically included are payments or receipts for damages and tax repayments resulting from losses.

Tables 4.1 and 4.2 are examples given by Macdonald, Bird and Climo. Table 4.2 classifies trading flows by principal activities. Within each such classification fixed outflows are shown separately from net variable flows. Where fixed outflows are not attributable to a particular class of activity they should be shown separately. Fixed outflows are those relating to transactions, the volume of which does not vary with the volume of trading.

In Tables 4.1 and 4.2, 'F' stands for forecasted cash flows; 'P' stands for previous forecasted cash flows; 'A' stands for actual cash flows; ' + ' stands for cash inflows; ' – ' stands for cash outflows. In these statements, the cash flow forecasts for the years 19X0, 19X1 and 19X2 are compared with the actual cash flows in those years, and any significant variance should be explained to investors. The reliability of forecasts would be accessible by reference to the size of any individual variances and the explanations given by management to investors. For the years 19X3 and 19X4 forecasts of cash flows are compared with previous forecasts. Here again, the reasons for variances should be explained.

It was noted earlier in this chapter that reliability is one of the important characteristics of financial reports mentioned by the Corporate Report. The recommendations noted above are clearly addressed to this normative requirement, in addition to being addressed to the provision of relevant information in the form of cash flow forecasts.

The ICAS reiterates the need to report both current and projected future cash flow, both as a tool for management and an important reference point for external users of accounts. It recommends that management should have access to cash flow forecasts for the next three years, and that outside users should have them for at least the next 12 months.

Advantages of publishing company forecasts

Financial reports tend not to disclose many specific details which reflect the management's view of the company's future prospects, their plans for the future and related matters. It has been argued that the disclosure of company forecasts of future profits or cash flows would be very advantageous to investors. The advantages perceived as attached to the disclosure of company forecasts are as follows:

1   Since investment decisions by management are made in the context of the expectations which they hold of the profitability of future

Table 4.1 Cash flow statement for a company with three principal trading activities

	19X0 F	19X0 A	19X1 F	19X1 A	19X2 F	19X2 A	19X3 P	19X3 F	19X4 P	19X4 F	19X5 F
Recurrent cash flows											
Net trading inflow before tax (see Table 4.2)	±	±	±	±	±	±	±	±	±	±	±
Non-trading inflow (by source)	+	+	+	+	+	+	+	+	+	+	+
Non-trading outflow	−	−	−	−	−	−	−	−	−	−	−
Taxation	−	−	−	−	−	−	−	−	−	−	−
(sub-total 1)											
Non-recurrent cash flows											
Realization of capital resources	+	+	+	+	+	+	+	+	+	+	+
Investment by investors	+	+	+	+	+	+	+	+	+	+	+
Acquisition and provision of capital resources	−	−	−	−	−	−	−	−	−	−	−
(sub-total 2)											
Extraordinary											
(sub-total 3)											
Total cash flows for the period (1+2+3)	±	±	±	±	±	±	±	±	±	±	±
Cash retained b/f	±	±	±	±	±	±	±	±	±	±	±
Cash available	±	±	±	±	±	±	±	±			
Distributions by investors											
Recurrent (by class)	−	−	−	−	−	−	−	−	−	−	−
Non-recurrent (by class)	−	−	−	−	−	−	−	−	−	−	−
Cash retained c/f	±	±	±	±	±	±	±	±	±	±	±

Table 4.2 Cash flow statement for a company with three principal trading activities

	19X0 F	19X0 A	19X1 F	19X1 A	19X2 F	19X2 A	19X3 P	19X3 F	19X4 P	19X4 F	19X5 F
Division A											
Net variable trading inflow	±	±	±	±	±	±	±	±	±	±	±
less: Fixed trading outflow	−	−	−	−	−	−	−	−	−	−	−
(sub-total 1)											
Division B											
Net variable trading inflow	±	±	±	±	±	±	±	±	±	±	±
less: FIxed trading outflow	−	−	−	−	−	−	−	−	−	−	−
(sub-total 2)											
Division C											
Net variable trading inflow	±	±	±	±	±	±	±	±	±	±	±
less: Fixed trading outflow	−	−	−	−	−	−	−	−	−	−	−
(sub-total 3)											
Net trading inflow before tax and fixed outflows common to all trading (1+2+3)	±	±	±	±	±	±	±	±	±	±	±
less: Fixed outflows common to all trading	−	−	−	−	−	−	−	−	−	−	−
Net trading inflow before tax	±	±	±	±	±	±	±	±	±	±	±

operations, the disclosure of their forecasts would represent the essential information needed by investors.

2 The disclosure of company forecasts would provide investors with the benefit of management's knowledge of company operations, and its views of the future outlook for such operations. Market efficiency does not imply clairvoyance. Therefore, since information concerning a company's future prospects and plans is not made public, it may be assumed not to be impounded already in share prices. Therefore, it may be argued that the publication of company forecasts would result in more efficient share prices. Such share prices would reflect more correctly the future prospects of the company, and the value of the company's shares. Patell (1976) examined the reaction of share prices to the voluntary disclosure of forecasts of annual earnings per share by 336 companies, and found that, on average, there was a significant share price reaction in the week when forecasts were disclosed.

3 The public disclosure of information relevant to investors' needs might help prevent abnormal returns accruing to privileged individuals having access to inside information.

4 The disclosure of corporate plans would provide investors with a better basis for evaluating managerial performance.

The ICAS report recommends that both management and investors should have access to the company's financial plans. In the case of management, information should cover the next three years; investors should have information about the next 12 months. The issues to be covered are:

- the entity's objectives;
- major assumptions used in preparing the plan;
- the plan itself.

Disadvantages of publishing company forecasts

Numerous objections have been made to the proposition that forecasts should be published to investors. The four major objections are as follows:

1 forecasts are uncertain and may mislead investors;
2 forecasts may be manipulated by unscrupulous managers;
3 forecasts are difficult to audit;
4 forecasts made known to competitiors may be harmful to the interests of the enterprise, and therefore to those of its investors.

1 It is true, of course, that forecasts are uncertain. This uncertainty stems from the variety of elements incorporated in forecasts which are themselves uncertain. However, this does not render forecasts valueless. Thus, budgetary control implies the necessity of forecasting, as do management decisions regarding production levels, manning levels, product development and many other factors relating to business life. Clearly, forecasts made and used within the firm by management are of critical importance to the quality of decision-making. Such forecasts will be regarded as reliable in this use to the extent that they are carefully prepared. Their quality will be higher than those which are attempted by outsiders. Indeed, it is for this reason that the publication of profit projections has been practised for more than a decade in prospectuses and in circulars issued during the course of mergers and takeovers. It follows that the real question at issue is not whether forecasts are sufficiently reliable in an absolute sense, but whether users of financial reports are likely to find such reports more useful if accompanied by forecasts. As the Trueblood Report stated, 'the important consideration is not the accuracy of management forecasts themselves, but rather the relative accuracy of users' predictions with and without forecasts in financial statements.'

2   It is also true that forecasts may be manipulated by unscrupulous management. However, if management were made accountable by the publication of the results obtained with the forecasts which had been published previously, the need to explain subsequently any material difference between forecasts and results would restrain any tendency to making wild forecasts.

3   It may also be true that forecasts are more difficult to audit than actual results. Auditors have been reluctant to get involved in the audit of forecasts, and the position of auditors as regards forecasts is confused, particularly in the United States where the danger of legal action against auditors is considerably greater than in the United Kingdom. The resistance of the accounting profession on reporting forecasts has diminished since the publication of the City Code and the Institute of Chartered Accountants' statement on the matter.

'The requirement to report publicly was initially accepted with reluctance at the insistence of the Panel. However, when asked if they would report publicly, if it were not for the Panel, an overwhelming number of accountants said "yes", they would report publicly. Many pointed out that they had been reporting privately on profit forecasts for some time and they felt that public reporting was not that different.' (Adelburg, 1976.)

The problem of verifying audits is a very controversial subject. It could be argued that although the accountant should have knowledge of forecasting techniques, it does not follow that he should be an expert in this field. Moreover, forecasting is not simply a matter of handling techniques: it requires an expert knowledge of the industry and the markets in which the firm is located. Tomkins (1969) has suggested that a solution to this difficulty lies in the accountant obtaining a second opinion on forecasts from individuals other than the company's officials. Experts in the field of business forecasting outside the firm could be employed to provide such second opinions. Consequently, the auditor would not be legally liable for the forecasts and would be responsible merely for verifying the opinions of the experts concerned.

The problem of verification becomes more complex when forecasts covering several years are involved. Forecasts for the year immediately ahead merely provide an extended view of current achievements. Ideally, investors would need to be provided with forecasts covering a longer period. There would seem to be no reason why five-year rolling forecasts should not be adopted as a framework for disclosure, thereby enabling investors to appraise current performance and plans in relation to the firm's attainment of long-term goals. It would be difficult, however, to propose standard procedures which would ensure the required objectivity for audit purposes, for in the face of an increasing time-span there could be a very wide divergence of opinion between management and expert forecasters of the forecasts formulated for disclosure purposes. For this reason, some writers have argued that there is little point in verifying these forecasts (Briston and Fawthrop, 1971).

The ICAS recognizes the problems posed by its advocacy of the use of forecasts. It suggests that it will be necessary to involve non-accountants in what it calls the 'independent assessment teams' which will be responsible for providing assurance on the quality of financial statements. It recognizes that the work of the independent assessor will be more judgemental than that of the present-day auditor. The report produced will need to be longer and more explicit than the present audit report, and tailored to the circumstances of the individual client rather than following a predetermined format.

4 The argument that the disclosure of forecasts to competitors would be harmful to the interests of the enterprise and its shareholders is the same argument which has been advanced for years against the increased disclosure requirements of the Companies Acts, the Stock Exchange and the Statements of Standard Accounting Practice. Forecasts of profits are currently made public during the course of a takeover or merger or issue of shares, when they are thought presumably to do more good than harm. If forecasts were mandatory for all comparable companies, it is difficult to see how an unfair advantage could be gained by a competitor. The only user likely to gain from having such information is the one who is better able to compare and evaluate the prospects of different firms.

The Sandilands Committee considered the case for cash flow forecasting and concluded:

'We doubt whether such a proposal is practicable, at least in the foreseeable future. Many companies by the nature of their business would find it difficult to forecast their cash requirements with sufficient accuracy. Moreover, the proposal would require companies to disclose forecasts of their future position which could be damaging to their prospects. In general, we do not think it reasonable or practicable to require predictions about future events to be disclosed as part of a company's published accounts. . . . We doubt whether such a fundamental change would be acceptable to British companies at the present time.' (The Sandilands Report, 1975.)

In making this statement, the Sandilands Committee revealed the attachment to sentiment which afflicts the question of financial reporting. Each sentence in the above paragraph is a denial of fundamental points which we have examined in this part. To assert that firms are unable to make sufficiently accurate forecasts of their cash requirements is to deny the usefulness and, indeed, existence of cash budgeting as a central tool of management. To proceed to assert, by implication, that firms do make cash forecasts but that their disclosure would be damaging to their interest exposes the weakness of the first assertion, and is a plea for secrecy and for discrimination in information supply. The third assertion, that it would not be reasonable or practicable to require predictions to be disclosed, is a rejection of our basic premise—that the relevance of financial reports is to be found in information which allows predictions to be made about future events.

Cash flow versus profit reporting

Cash flow statements have many advantages over traditional financial reports based on profit and loss accounts and balance sheets (Lee, 1984, Charitou and Venieris, 1990).

1. Cash is more objective than profit, since its measurement is free of subjective valuations. It is also more easily verified than historical-cost or current-value accounting measurements, for receipts and disbursements are evidenced by means of source documents.

2. The problem associated with distinctions between capital, revenue, income and expenditure, or with allocations of cost between a series of arbitrary time periods, do not arise under cash flow accounting. Hence, although forecasts of either cash flows or profit flows are subject to uncertainty, cash flow forecasts are more objective than forecasts of profit flows.

3. Comparability between firms is enhanced since a common measure, that is, cash, is applied to all the elements of the financial report. The problem of uniformity, discussed in Chapter 9, therefore disappears.

4. Cash is crucial to the survival and progress of an enterprise. The problem of solvency is necessarily tied to the availability of cash to meet current liabilities, whereas conventional accounting treats the problem of solvency as of secondary importance by focusing primarily on profit measurement. Many enterprises have shown book profits up to the day when a liquidator has been appointed, and equally, many enterprises have survived despite accounting losses owing to the availability of cash.

Despite the advantages of cash flow over profit measures, the cash flow statement is usually viewed as a complementary statement rather than a replacement of the profit and loss account. Although profit measurement is fraught with limitations, profit is still accepted to be the primary measure of enterprise performance. At the present time a great deal of evidence points to the fact that management, auditors and users are essentially profit oriented (Sprouse, 1978). For this reason the FASB's Concepts No. 1 states that users' 'interest in an enterprise's future cash flow and its ability to generate favourable cash flows leads primarily to an interest in information about its earnings'. Given this orientation towards profit, we advocate more comprehensive disclosures that would permit individual users of financial statements to make their own measure of profit. This kind of approach is supported by the empirical research discussed in the previous chapter which illustrates the usefulness of additional disclosures to the sophisticated investors.

Segment reporting

The ideal method of reporting discussed earlier on page 398 suggested that cash flow forecasts for all the segments of the enterprise should be made available to external users. Advocates of segment reporting argue that the separate segments of an enterprise are usually subject to different economic conditions, different degrees of risk and exhibit different growth rates. A single, all-inclusive report tends to average out these differences, thereby obscuring them. Accordingly, they argue that segment reporting would enable users of financial reports to make better decisions.

Progress towards segment reporting has already occurred in the United Kingdom, where the Companies Act 1967 requires the disclosure of:

1   the principal activities of the company and its subsidiaries and any significant changes in such activities during the year; and
2   with certain exceptions, an analysis of the turnover and profit or loss before taxation of the company or group between what are, in the opinion of the directors, substantially different classes of business.

There has been a wide variation in the manner in which these disclosure requirements have been interpreted. A significant number of companies does not appear to have complied with the statutory requirements mentioned above.

The ideal method of reporting discussed earlier (p. 399), which was suggested to be a basis for formulating a normative definition of the investor's information needs, does require segmental cash flow forecasts. Such a requirement becomes increasingly relevant when, as a result of diversification, many companies have major products and markets which differ with respect to profitability, growth potential and risk. These segments are likely to be affected differently by changes in general economic conditions, as well as changes in the conditions affecting industry sectors or regions. Consequently, the consolidation of the operating results of diversified segments undermines the reliability of consolidated financial reports for forecasting future profits.

The main argument against segment reporting is that a diversified enterprise is, in effect, one business as far as the investor is concerned. Since the investor cannot differentiate one segment of the business from another in respect of the investment he makes in the company's shares, financial reporting should be restricted to providing him with a view of the enterprise as one unit. However, investment analysts first seek to divide the business into segments in making their own forecasts (Gibbs and Seward, 1983).

In the United States, FSAB Statement No. 14 'Financial Reporting for Segments of a Business Enterprise' issued in 1976 required the disclosure of information about enterprise operations in different industries, foreign operations and export sales and major customers. The purpose of such disclosures was an intention to 'assist financial statements users in analysing and understanding the enterprise's financial statements by permitting better assessments of the enterprise's past performance and future prospects.' Research findings show that the standard has increased the usefulness of information to users (Baldwin, 1984).

Other aspects of the disclosure problem

The ICAS report concurs with earlier researchers in proposing cash flow reporting, forecasts and segmental reporting as important aids to investors in their decision making. It also makes a number of other suggestions for improving the usefulness of financial statements.

Corporate objectives

Investors can best judge an entity's performance by comparing its achievements with its intentions. The ICAS recommends that financial statements should contain a statement of corporate objectives, drawn up and periodically reviewed by management. This would allow investors to judge whether or not the organization had achieved its aims.

Market capitalization

The ICAS suggests that the market capitalization of a company—i.e. its quoted share price multiplied by the number of shares in issue—is likely to represent a conservative estimate of the value of the business. The underestimate is likely to be of the order of 15–20 per cent on the average share, as this is the average amount of the premium arising on a takeover. This is considerably less than the undervaluation arising if assets and liabilities are disclosed at historical book values. It is recognized that the market capitalization will be affected by at least three factors—the state of the equity market generally, the market's view of the industry within which a company operates, and the company's standing within that industry. Market capitalization is not, therefore, an infallible measure of a company's worth, but an argument can be made for its usefulness, and it has the advantage of being externally verifiable.

The ICAS advocates that the market capitalization of a company should be disclosed alongside the book value of net assets. This should be done on an Assets and Liabilities statement which would form part of the financial statements, corresponding to the present balance sheet. The difference between book values and market capitalization would be highlighted, and any movements in the difference would be explained.

Revised financial statements—the ICAS proposals

The ICAS suggests that the present combination of balance sheet, profit and loss account and funds flow statement should be replaced by four related but slightly different statements. It proposes:

1 *Assets and Liabilities Statement*. As mentioned above, this would show the total net realizable assets of the company and its market capitalization and would highlight the difference.

2 *Operations Statement*. This would calculate the financial wealth added to the business by trading. Its main difference from the present profit and loss account is that it would deal only with those exceptional or extraordinary items which arise from revenue transactions. Such gains or losses relating to fixed assets would be dealt with as part of the next proposed statement.

3 *Statement of Changes in Financial Wealth*. This would show how the wealth of the entity had increased or decreased and would analyse the movement between operations, changes in fixed asset values and changes in capital.

4 *Distributions Statement*. This would highlight the amount available for distribution by the entity, either out of the distributable change in financial wealth for the year or out of the undistributed surpluses of previous years, and show what had been distributed by way of dividend.

Interim financial reporting

Interim financial reports provide financial information for a period of less than one year. In the United Kingdom quoted companies have to deliver a six-monthly report of profitability and financial position to their shareholders. In the United States the disclosure requirement is on a quarterly basis. Interim reports are not audited.

One normative characteristic of the process of reporting to users discussed previously in this chapter was that of timeliness. The aim of interim reports is to provide users with more timely information about companies so as to alleviate the disadvantages of the significant time lag between annual reports. Research findings indicate that interim financial reports play an important role in security investment decisions. Changes in share prices, following the disclosure of quarterly earnings are greater than average share-price changes during the year (Foster, 1977).

The limitations which circumstances impose on the level of precision attainable in assigning the results of a company's operations to annual periods are severe. The limitations are even more severe when we undertake to assign results to shorter accounting periods. However, American experience indicates that a more extensive use of interim reports in the United Kingdom would enhance the predictability of company reports. Whether interim financial reports should be audited is a very controversial subject. At the present time it is doubtful that the benefits to investors justify the cost to the reporting companies.

Reporting cost details

As we shall see in Part 5, operating costs fall into categories which behave quite differently under changing volumes of business. Variable costs tend to vary in direct proportion to production levels; programmed costs are budgeted annually in corporate plans, for example advertising and research and development costs; long-run fixed costs change little in total with changes in output.

Some knowledge of a company's cost structure is needed by the investor if reliable forecasts are to be made which take account of the impact of changing output levels on profits. The ability of investors to make such forecasts is impeded by the omission in financial reports of information about a company's cost structure. This problem will be examined further in Part 5, where the effects of SSAP 9 'Stocks and Work in Progress' on investment decisions will be discussed.

Reporting realizable values

The ideal method of reporting mentioned earlier also suggested that estimates of the realizable values of assets should be disclosed. According to the Trueblood Report, 'of primary importance for predicting the risk associated with the firm's cash flows (but also for assessing returns) is the degree of flexibility and manoeuvrability that the management possesses in employing its resources.'

One alternative way of using a firm's resources is to dispose of them. This alternative may be quantified by using market exit values. Clearly, the more convertible into cash are the firm's resources and the greater the realizable value of these resources, the greater is the degree of flexibility and manoeuvrability that management has over the employment of resources. If the market exit values are small, the alternative uses of resources appear to be more restricted. Consequently, the utilization of resources inside the firm will be highly dependent on the marketability of the specific assets of the enterprise.

The ICAS strongly advocates the adoption of net realizable value (NRV) in reporting. It argues that NRV has a number of advantages:

- It is based on values which may be readily observed in the marketplace.
- It is readily understandable by investors.
- It removes the need for depreciation calculations.
- It produces values which are additive because they are all expressed in the same current terms.
- It provides a useful measure of an entity's liquidity.
- Its use would improve the comparability of financial statements between entities and between different periods.

Reporting the value added

There has been much discussion in the United Kingdom and elsewhere in Europe of the desirability of interpreting enterprise results not in terms of profits but in terms of the value added by the enterprise itself to the resources acquired in transforming those resources into the final product. Value-added financial reporting was discussed in the Corporate Report (Accounting Standards Committee, 1975), which suggested that such reports should include a value-added statement.

The concept of 'value added' is relatively easy to understand. It defines the income accruing to the enterprise after payments to external parties for goods and services supplied have been taken into account. It represents the value added to goods and services acquired by the enterprise, which results from the efforts of its own management and employees. In effect, the value added defines the income accruing to the enterprise which will be distributed among those who are involved in its activities as employees and shareholders. An example of a value-added statement given in the Corporate Report is shown below.

The value-added statement represents a move in a new and different direction for financial accounting. In recent years accounts have given much attention to the question, 'How should we measure income?' The value added statement asks a different question: 'Whose income should we measure?' Instead of restricting ourselves to reporting the shareholders' income we are reporting the income which has been earned for the whole team of co-operating groups which contribute to the company's performance. The value-added statement is directly relevant to the information needs of all parties with an interest in the company. They are all interested in the wealth the company creates, in how the wealth is shared and in productivity (Morley, 1979). The role of value added in pay bargaining is discussed in Chapter 24.

Statement of value added

	£m	19X0 £m	£m	19X1 £m
Revenue		90.0		100.0
Materials and services acquired		55.0		60.0
Value added		35.0		40.0
Applied as follows:				
To employees		27.0		30.0
To pay supplies of capital interest on loans	0.9		1.0	
Dividends to shareholders	0.8	1.7	1.0	2.0
To pay government		3.3		4.0
To provide for maintenance and expansion of assets:				
Depreciation	0.9		1.0	
Retained profits	2.1	3.0	3.0	4.0
Value added		35.0		40.0

The importance of educating users of financial reports

From the foregoing discussion of the problem of defining users' needs as a precondition to developing a normative theory of financial reporting, it is clearly important that a successful resolution of this problem lies in part in educating users of financial reports. This need is urgent in two respects. First, sophisticated decision makers know the nature of the information which is required. This perception is necessary to the definition of the information input to the decision models used. Second, educated users of financial reports know how to use the information which they contain. According to Sterling (1970), 'the accounting profession ought to devote some of its efforts and resources to the education of the receivers. The profession ought to tell the receivers which decision theories are correct and then supply the data specified by those theories.'

Summary

The purpose of this chapter has been to examine the problems implicit in providing investors with financial reports relevant to their needs. The difficulty in defining these needs by empirical research methods was revealed, and it was suggested that an alternative approach to this problem lay in formulating a normative theory of reporting to investors which could be based on the economics of decision making. A discussion of this suggestion revealed the importance of cash flows to investors, and the need to provide them with financial reports containing details of cash flows. Evidently, the most relevant information is that which is addressed to the future, and in this sense the publication of cash flow forecasts would seem to meet investors' needs.

Various aspects of the problem of disclosing information to investors were considered, in particular the disclosure of company forecasts, segment reporting, and the disclosure of cost details and realizable values of assets.

References

Accounting Standards Committee (1975). *The Corporate Report*, pp. 28–29, Institute of Chartered Accountants in England and Wales.

Adelburg, A. H. (1976). Forecasting and the US dilemma, *Accountancy*, October.

AAA (1966). *A Statement of Basic Accounting Theory*.

AAA (1969). An evaluation of external reporting practices—a report of the 1966–1968 Committee on External Reporting, *The Accounting Review*, Supplement to Vol. 44.

AICPA (1973). 'Report of the Study Group on Objectives of Financial Reporting', *The Trueblood Report*.

Arnold, J. and Hope, A. (1975). Reporting business performance, *Accounting and Business Research*, Spring.

Baldwin, B. A. (1984). Segment earnings, disclosure and the ability of security analysts to forecast earnings per share, *The Accounting Review*, July.

Briston, R. J. and Fawthrop, R.A. (1971). 'Accounting principles and investor protection', *Journal of Business Finance*, Summer.

Charitou, A. G. and Venieris, G. (1990). The need for cash flow reporting: Greek evidence, *British Accounting Review*, June.

Foster, G. (1977). Quarterly accounting data: time-series properties and predictive ability results, *The Accounting Review*, January.

Gibbs, P. M. D. and Seward, W. T. (1983). 'How an investment analyst uses a profit forecast and makes his own', in Westwick, C. A. (ed.), *Profit Forecasts*, Gower.

Institute of Chartered Accountants of Scotland, Research Committee (1988). *Making Corporate Reports Valuable*, Kogan Page.

Lee. T. A. (1984). *Cash Flow Accounting*, Van Nostrand Reinhold.

Macdonald, G., Bird, P. and Climo, T. (1974). 'Statements of Objectives and Standard Practice in Financing Reporting, *Accountancy Age*.

Morley, M. F. (1979). The value added statement in Britain, *The Accounting Review*, July.

Patell, J. M. (1976). Corporate forecasts of earnings per share and stock price behaviour: empirical tests, *Journal of Accounting Research*, Autumn.

Revsine, L. (1973). *Replacement Cost Accounting*, pp. 33, 34, Prentice-Hall.

The Sandilands Report (1975). *Report of the Inflation Accounting Committee*, p. 62, HMSO Cmd 6225.

Sprouse, R. T. (1978). The importance of earnings in the conceptual framework, *Journal of Accountancy*, January.

Sterling, R R. (1970). Theory construction and verification. *The Accounting Review*, July.

Tomkins, C. (1969). The development of relevant published accounting reports, *Accountancy*, November.

Questions

1 What information should be provided in order to meet the needs of the investor's normative model?
2 What are the advantages and disadvantages of publishing company forecasts?
3 How does cash flow reporting compare with profit reporting?
4 What additional disclosures are recommended by the ICAS report?

Chapter 24

Reporting to employees

Traditionally, the focal point of the literature of both accounting and economics has been the needs and the viewpoints of investors. Indeed, the concept of financial management and the theories with which it is associated are founded on the premise that the 'maximization of shareholders' wealth is an appropriate guide for how the firm should act' (van Horne, 1983). Equally, accounting research which has attempted to assess the importance and relevance of financial reports to decision makers has been confined largely to the decisions of investors and creditors.

The changing social environment has been concerned with the social imbalance between those having wealth and controlling society through the influence of wealth, and those whose political influence in numerical terms has secured the return of governments committed to reforms and the gradual redistribution of wealth.

In effect, this imbalance is reflected in the significance attached to the interests of investors in the literature of accounting and a major part of research in this field. The indications are that the process of redressing this imbalance has been engaged. Developments in reporting to employees in recent years is evidence of progress in recognizing the importance of employees in the activities of business enterprises. These developments have occurred as a result both of changes in social attitudes and changes in the law.

The purpose of this chapter is to analyse the development of financial reporting to employees in the context of their special interests as users of financial information.

Investor and employee reporting compared

Having already discussed the information needs of investors as users of financial reports, it is interesting to begin the analysis of the information needs of employees by establishing the extent to which they require similar information. The following comparison between the needs of investors and employees may be made:

1 In both cases, it is necessary to focus upon their needs as users rather than upon their wants. In this respect, the construction of a normative theory of financial reporting to employees is required to overcome the problems of theory construction mentioned earlier in Chapter 23.

2 The information needs of employees are more complex than those of investors, because employees require additional information on matters of special interest, for example matters of safety. At the same time, the information deemed in Chapter 23 to be relevant to investors is also relevant to employees. In this sense, both employees and investors are interested in cash flow forecasts.

3 In both cases, the disclosure of information has been regulated by law. The Companies Act 1985 prescribes the minimum level of information which should be disclosed to shareholders. The Employment Protection Act 1975 places an obligation on employers to disclose information to trade unions for the purpose of collective bargaining.

4 In both cases, traditional financial reports in the form of profit and loss accounts, balance sheets and funds flow statements have limited usefulness. If anything, the timing, presentation and content of corporate financial reports are less relevant to the needs of employees than they are to investors. Thus, these reports do not deal with matters of importance to employees, such as explanations of reductions in the amount of overtime pay and the effects of streamlining the product range.

5 The impact of management decisions falls more obviously and directly on employees than on investors. A shareholder who dislikes current management policy has the opportunity to sell his shares. An employee does not have such a simple choice, for he may find it difficult to transfer his labour elsewhere.

6 The role of the auditor has been traditionally to protect the interests of shareholders by ensuring that the financial reports present a true and fair view. The presentation of information to employees does not require auditing in the same sense. Reports to employees are devised and presented by management, and consequently may be discredited. Norkett (1977) noted that 'one problem which recently arose with employee accounts was when an accountant genuinely tried to simplify the presentation and omitted some figures shown in the accounts. The difference was noticed by an employee representative, and the employee accounts were subsequently dismissed as a management con-trick.'

7 One important difference between investors and employees in the area of financial reporting lies in the historical background to the different treatment accorded to these two groups. Financial reporting to investors originated in the nineteenth century, whereas there was very little interest in reporting to employees before 1970.

Financial reporting to employees

The accountant has been involved in the process of reporting to employees in two distinct ways:

1 direct reporting to employees in the form of employee accounts;
2 reporting as part of the process of collective bargaining.

Direct reporting

Section 57 of the Industrial Relations Act, 1971 imposed a statutory obligation on firms employing more than 350 persons to report directly to employees by means of an annual written statement. When the Industrial Relations Act 1971 was repealed, and the Trade Union and Labour Relations Act 1974 was enacted, neither the latter nor the Trade Union and Labour Relations Amendment Act 1976 re-enacted the obligation to report to employees. At the moment, therefore, there exists no legal obligation of firms to report to employees directly. Nevertheless, the interest in some form of reporting to employees remains very much alive, and the Department of Trade issued in 1976 a preliminary consultative document 'The Aims and Scope of Company Reports', which suggested reinforcing and extending the 'corporate report' proposals for employee reports.

Scope of employee reports

The purpose of employee reports is to inform employees in the context of a general communicative and consultative philosophy of the corporate environment in which they work. For example, there is a need to inform employees and correct any misunderstanding about the necessity for company profits and for explanations of the manner in which they are applied. Many companies have embarked upon the practice of informing employees about matters of which management believes they should be aware (Davenport, Elton and Middleton, 1984).

The emphasis in employee reports is on making information visually attractive and comprehensible. A general problem is the low level of interest of employees in company affairs, and to overcome apathy, colours, diagrams and cartoons are used. Financial information is shown in the form of bar charts, cakes or other diagrams which are easily understood. In view of the employee's interest in the performance of his own unit, there is a strong need for segment reporting.

Employee reports are not suitable for the purpose of wage negotiations. It is unlikely, for example, that wage negotiations will occur near the release of year-end financial information.

Advantages of employee reports

The main aim of reporting directly to employees is to promote goal congruence by explaining how the interests and efforts of employees relate to those of the firm. The intention is to improve communications and the employees' understanding of the manner in which the firm is being managed in the interests of all participants. For example, employees are more likely to accept technological change if direct reporting can create a climate of opinion in which the interests of employees are identified with those of management.

Another aim of reporting directly to employees is to improve public relations. Management realizes that employee reports have effects which extend beyond the firm. Employee reports are read by persons outside the firm, by members of the employee's family, and friends. They not only have public relations implications, but also may be helpful in the recruitment of personnel.

Disadvantages of employee reports

Two major disadvantages affect employee reports. First, as they are prepared by management for employees, they may be perceived by employees as being slanted towards giving employees only what the management wishes them to know. For this reason, employee reports may not be seen by employees as providing them with information directly relevant to their needs. Second, the desire to simplify employee reports so as to make them readily understandable may lead to misleading generalizations.

Reporting for collective bargaining

In the past, the release of information for collective bargaining purposes has depended on the strengths and abilities of the parties involved in the collective bargaining process. The Employment Protection Act 1975 altered this situation radically by placing a general duty on employers to disclose information for collective bargaining purposes that is both:

1. information without which the trade union representatives would be, to a material extent, impeded in carrying on with such collective bargaining;
2. information which would be in accordance with good industrial relations practice for the employers to disclose to trade union representatives for the purpose of collective bargaining.

Three views on disclosure for collective bargaining

The Employment Protection Act, 1975 did not specify the information which should be disclosed to trade unions. It was left to the Advisory Conciliation and Arbitration Service to give guidelines on this matter.

The first view on disclosure may be found in the Advisory Conciliation and Arbitration Service's Code of Practice (1977) which, while not more specific than others who had tried to specify guidelines for information disclosure, did state that the information disclosed should be relevant to matters under negotiation. The Code of Practice provides a list of 'information relating to the undertaking which could be relevant in certain collective bargaining situations'. The main heads of information listed were: pay and benefits, conditions of service, manpower, performance and financial. The Code of Practice stated that 'these examples are not intended to represent a checklist of information that should be provided for all negotiations. Nor are they meant to be an exhaustive list of the types of information, as other items may be relevant in particular negotiations.' The Code of Practice explained restrictions on the general duty to disclose information. These restrictions recognized the sensitive nature of some information, such as cost information on individual products, details of investment plans and details of pricing and marketing. Nevertheless, according to the Code of Practice, it is for the employer to prove that 'substantial injury' to the employer will occur if certain information is disclosed. Furthermore, the cost of providing information should not be disproportionately high in relation to its importance, and the disclosure of information should not be against the national interest. The Code of Practice suggested that a joint arrangement for the disclosure of information for collective bargaining be negotiated, as a means of pre-empting the necessity for employers to prove that disclosure might be substantially injurious.

The second view on disclosure for collective bargaining may be found in a booklet issued by the Confederation of British Industries in 1975 entitled 'The Provision of Information to Employees'. This booklet stressed the need for companies to provide employees with 'as much information as is relevant to their needs and wishes and which will assist them to identify with their company, paying due regard to constraints arising out of competitive requirements and confidentiality'. The booklet listed the type of information which could be provided under a number of headings called 'checklists', for example, information about the company as a whole, the organization of the company, finance, competitive situation and productivity, plans and prospects, and information relevant to employment.

The third view on disclosure is to be found in a number of recommended guidelines issued by the Trades Union Congress in a document in 1974 entitled 'Industrial Democracy'. This document identified information relating to collective bargaining as including manpower, earnings, costs, sources of revenue, directors' remuneration, performance indicators and the worth of the company.

The main limitations of these three sets of views on information disclosure is that they are in the form of checklists or guidelines giving lists of headings randomly brought together. They do not reflect a well-thought-out analysis of the information needs of users based on the normative approach to the construction of a theory of reporting to trade unions and employees, the applicability and merits of which were discussed earlier in Chapter 23. These three views reflect no considered analysis of the normative decision models which those engaged in collective bargaining should use. On the contrary, they reflect very generalized views of beliefs about the information which such users wish to have available.

A normative theory of pay bargaining information

The construction of a normative theory of financial reporting relevant to pay bargaining between employers and employees and their representatives ought to be based on the criteria suggested in Chapter 23. It will be recalled that these criteria, based on the Corporate Report, required information to be relevant, understandable, reliable, complete, objective, timely and comparable. The discussion of these criteria in Chapter 23 identified relevance as the most important criterion, and on the basis of that assumption proceeded to identify cash flows to investors as the most relevant information for the decisions which investors ought to make. Using the same type of analogy, the information which may be assumed to be most relevant to pay bargaining is related to two factors:

1   the minimum acceptable settlement which is based on considerations of equity, and is made up of a combination of factors including the cost of living, comparability with other industries, and value added;
2   the ability to pay, which determines whether the firm is in a position to afford to meet a pay claim without endangering profitability (Foley and Maunders, 1977).

The minimum acceptable settlement

The elements making up the minimum acceptable settlement may be analysed in more detail.

1   *The cost of living*. The need to take account of expected inflation rather than experienced inflation in assessing changes in the cost of living for pay bargaining purposes has been recognized in recent times when accelerating price rises occurred. Trade union negotiators have been conscious of the need to maintain living standards, and for this reason have attached significance to the maintenance of living standards in real terms. To this end, cost-of-living data has been used in pay bargaining to show that money wages and earnings have failed to keep up with the real cost of living, and that added compensation is required to regain lost ground.

2   *Comparability*. Trade union negotiators make use of two classes of information when engaged in pay bargaining—external and internal wage data. When negotiations are being conducted at a national level, that is, for all the divisions and plant of the same company or industry, external wage data relating to pay conditions existing in other companies or industries is important in establishing pay comparability. When negotiations are being conducted at a plant level, wage data relating to the wage policy of the entire company or industry is important in establishing pay comparability at the plant level. It follows that the process of pay bargaining might be improved considerably if more data on the relative earnings of workers were available, particularly on a company basis.

3   *Value added*. Given the sensitivity attaching to the term 'profit', the Corporate Report (Accounting Standards Committee, 1975) suggested that 'the simplest and most immediate way of putting profit into proper perspective *vis-à-vis* the whole enterprise as a collective effort by capital, management and employees is by the presentation of a statement of value added.'

Many companies are introducing value-added concepts into wage incentive schemes in order to improve productivity. The first step is to agree a target for the ratio of wages to value added. If performance exceeds this percentage a bonus will be payable, but if performance falls short of the target there will be no bonus and the deficit will be carried forward to reduce any future bonuses. The process of agreeing on the appropriate percentage which ought to accrue to employees is an important aspect of pay bargaining.

The ability to pay

The ability of the firm to meet a pay claim is defined as the distributable operating cash flows less the minimum required by those who have provided the capital. This measure signals that the firm:

1   is capable of surviving, and
2   has experienced a change in circumstances relative to the previous period which justifies a change in the level of real wages (Pope and Peel, 1981).

In the context of the firm's ability to pay, the reliability of future cash flow projections becomes very important. For this reason, cash flow statements containing comparisons of actual cash flows with forecast cash flows and explanations of deviations between these sets of figures would be as relevant to pay bargaining as they were seen in Chapter 23 to be relevant to the needs of investors.

Productivity data is also an important aspect of the definition of the firm's ability to pay. Management may be amenable to arguments that link pay increases to increases in productivity, for pay increases may be absorbed by increased productivity without affecting the firm's pricing policy. The government also tends to favour pay agreements based on productivity increases, for they are more likely to result in non-inflationary pay settlements. One crucial problem revolves around measuring productivity changes. For example, there are classes of employees in respect of whose activity the notion of productivity is difficult to express in numbers. This is true of personnel in research and development departments.

The cost structure of the firm is another factor which affects the firm's ability to pay. If a plant operates at a relatively low breakeven point, its ability to pay more will be greater at levels of output which exceed the break-even point. The plant which has a relatively high break-even point will have its ability to pay more restricted by the much longer range of output. The importance of the cost structure is discussed in detail in Part 5.

Advantage of disclosure in collective bargaining

The main advantage of disclosing information of the type listed above in the collective bargaining process is that it makes that process more rational. According to the Report of the Commission on Industrial Relations 1974, 'Trade Unions claim that certain advantages might result from improved disclosure of information—a speeding of the bargaining process because information is readily available, a greater likelihood of longer-term wage deals, and an increased chance of the employer obtaining greater co-operation from his employees.'

Disadvantages of disclosure in collective bargaining

Studies have shown that trade union officials do not understand the information in accounting reports (Sherer, Southworth and Turley, 1981). However, it may also be suggested that, in itself, this is not an argument against disclosure, but an argument for improving the financial knowledge of trade union negotiators. It may be argued that in certain circumstances management should themselves consider adopting the role of accounting educators since they may benefit if trade union officials are made more fully aware of the financial performance of the company.

A second argument against disclosure is that it may increase the bargaining strength of trade unions to the detriment of the long-term interests of the firm. However, trade unionists are only able to take a long-sighted view in wage negotiations if they are presented with all the relevant information.

A further argument against disclosure is that important information may be revealed during collective bargaining which could be harmful to the firm's negotiating position if leaked outside the firm. It seems, however, that the high level of disclosure which has existed in West Germany for many years in this context has not been associated with a problem of breaches in confidentiality.

Disclosure in collective bargaining and management style

Many of the arguments which revolve around the issue of the disclosure of information in pay bargaining are really issues about management style. It is evident that the successful communication of information during pay bargaining hinges to some extent on management–union relationships. According to the White Paper on Industrial Democracy (1978),

'People in industry have different interests, and differ about objectives and how they should be achieved. But part of the conflict is due to poor communication, lack of information and lack of trust. One way to change this is to create a framework for employees and their representatives to join in those corporate decisions which affect them and so encourage them to do so. Where decisions are mutually agreed both sides of industry must then share responsibility for them.'

The Employment Act 1982 adds a more formal dimension to this process by requiring a statement of 'employee involvement' to be included in the directors' report of companies with more than 250 employees in the United Kingdom. The requirement for this statement should lead management to examine its relationships with employees (Peat, Marwick Mitchell, 1983).

Summary

The purpose of this chapter has been to address the problem of reporting to employees as users of financial reports. Traditionally, the interests of investors have been recognized as paramount both in terms of

Company Law and in terms of accounting theory. Changes in the social environment and in political attitudes have begun to emphasize the importance of employees. This process may be seen in the context of the movement towards participation in decision making which has featured largely in the literature of management science, and in the discussion of the concept of industrial democracy which has excited the imagination of progressive elements in Western European countries.

The comparison between investors and employees as users of financial reports indicates a similarity of needs for information for decision making. Financial reporting to employees currently occurs at two levels. First, direct reporting by management to employees as part of the process of good staff/employees relations. Second, information disclosure in the course of pay bargaining.

It was seen that there exists a need for a normative theory of pay bargaining information, similar in its construction to that required for investors as users, which would be directed to establishing the information which those engaged in pay bargaining negotiations require to make efficient decisions.

References

Accounting Standards Committee (1975). *The Corporate Report*, Institute of Chartered Accountants in England and Wales.

Advisory Conciliation and Arbitration Service (1977). Disclosure of Information to Trade Unions for Collective Bargaining Purposes.

Confederation of British Industries (1975). *Guidelines for Action—The Provision of Information to Employees*.

Davenport, J., Elton, J. and Middleton, J. (1984). *The Illustrated Guide to Employee Reports*, The Industrial Society.

Foley, B. J. and Maunders, K. T. (1977). *Accounting Information Disclosure and Collective Bargaining*, Macmillan.

HMSO (1978). *Industrial Democracy*, White Paper, May.

Norkett, P. (1977). Stepping into a dangerous minefield, *Accountants Weekly*, 22 July.

Peat, Marwick Mitchell (1983). *Employee Involvement: After the Employment Act of 1982*.

Pope, P. F. and Peel, D. A. (1981). The optimal use of information, collective bargaining and the disclosure debate, *Managerial Finance*, Vol. 1, No. 2.

Sherer, M., Southworth, A. and Turley, S. (1981). An empirical investigation of disclosure, usage and usefulness of corporate accounting information, *Managerial Finance*, Vol. 7, No. 2.

The Future of Company Reports (1977). HMSO Cmd 6888.

Van Horne, J. C. (1983). *Financial Management and Policy*, 6th edn, Prentice-Hall.

Questions

1 How do the needs of employees for financial information compare with those of investors?
2 What are the advantages and disadvantages of direct reporting to employees?
3 What elements make up the minimum acceptable settlement?
4 What are the problems in estimating ability to pay?
5 What are the advantages and disadvantages of collective bargaining?

Chapter 25

Social responsibility accounting

We considered in Chapter 2 the several groups having vested interests in business organizations, with a view to determining the scope of the accounting problem, defined as the provision of information for making economic decisions having welfare implications. The review of the role of theory in accounting, conducted in Chapter 3, provided justification for approaching the definition of users' information needs by means of a normative specific approach to constructing theories about such users' needs. Accordingly, we were able to discuss the provision of information for shareholders, investors and employees in Chapters 23 and 24 by attempting to stipulate the information which such groups ought to be using in making economic decisions. In effect, we suggested that the needs of investors emphasized cash flow expectations in line with the hypothesis that investors were primarily concerned with maximizing their own welfare. Equally, we examined the information needs of employees in the same context, and came to the conclusion that such information as they should require related to matters affecting their welfare as a specific group of individuals.

The concept of social responsibility accounting raises initial problems of defining not only the users of such information, but their objectives in receiving such information. In effect, the concept of corporate social responsibility, which underlies the debate about social responsibility accounting, assumes that there exists a theory about the social role of business firms in modern society. Clearly, such a theory not only explains the public interest in the role of business in society, but would seek to monitor and influence the behaviour of firms in accordance with the value judgements on which such a theory might be considered to be founded.

In a very precise sense, the law exists as an institution having the objective of embodying and expressing those value judgements by which behaviour is to be regulated. In accordance with many Acts of Parliament and legal precedents, the accountability of business firms for matters affecting the social good is strictly laid down and enforced. For example, firms are liable at law for various offences in relation to harmful acts, such as allowing the escape of dangerous substances, failing to provide adequate safety precautions for employees etc. Equally, the law provides very clear rules for the manner in which the accountability of business firms to investors and employees is to be met.

The concept of corporate social responsibility extends beyond notions embodied in current law. Essentially, it represents an emerging debate having its source in political and social theory. In its present state of evolution, there is very real controversy in the following critical areas:

1   the nature of corporate social responsibility;
2   the objectives to which accounting information might be directed;
3   the scope of corporate social responsibility;
4   the manner in which information is reported.

In this chapter, we examine the problems stipulated above and review the development of social responsibility accounting. As we shall see, while there appears to be a great deal of uncertainty about the problems which we have indicated, business firms and governments have already committed themselves to this enlarged concept of business accountability.

The nature of corporate social responsibility

When considering the information needs of investors and employees in Chapters 23 and 24 respectively, the assumptions underlying the normative decision models of those users were based on notions of economic efficiency expressed in terms of cash flows. The concept of social responsibility introduces new dimensions and new problems.

First, there is as yet no generally accepted concept of the social responsibility of business enterprises. Almost everyone agrees that they should be socially responsible, though it may be argued that such a view is merely an extension of the universally accepted doctrine that individuals, either single or in groups, should weigh the impact of their actions on others.

Three approaches to the concept of corporate social responsibility may be distinguished:

1   The first approach originates in classical economic theory as expressed in the hypothesis that the firm has one and only one objective, which is to maximize profit. By extension, the objective of a corporation should be to maximize shareholders' wealth. It is asserted that in striving to attain this objective within the constraint of the existing legal and ethical framework, business corporations are acting in the best interests of society at large. This classical interpretation of the concept of corporate social responsibility has been advocated by Milton Friedman (1962) in the following terms:

'. . . there is one and only one social responsibility of business—to use its resources and engage in activities designed to increase its profit, as long as it stays within the rules of the game, which is to say, engages in open and free competition, without deception or fraud. . . . Few trends could so thoroughly undermine the very foundations of our free society as the acceptance by corporate officials of a social responsibility other than to make as much money for their shareholders as possible.'

2   The second approach developed in the 1970s, and recognizes the significance of social objectives in relation to the maximization of profit. In this view, corporate managers should make decisions which maintain an equitable balance between the claims of shareholders, employees, customers, suppliers and the general public. The corporation represents, therefore, a coalition of interests, and the proper consideration of the various interests of this coalition is the only way to ensure that the corporation will attain its long-term profit maximization objective.

3 The third view regards profit as a means to an end, and not as an end in itself. In this view, 'the chief executive of a large corporation has the problem of reconciling the demands of employees for more wages and improved benefit plans, customers for lower prices and greater values, shareholders for higher dividends and greater capital appreciation —all within a framework that will be constructive and acceptable to society' (Committee for Economic Development, 1971). Accordingly, organizational decisions should be concerned with the selection of socially responsible alternatives. Instead of seeking to maximize profit generally, the end result should be a satisfactory level of profit which is compatible with the attainment of a range of social goals (Schrader, 1987).

The change from the second to the third approach to social responsibility is characterized as a move from a concept of the business corporation based on shareholders' interests to one which extends the definition of 'stakeholder'. The former concept views the business enterprise as being concerned with making profits for its shareholders, and treats the claims of other interested groups, such as customers, employees and the community, as constraints on this objective. The latter concept acknowledges that the business enterprise has a responsibility to all stakeholders, that is, those who stand to gain or lose as a result of the firm's activities.

Second, the acceptance of the third view expressed above that 'organizational decisions should be concerned with the selection of socially responsible alternatives' requires clarification of the meaning of 'socially responsible alternatives'. It is evident that unless firms are able to develop clear views of society's preferences and priorities, they will be unable to plan activities which will make a social impact, and much less report in a meaningful way on their social performance. Therefore, without a precise knowledge of such preferences and priorities, much of the discussion of what is socially desirable must pass for subjective judgements, or at worst pure guesswork.

Third, it has been argued that both from a theoretical standpoint and from the standpoint of welfare economies, it is impossible to make public decisions about the social good. According to Arrow's general impossibility theorem, 'if we exclude the possibility of inter-personal comparisons of utility, then the only methods of passing from individual tastes to social preferences which will be satisfactory and which will be defined for a wide range of sets of individual orderings are either imposed or dictated' (Arrow, 1963).

Fourth, at the operational level, there is the problem of the ever-changing nature of the ordering of social preferences, were such ordering ever possible. Social costs, as well as social benefits, are a function of social perception of what is bad and good about business activity. As a result, the nature of corporate social responsibility is not a static concept. Rather, it is concerned with moving targets many of which are the subject of government action. Such action may take three forms:

1 Legislation which outlaws undesirable social activities. Many examples exist of public concern with undesirable features of business activity, and of legislation to suppress such activities. One early example in the United Kingdom was the legislation relating to child labour in the nineteenth century which was made illegal.

2 Licensing systems may be employed to limit the extent of activities which are useful to society, but present a potential social problem. The licensing of lorries, for example, has been made the subject of certificates of road-worthiness, and attention is now paid to the control of exhaust emission. Thus, licensing may be qualitative as well as quantitative.

3 It has been argued that taxation is a convenient manner of internalizing external social costs of activities having negative effects on society. The objective is to impose taxes on the firm equal in magnitude to the damage sustained by society from the firm's activities. The obvious purpose of such taxes would be to encourage firms to abate the effects of such activities, or alternatively to finance public programmes for controlling these effects. According to some advocates of the taxation approach to dealing with social costs, business firms would be free to choose between abating the social nuisance and avoiding tax, or continuing as before and paying the tax. According to other advocates of this approach, there should be a tariff of taxes designed to encourage firms to locate in areas where their methods of production would do least harm to the environment. Many environmentalists would probably argue, however, that such by-products as pollution do harm wherever they occur, and that suppression through legislation is the only appropriate course of action for society to take.

From the foregoing discussion of the nature of externalities and the role of government in solving social problems, it is apparent that corporate social responsibility is difficult to define. The question may be asked— to what extent should business enterprises be responsible for dealing with all social problems left unsolved by government? Should they concentrate on solving some of these problems? Or should firms merely operate within a strict interpretation of the letter of the law, and if so, would this adherence to the letter of the law frustrate any claim that their behaviour towards externalities could be antisocial?

In the absence of a clear definition of corporate social responsibility by legislation, individual firms must decide for themselves the nature of their social responsibility as a management concept and constraint. The only guidelines available to a firm in this respect is legislation on the one hand and public opinion and pressure on the other. Subject to these constraints, it is evident that corporate social responsibility may be broadly or narrowly defined, and that individual firms have a fair margin of choice as to the standard of corporate social responsibility which they may be willing to accept.

The objectives of users of social accounting information

The Corporate Report (ASC, 1975) identified seven groups of users as having a reasonable right to receive information from companies. It did not specify, however, the decision models of these several groups of users, nor did it consider it to be practicable to publish information of a social accounting nature. Clearly, much of the information described above is of a qualitative rather than of a financial nature, and as such would be subjected to use by groups concerned with making value judgements about the firm's social contributions. In effect, identifying such groups of users as having distinctly different objectives from those already considered in the Corporate Report, namely, equity investors, loan creditors, employees, analysts, business contacts, government and public, poses complex problems of identifying what objectives such further groups might have in using social accounting information. For example, it might be considered by one group to be undesirable to conduct trade with another country having a political system with which that group is not in sympathy. Consequently, it might wish to have detailed information about trading activities and customers of the company for the purposes of conducting a political campaign to dissuade the company from conducting such trade. At the same time, of course, the group likely to be affected is already a customer and might consider it as inequitable that it should be penalized for activities beyond its own control as a customer group. Moreover, the objectors might conceivably be a caucus within a group, whose purposes are not identical with those of the majority of the group. The problem is that it becomes extremely difficult not only to identify the objectives for which social accounting information might be required, but also to establish stable patterns of value judgements about the activities reported upon, and stability in the 'opinions' of the individuals forming a group of users.

These theoretical problems are implicitly recognized in the debate about corporate social accountability. The need to find a way forward has prompted some authors to state the objectives toward which social accounting information might be directed. For example, Ramanathan (1976) suggests the following three objectives for social accounting information:

1   to identify and measure the periodic net social contribution of an individual firm, which includes not only the social costs and benefits internalized to the firm, but also those arising from externalities affecting different social segments;

2   to help determine whether an individual firm's strategy and practices which directly affect the relative resource and power status of individuals, communities, social segments and generations are

consistent with widely shared social priorities on the one hand and individuals' legitimate aspirations on the other; and

3   to make available in an optimal manner to all social constituents relevant information on a firm's goals, policies, programmes, performance and contribution to social goals.

The first two objectives may be viewed as measurement objectives for social acccounting. It is necessary to attain these measurement objectives if the third objective, which is a reporting objective, is to be realized. The development of measurement objectives encounters the problems discussed at the beginning of this chapter in that there is an apparent inability at this stage in time to develop measurements of performance everyone will accept. In this sense, the uncertainty as to the meaning and extent of corporate social responsibility may be seen as impeding agreement on dimensions of the measurement problem as a first stage in the search for appropriate measurements. Second, there is an apparent inability to make creditable cost-benefit and cost-effectiveness analyses to guide decision makers. This problem may be seen as related to the two previous problems, for if the objective of measurement is unclear, measurement standards cannot be developed and analyses cannot be conducted (Dierkes and Antal, 1985).

The scope of corporate social responsibility

Ernst and Ernst (1978) identified six areas in which corporate social objectives may be found:

1   Environment.
2   Energy.
3   Fair business practices.
4   Human resources.
5   Community involvement.
6   Product.

Environment

This area involves the environmental aspects of production, covering pollution control in the conduct of business operations, prevention or repair of damage to the environment resulting from processing of natural resources and the conservation of natural resources.

Corporate social objectives are to be found in the abatement of the negative external social effects of industrial production, and in adopting more efficient technologies to minimize the use of irreplaceable resources and the production of waste.

Energy

This area covers conservation of energy in the conduct of business operations and increasing the energy efficiency of the company's products.

Fair business practices

This area concerns the relationship of the company to special interest groups. In particular it deals with:

Employment of minorities.
Advancement of minorities.
Employment of women.
Advancement of women.
Employment of other special interest groups.
Support for minority businesses.
Socially responsible practices abroad.

Human resources

This area concerns the impact of organizational activities on the people who constitute the human resources of the organization. These activities include:

recruiting practices,
training programmes,
experience building—job rotation,
job enrichment,
wage and salary levels,
fringe benefit plans,
congruence of employee and organizational goals,
mutual trust and confidence,
job security, stability of workforce, layoff and recall practices,
transfer and promotion policies,
occupational health.

Community involvement

This area involves community activities, health-related activities, education and the arts and other community activity disclosures.

Products

This area concerns the qualitative aspects of the products, for example their utility, life-durability, safety and serviceability, as well as their effect on pollution. Moreover, it includes customer satisfaction, truthfulness in advertising, completeness and clarity of labelling and packaging. Many of these considerations are important already from a marketing point of view. It is clear, however, that the social responsibility aspect of the product contribution extends beyond what is advantageous from a marketing angle.

Corporate social reporting in the UK

Companies are required by law to disclose the following information:

Fair business practices

1 Companies with more than 250 employees are required to state the policy regarding the employment, training, career development and promotion of disabled people.

2 Information about employment practices of subsidiaries and associated companies with respect to black workers in South Africa.

Human resources

1 For companies which employ 100 or more the Directors' Report is required to state the average number of UK employees and their related remuneration during the year.

2 The Health and Safety at Work Act, 1974, provides for regulations to be made requiring companies to disclose information about 'arrangements in force for securing the health, safety and welfare at work of employees of the company and its subsidiaries.'

3 The Directors' Report is required to include action with regard to informing employees, consulting employees, encouraging involvement (e.g. share ownership schemes).

Charitable and political gifts which must be disclosed in the Directors' Report.

Several surveys have been undertaken in the UK in order to establish the nature and extent of social responsibility disclosures in the annual accounts. Maunders (1982) surveyed the published accounts of 300 large companies for 1981/82. Mirza (1987) examined the annual reports of 131 top companies for 1984/85. Gray (1989a) has conducted a longitudinal survey of 200 large companies for 1978/87. All three surveys raise the issue of the possible measurement levels that are feasible in relation to social reporting:

1 identification and description of efforts (e.g. general policy statements);

2 physical but non-financial quantification (e.g. employee man-hours in training); and

3 financial quantification (e.g. expenditure on pollution control).

Most social reporting was found to be of type 1 with the exception of human resource information. Gray (1989a) found that the trend of mandated disclosure is upward, reflecting an increased response to legislation. No such conclusion could be drawn from the voluntary disclosures, although over 60 per cent of the companies surveyed made voluntary disclosures of some sort.

Maunders (1982) found that the voluntary disclosures by his sample of companies for 1981/82 by categories of information were as follows:

	%
Human resources	40
Fair business practice	19
Energy	15
Community involvement	12
Product-related	10
Environmental	9

The largest incidence of voluntary disclosure is in the category of human resources which includes items such as employee training and development. Fair business practice concerns the disclosure by companies of information about women and persons of various ethnic groups in their employment. Mirza (1987) found that 15 per cent of his sample included information about environmental protection including the reporting of activities like treatment of effluent water, following stringent nuclear safety standards, restoration of mining areas and maintenance of trees. However, Gray (1989a) shows that there has been no significant increase in environmental and energy disclosures during the five years following the Maunders' survey.

The two categories where voluntary disclosures appear to have shown an upward trend in recent years are 'community involvement' and 'product-related'. According to Gray's (1989a) sample, product safety disclosures have increased over the nine years in question and community involvement disclosures had increased to nearly 40 per cent by 1987.

The greening of accounting

The recent escalation in concern for environmental issues has increased considerably attention to business social responsibility. In particular, the accounting literature has recently devoted more space to two issues:

1   environmental reporting;
2   the environmental audit.

Environmental reporting

Calls for environmental company reports have increased with the publication of *Blueprint for a Green Economy* (Pearce et al, 1989). This report, which was commissioned by the Department of the Environment, stresses the need to account for the use of environmental resources and for the use of substances which may damage the environment. According to Doherty (1989) this report 'could radically change the entire nature of company reporting in the UK'. It could lead to the requirement to publish, as part of the normal yearly report, an environmental report which would show:

1   the resources used by the company; and
2   the pollution and other effects, of the company on the environment (Dewhurst, 1989).

The environmental resources used by a business can be categorized as water, energy, raw materials and hazardous chemicals. The quantities of these resources used should be disclosed. The second part of the report would measure a company's pollution of the environment in the form of the effect on air, water, industrial and hazardous waste, noise and land. The effects of the outputs of a company on the environment can be substantial. These outputs are rarely measured and, as we have noted previously, are never expressed in money terms. Furthermore, disclosures by entities refer only to the positive impact of their activities on the environment. It is argued that requiring companies to report publicly both the positive and negative impact of their operations on the environment and wider community will urge them to improve their social responsibilities (Derwent, 1989).

The environmental audit

As green consciousness grows and develops, more companies are beginning to evaluate both its commercial implications and the impact any legislation and regulation could have for their operations. The environment audit is essentially a management tool. It implies that companies should not wait for restrictive legislation to bring about change.

The audit comprises a number of stages (Gray, 1989b):

1 Existing legislative requirements, health and safety practices and forthcoming regulatory developments are analysed.
2 Internal procedures and external requirements are examined, compared and contrasted. The implications of external requirements on production processes and equipment are assessed and the impact in terms of waste and emission are evaluated (Newell et al, 1990). Employee safety will also be examined.
3 The organisational structure, administrative and communication processes of the company are analysed to determine the extent to which management is informed of (and can therefore control) the environmental impact of the company's activities. Gaps are identified and remedies suggested.

Summary

The concept of corporate social responsibility emerged in the 1960s when changing social values and expectations gave rise to a debate about the role of business in society. This debate focused on the nature of corporate social responsibility, and gave rise to the possibility that this responsibility could be discharged through a method of social responsibility accounting. It was argued that such a method of accounting would indicate the nature and the manner of the firm's social contributions or outputs. Corporate social objectives may be found in six areas of enterprise activity. Most social reporting disclosures are descriptive in nature. Although the trend of mandated disclosure in the UK has been upwards in recent years, no such conclusions can be drawn from voluntary disclosures. The recent concern for environmental issues may have a dramatic effect on future corporate social accounting systems.

References

Accounting Standards Committee (1975). *The Corporate Report*, Institute of Chartered Accountants in England and Wales.

Arrow, K. J. (1963). *Social Choice and Individual Values*, Yale University Press.

Committee for Economic Development (1971). *Social Responsibilities of Business Corporations*.

Derwent, R. (1989). A mandate for green reporting, *Accountancy*, October.

Dewhurst, J. (1989). The green resource audit, *The Accountant*, December.

Dierkes, M. and Antal, A.B. (1985). The usefulness and use of social reporting information, *Accounting, Organizations and Society*, Vol. 10, No. 1.

Doherty, J. (1989). The greening of accountancy, *The Accountant*, December.

Ernst and Ernst (1978). *Social Responsibility Disclosure: 1978 Survey*, Ernst and Ernst, Cleveland, Ohio.

Friedman, M. (1962). *Capitalism and Freedom*, p. 133, University of Chicago Press.

Gray, R. H. (1989a). *Corporate social reporting by UK companies: a cross-sectional and longitudinal study*, Draft Working Paper, December.

Gray, R. H. (1989b). Social audit: responding to change? *Management Accounting*, UK, December.

Maunders, K. T. (1982). 'Social reporting and the employment report', in Skerratt, L. C. L. and Tonkin, D. J. (eds) *Financial Reporting 1982–83: A Survey of UK Published Accounts*, The Institute of Chartered Accountants in England and Wales.

Mirza, A. M. (1987). Social reporting by the UK companies, *Business Graduate Journal*, April.

Newell, G. E., Kreuze, J. G. and Newell, S. J. (1990). Accounting for hazardous waste, *Management Accounting USA*, May.

Pearce, D. W., Markandya, A. and Barbier, E. B. (1989). *Blueprint for a Green Economy*, Earthscan.

Ramanathan, K. V. (1976). Towards a theory of corporate social accounting, *The Accounting Review*, July.

Schrader, D. F. E. (1987). The corporation and profits, *Journal of Business Ethics*, 6.

Questions

1 'There is as yet no generally accepted concept of the social responsibility of business enterprises.' Discuss.
2 What six areas in which corporate social objectives may be found were identified by Ernst and Ernst?
3 Examine the recent trends in corporate social reporting in the UK.
4 What are the implications for accounting of the increasing concern with green issues?

Part 5

Planning and control

Introduction

The significance of the role which the management accountant fulfils today lies in his contribution to the overall management of business operations rather than in the set of procedures for which he is responsible and which relate purely to the financial aspects of management control. Accordingly, an appreciation of management accounting as a field of knowledge is more appropriately developed through the systems approach, which as we noted in Chapter 2 is really a way of viewing accounting in the context of the organization as a whole.

The objective of this part is to provide our readers with a coherent and intelligible management framework in which the importance of accounting information may be understood.

One difficulty which arises in this respect is that there is a great deal of controversy about management theory itself. For example, writing in the early 1960s Harold Koontz described management theory as a jungle in which he could identify six different schools of thought. Today, the position remains just as confused and there does not exist a coherent theory of management in which the role of accounting could be unambiguously analysed.

Another difficulty arises from conflicts with regard to the theory of the firm itself. For example, classical economic theory assumed that the firm had the sole objective of profit maximization. This theory provided a purpose for management decision making which was clearly defined, and a need for a type of management accounting information which was unambiguously stated. The subsequent erosion of the supremacy of the classical theory of the firm by the appearance of either modified assumptions about profit maximization or different assumptions about the objectives of the enterprise has destroyed the basis for a coherent view of the objectives for which accounting information might be required by decision makers within the enterprise. Thus, neo-classicists assume that profit maximization cannot be achieved and that the objective of management ought to be to 'satisfice' a profit requirement. Behavioural theories of the firm assume that the firm seeks to expand through the maximization of sales, or alternatively that the objectives of the firm can be defined only from the objectives of the dominant personalities in the enterprise. Finally, there are now radical theories which redefine the role of the business enterprise within society in terms of socially oriented objectives, which may be assumed either to be free enterprise in the process of adjustment to social change or to be imposed by political diktat.

It follows that the absence of coherent theories of the firm and coherent theories of management prohibits the formulation of a normative theory of users' needs for accounting information which would define the informative objectives to which accounting might be addressed in the context of decision making within the firm. Consequently, in this part the analysis of accounting information in the context of management decision making is constrained and suffers from the immaturity of extant theories.

There remains, however, the need for some kind of framework in which the contribution of accounting to the management process could be examined. Many would agree that the following factors are important in this regard:

1 The best way to understand the complexities of enterprise decision making is to recognize that each separate situation requires its own organized solution. Accordingly, companies should be managed in the context of their own peculiar circumstances. Moreover, different companies are, in effect, trying to accomplish different things. They are so diverse in such respects as markets, production methods, ownership and size that they inevitably have a diversity of objectives.

2 Regardless of the variety of theories about the firm or about management, it is generally accepted that management has a set of specific functions to perform such as planning, organizing, controlling, communicating and motivating people.

3 The decision-making process integrates all the management processes, for all managerial functions involve decision making. Hence, the key to understanding management behaviour is the decision-making process. In Part 4, we examined investors' and employees' decisions and developed criteria for information relevant to their decisions. These criteria, which were discussed in Chapter 23 and which emphasized— among others—relevance and understandability, are applicable to management decisions. Accordingly, these criteria suggest that our concern should be with such questions as:

- What decisions do management make?
- What information is relevant to particular decisions?

4 Managers of business enterprises are faced with constant changes in the environment within and outside the firm. To survive, business enterprises must themselves be susceptible to change. The ability to evaluate past decisions, to react to current situations and to predict future events should be regarded as critical success factors. Management accountants may be seen to be concerned with the process of change by the analysis of past decisions, the provision of information that appreciates current trends, and participating in the decisions that will affect the future of the enterprise by ensuring that the information that is needed will have relevance to those decisions.

Given this definition of the problems of accounting for management decision making, our scheme of work in the subsequent chapters is as follows:

Section 1
A framework for
planning and control

In this section, we examine the concepts of planning and control as they are applied to business organizations. We will see that central to this analysis is the selection of the goals towards which the activities of such organizations are to be directed. These goals, therefore, provide the focus to the decision-making process.

We examine the management process in some detail so as to establish the role of information in this context. Cost plays an important role in the planning and control process. The problems of ascertaining unit product costs are examined in this section.

Section 2
Planning

This section is concerned with a relatively detailed analysis of the planning process. It begins with a discussion of long-range planning as a means of attaining the organization's long-term goals. We proceed with an examination of the stages by which these goals may be realized. This involves, on the one hand, providing the assets which will enable the firm to operate and involves capital expenditure, and, on the other, realizing long-range plans in annual stages by means of the activities envisaged in the annual budget.

Planning decisions are made in the face of uncertainty. We devote a chapter, therefore, to the analysis of risk and the means by which this problem may be reduced to some extent.

Our discussion of the nature and importance of the annual budget leads us to such problems as the relationship between costs, volume of output and profit, and pricing. Lastly, we examine those types of decisions which tend to be made on a 'once-and-for-all' basis and do not form part of the long-range planning process, for example, such decisions as the acceptance of special offers, dropping product lines and making-or-buying decisions.

Section 3
Control

We begin this section by relating control to planning and establishing in this way that the purpose of control is to ensure that the firm's activities conform with its plans. We relate the concept of control also to an organizational framework aimed at securing the performance of the tasks involved in implementing plans. This enables us to introduce the concept of responsibility accounting.

The importance traditionally attached in accounting to the control of costs, and the use of costs in the control of performance are considered in a chapter on standard costing and associated techniques such as flexible budgeting.

Since the publication of the third edition of this text, there have been a number of new developments, both in the discussion of theories relating to management accounting, and also an extension of the subject matter of management accounting in the area of production control. Thus, the interest in agency theory has stretched the intellectual boundaries in accounting research, and in some important respects the area of management control (Antle Rick on Intellectual Boundaries in Accounting Research, *Accounting Horizons*, American Accounting Association, June 1989, pp. 103–109). Significantly, also, has been the evolution of advanced manufacturing techniques, such as just-in-time accounting, that have provoked discussions of the need to develop appropriate cost accounting systems for high technology industries. At the same time, conventional cost accounting methods have been exposed to the pressures of a highly competitive business environment. This has led to greater stress on cost reduction, of which the development of JIT inventory management and target costing are direct consequences.

Throughout this section, we stress the importance of information feedback as a means of ensuring that actual performance conforms with planned and required performance. We devote a chapter to performance appraisal in which we stress the importance of behavioural factors related to the influence of the human element in organizations. We argue also that the accountant should play a larger role in the design of management information systems.

<table>
<tr>
<td>

Section 1

A framework for planning and control

</td>
<td>

Chapter 26

The meaning of planning and control

</td>
</tr>
</table>

There are two conflicting schools of thought regarding the extent to which the firm is in charge of its own destiny. Market theory postulates that the firm is solely at the whim of prevailing economic and social forces, so that successful management depends upon the ability to 'read' the environment. By contrast, planning and control theory asserts that management has control over the firm's future and believes that the firm's destiny may be manipulated and hence planned and controlled. In this view, the quality of managerial planning and control decisions is the key factor for success.

In reality, business organizations normally operate somewhere in between these two extreme views: many elements, such as raw material prices, are completely outside their control; on the other hand some elements, such as the selling price of its product, are determined by the organization itself. One may make a distinction, therefore, between controllable and non-controllable items. It is the function of management to manipulate the controllable items to the firm's best advantage, and to ensure that it is prepared to meet changes in the non-controllable ones, so as to take full advantage of favourable changes and minimize the impact of unfavourable ones. Planning is essential for all the factors which affect the organization, irrespective of whether or not they are controllable or non-controllable. We may infer from this fact that the greater is the degree to which a firm's management reflects the views of control theorists the greater are its chances of success.

The processes of management

Although there are different schools of thought as to what may be understood by the term 'management' and how it should be practised, it is generally accepted that management has five main functions: planning, organizing, controlling, communicating and motivating.

Planning

Planning is the most basic of all management functions, and the skill with which this function is performed determines the success of all operations. Planning may be defined as the thinking process that precedes action and is directed towards making decisions now with the future in mind. Theoretically, the function of planning is to improve the quality of decision making by a careful consideration of all the relevant factors before a decision is made, and ensuring that decisions conform with a rational strategy by which the firm's future is to be shaped. Planning may be seen as consisting of five stages:

1 Setting organizational objectives.
2 Assessing the environment in which the organization will be operating, by reference to the external factors which are likely to affect its operations. For this purpose, forecasts have to be made which attempt to predict what will happen in the future, with and without policy changes on the part of the planning organization.
3 Assessing existing resources, for management is concerned with making the most efficient use of those scarce resources, often called the four M's: men, machines, materials and money. This aspect of the planning function involves making an estimate both of external resources which are accessible, and resources already held which are either idle or which might be more efficiently utilized.
4 Determining the strategy for achieving stated objectives by means of an overall plan which specifies strategic goals. Strategic decisions are concerned with establishing the relationship between the firm and its environment.
5 Designing a programme of action to achieve selected strategic goals by means of both long-range programmes and short-range programmes, the latter covering a period of a year or less and containing sets of instructions of the type found in annual budgets.

Thus, decisions are essential at every stage of the planning process, and the key areas may be stated as deciding 'what should be done, when it should be done, how it should be done and who should do it'.

The importance of environmental factors to the planning process is obvious; and it is equally clear that environmental information should not be subjected to a less disciplined treatment than the internal or analytical information, which an organization itself provides. There may sometimes be important areas in which one may criticize the quality of analytical information as being inadequate for the purpose of efficient decision making. Deficiencies in the nature and quality of analytical information will be examined in much greater detail elsewhere in this book. However, there is a need for a continuous flow of information on the environment, for the most important determinant of a firm's potential for growth and improved efficiency is the ability of its management to learn about this aspect. Information systems are now moving away from a heavy emphasis on internal or analytical information and incorporating much more environmental data. As surveys in the United States have shown, the scan of environmental data in which management is interested ranges from market potential of new and existing product lines, to new processes and technology, the actions of competitors, sales regulations, resources and supplies available to government actions and policies.

We may distinguish three kinds of planning activities:

1   Strategic planning which is concerned with a period from three to ten years ahead and which is usually called long-range planning.
2   Project planning is an activity which follows the long-range plan, and involves developing plans for the capital expenditures necessary to meet long-term objectives.
3   Budgetary planning which converts the firm's long-range plan to the needs of the immediate future. This is usually described as budgeting, and is generally carried out on a one-year basis. The annual budget is then broken down into months, and in some cases into weeks, to chart the path the firm should take in the immediate future.

Organizing

Organizing involves setting up the administrative structure for implementing strategic decisions. The administrative design area is concerned with establishing the structure and the shape of the firm or organization, and defining responsibilities and lines of authority. It involves a definition of the tasks necessary to achieve strategic goals, determining who is to perform these tasks and assigning responsibility for their performance. The function of organizing is to co-ordinate these tasks in such a way that the organization is able to work efficiently in fulfilling its objects. The process of organizing is achieved through departmentalization, by which different specialisms are hived off into separate departments. These departments are linked in a hierarchy, a formal communication structure that enables instructions to be passed downwards and information to be passed upwards to senior management. Figure 5.1 shows a partial organization structure for a firm which is concerned with two main activities—furniture and floor covering.

A manager may be allotted the task of managing the activities in each of these boxes, which then represent executive positions; the lines represent the formal channels of communication between them. The top five boxes represent the five major functions of this firm—marketing, manufacturing, finance, personnel and research and development. For administrative purposes, the firm is organized according to its product categories; therefore, two divisions—furniture and floor covering—are established.

At the bottom of the pyramid in the figure are the basic organizational units, known as departments; this illustrates the six departments belonging to the furniture division. Departments form an occupational classification—in this case they are divided into production and service departments.

A major purpose of any organizational structure is to facilitate the flow of information to and from decision makers. Since management may be said to be the process of converting information into action, organizations should be designed around information flows. Each decision point in this process is a sub-information system having its own elements

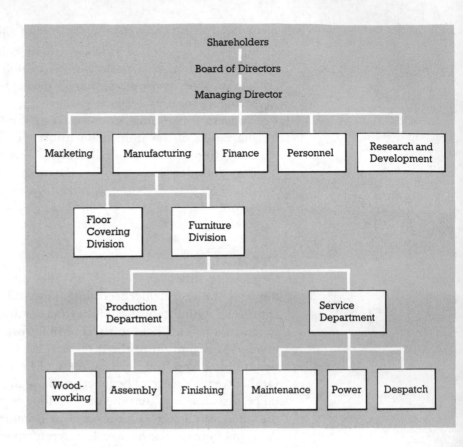

Fig. 5.1

at input, processor and output. Hence, information networks shape the structure of the organization.

Control

In their discussion of 'control', some writers make no distinction between 'planning' and 'control', thereby giving a much wider meaning to their concept of control. We shall discuss the extended meaning of 'control' later in this chapter. For the purpose of our own analysis of the management process, we propose to make a distinction between 'planning' and 'control'. This distinction enables us to examine the management process as a cycle of activities as shown in Fig. 5.2.

The decisions involved in this area stem from two main activities, first, comparing actual performance against that stipulated in the plan, and second, determining whether the plan itself should be modified in the light of this comparison.

Control is closely linked to the planning function in that its purpose is to ensure that the firm's activities conform to its plans. It is effected by means of an information feedback system which enables performance to be compared with planned targets. Control is essential to the realization of long-range and short-term plans.

In long-range planning, information feedback enables management to assess what progress has been made towards the realization of the

Fig. 5.2

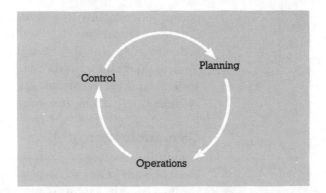

long-range objectives specified in the long-range plan. Additionally, it allows management to review long-range objectives in the light of new circumstances which may have rendered those objectives unrealistic.

In practice, by far the greatest emphasis is attached to the control of operations so as to meet the objectives contained in the annual budget which, as we noted earlier, should be seen as part of the long-range plan. Information feedback is an integral part of budgetary control procedures which are intended to be highly sensitive to operational variations on a day-to-day basis. Their aim is to highlight deviations from the budget plan as soon as possible so that remedial action may be taken immediately.

A prerequisite of the successful performance of the control function is an efficient information system which will reveal the need for corrective action at an appropriate time, enabling managers to judge whether their targets are still appropriate as the environment changes month by month and year by year. The control function is closely linked to the planning function by means of a feedback system which provides information on the results of past decisions. Such a system is necessary to the assessment of the quality of the decision-making process and to its improvement, and is illustrated in Fig. 5.3.

The feedback system provides the great bulk of analytical information used in the planning process. It provides a means also of evaluating planned objectives. Should, for example, the economic climate change, the efficiency of the organization's operations will depend on the swiftness of its reaction to this change by way of alterations to the planned objectives. The feedback system is also instrumental to the making of control decisions, for it provides a means of continuously assessing current

Fig. 5.3

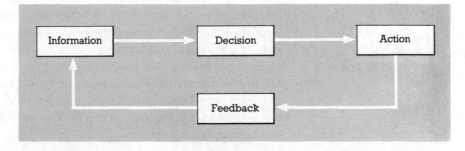

performance against the strategic plan. Decision making in this sense thus involves making day-to-day adjustments to changing conditions in order to map out the most appropriate course of action needed to implement strategic decisions. Thus, information is the lifeblood of any system, and the responsibility for the design of adequate information systems is of paramount concern to management.

Communication

Communication is an exchange of facts, ideas and opinions by two or more persons. The exchange is successful only when actual understanding results. Merely saying is not enough; a receiver of information must understand the message which the sender is trying to communicate. Communication occurs when the former understands what the latter means to convey.

Communication involves linking all the management functions by transmitting information and instructions within the organization. Additionally, the communication process relates the organization to its environment by linking it to suppliers of resources, and to the consumers for whom its products are intended.

In any organization, the specialization of tasks and the consequent division of labour creates a situation in which an unrestricted flow of ideas and facts is necessary if it is to function efficiently. A high degree of communication binds the various members of the organization together, uniting them in the pursuit of organizational goals. Hence, an organization may be viewed not only as a decision-making system, but also as a communication system.

The major components in the communication system are the sender, the message and the receiver. The *sender* may be an individual or a computer or other device which is capable of sending a message. The *message* is the information transmitted to the receiver. The medium used for transmitting a message may be written, oral, visual or other forms of communicating meaning. A red light on operating equipment, for example, is often used to indicate a breakdown or a danger. From a management viewpoint, written communication has special advantages in that information may be planned and incorporated into formal procedures, forms, reports etc., by which means communication is effected. Essentially, procedures which are designed to communicate information should focus on what is important, so as to maximize the possibility of effective communication occurring. This requires a limitation on the number of messages communicated so that the really important information is perceived. The principle of communicating only 'exceptional' information, that is, information about a variance from a predetermined plan which requires immediate attention, is a feature of successful communication systems. Moreover, the frequency of communication should be considered in the light of the needs of the receiver, having regard to the effective action which may result from the communication.

Fig. 5.4

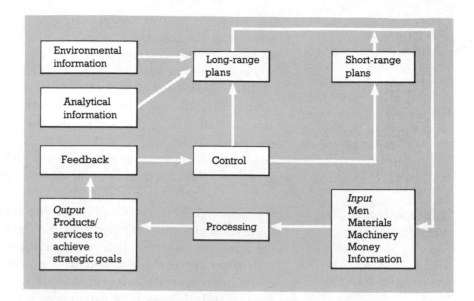

Occasionally, the context or situation surrounding communication may affect its transmission or reception. This occurs when interference, such as static on a radio message, prevents the message from being transmitted or distorts the manner in which it is received. The 'gap' or 'noise' is the result of factors causing distortions or loss of meaning, and one of the tasks of the designers of information systems is to minimize noise and prevent it from being accepted as true information.

Lastly, the *receiver* must recognize the context in which the message is sent and received in order that he may interpret the message correctly. The last stage in the communication process involves a human factor, in that the reception of information should produce the correct response. Behavioural factors which impede the required response may render the entire process of communication futile.

The way in which information is communicated and related to planning and control may be illustrated as in Fig. 5.4.

Figure 5.4 shows how environmental and analytical information is combined in the plans which are designed to meet the organization's objectives. These plans are implemented as resources become inputs which are converted into products and services. The feedback and control systems should function so as to ensure the effectiveness of the plans.

Motivation

This involves getting all the members of the organization to pull their full weight, and finding ways in which individual performance may be improved. When we study motivation, we are studying the influences on a human being and what affects his behaviour. For example, when we ask someone to perform a certain task which we know to be within his capability and experience and it is not done satisfactorily, this failure may well be the result of poor motivation rather than lack of ability.

Some motivating factors are basically biological or physiological and may be looked upon as natural or inherent such as the need for air, water, food, sleep, clothing and housing. Some motivating factors are learned, for example, the combination of needs associated with the individual's ego and a correct evaluation of himself.

Other motivating factors are related to social needs, and these are influenced by the organization of the work situation. Many studies have examined the effects of these needs, and they illustrate how the size, cohesiveness and motives of the group act as controls on the members' own motives. Hence, the organization should create a situation in which group and individual goals coincide to as great a degree as possible.

Information and decision making

Decision making has received increasing attention in recent years, and some authorities have argued that management and decision making are synonymous terms. Indeed, there is very little managerial activity which does not involve decision making in some form. Since the quality of information available is crucial to the quality of decision making, an efficient and adequate information system is a prerequisite of managerial success. The hallmark of efficient management may thus be seen in the ability to specify accurately the information needed, and this ability is in itself a function of clear definition of objectives, sound planning and control capability and satisfactory organizational arrangements.

Information is an integrating force which combines organizational resources into a cohesive whole directed towards the realization of organizational objectives. Since information affects the fortunes of an organization in such a fundamental way, it is important that information should be effectively organized and efficiently handled, and this is achieved through what has become known as a management information system. A management information system provides individual managers with the information required for making decisions within their own particular areas of responsibility. It may be likened to the central nervous system of an organism in that it consists of a network of information flows to which each decision may be related.

Within this information network, decision points may be identified at three levels—strategic planning, management control and operational control (Anthony, 1965).

Strategic planning involves the determination of corporate objectives and goals, as well as the development of broad policies and strategies by which they may be achieved. This activity relies heavily on information about the environment, and has an irregular pattern. Management control is a lower-level activity which is concerned with the implementation of the strategic plan; it assures that the necessary resources have been obtained, also that they are being used effectively and efficiently. This activity is rhythmic, and follows a weekly, monthly or quarterly pattern. Operational control is the process of ensuring that specific tasks are being carried out effectively and efficiently. It is an activity which focuses on individuals' jobs and transactions, and its tempo is 'real time' (that is, data reported as events occur). Operational control

Fig. 5.5

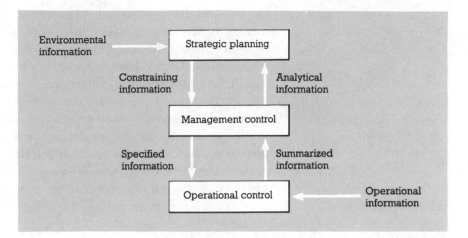

is thus exercised over operating systems, and these include stock records, personnel records, data handling and maintenance records. Examples of the relationship between these levels of activity are illustrated as follows:

Strategic planning	Management control	Operation control
Setting marketing policies	Formulating advertising programmes	Controlling the placement of advertisements
Setting personnel policies	Planning staff levels	Hiring and controlling staff

The relationship between these three levels of activities and the information flows is shown in Fig. 5.5.

Strategic planning decisions are based upon data derived both from outside and within the system in the form of environmental and analytical information; the latter identifies the organization's strengths and weaknesses, and the former enables it to formulate its strategy.

The constraints imposed upon management control decisions emanate from the strategic decisions incorporated in the strategic plan, and for the purposes of management control decisions these constraints are contained in long- and short-term plans. These plans themselves are broken down into detailed programmes for the various operational subsystems, and into specified information for the purposes of operational control. Hence, management control decisions are based on summarized information which compares the actual performance of cost and profit centres against their planned performance. In order that management should not be inundated with irrelevant information, reports to management should be in the form of statements of variances from the budget plan, and the reasons why these variances have occurred. Management control exercised in this way is known as management by exception. Management control decisions are thus concerned with investigating variances, and issuing instructions to operating managers on how to deal with them. Alternatively, management may recognize that the variances are inevitable and uncontrollable, and therefore recommend that the strategic plan should be altered to take account of this fact. In such a case, the decision will take the form of a recommendation of an adjustment to the strategic plan.

Operational control decisions are made at the meeting point between specified and operating information associated with the various subsystems. Specified information sets up standards of performance in terms of volume and costs of production and allocated time. Operating information discloses the results in the form of items produced, and production performance in terms of and time actually taken. Operational control decisions, unlike management control decisions, are concerned with day-to-day variances occurring in detailed operations, such as the time taken to perform individual tasks.

Extended meanings of 'control'

The term control has acquired a variety of uses in our daily language. We speak, for example, of traffic control, arms control and pest control. It is evident, however, that in applying the term control to different situations, we are thinking of different kinds of actions. Thus, when we speak of traffic control, we are really thinking of traffic regulation; when we speak of arms control, we have in mind arms limitation; and when we are speaking of pest control, we mean pest eradication. A similar flexibility of use in the term control is to be observed in the manner in which it is employed in the context of business affairs. Control is used to describe key functions, such as production control, quality control and budgetary control. These functions, however, represent quite different types of activities; production control refers to the production process and the need to regulate that process; quality control implies the rejection of substandard work; and budgetary control is concerned with keeping expenditure within a firm in line with a budget plan.

The term control also may be given both a narrow and a broad definition. A narrow definition of control is associated often with the maintenance of standards and the imposition of penalties. The broad concept of control which is to be found in the literature of management science treats the term control as synonymous with management itself. In this sense, control embraces the various processes by which management determines its objectives, draws up plans to attain those objectives, organizes and supervises the operations necessary for the implementation of plans, and appraises performance. Control also implies the investigation of deviations from planned objectives, so that performance levels may be brought into line with planned levels. Where necessary, plans and objectives may be changed to meet new circumstances.

One may subject the concept of control to a more complex theoretical analysis, which suggests that both normative and descriptive theories of control may be developed. In either context, the crux of control is in measurement. Measurements are required in setting objectives as targets for plans, and since plans are directed towards the future, such measurements are based upon predictions. Prediction is an integral part of control, which in this sense contemplates a future course of action. A normative theory of control recognizes that numerous possible courses of action may exist, each requiring its own control procedure if a system is not to get out of control. Control theory in this sense is based upon what is known as the *law of requisite variety* which states that there must be at least as many variations in the controls to be applied as there are ways for a system to fall out of control. The following example illustrates this principle.

Example

A firm is experiencing a decline in sales and hence has cut back its level of production. Stocks of raw materials, however, are increasing because the purchasing function uses decision rules which are appropriate only for normal conditions, and is not scaling down its levels of purchases. Hence, the control system operating within the firm may be said to be not flexible enough to take into account abnormal circumstances, that is, it has not enough variety to cope with the range of situations with which the system is faced. To remedy this defect, two alternative steps are open to management; either new decision rules must be formulated for the purchasing function which take into account abnormal situations, or the purchasing function must be free to generate its own response to changing circumstances.

The law of requisite variety has important implications for the design of information systems. It implies that decision rules should be devised for making routine decisions. As we saw in Part 1, such decisions may be programmed, and, as a result, they may be automated. On the other hand, where decisions involve judgement and experience, the law of requisite variety requires that enough information be provided so that the decision maker himself may generate appropriate responses.

Summary

Planning occurs at all management levels, and the success of other management functions depends upon the quality of planning.

Planning is concerned with both controllable and uncontrollable factors which affect the organization. Controllable factors should be manipulated to the organization's advantage, and the effects of uncontrollable factors should be minimized.

Management is also concerned with such functions as organization, control, communication and motivation. Since decision making is a key characteristic of all management functions, decision making has become synonymous with management.

Information is necessary for decision making, and the quality of information will affect the quality of decisions. Hence, an adequate and efficient information system is a prerequisite of managerial success.

Decision making may be classified according to the following areas:

1 strategic planning—which involves the determination of corporate objectives and goals as well as the broad policies and strategies by which they may be achieved;

2 management control—which is concerned with implementing the strategic plans;

3 operational control—which is the process of ensuring that specific tasks are carried out effectively and efficiently.

In this part we shall consider the role of accounting as the most important element of a management information system, and we shall also examine the manner in which accounting information assists management in its various functions.

Reference

Anthony, R. N. (1965). *Planning and Control Systems: A Framework for Analysis*, p. 24, Harvard Business School.

Questions

1 State the main functions of management.
2 Define the term 'planning' as a management function, and refer your definition to the planning process.
3 Distinguish three kinds of planning activities, and comment on their relative importance.
4 Explain what is meant by 'organizing' as a management function.
5 What is the significance of an 'organizational structure'?
6 What is meant by 'control'?
7 Why is communication viewed as of critical importance in the management process?
8 Discuss motivation in a management context.
9 Discuss the role played by information in the management decision making.
10 Explain the different levels of management activity, and comment on their relative importance.

Chapter 27

The cost accounting framework

Costs represent money measurements of the efforts that an organization has to make to achieve its objectives. Consequently, costs play a very important role in management decision-making.

Different costs are used for different types of decision. For example, costs required for the purpose of product costing are analysed as direct costs and indirect costs. Costs that reflect the impact of different activity levels and are relevant to decisions relating to activity volume are presented in the form of fixed costs and variable costs. Accordingly, the various cost terms that are used in accounting, such as direct and indirect costs, fixed and variable costs, sunk costs, differential costs, all have a specific meaning and a specific decision use. These terms will be examined in this chapter and subsequent chapters.

Objectives of cost analysis

Costs are collected for four major purposes:

1 To assist in planning decisions, such as the determination of which products to manufacture, the quantities which should be produced and the selling prices. Since planning is addressed to the future, we are interested in future costs for this purpose. Historical costs are useful only in so far as they are reliable indicators of future costs.

2 To assist in the control of operations by maintaining and improving the efficiency with which resources are employed. Control involves comparing the actual costs of current operations against their planned costs. It follows that since actual costs are monetary surrogates of the resources which have been exhausted in current operations, we should be interested in replacing those resources. Hence, for this purpose, we require replacement costs. The control process assists in keeping current costs in line with planned costs by highlighting inefficiencies. It may also lead to a revision of planned costs.

3 To assist in the measurement of reported profits.

4 To assist in the collective bargaining processes.

Costs are accumulated in two forms: in terms of their relationship to a person (responsibility accounting) and in terms of product. Responsibility accounting, which uses costs accumulated in the first form, is directed at the control of costs by associating them with individuals in the management hierarchy. This form of accounting plays a central role in the control of operations, which is dealt with in Chapter 35.

Here we deal with the accumulation of costs in order to calculate full product costs, that is, all the manufacturing costs incurred in bringing the product to a marketable state. One application of full product costs is computing inventory values. Sometimes, non-manufacturing costs such as administrative and marketing costs are added to the full product costs for the purpose of determining the profitability of products and for establishing pricing policies. These product costs are also used in government contracts which seek to establish a 'fair price' by basing the price on total costs.

The elements of cost

The costs of transforming raw materials into finished products are classified into two major categories—manufacturing and non-manufacturing costs.

Manufacturing costs

These costs comprise three elements:

1   direct material costs;
2   direct labour costs;
3   factory overhead costs.

The term 'direct' cost is applied only to those costs which can be readily identified with the product. Therefore, direct material costs include only those costs which can be directly associated with the finished product. Similarly, if an employee performs a task connected with the making of the product, his wage is considered as a direct labour cost. Direct material and direct labour costs are referred to as prime costs.

In deciding which costs to treat as direct costs, the accountant has to take into consideration the materiality of the item. The expense of determining that some item is a direct cost rather than regarding it as a factory overhead cost may outweigh any benefit attached to such information. Thus, the expense of recording as direct costs such small items as washers, nuts and bolts far outweighs any benefit which may be derived from this exercise.

Factory overhead costs include all the remaining production costs, after direct costs have been determined. They include indirect material costs such as lubricants, and supplies of materials for repairs and maintenance. They also include indirect labour costs such as the salaries and wages of inspectors, timekeepers and workmen who do not work on specific products. Factory overhead costs also include other indirect costs such as heat, light, power and the depreciation of factory buildings, plant and equipment.

The manufacturing cost is the total of all direct and indirect costs. It is the cost of manufacture which is recorded as the stock value of the finished product while it is awaiting sale. Upon sale, the manufacturing cost forms part of the cost of sale for the purpose of calculating the trading profit.

Non-manufacturing costs

These costs are not included in the cost of manufacturing the product, and they are not included, therefore, in the cost of sales. Hence, they are assumed not to attach to the product costs for income measurement purposes. Non-manufacturing costs are 'period' rather than 'product' costs, and they are associated with accounting periods rather than with output. Non-manufacturing costs include administrative and marketing costs. Administrative costs are defined as the costs incurred on executive salaries, head office staff expenses including all clerical and secretarial staff, legal expenses and depreciation on office equipment, furniture etc. Marketing costs include the activities associated with obtaining orders, such as advertising and selling costs, and activities concerned with fulfilling orders, such as warehousing, packing and delivery.

Full product costs

The elements of cost involved in the calculation of full product costs for a unit of a product may be summarized by the following ascertained unit costs:

	£
Direct material costs	4
Direct labour costs	6
Direct cost per unit	10
Factory overhead costs	8
Manufacturing cost per unit	
Full product cost	18

In calculating full product costs, the accounting problem is to find means of attributing to units of products their appropriate costs for the various decisions which management has to make. The task of calculating the direct material and direct labour costs attributable to individual products is relatively easy. The direct material costs are calculated by ascertaining the quantities of materials used in the product, making due allowance for normal waste, and multiplying the quantity by the raw material purchase price. Similarly, the direct labour costs are obtained by specifying the operations involved in production and the time taken, and multiplying the time factor so derived by the appropriate labour rates. It is in the calculation of total overhead costs per unit that the major accounting problem of cost determination lies.

The problem of overhead costs

The problem of ascertaining the overhead costs applicable to a unit of a product is first and foremost a function of the number of different products which the firm manufactures. Where the firm manufactures only one product, the problem is relatively simple. If, for example, the firm produces 1000 units of the product, and the overhead costs total £2000, the total overhead costs per unit is £2.

Where the firm manufactures more than one product, however, many problems arise in computing unit overhead costs of production. We shall discuss these problems in terms of the undermentioned stages in the ascertainment of full-product costs:

1   The allotment of factory overhead costs to production cost centres.
2   The allotment in turn of the costs of production cost centres to individual products.
3   The selection of an appropriate level of activity for calculating unit product costs. This is necessary because unit costs vary with activity levels, and a choice has to be made as to the activity level which is applicable to future output.

The allotment of factory overhead costs to production cost centres

Cost centres are locations with which costs may conveniently be associated for the purpose of product costing.

Basically, there are two types of cost centres for which costs are accumulated—production and service cost centres. Production cost centres are those actually involved in production, such as machining and assembling departments. Service cost centres are those which exist to facilitate production, for example, maintenance, stores and canteen.

The first stage in the allotment of factory overhead costs to production cost centres is to collect and classify factory overhead costs as between indirect material, indirect labour or other identifiable cost headings. The next stage is to allocate these costs, where possible, to production and service cost centres. The term 'cost allocation' has a special meaning, being used to refer to the allotment of whole items of cost to cost centres. For example, the salaries of foremen in charge of individual cost centres may be allocated to those cost centres. Items of costs which cannot be allocated to cost centres must be apportioned. The term 'cost apportionment' means the allotment of proportions only of items of cost to cost centres. For example, the cost of rates cannot be allotted to any particular cost centre and must be apportioned between cost centres.

The third stage is to apportion the costs of the service cost centres to the production cost centres. If we assume that a firm has three service cost centres and two production cost centres, as in Fig. 5.6, the

Fig. 5.6

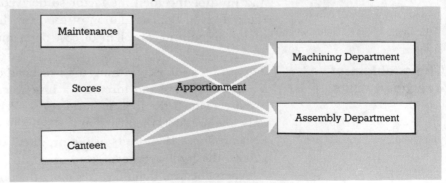

apportionment of the service cost centre costs involves selecting appropriate methods for apportioning these costs to the production cost centres.

When the apportionment is completed, the major production cost centres will have accumulated both prime costs and factory overhead costs.

Example

The production process of Simplex Ltd is based on a machining department and an assembly department, which are supported by one service department which is a maintenance department. Consider the following cost information.

Departmental cost data

Direct (or allocated overheads)	Total	Machining	Assembly	Maintenance
	£	£	£	£
Indirect materials	15 000	8 000	5 000	2 000
Indirect labour	6 000	4 000	1 000	1 000
Depreciation of machinery	7 000	2 500	4 500	—
Total direct overhead costs	28 000	14 500	10 500	3 000
Indirect (or unallocated overheads)				
Supervisory salaries	6 000			
Rates	10 000			
Total overhead factory costs	44 000			

From this information, we may observe that the first stage in the treatment of overhead factory costs has been completed, since those factory overhead costs which may be directly associated with cost centres have already been allotted. In this connection, it should be mentioned that the direct overhead factory costs are said to be direct to the cost centres concerned, but they remain indirect to the units of the product.

The next stage, therefore, is to apportion the indirect overhead factory costs as between the three cost centres. It will be recalled that indirect factory overhead costs are those which cannot be directly associated with any particular cost centres, but are attached to the factory as a whole. Bases are needed, therefore, to apportion them to the three cost centres in question. These bases should reflect the benefits received by the three departments from these costs. For example, since rates are related to the area occupied by the factory, the area occupied by each cost centre may serve as a basis for apportioning rate charges.

Simplex Ltd has adopted the undermentioned bases for the apportionment of indirect factory overhead costs:

Basis of apportionment	Total	Machining	Assembly	Maintenance
	£	£	£	£
Number of employees	60	30	20	10
Square feet of floor space	100 000	50 000	40 000	10 000
Maintenance man hours	2 500	1 500	1 000	—
Direct labour man hours	10 000	5 000	5 000	—

Applying these bases to the apportionment of indirect factory overhead costs to the three cost centres, the following distributions are obtained:

Apportionment of factory overhead costs

Overhead costs	Basis	Total	Machining	Assembly	Maintenance
		£	£	£	£
Indirect materials	Direct	15 000	8 000	5 000	2 000
Indirect labour	Direct	6 000	4 000	1 000	1 000
Depreciation of machinery	Direct	7 000	2 500	4 500	—
Supervisory salaries	No. of employees	6 000	3 000	2 000	1 000
Rates	Floor space	10 000	5 000	4 000	1 000
		44 000	22 500	16 500	5 000
Apportionment of maintenance cost centre overheads	Maintenance man hours	—	3 000	2 000	(5 000)
		44 000	25 500	18 500	—

We may note from the foregoing example that the final stage in apportioning factory overhead costs to production cost centres was the apportionment of the service cost centre overhead costs. The basis used was the number of maintenance man hours expended in each of the production cost centres. Among other methods commonly used in respect of other service cost centres are the following examples:

Service cost centres	Basis of apportionment
Purchasing	Cost of materials purchased or number of orders placed
Stores	Cost of materials used, or the number of stores requisitions
Personnel } Canteen	Number of employees
Building maintenance	Space occupied

The allotment of production cost centre costs to products

This stage is the second major step in the ascertainment of full-product costs. As we mentioned earlier, difficulties arise where production cost centres produce more than one product, which is usually the case. It is necessary in such cases to establish a method for attributing to each product an equitable proportion of the production cost centre's overhead costs. The method to 'recover' or 'absorb' these costs relies on the calculation of an 'overhead rate', which is usually linked to one of three factors:

1   direct labour costs;
2   direct labour hours;
3   machine hours.

A prerequisite for the calculation of an 'overhead rate' is the selection of an appropriate base for this purpose.

Example

Having completed the apportionment of factory overhead costs to the two production cost centres—machining and assembly—the next problem facing Simplex Ltd is to select an appropriate overhead base for apportioning overhead costs to the products manufactured in these two centres. The following information relates to the machining cost centre:

	£
Direct labour costs	5 000
Direct labour hours	10 000
Machine hours	15 000

On the basis of this information, we are able to calculate three different 'overhead rates' for absorbing overhead costs into the full-product costs of each unit of the different products manufactured by Simplex Ltd. The calculations are as follows:

Overhead rate based on direct labour costs

$$\frac{\text{cost centre overhead costs}}{\text{cost centre direct labour costs}} \times 100$$

$$= \frac{\pounds 25\ 000}{\pounds 5\ 000} \times 100$$

$$= \underline{510\%}$$

Thus, for each £1 of direct labour cost which each unit of a product has incurred in the machining cost centre, that unit will also attract £5.1 of the cost centre's overhead costs. Given that the prime costs incurred by Product A in the machining cost centre are:

	£
Direct labour costs per unit	1.00
Direct material costs per unit	2.00

The full-product costs per unit of Product A at the end of processing through the machining department would be:

	£
Direct costs as above	3.00
Factory overhead costs	5.10
	8.10

Overhead rate based on direct labour hours

$$\frac{\text{cost centre overhead costs}}{\text{cost centre direct labour costs}}$$

$$= \frac{£25\ 000}{£10\ 000}$$

$$= \underline{£2.55 \text{ per direct labour hour}}$$

Thus, for every hour of direct labour spent on making a unit of a particular product in the machining department, that unit will attract £2.55 of that cost centre's overhead costs. Hence, if Product A needs 2½ direct labour hours, the overhead costs apportioned would be £6.375 per unit.

Overhead rate based on machine hours

$$\frac{\text{cost centre overhead costs}}{\text{cost centre machine costs}}$$

$$= \frac{£25\ 000}{£15\ 000}$$

$$= \underline{£1.70 \text{ per machine hour}}$$

Thus, for every hour which is spent on machining a unit of a product in the machining department, that unit will attract £1.70 of that cost centre's overhead costs. Hence, if product A needs 3½ hours of machining, the overhead costs apportioned would be £5.95 per unit.

The choice of one particular overhead rate as against the others may substantially affect the amount of overhead costs apportioned to a unit of product. Consequently, variations in full-product costs may result simply from the manner in which the overhead rate is selected. The 'best' rate to use depends on the particular circumstances facing the firm. The 'direct labour cost' base is easy to use since the necessary information is usually readily available. There may be no relationship, however, between direct labour costs and overhead costs: indeed, most factory overhead costs are incurred on a time basis and are not related to the labour payroll. A further problem resulting from the use of this overhead base is that there will be distortions in the absorption of overhead cost by different products if the rate of pay for similar work is not comparable. The 'direct labour hour' base is usually found to be a better method because most factory overhead costs are more related to time than any other factor. Where, however, there is a greater reliance on machinery rather than on labour, the 'machine hour' base may be the most suitable overhead base for absorbing costs into full-product costs.

Plant-wide versus department overhead rates of recovery

In our discussion so far, we have examined methods of calculating overhead rates which were related to departmental overhead bases. We took the information for the machining department, for example, as a means of calculating overhead rates for the absorption of its own factory overhead costs into the costs of various products processed in that department. It may be felt that an easier and less extravagant method would be to select an overhead base for use by every department, rather than having different overhead bases used by different departments. The argument in favour of departmental overhead rates is that different departments do not incur the same amount of factory overhead costs, as we have already seen, and do not necessarily use the same number of labour or machine hours, nor do they have the same labour costs. It follows, therefore, that the use of a plant-wide overhead rate will not produce an accurate measure of the departmental costs associated with each unit of product. Departmental overhead rates, by contrast, lead to more accurate measurement, as may be seen from the following example.

Example

Eastlands Carburettors Ltd manufactures two types of carburettor, Type X and Type Y, both of which are processed in two departments— Department A and Department B. The following cost information is available:

	Type X	Type Y
	£	£
Direct factory costs per unit	8	8
Direct labour hours		
Department A	4 hours	1 hour
Department B	1 hour	4 hours
Total hours	5 hours	5 hours

Overhead rates based on direct labour hours are given as follows:

Overhead rates	Per direct labour hour
Department basis	
Department A	6
Department B	1
Plant-wide basis	
Department A	3
Department B	3

This information enables us to compare the costs per unit which would result from the use of a plant-wide overhead rate as against departmental overhead rates.

Unit costs using a plant-wide overhead rate

	Type X	Type Y
	£	£
Direct factory costs per unit	8	8
Add: Overhead charge per unit		
(5 hours at £3.00)	15	15
Manufacturing costs per unit	23	23

Unit costs using departmental overhead rates

	Type X	Type Y
	£	£
Direct factory costs per unit	8	8
Add: Overhead charge per unit		
Department A (at £6 per hour)	24	6
Department B (at £1 per hour)	1	4
Manufacturing costs per unit	33	18

It is noteworthy that:

1 Product X, which spends more processing time in Department A which has the higher overhead rate, is undercosted by £10 when a plant-wide overhead rate is used.

2 Product Y, however, which spends more processing time in Department B, which has the lower overhead rate, is overcosted by £5 when a plant-wide overhead rate is used.

These wide differences highlight the dangers of using cost measurements which do not lead to accurate statements of unit costs. The absorption of factory overhead costs by means of departmental overhead rates rather than a plant-wide overhead rate yields a more accurate measurement of the costs incurred in manufacturing products. Management decisions which require accurate cost measurements for such purposes as pricing policies and production-mix decisions would be made incorrectly where a plant-wide rather than departmental rate is employed.

The selection of an appropriate level of activity
So far we have classified costs into two categories—direct costs and overhead costs. This classification is helpful in understanding how costs are related to products for the purposes of measuring unit costs of production. We mentioned earlier in this chapter that different cost concepts perform different functions. In order to understand the manner

in which costs are affected by different levels of activity, we use another classification. This classification requires that costs be categorized into fixed and variable costs, and its purpose is to define how particular items of costs are affected by changes in activity levels.

Fixed costs are those costs which do not vary with changing levels of activity, for example, factory rent, insurance and rates. Variable costs are those costs which do change directly with changes in the level of activity, for example raw material costs and direct labour costs. There are costs, however, which are partly fixed and partly variable, for example, maintenance and repairs of machinery and plant equipment, heat, light and power. These are called mixed costs.

The level of activity, therefore, is an economic factor which affects the calculation of the unit cost of output produced. Since fixed costs remain constant as output fluctuates, the greater the output, the lower will be the fixed cost per unit. For example, if fixed costs for the period are £10 000, the fixed cost per unit will depend upon the total number of units produced. If 10 000 units are produced, the fixed cost per unit will be £1; if 5000 units are produced the fixed cost per unit will be £2. This problem does not affect the variable costs, for, as we have already noted, variable costs per unit of output remain constant at all levels of activity, assuming always that prices remain stable. For management decision making based on full unit costs, however, the level of activity is an important ingredient which must be taken into account when providing relevant information for such decisions.

The table below illustrates the behaviour of costs as volume changes.

Units pro-duced	Total fixed costs £	Total variable costs £	Total costs £	Average fixed cost per unit £	Average variable cost per unit £	Average total cost per unit £
1	300	100	400	300	100	400
2	300	200	500	150	100	250
3	300	300	600	100	100	200
4	300	400	700	75	100	175
5	300	500	800	60	100	160

From the foregoing discussion, we must examine the usefulness of the actual—that is current—volume of output as a level of activity upon which to base calculations of full unit costs. Current unit costs will fluctuate according to the actual level of activity; here costs are of little use for decisions regarding the future. Thus, pricing decisions require a more stable view of full costs than that provided as a result of fluctuating levels of output. Moreover, cost control implies that full unit costs incurred in one period are compared with those of other periods. Comparisons based on actual levels of output are unreliable because fixed costs per unit will be different where the output levels are different. Even for stock valuation purposes, which, as we mentioned, was central to profit measurement, calculations based on actual volume will introduce distortions. Finally, since the calculation of unit costs based on actual volume can be effected only at the end of an accounting period, such unit costs are not relevant to its decision problems, which are more concerned with future than with past costs.

Since actual volume is not a satisfactory basis for calculating a fixed overhead rate which will be useful for the purposes we have mentioned, the following alternative bases may be considered:

1   theoretical capacity, which is the capacity of a particular department to maintain output at a 100 per cent level without interruption;
2   practical capacity, which is the result of making allowances against the theoretical capacity in respect of unavoidable interruptions to output such as time lost for repairs and holidays;
3   expected capacity as a short-run view of capacity, which is determined by immediate expectations of output levels;
4   normal capacity, which is an estimate of output capacity based on a period of time long enough to level out peaks and troughs of cyclical fluctuations.

Normal capacity, as defined above, is the most useful level of activity for the purpose of determining a fixed overhead rate which will be relatively stable over a number of years. It will be appreciated that there is an element of subjectivity in the assessment of normal capacity, and it will lead invariably to some under- or over-absorption of fixed factory overhead costs, depending on whether the actual level of activity is under or over the normal level. We will deal with this problem in Chapter 36. Normal capacity often does provide, however, the most reliable and stable basis for calculating full-product costs for decision-making purposes.

Limitations of full cost calculations

It is clear from the foregoing examination of the problems associated with overhead costs that full-product costs cannot be measured with complete accuracy. To some extent, all methods used for apportioning overhead costs are arbitrary, and are based upon assumptions which are subjective to a degree. We stated that the 'benefit received' should be the main criterion for apportioning factory overhead costs to cost centres. It is difficult, however, to find bases which are suitable for this purpose. For example, the cost of the factory personnel department may be apportioned to cost centres on the basis of the relative number of their employees, but this base assumes that all employees will benefit equally from the services of this department. This example is, of course, a gross simplification of the general problem of apportioning overhead costs. Labour turnover and the difference in skills between different classes of employees will influence the time and the effort expended by the personnel department.

We have referred already to the element of subjectivity which enters into the selection of the methods of apportioning overhead costs. This is exacerbated by the degree of subjectivity which may be attached to the selection of the level of activity selected from recovering overhead costs. Indeed, two equally competent accountants may arrive at very different product costs simply because their views of what constitutes a 'normal level' of activity may differ. This problem applies similarly to the allotment of administrative costs. The bases for allotting these costs we mentioned may be rationalized but may not be defended as being adequate cost accounting procedures. The cost of operating the purchasing department cannot be related, for example, to any of the bases which we mentioned.

It is apparent that the main difficulty in computing full product costs stems from the presence of fixed overhead costs. The allotment of these costs to product costs on bases which are arbitrary renders the end result of doubtful accuracy. As we shall see elsewhere in this book, incorrect decisions may arise from the inclusion of fixed costs in product costs. For the purpose of external financial reporting, for example, we argue in Chapter 32 that more useful information may be provided if fixed overhead costs are not absorbed in output, but are treated as period costs. Moreover, their inclusion in product costs may give a misleading view of profit results. It is often claimed that for the purpose of long-range planning, product cost information should reflect total costs. However, as we shall see in Chapter 33, there is a case for directing attention away from a narrowly conceived view of price determination based on mark-up percentages on costs to the broader implications of cost–volume–profit relationships. As we shall also see, because of the behaviour of fixed and variable costs over different volumes of output, product cost information based on full costs is irrelevant to the problem of control. A distinction has to be made, therefore, between fixed and variable cost information for control purposes.

It follows that the limitations inherent in full-cost computations should be appreciated by all those using such information for decision making. From an accountant's point of view, specific instruction from management should be awaited for the calculation of product costs inclusive of fixed costs. Even then, a clear distinction should be made between fixed and variable cost components.

Costing systems

Costs are accumulated in costing systems. The development of costing systems reflects the manner in which accounting methods have been adapted to the needs of different forms of activity and technology, and also to the appearance of advanced manufacturing techniques that have been a feature of recent years.

In effect, the objective of costing systems has remained constant in the sense that the accumulation of costs has the ultimate purpose of ascertaining product or service costs. However, the need to render this information relevant for decision making has shifted the emphasis from recording costs *incurred* to costs that *will be incurred* in producing goods and services. The competitive nature of the markets in which goods and services are sold has placed further stress on the efficient management of costs, and this has shifted costing systems to record costs that *should be incurred*.

Today, advanced manufacturing techniques have focused on the utilization of *time* as a critical factor in incurring costs. In this regard, economies of production are now sought from reducing the financial costs of holding inventories and eliminating delays in the production process. This has given rise to costing systems in which a further refinement is added to determine *when costs should be incurred*. Just-in-time accounting for constant-flow manufacturing is an outcome of the continuing search for product costs economies.

Significantly, these developments have brought accountants and engineers much closer together in recent years by reason of their mutual concern with manufacturing operations. Production engineers and cost accountants are required to collaborate in installing and operating cost control systems that ensure financially efficient methods of production.

Although cost control systems share the same objectives, reference commonly is made to three major types of systems, namely:

1 product costing;
2 activity-based costing;
3 just-in-time (JIT) production.

Product costing systems

Product costing represents the classical tradition in cost accounting in the manner in which costs are analysed and recorded. Its objective is to allow product costs to be determined as accurately as possible in order to permit efficient management decisions in various areas, for example in pricing and in seeking to improve the efficiency in use of scarce resources.

The identification of costs with products has focused attention on the identification of costs with products and has relied on the classification of costs as between direct costs and indirect costs. As we have seen, the major problem in determining full product costs is the need to find reliable allocation keys with which to apportion indirect costs to products, thereby accumulating direct costs and indirect costs into 'full product costs'.

The suitability of product costs is also the function of two other criteria:

1 the technology used for providing the goods or services,
2 the time reference of the cost data itself.

Cost accounting systems for different technologies

Cost accounting systems allow full product costs to be accumulated in accordance with the type of technology employed. Five major costing systems commonly found are:

1 job order costing;
2 contract costing;

3   process costing;
4   operations costing;
5   service.

Job order and contract costing share the similarity that the product or contract is undertaken upon receipt of the client's order and is completed in accordance with his specifications. Costs are accumulated to the job or contract until it is completed. The essential difference between job order and contract costing lies in the time taken to fulfil the order. For this reason, job order costing is found where production is completed in the short term: contract costing is used where completion extends over one or more years. Accordingly, the major accounting problem associated with contract costing system is the determination of periodic profit. This is because contract costing involves carrying forward substantial work-in-process costs across accounting year-end, until work is delivered to the client in accordance with the terms of the contract. For example, a major road construction contract may take two years to complete, during which only costs are incurred. Hence, at the end of the first year, the question is—can the contractor show a profit if he is not entitled to full payment for the work done in that year?

Process costing is a method of product costing used by manufacturing concerns engaged in the mass production of standardized products. Production is undertaken in anticipation of demand, and hence finished products are stocked until they are sold. Process costing is used in such industries as cement, flour, sugar, cars, oil and chemicals. Product costs are accumulated by reference to a standard quantity of a homogeneous product, expressed in a conventional cost unit, either by quantity, volume or weight, as the case may be.

Operations costing is a form of costing that lies somewhere in between job-order and process costing. It is found in situations where the technology of production does not rely upon a job-order specification, nor is process costing applicable by reason of the homogeneity of the product. In effect, it consists of accumulating product costs by reference to the cost of operations, as such, that batches of slightly dissimilar products undergo.

Service costing is a special application of process costing, used where services rather than products are supplied, for example, computer services, transport, canteens, maintenance etc. The particular problems that are involved in setting up service costing systems are:

1   selecting cost units in relation to which the cost of services can be accumulated. For transport services, for example, a suitable cost unit could be ton/mile;
2   selecting a charging rate for services.

The time reference of the cost data itself

Two different time references are used with respect to cost data. Cost systems that record invoiced product costs, in effect, accumulate actual costs, defined in accounting as 'historic costs'. These costs are useful for accounting purposes, but have limited usefulness for the control of product costs. The development of the concept of 'standard' or 'predetermined' costs is associated with the concept of cost for control purposes. Standard costs reflect a desire to discover efficient product costs, as a basis for controlling product costs. Standard costs are discussed in Chapter 36.

Activity-based costing systems

Organizations achieve their objectives through activities. These activities manifest themselves in the form of specific tasks or of specific operations. The implementation of tasks or operations results in an output in the form of a product, service, information, or a treatment of a particular nature.

Activity-based costing seeks to analyse organizational activities in terms of functions, in which activities leading to a specific output are grouped. This done, activity costing seeks to identify causal factors defined as 'cost drivers' that influence cost levels in relation to activity levels, and to cost output, in whatever guise, in terms of the cost of the activities implied.

Just-in-time production systems

Just-in-time systems are concerned with reducing production costs by eliminating as far as possible inventories and production delays. Terms that describe just-in-time systems include MIPS (minimum inventory production systems), ZIPS (zero inventory production systems), MAN (materials as needed production systems).

JIT systems are, in effect, manufacturing systems with zero inventories and constant production flows.

JIT systems imply a radical change in the manufacturing environment, since their successful implementation requires an environment concerned with the following:

- elimination of waste;
- zero inventories;
- zero idle production time;
- constant production rate;
- balanced capacity;
- emphasis on zero waste/faulty work;
- increased personnel involvement.

As we saw earlier, traditional product costing systems define the objective of costing systems as being concerned with three elements of costs, namely, raw materials, direct labour and overhead costs, recorded in three separate stock accounts, namely, raw materials, work-in-process and finished goods.

The concern with the elimination of inventories implies a radical alteration in the tracking of inventories through inventory accounts, as seen in conventional product costing systems. Consequently, the control of materials focuses on the points of materials utilization, rather than on inventory control. The concern of JIT materials accounting is with the following two aspects of materials control:

1   estimating materials requirements for actual production;
2   eliminating usage variances at the point of usage.

JIT systems also imply radical changes in the tracking of direct labour costs as product costs. Since JIT systems aim to secure constant manufacturing conditions, many of the objectives involved in obtaining direct labour cost information have been superseded. For this reason, JIT direct labour accounting systems are also greatly simplified, and the significance attached to accounting separately for direct labour cost has also decreased. For example, conventional labour utilization and efficiency measures are largely redundant when emphasis is given to constant work flows.

In many industries, the proportion of direct labour costs in total production costs is decreasing. In some companies, the implementation of JIT has seen the introduction of the following methods of accounting for direct labour costs:

1   expensing direct labour at source;
2   recovering direct labour costs in the form of a product overhead rate, thereby eliminating direct labour costs as a separate cost element;
3   retaining direct labour as a separate production cost, but allocating such costs over time.

The introduction of advanced manufacturing techniques has changed considerably the relative importance of conventional cost elements in total product costs. In effect, the importance of direct material and direct labour costs has decreased relatively to factory overhead costs that have themselves increased.

Under conventional product costing methods, the major problem is finding a suitable allocation key for apportioning factory overhead costs to products. Labour cost and labour hour rates are frequently utilized for apportioning overhead costs.

The introduction of JIT systems has had three important consequences in accounting for overhead costs. First, direct labour cost is seen as less relevant for the recovery of overhead costs. Second, JIT systems are concerned with eliminating waste. Therefore, accounting for overhead costs is concerned with functional relationship between level of overhead expenditures and production activity levels. Third, the search for suitable allocation keys has moved emphasis to multiple recovery rates based on direct material costs, total direct costs and cycle times.

Summary

Cost information is required for four main purposes:

1 for planning decisions;
2 for control decisions;
3 for the measurement of reported profits;
4 for reporting to employees.

The type of cost information required may be different in each of these cases. We analyse the nature and the use of various cost measurements in this part.

This chapter has been concerned with the accounting problems involved in the measurement of unit costs of production. The major difficulty in the measurement of full product costs lies in the calculation and assignment of factory overhead costs. The process of assigning factory overhead costs to units of product occurs in the following stages:

1 allotting factory overhead costs to production cost centres and finding appropriate levels of activity for this purpose;
2 allotting the costs of production cost centres to units of product and finding appropriate methods for this purpose.

The use of cost information for planning and control decisions implies that such cost information should reflect the future rather than the past. For this reason, standard costs—which are predetermined costs—are used. They not only reflect expectations about the costs which will be current in the period ahead, but are intended to deal with the uncertainties implicit in decision making.

Costs are accumulated in costing systems. Reference is commonly made to three major types of costing systems, namely, product costing, activity-based costing and JIT production costing systems. They are all concerned with the objective of establishing product costs. These different product costing systems reflect an adaptation to different technologies and problems of recording costs. They also reflect the adaptability of accounting methods under changing conditions and the recognition of new management requirements. In particular, the development of advanced manufacturing techniques has seen the appearance of just-in-time production costing systems.

Questions

1 State the four purposes for which costs are collected.
2 Describe the three elements of product costs.
3 What is the significance for product costing of the difference between manufacturing and non-manufacturing costs?
4 What is meant by the term 'full product cost'?
5 What problems are involved in determining factory overhead costs per unit?
6 What methods are commonly used for recovering overhead costs?
7 What are the advantages of departmental rates, as against plant-wide overhead rates?
8 Describe five major types of product costing systems.
9 What do you understand by 'activity-based costing'?
10 What are JIT production systems?

Problems

1 As the accountant of the Northumberland Engineering Co. operating in a very competitive industry by means of special jobs to each customer's requirements, you are required to:

(a) Calculate the (estimated) cost of job enquiry number 876, for which details are given below.

(b) On the basis of your cost figures, indicate the price you feel should be charged to the customer for job 876; or, if you feel unable to do this, indicate what further information you would need in order to arrive at a price.

All calculations should be clearly shown and figures justified.

Job Enquiry Number 876

(a) Estimated direct material cost: £1 000

(b) Estimated direct labour input:

	Hours	Rate per hour £
Plating department	81	4.00
Welding department	14	3.00
Assembly department	10	2.00

(c) Indirect departmental costs:

	Plating	Welding	Assembly
Total indirect costs:			
Last year's actual	£20 000	£8 000	£4 000
This year's budget	£22 000	£9 000	£5 000

(d) Activity levels (labour hours):

	Plating	Welding	Assembly
Last year's actual	10 000	8 000	4 000
This year's budget	9 000	10 000	4 000

2 Byfokal Product Ltd uses a predetermined overhead rate for the purpose of job-order costing. This rate is based on machine hours with regards to the machining department and on direct labour cost with respect to the assembly and finishing department.

The following forecasts have been used to calculate the predetermined overhead rate for these two departments:

	Machining department	Assembly and finishing department
Machine hours	100 000	30 000
Direct labour hours	60 000	150 000
Direct labour cost	£500 000	£1 250 000
Factory overhead costs	£2 500 000	£2 000 000

The job-order cost sheet for Job Number 35 showed the following information:

	Machining department	Assembly and finishing department
Direct materials used	£3 500	£1 000
Direct labour cost	£20 000	£28 000
Direct labour hours	2 400	3 360
Machine hours	4 000	672

Required

(a) What is the predetermined overhead rate for each department?

(b) Calculate the total overhead cost for Job 35.

3   The managing director of Marco Fabrication is concerned about the reliability and relevance of the product unit costs which have been used to date for general purposes. Shortly after your appointment as the firm's accountant you are required to write him a report explaining your general approach to the use of cost accounts and in particular the problems of overhead costing. You derive the following information for this purpose:

The company has two producing departments, machining and assembly, and one service department, canteen. Direct departmental overhead for the coming year is estimated as machining £50 000, assembly £40 000 and canteen £10 000. Details of estimated indirect overhead are as follows:

Rates	£1 000
Depreciation	£9 300
Light and power	£600

Departmental data

	Kilowatt hours	No. of employees	Cost of equipment	Square feet
Machining	600	20	£10 000	600
Assembly	1 100	10	£20 000	1 200
Canteen	300	5	£1 000	200

	Estimated direct labour cost	Estimated direct labour hours	Estimated machine hours
Machining	£10 000	18 000	8 000
Assembly	£15 000	12 000	20 000

The above activity levels are based on what could be attained if production was at full capacity. Expected activity for the coming year is estimated to be 70 per cent full capacity, and normal activity at 80 per cent.

Section 2	Chapter 28
Planning	**Long-range planning**

Long-range planning is not a single technique, nor is it just one area of management responsibility. It is a systematic attempt to plan the entire behaviour of the organization in the long run. In the case of profit-making organizations, it has a particular focus on profitable growth and aspects of corporate strategy that are associated with this primary objective.

In this chapter, we shall examine the stages involved in long-range planning, and we shall discuss the accountant's role in that process.

Long-range planning is concerned with:

1 setting long-range objectives and goals;
2 preparing the position audit;
3 formulating strategy;
4 preparing and implementing the plan;
5 continuous review and updating of the plan.

Setting long-range objectives and goals

Given that long-range planning is concerned with the totality of the enterprise's strategy in every sphere of action, it is evident that the information that is needed goes much beyond that which normally is defined as accounting information.

Long-range planning focuses on objectives and goals. Common usage sometimes treats these two terms as synonymous, but in their reference to long-range planning, they have a specific meaning as they are used to identify two basic types of organizational objectives:

1 Broad corporate objectives which are general statements of policy which represent the ideals of the organization.
2 Goals which are derived from these objectives and which establish specific targets for the organization. They include also lesser goals such as targets for subunits, such as departments, and performance standards for managers and employees.

It follows, therefore, that there exists a hierarchy of goals applicable to every level of the organization, which are subordinated to the main goals and which interpret those goals. The management problem is not simply setting goals, but securing the attainment of those goals. We shall examine the behavioural aspects of the latter problem in Chapter 38 where we discuss the manner in which the style of management known as 'management by objectives' attempts to create a high degree of goal congruence between the personal objectives and organizational goals.

For the moment, we shall concern ourselves with the analysis of organizational objectives and organizational goals.

Organizational objectives

These objectives serve as guidelines for establishing goals.

Example

Hygrade Cutlery Ltd has the following objectives:

1 Profit objective—to achieve a profit level sufficient to reward shareholders adequately and to protect the interests of creditors.
2 Financial objectives—to secure adequate financial resources and to report to management on the utilization of these resources.
3 Market objective—to build public confidence and to create goodwill for products bearing the company's name, thereby increasing customers' preference for the company's goods.
4 Production objective—to increase the efficiency of production of high-quality products.
5 Employee objective—to provide good jobs, wages and working conditions, work satisfaction, stability of employment and opportunity for advancement, in return for loyalty, skills, initiative, effort and teamwork.
6 Innovation objective—to develop new and better products.

Organizational goals

Goals are objectives which have been quantified and set as targets. Whereas objectives may sound rather vague or obvious, goals are targets which are intended to apply to the time-span of the planning period.

Example

The goals established by Hygrade Cutlery Ltd for the next five years are as follows:

1 Profit goals—to attain a profit level of 20 per cent before tax on the market value of the shareholders' equity by the end of the fifth year; to attain a profit level of 16 per cent on total assets by the end of the fifth year; to achieve a profit before tax/sales ratio of 12 per cent for each year; to increase after tax earnings per share by at least 10 per cent per year.
2 Financial goals—to improve the present cash position; to reduce debtors by 5 per cent; to secure a return of 14 per cent after tax on new capital expenditure.
3 Market goals—to increase total sales of stainless steel cutlery over the period by 30 per cent; to increase marketing facilities abroad so that the number of customers served by the company will be 20 per cent higher in five years' time.

4 Production goal—to increase output per employee by 16 per cent over the next five years.

5 Employee goals—to reduce labour turnover by 15 per cent; to improve the current management development scheme; to introduce management by objectives within two years.

6 Innovation goal—to introduce a new range of stainless steel family-size teasets within one year.

The importance of cash flows

In the final analysis, cash flows into and out of a business enterprise are the most fundamental events upon which accounting measurements are based. Management and investors, in particular, are very concerned with the cash flows generated by corporate assets. These cash flows are not only central to the problem of corporate survival, but they are essential to the attainment of corporate objectives. In this part, we are concerned with the management of corporate assets with the view to generating cash flows. The size, timing and risks inherent in estimating future cash flows are critical aspects of this analysis. In Part 4, we argued that the purpose of profit measurement is to enable shareholders and investors to predict future cash flows.

The recognition of the importance of future cash flows has led many writers to define *the* objective of business corporations in terms of maximizing corporate wealth, defined as the present value of the future stream of net cash flows to be earned by corporate assets. This objective is also expressed as the maximization of shareholders' wealth, since they are deemed in law to be the owners of the enterprise.

In Part 1, we explained that the distinctive feature of the modern business corporation as an 'entrepreneurial unit' is the separation of ownership from management. The power of shareholders to control management is limited to a number of issues, which is the business reserved by law to the annual general meeting of shareholders. This business includes the election of directors, the appointment of auditors, and the approval of annual financial reports and of dividend recommendations. In the process of adjusting to social pressures both external and internal to the firm, management has tended to utilize its relative freedom from ownership control to redefine the concept of managerial responsibility. Responsibilities to employees, consumers and to society at large may conflict with responsibilities to shareholders. Nevertheless, profit remains the most widely understood index of business success. Accordingly, profit making, which is regarded as the ability to generate cash flows, remains the basic objective of management.

The position audit   In estimating future cash flows, which are intended to result from a planned course of action, managers are able to draw on a great deal of inside information which is at their disposal. Top managers are placed in a unique position to assess a wide range of opportunities open to the firm, and to relate its present or potential technological, production and financial resources to these opportunities in the process of selecting the best strategy for attaining corporate objectives. This process of assessment is conducted by means of a position audit, which has an external and an internal aspect.

The external audit

The external audit is concerned with the environment in which the firm exists. It is also concerned with identifying opportunities and dangers facing the organization, and in particular in assessing changes in the economic, political, social, technological and industrial environment. If management is able to forecast significant changes in these various aspects of the firm's environment, it will be in a better position to deal with the opportunities and the problems these changes present.

Forecasting plays a crucial role in the external audit. Two techniques are useful in this respect—economic forecasting and technological forecasting. Economic forecasting is concerned with predicting economic conditions which may have important implications for the firm. Technological forecasting is concerned with predicting changes in technology, so as to anticipate the nature of technological innovation to the advantage of the firm.

The usefulness of forecasts is realized only when they influence decisions, that is, when predictions are assumed to be part of the firm's environment in formulating objectives and goals, and preparing a strategy for attaining them.

The internal audit

The internal audit is focused on the organization's own strengths and weaknesses. It involves an appraisal of every aspect of the organization, including management, labour, products, markets, distribution channels, finance, assets and research and development. The purpose of this appraisal is to discover the reasons for present successes and failures, and to identify key success factors for the future. In conducting the internal audit, management will have much to learn from the experience of its competitors, and in identifying key success factors it will seek to compare its own strengths and weakneses with those of its competitors.

The main purpose of both external and internal audits is to relate the organization's prospects with the prospects of the industry in which it is operating. The outlook for the industry affects the demand for the products or services of the industry; the supply of products or services is affected not only by productive capacity in the industry, but by labour and material costs peculiar to the industry. The firm's prospects within the industry are a function of its own position in the industry, the degree of competition existing in the industry and the firm's own cost structure. The position audit is, therefore, a learning exercise for the firm.

The formulation of strategy

The position audit outlines the array of factors which should be considered when formulating a strategy for attaining organizational objectives and

Fig. 5.7

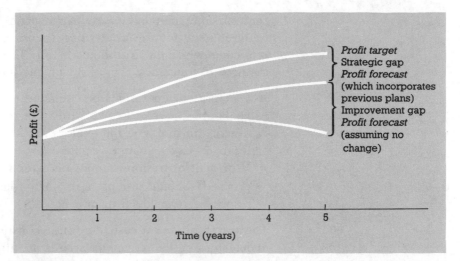

goals. The role of strategy, therefore, is to select the best way of getting from the present position to the goals which have been derived from the organization's objectives. The first stage in the formulation of a strategy is an analysis of the gap between the present position and the desired position, which takes into account the forecasts which will have been made. Gap analysis involves the following questions:

1   What will happen if nothing is done?
2   What will happen if we pursue present policies?
3   What should be done to attain organizational goals?

Gap analysis and the profit goal

The effects of alternative policies on profits is a very good example of gap analysis. Once the profit goal has been determined, it may be compared with the level of earnings for the business as it is presently operated. If no changes were made, present earnings would probably begin to decline after a period of time. This is because, as technology changes, as market demand and tastes change, as competitors improve performance etc., existing products are likely to become less profitable.

Previous long-range planning exercises, however, will have built into the operations of the firm tactics to counter the fall-off in performance which would have occurred due to the causes mentioned. The difference between these two forecasts may be called the 'improvement gap'. It illustrates the value to the firm of former plans. The difference between the profit improvement figure and the profit goal is called the strategic gap. This represents the profit which the firm is required to make to meet the shortfall in its profit goal, and may be illustrated as in Fig. 5.7.

Long-range planning and gap analysis

The essence of long-range planning is really one of gap analysis. The problem involved in this analysis is the evaluation of alternative strategies for closing the strategic gap and selecting that strategy which is seen as the best one. Future cash flows, and consequently profits, are highly constrained by past and present capital expenditure decisions. Therefore, a prerequisite for gap analysis is a *search* process to discover suitable projects in which the firm should invest. Throughout the search process, the firm is concerned typically with the following questions:

- Can present operations be extended to meet organizational goals? If so, what does this mean in terms of greater penetration of existing markets, the exploration of new markets, the need for finance, assets, manpower etc.?
- If present operations cannot be extended, how should the firm proceed? Should less profitable activities be abandoned and resources redeployed in new activities?

The search process is costly and time-consuming. An influential factor in determining the scope of search is the affinity between search areas and the present activities of the organization. Areas of search should be chosen which will complement current areas of activity, thereby providing synergistic opportunities. Synergy arises when two activities or actions performed jointly produce a greater total effect than if they had been performed separately. For example, the addition of a restaurant to the activities of a departmental store produces a synergistic effect in that the restaurant makes the store a more convenient place in which to shop, and the store provides a ready clientele for the restaurant. Hence, the total volume of business enjoyed by both the store and the restaurant is greater than if they had been established and maintained as separate businesses in different locations.

The preparation and implementation of the plan

The selected strategy for the long run will concentrate on the key factors for success and on the major decisions required. In particular, it will be concerned with basic issues such as the selection of the kinds of products or services which should be produced, their markets, the production process and its location, and the asset structure required.

Once the strategy has been selected, it has to be expressed in more detailed plans which then become the basis for action. Responsibility for implementing the plan will fall upon the management personnel in the various divisions and departments of the organization. In this chapter, we examine briefly a small aspect of the planning process, namely financial planning. The reader should bear in mind that long-range planning covers every spectrum of the firm's activities, and detailed plans for all these activities will be drafted.

The continuous review and updating of the plan

Corporate planning is a continuous process which responds to feed-back information. Updating may occur both on a continuous and on an annual basis. Corporate planning departments will be continually accumulating information and interpreting the significance of that information to the plan. The time-period envisaged by different firms for long-range planning purposes does vary, but it is quite normal to review the plan at the end of each year, and to incorporate those changes deemed to be necessary. This allows changes of every kind to be recognized and so introduces a degree of flexibility into the corporate planning process. At the end of each year, the plan must be extended for a further year so that the roll-over maintains a view of a constant time-period associated with long-range planning. The relationship between the long-range plan and the annual budget plan is very significant, and we consider this problem in Chapter 30.

The importance of the long-range profit goal

We stated at the beginning of this chapter that the firm's success depends on its ability to generate a sufficiency of cash flows, symbolized by profit. The selection of a profit target for long-range planning purposes is not just a matter of fixing an arbitrary figure such as £5 million. A profit target of itself has little meaning: its significance appears when it is related to some other measurement, such as total assets employed, when it becomes a meaningful measure of performance. Thus, the return on capital employed (ROCE) which relates profits to assets employed provides an assessment of the significance of a profit target by means of the following formula:

$$ROCE = \frac{planned\ net\ profit}{planned\ total\ assets}$$

There is a general agreement that the ROCE is the most important performance measurement for long-range planning and for setting long-range profit targets. It is a common practice to compute the ROCE for each year covered by the long-range plan in order to show whether planned increases in annual profits will keep pace with annual increases in assets. This analysis also indicates the effectiveness with which management will be required to use corporate assets.

In recent years, the usefulness of ROCE measures has been questioned. We shall discuss the controversies involved in the use of ROCE in Chapter 35 of this part. Further difficulties are caused by the manner in which profits and assets might be defined and measured. These difficulties were considered in Part 4.

There are eight areas of activity to which the firm should direct its attention when formulating its objectives—market standing, innovation, productivity, physical and financial resources, profitability, manager performance and development, worker performance and attitude, and public responsibility. It is in these areas of activity that the several parties having a stake in the firm—shareholders, management, employees, government, customers and suppliers, and the local community—have vested interests. Of the eight areas listed above, profitability is the most important because it provides a means of achieving objectives in the other seven areas. Unless a firm achieves a satisfactory profit goal, it may not survive in the long term.

The accountant's task is not to attempt the impossible by deciding what should be the maximum possible long-range profit on the basis of assumed long-range resources for planning purposes: his job is to quantify the size of the profit which is required as the profit objective. The required profit as a planning goal is never a theoretical ideal, such as 'the maximum long-term profit' or 'the maximum long-term return to shareholders', but represents rather the outcome of discussion as to what is a possible and desirable target for the time-span considered.

The longer the time-span envisaged as a planning period, the less reliable is the profit target selected as a planning objective. It is for this very important reason that we suggested earlier that the 'maximum long-term profit' is never a planning goal, for it falls beyond a planner's vision. Instead a firm aims to earn a 'satisfactory' profit over the planning period.

As a guide to selecting the profit target, one of the most influential factors is the minimum rate of return expected by investors and creditors. A satisfactory profit ensures that debt and dividend payments may be made, thereby reducing the risks attached to investing in the firm.

If the profit target is set too low to provide a fair dividend for shareholders and sufficient retained profit to finance future expansion, the Stock Exchange's dissatisfaction with performance will be reflected in the company's share price, which in turn will impede the firm's ability to raise fresh capital and undermine its financial standing with creditors. It is, therefore, desirable that the share price should reflect a satisfactory profit target, for the value of a company is represented by the market price of its shares. It is through capital gains, as these shares appreciate in value, that shareholders receive much of their return. The amount of takeover activity in recent years has drawn attention to the fact that management should be aware of the importance of the behaviour of share prices.

Another important factor in long-range profit planning arises from the need of firms to generate capital to finance expansion. Capital generated in this way represents a substantial portion of the capital required by established companies, and profit retentions for this purpose often amount to 50 per cent of net profits.

The firm is faced, therefore, with the unavoidable problem of selecting a long-range profit target which will be satisfactory as regards the various points we have just discussed. This is a minimum requirement, and unless an attempt is made to attain this profit objective in the long-range plan, the plan itself cannot be regarded as satisfactory.

Before we can calculate a target return on capital employed we must first estimate the returns shareholders are likely to expect over the planning period. The following factors will affect these returns:

1 The rate of return shareholders have had in recent years.
2 The rate of return they could earn elsewhere. If a better rate of return is obtainable from similar companies, there will be pressure from management to increase the profit target.
3 The impact of inflation on the rate of return. The rate of return may have to be increased to compensate shareholders for the falling value of money.

4 The effects of changes in government policy with regard to taxation. For example, the introduction of capital gains tax, and the restrictions governments have imposed on dividends in recent years have had serious repercussions on shareholders.

5 The effects of changes in gearing. It may be possible to increase the return on shareholders' funds by altering the capital structure.

6 The character of the firm's dividend policy. There are two methods by which the risk borne by ordinary shareholders may be rewarded. The first method emphasizes a high annual rate of dividend, and the second stresses the capital gain which accrues as a result of the increased value of the shares where a company retains and reinvests a high proportion of its profit. There are some who argue that the interests of investors and of the community would best be served by the total distribution of profit as dividends, and that individual companies should go to the market for any capital which is needed for expansion. In practice many companies attempt to strike a balance, distributing approximately half their profits as dividends and retaining and reinvesting the balance in their capital expansion plans. As a result, most ordinary shareholders receive a return which is a mixture of annual dividend and capital gain.

Setting profit targets

Once having agreed the returns to shareholders, the next step is to incorporate the results of these calculations in a return on capital employed. This takes into account the amount to be retained in the business and the tax liability.

Consider the position of a firm for which it is calculated that a necessary return to shareholders of £50 000 has been calculated; while it is estimated that £20 000 should be retained in the business.

From the figures listed below it is apparent that an earnings figure of £100 000 is required in order to provide for these estimates:

	£
Returns to shareholders	50 000
Retained in business	20 000
Tax (30%)	30 000
Earnings required	100 000

If the firm's total assets are forecast at £500 000, then a return of 20 per cent on capital employed is required, viz:

$$\frac{\text{earnings required}}{\text{total assets}} = \frac{£100\ 000}{£500\ 000} \times 100 = \underline{20\%}$$

Divisional profit targets

Once the company's overall long-range profit target has been agreed, the next task is to apportion it across the separate parts of the enterprise, whether these be divisions or subsidiary companies. It is not necessary, nor indeed desirable, that the overall profit target be evenly spread across the enterprise, for different growth rates and different profit targets are perfectly compatible with sound strategic planning. Thus, it is possible to select a distribution showing an expected rate of return on investments of 30 per cent in respect of one division as against a 10 per cent rate for another division. The reasons for a diversity among planned divisional profit targets may lie in the type of market in which the divisions operate: fast-growing markets may offer higher return prospects than mature and established markets. Equally, varying rates of return may reflect the different degrees of risks attached to the different types of activities in which the several divisions may be engaged.

In the discussions leading to the formulation of the overall profit target, the various divisions will have submitted their estimates of the possible profit targets. Should a gap have existed between the aggregated divisional profit recommendations and the overall target which top management sought to attain, it may have been necessary to revise the corporate strategy and re-examine both the company and divisional profit targets.

Financial planning

We have seen how the main objectives of the firm are expressed in financial form. Detailed financial analysis is necessary to support these financial targets. Since this type of analysis is dealt with throughout this book, this chapter is not detailed in this respect. Indeed, the purpose of this chapter is to emphasize the necessity of setting long-run objectives and of relating short-term decisions to these objectives.

In the field of long-range planning, the accountant's role is to contribute to the management team. The importance of this role should be apparent from our discussions earlier in this chapter of the way profit targets are set.

The accountant's role in this regard may be defined as embracing the following activities:

1 Providing background information which serves as a prelude to planning. A valuable contribution which the accountant may make in this respect is the preparation of preliminary studies in the form of reviews of past performance, product-mix studies, surveys of physical facilities, and estimates of capital expenditure requirements. Moreover, he has special skills in the analyses of cost–volume–profit relationships, profit margins by product lines, cash flows and so on.
2 Assisting in the evaluation of alternative courses of action which are being considered, and assessing the financial feasibility of the proposed course of action. This requires the accountant to decide what data is relevant, prior to its analysis and expression in financial terms, so that the database of the long-range plan shall be reliable.
3 Assembling, integrating and co-ordinating detailed plans into a corporate master plan. In this respect, the accountant has a traditional skill in aggregating data which is particularly relevant.

4   Translating plans into overall schedules of costs, profit and financial conditions. These schedules may subsequently be used to prepare detailed operating budgets.

5   Presenting the anticipated results of future operations in financial terms.

6   Assisting in the critical appraisal and, where necessary, the revision of long-range plans to ensure that they do constitute a realistic basis for directing and controlling future operations.

7   Establishing and administering the network of operational controls that are necessary to the attainment of the planned objectives. This vital phase of the planning process requires the integration of long- and short-run profit plans, the monitoring of current performance against that planned for the long term and reporting to management on the realization of the long-term plan.

Summary

The purpose of this chapter has been to emphasize the necessity of setting long-run objectives and of relating short-term decisions to these objectives. Long-range planning has received increasing attention in recent years due to rapidly changing business conditions, which have persuaded management to take a longer view of the firm's activities than has hitherto been thought necessary. It is becoming widely recognized that effective long-range planning should result in a firm being always in the best position with products, resources and processes deployed in such a way as to take advantage of all the opportunities which present themselves. Long-range planning is seen as providing a systematic way of running a company so that not only can it anticipate change, but it may actually profit from change. The absence of long-range planning may be detrimental to a firm in a number of ways: for example, current profitability may induce so much complacency that danger signals may be ignored, and in due course, valuable opportunities may not be seized. Equally, an excessive concern with short-term planning may encourage actions in the short term which are detrimental to the long-term interests of the firm.

A long-range plan may be damaging, however, if it is badly implemented. Thus, a rigid long-range plan may turn out to be inappropriate for new circumstances. It is necessary, therefore, that long-range planning should have a degree of flexibility, so as to allow for adjustments to changing circumstances. Long-range planning should include a continuous scanning process aimed at discovering opportunities, defining constraints and assessing risks.

The accountant has an important role to play in long-range planning, particularly in long-range financial planning.

Questions

1   Why are cash flows so important to an enterprise?
2   Distinguish between objectives and goals.
3   Name six typical areas in which a firm may set objectives and goals.
4   What is a position audit?

5   How is strategy formulated?
6   What factors does management take into account in calculating the returns which shareholders are likely to expect over the planning period?
7   What is the role of the accountant in long-range financial planning?
8   What are the main components of a long-range financial plan?

Chapter 29

Planning capital expenditure

The level of a firm's profits depends upon the success with which it is able to employ all its assets—human and non-human. The firm's future profitability depends on two factors, first, maintaining and enlarging its asset structure and, second, devising a successful strategy for that asset structure. The previous chapter drew attention to the fact that preparing the capital expenditure plan is part of the long-range planning process. The activity of investing in new assets, often termed *capital budgeting*, involves planning capital expenditure and arranging the financing of this expenditure. It is an area of management decison making which has attracted a great deal of interest among accountants and economists in recent years, and much research has been devoted towards evolving methods for improving the quality of these decisions.

In this chapter, we deal mainly with capital expenditure decisions, and examine the relevant factors and the methods which are currently employed for making capital investment decisions.

Capital investment decisions

Probably the most significant factor affecting the level of profitability in a business is the quality of managerial decisions affecting the commitment of the firm's resources to new investments within the firm. The reasons which render such strategic decisions so important may be listed as follows:

1 They involve the commitment of substantial sums of money.
2 This commitment is made for a long period of time, and the element of uncertainty is therefore much greater than in the case of decisions whose effects are limited to a short period of time.
3 Once made, capital investment decisions are almost impossible to reverse should they appear subsequently to have been wrongly made.
4 Occasionally, the success or the failure of a firm may depend upon a single decision. In all cases, the future profitability of the firm will be affected by the decision.
5 Not only is capital expenditure policy of major importance to a firm, but it is of great significance to an industry as well as to the national economy.

Types of capital investment decisions

A capital investment may be defined as an investment which yields returns during several future time periods, and may be contrasted with other types of investments which yield all their return in the current time period. Capital investment decisions may concern the following:

1 the acquisition or replacement of long-lived assets, such as buildings and plant;
2 the investment of funds into another form from which revenues will flow;
3 a special project which will affect the firm's future earning capacity, such as a research project or an advertising campaign;
4 the extension of the range of activities of the firm involving a capital outlay, such as a new production line or indeed a new product.

Capital investment decisions encompass two aspects of long-range profitability: first, estimating the future net increases in cash inflows or net savings in cash outlays which will result from the investment; and second, calculating the total cash outlays required to effect the investment.

The analysis of capital investment proposals

In the analysis of capital investment proposals, many of the important facts are uncertain, so that the first problem is to reduce the area of uncertainty before a decision is made. The second problem is to ensure that all known facts are correctly assessed and quantified. Both known and uncertain facts are estimated in cash terms, and methods of capital investment appraisal focus on cash flows.

The selection of investment projects is always a question of considering which of several competing alternatives is the best from the firm's point of view. By quantifying the cash inflows and the cash outlays which are involved in the various alternatives, a decision may be made by selecting that alternative which is preferred by the firm.

Example 1

Wall Street Finance Ltd is offered the opportunity of selecting two investments, each of which will yield £500 000 yearly. Investment A requires a total cash outlay of £5 000 000—hence it promises a rate of return of 10 per cent. Investment B requires a total cash outlay of £50 000 000—and therefore offers a rate of return of 1 per cent per annum. The firm would prefer investment A. However, if the firm has a minimum acceptable rate of return of 15 per cent, neither project would be acceptable.

We may conclude, therefore, that there are three major factors affecting capital investment decisions:

1 The net amount of the investment required, expressed as the total cash outlay needed to support the project during its entire life.
2 The net returns on the investment, expressed as the future expected net cash inflows. These may be actual cash flows, or cash savings.
3 The rate of return on investment, expressed as a percentage. The determination of the lowest acceptable rate of return on investment

will be influenced by a number of factors, among which are the firm's rate of return on its other investment opportunities and the cost of capital to the firm.

The relevant cash flows

Before we proceed to examine the methods of selecting investment projects, let us briefly define the meaning of the terms which we shall be employing.

Net investment outlays

These consist of initial investment outlays required to establish the project, and the subsequent investment outlays which are envisaged at the outset, and are distinguishable from operating cash outlays. Thus, initial investment outlays may compromise expenditure on equipment, installation costs, manpower training, working capital etc. Subsequent investment outlays may include 'second stage' developments, plant extensions etc. The analysis of a capital project is in terms of net cash costs to the firm, so that where tax credits are allowable, these credits must be deducted from the total cash costs to obtain the relevant cash outlay.

Net cash inflows

These are the operating cash flows associated with the investment over the period of its useful life. They are calculated after deducting operating cash expenditure and taxation. Since there may be year-to-year variation in the profile of these net cash flows, and since their periodic pattern is largely guesswork, they are the most difficult cash flows to quantify.

All cash-flow calculations are made on the basis of the estimated useful life of the investment, which is defined as the time interval that is expected to elapse between the time of acquisition or commencement and the time at which the combined forces of obsolescence and deterioration will justify the retirement of the asset or project. The useful life of the investment may be shortened by market changes which will diminish its earnings.

Methods of appraising capital investments

The more commonly used methods of evaluating capital investment proposals are:

1   the payback period;
2   the accounting rate of return;
3   the discounted cash flow techniques, of which there are two main forms:
    (a) the net present value method (NPV),
    (b) the internal rate of return (IRR).

The payback period

This method attempts to forecast how long it will take for the expected net cash inflows to *pay back* the net investment outlays. The payback period is calculated as follows:

$$\text{payback period (years)} = \frac{\text{net investment outlays}}{\text{average net cash inflows}}$$

Example 2

Northend Engineering Co. Ltd is considering the acquisition of machinery which will considerably reduce labour costs. The following are the relevant facts:

Net investment outlays	£200 000
Estimated annual cash savings (after tax)	60 000
Estimated useful life	5 years
Salvage value	nil

The payback period is as follows:

$$\frac{£200\ 000}{60\ 000} \text{ i.e. } 3\tfrac{1}{3} \text{ years}$$

The payback method has the advantage of simplicity. By advocating the selection of projects by reference only to the speed with which investment outlays are recovered, it recommends the acceptance of only the safest projects. It is a method which emphasizes liquidity rather than profitability, and its limitations may be stated to be:

1 It lays stress on the payback period rather than the useful life of the investment, and ignores the cash flows beyond the payback period. Hence, it focuses on breakeven rather than on profitability.
2 It ignores the time profile of the net cash inflows, and any time pattern in the net investment outlays. Any salvage value would also be ignored. This method, therefore, treats all cash flows through time as having the same value, so that in the example given, the value of £200 000 invested now is equated with £200 000 of net cash inflows over $3\tfrac{1}{3}$ years.

These problems may be illustrated as follows.

Example 3

Multiplexed Ltd is considering four different investment projects each costing £20 000. The following information relates to these projects:

Project No.	1	2	3	4
	£	£	£	£
Initial investment outlay	20 000	20 000	20 000	20 000
Cash inflows				
Year 1	9 000	11 000	3 000	10 000
Year 2	11 000	9 000	6 000	6 000
Year 3	—	—	8 000	4 000
Year 4	—	—	10 000	4 000
Year 5	—	—	10 000	3 000
Payback period (years)	2	2	3⅓	3

A crude application of the payback method would select projects 1 or 2 but would be unable to decide between these two projects.

The accounting rate of return

The accounting rate of return method seeks to express the average estimated yearly net inflows as a percentage of the net investment outlays. As, however, it is possible to recover depreciation from the yearly net inflows, the formula is expressed as follows:

$$R = \frac{C - D}{I}$$

where R = the accounting rate of return
C = average yearly net inflows
D = depreciation
I = net investment outlays

Substituting the figures given in our example on p. 486, the accounting rate of return would be calculated as follows:

$$R = \frac{£60\ 000 - £40\ 000}{£200\ 000} \times 100\%$$
$$= 10\%$$

It may be argued, however, that the recovery of depreciation over the useful life of the investment reduces the value of the net investment outlays through time. Assuming an average recovery through depreciation at the rate of £40 000 per year, the average net investment over the estimated useful life of 5 years is £100 000, calculated by using the arithmetic mean method as follows:

$$\text{Average lifetime investment} = \frac{£200\ 000}{2}$$
$$= £100\ 000$$

The average lifetime investment may be calculated graphically in Fig. 5.8.

Fig. 5.8

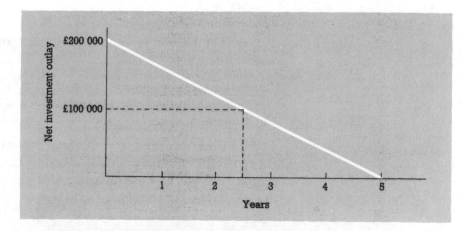

In the light of this argument, the accounting rate of return on investment should express the annual net cash inflows as a percentage of the average annual net investment outlays, so that, substituting the values given in our example, the average return on investment is:

$$R = \frac{£60\ 000 - £40\ 000}{£100\ 000} \times 100\%$$

$$= 20\%$$

This method of evaluating investment projects overcomes the disadvantage of the payback method in that it attempts to calculate the profitability of the various projects under study. Its main disadvantage is that it fails to consider the changing value of money through time, and treats the value of £1 in the future as equal to £1 invested today. Moreover, it ignores also the differences which may occur through time in the rate of net cash inflows. In both these senses, it suffers from the same defects as the payback method.

Discounted cash flows

The methods of investment appraisal we have just examined are generally regarded as producing misleading results. The DCF method has gained widespread acceptance, for it recognizes that the value of money is subject to a time preference, that is, that £1 today is preferred to £1 in the future unless the delay in receiving £1 in the future is compensated by an interest factor. This interest factor is expressed as a discount rate.

In simple terms, the DCF method attempts to evaluate an investment proposal by comparing the net cash flows accruing over the life of the investment at their present value with the value of funds about to be invested. Thus, by comparing like with like it is possible to calculate the rate of return on the investment in a realistic manner.

To find the present equivalent value of £1 receivable one year hence, one applies the rate of interest to discount that £1 to its present value. This is the same thing as asking 'what sum of money invested today at the rate of interest would increase in value to £1 a year hence?'

Example 4

Given that the rate of interest is 10 per cent per annum the following calculations may be made;

£1 invested now at 10 per cent will amount to £1.10 in a year. Conversely, the value of £1.10 a year's hence is worth £1 now if the rate of interest is 10 per cent.

Using this principle, discount tables may be constructed for the value of £1 over several time periods ahead by compounding the interest rate through time, i.e., £1.00 invested for 1 year at 10 per cent will be worth £1.10 at the year end, £1.10 then reinvested for another year at 10 per cent will be worth £1.10 + 0.11 = $1.21 at the end of the second year.

Example 5

The value of £1 at the end of 1 year at 10% is £1 + .10 = £1.1

£1	2 years	$(£1.1)^2 = £1.21$
£1	3	$(£1.1)^3 = £1.331$
£1	4	$(£1.1)^4 = £1.464$
£1	5	$(£1.1)^5 = £1.611$

Conversely, the present value of £1 receivable at a future date is:

£1 receivable in 1 year's time is $\dfrac{£1}{1.1}$ = £0.9091

£1	2	$\dfrac{£1}{1.21} = £0.8264$
£1	3	$\dfrac{£1}{1.331} = £0.7513$
£1	4	$\dfrac{£1}{1.464} = £0.6831$
£1	5	$\dfrac{£1}{1.611} = £0.6208$

The value of money is, therefore, directly affected by time, and the rate of interest is the method which is used to express the time value of money. Compound interest tables and discount tables are available which show the value of money at different interest rates over a number of years, so that in actual practice, it is a simple matter to apply the DCF method to the evaluation of an interest.

The net present value

This method is based on an assumed minimum rate of return. Ideally, this rate should be the average cost of capital to the firm (see p. 495) and it is this rate which would be used to discount the net cash inflows to their present value. The net investment outlays are subtracted from the present value of the net cash inflows leaving a residual figure, which is the net present value. A decision is made in favour of a project if the NPV is a positive amount. This method may likewise be applied to the comparison of one project with another when considering mutually exclusive investments.

The rule may be stated as follows:

Accept the project if:

$$\frac{a_1}{(1 + i)^1} + \frac{a_2}{(1 + i)^2} + \ldots + \frac{a_n}{(1 + i)^n} > A$$

where A is the initial project cost

a are the net annual cash inflows

i cost of capital

n expected life of project

Example 6

Corween Ltd is considering a project which has a life of 5 years and which will produce an annual inflow of £1000. The investment outlay is £3000 and the required rate of return is 10 per cent.

Year	Inflow	Discount factor (at 10%)	Present value of inflow
1	£1 000	0.9091	£909.1
2	£1 000	0.8264	£826.4
3	£1 000	0.7513	£751.3
4	£1 000	0.6831	£683.1
5	£1 000	0.6208	£620.8
Present value of net inflows			£3 790.7
Cost of investment outlay			£3 000.0
Net present value of the project			£790.7

Since the net present value of the cash inflows (a) is greater than the present value of the cash outlay (A), the project should be accepted.

The internal rate of return

This method requires us to calculate that rate of interest which used in discounting will reduce the net present value of a project to zero. This enables us to compare the internal rate of return (IRR) with the required rate.

The rule may be stated as follows:

Accept the project if:

$$A = \frac{a_1}{(1+r)} + \frac{a_2}{(1+r)^2} + \ldots + \frac{a_n}{(1+r)^n}$$

and $r > i$

where A is the initial project cost

$\quad a$ are the net annual cash inflows

$\quad r$ is the solution discount rate

$\quad i$ is the required rate of return

Example 7

Let us return to the example given above and assume that Corween Ltd applies the internal rate of return analysis to the project under consideration. The analysis would be as follows:

Year	Inflow	Discount factor at 19%	Present value at 19%	Discount factor at 20%	Present value at 20%
	£		£		£
1	1 000	0.8403	840.3	0.8333	833.3
2	1 000	0.7062	706.2	0.6944	694.4
3	1 000	0.5934	593.4	0.5787	578.7
4	1 000	0.4987	498.7	0.4823	482.3
5	1 000	0.4190	419.0	0.4019	401.9
Present value of net inflow			3 057.6		2 990.6
Cost of investment outlay			3 000.0		3 000.0
Net present value of the project			+57.6		−9.4

We can see that the IRR is almost 20 per cent. (It is often possible to approximate the true rate more closely by assuming a linear relationship and interpolating between the two nearest points.) The ascertainment of the IRR at 20 per cent enables us to compare the IRR with the required rate of return on investment by the company.

Net present value and internal rate of return compared

When dealing with simple investment appraisal projects, that is, those involving a once-and-for-all investment outlay followed by a stream of cash inflows, both the NPV and the IRR methods produce the same YES or NO decisions.

But the advantage of the NPV method is the simplicity with which the results are stated. Our example shows that with the NPV method, the expected results arc expressed in terms of pounds which directly reflect the increased wealth position. The internal rate of return, on the other hand, produces a result which is shown as a percentage, and this result has to be compared with a minimum required rate of return before a decision may be made.

Example 8

Norwell Industries Ltd is studying two projects, each of which requires a net investment outlay of £3000. Both have a useful life of 5 years, and the estimated profile of the net cash inflows are:

End of year	Project A	Project B
	£	£
1	500	2 000
2	1 000	1 500
3	1 500	1 500
4	2 000	1 000
5	2 000	500
	£7 000	£6 500

The desired minimum rate of return is 10 per cent.

Analysis—net present value

The present value of the two projects may be calculated by using the desired minimum rate of return as a discount factor.

End of Year	Discount factor 10%	Project A	Present value	Project B	Present value
		£	£	£	£
1	0.9091	500	454.6	2 000	1 818.2
2	0.8264	1 000	826.4	1 500	1 239.6
3	0.7153	1 500	1 073.0	1 500	1 073.0
4	0.6831	2 000	1 366.2	1 000	683.1
5	0.6208	2 000	1 241.6	500	310.4
Present value of total cash inflows			£4 961.8		£5 124.3
less: net investment outlay			£3 000.0		£3 000.0
Net present value			£1 961.8		£2 124.3

Both projects are acceptable to the firm, and if a choice has to be made between them, Project B would be selected since it produces the highest net present value of the two. The time profile of the net cash inflows is seen to be a determining influence on the result, for although the total cash inflows before discounting are higher with Project A, the cash flows associated with Project B are concentrated in the earlier years and, when discounted, have a higher net present value than A's.

Analysis—the internal rate of return

Taking the net cash inflows estimated for Project A, the rate which will discount the net cash inflows to £3000 is found once again by trial and error. Using discount tables, we establish in this way that the discount rate is between 28 per cent and 29 per cent, as follows:

Cash inflows	Discount factor at 29%	Present value at 29%	Discount factor at 28%	Present value at 28%
£		£		£
500	0.7752	387.7	0.7813	390.7
1 000	0.6009	600.9	0.6104	610.4
1 500	0.4658	698.7	0.4768	715.2
2 000	0.3611	722.2	0.3725	745.0
2 000	0.2799	559.8	0.2910	582.0
		£2 969.3		£3 043.3
Original investment outlay		£3 000.0		£3 000.0
		−30.7		+43.3

Using the same approach, the IRR from Project B may be calculated as 39 per cent.

The crucial test upon which the final acceptance of a project depends is whether or not the IRR compares favourably with the required rate of return. If the required rate of return is 20 per cent then both projects qualify.

One of the problems of comparing rates of return on projects is that direct comparisons between two percentages are meaningless unless referred to the initial outlays, so that their true dimensions may be perceived. This problem should never be lost sight of when using IRR percentages.

With more complicated investment problems, for example, those which require that cash surpluses be set aside to meet an obligation arising at the end of the project's life, both methods assume that those cash surpluses are reinvested at the appropriate rate of return. Thus, where a loan has been raised to finance the project,* the IRR method envisages that the cash surpluses will be reinvested at the IRR discounting rate, whereas the NPV method envisages that they will be reinvested at the minimum acceptable rate of return used in that method. Thus, the advantage of the NPV method is that it makes more realistic assumptions about reinvestment opportunities.

More complex problems arise when applying the IRR method to investment projects which do not have the simple pattern of cash flows of the above examples, but we regard these problems as beyond the scope of this text.

Taxation and other factors

In order that DCF calculations should lead to correct results, it is important that all factors affecting the calculations of cash flows should be taken into account. The most important of these factors is, of course, taxation. Indeed, we have assumed from the outset that the cash flow figures were net after tax. Apart from the direct effects of taxation, we should also adjust our figures for indirect aspects of taxation, such as investment grants, and the reader will recall that in calculating the net investment outlay, any recoveries in the form of investment incentives must be deducted from the amount brought into the DCF calculation. The effects of these incentives vary from project to project.

The cost of capital

The evaluation of an investment project by DCF analysis requires a firm to calculate its cost of capital. This is true in selecting the discount rate for appraisal by means of the net present value method, or for establishing the acceptability of the internal rate of return.

A full discussion of the concept of the 'cost of capital' is beyond the scope of this book; indeed, the subject is perhaps the most difficult and

---

* The simplifying assumption which we are making for the purpose of illustrating the point is that the firm's finances are linked to specific investment projects, which in reality is not perhaps the case.

controversial topic in the whole theory of finance. Our discussion will be a very elementary one so as to provide the reader with some understanding of investment planning.

The first problem in discussing the cost of capital lies in different meanings which the term has acquired. From a lender's point of view, the cost of capital represents the cost to him of lending money which may be equated to the return he could have obtained by investing in a similar project having similar risks. This concept of the cost of capital is founded on its 'opportunity cost'. The opportunity cost approach to the assessment of the cost of capital is one which a firm must always consider when evaluating an investment project. A firm may find, for example, that investing funds outside the firm may produce higher returns than an internal project. The main obstacle to a more widespread use of the opportunity cost concept is that of identifying investment of equal risks and hence measuring the opportunity cost.

Another concept in use is the actual cost incurred by a firm in borrowing money. A firm may obtain funds in a variety of ways: and each way has a different cost attached to it. Thus, a firm may issue shares and will pay a dividend on those shares, which must represent the cost of raising funds in that way. It may also borrow by the issue of debentures or by bank or other methods, and in these cases interest is payable. The fact that the firm may have raised its finance in several different ways makes it more realistic to use the 'average cost of capital' which is based on an analysis of its capital structure.

Example 9

The Keystone Corp Ltd has a capital structure distributed as to 80 per cent share capital and 20 per cent loan capital. The dividend rate is 10 per cent and the interest payable on the loan capital is 8 per cent. Calculate the average cost of capital.

Source of funds	Proportion of total funds %	Cost of capital %	Product
Share capital	80	10	£800
Loan capital	20	8	160
	100		£960

The weighted average cost of capital is: $\dfrac{960}{100} = 9.6\%$

The average cost of capital so calculated would in the case of this firm represent the minimum acceptable rate of return.

Gearing and the cost of capital

It will be recalled from Part 2 that the distribution of a firm's capital structure as between share capital (equity capital) and fixed-interest stock (preference shares and debentures) is known as the gearing. A firm which is highly geared has a higher ratio of fixed-interest stock to equity capital. By changing its gearing, a firm may alter its average cost of capital.

Example 10

The firm in the above-mentioned example increases its gearing by raising the proportion of loan capital to share capital from 20 per cent to 40 per cent. Its average cost of capital, as a result, is reduced to 9.2 per cent:

Source of funds	Proportion of total funds %	Cost of capital %	Product
Share capital	60	10	£600
Loan capital	40	8	320
	100		£920

The average cost of capital is: $\dfrac{920}{100} = 9.2\%$

It should be noted that financial theorists have argued that it is due only to the influence of a corporation tax system which allows loan interest as a tax deductible expense that gearing is of any significance.

Financial planning requires a firm to give very serious consideration to its capital structure and to its gearing. Very complex issues are involved in planning an appropriate capital structure. Circumstances may make it advantageous to attempt to increase the proportion of loan capital, that is, increase the gearing, such as the tax deductibility of loan interest which we have already mentioned. There is an upper limit to debt finance, however, for not only are there obvious dangers in the presence of large fixed-interest charges against corporate income, but there are practical limits to the amount of funds which may be borrowed for long-term purposes.

Investment appraisal and inflation

As the cash flows associated with a particular project may span a considerable period of time, it is evident that the level of inflation during that time will affect considerably the profitability of the project. We pointed out in Chapter 27 that estimates of future events should take inflation into account, and in Part 3 the distinction between general price level and specific price changes was discussed. We indicated the need to adjust cash-flow forecasts for specific price changes which would affect the enterprise, so as to maintain its operating capability. Accordingly, it is the inflating cost of specific items which are to be taken into account in investment appraisal. The cost of these specific items will exhibit different rates of change, as will the prices of the products containing elements of the specific items of costs. In effect, the existence of a lag between increases in cost and increases in prices may considerably reduce the profitability of a project under conditions of inflation. As the rate of inflation increases, so this problem becomes more acute. For thi reason, firms entering into fixed-price contracts extending over a lon period of time should arrange for cost-escalation clauses to mitigate th impact of inflation.

The most appropriate method of incorporating the effects of inflation into DCF calculations is to adjust cash flow forecasts for specific price increases. Such adjusted cash flows are then discounted by the monetar cost of capital.

Example 11

In the earlier example (p. 490), Corween Ltd had annual net cash flow of £1000 for a period of 5 years, and the discount rate was given as 1 per cent. It may now be assumed that the annual net cash flows wer derived as follows:

	£	£
Cash inflows from sales		5 00
Cash outflows:		
Materials	3 000	
Labour	1 000	
		4 00
Annual net cash flow		1 00

The impact of inflation is considered in the following terms:

1 Sales revenues are expected to be adjusted for price changes at th rate of 15 per cent per annum. The adjustment to the annual expecte cash inflows from sales is shown below.
2 Material costs are expected to increase at the rate of 18 per cent pe annum. The adjustment for this increase is also shown below.
3 Labour costs are expected to increase at the rate of 10 per cent pe annum. The adjustment is also shown below.

	Annual rate of change	Year 1	Year 2	Year 3	Year 4	Year
	%	£	£	£	£	£
Sales revenue	15	5 750	6 613	7 605	8 746	10 05
Materials	18	3 540	4 177	4 929	5 816	6 86
Labour	10	1 100	1 210	1 331	1 464	1 61
		4 640	5 387	6 260	7 280	8 47
Net cash flows (adjusted)		1 110	1 226	1 345	1 466	1 58

These annual expected future net cash flows may now be discounte at the appropriate discount rate. For simplicity, if it is assumed that th discount rate is 10 per cent, these annual net cash flows have a present value of £5017, as follows:

Year	Net cash flow	Discount factor at 10%	Present value
	£	%	£
1	1 110	0.9091	1 009
2	1 226	0.8264	1 013
3	1 345	0.7513	1 010
4	1 466	0.6831	1 001
5	1 585	0.6208	984
			5 017
less: Initial investment outlay			3 000
Net present value of the project			2 017

The foregoing example shows the manner in which inflation adds a new dimension to the problem of calculating present values. More calculations are involved, and the degree of uncertainty is increased. Many accountants feel that, under conditions of rapid and high inflation, the task of forecasting cash flows over the lifetime of a project covering several years seems somewhat academic. Research has shown that the most popular method of investment appraisal is the payback method, which emphasizes the rate of recovery of investment outlays. During periods of inflation, the payback method places emphasis on projects which have shorter payback periods.

Summary

Preparing the capital expenditure plan is part of the long-range planning process. The quality of managerial decisions committing the firm's resources to new investments is probably the most significant factor affecting the level of future profitability.

Capital investment decisions encompass two aspects of the long-range profit plan—first, estimating the future net increases in cash inflows or net savings in cash outlays which will result from an investment; second, calculating the total cash outlays required to carry out an investment.

There are three well-known techniques for appraising investment proposals from a financial viewpoint:

1 the payback method, which emphasizes the length of time required to recoup the investment outlay;

2 the accounting rate of return, which seeks to express the average estimated yearly net inflows as a percentage of the net investment outlays for the purpose of assessing the profitability of a proposed investment;

3 discounted cash flow methods, which attempt to evaluate an investment proposal by comparing the present value of the net cash inflows accruing over the life of the investment with the present value of the funds to be invested.

Discounted cash flow techniques provide the most useful procedures for evaluating capital investment proposals. They comprise two methods— the net present value and the internal rate of return. Both methods take into account the time value of money, unlike the other methods mentioned which ignore this factor.

In many situations it is difficult to forecast the time profile of future cash flows with any degree of certainty. The next chapter considers risk analysis as a means of handling the problem of uncertainty.

Questions

1 What do you understand by capital investment decisions? State briefly the reason for their importance.
2 Give four examples of capital investment decisions.
3 Explain briefly the type of information used in making capital investment decisions.
4 State the three major factors affecting capital investment decisions.
5 What are the advantages and disadvantages associated with the pay-back period?
6 Do you consider the accounting rate of return method to be more useful than the pay-back period in evaluating capital investment?
7 Explain briefly the discounted cash flow method, and discuss its advantages and disadvantages when applied to investment appraisal.
8 Compare and contrast present value and internal rate of return methods.
9 What is the significance of the cost of capital in investment appraisal?
10 Suggest possible ways in which inflation may be taken into account in making capital investment decisions.

Problems

1 The purchase of a machine is contemplated and the relevant facts concerning two possible choices are as follows:

	Machine A	Machine B
Capital expenditure required	£50 000	£60 000
Estimated life—years	3	4
Residual value	nil	nil
Cash flow after taxation— constant each year at	£25 000	£24 000

Assume a rate of interest of 10 per cent for which the reciprocals are:

Year 1	0.9091	Year 2	0.8264
Year 3	0.7513	Year 4	0.6830

Required:
Set out calculations illustrating and comparing the following methods of evaluating the return from these investments:

(a) Payback period
(b) Accounting rate of return
(c) Discounted cash flow.

Comment on the results.

2 Jazz Ltd is considering replacing three of its record-pressing machines with one machine which has just come onto the market. The three existing machines are two years old and cost £1500 each. They are being depreciated on a straight-line basis over twelve years. It was expected that their final scrap value would be £600

each. Their replacement is being considered because a fault has developed in their operation which can only be corrected at a total cost of £5000 for the three machines. The current secondhand market value of the machines is £1000 each.

The annual operating costs of the exisiting and new machines are as follows:

Existing machines; costs per machine:

		£
Materials		60 000
Labour: one operator at 1800 hours		1 350
Variable expenses		925
Maintenance (excluding exceptional items)		2 000
Fixed		expenses:
Depreciation	75	
Fixed overheads absorbed	2 700	2 700

New machine:

		£
Materials		162 000
Labour: two operators at 1500 hours	3 000	
one assistant at 1500 hours	900	3 900
Variable expenses		2 275
Maintenance		4 500
Fixed expenses:		
Depreciation	9 550	
Fixed overheads absorbed	7 800	17 350

The new machine's estimated life is 10 years and will cost £100 000.
The company's cost of capital is 10 per cent.

Required:

(a) Advise the management of Jazz Ltd on the most profitable course of action to undertake.
(b) Comment on the method you have used and the other factors which might influence the decision.

Chapter 30

Budgetary planning

The process of budgeting focuses on the short term, normally one year, and provides an expression of the steps which management must take in the current period if it is to fulfil organizational objectives. It is useful to distinguish between the two functions—planning and control. Applying a similar distinction to budgeting, we may examine in turn the functions of budgetary planning and budgetary control. In this chapter, we deal with the technical aspects of budgeting. The analysis of the budgeting problem, in terms of the relationships between costs, volume and profits, is discussed in Chapter 31.

The nature of budgetary planning

Long-range planning involves the determination of corporate objectives and the determination of a suitable plan for attaining these objectives. The budget represents the expression of this plan in financial terms in the light of current conditions. Therefore, the long-range plan is the guide for preparing the annual budgets and defines actions that need to be taken now in order to move towards long-term objectives. Indeed, the budget represents the first one-year span of the long-range budget.

The reader will recall that one important feature of planning is the co-ordination of the various activities of an enterprise, and of its departments, so that they are harmonized in the overall task of realizing corporate objectives. For example if the marketing function were to increase sales massively over a short period of time, the manufacturing function would have to increase output substantially—probably through the use of costly overtime labour, or by buying goods from an outside supplier at high prices. Conversely, excessive production may force the marketing function to sell at unrealistically low prices in order to avoid excessive investment in stock. The function of budgetary planning is to co-ordinate the various activities of an organization in order to achieve company rather than divisional or departmental objectives. There it is necessary to establish objectives for each section of the organization which are in harmony with the organization as a whole.

The need for flexibility

Because business conditions are always changing, it is necessary to view the budgeting process as a guide to future action, rather than a rigid plan which must be followed irrespective of changing circumstances. The latter approach may place the manager in a strait-jacket in which he is forced to take decisions which are not in accordance with company objectives. For example, a departmental manager may find, due to changing conditions, that he has not spent all of his budget on a particular item. In order to spend all his budget allowance, so as to prevent the possibility of a cut in his allowance next year, he may squander funds which could have been put to better use in other sections of the organization.

More importantly, management must plan for changing business conditions, in order that appropriate action may be taken to deal with changes that may occur should any of the assumptions underlying plans be affected by such changes. This implies that contingency plans should be available to deal with changes which were unforeseen at the time when the budget was originally prepared.

Some firms relate their planning budgets to changing conditions by means of a rolling budget which is prepared every quarter, but for one year ahead. At the end of each quarter the plans for the next three quarters are revised, if this is necessary, and a fourth quarter is added. By this process the budgets are kept continually up to date.

Flexibility is also required if budgetary control is to be effective. Indeed the type of budget which may be suitable for planning may be inappropriate for control purposes. Therefore, budgets should be established for control purposes which reflect operating conditions which may be different from those envisaged in the planning stages. This is essential if individual managers are to be held responsible only for those deviations over which they have control. Such a requirement is called for by the use of a responsibility accounting system, which is discussed in Chapter 35.

The organization of budgeting

The budgeting process itself requires careful organization. In large firms, budgeting is often in the hands of a budgeting committee which acts through the budget officer whose function it is to co-ordinate and control the budgeting process for the whole organization. Departmental budget estimates are requested from divisional managers, who in their turn collate this information from estimates submitted to them by their own departmental managers. Hence, budget estimates are based on information which flows upwards through the organization to the budget committee. The budget committee is responsible for co-ordinating this information, and resolving any differences in consultations with the managers involved. The final budget proposal is presented to the board of directors for its final approval.

Steps in budgeting

The first stage of a budgeting exercise is the determination of the 'key' factors or constraints which impose overall limits to the budget plan. Among these factors are the productive capacity of the plant, the finances available to the firm, and, of course, the market conditions which impose a total limit on the output the firm is able to sell. Normally from a management point of view, the critical question is 'what is the firm able to sell in the budget period?', and this question summarizes all the limits

Fig. 5.9

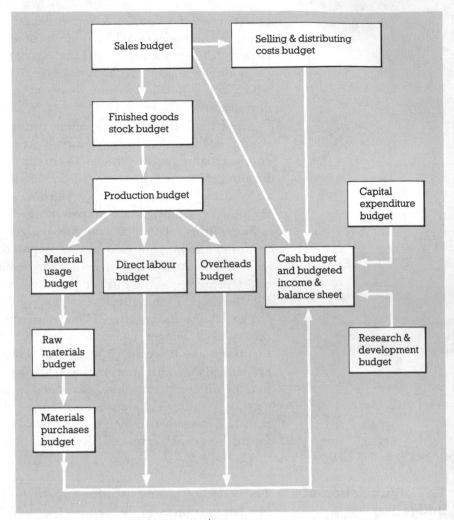

to the budget plan. It is for this reason that the sales budget is at once the starting point and the fulcrum of the budgeting process.

Figure 5.9 illustrates how the various resources and activities of an enterprise are co-ordinated.

The arrows indicate the flow of relevant information. Once the level of sales is established, selling and distribution cost may be ascertained. The production budget itself is determined by the sales forecast, the desired level of stock of finished goods and plant capacity. From the production budget may be estimated the production costs, and the cost schedules for materials, labour and overheads.

In addition, the budgeting process for capital expenditure reflects decisions taken in developing the long-range plan. The capital expenditure budget is concerned with expenditure during the budget period on the maintenance and improvement of the existing productive capacity. Associated with this budget are research and development costs for improving methods of production and product improvement as well.

From a financing point of view, the cash surplus of deficits arising out of the overall budget are revealed by the cash budget which incorporates all cash revenues and cash expenditures. This enables the firm to arrange its financial needs accordingly.

Finally, the projected results in terms of the overall net profit, and the changes in the structure of the firm's assets and liabilities are expressed in the budgeted profit and loss account and the budgeted balance sheet at the end of the budget period.

This description of the manner in which the budget co-ordinated the various activities of the firm is a simplified one. Budgetary planning is an activity which is of critical importance to the firm, and the problems involved are often complex and difficult ones to resolve. A firm's sales policy, for example, cannot be considered in isolation from its pricing policy and its cost structure. The firm's planned costs in relation to the required output may be too high to reach the profit target. If this should be the case, pricing and advertising policies may require further scrutiny, both planned and development costs may have to be reduced, and the final product itself may have to be modified. The role of the budget committee is, therefore, a very important one: not only has it to harmonize all the divisional budgets into an overall planning framework, but it has to deal with the numerous adjustments which may have to be made if the overall budget fails to meet some of the firm's stated objectives. Hence, the role of the budget committee is not only important in a practical sense: it affects important and sensitive areas of policy making and management.

Forecasting sales

A major problem in budgeting is forecasting sales, for many factors affecting sales are outside the firm's control, for example the behaviour of the firm's competitors and the future economic climate.

The importance of an accurate sales forecast cannot be over-emphasized. If the sales forecast is too optimistic, the firm may be induced to expand its capital expenditure programme and incur costs which may not be recoverable at a later date. In the meantime the production target may be set too high, resulting in the pile-up of stock of finished goods, which in itself has important financial consequences. Moreover, an optimistic sales forecast may disguise a deteriorating sales position, so that the necessary economies are not made which would produce a satisfactory profit. If, on the other hand, the sales forecast is pessimistic, the firm will miss the opportunity of larger current profit and may be misled as to its future prospects. The firm may, as a result, not undertake the necessary capital expenditure which would place it in a good position to exploit the market.

The sales forecast is the initial step in preparing the sales budget. It consists of not only analysing the market for the firm's products, but also forecasting the levels of sales at different prices. Hence, the study of the firm's pricing policy is an integral aspect of sales forecasting. Once the sales forecast is completed, the sales budget may be derived from the target sales established both as regards price and sales volume.

There are various methods of forecasting sales, for example:

1 *The sales force composite method.* This method places responsibility upon individual salesmen for developing their own sales forecasts. The advantage of this method is that if participative budgeting is to be encouraged, the sales staff should assist in the preparation of the sales forecast.

2 *The analysis of market and industry factors.* This method recognizes the importance of factors not within the knowledge of the sales force, such as forecasts of the gross national product, personal incomes, employment and price levels etc. The salesmen's estimates are modified by the information so obtained.

3 *Statistical analysis of fluctuations through time.* Sales are generally affected by four basic factors: growth trends, business cycle fluctuations, seasonal fluctuations and irregular variations in demand. A time series analysis of sales is a statistical method of separating and analysing the historical evidence of the behaviour of sales to identify these several effects and their impact on sales. The results of this analysis are applied to the sales forecast, and are means of testing the quality of the forecast.

4 *Mathematical techniques for sales forecasting.* Of recent years, mathematical techniques have been applied to the study of the relationship between economic trends and a firm's sales pattern through time, to arrive at a projection of future sales. These techniques usually involve the use of computers. One such technique is known as exponential smoothing, which is really a prediction of future sales based on current and historical sales data, weighted so as to give a greater importance to the latest incoming information.

An illustration of the budgeting process

Once the sales forecast is known, a firm may begin to prepare the budget. We believe that the reader will obtain a better understanding of budgeting if we work through a simple example. In the following example, we focus on the technical problems of budget construction, and we assume that the problem of changing price levels is not present. This assumption allows us to treat asset values as remaining constant.

Example

The Edco Manufacturing Co Ltd manufactures two products, A and B.

A formal planning system had been introduced some time ago as a means of steering the company into more profitable levels of operation. Considerable progress had already been made in streamlining production and reducing costs. The budgeting process normally began in October, prior to the end of the accounting year on 31 December.

The Edco Manufacturing Co Ltd
Forecast results for the year ending 31 December 19X0
profit and loss account

	£	£	£
Sales		135 000	
Cost of goods sold		80 000	
Gross margin		55 000	
Selling and administrative expenses		25 000	
Profit before tax		30 000	
Tax at 40%		12 000	
Profit after tax		18 000	

Balance sheet

Fixed assets	Cost	Depreciation	
	£	£	£
Plant and machinery	250 000	30 000	220 000
Current assets		£	
Stocks:			
Raw materials		1 650	
Finished goods		6 025	
		7 675	
Debtors		20 000	
Cash		5 325	
		33 000	
less: Creditors: amounts falling due within one year:			
Creditors	5 000		
Tax	12 000		
		17 000	
Net current assets			16 000
Total assets less current liabilities			236 000
Capital and reserves			£
Called-up share capital			210 000
Profit and loss account			26 000
			236 000

The expected results for the current year ending on 31 December 19X0 were as shown above.

From these forecast results, the expected performance for the current year may be calculated as follows:

return on shareholders' equity: $\dfrac{£18\ 000}{£236\ 000} = 7.6\%$

return on capital employed: $\dfrac{£18\ 000}{£253\ 000} = 7.1\%$

The following additional information was obtained for the purpose of preparing the budget for the year ending 31 December 19X1.

The sales forecast

	Product A	Product B
Expected selling price per unit	£11	£14
Sales volume forecast		
1st quarter	1 500 units	2 000 units
2nd	1 000	2 000
3rd	1 000	2 000
4th	1 500	2 000
Total for the year	5 000	8 000

Factory costs forecast

Two departments are concerned with production: the preparation department and the machining department. The following analysis relates to the production of these departments:

1   *Direct costs*

	Direct labour required per unit of product (in labour hours)		Departmental wage rate	Direct labour cost per unit of output	
	A	**B**		**A**	**B**
Preparation department	⅕	½	£2 per hour	£0.40	£1.00
Machining department	½	½	£2 per hour	£1.00	1.00
				£1.40	£2.00

2   *Raw material requirement forecast*

The standard quantities of the two raw materials, X and Y, which should be used in the manufacture of the two products, and the prices of these raw materials have been estimated as follows:

Standard quantities:
    Raw material X—2 units for each unit of product A
    Raw material Y—3 units for each unit of product B

Estimated costs:
    Raw material X—£0.50 for each unit of X
    Raw material Y—£0.30 for each unit of Y

3 *Overhead costs*

Factory overheads are classified into fixed and variable costs. The fixed overhead costs are deemed to be incurred in equal amounts quarterly for the purpose of allocation, whereas the variable overheads vary according to the level of production. The following estimates are available:

Fixed overheads:

Depreciation	£10 000 per annum
Rates and insurances	4 000
Supervisory salaries	6 000
	£20 000

Variable overheads:

	Cost per unit of output	
	A	B
	£	£
Indirect labour		
Indirect material		
Repairs and maintenance	£0.50	£1.00
Power		

Stock forecasts

Finished goods:

Product A—estimated opening stock: 750 units
Product B—estimated opening stock: 1000 units

It was planned that the closing stock level at the end of each quarter should be maintained at a level equal to half the expected sales for the next quarter for both products.

For the purposes of calculating the expected profit, the closing stock is to be valued on a variable costing basis, as follows:

	A	B
Raw materials	£1.00	£0.90
Direct labour	1.40	2.00
Variable overheads	0.50	1.00
Total variable costs per unit	£2.90	£3.90

Raw materials:
  Raw material X—estimated opening stock: 1500 units
  Raw material Y: 3000 units

Administrative and selling costs forecast

1 Administrative costs:		
Office salaries	£18 000	
Stationery	1 000	
Other	1 000	
		£20 000
2 Selling costs:		
Salaries	15 000	
Advertising	5 000	
		20 000
Total		£40 000

Cash flow forecast

1 Sales receipts
50 per cent of sales received in cash during month of sales
50 per cent of sales received in cash in the following month

2 Cash expenditure
Production costs
Direct labour, direct materials and variable overheads paid in the month in which incurred
Fixed overheads paid in equal amounts quarterly
Administrative and selling costs
Paid in equal amounts quarterly
Other costs
Tax outstanding amounting to £12 000 will be paid off in equal instalments quarterly over the year
Capital expenditure
Expenditure on the acquisition assets is planned as follows:

1st quarter	£10 000
2nd	15 000
3rd	8 000
4th	20 000
	£53 000

Sundry creditors balance

The amount outstanding to sundry creditors will remain at a constant amount of £5000 throughout the year.

Preparing the budget for the year ending 31 December 19X1

The task of preparing the overall budget involves a sequence of steps:

Step 1 The sales budget
　　 2 The production budget

3   The direct materials usage budget
4   The materials purchases budget
5   The budgeted direct labour costs
6   The overhead costs budget
7   The closing stock budget
8   The selling and administrative costs budget
9   The capital expenditure budget
10   The cost of goods sold budget
11   The cash budget
12   The budgeted profit and loss account
13   The budgeted balance sheet

Step 1   The sales budget

The sales budget is prepared from the sales forecast as follows:

	1st quarter	2nd quarter	3rd quarter	4th quarter	Total
Units:					
Product A	1 500	1 000	1 000	1 500	5 000
Product B	2 000	2 000	2 000	2 000	8 000
Value:					
Product A (£11)	£16 500	£11 000	£11 000	£16 500	£55 000
Product B (£14)	28 000	28 000	28 000	28 000	112 000
	£44 500	39 000	£39 000	£44 500	£167 000

Step 2   The production budget

The production budget is designed to plan the resources required to produce the output envisaged by the sales forecast. A precondition for an agreement as to the size of the sales budget is the adequacy of the productive capacity of the plant to provide the required output. If existing capacity is inadequate, decisions will have to be made as to the advisability of introducing overtime working, of subcontracting production, or of hiring or purchasing additional plant and equipment. If, on the other hand, the sales forecast falls short of productive capacity, sales promotion schemes may be considered as a means of closing or reducing the gap. With the tendency of businessmen to use stock levels as buffers to insulate an efficient rate of production from variations in sales, the production budget is also dependent upon the planned levels of closing stock.

Using the information given in our example, the following production budget may be prepared:

	1st quarter	2nd quarter	3rd quarter	4th quarter	Year
Product A:		(UNITS)			
Desired closing stock (units)	500	500	750	750	750
add: Sales	1 500	1 000	1 000	1 500	5 000
Total required	2 000	1 500	1 750	2 250	5 750
less: Opening stock	750	500	500	750	750
Production required	1 250	1 000	1 250	1 500	5 000
Product B:					
Desired closing stock (units)	1 000	1 000	1 000	1 000	1 000
add: Sales	2 000	2 000	2 000	2 000	8 000
Total required	3 000	3 000	3 000	3 000	9 000
less: Opening stock	1 000	1 000	1 000	1 000	1 000
Production required	2 000	2 000	2 000	2 000	8 000

Step 3 The direct materials usage budget

The rate of usage of raw materials is known, so that the direct materials usage may be budgeted by multiplying the usage rate by the production required.

	1st quarter	2nd quarter	3rd quarter	4th quarter	Year
Material X (2 units for A)	2 500	2 000	2 500	3 000	10 000
Material Y (3 units for B)	6 000	6 000	6 000	6 000	24 000

Step 4 The direct materials purchase budget

The purpose of this budget is to determine both the quantities and the values of raw material purchases necessary to meet the production levels stipulated in the production budget. The information required for this budget is found in the direct materials usage budget, stock forecasts and raw materials purchase prices.

	1st quarter	2nd quarter	3rd quarter	4th quarter	Year
Raw material X					
Desired closing stock	1 000	1 000	1 500	1 500	1 500
add: Material usage (Step 3)	2 500	2 000	2 500	3 000	10 000
Total required	3 500	3 000	4 000	4 500	11 500
less: Opening stock	1 500	1 000	1 000	1 500	1 500
Purchases required (units)	2 000	2 000	3 000	3 000	10 000
Price per unit	£0.50	£0.50	£0.50	£0.50	£0.50
Total purchases (value)	£1 000	£1 000	£1 500	£1 500	£5 000

Raw material Y

Desired closing stock	3 000	3 000	3 000	3 000	3 000
add: Material usage (Step 3)	6 000	6 000	6 000	6 000	24 000
Total required	9 000	9 000	9 000	9 000	27 000
less: Opening stock	3 000	3 000	3 000	3 000	3 000
Purchases required (units)	6 000	6 000	6 000	6 000	24 000
Price per unit	£0.30	£0.30	£0.30	£0.30	£0.30
Total purchases (value)	£1 800	£1 800	£1 800	£1 800	£7 200
Total purchases (value)	£2 800	£2 800	£3 300	£3 300	£12 200

Step 5 Budgeted direct labour costs

This budget is based upon calculations of the manpower requirements necessary to produce the planned output. The direct labour costs are computed by multiplying the manpower requirements by the forecast of wage rates payable during the budget period.

	1st quarter	2nd quarter	3rd quarter	4th quarter	Year
Production (Step 2—units)					
Product A	1 250	1 000	1 250	1 500	5 000
Product B	2 000	2 000	2 000	2 000	8 000
Labour hours					
Preparation department					
Product A ($\frac{1}{5}$)	250	200	250	300	1 000
Product B ($\frac{1}{2}$)	1 000	1 000	1 000	1 000	4 000
Total	1 250	1 200	1 250	1 300	5 000
Machining department					
Product A ($\frac{1}{2}$)	625	500	625	750	2 500
Product B ($\frac{1}{2}$)	1 000	1 000	1 000	1 000	4 000
Total	1 625	1 500	1 625	1 750	6 500
Direct labour costs					
Preparation department					
Labour hours	1 250	1 200	1 250	1 300	5 000
Wage rate/hour	£2	£2	£2	£2	£2
Direct labour cost	£2 500	£2 400	£2 500	£2 600	£10 000
Machining department					
Labour hours	1 625	1 500	1 625	1 750	6 500
Wage rate/hour	£2	£2	£2	£2	£2
Direct labour cost	£3 250	£3 000	£3 250	£3 500	£13 000
Total direct labour cost	£5 750	£5 400	£5 750	£6 100	£23 000

Step 6 The overhead costs budget

Having disposed of the direct costs of production in the form of materials and direct labour, we now come to the preparation of the estimates of the overhead costs of production. These costs are divided into the two

categories mentioned earlier. We are told that the fixed overheads ar
incurred in equal amounts quarterly, and we may calculate the tota
variable costs per quarter by multiplying the expected variable costs pe
unit by the planned quarterly output.

	1st quarter	2nd quarter	3rd quarter	4th quarter	Year
Production (Step 2)					
Product A (units)	1 250	1 000	1 250	1 500	5 00
Product B (units)	2 000	2 000	2 000	2 000	8 00
Variable costs					
Product A (£0.50 per unit)	£625	£500	£625	£750	£2 50
Product B (£1.00 per unit)	2 000	2 000	2 000	2 000	8 00
Total	2 625	2 500	2 625	2 750	10 50
Fixed costs					
Depreciation	2 500	2 500	2 500	2 500	10 00
Rates and insurance	1 000	1 000	1 000	1 000	4 00
Supervisory salaries	1 500	1 500	1 500	1 500	6 00
Total	5 000	5 000	5 000	5 000	20 00
Total overhead costs	£7 625	£7 500	£7 625	£7 750	£30 50

Step 7   The closing stock budget

The closing stock budget consists of an estimate of the value of planne
closing stock of raw materials and planned stocks of finished goods.
is arrived at by calculating the budgeted unit cost of stock and multiplyin
the result by the planned stock level.

1   Budgeted closing raw material stock

Raw material	**X**	**Y**	
Closing stock (units)	1 500	3 000	
Cost per unit	£0.50	£0.30	
Value of closing stock	£750	£900	
Total			£1 65

2   Budgeted finished goods stock

We are told that the accountant values the stock of finished goods o
a variable costing basis, and that the unit cost of Products A and B ha
been calculated to be £2.90 and £3.90 respectively. These values ar
applied to the budgeted closing stock figures as follows:

Product	**A**	**B**	
Closing stock (units)	750	1 000	
Cost per unit	£2.90	£3.90	
Value of closing stock	2 175	3 900	
Total			£6 07

Step 8 The selling and administrative expenses budget

Selling expenses:		
Salaries	£15 000	
Advertising	5 000	£20 000
Administrative expenses:		
Office salaries	18 000	
Stationery	1 000	
Other expenses	1 000	20 000
Total		£40 000

Step 9 The capital expenditure budget

We devoted Chapter 29 to a discussion of capital budgeting as an aspect of long-range planning. The annual capital expenditure budget must be seen, therefore, as a one-year slice of the long-term capital budget. The purpose of the annual capital expenditure is to make provision in the current budget for the planned capital expenditure in the current year. This information has been provided as follows:

Capital expenditure:	
1st quarter	£10 000
2nd	15 000
3rd	8 000
4th	20 000
Total for the year	£53 000

Step 10 The cost of goods sold budget

The reader will recall that all the previous budgets mentioned have dealt with the various aspects of the production process, in unit and value terms, including the expenses associated with selling and administration and the valuation of closing stock. The purpose of this budget is to bring all these items together to arrive at an estimate of the cost of the goods sold. This estimate will be used in the budgeted profit and loss account. It is compiled as follows:

Opening raw materials stock (balance sheet 31.12.19X0)	£1 650
add: Materials purchases (Step 4)	12 200
Raw materials available for production	13 850
less: Planned closing stock of raw materials (Step 7)	1 650
Cost of raw materials to be used in production	12 200
Cost of direct labour (Step 5)	23 000
Factory overhead costs (Step 6)	30 500
Cost of goods to be manufactured	65 700
add: Opening stock of finished goods (balance sheet 31.12.19X0)	6 025
	71 725
less: Planned closing stock of finished goods	6 075
Budgeted cost of goods sold	£65 650

Step 11   The cash budget

The cash budget consists of the estimates of cash receipts and cash payments arising from the planned levels of activities and use of resources which are considered in the various budgets we have examined. The cash budget is a complete survey of the financial implication of expenditure plans of both a current and a capital nature during the year. Moreover, by comparing the anticipated outflows of cash with the expected inflows, the cash budget enables management to anticipate any deficits so that the necessary financing arrangements may be made, and to decide upon a policy for placing any cash surpluses.

As its name implies, the cash budget deals only with 'cash' flows—it excludes expenses of a non-cash nature, such as depreciation. The cash budget is one of the last budgets to be prepared because it depends upon the other budgets which form part of the budgeting process.

	1st quarter	2nd quarter	3rd quarter	4th quarter	Total
	£	£	£	£	£
Opening cash balance	5 325	10 900	11 450	15 275	5 325
Receipts:					
Debtors (balance sheet)	20 000	—	—	—	20 000
50% of current sales (Step 1)	22 250	19 500	19 500	22 250	83 500
50% of previous quarter (Step 1)	—	22 250	19 500	19 500	61 250
Total receipts	42 250	41 750	39 000	41 750	164 750
Total cash available	47 575	52 650	50 450	57 025	170 075
Payments:					
Purchases (Step 4)	2 800	2 800	3 300	3 300	12 200
Direct labour (Step 5)	5 750	5 400	5 750	6 100	23 000
Factory overheads (Step 6) (excluding depreciation)	5 125	5 000	5 125	5 250	20 500
Selling and administrative expenses (Step 8)	10 000	10 000	10 000	10 000	40 000
Capital expenditure (Step 9)	10 000	15 000	8 000	20 000	53 000
Tax (balance sheet)	3 000	3 000	3 000	3 000	12 000
Total payments	36 675	41 200	35 175	47 650	160 700
Closing cash balances	10 900	11 450	15 275	9 375	9 375

Note that the cash budget is planned through time: for the time profile of cash receipts and cash payments is critical to the analysis of a firm's cash needs at any given point of time.

In practice, determining the level of cash which is required at any point in time may not be an easy matter. The dilemma of cash management lies in the conflict of liquidity with profitability. If a firm holds too little cash in relation to its financial obligations, a liquidity crisis may occur and may lead to the collapse of the business. On the other hand, if a firm holds too much cash it is losing the opportunity to employ that cash profitably in its activities. Idle cash balances usually earn very little profit for the firm. A reasonable balance must be found, therefore, between the financial objectives of maintaining a degree of liquidity and of minimizing the level of unproductive assets. The problem of ascertaining optimal balances of physical stocks has for long attracted the attention of operational researchers, and certain of the ideas which they have developed may have applicability as regards the holding of optimal cash balances. Essentially these relate the cost of holding cash with the cost of obtaining cash: total costs are minimized when the two are equated.

The effects of inflation on business enterprises are manifested in a growth in monetary terms, which may be in some direct relationship with the rate of inflation, while at the same time undergoing no growth at all in real terms, or even shrinking in profitability and value. The financing problem resulting from the monetary growth associated with inflation lies in the need to finance higher levels of stocks and debtors. If a firm is unable to finance the higher level of working capital required from adjustments to its prices and sales revenues, it must either borrow or reduce its level of activity. In effect, the rapid inflation which business firms experienced in the 1970s caused severe liquidity problems and many cases of insolvency.

The problems of cash budgeting under conditions of inflation require that special attention be given to the timing of cash inflows and outflows, which should be adjusted for changes in specific price changes affecting the firm. In this connection, adjustments to budget figures for changes in the general purchasing power of money will not reflect the impact of inflationary changes as they affect individual firms.

Among the special problems associated with budgeting under conditions of inflation is the loss of purchasing power exhibited by holdings of net monetary assets. This implies that losses in the value of net monetary items should be minimized in a manner consistent with the overall objectives of the firm by the reduction of holdings of net monetary assets. In effect, particular attention should be given to cash and debtor balances, and the impact of changes in selling prices on cash inflows should be carefully monitored. At the same time, gains resulting from the impact of inflation on creditor balances should encourage more aggressive borrowing policies.

Step 12   The budgeted profit and loss account

The purpose of the budgeted profit and loss account is to summarize and integrate all the operating budgets so as to measure the end result on the firm's profit.

	£
Sales (Step 1)	167 000
Cost of goods sold (Step 10)	65 650
Gross profit	101 350
Selling and administrative expenses (Step 8)	40 000
Net profit before tax	61 350
Tax (40%)	24 540
Net profit after tax	36 810

Step 13 The budgeted balance sheet

The final stage is the projection of the budgeted results on the firm's financial position at the end of the year. The following balance sheet reflects the changes in the composition of assets and liabilities as a result of the planned activities:

Budget balance sheet as at 31 December 19X1

Fixed assets	Cost	depreciation	
	£	£	£
Plant and machinery	303 000	40 000	263 000
Current assets	£	£	
Stocks:			
Raw materials	1 650		
Finished goods	6 075		
		7 725	
Debtors		22 250	
Cash		9 375	
		39 350	
less: Creditors: amounts falling due within one year:			
Creditors	5 000		
Tax	24 540		
		29 540	
Net current assets			9 810
Total assets *less* current liabilities			272 810
Capital and reserves			£
Called-up share capital			210 000
Profit and loss account			62 810
			272 810

Evaluating the budget proposals

As a means of comparing the planned performance for the coming year with the results of the curent year, the planned performance may be interpreted as follows:

Return on shareholders' equity: £36 810 ÷ £272 810 = 13.5% (previous 7.6%)

Return on capital employed: £36 810 ÷ £302 350 = 12.2% (previous 7.1%)

It is evident, therefore, that the firm is expected to make considerable improvements in the forthcoming period. If the budgeted results are considered to be satisfactory the final stage is a recommendation that the budget proposal be accepted by the Board of Directors as its policy, and as conforming with its view of the future.

Budgetary control

Planning alone does not necessarily ensure the realization of plans. It is also necessary to have control. This process necessitates the establishment of standards of performance which will act as day-to-day guidelines for the successful realization of the budget plan. In effect, the annual budget is subdivided into shorter periods for control purposes—into months and weeks. For these periods, the budget is compared with actual costs, the reasons for deviations are established and corrective action is taken if necessary.

As with budgetary planning, budgetary control is geared to the long-range plan. The continuous review of current progress indicates the extent to which the organization is moving towards the long-range plan.

Inflationary conditions place severe stress on budget planning and control systems. The phenomenon of rapidly changing costs distorts all the assumptions which may have shaped the budget. Thus, more importance should be attached to the latest forecasts and the analysis of changes which are occurring, if budgets are to be effective for both planning and control purposes. Once effective forecasting procedures have been established, the significant comparisons are no longer between planned and actual costs, but between forecasts, as follows:

1 Latest forecast *v.* previous forecast. This comparison becomes the prime action mover, and leads to the following questions:
    (a) Why has the forecast changed?
    (b) How does the latest forecast affect the net cash flow?
    (c) What actions should be taken to improve the situation?
2 Actual *v.* previous forecast. This comparison leads to the following questions being asked:
    (a) Was the previous forecast effective as regards identifying the events now facing the firm?
    (b) If not, why was the previous forecast wrong?
    (c) Are the errors in forecasting due to excessive pessimism or optimism and can these errors be corrected?

Summary

Budgetary planning is an activity which should be seen as being concerned with the implementation of a yearly segment of the long-range plan. The budget expresses this plan in financial terms in the light of current conditions.

Successful budgetary planning depends on a number of other factors, for example, a sound formal organizational structure which designates clearly areas of authority and responsibility, as well as an accounting information system which allows effective financial control.

A major problem in budgetary planning is the forecasting of sales. The budget plan itself consists of some thirteen stages as follows:

1 the sales budget
2 the production budget
3 the direct materials usage budget
4 The materials purchases budget
5 the budgeted direct labour costs
6 the overhead costs budget
7 the closing stock budget

8 the selling and administrative costs budget
9 the capital expenditure budget
10 the cost of goods sold budget
11 the cash budget
12 the budgeted profit and loss account
13 the budgeted balance sheet

Budget plans may be evaluated by means of financial ratios such as the return of shareholders' equity and the return on capital employed.

Questions

1 Describe the nature of budgetary planning.
2 Outline the organization of the budgeting process.
3 Outline the series of steps that are implied in orderly budgeting.
4 Discuss the importance of the sales forecast.
5 State the various methods used for forecasting sales.
6 State how budgeted performance may be expressed in terms of overall goals, and how budget proposals may be evaluated.
7 Describe a budgeting process.
8 Examine the relationship between the sales budget and the production budget.
9 Comment on the significance of the cash budget.
10 Examine the functional relationship between budgetary planning and budgetary control.

Problems

1 Dafa Ltd is a trading company dealing in a single product. It is preparing its annual budget for the twelve months ending 30 June 19X9. So far, the following budgets have been prepared:

	July– Sept.	Oct.– Dec.	Jan.– Mar.	April– June
Sales (at £3 per unit)	15 000	18 000	21 000	12 000
Purchases (at £2 per unit)	12 000	14 000	10 000	8 000
Sundry expenses				
Distribution	500	800	1 100	200
Administration	1 000	1 000	1 000	1 000
Depreciation	500	500	500	500
	2 000	2 300	2 600	1 700

Notes:
(a) Sales are made on one month's credit. It may be assumed that debtors outstanding on sales at the end of each quarter are equivalent to one-third of sales in that quarter, and that this is received the following quarter.

(b) All purchases are for cash. No credit is received.
(c) Distribution and administration expenses are paid in cash as incurred.
(d) The company has no expenses apart from those given.
(e) Opening balances at 1 July 19X8 are:

Debtors £3000
Cash £2000
Stock 1000 units

Required:

Complete Dafa Ltd's annual budget by preparing
(a) a debtors' budget
(b) a cash budget, *and*
(c) a stock budget to show the number of units in stock at the end of each quarter.

2 A small private company, after several years of unprofitable trading, was taken over by a new management on 31 December.
The accounts for the following year were summarized thus:

	£
Direct materials	78 000
Direct wages	31 200
Variable overheads	15 600
Fixed overheads	30 000
Profit	1 200
Sales	156 000

The balance sheet as at the end of the first twelve months of trading was as follows:

	£	£	£
Fixed assets			24 000
Current assets			
Stocks		26 000	
Debtors		26 000	
Cash		52 000	
less: Creditors: amounts falling due within one year			
Bank overdraft	26 500		
Creditors	19 500		
		46 000	
Net current assets			6 000
Total assets *less* current liabilities			30 000
Capital and reserves			£
Called up share capital			40 000
Profit and loss account			(10 000)
			30 000

The budgeted sales for the second year of trading are as follows:

	£
1st quarter	42 000
2nd quarter	45 000
3rd quarter	48 000
4th quarter	51 000

It is anticipated that the ratios of material consumption, direct wages and variable overheads to sales are unlikely to change; that the fixed overheads (incurred evenly during the year) will remain at £30 000 per annum; and that creditors can be held at three months' direct material usage. Both stocks and debtors can be maintained at two months' sales.

Bank interest and depreciation, the latter at 10 per cent per annum on fixed assets, are included in the overheads.

Required:
Prepare quarterly budgets for the second year of operation to indicate to management:
(a) Whether the results are likely to be satisfactory.
(b) Whether the overdraft facilities (which are normally limited to £25 000) are sufficient, or whether further capital must be introduced.

3   Jones is considering whether to open up his own wholesaling business. He makes the following estimates about the first six months' trading:

(a)	*Sales on credit*	● For first two months £50 000 per month.
		● Thereafter £80 000 per month.
		● One month's credit allowed to customers.
(b)	*Gross margin*	● The cost of goods bought for resale is expected to be 75 per cent of the selling price.
(c)	*Closing stock*	● £75 000.
(d)	*Purchases creditors at end*	● £50 000.
(e)	*Wages and salaries*	● Paid for period £40 000.
		● Owing at end of period £2500.
(f)	*Warehouse expenses*	● Cash paid for rent, rates, lighting, heating etc. £50 000.
		● In addition £5500 of warehouse expenses will be owing at end of six months.
		● Of the cash paid, however, £3500 will be rent and rates paid in advance.
(g)	*Furniture, fixtures and fittings*	● Amounting to £50 000 to be purchased on opening of business and will be subject to 10 per cent p.a. depreciation.
(h)	*Delivery vehicles*	● Three vans costing £2000 each will be purchased at once and will be subject to 25 per cent p.a. depreciation.
(i)	*Loan interest*	● Long-term loans can be raised at an interest rate of 10 per cent p.a.
(j)	*Jones*	● Expects to draw from the business accounts his own 'wages' at a rate of £300 per month.

Required:
(a) A budgeted cash account for the period on the basis of the above information (see part (c) below).
(b) Budgeted profit and loss account for the period and balance sheet as at the end on the basis of the above information (see part (c) below).
(c) Advise Jones as to how much capital should be introduced initially into the business. Jones, however, has only £50 000 available as capital. Complete the accounts on the assumption that he accepts your advice.
(d) Jones asks you whether the business appears to be a worthwhile one. Give a *brief* reply to this question.

Chapter 31

Cost–volume–profit analysis

Much of the discussion in the previous three chapters was concerned with the importance of the distinction between the long term and the short term for decision making, and consequently of the nature of the accounting problem of providing relevant information for decisions affecting different time periods.

The essential qualitative difference between the long term and the short term is that the long term may be defined as planning for change, whereas the short term implies adapting to change. In this sense, the firm's resources may be planned in the long term to take advantage of changing opportunities in such a way that not only its structure may be altered but its objectives as well. In the short term, however, the firm's output capacity is fixed, so that the firm's freedom of action is limited.

Short-term planning, which is the subject of this chapter, considers the most desirable course of action to take to achieve a planned profit given that the firm's output range is relatively fixed. Cost–volume–profit analysis is an important tool in short-term planning for it explores the interrelationship which exists between the four principal variables— cost, revenue, volume of output and profit. In planning its short-term strategy management will require to know what will be the effect of changing one or more of these variables, and the effect of this change on profit.

Applications of cost–volume–profit (c–v–p) analysis

Cost–volume–profit analysis lies at the centre of short-term profit planning because it has a wider application to a whole series of decision problems. In view of the relationship between costs and volume of output, c–v–p is helpful in establishing a pricing strategy. C–v–p is also relevant to the selection of the best sales mix, where a firm produces several different products. In such a case, it is essential to select the most profitable combination of the different products having regard to their costs of production and the prices which are obtainable. A decision to produce a sales mix which is less profitable may be made, for example, in order to penetrate a market or to establish a stronger position in a particular market from a sales point of view, and in such a case c–v–p will enable management to assess the cost of that strategy in terms of lost profit. Other applications include the study of product alternatives, the acceptance of special orders, selecting channels of distribution, the strategy for entering a foreign market and changing plant layout.

C–v–p analysis lays emphasis on cost behaviour patterns through different volumes of output as a guide to the selection of profit targets and the adoption of an appropriate pricing policy. By uniting the behaviour of all four variables together in one short-term model, c–v–p analysis provides management with a sweeping overview of the planning process.

Cost analysis and profit planning

The response of cost to a variety of influences is invaluable to management decision making. As we saw in Chapter 27, some costs are constant, or fixed, in a given time-span, whereas other costs vary. Cost–volume–profit analysis focuses on the distinction between 'fixed' and 'variable' costs: the former being defined for this purpose as the costs which do not change over a range of output, and the latter being those which change directly with output.

C–v–p analysis requires that the fixed and variable elements be segregated and calculated so that all costs may be divided into simply fixed and variable costs.

One of the most important uses of the distinction between fixed and variable cost lies in the analysis of these costs through different levels of production.

Example

Unit sales	40 000 Total	40 000 Unit	50 000 Total	50 000 Unit
		£		£
Revenue	400 000	10.0	500 000	10.0
Variable costs	160 000	4.0	200 000	4.0
Contribution margin	240 000	6.0	300 000	6.0
Fixed costs	150 000	3.8	150 000	3.0
Net profit	90 000	2.2	150 000	3.0

Duofold Ltd produces an article which it sells for £10. Fixed costs of production are £150 000 per year, and variable costs are £4 per unit. The present yearly volume of output is 40 000 units, but could be increased to 50 000.

Problem: What will be the effect on total costs of the projected increase in output, and the impact of profit?

The analysis shows that total variable costs increase proportionally with output while unit variable costs are constant. Total fixed costs, however, remain constant at both levels of output so that unit fixed costs fall as output rises and vice versa. It is because unit fixed costs are falling that total unit costs are less for an output of 50 000 units than for one of 40 000 units.

Fig. 5.10

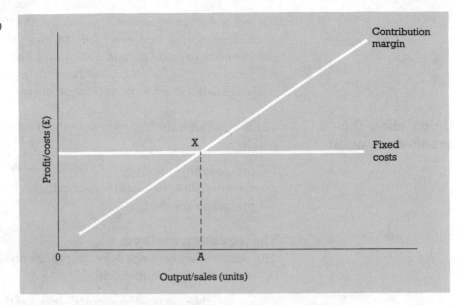

If we assume that selling prices remain unaltered, cost savings themselves will lead to increased profitability. The contribution margin is an important concept in cost-profit analysis. As may be seen from the example above, the contribution margin is calculated by deducting the variable costs from revenue. It is the first stage in calculating the net profit and measures the profit which is available to cover fixed costs. Since fixed costs are incurred irrespective of sales, a firm will make a loss if the contribution margin is insufficient to cover fixed costs. At low levels of output the firm will make a loss because fixed costs are greater than the contribution margin. As output increases, so does the contribution margin which will ultimately equal and then exceed fixed costs. The relation between fixed cost and the contribution margin may be illustrated as in Fig. 5.10. The critical point at which the contribution margin is equal to fixed costs is known as the break-even point which indicates that level of output (OA) at which the firm makes zero profits, that is, where total costs are equal to total revenues.

Break-even analysis

Break-even analysis focuses on the measurement of the break-even point. Before we attempt any calculations, it is necessary to make certain assumptions about the behaviour of costs and revenues. Thus, we assume that costs and revenue patterns have been reliably determined and that they are linear over the range of output which is being analysed. These assumptions also imply that costs may be resolved without difficulty into fixed and variable costs; that fixed costs will remain constant, that variable costs will vary proportionally with volume of output; and that all other factors will remain constant, that is, that selling prices will remain unchanged, that the methods and the efficiency of production will not be altered and that volume is the only factor affecting costs. It is because these assumptions are difficult to maintain in a 'real life' situation that break-even analysis cannot pretend to be anything but a rough guide.

Its real value to management lies in the fact that it highlights the interrelationships between the factors affecting profits, allowing management to make certain assumptions about these factors and seeing the likely effects of changes in these assumptions. Hence, break-even analysis is useful as a management decision model.

Calculating the break-even point

There are three methods commonly employed in solving break-even problems:

1   the equation method;
2   the contribution margin method;
3   the graph method.

The equation method

The relationship between sales, variable and fixed costs and profits may be expressed as an equation:

sales = variable costs + fixed costs + net profit

Example

Take the values given in the previous example, that is, that the unit sale price is £10, variable costs are £4 per unit and fixed costs £150 000 per year.

Problem 1   How many units must be produced to break even?

Analysis Let x be the number of units required. Our equation will be:

$$£10x = £4x + £150\ 000 + £0$$
$$\text{and } £10x - £4x = £150\ 000 + £0$$

so that

$$x = \frac{£150\ 000}{6}$$

$$= \underline{25\ 000\ \text{units}}$$

Problem 2   Alternatively, the problem may be calculating the sales revenue required to break even.

Analysis   Since net profit is zero, our formula remains:

sales = variable costs + fixed costs

Let the unknown level of sales revenue be x, and knowing that variable costs are four-tenths of x, we can substitute:

$$x = \tfrac{4}{10}x + £150\ 000$$
$$\text{and } x - \tfrac{4}{10}x = £150\ 000$$
$$\tfrac{6}{10}x = £150\ 000$$
$$x = \underline{£250\ 000}$$

The break-even sales revenue can be equally derived from the break-even volume of sales (25 000 units at £10 = £250 000), but the calculations are intended to show that the results can be calculated independently.

The contribution margin method

This method makes use of the variable profit or contribution margin per unit of output which is required to cover fixed costs.

Problem 1   On the basis that the unit sale price is £10, that the variable costs are £4 per unit and that fixed costs total £150 000 a year, calculate the break-even volume of sales.

Analysis   Let x be the number of units required. We know that the unit contribution margin is the difference between unit sale price and unit variable costs. Our formula is:

$$x = \frac{\text{fixed costs} + \text{net profit}}{\text{unit contribution margin}}$$

$$x = \frac{£150\ 000 + 0}{(£10 - £4)}$$

$$= \frac{150\ 000}{6}$$

$$= \underline{25\ 000\ \text{units}}$$

Problem 2   Using the same values calculate the break-even sales revenue.

Analysis   In this case, we make use of the contribution margin ratio to calculate the sales revenue required to cover fixed costs. The contribution margin ratio is:

$$\frac{\text{unit contribution margin}}{\text{revenue per unit}}\%$$

Our formula may be expressed as follows:

$$x = \frac{\text{fixed costs} + \text{net profit}}{\text{contribution margin ratio}}$$

Substituting the given values we have:

$$x = \frac{150\ 000 + 0}{60\%}$$

$$= \underline{£250\ 000}$$

Alternatively, the break-even revenue may be found from the following formula:

$$x = \frac{\text{fixed costs} + \text{net profit}}{1 - \dfrac{\text{total variable costs}}{\text{total sales revenue}}}$$

$$= 1 - \frac{\dfrac{150\ 000}{160\ 000}}{400\ 000}$$

$$= \underline{\underline{£250\ 000}}$$

It is clear that both the equation method and the contribution margin method can be applied to profit planning by the substitution of the net profit figure, which for the purpose of our analysis of the break-even point we have taken to be zero.

The graph method

This method involves using what is usually called a break-even chart. This description is not very satisfactory because it gives undue emphasis to the break-even point whereas other points on the graph are just as important.

A break-even chart is easy to compile, but the accuracy of the readings will depend on the accuracy with which the data are plotted. The output or sales in units may be drawn on the horizontal axis and the vertical axis is used to depict money values.

Method Using the values given for the previous examples, the stages in compiling the break-even chart are as follows:

1 Using suitable graph paper, draw a horizontal axis to measure total output in units (50 000 units). Draw a vertical axis representing this output at its selling price of £10 per unit (£500 000).
2 Draw the variable-cost curve as a straight line from zero to £200 000 at 50 000 units of output (50 000 at £4).
3 Draw the fixed-cost curve parallel to the variable-cost curve but £150 000 higher, so that total costs including variable costs will be represented by the area below this curve.
4 Insert the total revenue curve from zero to £500 000 at 50 000 units.

Figure 5.11 vividly depicts the relationship between costs, revenues, volume of output and resultant profit. The area between the revenue curve and the variable cost curve represents the contribution to fixed costs and profit at each level of output. The point at which the revenue curve crosses the total cost curve is the break-even point. As output expands from zero, fixed costs are gradually recovered until the break-even point, and thereafter each unit of output contributes to profit.

The excess by which actual sales exceed break-even sales amounts to £250 000, so that sales could be reduced by £250 000 before losses start to be incurred. This excess is known as the margin of safety. The margin of safety ratio is the percentage by which sales revenue may fall before a loss is incurred and is expressed as follows:

$$\text{margin of safety ratio} = \frac{\text{margin of safety revenue}}{\text{actual sales}}$$

Fig. 5.11

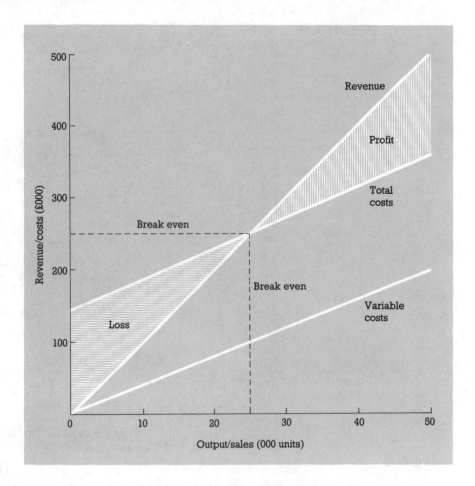

Hence, in the example given, the margin of safety ratio is

$$\frac{£250\ 000}{£500\ 000}, \text{ i.e. } 50\%$$

Clearly, the higher the margin of safety ratio, the safer the firm's position.

An alternative way of constructing the break-even chart is as in Fig. 5.12. The disadvantage of this form of presentation is that unlike Fig. 5.11, it does not emphasize the importance of the contribution margin to fixed costs.

The profit–volume chart

The profit–volume chart is a special type of break-even chart. It is concerned with analysing profit and loss at different levels of activity. As in the break-even chart, the horizontal axis is used to measure the volume of output or sales in units, but the vertical axis is employed to measure the profit or loss at any given level of output or sales.

Using the same information as above, Fig. 5.13 shows the profit–volume chart. Only three items are needed to plot this chart—the fixed costs, DC, which are £150 000, and which must be recovered before a profit is made, the break-even point, E, which represents sales

Fig. 5.12

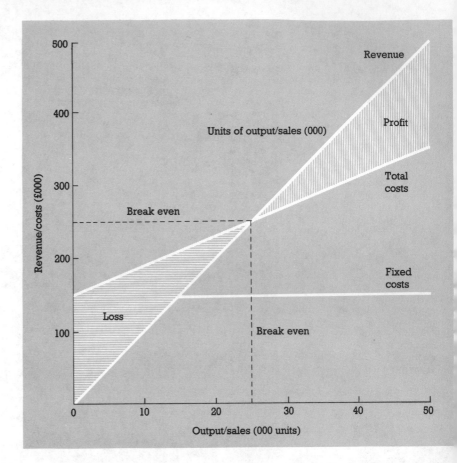

Fig. 5.13

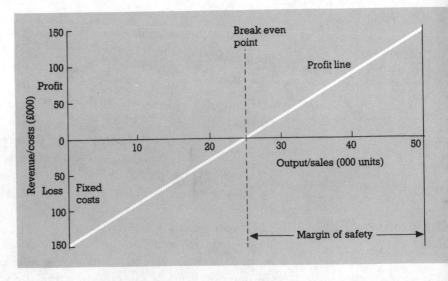

of £250 000 necessary to cover fixed costs, and the profit at an assumed
level of activity (which in this case is 50 000 units yielding a profit of
£150 000).

The profit–volume chart (Fig. 5.13) is simply the conventional break-
even chart rearranged to show changes in profit or loss which occur

through volume changes either of sales or of output. It is less detailed since it does not show separate curves for costs and revenues, but its virtue lies in the fact that it reduces any changes down to two key elements—volume and profit. For this reason, the volume–profit chart is useful for illustrating the results of different management decisions.

Insofar as the volume–profit chart focuses simply on the relationship between volume and profit, it allows for an extended analysis of this relationship. Thus, the slope of the curve DA indicates the contribution margin ratio, which may be measured by AB/BE or DC/CE—either calculation giving the same results in this case (60 per cent).

The slope of the curve DA also indicates the rate at which changes in volume assist in the recovery of fixed costs and affect profit: the greater the slope the greater will be the effect of changes in volume on profits. Equally, the steeper the slope of the profit curve the quicker will the margin of safety be eroded and the break-even point reached as the volume of output or sales falls, as may be seen from the three cases in Fig. 5.14.

Fig. 5.14

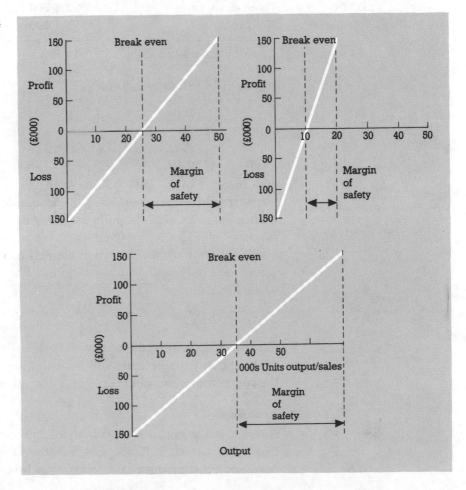

Profit planning through change

Profit planning is related to a consideration of four factors—fixed costs, variable costs, selling price and sales volume. Any change in one or several of these factors will affect planning profit. Cost–volume–profit analysis enables management to consider the effects of these changes.

Changes in fixed costs

Assuming that all other factors remain unchanged, a change in fixed costs will affect only the break-even point.

Example

The consequential effect of an increase of £15 000 in head office costs on the break-even level is as follows:

	Original	After increase in fixed costs
	£	£
Sales	500 000	500 000
Variable costs	200 000	200 000
Contribution margin	300 000	300 000
Fixed costs	150 000	165 000
Net profit	150 000	135 000
Contribution margin ratio	60%	60%

The new break-even point is:

$$\frac{\text{fixed costs}}{\text{unit contribution margin}} = \frac{165\ 000}{£6} = 27\ 500 \text{ units}$$

Hence, a 10 per cent increase in fixed costs has resulted in a 10 per cent increase in the sales volume (and sales revenue) required to break even from 25 000 units (£250 000) to 27 500 units (£275 000). Thus, additional sales of 2500 units at £10 a unit are required to cover an increase of £15 000 in fixed costs. It should be noted that as the contribution margin ratio has remained constant, the change in fixed costs is the only factor affecting profit. The change may be illustrated as in Fig. 5.15.

Changes in variable costs

A change in variable costs will have the immediate effect of changing the contribution margin ratio, and consequently the break-even point.

Example

It is decided to improve the quality of a product by incorporating more expensive materials. As a result, variable costs are increased by 10 per cent, and the consequential effects on the break-even level are as follows:

Fig. 5.15

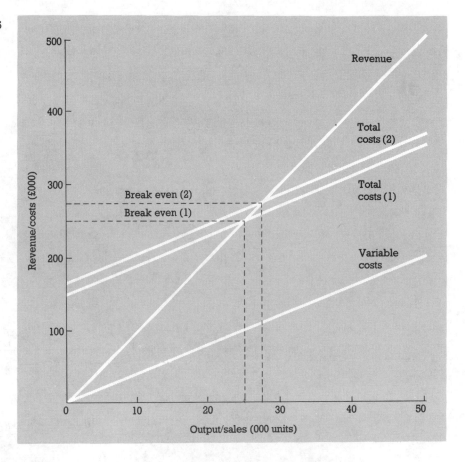

	Original	After increase in variable costs
	£	£
Sales	500 000	500 000
Variable costs	200 000	220 000
Contribution margin	300 000	280 000
Fixed costs	150 000	150 000
Net profit	150 000	130 000
Contribution margin ratio	60%	56%

The new break-even point will be:

$$\frac{\text{fixed costs}}{\text{contribution margin per unit}} = \frac{£150\ 000}{5.6} = 26\ 786 \text{ units.}$$

Note that whereas a 10 per cent increase in fixed costs led to a 10 per cent increase in the sales volume (and sales revenue) required to break even in this instance, a 10 per cent increase in variable costs has led to a proportionately smaller increase in the sales volume required to break even, that is, 1786 units of 7.14 per cent. We may illustrate the change as in Fig. 5.16.

Fig. 5.16

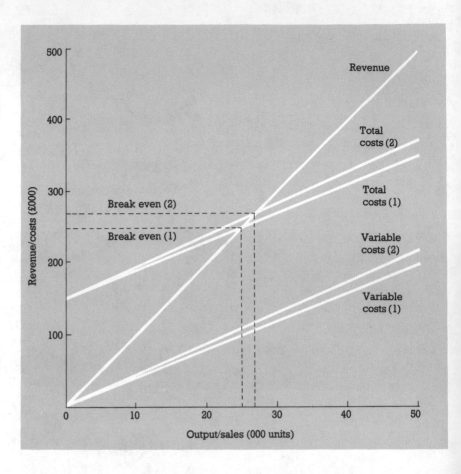

Changes in selling price

Successful profit planning through changes in selling prices depends upon management knowing how the market will react to these price changes. If the price is reduced will customers buy greater quantities of the product so as to increase the total revenue derived from sales? In other words it is important to know the effect upon total revenue of changes in selling prices. This effect is measured through the price elasticity of demand.

Let us assume that a 10 per cent increase in selling price will lead to a 10 per cent reduction in the volume of sales. Assuming all other factors remain constant, the result of the price change will be as follows:

	Original	After increase in selling price
Sales in units	50 000	45 000
Sales revenue	£500 000	£495 000 (45 000 @ £11)
Variable costs	200 000	180 000 (45 000 @ £4)
Contribution margin	300 000	315 000
Fixed costs	150 000	150 000
Net profit	150 000	165 000
Contribution margin ratio	60%	63.6%

The break-even point will, as a result, be lowered from 25 000 units to 21 429 units as follows:

$$\frac{\text{fixed costs}}{\text{contribution margin per unit}} = \frac{£150\ 000}{£7} = 21\ 429 \text{ units}$$

Thus, a 10 per cent increase in the selling price has led to a much greater adjustment in the sales volume required to break even, that is, 3571/25 000 or 14.3 per cent. We have assumed, however, that the elasticity of demand for the product was unity, that is, that a percentage alteration in the price would lead to the same proportionate alteration in the volume of sales. In most situations this would be an unreal assumption to make, so that it becomes crucial to management to know the slope of the demand curve for the commodity, that is, the elasticity of demand if their analysis of the impact of a price change on the net profit is to be valid. We may compare the three different results that would be obtained by the same price change under three different demand conditions for the commodity as follows:

1 Where the demand is *elastic*, i.e., elasticity is greater than unity. In this case we assume that a 10 per cent increase in selling price will lead to a 20 per cent reduction in sales.
2 Where the elasticity of demand is unity. In this case we assume, as in the example above that a 10 per cent increase in selling price will lead to a 10 per cent reduction in sales.
3 Where demand is inelastic. We assume a 10 per cent increase in selling price will lead to a 5 per cent reduction in sales.

This example illustrates the importance to management of knowing the nature of the demand for their products. In the example, where demand is elastic, we witness a sharp fall in net profit from the original £150 000 to £130 000. On the other hand, a unitary or inelastic demand schedule results in an increase in net profit.

	Elastic	Unity	Inelastic
Sales units	40 000	45 000	47 500
Sales revenue (£11)	£440 000	£495 000	£522 500
Variable costs (£4)	160 000	180 000	190 000
Contribution margin	280 000	315 000	332 500
Fixed costs	150 000	150 000	150 000
Net profit	£130 000	£165 000	£182 500

The sales mix

We mentioned at the beginning of this chapter that c–v–p was important to short-term profit planning, and that it was helpful also to the solution of other types of managerial problems. One such problem is that of selecting the best sales mix. So far in our discussion, we have assumed that the firm had only one product so that profit planning involved a consideration of only four factors, that is, fixed and variable costs, selling price and sales volume. Most firms, however, either produce or sell more than one product and management has to decide in what combination these products ought to be made or sold. It may be possible, for example, that by altering the existing sales mix by selling proportionately more of the product which has the highest contribution margin, the overall contribution margin and the break-even point may be improved.

Example

Assume that Maximix Ltd has data concerning the three products which it markets as follows:

Product	A	B	C	Total
	£	£	£	£
Sales	100 000	100 000	50 000	250 000
Variable costs	50 000	30 000	20 000	100 000
Contribution margin	50 000	70 000	30 000	150 000
Fixed costs				150 000
Net profit				Nil
Contribution margin ratio	50%	70%	60%	60%

If the firm could switch its sales so as to sell more of product B, which has a higher contribution margin ratio than the other two, it would succeed in improving its profitability. At the present moment, the firm is just breaking even. Let us assume that it maintains the present total sales of £250 000, but that the sales mix is altered as shown below:

Product	A	B	C	Total
	£	£	£	£
Sales	50 000	175 000	25 000	250 000
Variable costs	25 000	52 500	10 000	87 500
Contribution margin	25 000	122 500	15 000	162 500
Fixed costs				150 000
Net profit				12 500
Contribution margin ratio	50%	70%	60%	65%

Hence the new product mix has raised the contribution margin ratio by 5 per cent, leading to a profit of £12 500 and a lowering of the break-even point from £250 000 to £230 769 as follows:

$$\frac{\text{Fixed costs}}{\text{Contribution margin ratio}} = \frac{£150\ 000}{65\%} = £230\ 769$$

The effect of the change in the product mix may be depicted graphically as in Fig. 5.17.

Fig. 5.17

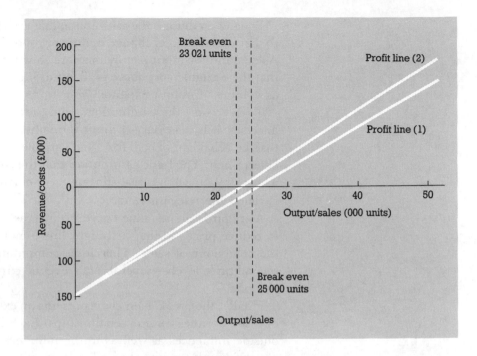

Cost–volume–profit analysis: some limitations

C–v–p analysis, though it is a very useful tool for decision making, is based upon certain assumptions which can rarely be completely realized in practice. Hence the fragility of these assumptions places limits on the reliability of c–v–p analysis as a tool in decision making. For example, it is assumed that fixed costs are constant, and that both the variable cost and the revenue curves are linear over the relevant volume of output. It is also assumed that volume is the only factor affecting costs, and that both the price of cost factors and of the product produced or sold remains unaffected by changes in the volume of output.

All these assumptions may be challenged. Fixed costs may not remain constant over the entire output range considered in the analysis, that being particularly true if the volume range considered is fairly extensive. Fixed costs may indeed be constant over a band of output, but then will rise sharply and remain constant for another stage, as indicated in Fig. 5.18.

Fig. 5.18

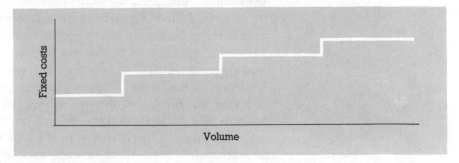

Equally doubtful is the assumption that the variable cost curve is linear so that variable costs change in direct proportion to changes in volume. As demand for input factors increase so will their price, with the effect that the variable-cost curve is likely to increase proportionately faster as volume of output expands.

To overcome these limitations, and to retain the usefulness of c–v–p analysis, it is necessary to limit the volume range to be examined so that the behaviour of both fixed and variable costs may be more accurately determined. The basic assumption that the cost–volume relationship is a linear relationship is realistic only over narrow ranges of output which is called the relevant range.

As regards the revenue curve, to increase sales it may be necessary to reduce price, so that a straight line is not an accurate portrayal of the behaviour of sales. Therefore, computations are often needed at several price levels—several total-revenue curves are needed instead of just one.

Finally, the break-even chart presents an extremely simplified picture of cost–revenue–volume relationships. Each of these three is subject to outside influences as well as to the influence of the other two. Above all, the break-even analysis should be viewed as a guide to decision making, not a substitute for judgement and common sense.

Despite its limitations, the real usefulness of c–v–p is that it enriches the understanding of the relationship between costs, volume and prices as factors affecting profit, enabling management to make assumptions which will assist the decision-making process in the short-run planning period.

Summary

In the short run, the firm's output is fixed, so that its freedom of action is limited in this respect. Given this condition, short-range planning considers the most desirable action to take to achieve a planned profit. Cost–volume–profit analysis (c–v–p) has an important role to play in short-run planning by providing an insight into the relationships between costs, volume of output, revenue and profit. In particular, c–v–p analysis highlights the significance of the distinction between fixed and variable costs and the behaviour of these two types of costs through changes in the volume of output.

C–v–p analysis makes an important contribution to short-run profit planning by providing an understanding of the conditions required to break even. It does not assist in the discovery of the conditions required to maximize profits, in sharp contrast to economic theory which pays particular attention to this aspect of profit planning. Its advantage to management is that it is a method which is operationally useful. Moreover, it deals with the most important consideration—the avoidance of losses. In this sense, c–v–p analysis reflects the assumption of risk analysis that decision makers are risk-averse.

C–v–p analysis has limitations as a result of the assumptions that it incorporates. Many of these assumptions may be challenged, for example, the linearity of the behaviour of costs and revenues over a range of output. Although some of the criticism of c–v–p analysis may be partially refuted, its real usefulness lies in the manner in which it enriches the understanding of the relationship between cost, volume of output and revenue for profit planning purposes in the short run, thereby assisting management in the making of short-run profit-planning decisions.

<table>
<tr><td>**Questions**</td><td>1</td><td>Explain briefly the significance of the terms 'long-term' and 'short-term' in the context of planning and control.</td></tr>
</table>

Questions

1 Explain briefly the significance of the terms 'long-term' and 'short-term' in the context of planning and control.
2 Give some examples of the type of information that is relevant to long-term planning.
3 What variables are relevant to short-term planning?
4 Explain what is meant by c–v–p analysis.
5 Describe how c–v–p analysis is used in profit planning.
6 What is the significance of the break-even point?
7 Describe various ways in which the break-even point may be calculated.
8 What is a profit–volume chart?
9 List a number of possible ways in which short-term profitability may be improved.
1 0 What difficulties are implied in using c–v–p analysis for short-term decision making?

Problems

1 The Carbon Ink Company's profit statement for the preceding year is presented below. Except as noted, the cost and sales relationship for the coming year is expected to follow the same pattern as in the preceding year.

	£
Sales (2 000 000 bottles at £0.25)	500 000
Variable costs	300 000
Fixed costs	100 000
Total costs	400 000
Profit	100 000

Required:
(a) What is the break-even point in sales value and units?
(b) An extension to the factory will add £50 000 to the fixed costs and increase production capacity by 60 per cent. How many bottles would have to be sold after the extension to break even?
(c) The management of the company feels that it should earn at least £10 000 on the new investment. What sales volume is required to enable the company to maintain existing profits and earn the minimum required on the new investment?
(d) If the factory operates at full capacity after extension, what profit will be earned?
(e) What are the weaknesses in the use of break-even analysis?

2 An accountant and an economist were having an argument. The economist accused the accountant of using a naive, over-simplified model of cost–volume–profit relationships by assuming linear patterns in variable costs. Since costs do not behave in this simplistic way, the accountant, argued the economist, should be more realistic in his assumptions.

The accountant countered by saying that the economist was just as bad, if not worse, because most economic models ignore variations in fixed costs. Although the accountant agreed that in the long run all costs are variable, a firm had to make decisions in the short run in order to survive. And, argued the accountant, in the short run some costs are definitely fixed.

The economist was becoming somewhat agitated and accused the accountant of not using a dynamic analysis for solving business problems. The economist claimed, for example, that the static nature of cost–volume–profit analysis often produced misleading information. The accountant thought this a case of the pot calling the kettle black, and accused the economist of using unrealistic models which never exist in practice.

Required:

Both men turn to you for support; what would be your reply? Use the case below to illustrate your answer.

The Malplaquet Company cans fresh orange juice. The company's budget at 80 per cent capacity for 19X8 was as follows:

	£
Sales	250 000
Cost of oranges and other materials used	60 000
Cost of cans	30 000
Direct labour	60 000
Manufacturing expenses:	
Fixed	20 000
Variable	30 000
Administration, selling and other indirect expenses:	
Fixed	10 800
Variable	8 000

The directors of the company anticipate the following in costs during 19X9:

Price of oranges and other materials used	5% increase
Price of cans	No change
Rates for direct labour	10% increase
Manufacturing expenses: fixed	£800 decrease
Administration, selling and other indirect expenses:	
Fixed	No change

Manufacturing variable expenses will maintain the same ratio to wages paid, and administration, selling and other indirect variable expenses will vary only with quantity sold.

In 19X9 sales quantity and selling price are expected to remain constant.

Chapter 32

Variable costing

The cost–volume–profit relationships considered in the preceding chapter emphasize the usefulness of variable cost data for profit planning purposes. It indicates the significance of a knowledge of cost behaviour for management decision making. Nevertheless, there is considerable controversy about the use of the variable costing system for product costing and profit determination purposes. In effect, the use of product costs based on variable cost only, has significant effects on the valuation of stock, and implicitly on the measurement of periodic profit. The purpose of this chapter is to examine the implication of variable costing as compared to the conventional method of product costing based on full or absorption costing.

The case for variable costing for stock valuation

As we saw in Part 2, periodic profit measurement and the matching principle constitute the core of financial accounting. According to SSAP 2 'Disclosure of Accounting Policies', 'revenues and costs are matched with one another so far as their relationship can be established or justifiably assumed.'

Different methods of matching

The logic behind the matching principle springs from a desire to provide a rule which will secure uniformity in the preparation of profit and loss accounts. Investors require uniformity in accounting practices if they are to be able to evaluate the performance of one firm against another. As far as the matching principle is concerned the problem is to develop suitable methods for matching costs to revenues. Two such methods have been developed: product costing and period costing.

Product costing

Accountants long ago recognized the product itself as a convenient vehicle for matching costs with revenues. Product costing involves attaching all costs, whether direct or overhead costs, to the product. In measuring the cost of goods produced and sold to be matched against revenues from sales, product costing requires the inclusion of those manufacturing costs which are incurred irrespective of production. Thus, costs such as rent, insurance and rates which are incurred on a time basis rather than on the rate of production are recovered against the units produced.

The proponents of product costing as the only method of matching costs to revenues argue that all manufacturing costs are product costs, and that there is no such thing as a period cost because 'ideally all costs incurred should be viewed as absolutely clinging to definite items of goods sold or services rendered. . . . The ideal is to match costs incurred with the efforts attributable to or significantly related to such costs' (Paton and Littleton, 1940). They argue, therefore, that manufacturing costs are incurred solely to make possible the creation of a product.

Period costing

Period costing recognizes that certain costs are incurred on a time basis, and that the benefit derived from these costs is not affected by the actual level of production during a period of time. Since rent, insurance and salaries are items which are incurred on a time basis, their deteriorating effect on a firm's cash resources are not halted by the lack of revenue.

Period costing is a method of costing which conflicts with the traditional view of costing expressed by product costing, and has given rise to the variable or marginal costing controversy. The issue between the two schools of thought revolves round the question of whether fixed manufacturing costs, that is those costs incurred irrespective of production, should be charged as the costs of the product or charged against the revenue of the period. According to the supporters of product costing, who employ absorption or full costing, all manufacturing costs should be absorbed by the product. Variable costing assigns only the variable costs, that is the costs which vary with the level of production, to the products, and fixed manufacturing costs are written off each year as period costs.

One advantage of variable costing over absorption costing which is often advanced by its advocates is its superiority for management decision making. Because the distinction between fixed and variable costs is 'built into' the accounting system, it assists profit planning, product pricing and control. However, the controversy which surrounds variable costing is whether or not it should be used for external reporting. The advocates of absorption costing argue that figures prepared on a variable costing basis for the use of management should be adjusted to an absorption costing basis before they are released to external users.

Both management and investors are concerned primarily with the future outcome of present decisions. Accountants who advocate the use of absorption costing for external financial statements deprive investors of a useful, analytical device and make the task of interpreting the results more difficult.

Variable costing emphasizes the behaviour of fixed and variable costs, which is of utmost importance to investors. Variable costing helps to predict cash flows in relation to volume changes; the isolation of fixed costs in the profit statement permits more accurate forecasts of claims on cash in meeting current outlays on fixed expenses. Variable costing also helps to correlate fluctuations in cash flows with fluctuations in sales volume.

We argued earlier that management should not receive the credit for increasing the net worth of business before the critical event has occurred, and we conceded that in almost every case, the sale was the critical event. Since profit should vary with a company's performance (which really means accomplishing the critical event) where profit is related to sales, it is logical that there should be a direct relationship between the two. Variable costing should therefore be used in these cases. Absorption costing, being based on the product concept, does not provide this relationship between profit and sales, because under this method, profit variation is partly related to production.

Variable costing also permits more accurate profit forecasts because net profit will have a direct relationship with sales, instead of confusing the picture with the impact of the two activities of producing and selling.

The treatment of overheads

SSAP 9 'Stocks and Work in Progress' restated the traditional accounting view that the aim should be to match costs and revenues 'in the year in which revenue arises rather than the year in which cost is incurred', cost being defined for this purpose as including 'all related overheads, even though some of these may accrue on a time basis'.

Absorption and variable costing compared

Let us assume the following basic data:

Total sales and production over 4 years (500 units per year)	2000 units
Direct material costs per unit	£1
Direct labour costs per unit	£1
Variable overhead costs per unit	£0.5
Fixed overhead costs	£1000 p.a.
Sales price per unit	£6

Let us further assume that the volume of sales and of production are constant in time.

The volume of production, sales and the level of stocks in units is as follows:

Year	1	2	3	4	Total
Opening stock (units)	40	40	40	40	40
Production (units)	500	500	500	500	2 000
Sales (units)	500	500	500	500	2 000
Closing stock (units)	40	40	40	40	40

The results under the two forms of costing would appear as follows:

Year	1	2	3	4	Total
Variable costing	£	£	£	£	£
Sales	3 000	3 000	3 000	3 000	12 000
Cost of goods produced	1 250	1 250	1 250	1 250	5 000
add: Opening stock	100	100	100	100	100
Available for sale	1 350	1 350	1 350	1 350	5 100
less: Closing stock	100	100	100	100	100
Cost of goods sold	1 250	1 250	1 250	1 250	5 000
Contribution margin	1 750	1 750	1 750	1 750	7 000
Fixed overheads	1 000	1 000	1 000	1 000	4 000
Net profit	750	750	750	750	3 000
Absorption costing	£	£	£	£	£
Sales	3 000	3 000	3 000	3 000	12 000
Cost of goods produced	2 250	2 250	2 250	2 250	9 000
add: Opening stock	180	180	180	180	180
Available for sale	2 430	2 430	2 430	2 430	9 180
less: Closing stock	180	180	180	180	180
Cost of goods sold	2 250	2 250	2 250	2 250	9 000
Net profit	750	750	750	750	3 000

The above example illustrates the effects on profits of using absorption and variable costing methods for a firm in which everything stayed exactly the same in four consecutive years. Therefore, sales and levels of production are constant in each period and both opening and closing stocks remain unchanged. Under these conditions profit figures for each year remain the same under both methods of calculating profit.

In reality, the effect on production of shortages of materials, or the effect on sales of credit squeezes and changes in indirect taxation distorts the relationship between sales and production and stock levels act as buffers. Stock levels, therefore, are not stable; they are in fact very volatile. Moreover, modern methods of production require a constant rate of production, not only to maintain the efficiency of operations but also to prevent lay-offs and so assist in the preservation of good industrial relations. Flexible stock level standards are normally established for the purpose of planning for a reasonably uniform level of production.

We shall now examine the different results obtained under variable and absorption costing under the following circumstances:

1 where sales fluctuate but production remains constant
2 where sales are constant but production fluctuates.

Results where sales fluctuate but production is constant

As soon as the rate of sales begins to differ from the rate of production the use of different methods of allocating overheads to costs of production starts to affect profit calculations. Let us take the figures given in the earlier example, but keeping the level of production constant against varying levels of sales as follows:

Year	1	2	3	4	Total
Opening stock (units)	40	140	340	240	40
Production (units)	500	500	500	500	2 000
Sales (units)	400	300	600	700	2 000
Closing stock (units)	140	340	240	40	40

The results under the two methods of costing would appear as follows:

Year	1	2	3	4	Total
Variable costing	£	£	£	£	£
Sales	2 400	1 800	3 600	4 200	12 000
Cost of goods produced	1 250	1 250	1 250	1 250	5 000
add: Opening stock	100	350	850	600	100
Available for sale	1 350	1 600	2 100	1 850	5 100
less: Closing stock	350	850	600	100	100
Cost of goods sold	1 000	750	1 500	1 750	5 000
Contribution margin	1 400	1 050	2 100	2 450	7 000
Fixed overheads	1 000	1 000	1 000	1 000	4 000
Net profit	400	50	1 100	1 450	3 000
Absorption costing	£	£	£	£	£
Sales	2 400	1 800	3 600	4 200	12 000
Cost of goods produced	2 250	2 250	2 250	2 250	9 000
add: Opening stock	180	630	1 530	1 080	180
Available for sale	2 430	2 880	3 780	3 330	9 180
less: Closing stock	630	1 530	1 080	180	180
Cost of goods sold	1 800	1 350	2 700	3 150	9 000
Net profit	600	450	900	1 050	3 000

It becomes evident why there is a controversy between the two schools of thought as regards the measurement of profit for the purpose of financial reporting for under the circumstances outlined above wide differences appear in net profit figures. These differences may be illustrated graphically below, and it may be seen that the profit profile fluctuates more widely when overheads are excluded, as they are under variable costing, than when they are included as under absorption costing.

Results where sales are constant but production fluctuates

Let us now keep the figures for sales constant, and compare results under the two methods of costing when levels of production vary.

Year	1	2	3	4	Total
Opening stock (units)	40	140	340	240	40
Production (units)	600	700	400	300	2 000
Sales (units)	500	500	500	500	2 000
Closing stock (units)	140	340	240	40	40

Fig. 5.19

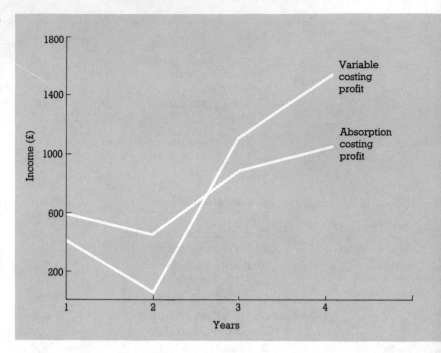

The results under the two methods would be calculated as follows

Year	1	2	3	4	Total
Variable costing	£	£	£	£	£
Sales	3 000	3 000	3 000	3 000	12 000
Cost of goods produced	1 500	1 750	1 000	750	5 000
add: Opening stock	100	350	850	600	100
Available for sale	1 600	2 100	1 850	1 350	5 100
less: Closing stock	350	850	600	100	100
Cost of goods sold	1 250	1 250	1 250	1 250	5 000
Contribution margin	1 750	1 750	1 750	1 750	7 000
Fixed overheads	1 000	1 000	1 000	1 000	4 000
Net profit	750	750	750	750	3 000
Absorption costing	£	£	£	£	£
Sales	3 000	3 000	3 000	3 000	12 000
Cost of goods produced	2 700	3 150	1 800	1 350	9 000
add: Opening stock	180	630	1 530	1 080	180
Available for sale	2 880	3 780	3 330	2 430	9 180
less: Closing stock	630	1 530	1 080	180	180
Cost of goods sold	2 250	2 250	2 250	2 250	9 000
Over- (or under-) absorbed overhead	200	400	(200)	(400)	—
Total cost of goods sold	2 050	1 850	2 450	2 650	9 000
Net profit	950	1 150	550	350	3 000

In order to simplify the calculations under the absorption costing method we have assumed a normal level of production of 500 units year. Since total fixed cost is £1000 per year, a recovery rate of £2 per unit is used. We have assumed, also, that selling prices and costs remain unchanged over the four years. By using a normal overhead rate for recovering fixed overhead, the value of opening and closing stock per unit remains constant at £4.5 (£2.5 variable + £2.0 fixed). In the first two years the normal output level is exceeded by 100 and 200 units respectively, with shortfalls in the last two years. The cost of goods sold is adjusted by the over- or under-recovery of fixed overhead resulting from those differences in deriving profit under absorption costing.

In this example, where sales have remained constant but production has fluctuated, we note that profit results obtained under variable costing remain constant, but those based on absorption costing show wide fluctuation—£1150 in year 2 and £350 in year 4.

Variable and absorption costing: their impact on profit summarized

The various examples we have considered enable the following generalizations to be made on the impact on profit of these two different methods of costing:

1   where sales and production levels are constant through time, profit is the same under the two methods;
2   where production remains constant but sales fluctuate, profit rises or falls with the level of sales, assuming that costs and prices remain constant, but the fluctuations in net profit figures are greater with variable costing than with absorption costing;
3   where sales are constant but production fluctuates, variable costing provides for constant profit, whereas under absorption costing, profit fluctuates;
4   where production exceeds sales, profit is higher under absorption costing than under variable costing for the absorption of fixed overheads into closing stock increases their value thereby reducing the cost of goods sold;
5   where sales exceed production, profit is higher under variable costing. The fixed costs, which previously were part of stock values, are now charged against revenue under absorption costing. Therefore, under absorption costing the value of fixed costs charged against revenue is greater than that incurred for the period.

The variable costing controversy

We have seen in this chapter how profit may be affected by the manner in which costs are matched against revenues, so that the selection of one accounting procedure rather than another may, according to prevailing circumstances, affect the outcome of profit plans. Advocates of variable costing base their case on the superiority of this method for planning and control purposes. It does so by clarifying the relationship between costs, volume and profit by identifying the contribution margin, that is the excess of sales revenue over variable costs of production, linking profit to the level of sales which is the most critical event affecting a firm's financial performance.

The arguments in favour of providing variable costing information for assisting decision making by external users are overwhelming. Some opponents of variable costing assert that it is incorrect to suggest that information which is useful for management decision making is relevant for all business purposes, although it is difficult to accept the contention that variable costing information may be helpful to management but not to external users, for both management and investors are faced with the same task, that is, decision making.

Some accountants have been concerned by the fluctuations which are imported in profit measurement by the exclusion of fixed costs, and to secure a certain stability in profit, advocate the retention of the absorption costing method of valuing stocks. A further controversy arises from the effects of variable costing on the balance sheet of omitting fixed factory overheads from stock values. The real argument on this issue is whether the balance sheet should show stocks at actual cost or at a value to the current period of the resources transferred from the period just ended. Variable costing is said to have a 'profit and loss account emphasis', whereas absorption costing is said to have a 'balance sheet emphasis'.

The need for a definition of assets

The variable costing controversy stresses the need in accounting theory for a comprehensive definition of assets. Assets are not usually defined, and where they are, the definition is restricted to a vague description. Instead, considerable time is spent on discussing the classification of assets, and how one type of asset may be distinguished from another. Classifications which do not specify the tests to be applied in identifying assets are inadequate for an understanding of their basic nature.

Recently, there have been attempts to define assets as 'rights to service potentials' or 'rights to future benefits'. There remains the problem of interpreting these definitions, and some have taken the 'service potential' of an asset to mean its capacity to contribute to revenue-earning in the future. If one distinguishes unexpired and expired costs, according to whether or not they will contribute to revenue in the future, such a definition of assets would imply adherence to an absorption costing method of valuing assets.

A more recent interpretation of 'service potential' is one which considers assets as having a service potential to the extent that they avert the need to incur future costs. This 'cost obviation' interpretation has led some to believe that the variable costing method of valuing stocks is superior to the absorption costing method for the purposes of measuring stocks in terms of future benefits. The most detailed discussions of the cost obviation concept approach the problem of stock valuation from the standpoint of relevant costs. Relevant costs are those which differ when two or more courses of action are contemplated, and they are those costs which will be avoided by not undertaking a given alternative. Irrelevant costs are those which have no influence on a decision because they remain the same under all the alternatives considered. The concept of relevant costs is not a new one. This text considers the concept fully in Chapter 34. This concept should be applied to asset valuation because the main purpose in providing accounting measurements is to influence decision making. Therefore, stocks should consider only of costs that will influence future results.

Summary

Accountants are more likely to agree on the nature of measurement if they agree on the purpose of accounting. If the central purpose of accounting is to make possible the periodic matching of costs and revenues, and if the matching principle is the 'nucleus of accounting theory', then clearly the absorption costers are correct in their view. But if, as we argue in this book, the prime objective of accounting is to provide information which is useful for decision making, then the case for variable costing seems to be very strong.

Reference

Paton, W. A. and Littleton, A. C. (1940). *An Introduction to Corporate Accounting Standards*, Monograph 3, AAA.

Questions

1 What do you understand by variable costing?
2 Review, briefly, the importance of variable cost information for c–v–p analysis.
3 Explain how accountants conventionally match costs with revenues.
4 What would be the logical implication for product costing of using variable cost information?
5 Compare and contrast absorption costing and variable costing.
6 Explain the treatment of overhead costs under absorption costing and variable costing.
7 Is there any significant difference as regards reported profits using absorption costing and variable costing when periodic sales and periodic production remain constant?
8 Discuss the different profit results that are obtained using absorption costing and variable costing under the following circumstances:

(a) where sales fluctuate but production remains constant,
(b) where sales are constant but production fluctuates.

9 What do you understand by the 'variable costing controversy'?
10 Identify a number of cases where you believe firms do use variable costing.

Problems

1 Computer Limited was formed three years ago to produce a single product, the 'Mini'. The directors are receiving the financial results of the first three years presented by the company accountant, and are concerned with the decline in profits in the year 19X3 despite a substantial increase in sales.
Summarized results are shown below:

	19X1	19X2	19X3
Production: Budget (units)	1 000	1 000	1 000
Actual (units)	900	1 100	800
Sales (units)	800	800	1 000
Selling price per unit	£80	£80	£80
Variable production cost per unit	£10	£10	£10
Fixed production overheads	£40 000	£40 000	£40 000
Fixed selling and administrative overheads	£20 000	£20 000	£20 000
Net profit	nil	£8 000	£2 000

Fixed overheads are absorbed on the basis of budgeted annual production. Under- or overabsorbed are charged to cost of goods sold.

Required:

(a) Prepare a statement showing the profit figures derived by the company accountant.

(b) Prepare profit and loss accounts using a variable costing approach.

(c) Reconcile the profits calculated in parts (a) and (b) above.

(d) Explain the rationale behind the approaches adopted in parts (a) and (b).

2   The Sherwood Co Ltd is a single-product manufacturing company, which uses a variable costing system for internal management purposes. The year-end external reports are converted to absorption costs. Variances are charged to the cost of goods sold.

The following data refers to the years ended 31 December 19X5 and 19X6:

	19X5	19X6
	£	**£**
Sale price per unit	80	90
Standard variable costs per unit:		
Direct materials	21	23
Direct labour	19	22
Variable factory overheads	8	10
Variable selling and administrative expenses	2	3
Fixed factory overheads	170 000	180 000
	Units	**Units**
Opening stocks	1 500	2 000
Closing stocks	2 000	1 500
Sales	20 000	25 000

The normal volume used for the purpose of absorption costing is 28 000 units in both years.

Required:

(a) Prepare profit and loss accounts for the year ended 31 December 19X6 on a variable costing and on an absorption costing basis.

(b) Discuss any differences which you may find between these two profit and loss accounts.

(c) State what advantages and disadvantages attach to the variable costing approach for internal management purposes.

Chapter 33

Pricing

It is generally assumed that capitalist enterprises are sales-led, and that the ability to sell under competitive conditions is a critical success factor on which the production process is significantly dependent.

One of the key factors in selling products under competitive market conditions is product pricing. The significance of pricing goes much beyond the simple question of determining product profitability. The complex set of notions that are involved in pricing have their fundamental roots in the strategic decisions that are concerned with capital investment, as well as those that relate to the immediacy of current operating profitability.

If a firm develops a pricing policy that affects its position in the market, it is evident that such a policy has long-term implications, for in the long term, any change in the volume of demand for products will affect the capital budgeting.

Equally, pricing policy has a direct influence on market demand, and, given cost–volume–profit relationships discussed in Chapter 31, current profitability also will be directly affected.

The purpose of this chapter is to discuss these problems, with particular reference to the costing approach to pricing with which traditionally accountants have been concerned.

The nature of the pricing problem

The firm's long-term survival depends on its ability to sell its products at prices that will cover costs as well as providing a profit margin that will ensure a reasonable rate of return to investors. This simple statement of the pricing problem suggests that it is sufficient for accountants to accurately measure costs, and then add a profit margin that will provide the return on capital that investors expect.

The truth is that the pricing problem is much more complex than simply estimating costs. In the short term, the firm's cost structure will determine whether a given price will produce a profit or a loss at product unit level, but total profit may be affected also by changes in consumer demand, and the firm's business environment. Competition and economic policies that affect the aggregate level of demand frequently are more significant to the pricing problem than the firm's total costs per unit. Moreover, a variety of circumstances call for different pricing policies, implying alternative cost concepts and cost measurements.

Pricing is only one of the ways through which the firm can influence the demand for its products. For example, sales can be expanded by advertising, increasing the sales force, improving the selling style, and improving product presentation, as well as by lowering price. In effect, altering pricing policy may not necessarily be the best way of expanding sales and improving total profits. Equally, a fall in demand for a product may be remedied by improvements in selling methods rather than increasing its price competitiveness. Therefore, in focusing on the pricing problem, we are focusing on only one of the factors that may influence the level of sales.

Recent years have seen a remarkable shift in the relative importance of long-term rather than short-term considerations in developing pricing policies. Whereas traditional approaches to pricing utilized by US and European enterprises have involved pricing by reference essentially to short-run cost analysis, Japanese enterprises have categorized pricing policies as a long-term, rather than a short-term, problem. In this regard, the concept of 'target pricing' involves deliberately determining prices in the context of long-range planning, and forcing down planned production costs to targeted costs.

The nature of pricing theories

Two distinct influences are seen at play in various pricing theories. First, the influence of classical economic theory that is concerned with guidelines for finding the best or optimal price. Second, the influence of business traditions of conservatism and sound management, that looks to costs as setting a minimum level in price determination.

In sharp contrast to classical economists, businessmen and accountants have been less concerned with finding the best price than with establishing a price that covers an agreed measure of costs and provides a sufficient profit. Hence, pricing is part of both long-range and budgetary planning.

Pricing theory in economics

Classical theorists hold that the firm should determine the optimum price, which is that price that will maximize the firm's profits. From their point of view, the price which maximizes profits implies the most efficient use of the economic resources held by the firm. Furthermore, such a pricing policy is necessary if capitalist enterprise is to reflect correctly the tenets of classical philosophy of capitalism, that is, that the objective of the firm is to maximize the returns accruing to the owner of its capital. The efficient allocation of resources through the economy is secured by the assumption that every owner of capital will seek to maximize the return on invested capital. Accordingly, scarce economic resources will be distributed between competing ends in a manner which will produce the greatest national wealth.

The price which maximizes profits is found at that level of sales where the addition to total revenue resulting from the sale of the last unit (the marginal revenue) is equal to the addition to total costs resulting from the production of that last unit (marginal cost).

It is clear that economic theory imposes very exacting conditions on the analysis of the optimum price, and in particular makes demands for information which are extremely difficult to meet. Classical theorists argue, nevertheless, that this principle is a useful guide to profit maximization.

Example

Let us assume that a firm producing Widgets in large numbers has sufficient knowledge of the revenue and cost schedules at different volume levels associated with different selling prices. The accountant is able to produce the undermentioned data:

Selling price per unit	No. of units which may be sold	Total sales revenue	Total variable costs	Fixed costs	Profit (loss)
£		£	£	£	£
30	100 000	3 000 000	1 800 000	800 000	400 000
32	90 000	2 880 000	1 620 000	800 000	460 000
34	80 000	2 720 000	1 440 000	800 000	480 000
36	70 000	2 520 000	1 260 000	800 000	460 000
38	60 000	2 280 000	1 080 000	800 000	400 000
40	50 000	2 000 000	900 000	800 000	300 000

It is clear that the price of £34 a unit yields the maximum profit, and that is the price which the firm should establish. At this price, marginal revenue equals marginal costs.

The limitations of the classical theorists' approach arise from the failure to appreciate the many practical problems with which managers are faced. In particular, it is extremely difficult to estimate the exact shape of the demand curve, that is, how much will be sold at any particular price.

There are further reasons for doubting the assumptions of classical theory. It is not only myopic in ignoring the information problem completely, but it assumes that the volume of sales is solely a function of price. As we mentioned earlier, expenditure on sales promotion may well affect the demand curve without the need to adjust the price of the product.

There is little doubt that businessmen are not as a general rule profit-maximizers. Indeed, the businessman is a human being, whose decisions are influenced by moral, social, political considerations as well as by financial ones. As we saw in Chapter 28 the required profit as a planning goal is never a theoretical ideal such as the maximum long-term profit but represents what is thought to be a possible and desirable target for the time span considered.

Economic theory makes an important contribution to pricing theory, despite the criticisms we have just mentioned, because it draws attention to the factors which are relevant to the pricing decision, in particular the importance of the interaction of revenue and cost information for deciding upon a 'good' price, and draws attention to those cost elements relevant to such a price. It has most certainly encouraged the idea of variable or marginal cost pricing, and the formulation of flexible pricing strategies.

Cost-based pricing theories

Businessmen have for long been aware that pricing a product is one of the most important and complicated problems which they have to face. In attempting to resolve this problem, and in trying to find some general guidelines by which to establish a sound pricing policy, they are in agreement that cost is one of the factors which must be taken into account. Consistently selling below full costs will lead to bankruptcy, while if the firm is to survive it must try to sell at prices which will not only cover costs but yield a sufficient profit. No hard and fast rules may be laid down since each firm's product and market situations have features which themselves may be unique.

The influence of costs on pricing decisions varies according to circumstances. Where firms are under contract to supply on a cost-plus basis, their costs are all-important in deciding the contract price. In other situations, for example a liquidation sale, costs are irrelevant because the prices at which the goods are sold are not related to their costs. Normally, the importance of the firm's costs lies somewhere between these two extremes.

The relevance of costs to pricing decisions is influenced also by the firm's drive to meet certain objectives, for example, earning a specified rate of return, increasing its share of the market, or penetrating a new market. Moreover, the firm's relative marketing strength in a particular market may be a more dominant influence on pricing than its costs. Thus, a firm may be so strong as to be a price maker, so that it is able to fix a price which other producers will have to follow. Conversely, a firm may be a price taker, that is, its position in the market is so weak that it cannot influence the price.

In general, cost-based pricing theories are concerned with two elements of price. The first is the relevant costs which should be included in the price, and the second is the profit margin which must be added to reach the price. The profit margin will reflect a degree of caution about the likely reactions of customers or the nearness of a substitute if the firm is contemplating improving its profitability. Its relationship with near competitors may affect the firm's views on the size of its profit margin. Price cutting through the reduction of profit margins may lead to a price war, and profit margins may be safeguarded and increased by means of trading agreements. Some of these agreements in restraint of trade, which were really agreements in restraint of competition, are now illegal.

Cost-based pricing theories have a moral quality which economic theory does not reflect. In the sense that cost-based pricing reflects the notion that a cost-plus formula is 'fair', it reflects that medieval notion of a 'just price' which was such an important part of the teaching of such men as St Thomas Aquinas, and which still dominates our own conception of fair trading. It is incorrect to suggest, as does economic theory, that business theories and the actions of businessmen may be divorced from the rules of morality by which their behaviour as individuals is affected. It is evident that businessmen are concerned with finding a 'fair' price, and that this 'fair price' is one which on the one hand will cover their own costs and on the other will contain that measure of reward the buyer will regard as reasonable. In this sense, cost-based pricing theories do reflect the interaction of demand and supply, but unlike economic theory, do so in a way which reflects behavioural realities.

Cost-based pricing theories present themselves in two distinct forms:

(a) cost-based pricing relying on budgeted costs,
(b) target pricing relying on target costs.

Cost-based pricing and budgeted costs

1 Full-cost pricing

This theory requires that all the costs both fixed and variable of bringing the product to the market be included in the selling price. Once the full costs have been established, it suffices to add the agreed profit margin.

Example

High Speed Castings Ltd produces two castings, Type A and Type B. The total unit costs are as follows:

	Type A	Type B
	£	£
Direct materials	4	12
Direct labour	6	4
Factory overheads:		
Variable	6	3
Fixed	4	1
Total manufacturing costs	20	20
Marketing and administrative costs:		
Variable	2	3
Fixed	4	3
Full costs per unit	26	26

To calculate the selling price under this method, we simply add the required profit margin, as follows:

	£	£
Full costs per unit	26	26
add: Mark-up (50% on costs)	13	13
Selling price	39	39

Full-cost pricing appears on the surface to be an easy method. By ignoring demand considerations completely and concentrating on costs, it avoids one of the major problem areas of pricing. Nevertheless, there are problems in calculating full costs which are not easy to resolve. By and large, one may assume that the calculation of unit variable costs presents no serious measurement difficulties. By contrast, the assignment of fixed costs to units of output is an extremely complex matter.

Indirect costs and full-cost pricing

Many factory, administrative and marketing costs cannot be identified clearly with a particular cost centre. Furthermore, there is the problem of selecting an appropriate basis for assigning them to individual products. Under full-cost pricing, this problem is critical to the determination of the selling price.

Consider the previous example of High Speed Castings Ltd and let us assume that the demand for Product B is buoyant whereas the demand for Product A is slack. In these circumstances, it may be a good idea to transfer a higher proportion of fixed costs to Product B, and so enabling the price of Product A to be lowered to encourage more sales. By introducing such considerations to the problem of the allocation of fixed costs in multiproduct firms, one is introducing a new principle to full-cost pricing, that is, the ability of the market to accept costs. Consequently, one is moving away from the essence of full-cost pricing.

Fixed costs and volume changes

The impact of changes in the sales volume upon unit fixed costs leads to a circular discussion, because price changes affect the volume of sales which in turn affect unit fixed costs which finally open up the possibility of further price changes. Since full-cost pricing implies flexible pricing in this sense, it is difficult to see its usefulness to those businessmen who instead of wanting a 'safe' price are looking for an aggressive price which will encourage the expansion of sales. Hence, they will tend to select a price which will be below full costs and look to the expanded volume of sales to cover total costs ultimately. It is in the nature of things that until such men are satisfied with their market position, price will always be below full costs. This is explainable in terms of the wish of businessmen to achieve market as well as profit objectives.

The following table shows the relationship of fixed costs and volume changes. Given that the percentage mark-up remains constant, there is a range of selling prices which will cover costs at a particular volume of sales.

No. of units (thousands)	100	200	300	400	500
Variable cost per unit	£4.00	£4.00	£4.00	£4.00	£4.00
Fixed cost per unit	2.00	1.00	0.67	0.50	0.40
Full cost per unit	6.00	5.00	4.67	4.50	4.40
10% mark-up	0.60	0.50	0.47	0.45	0.44
Selling price	6.60	5.50	5.14	4.95	4.84

It is also interesting to note the resulting aggregate profits which these different prices produce.

No. of units (thousands)	100	200	300	400	500
Selling price	£6.60	£5.50	£5.14	£4.95	£4.84
Profit per unit (at 10%)	0.60	0.50	0.47	0.45	0.44
Aggregate profit (£000)	60.00	100.00	141.00	180.00	220.00

Clearly, faced with these production possibilities, management would wish to pursue an aggressive pricing policy which would place the highest aggregate profits within the firm's reach. As explained above, full-cost pricing would stand in the way of such a pricing policy because of the decreasing nature of fixed costs per unit as output expands. A stage will be reached, of course, when the firm has reached the limit of production under existing capacity. In other words, a point exists where the firm must stabilize production or incur further capital expenditure on the expansion of productive capacity. This would involve the firm in a capital investment decision and a complete reconsideration of its pricing policy.

The price which the firm would wish to establish under full-cost pricing, therefore, is that price which will not only be the best price from the point of view of profit, but one which is related to the best output capacity which the firm can maintain. It is for this reason that a 'normal volume' of output must be established so that the firm may decide the appropriate full costs which are to form the basis of the price. This is a most important consideration, for customers do not like frequent price changes.

Full-cost pricing and the mark-up percentage

Having gone through the complicated process of ascertaining the full cost per unit, one moves to the final problem of determining the mark-up percentage which, when added to full costs, will yield the price.

We have already mentioned that there are a number of influences which bear upon the size of the percentage mark-up. First, there is the notion of the 'fair price', and businessmen will argue strongly that such-and-such a percentage is a 'fair profit' for a given trade. There is a connection between the rate of turnover and the mark-up percentage; for example, it is quite normal to expect jewellers to impose a higher mark-up percentage on their goods than butchers. Second, the mark-up is influenced by the elasticity of demand for the product, and market conditions generally. Third, as we have already mentioned, the mark-up is influenced by the nature of the firm's long-term strategy. Fourth, although businessmen argue that they seek a reasonable profit, it is evident that they mean the highest profit which they can 'reasonably' make. Finally, there is evidence also in the pricing policies of large firms, and particularly state corporations, that the need to generate capital to finance expensive capital projects influences the profit mark-up, and hence the price.

2 Conversion-cost pricing

Unlike full-cost pricing, conversion-cost pricing takes into account only the costs incurred by the firm in converting raw materials and semifinished goods into finished products. One of the limitations of full-cost pricing is that where the firm is selling two products which require different degrees of effort to convert to a marketable state, no distinction is drawn between them.

Conversion-cost pricing, therefore, excludes direct materials and may be calculated easily from the example given on page 553 which is repeated below.

	Product A		Product B	
	£	£	£	£
Direct materials		4		12
Conversion costs:				
Direct labour	6		4	
Factory overheads	10		4	
		16		8
Total factory costs		20		20

Under full-cost pricing, both products were priced at £39 as follows:

	Product A	Product B
	£	£
Total factory costs	20	20
Selling and administrative costs	6	6
Full costs	26	26
Mark-up at 50%	13	13
Selling price	39	39

The objective of conversion-cost pricing is to provide a pricing policy which will relate the cost or effort required by the firm to convert raw material into a marketable product to the selling price of the product. From the foregoing example, it is evident that Product A takes twice the effort to produce (£16) as Product B (£8). Hence, the firm should wish to formulate a pricing policy which will encourage the expansion of Product B, two units of which may be reproduced for the same production effort as Product A. This may be achieved by conversion-cost pricing, which will establish a lower price for Product B than for Product A. Under conversion-cost pricing, the mark-up is calculated on the conversion costs, as shown below.

It will be recalled from Chapter 32 that in selecting an appropriate sales mix from a profit planning point of view, the firm is attempting to plan production in such a way as to have that mix of product which will produce the best aggregate profit situation. Conversion-cost pricing will assist the firm which is faced with such a problem. If the demand for Product B were such that the firm could switch entirely to that product, the firm would simply cease manufacturing Product A. It is owing to the fact that the firm is compelled to produce both products because demand is limited that the sales-mix problem arises. It is equally for this reason that conversion-cost pricing is useful in such situations.

	Product A	Product B
	£	£
Conversion costs:		
Direct labour	6	4
Factory overheads	10	4
	16	8
Mark-up at 100%	16	8
	32	16
Other costs:		
Direct materials	4	12
Selling and administrative costs	6	6
Selling price	42	34

3 Return on investment pricing

The cost-based pricing theories which we have examined so far focus on costs of production. Although such costs will include depreciation, they exclude any consideration of the capital employed by the firm. The firm has profit expectations, of course, and these are stated in terms of a percentage mark-up on costs of production. Return on investment pricing attempts to link the mark-up to the capital employed, and so set a price which includes a return on capital employed. Research has shown that many firms have pricing policies which reflect a target rate of return. The formula used is as follows:

Selling price

$$= \frac{\text{total costs} + (\text{desired \% return on capital} \times \text{capital employed})}{\text{volume of output}}$$

Example

Let us assume that High Speed Castings Ltd, which produces the two products Type A and Type B has a 'normal' output of Product A amounting to 20 000 units a year. Let us assume also that the capital employed by the firm is £1½ million, of which £1 million is employed in the production of Product A. The desired rate of return which the firm has imposed on all its capital investment decisions is 20 per cent. Accordingly, the firm seeks a profit mark-up which reflects this objective. The selling price may be calculated as follows:

	Product A
	£
Total costs of production (20 000 × £26)	520 000
Desired return on capital employed (20% of £1 m.)	200 000
Expected sales revenue	720 000
Selling price per unit (£720 000 ÷ 20 000)	£36

The attraction of this method of establishing a mark-up to costs is that it relates the problem of pricing to financial objectives and criteria, and integrates pricing decisions with the firm's overall planning objectives. It is clearly superior from a rational point of view to simply deciding upon a percentage mark-up on the basis of what is considered to be 'fair'. At the same time, return on investment pricing has all the tendencies to rigidity which are the features of full-cost pricing policies.

Since pricing decisions are generally short run in nature, their effects on long-range objectives require that these objectives be considered. A firm which has a long-range target rate of return may find that, in attempting to apply such a target to short-run pricing policies, it may be forced from the market by competition. Thus, the firm may be compelled to price below its target rate of return to retain its share of the market, and thereby ensure the attainment of its long-range objectives in the broad sense.

Return on investment pricing may, in practice, invert the relationship of costs to price, in that costs are tailored to fit selling policies. This means that more complete knowledge of the market is possessed, for example the likely size of the market, its sensitivity to quality and packaging. In these circumstances, a firm may ensure that a specific rate of return on investment is obtained by selling a commodity at a price not exceeding a predetermined cost.

4 Variable-cost pricing

Sometimes referred to as the contribution method of pricing or marginal pricing, this method of pricing is related to the ideas which we discussed in Chapter 31. No one seriously disputes that in the long term a firm's pricing policy must cover full costs, whether these are interpreted as full production costs or the replacement of the capital invested, as well as providing an acceptable margin of profit. As we saw earlier, this is the main argument put forward by the supporters of full-cost pricing. For short-term decisions, however, no one can doubt the usefulness of variable-cost pricing.

There are many situations in which a price which covers variable cost but not full costs will nevertheless make a contribution to profits. Thus if a firm has spare capacity and has covered its fixed costs at the price set for its regular customers, and no further sales can be made to this market, the firm may attempt to reach another market by selling the article at a lower price with a slight alteration to the product presentation. Price discrimination, as this practice is known, enables the firm to sell the same product in different markets at different prices. The firm's total profits will be much greater as a result. This aspect of imperfect competition is commonly treated in economic textbooks. Similarly, where the firm is facing a fall in demand for its product due to a temporary market recession with the result that it is operating at a loss, any sales at a price which is above variable costs will contribute to the recovery of fixed costs.

Variable-cost pricing enables the firm to pursue special marketing policies, such as the penetration of a new market, or the development of an export market, by imposing upon the home market a price which recovers fixed costs so as to permit sales at variable costs in the new market. Variable-cost pricing is useful, therefore, because it indicates the lowest limit for a price decision. For example, the variable costs of the two products of High Speed Castings Ltd are as follows:

	Product A	Product B
	£	£
Direct materials	4	12
Direct labour	6	4
Variable factory overheads	6	3
Variable selling and administrative overheads	2	3
Minimum price—variable costs	18	22

Although variable-cost pricing is useful for dealing with temporary market difficulties or for exploiting new marketing strategies, there may be a danger that variable-cost pricing becomes the established method of pricing. The firm should therefore try to evolve both long-term and short-term pricing strategies, and return to a long-term pricing strategy once the short-term situation has been cleared.

In this section we have discussed the advantages of variable-cost pricing for short-term situations. It also has advantages for the long term. Full-cost pricing, as we have already suggested, may inhibit the firm from developing sales and production strategies which management considers to be desirable from a profit planning point of view. Variable-cost pricing takes account of the relationship between price, volume and costs, and in this sense it enables better profit planning decisions to be made.

5 Going-rate pricing

Where the price for a product is determined by the market, so that the firm is faced with a 'going rate', the major problem for the firm is how much to produce. In these situations, the volume produced is determined by the firm's costs and its profit planned accordingly. The classic examples where firms are faced with the going rate are the various commodity markets. Producers try to solve the price uncertainty by

Target pricing and target costs

Until recently, the development of cost-based pricing theories have assumed that product cost measurements were needed as the starting point from which to build up prices by adding required profit margins. Accountants have been concerned with improving the accuracy of cost measurements. In this regard, the most significant innovation of this century was the shift from historic to standard costs. This enabled cost measurements to be predetermined by the anticipation of changes in cost elements in the annual budgeting process.

As indicated earlier, the concept of target pricing is a radical development that seeks to improve price competitiveness by imposing a target price in the long-range product planning process. The objective of target pricing is to seek the required profit margin through product cost economies. Hence, target costs are used to attempt to compress cost principally by searching for ways of improving resource utilization and thereby reducing costs.

Summary

Pricing decisions form an integral part of the firm's planning process and are related directly to its objectives. The nature of the firm's product, the market situation and the firm's short-term and long-term objectives are all factors relevant to pricing decisions.

Pricing policies must be examined in terms of the particular objective which they seek to achieve, and we have already said that occasions may arise where a short-term objective requires a policy which would be unacceptable in the long term. Numerous examples may be given of business objectives which require their own tailor-made pricing policies. The introduction of a new product may require a 'skimming price policy', that is, setting a high price initially and lowering the price as the product gains acceptance and popularity and permits the firm to expand the scale of production, so reducing its costs. Ballpoint pens, nylons, television sets have all undergone this process. 'Penetration price policies', on the other hand, have been a popular way of entering a foreign market and call for low prices to encourage rapid acceptance of the product.

For all these reasons, the only general rule that can be laid down is that unit costs provide a means of determining the lowest limit of an acceptable short-term price, while in the long term the price should cover all costs and provide the margin of profit required by management.

Questions

1 Review briefly some of the business objectives involved in pricing policies.
2 Discuss briefly the objective of pricing policy in classical economic theory.
3 Explain the nature of cost-based pricing policies.
4 What do you understand by 'full-cost' pricing?
5 What kind of accounting information do you consider to be relevant to making full-cost pricing decisions?

6 Comment on the statement that 'since prices are determined by supply and demand factors, accounting data is irrelevant in determining a firm's pricing policy'.

7 Explain what is implied by:

(a) conversion-cost pricing,
(b) return on investment pricing.

8 What do you understand by 'variable cost' pricing? In what circumstances do you consider this method of pricing useful to pricing decisions?

9 Explain the objectives of target pricing.

10 Consider the view that long-term factors are more significant than short-term ones in determining pricing policies.

Problems

1 Schlutz and Co Ltd manufactures a product which it distributes through its own branches in England and Wales. The managing director was recently approached by McTosh and Co Ltd, a Glasgow-based company interested in obtaining sole distributor rights in Scotland. McTosh proposes to purchase the product from Schlutz at a price of £32.50 and to offer it for sale to retailers in Scotland at £42.50 and would pay the transport charges to Scotland averaging £3.50 per unit. No commission would be payable to McTosh on these sales. Schlutz and Co undertook to consider this offer. Given the undermentioned information, would you advise Schlutz and Co to accept the offer?

(a) The products now sold to retailers in England and Wales at a price of £44 inclusive of delivery charges.

(b) Sales commissions paid to retailers are computed at 5 per cent of sales.

(c) Transport costs average £1.50 per unit.

(d) Other selling and administrative costs are regarded as fixed and amount to £4.50 per unit.

(e) Manufacturing costs amount to £29.50 per unit as follows:

Materials	£18.70
Labour	3.00
Variable overheads	3.30
Fixed overheads	4.50
	£29.50

(f) Manufacturing capacity is adequate to handle the increased volume which is estimated to amount to 1000 units a month, but fixed factory overheads would probably increase by £1500 a month.

2 A standard unit of the Whitmore Manufacturing Company contains the following variable costs:

	Per unit
Direct materials	£5.60
Direct labour cost	1.50
Variable factory overhead	0.40
	£7.50

Fixed factory overhead is budgeted at £280 000 for a normal sales volume of 400 000 units. Factory capacity is 500 000 units. Distribution and administrative expenses are budgeted at £180 000.

Capital employed is considered to consist of 50 per cent of net sales for current assets and £450 000 for fixed assets.

Additional analysis indicates:

(a) Direct material prices will increase £0.40 per unit.
(b) An unfavourable direct labour variance of approximately 6 per cent has been experienced for the past two years.
(c) Customers' discounts average to about 2 per cent of the gross sales price.

Required:

Determine a sales price which will yield 16 per cent return on capital employed.

Chapter 34

Short-run tactical decisions

We discussed in Chapter 31 the importance of the relationship between cost and volume of output for profit planning purposes. Cost behaviour is a crucial element in profit planning, but a knowledge of the behaviour of future costs is equally important for a whole range of other decisions which management has to make.

We may divide the accountant's task of providing information as to costs for decision making into two parts. First, when planning the volume of output in the short term, the accountant has to provide information as to the behaviour of fixed and variable costs over the planned range of output. Second, for a number of 'special decisions' relating to alternative courses of action, such as the acceptance or rejection of a special order, he has to provide cost information which will guide management towards making the best, that is the most profitable, decisions.

The analysis of special decisions not only requires costs that are relevant to these decisions, but focuses on the size of the contribution margin that is associated with different alternatives. The usefulness of the contribution margin is not limited to one-off special decisions, but is applied also to handling problems resulting from limiting factors that exist as on-going problems.

The purpose of this chapter is to examine the nature of relevant costs, and the importance of the contribution margin in these areas of decision-making.

The nature of relevant costs

The nature of the costs which are relevant for short-run tactical decisions will depend on the type of decision problem for which they are required. We shall examine several different types of decision problems, and in this way ascertain the type of cost information which ought to be supplied by the accountant. In general, however, the relevant costs have two important characteristics:

1 They are future costs, that is, they are costs not yet incurred. This is a most important point, for it is easy to fall into the error of believing that costs which have already been incurred must be recovered. Past cost, that is sunk costs, are irrelevant costs: their only usefulness is the extent to which they may help the accountant to estimate the trend of future costs.

Example 1

Excelsior Ltd has spent £5000 on developing a new process. A revised estimate of further expenditure required to complete the development work shows an increase of 20 per cent on the original total estimate of £10 000. The cost which is relevant to the decision to continue with the development work is £7000, that is, the future cost which will be incurred, and not the new estimate of total costs of £12 000. Hence, the costs already incurred are irrelevant to the decision to be made concerning the completion of the development work.

2   Relevant costs are differential costs. Not all future costs are relevant costs: differential costs will be different under the alternative courses of action under examination.

Example 2

John Brown has decided to go to the cinema, and he is considering whether to go by bus or by car. The price of the cinema ticket is not a relevant cost, for it is not affected by the manner in which he travels to the cinema. Likewise, since cars tend to depreciate over time, the additional mileage on the car is also not a relevant cost. Although Brown's decision on his mode of travel will be influenced by his individual preference, the relevant cost is the cost difference between the cost of using the car, that is, petrol and parking, and going by bus. This cost difference is the differential cost.

From the foregoing examples, it might appear that only variable costs will be relevant costs, and that fixed costs cannot be relevant costs, since by definition they are not susceptible to change. The examples show that not all variable costs are relevant costs, for this depends on whether in the circumstances under review they are also differential costs.

In the long term, of course, fixed costs do become variable costs, so that in decisions affecting the long term, fixed costs may be differential costs and so will become relevant costs.

For short-run tactical decisions, however, it is possible, as we shall see, for fixed costs to be relevant costs. Thus, if a decision affects the short-run activity level, requiring further capital expenditure, the extra fixed costs so incurred will be relevant costs as regards that decision.

The importance of the contribution margin

Usually, short-run tactical decisions are aimed at making the best use of existing facilities. The contribution margin is an important concept in this analysis. It is defined as the excess of the revenue of any activity over its relevant costs, which is available as a contribution towards fixed costs and profits. Profits, of course, will not be made until all fixed costs have been covered, but under certain circumstances the expectation of a contribution margin will be sufficient to justify a particular decision.

One decision problem with which a businessman is frequently faced is the acceptance of a special order, which may be a large order at a price below the usual selling price, and sometimes below total manufacturing costs.

Example 3

Minnies Kurt Ltd manufactures a garment which is sold under the trade name of Withitog. Its total productive capacity is 100 000 units in the current period, and actual production is running at 80 per cent of productive capacity. The product sells at £1.00 per unit, and the firm's cost of production are as follows:

Fixed costs	£25 000
Variable costs	£0.50 per unit

The firm receives a special order for 10 000 Withitog from a mail order firm, subject to the firm agreeing to sell the product at £0.60 per unit. The managing director is reluctant to accept the order because the selling price is well below the manufacturing costs, which he has calculated as follows:

Fixed costs per unit (allocated over 90 000 units)

$$\frac{£25\ 000}{90\ 000} \qquad £0.28$$

Variable costs per unit	0.50
Total manufacturing costs per unit	£0.78

The contribution margin approach to the solution of this decision problem leads to a different conclusion. The revenue per unit is £0.60, and the relevant costs associated with the decision are the variable costs of production only, that is £0.50 per unit. Hence, there is a unit contribution margin of £0.10 per unit, and on that basis, the firm should accept the special order. The fixed costs are not relevant costs for two reasons: first they are sunk costs, that is they are not future costs, and second they are not affected by the decision to accept the special order, that is they are not differential costs.

The result of accepting the special order on the firm's total profit may be seen from the calculations below.

It is clear, therefore, that it is advantageous to the firm to accept the special order, since overall profits will be improved by £1000, which is the amount of the contribution margin resulting from the acceptance of that order.

It is evident, too, that the widespread belief that all costs should be covered may influence businessmen in considering special offers. Absorption costing is useful in determining the full costs of production, but leads to erroneous conclusions if indiscriminately applied.

	Without the special order		With the special order		Contribution margin
	(80 000 units)		(90 000 units)		—
	£	£	£	£	£
Sales revenue:					
80 000 units @ £1.00		80 000		80 000	
10 000 units @ £0.60		—		6 000	
		80 000		86 000	6 000
Manufacturing costs:					
Fixed costs	25 000		25 000		—
Variable costs @					
£0.50 per unit	40 000		45 000		
		65 000		70 000	5 000
Net profit		£15 000		£16 000	£1 000

Example 4

Speedo Engineering Ltd manufactures an electrical component widely used in the motor industry. It is currently producing 5000 units selling at £10 a unit. Its total productive capacity is 8000 units, and budgeted costs at different levels of output have been estimated as follows:

Output (units)	5 000	6 000	7 000	8 000
Variable costs	£30 000	£36 000	£42 000	£48 000
Fixed costs	10 000	10 000	10 000	10 000
Total costs	£40 000	£46 000	£52 000	£58 000
Total costs per unit	£8.00	£7.67	£7.43	£7.25

The firm receives three offers for three lots of 1000 units at selling prices of £8, £7 and £6.50 per unit respectively. Should these offers be accepted or rejected?

The unit costs of production under the absorption costing method may be calculated and compared with the respective offers, as shown below:

Output (units)	6 000	7 000	8 000
Total costs per unit	£7.67	£7.43	£7.25
Selling price per unit	8.00	7.00	6.50
Profit (loss) per unit	£0.33	£(0.43)	£(0.75)

From these calculations one might deduce that the firm should accept the order at £8 per unit, which will produce a profit of £0.33 per unit, but should reject the other two offers of £7 and £6.50 since they would result in losses.

An examination of the relevant costs leads to a different conclusion. The fixed costs are not relevant costs, since they will be incurred irrespective of the level of output. By comparing the relevant costs with the three offers, we may calculate the differential profits as under:

Output (units)	6 000	7 000	8 000
Differential units	1 000	1 000	1 000
Differential selling price	£8.00	£7.00	£6.50
Differential unit cost	6.00	6.00	6.00
Differential profit per unit	2.00	1.00	0.50
Differential total profit	£2 000	£1 000	£500

These figures illustrate the misleading effect of using absorption costing methods for decision making, and the necessity for using the relevant cost analysis. Using this latter method, it is clear that all three offers should be accepted, for in each case they provide a contribution margin towards fixed costs and profits.

Opportunity costs

Opportunity costs are not recorded in the accounting process, and although they are favoured by economists as appropriate costs for decision making, they are difficult to identify and to measure in practice. Hence, accountants prefer to record and use more objective measures of costs, such as past costs or budgeted future costs, as guidelines for decision making. There are a number of decision problems, however, in which the only relevant cost is the opportunity cost. The opportunity cost may be defined as the value of the next best opportunity foregone, or of the net cash inflow lost as a result of preferring one alternative rather than the next best one. In cases where it is clear that only the opportunity cost will assist in making the decisions, the accountant is often able to attempt its measurement.

Example 5

The Nationwide Investment Corporation Ltd seeks to invest £1 million. It has selected two investment projects for consideration: project A which is estimated to produce an annual return of 15 per cent, and project B which is expected to yield 20 per cent annually.

On the basis of these facts it is clear that the Corporation will select project B. The additional gain resulting from that decision may only be measured in terms of the opportunity costs of sacrificing project A, as follows:

Estimated annual return from project B	£200 000
less: Opportunity cost (the sacrifice of the estimated annual returns from project B)	150 000
Advantage of project B	£50 000

The opportunity cost is always a relevant cost concept when the problem facing the firm is a problem of choice: the measure of the cost of the decision is the loss sustained by losing the opportunity of the second best alternative. It is the opportunity cost which must be taken into account in calculating the advantage of choosing one alternative rather than the other.

The use of the opportunity cost concept is illustrated in the following situations:

1   dropping a product line;
2   selling or further processing a semi-manufactured product;
3   operate or lease;
4   make or buy a product.

Dropping a product line

Invariably, the reason for wishing to drop a product line is that it is unprofitable, or it is less profitable than another product line to which the firm could switch resources.

Example 6

Mechanical Toys Ltd manufactures three products, whose contributions to total profits for the year just ended are as under:

Products	A	B	C	Total
	£	£	£	£
Sales	200 000	100 000	150 000	450 000
Variable costs	100 000	70 000	80 000	250 000
Contributions	100 000 (50%)	30 000 (30%)	70 000 (47%)	200 000 (44%)
Fixed costs	60 000	40 000	50 000	150 000
Net profit (loss)	40 000	(10 000)	20 000	50 000

The company is considering dropping product B as it is showing a loss. By dropping product B, fixed costs could be reduced by £10,000, though the remaining balance of fixed costs of £30 000 being overhead fixed costs allocated to the product would have to be reallocated to products A and C.

The only choice facing the company is to continue or to cease making product B, and the financial consequences of that choice may be shown as follows:

	Keep product B	Drop product B
	£	£
Sales	450 000	350 000
Variable costs	250 000	180 000
Contribution	200 000	170 000
Fixed costs	150 000	140 000
Net profit	50 000	30 000

It is clear that although an overall loss appears to result from producing product B, the contribution which product B makes to the firm's fixed costs would be lost if the decision were made to drop product B. The net cost of dropping product B would be £20 000, that is, the contribution margin less the fixed costs of £10 000 incurred solely as a consequence of its production.

Expressed in terms of opportunity cost analysis, the company has the choice between a profit of £50 000 associated with a decision to keep product B, and a profit of £30 000 associated with a decision to drop product B. Clearly, it cannot have both: hence the cost of selecting the profit of £50 000 is the sacrifice of the opportunity of the alternative profit of £30 000. Hence, the opportunity cost of the decision to keep product B is £30 000, and the advantage of this decision over the alternative of dropping product B is £20 000.

There may be other alternatives open to the firm, of course, besides the two alternatives which we have discussed, such as replacing product B by a more profitable product. In such a case, all the available alternatives must be examined and their outcomes accurately estimated if the best decision is to be made.

Selling or further processing

On occasions, it is possible for a firm to bring a product to its semi-finished state and then sell it, rather than proceed to complete the production process and sell the finished article.

Example 7

Product A, which cost £4.8 per unit to produce, is sold as a refined petroleum product at £8 a unit. It could be put through a further processing stage after which it may be sold for £12 a unit. The costs associated with the further processing stage are estimated at £2 per unit.

The outcome of the two alternatives facing the firm, to sell or to further process the product, may be stated in the following terms:

	To sell	To process further
Revenues associated with the decision	£8	£4
Costs associated with the decision	4.8	2
Differential profit per unit	£3.2	£2

It is clear that if the firm decides to sell rather than to process further, it will lose the additional profit of £2 per unit. Hence, the opportunity cost of the decision to sell is £2 and the advantage of selling over further processing is £1.2.

Operate or lease

The decision as to whether to operate or lease assets is another example of the importance of opportunity costs for decision making.

Example 8

Betashoes Ltd owns a desirable freehold in Puddingford High Street, which it uses as a selling outlet. The Managing Director receives an offer to lease the property to a local company willing to pay an annual rent of £30 000. The net contribution of the selling outlet in Puddingford to the group profits of Betashoes Ltd is £40 000, after deducting the expenses attributable to it. The information which is relevant to the decision to continue to use the selling outlet may be set out as under:

Contribution to group profits	£40 000
Opportunity cost (rent)	£30 000
Net advantage of operating	£10 000

In the absence of other factors which may induce Betashoes to sell the site, the offer to lease the premises should be rejected and Betashoes should continue to use them as a selling outlet.

Make or buy

It is quite common for firms to subcontract the making of components to specialist firms. This practice does increase their dependence on outside suppliers and reduce to some extent their control on the quality of the components. The opportunity cost approach to this type of decision enables the firm to consider the advantages which could be obtained from alternative uses of the productive capacity released as the result of subcontracting the making of components.

Example 9

Highperformance Motors Ltd specializes in the manufacture of sports cars, making some of the components which are required and buying others. Alparts Ltd offers to supply a part currently made by Highperformance Motors Ltd at a price of £7. The costs incurred by Highperformance Motors in making the part are as follows:

Variable costs	£4
Traceable fixed costs	2
Allocated fixed costs	3
Total unit costs	**£9**

Let us assume for the moment that the productive capacity released as a result of accepting the offer will remain idle. On the basis of a monthly production of 5000 units a month, the relevant monthly costs, that is, those which would be affected by the decision to buy the units, are as follows:

Variable costs	£20 000
Traceable fixed costs	10 000
Relevant costs	30 000
Cost of buying	35 000
Advantage in making	**£5 000**

The allocated fixed costs are irrelevant to the decision since they are not affected, and will continue to be incurred by Highperformance Motors irrespective of whether the parts are made or bought. Since the relevant costs of making are less than the costs of buying, the firm should reject the offer and continue to make the parts.

Let us now consider the possibility that if the firm accepted the offer, the productive capacity released as a result will not remain idle, and will be used to extend the production line of motor cars. It is calculated that an additional four cars a month could be produced, leading to an increase in profits of £10 000. The opportunity costs of not accepting the offer, therefore, amount to £10 000. Hence, the information which is now relevant to the decision as to making or buying the part is as under:

Cost of making	
Relevant manufacturing costs	£30 000
Opportunity cost	10 000
	40 000
Cost of buying	35 000
Advantage of buying	£5 000

The introduction of the opportunity cost of not accepting the offer has altered the nature of the decision completely, and reversed the previous conclusion that it was an advantageous to make the part.

Decision making in the face of limiting factors

In the examples examined so far, a course of action has been selected on the basis of seeking the most profitable result. Business enterprises are limited in the pursuit of profit by the fact that they have limited resources at their disposal, so that quite apart from the limitation on the quantities of any product which the market will buy at a given price, the firm has its own constraints on the volume of output. Hence at a given price, which may be well above costs of production, the firm may be unable to increase its overall profit owing simply to its inability to increase its output.

The limiting factors which affect the level of production may arise out of shortages of labour, material, equipment and factory space to mention but a few obvious examples. Faced with limiting factors of whatever nature, the firm will wish to obtain the maximum profit from the use of the resources available; and, in making decisions about the allocation of its resources between competing alternatives, management will be guided by the relative contribution margin which they offer. Since the firm will be faced with limiting factors, however, the contribution margins must not be calculated in terms of units of product sold which fail to reflect constraints on the total volume of output, but should be related to the unit of quantity of the most limited factor. A simple example will serve to explain this point.

Example 10

Multiproduct Ltd manufactures three products about which is derived the following data:

Product	Machine hours required per unit of product	Contribution margin per unit	Contribution margin per machine hour
A	3 hours	£9	£3.0
B	2 hours	£7	£3.5
C	1 hour	£5	£5.0

The three products can be made by the same machine, and on the basis of this information, it is evident that product C is the most profitable product, yielding a contribution of £5 per machine hour, as against product A, which shows the smallest contribution per machine hour. Hence, in deciding how to use the limiting factor the firm should concentrate on the production of product C, rather than products A and B. If there were no limits to the market demand for product C, then there would be no problem in deciding which product to produce—it would be product C alone.

Firms undertake the manufacture of different products because the market demand for any one product is limited, so that they seek to find that product-mix which will be the most profitable. Let us assume that the maximum weekly demand for the three products and the total machine capacity necessary to meet this demand is as follows:

Product	Maximum demand in units	Machine hours equivalents
A	100	300
B	100	200
C	100	100
		600

Machine capacity is limited to 450 hours per week, so that the most profitable product-mix is a function of both machine capacity and market demand. The following product-mix would maximize profits:

Product	Output units	Machine hours	Contribution per machine hour	Total contribution
C	100	100	£5.0	£500
B	100	200	£3.5	£700
A	50	150	£3.0	£450
		450		£1 650

This product-mix reflects the order of priority in allocating machine use to the products with the highest contribution margin per hour. Product C receives the highest priority, then product B, and lastly product A. If machine hours were further limited to 300 hours, the firm would cease to make product A.

Linear programming and decision making

Linear programming is a mathematical technique which seeks to make the best use of a firm's limited resources to meet chosen objectives, which in accounting terms may take the form of the maximization of profits or the minimization of costs. In those situations, for example, where a manufacturer has a limited plant capacity, the level and cost of output will be determined by such capacity.

Example 11

Blackamoor Steels Ltd manufactures two high-quality steel products in respect of which the following information is available:

	Product A	Product B
	£	£
Selling price per unit	30	20
Variable costs per unit	15	10
Contribution margin	15	10

Milling and grinding machines are used in the manufacturing process, and the total machine hours necessary to produce one unit of each product are:

	Product A	Product B
Milling	5 hours	1½ hours
Grinding	2	2
	7	3½

Both products are in great demand, and the only constraint on expanding output is machine capacity. The total machine hours available per month are:

Milling (3 machines at 200 hours a month)	600 hours
Grinding (2 machines at 200 hours a month	400 hours

On the basis of the facts given above, the problem facing management is to ascertain that combination of output of products A and B which will maximize the total contribution margin to overheads and profits. The problem is similar to the example discussed in the previous section (see p. 572). At first glance, it would appear that the firm should maximize the production of product A since that product yields the highest unit contribution margin. Analysed in terms of the machine capacity limit, the total number of units of *either* product A *or* product B which could be manufactured is as follows:

Product A	600 hours ÷ 5 hours = 120 units
Product B	400 hours ÷ 2 hours = 200 units

These output limits are derived in the case of product A by the fact that output is limited to the capacity of the milling machines, for product A requires 5 hours of milling as against only 2 hours of grinding. Product B, however, is limited in output by the capacity of the grinding machines of which it requires 2 hours per unit, as against 1 ½ hours of milling time.

By relating the calculation of the contribution margin to the machine capacity limits, the total contribution to overhead costs and profits which will be obtained by the production of *either* A *or* B is as follows:

Product A: 120 units × £15 = £1 800
Product B: 200 units × £10 = £2 000

It follows, therefore, that given the option of making either product A or product B the firm should concentrate on the making of product B.

The approach to the solution of this problem under linear programming consists, first, of formulating the problem in simple algebraic terms. There are two aspects to the problem, the first being the wish to maximize profits and the second being the need to recognize the production limits. The two aspects may be stated algebraically as follows:

1   The objective is to maximize the contribution to fixed overheads and profit. This objective is called the objective function, and may be expressed thus:

Maximize $C = 15A + 10B$

where C is the total contribution and A and B are the total number of units of the two products which must be manufactured to maximize the total contribution. This equation is subject to the limits that:

$A \geqslant 0$
$B \geqslant 0$

for it is not possible to produce negative quantities of either A or B.

2   The constraints on production arising from the machine capacity limits of the milling department (600 hours) and of the grinding department (400 hours) may also be expressed in algebraic terms as follows:

$5A + 1 \tfrac{1}{2} B \leqslant 600$
$2A + 2B \leqslant 400$

The first inequality states that the total number of hours used on milling must be equal to or less than 600 hours; the second inequality states that the total hours used on grinding machines must be equal to or less than 400 hours.

The problem may now be summarized in the form:

Maximize C = 15A + 10B

subject to the constraints:

$$5A + 1\tfrac{1}{2}B \leqslant 600$$
$$2A + 2B \quad \leqslant 400$$
$$A \geqslant 0$$
$$B \geqslant 0$$

It is possible to solve the problem by means of a graph (Fig. 5.20) showing the manufacturing possibilities for the two departments, viz.:

Milling department:
Product A	600 ÷ 5 = 120 units
or Product B	600 ÷ 1½ = 400 units

Grinding department:
Product A	400 ÷ 2 = 200 units
or Product B	400 ÷ 2 = 200 units

Fig. 5.20

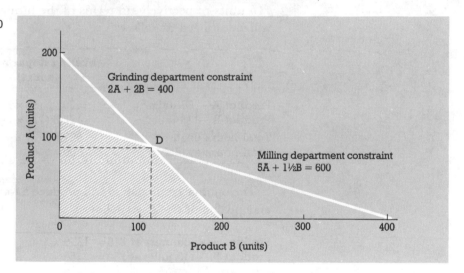

The shaded region contains all the combinations of products A and B which are feasible solutions to the problem, hence its name—the feasibility region. The optimal solution, that is, the product combination of A and B which is the best of all the feasible solutions, lies at the intersection of the lines at point D, and may be read off as 85 units of A and 115 of B. It will be observed that the optimal solution lies on a tangent which is the furthest away from the point of origin. The graphical method of solving the problem is susceptible to error unless carefully plotted, and a more reliable answer may be obtained by solving the problem mathematically.

The optimal combination of products A and B may be found by solving the simultaneous equation given above, that is,

1 5 A + 1 ½ B = 6 0 0
2 2 A + 2 B = 4 0 0

The solution is obtained by multiplying (1) by 4 and (2) by 3 to give us the value of A, as follows:

$$
\begin{array}{ll}
20A + 6B = 2\ 400 \\
-\ 6A + 6B = 1\ 200 \\
\hline
14A \qquad\ = 1\ 200 \\
A \qquad\ \ = 85\tfrac{5}{7}
\end{array}
$$

Since we are concerned only with completed units of A, the optimal production of product A is 85 units. The optimal number of units of B may be calculated by inserting the known value of A into the equation, as follows:

$$
\begin{array}{ll}
& 6 \times 85 + 6B = 1\ 200 \\
\text{i.e.,} & 510 + 6B = 1\ 200 \\
& 6B = 1\ 200 - 510 \\
& B = 115
\end{array}
$$

Hence, the optimal combination of products A and B is 85 units and 115 units respectively, in terms of the limited machine capacity which will be utilized as follows:

	Milling department (hours)	Grinding department (hours)
Product A— 85 units	425 (85 × 5)	170 (85 × 2)
Product B —115 units	172.5 (115 × 1½)	230 (115 × 2)
Total hours used	597.5	400
Total hours available	600	400

The optimal combination will produce a total contribution to overheads and profits of £2425 as follows:

Product A:	85 units at £15 =	1275
Product B:	115 units at £10 =	1150
		£2425

We may verify that this combination of products is the optimal one in terms of profits and available machine capacity, as follows:

1 Altering the product combination from 85 units of A and 115 units of B to 84 units of A and 116 units of B, which would affect machine use as follows:

	Milling department (hours)	Grinding department (hours)
Product A— 84 units	420 (84 × 5)	168 (84 × 2)
Product B —116 units	174 (116 × 1½)	232 (116 × 2)
Total hours used	594	400
Total hours available	600	400

Hence, this combination is as efficient in the utilization of the grinding department but less efficient in the utilization of the milling machines. It is also less profitable, yielding a contribution of only £2420 as against £2425 as follows:

Product A: 84 units of £15 = 1260
Product B: 116 units of £10 = 1160
                                 £2420

2 Altering the product combination from 85 units of A and 115 units of B to 86 units of A and 113 units of B, which would affect machine use as under:

	Milling department (hours)	Grinding department (hours)
Product A— 86 units	430 (86 × 5)	172 (86 × 2)
Product B —113 units	169½ (113 × 1½)	226 (113 × 2)
Total hours used	599½	398
Total hours available	600	400

Hence, whereas this combination is more efficient in the use of the milling machines than the optimal combination, it is less efficient in the use of the grinding machinery. Moreover, to keep within the capacity limits of the milling department we have had to forgo the production of 2 units of product B to expand the manufacture of product A by one unit. The consequential contribution to profits is also only £2420 as against the optimal contribution of £2425, which may be calculated as follows:

Product A: 86 units at £15 = 1290
Product B: 113 units at £10 = 1130
                                 £2420

It is noteworthy, also, that the linear programming approach to the best product combination mix gives a solution which is more profitable than the one which relates the contribution margin to the machine capacity limits, which we discussed on page 574, and which suggested that only product B should be made so that 200 units of B would be manufactured to yield a contribution for £2000.

We have so far discussed only simple cases involving at the maximum only two resource constraints. In real life, a firm may be faced with more than two constraints, but mathematical techniques exist for coping with larger numbers of limits. The Simplex Method, for example, which is based on matrix algebra may be employed in such cases and it is ideally suited for solutions using a computer.

Summary   In addition to providing information for short-run profit planning purposes, the accountant also often has to provide information for a number of short-run tactical decisions such as dropping a product line or choosing between selling or further processing a semi-manufactured product. As in other areas of accounting, cost information plays an important role in short-run tactical decisions. The costs which are relevant for such decisions are future differential costs.

Although opportunity costs are not recorded in the accounting process, there are a number of decision problems where opportunity costs are the only relevant costs. Opportunity costs may be defined as the value of the next best opportunity forgone, or of the net cash inflow lost as a result of preferring one alternative rather than the next best one.

Limits placed on resources have to be recognized in decision making. Product-mix decisions illustrate the nature of this problem and the manner in which the best use of limited resources may be made. In this connection, linear programming affords a useful technique for maximizing profits or minimizing costs in the face of constraints on resources.

Questions

1 Define the nature of relevant costs.
2 State what you understand by the following terms:

(a) future costs,
(b) sunk costs,
(c) differential costs.

3 Give examples of future, sunk and differential costs, and state the conditions required for such costs to be relevant costs.
4 Define the contribution margin.
5 What do you understand by 'opportunity costs'? Are opportunity costs also relevant costs?
6 Name four major classes of special decisions, and review the impact of these decisions on the enterprise in the short and the long term.
7 Explain how opportunity costs may be relevant costs in the four major classes of special decisions referred to in (6) above.
8 Define a limiting factor, and give four examples of limiting factors.
9 Explain how the contribution margin may be applied to decision making in the face of a limiting factor.
10 What do you understand by linear programming, and explain the usefulness of this method in decision making.

Problems

1 Heating Products Ltd has a division which manufactures radiators. The standard radiator is the Radwarm, but the company also produces radiators to customers' specification. Such radiators are described in the firm as Specials. The forecast results of the division for the year ending 31 December 19X0 are shown below:

	Radwarm	Specials	Total
Sales	50 000	100 000	150 000
Materials	16 000	20 000	36 000
Labour	18 000	40 000	58 000
Depreciation	7 200	12 600	19 800
Power	800	1 400	2 200
Rent	2 000	12 000	14 000
Heat and light	200	1 200	1 400
Miscellaneous costs	1 800	800	2 600
	46 000	88 000	134 000
Net profit	4 000	12 000	16 000

The expenses have been arrived at as follows:

(a) Depreciation is calculated on the book value of machinery used during production of each of the two groups of products.
(b) Rent is based on the space occupied in the division by each of the product lines. The building housing this division is rented at £14 000 p.a. on a ten-year lease.
(c) Heat and light for the building is apportioned on the basis of area occupied by the two groups of products.
(d) All other costs are traced directly to the product lines.

The divisional manager has receivd an order to supply 1000 Special radiators. To accommodate this order, the division would have to switch half of its Radwarm production capacity. The customer has offered a price of £70 per radiator for these Specials and each radiator would take £20 of materials and £36 of labour.

A special press would need to be purchased for this order at a price of £4000. There would be no further use for this once this order is finished and it would be discarded.

Required
(a) Calculate (i) the differential cost of the special order;
　　　　　　(ii) the full cost of the order; and
　　　　　　(iii) the opportunity cost of accepting this order.
(b) Write a report explaining whether Heating Products Ltd should accept the special order.

2　It is three months since William Wright was appointed accountant at Broomhill Manufacturing Company. During this period he has become increasingly dissatisfied with the company's accounting system. In particular, overheads are not analysed into fixed and variable elements. Wright believes that profit planning requires an understanding of the characteristics of cost and their behaviour at different operating levels. He resolved to write to the managing director and explain his new approach. To support his case Wright searched for examples which could be used to illustrate his arguments. One such example is given below.

Example
The profit and loss account for 31 December 19X7, Wright believed, could be improved for making the predictions implied in the profit planning process. This showed the following results:

	£
Sales revenue	100 000
Cost of sales:	
Materials	15 000
Labour	20 000
Factory overheads	20 000
	55 000
Gross margin	45 000
Selling and administrative expenses	35 000
Net profit	10 000

Wright estimated that fixed factory overheads amounted to £5000 and fixed selling and administrative expenses to £25 000.

The accountant of Broomhill Manufacturing, previous to Wright's appointment, had analysed the results for 19X7 by product groups and this had led the managing director to consider eliminating Product B, a loss-making product. The analysis by product is given below:

	A	B	C
	£	£	£
Sales revenue	60 000	15 000	25 000
Cost of sales:			
Materials	10 000	2 000	3 000
Labour	11 000	4 000	5 000
Factory overheads	11 000	4 000	5 000
	32 000	10 000	13 000
Gross margin	28 000	5 000	12 000
Selling and administrative	20 000	8 000	7 000
	8 000	(3 000)	5 000

Factory overheads were allocated to products at a rate of 100 per cent direct labour cost. Wright estimated that fixed factory overhead elements of the assigned costs were as follows:

A	£3 000
B	£1 000
C	£1 000

Selling and administrative expenses had been assigned to products on an arbitrary basis. Wright estimated the fixed elements as below:

	£
A	15 000
B	6 000
C	4 000

Required:
To what extent is Wright justified in seeking a reappraisal of the situation?

The integration of planning and control

We mentioned in the introduction to Part 5 that control may be related to planning by defining the purpose of control as being to ensure that the organization's activities conform with its plans. Control is itself an activity, therefore, and it should and does affect every aspect of the organization. We may depict the control cycle in the form of a generalized model as shown in Fig. 5.21.

The control cycle illustrated therein shows that the origin of control is in the objectives of the organization from which plans are developed. These plans, as we saw in Section 2, consist of both long-range and annual plans. The control cycle integrates both the long-range and the annual plan. Information feedback enables actual performance to be compared with the planned performance required by the annual plan, thus enabling management to control operations and the resources allocated to those operations. At the end of the year, the results may be compared with those envisaged in terms of the long-range plans, thereby providing information feedback for the purposes of reviewing the long-range plan. Finally, the control process allows achievements to be compared with the organization's desired objectives, thereby enabling new goals and new objectives to be formulated.

The control model illustrates the multidimensional nature of the control process, and the coincidence of the control process with the planning processes. It is this coincidence which allows the planning and the control process to be integrated into one model which is focused on organizational objectives and the goals derived from those objectives. Overall control is concerned with measuring progress towards the realization of organizational objectives and the strategic goals defined in the strategic plan. This aspect of control is exercised by top management. Using the terminology adopted in Chapter 26, management control is a subordinate activity concerned with the efficient use of resources committed to the realization of organizational goals. Finally, operational control is concerned with ensuring that the tasks defined in the operational plan are carried out effectively. Specific performance standards are attached to these tasks, and information feedback allows actual performance to be compared with the required performance.

From the foregoing, it follows that control standards are designed in the planning process. They are used as indices by which the effectiveness and the result of organizational activities are to be assessed, for they provide the basis by which actual and planned performance are to be

Fig. 5.21

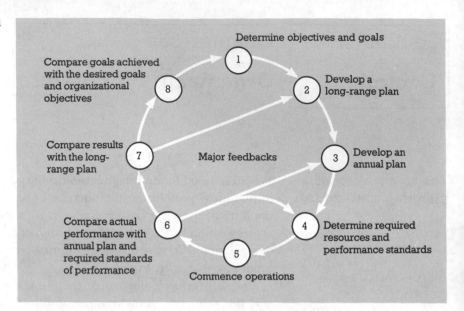

compared. Moreover, since organizational activities emanate from the planning process, plans themselves also constitute performance standards.

There remains, however, a perceptible distinction between planning and control in the sense in which we consider these terms in this text. A plan reflects the expectations and the means of achieving stipulated goals during a specified period. If such a plan is to be useful for control purposes as well, it should reflect adequately the extent to which those expectations and those means are subject to organizational control. Hence, it should provide the basis for the system of responsibility accounting which requires a clear definition of the controllable elements at every level of responsibility.

Responsibility accounting

Control depends on the existence of an organizational framework which will define the responsibility for securing the performance of individual tasks. This is achieved by establishing responsibility centres throughout the organization, and defining the responsibilities of managers accordingly.

A responsibility centre may be defined as a segment of the organization where an individual manager is held responsible for the segment's performance.

The nature of the organizational framework and the kinds of responsibility centres established will depend partly on the size of the organization and partly on the style of management adopted.

As organizations grow, top management faces two continuing problems:

1 how to divide activities and responsibilities;
2 how to co-ordinate subunits.

Inevitably, authority for decision making has to be allocated to various managers, and as soon as this occurs the result is the decentralization of the decision-making process. In essence, therefore, decentralization is the process of granting the freedom to make decisions to subordinate managers. In theory, there are two extreme states: total decentralization, meaning a minimum of constraint or control on managers and a maximum of the freedom to make decisions even at the lowest level of the management hierarchy, and total centralization, implying the maximum of constraint or control on managers and the minimum freedom to make independent decisions. In practice, total centralization and total decentralization rarely occur. Total centralization is not feasible because it is impossible for top management to attend to all the decisions which are required to be made. Equally, total decentralization is rarely found because the degree of freedom which it implies would result in an organizational structure consisting of a collection of completely separate units all aiming at their own individual goals. The extent to which an organization will be decentralized depends upon the philosophy of its top management, and the benefits and costs associated with decentralization.

Having decided to decentralize to a greater or lesser extent, the problem of control nevertheless remains. It may be resolved by establishing new responsibility centres called 'divisions'. These divisions may take the form of profit or investment centres. We shall consider these responsiblity centres later in this chapter.

The problem of controlling divisional operations is more complex than that of controlling a single activity within an organization. Where decision making is centralized, for example, it is possible to establish expense centres and to control their activities by means of budgetary control. Some of these expense centres may be cost centres, which are smaller segments of activity or areas of responsibility in respect of which costs are accumulated. Control may be exercised, therefore, by means of information feedback about the level of costs arising from the activities of these responsibility centres. Indeed, cost control has been the traditional means of securing the control of operations, although, as we shall see later, the failure to recognize behavioural factors affecting performance has implications for the effectiveness of cost control. Where decision making is decentralized, however, the control of divisional performance is made more difficult for a number of reasons. The range of decisions over which divisional managers have authority is much more extensive. Thus, they may have authority over the determination of the pricing of products, make-or-buy decisions and some investment decisions. The problem goes beyond the control of costs, therefore, to the control of profits and to ensuring that there is a high degree of goal congruence between the various divisions and the organization's top management.

Our analysis of the problem of control through responsibility accounting should recognize the problems created by the degree of centralization and decentralization of authority. The first category of responsibility centre which we shall examine, namely expense centres, are appropriate to highly centralized organizations or units. The second and third categories of responsibility centres, namely profit and investment centres, are appropriate to those organizations where the authority for decision making has been decentralized to some extent, and where the problem of control is necessarily more complex. We deal with the behavioural aspects of control which such a degree of centralization creates in Chapter 38. For the time being, we focus attention on the accounting problems stemming from the establishment of these various types of responsibility centres.

Expense centres

An expense centre may be defined as a responsibility centre in which the manager has no control over revenue but is able to control expenditure. It will be recalled that in Chapter 27 we drew a distinction between the accumulation of costs for product costing purposes and that for control purposes. In product costing, we noted that costs are first allocated and apportioned to service departments and production departments; next, that service department costs are apportioned to the production departments; finally, overhead recovery rates are computed to enable overhead costs to be absorbed into product costs. Since the production departments are the focal points on which the process of cost accumulation converges, these departments are known as 'cost centres'.

From the foregoing, we may distinguish an expense centre from a cost centre. An expense centre is a department which incurs expenditure. A cost centre is a production department in which product costs are accumulated.

As we stated earlier, a prerequisite for an effective responsibility accounting system is the establishment of an organizational framework which will define the formal relationships which link the different executive roles in the organization. Levels of responsibility may be delineated for foremen, departmental managers, works managers and upwards to director level. Figure 5.22 is an organizational chart applied to a centralized organization and shows that the three foremen are responsible to the manager of department B, who in turn reports to the works manager. The works manager is responsible to the board.

An important facet of a comprehensive planning and control programme is a system of performance reports incorporating comparisons of actual performance against planned performance for individual responsibility centres throughout the enterprise. These reports provide a means of instituting responsibility accounting, which is a method of cost control in which the costs of responsibility centres are identified with individual managers who are given authority over such costs and responsibility for them. The nature of the relationship existing between various levels of management and the flow of information between these levels may be illustrated as in Fig. 5.23.

Responsibility budgets deal only with the costs for which each manager is to be held responsible, and their performance as managers is evaluated

Fig. 5.22

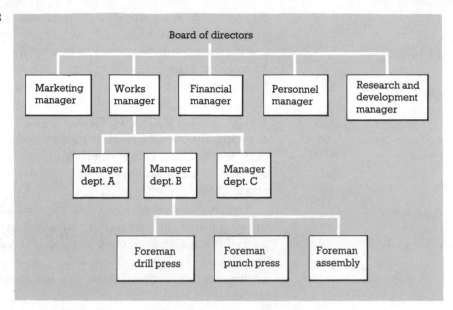

by reference to the success with which they have managed their own area of responsibility. It is important, therefore, to make a distinction between those costs which are under the control of a particular manager and those for which other managers are responsible. For example, the foreman of the assembly department may be responsible for the amount of direct labour used, but he will certainly not be responsible for the wage rate which is paid to these workers. This is determined by collective bargaining and is outside his sphere of influence. In assessing managerial performance under systems of responsibility accounting, a manager should not be held responsible for costs which are outside his control. An inference which may be drawn from our diagram is that the higher one ascends the pyramid of control, the greater is the proportion of total costs which is defined as controllable costs: at board of directors level

Fig. 5.23

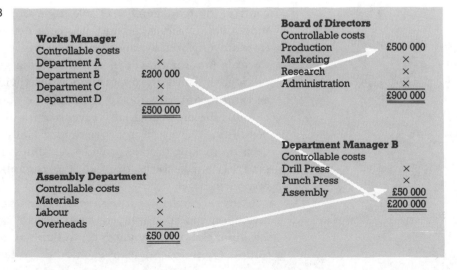

all costs are by definition controllable as the board is ultimately responsible for all costs.

There are conflicting views as to whether non-controllable costs should be included in performance reports. One view is that, if they are included, managers will be informed of all the costs affecting their departments. Their inclusion also enables department managers to appreciate the size and the costs of the organizational support upon which their department depends. If non-controllable costs are included in performance reports, they should be distinguished from the costs which fall within the manager's responsibility, that is, those costs which are defined as controllable.

The manager in charge of an expense centre has the responsibility for seeing that the expenditure incurred by his department should not exceed the limits contained in his budgeted expenditure. Clearly, his ability to control expenditure will be an important consideration in the evaluation of his effectiveness as a manager. It follows, therefore, that the use of budgets for evaluating the performance of managers has implications for the manner in which budgets are organized. We discuss this problem in the next chapter.

Profit centres

In recent years, there has been a tendency for organizations to grow in size, and the problem of control which this growth has created has encouraged the devolution of authority in large organizations by the creation of organizational structures based upon the concept of 'divisions'. The rationale underlying this process of decentralization is founded on the belief that divisionalization enhances overall corporate profitability. Several reasons are adduced for this belief. First, responsibility for decision making is transferred to executives who are 'on the spot', and who are directly concerned with the particular problems of manufacturing and marketing divisional products. Hence, they are able to devote all their energies to these problems, whereas under systems of centralized control, top management is able to devote less time to the problems of individual divisions. Second, it is considered that the greater degree of freedom enjoyed by divisional executives increases their motivation towards the attainment of organizational goals, and in particular the profit goal. Third, the opportunity which divisionalization affords of using accounting information to measure the contribution of each division towards the profit goal, also reveals areas of weakness and may suggest possibilities for profit improvement. Finally, the decentralization of the decision-making process provides a training ground for managers as they progress successively through the organization to higher levels of responsibility.

Conventional accounting measurements of performance, such as the return on capital employed, may serve a useful purpose in evaluating the financial performance of individual divisions, where they are completely independent of each other. Where, however, the activities of individual divisions are interrelated, so that the output of one division provides a substantial part of the input of another division, the usefulness of conventional accounting measurements of financial performance is less clear. Under these circumstances, there is a need to establish a price for transferring these so-called intermediate products between the divisions, and this price will clearly affect their profits.

Transfer pricing

From the foregoing, the use of profit centres for the control of divisional performance may give rise to the problem of determining the price at which the product of one profit centre should be transferred to another profit centre. The transfer price is critically important to the profit of both centres, being at once revenue to the selling centre and cost to the buying centre. The evaluation of managerial performance based on the size of the divisional profit requires that the transfer price should be so calculated as to reflect accurately the value added to the product by the selling centre. If it is set too high, it will reflect too favourably upon the selling centre and too unfavourably upon the buying centre, and vice versa. Hence, financial results may be heavily biased by the prices adopted for the transfer of intermediate goods. Defects in the transfer price mechanism may frequently invalidate the conclusions which divisional profit figures might seem to suggest. In such cases, these figures may not merely fail to produce the right decisions: they may actively promote wrong ones.

In Chapter 33, we examined pricing as a means of regulating the exchange of the firm's products with the outside world. In this chapter, we examine transfer pricing as a method of controlling the activities of profit centres within the firm. Hence, we see that the distinction between pricing and transfer pricing lies in their different purposes.

Transfer prices should satisfy the following three criteria:

1 They should promote goal congruence within the organization by harmonizing the interest of individual divisions with the interest of the organization as a whole, by preventing divisional managers from optimizing divisional profits by policies which are harmful to the rest of the organization.
2 They should make possible reliable assessments of divisional performance for the following purposes:
(a) making predictions for decision-making purposes
(b) appraising managerial performance
(c) evaluating the divisional contribution to corporate profits.
3 They should ensure that the autonomy of the individual divisions is respected, and that their profits are not dependent upon the actions of other divisions.

Transfer pricing methods

There are three main methods for establishing transfer prices:

1 market-based transfer pricing;
2 cost-based transfer pricing;
3 negotiated pricing.

Market-based transfer pricing

Where external markets do exist for the selling centre's products, it is preferable to use market prices rather than cost-based prices. This is because market price is a better guide to the value added to products than a cost-based price which incorporates a profit element. If the external market is competitive and divisional interdependence is minimal, the market price generally leads to optimal decisions within the organization, that is, decisions which satisfy the three criteria stipulated above. Where market prices can be used with a large measure of success, the divisions are effectively separate business entities.

When using market prices, it is essential that the transfer price should be no higher than the buying centre would have to pay on the market. Otherwise, it is evident that an imbalance will be created between the interests of the selling and the buying centres. The existence of an independent market price imposes an upper limit to the transfer price, for given that the selling centre is able to sell at that price, the buying centre should be compelled to buy internally rather than to purchase from external suppliers.

A number of problems arise from the use of the market price as the basis for the transfer price. Thus, changes in supply may lead to large price changes, and the recognition of these changes will cause large variations in the transfer price. As a result, a degree of instability will be introduced in the control mechanism. Further problems are associated with the weight which should be attached to different market price rulings during the transfer period, and to such other factors affecting market prices, such as quantity discounts, area and trade channel differentials, transportation and delivery allowances and service factors. The market price also reflects the result of a bargain, and a reconciliation between what one has to accept to effect a sale, and what one has to pay to effect a purchase. The effects of relative bargaining positions on the market price have implications for the transfer price selected—should it favour the selling or the buying division?

Hence the determination of a fair market price for establishing a viable transfer pricing system which will satisfy the three criteria which have been stipulated, calls for a solution to the various problems mentioned above. In many cases, the solution may be arrived at only by an independent arbitrator. This process immediately undermines the third criterion—the preservation of the autonomy of individual divisions— and results in the establishment of a negotiated price.

Cost-based transfer pricing

In many cases, the transfer of products beween profit centres involves intermediate goods in respect of which an external market does not exist. In such cases, it is necessary to use cost-based transfer prices.

A common problem which may arise in employing cost-based transfer prices is that they may conceal inefficiencies in the activities of the selling centre. It is essential, therefore, that the transfer price should be based on standard costs rather than actual costs. As we shall see in the following chapter, the standard cost represents what an item should cost to produce rather than what it does cost, that is it excludes inefficiencies which have arisen in production. Hence, the use of standard costs prevents inefficiencies which have occurred in one profit centre from being transferred to another profit centre.

As we mentioned in Chapter 33, there are different kinds of cost-based prices. Two commonly used cost-related prices are full-cost and variable- (or marginal-) cost prices.

Full-cost transfer pricing

The major disadvantage of using full cost, or rather full cost plus a profit percentage, as a transfer price is that this method may encourage managers to make decisions which are not in the interest of the firm as a whole.

Example

The following data relates to profit centre A which sells to profit centre B at full cost plus a profit percentage:

Profit centre	A	B	
	£	£	£
Variable costs	10	30 +	10
Fixed costs	10		10
Mark-up (50%)	10		25
Total unit cost	30		75

Profit centre B treats the input of £30 from profit centre A as a variable cost. Hence, before profit centre B is able to have a contribution margin (defined, it will be remembered, as the excess of sales revenue over variable costs which contributes to fixed costs and profits) it must be able to sell its own output at £40 a unit. It is clear, however, that as far as the firm as a whole is concerned, total variable costs per unit are only £20. Given that both profit centres have spare capacity, it is in the firm's interest that profit centre B should produce and sell if it can obtain a price of £20 or over per unit for its output. If it regards £40 as its minimum acceptable price, the firm will lose the benefit of a contribution margin which otherwise it would have had.

In addition to the limitations of full-cost transfer pricing illustrated by the previous example, the use of full costs as a basis for transfer pricing may import a rigidity in an organization which contradicts the rationale for establishing profit centres. Managers should be able to control all the determinants of profits (selling price, volume, fixed and variable costs) if they are to be held responsible for profits. Thus, in the example given above, the manager of profit centre A may feel that his output is constrained by the obligation to sell to profit centre B at a transfer price of £30 a unit. Furthermore, his production is also dependent upon the sales volume attained by profit centre B. This volume may be too low to enable profit centre A to achieve a satisfactory profit, and the manager of that profit centre may well wish to sell his output outside the firm, if he is able to, at varying prices.

Therefore, the rigidity imposed on a firm by virtue of the inflexibility of an agreed full-cost transfer pricing system does not provide a sound basis for the delegation of decisions to profit centres.

Variable-cost transfer pricing

Transfer prices based upon variable cost are designed to overcome some of the problems stemming from the use of full-cost measurement. Thus, in the aforementioned example, profit centre A would have transferred to profit centre B at a unit price of £10. In the short run, when both profit centres have surplus capacity, this would enable centre B to adopt a more realistic pricing policy to the benefit of the organization as a whole. Such a decision, however, applies only in special circumstances. In the long run, transfer prices based upon variable costs are of little value for the purpose of performance evaluation, for they result in a loss to the selling division, and would impair the degree of motivation which is one of the reasons for decentralizing.

As we saw in Chapter 33, pricing policies should be based on differential costs and revenues of the company as a whole in order that better profit planning decisions may be made. This implies that decisions about the output volume of divisions cannot be determined independently, thereby undermining the autonomy of individual divisions.

Negotiated pricing

Whatever method the firm adopts for determining transfer prices, it is evident that some form of negotiated price must be agreed between the managers of profit centres if the transfer pricing system is to operate satisfactorily. It is assumed that independent negotiations between managers will produce results which are beneficial to the firm as a whole, and that the resolution of conflicts of interests will not reflect any bias in favour of any particular groups. These assumptions are probably questionable for a number of reasons. First, transfer price negotiations are very time-consuming, and may lead to a diversion of managerial interest from their own work as they get more involved in the negotiations. Second, conflicts which undoubtedly will occur may lead to recriminations and the involvement of top management as arbitrators may be required.

The advantages of transfer pricing

The various transfer pricing systems we have examined seem fraught with problems and drawbacks. Nevertheless, these difficulties should be weighed against the advantages which may be derived from setting up profit centres. Equally, these difficulties do not amount to a substantial case for abandoning the practice of assigning transfer prices to interdivisional products. Some value must be found and attached to each element of input and output for the purpose of effective organizational control. Without some form of transfer pricing, the whole structure of intradepartmental analysis and control would collapse.

Very few aids for planning and control are perfect. This is certainly true of transfer pricing. It should be recognized that no available transfer pricing system is likely to serve all the purposes for which it is needed. The limitations found present in any transfer pricing system should be recognized, and any results obtained should be interpreted in the full knowledge of those limitations.

Investment centres

Investment centres represent the ultimate stage in the decentralization of the decision-making process. Divisional managers are made responsible not only for cost goals (expense centres), profit contribution goals (profit centres), but also for elements of the capital invested in the division.

Investment centres extend the principles underlying profit centres by associating divisional profits with the capital invested in the divisions. The criterion most commonly employed for assessing the financial performance of investment centres is the return on capital employed (ROCE). It is a comprehensive measure of financial performance which enables comparisons to be made between companies and divisions for the purpose of evaluating the efficiency with which assets are utilized. The ROCE is calculated as follows:

$$ROCE = \frac{\text{net profit before interest and tax}}{\text{average capital invested}} \times 100$$

This formula may be extended so as to incorporate the ratio of net profit to sales, and the ratio of sales to capital employed (the rate of asset turnover).

$$ROCE = \frac{\text{NP PBIT}}{\text{sales}} \times \frac{\text{sales}}{\text{average capital invested}} \times 100$$

The expanded formula is useful for focusing attention on the important elements which affect the ROCE. It implies that profitability may be improved in the following ways:

1 by increasing the volume of sales;
2 by reducing total assets;
3 by reducing costs;
4 by improving the profit mark-up, for example by raising selling prices or improving the product mix.

The asset turnover will be improved by *1* and *2* and the profit margin by *3* and *4*.

Example

The following table compares the sales, profit and capital employed for three divisions of a large organization. Their profit contribution is £50 000 in each case.

	Division A	Division B	Division C
Sales	£500 000	£500 000	£1 000 000
Net profit PBIT	£50 000	£50 000	£50 000
Capital employed	£250 000	£500 000	£500 000
Return on sales	10%	10%	5%
Asset turnover	2	1	2
ROCE	20%	10%	10%

It is clear that division A has the most effective financial performance since its ROCE of 20 per cent is higher than the ROCE of the other two divisions. Division B's return on sales, that is its profit margin, is equal to that of division A, but its asset turnover is half as high as A's, implying that it employs twice as much capital as A to earn the same profit. This position indicates that either sales could be improved or that excessive capital is being carried by division B, and that an investigation of asset use may reveal that plant and stocks could perhaps be reduced. Division C has the same ROCE as division B. Its margin on sales, however, is inferior to that of both other divisions, thereby indicating that selling prices may be too low or that operating costs may be too high.

The foregoing example shows that a ROCE analysis may isolate factors requiring investigation. These factors are illustrated in Fig. 5.24.

Problems associated with ROCE measurements of performance

Three major problems arise as a result of employing ROCE measures for assessing divisional performance. They stem from the following factors:

Fig. 5.24

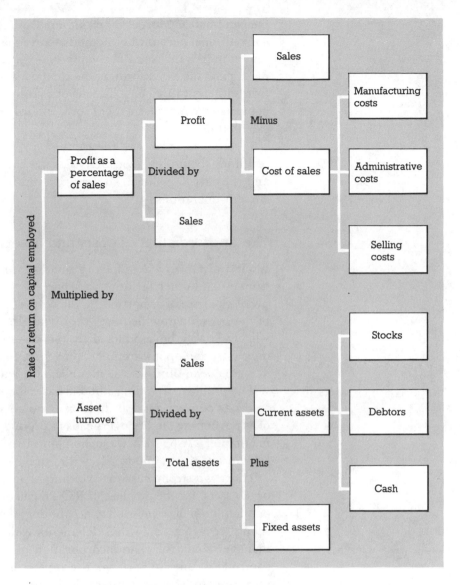

1 the measurement of profit and capital employed;
2 the appropriation of costs and assets as between divisions;
3 the limitations inherent in ROCE.

The measurement of profit and capital employed

The use of ROCE measures of performance for comparing the performance of similar divisions requires measurements of profit and capital employed which are free from any accounting bias. Thus, uniform accounting procedures should be established for valuing stock, and charging against profit such costs as depreciaion, research and development and advertising costs. If comparisons are to be meaningful, the effect of price level changes should also be eliminated from accounting measurements. Moreover, profit and capital employed as measured by conventional accounting methods tend to reflect a much better rate of return than is the case. The valuation of assets on a historical cost basis means that the assets forming the capital investment base are a composite from different monetary dimensions. It follows that the same problem applies to the measurement of costs applied to current revenues for profit calculation.

In order to overcome these problems, therefore, current operating revenues should be associated with the current costs of earning them, and the current value of the assets comprising the capital employed in current operations.

The appropriation of costs and assets as between divisions

In circumstances where factory buildings, production facilities, office, canteen and other facilities are shared by more that one division, the problem arises of apportioning the costs of these facilities and the value of the investment which they represent. In any event, certain facilities will invariably be conducted by the organization on behalf of all the divisions, and apportionments may have to be made in respect of such items as head-office costs, management and technical services, etc.

The problem of finding suitable bases for apportioning such costs and assets as between several divisions bears a strong resemblance to that of apportioning factory overheads to product costs, which we examined in Chapter 27. As we saw, such appointments tend to be arbitrary, and seldom are the methods selected entirely immune from criticism.

There is a strong case for avoiding apportionments, whether of costs or of assets, for the purpose of ROCE calculations. In accordance with our definition of responsibility accounting, the evaluation of performance should recognize only those elements which are under the divisional manager's control. The incorporation of non-controllable items with controllable ones in performance reports is admissible for information purposes, so long as they are distinguished from each other, and the fundamental principles enshrined in responsibility accounting are maintained.

Limitations inherent in ROCE

The main disadvantage of ROCE measures of performance is that they contain a conceptual weakness. This stems from the fact that different investment centres will have different ROCE measurements. Thus, the ROCE for the whole organization may be 10 per cent, whereas the various investment centres may have ROCEs ranging from under 10 per cent to over 10 per cent. The manager of an investment centre enjoying a ROCE of 15 per cent will be unwilling to consider any project offering a rate of return on investment of less than 15 per cent, even though it offers a rate of return of over 10 per cent. This is because the evaluation of his own performance will be made in terms of the current ROCE for his own investment centre. Hence, the use of ROCE for the evaluation of divisional performance may well motivate divisional managers to act in a way inconsistent with the financial objectives of the organization as a whole.

It was to deal with this difficulty that the General Electric Company introduced the residual-profit method of performance appraisal in the 1950s. Under this method, the performance of investment centres is evaluated by the residual profit after charging an appropriate amount calculated by reference to the rate of return on investment being earned by different types of assets. Because the residual profit is an absolute figure and not a ratio, a division which is trying to improve its residual-profit figure will undertake investment programmes even where the expected rate of return is less than the current ROCE.

Example

The net assets (total assets – current liabilities) of a division are valued at £1000. The company has decided that a return of 10 per cent on these net assets is an appropriate target. The division's profit statement for the current year is given below:

Revenue	£1 000
less: Costs	700
	300
less: Taxes	150
Profit after taxes	150
Capital charge (10%)	100
Residual profit	£50

If the manager of this division were evaluated on the ROCE basis, he would not invest in a project which produced a return of below 30 per cent, i.e.

$$\frac{£300}{£1000} \times 100$$

However, if he were evaluated on residual profit he would invest in a project which gives a reurn above 10 per cent because this will increase residual income. This action will be beneficial to the company.

Summary

Control and planning are integrated processes which affect every aspect of organizational activity, including the determination of objectives and the development of long-range and short-range plans. The comparison of actual performance with the goals stipulated in these plans discloses the extent to which they have been attained.

Responsibility accounting underpins the control process, and requires the establishment of responsibility centres throughout an organization.

A responsibility centre is a segment of an organization where an individual manager is held responsible for the segment's performance. Responsibility centres may take three forms:

1 expense centres in which the manager has no control over revenue but is able to control expenditure;
2 profit centres where the manager has control over both revenue and costs;
3 investment centres where the manager has responsibility not only for revenues and costs but also for the capital invested.

The control problem is made more complex by the size of business organizations and the occurrence of transactions between various divisions of such organizations. In order that divisional performance should be accurately assessed for control purposes, transfer prices should be established which will be useful in this respect. If transfer pricing systems are to operate satisfactorily, some form of negotiated pricing must be agreed by divisional managers. Investment centres pose additional problems as regard the assessment of financial performance. The ROCE is a comprehensive measure of performance, but its limitations should be understood.

Questions

1 State what you understand by 'control'.
2 Examine the nature of the control process.
3 What is meant by 'responsibility accounting'?
4 What is the difference between an 'expense centre' and a 'cost centre'?
5 Discuss the significance of the distinction between 'controllable' and 'non-controllable' costs.
6 What is meant by a profit centre? Give some examples of organizational segments that would be able to function as profit centres.
7 State what criteria are relevent for evaluating transfer pricing policies.
8 Review three main methods used for establishing transfer prices.
9 What is meant by an 'investment centre'. Identify types of organizational segments that would be able to function as investment centres.
1 0 'ROCE is a comprehensive measure of performance, but its limitations should be understood.' Discuss this statement.

Problems

1 Electrical Products Company consists of four operating divisions. Divisional managers are granted considerable discretion in setting employment, sales and production policies. For some time the Chairman, Ronald Jackson, has been concerned with the method of evaluating divisional performance. On 1 June 19X2, he wrote the following letter to Miles French, a management consultant:

Dear Mr French
We have been trying to develop a system which will provide an incentive to our division managers and act as a basis for evaluating their effectiveness. Originally we used profit as an index for evaluation. Then we realized that, in order to be meaningful, profit should be related to another index such as profits of prior periods. After giving the matter much thought I have now become convinced that only a composite index, as shown below, will give equal weights to the three principal objectives of a division.

Composite index for evaluating division performance

Objective	Criterion	Last year	This year	% Change
Minimize capital	Capital turnover	1.5	1.7	+ 13
Profitability	Return on sales	10.0%	9.0%	– 10
Growth	Share of market	15.0%	15.6%	+ 4
	Net composite change			+ 7%

I propose to offer each division manger a bonus of £200 for each one per cent increase in the composite index. I aim to present this proposal to the board at the October meeting, and, if approved, start the system next year.

Please let me have an evaluation of this plan in writing.

Yours sincerely,

Ronald Jackson.

Required:
Assuming you are the consultant, write a letter to Mr Jackson evaluating the proposal.

2   The Akroid Corporation Ltd is a divisionalized enterprise manufacturing specialized equipment for the construction industry. Division A makes one of the basic components—the Spikron—which is used by Division B in the manufacture of the Akroid Scraper, which is then sold as a final product. Division B absorbs about three-quarters of the total output of Division A. The Spikron has other applications, and Division A has been selling the remaining 25 per cent of its output to outside firms. The annual profit of Spikrons is 16 000 units. The Spikron is transferred at £350 to Division B, and is sold at £400 to outside firms.

The following costs are associated with the Spikron produced in Division A:

	£
Variable costs at £300 per unit	4 800 000
Fixed costs	200 000
Total costs	5 000 000

A German company makes a similar product to the Spikron, which could be adapted for integration into the Akroid Scraper, and has offered to supply Division B with the adapted product at a cost of £320 per unit.

The Manager of Division B wishes to buy the German product as this will substantially reduce his costs, and make his own product more competitive on the market. The Manager of Division A argues that he would not be able to expand his sales of the Spikron to outside firms, and that, as a result, the profitability of his division would be seriously affected.

Required:
Discuss the implications of the German offer from the point of view of the Akroid Corporation Ltd and of both divisions.

Chapter 36

Standard costs and variance analysis

We turn now to a consideration of an important method of establishing standards of performance by the use of standard costs. The difficulty about using data recorded in the financial accounting system for planning purposes is that it relates to the past and although managers are interested in the results of previous decisions, they are primarily concerned with decisions which will affect the future.

For control purposes, historical costs are of little use. Particularly in times of inflation, past experience will not inform management whether an operation, a job or a department costs too much. Indeed, what management wishes to know is not what costs were in the past but what they ought to be in the present. Once it has been determined what these costs ought to be, actual costs can be compared with them and any difference analysed.

Standard costing has been evolved as a method to meet this need. It relies upon predetermined costs which are agreed as representing acceptable costs under specified operating conditions.

Standard costs and budgeted costs

The principal differences between standard costs and budgeted costs lie in their scope. Whilst both are concerned with laying down cost limits for control purposes, budget costs impose total limits to costs for the firm as a whole, for departments or for functions for the budget period, whereas standard costs are attached to products and to individual manufacturing operations or processes. For example, the production department's budget for the period ahead may envisage a total production of 100 000 units at a cost of £10 a unit, so that the production department will be allocated an expenditure ceiling of £1 million. The unit cost of £10 will have been based upon the established standard costs relating to material usage and price, labour usage and labour costs as well as allocated overhead costs. Standard costs are revised when it is clear that they have ceased to be realistic in terms of current costs.

The relationship between budgeted costs and standard costs is clear: the setting of standard costs as performance standards for control purposes implies that they must be used as a basis for drawing up budget statements and calculating budget costs, for otherwise there can be no confidence in their use as a basis against which actual performance may be measured.

Applications of standard costing

Standard costing is a useful method of control in a number of ways. First, the process of evaluating performance by determining how efficiently current operations are being carried out may be facilitated by the process of management by exception. Very often the problem facing management is the time lost in sifting large masses of feedback information and in deciding what information is significant and relevant to the control problem. Management by exception overcomes this problem by highlighting only the important control information, that is the variances between the standard set and the actual result. This process allows management to focus attention on important problems so that maximum energy may be devoted to correcting situations which are falling out of control.

Second, a standard costing system may lead to cost reductions. The installation of such a system demands a reappraisal of current production methods as it necessitates the standardization of practices. This examination often leads to an improvement in the methods employed which is reflected in a reduction of the cost of the product. One example of cost reductions through increased efficiency may be seen in the simplification of the clerical procedures relating to stock control. All similar items of stock may be recorded in the accounts at a uniform price; this eliminates the need which arises under historical costing for recalculating a new unit price whenever a purchase of stock is made at a different price.

Third, standard costs are used as a basis for determining selling prices. Standard costs represent what the product should cost, and are a much better guide for pricing decisions than historical costs which may contain purchasing and production inefficiencies which cannot be recouped in competitive markets.

Finally, perhaps the most important benefit which may be derived from a standard costing system is the atmosphere of cost consciousness fostered among executives and foremen. Each individual is aware that the costs and output for which he is responsible are being measured, and that he will be called on to take whatever action is necessary should large variances occur. As we concluded earlier in this chapter, if the philosophy of top management is positive and supportive, standard costing may work as an incentive to individuals to act in the best interest of the firm. Moreover, a standard costing system which allows subordinates to participate in setting the standards fosters a knowledge of costing down to shop floor level, and assists in decision making at all levels. Thus, if there should occur spoilt work necessitating a decision from the foreman in charge on whether to scrap or rectify the part involved, a knowledge of costs will enable him to make the best decision.

Setting cost standards

To be effective for the purpose of cost control, standard costs should reflect attainable standards of cost performance. This means that the process of setting standard costs is of critical importance if a standard costing system is to be effective as a means of cost control.

Setting standard costs implies:

1 establishing procedures for setting standards with respect to the price at which resources are acquired and their usage. This suggests the employment of specialist engineers and consultants for determining relative levels of cost efficiency that should be within the firm's reach;
2 establishing procedures for allowing participation by cost centre managers in setting attainable standards. This suggests that there may be resistance to cost standards that are too harshly set, in the form of negative reactions by personnel.

Cost standards are set for all categories of costs and for all cost centres. Setting cost standards for direct costs, such as direct material and direct labour costs, focuses upon price and usage as the two key cost components.

Setting cost standards for indirect costs is relatively more difficult since there is no direct output against which standard costs can be set. This problem is resolved by a surrogate measure of output in respect to which overhead costs can be related.

Overhead costs are considered to vary with activity levels, which are expressed in standardized measures, such as standard labour hour, standard machine hour or standard labour cost.

Further problems associated with standard overhead costs are as follows:

1 an appropriate overhead rate must be selected for allocating standard variable and standard fixed costs per unit;
2 in the case of fixed overhead costs, the overhead rate selected must be calculated by reference to a standard activity level for the budget period.

Setting standard costs for direct material and direct labour

Setting standard costs for direct material and direct labour involves two aspects:

1 quantifying an efficient input of resources;
2 acquiring that input at the best price.

1 Standard direct material costs

The quantity of raw material required for a standard unit is determined by engineers. The standard quantity should include an appropriate allowance for normal wastage in production.

Responsibility for purchasing rests with the purchasing department. The standard price should reflect the best price that the purchasing department can obtain, and be the price expected to be paid during the budget period.

2 Standard direct labour costs

Before standard labour costs can be set, operatives have to be graded according to standardized categories of skills. Labour time standards are set by time and motion study engineers. The standard wage rates are those that are expected to be paid during the budget period.

Variance analysis for direct costs

The control of direct costs through variance analysis is based on two principles:

1 *Management by exception.* Actual expenditure is assumed to be in line with standard costs, unless this is contradicted by information showing that variances are occurring between the budget allowance, based on standard costs, and actual expenditure being recorded in the financial accounting through the process of recording invoices.
2 *Accounting responsibility.* Responsibility for the control of costs is located with the manager having the responsibility for cost centre costs.

The first sign that standard costs are not being respected is the appearance of a *budget variance* on direct material or direct labour. A budget variance is *defined as a difference between the budget allowance for the output achieved and actual spending on the output achieved.* It requires further analysis, before its causal factors may be identified, investigated and, if possible, corrected.

The analysis of the budget variance necessitates splitting up the budget variance into the two components of standard costs, namely the quantity standard and the price standard. As a result, it is possible to attribute the problem to the occurrence of excessive usage or excessive price, or both.

Variances fall into two categories:

1 *unfavourable variances* that arise when the standard allowance is exceeded by actual expenditure;
2 *favourable variances* that are due to actual expenditure being less than the standard allowance.

Clearly, management will be more immediately concerned with possible inefficiencies arising as a result of *unfavourable* variances. *Favourable variances* may arise out of fortuitous events occurring in the firm's favour, for example, a fall in market prices for raw materials. However, favourable variances may also indicate that standards should be adjusted upwards to reflect actual performance more accurately. The truth remains that, under ideal conditions, favourable or unfavourable variances should not occur if standards have been correctly set.

Direct material variances

The analysis of the direct material variance begins by identifying the direct material budget variance. The material budget variance is *the difference between the actual expenditure and budgeted expenditure.* It provides a measure of the overall difference that has to be investigated. It is composed of two elements:

1 price variance, that explains the proportion of the budget variance

that is caused by paying more or less than the standard price for actual purchase;

2 usage variance, that explains the proportion of the budget variance that is due to using more or less material in production than the standard quantity.

The principle of accounting responsibility means that responsibility for the price variances is laid on the purchasing department, whereas responsibility for the usage variance lies with the manager of the appropriate production cost centre.

Example

Ragon Ltd is a small manufacturing company making a product known as Platron. It has a standard costing system, and standard direct material costs per unit of Platron have been set for the budget year 19X6 as follows:

Standard material quantity per unit   3 kilos
Standard price per kilo   0.50

During the month of January 19X6, 4000 units of Platron were produced. This was the budgeted output volume. The following information was obtained by the costing department:

Quantity used during January   11 000 kilos
Quantity purchased during January   15 000 kilos
Budgeted expenditure for January   £6 000
Actual expenditure for January   £8 250

The analysis of the direct material budget variance into its two components is as shown in Fig. 5.25.

Fig. 5.25 Analysis of direct material variances

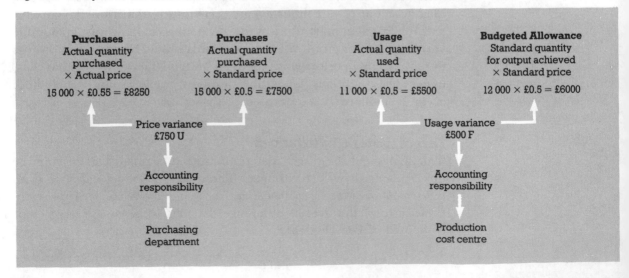

It should be noted that the effects of the price variance have been magnified due to excessive purchasing over usage. Responsibility for the price variance falls on the purchasing department, that may well have acted rationally and in the best interests of the firm in stocking up in anticipation of rising prices. By contrast, responsibility for the usage variance falls entirely on production cost centres.

Direct labour variances

The analysis of the direct labour variance begins by determining the *direct labour budget variance* defined as *the difference between the actual payroll and the budgeted payroll*. The major difference between the analysis of direct material and direct labour variances is in the stocking of direct materials in excess of usage. The terminology is slightly different, though the same meaning is retained. The notion of price is expressed in the labour wage rate; and the notion of usage is stated in labour efficiency. Accordingly, once the direct labour budget variance has been calculated, it is split into *the direct labour wage rate variance* and *the direct labour efficiency variance*.

Example
Standard costs established by Ragon Ltd for the 19X6 budget year were as follows:

Standard direct labour hour per unit	0.25 hour
Standard direct labour rate per unit	£4.00 per hour.

The actual output for the month of January 19X6 was 4000 Platron. This corresponded to the budgeted volume. The following additional information is given:

Actual hours	900
Actual expenditure	£3 690

The direct labour budget variance is analysed into its two components, as shown in Fig. 5.26.

Setting standards for overhead costs

Setting standard overhead costs poses more difficult and complex problems than the setting of standard direct costs in the following respects:

1 setting cost standards;
2 selecting an overhead rate for both standard fixed and variable overhead cost allocation;
3 determining the standard volume for the purpose of recovering standard fixed overhead costs.

Setting cost standards

The setting of efficient cost standards for overheads requires ensuring that the resources classified as fixed and variable overheads have been

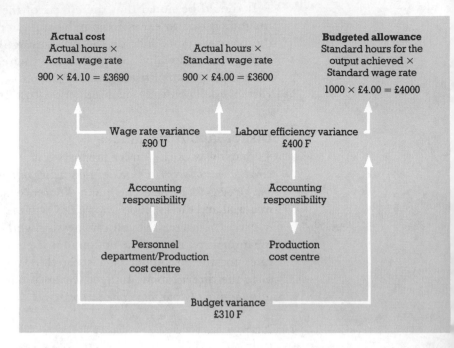

Fig. 5.26 Analysis of direct labour variances

acquired by means of efficient purchasing, and that the usage of these resources corresponds to an efficient utilization.

Efficient purchasing implies that the responsible departments will have secured resources at the best price, and that the budget allowance is a spending level that reflects such purchasing. In this respect, the budget allowance for fixed and variable overheads has a component element that is similar to the standard price and standard wage rate used for setting standard direct material and direct labour costs.

The budget allowance also has another component that assumes that there will be an efficient usage made of variable and fixed costs. This implies that such costs will support a standard level of activity. Therefore, setting efficient usage levels for variable overheads consists in finding what type of activity provokes variations in variable overheads, and then attempting to impose expenditure limits on variable overheads with respect to activity. For example, if the simplifying assumption is made that machine repair and maintenance costs vary with machine hours, the problem is not simply to ensure that repair charges are the best obtainable, but that in relation to machine hours, repairs themselves are not excessive but reflect good machine usage.

Selecting a standard overhead rate

The difficulty in establishing an appropriate level of activity in relation to variable and fixed costs lies in that overhead costs are not directly related to output expressed as units of product. As discussed earlier in

Chapter 27, an overhead rate has to be selected for the purposes of allocating standard variable and fixed overheads to products.

The most convenient overhead rate is the *standard hour* defined as *a unit of measurement representing the quantity of any product or service which can be produced or performed in one hour by any process, machine or operative.*

The standard hour is not a measure of time but a measure of performance in a period of one hour.

Example

If the estimate time required to write 200 letters is 20 hours, a standard hour represents 10 letters. Similarly, if 48 units of product A can be produced in 12 hours, a standard hour of that product represents 4 units.

The standard hour constitutes not only a convenient base for establishing standard overhead rates, but can also be applied to all types of cost centres where it is useful to have a common measure through which the output of diverse products can be expressed.

The standard hour may also be used to develop overhead rates both for variable and fixed overheads.

Three production control ratios are derived from the standard hour:

1   *The efficiency ratio* that measures the efficiency of direct labour and is expressed as follows:

$$\text{Efficiency ratio} = \frac{\text{Standard hours of production achieved}}{\text{Actual direct working hours}} \times 100$$

2   *The production volume ratio* that compares actual output with budget and is expressed as follows:

Product volume ratio

$$= \frac{\text{Standard hours of production achieved}}{\text{Budgeted standard hours}} \times 100$$

3   *The capacity ratio* that compares actual hours with budgeted hours and is expressed as follows:

$$\text{Capacity ratio} = \frac{\text{Actual hours worked}}{\text{Budgeted hours}}$$

Example

Tafel Ltd manufactures tables and chairs. It is estimated that 2 hours are required for one table and 1 hour for one chair. In March, 19X2, actual production was 50 tables and 150 chairs. Budgeted production for the period was 40 tables and 160 chairs. Actual hours worked were 230 and actual output in terms of standard hours was:

Tables: 50 units × 2 hours per unit = 100 hours
Chairs: 150 units × 1 hour per unit = 150 hours
                                   250 standard hours

Budgeted production in terms of standard hours:

Tables: 40 units × 2 hours per unit = 80 hours
Chairs: 160 units × 1 hour per unit = 160 hours
250 standard hours

$$\text{Efficiency ratio} = \frac{250}{230} \times 100 = 108.7\%$$

$$\text{Production volume ratio} = \frac{250}{240} \times 100 = 104.2\%$$

$$\text{Capacity ratio} = \frac{230}{240} \times 100 = 95.8\%$$

These results may be checked as follows:

$$\text{Production volume ratio} = \text{Capacity ratio} \times \text{Efficiency ratio}$$

$$104.2\% = \frac{230}{240} \times \frac{250}{230}$$

Determining the standard volume for fixed overhead cost recovery

Variable overhead costs vary directly with output. Hence, if the output is expressed in standard hours, variable overheads will be applied to actual output in accordance with the predetermined rate.

Fixed costs, however, do not vary with output. Hence, a normal or standard output must be budgeted to enable a fixed overhead rate to be calculated. The standard fixed overhead rate will be applied to the number of standard hours fixed in the budget.

The term *fixed budgeting* refers to budgets prepared on the basis of a standard output for the purposes of establishing budget allowances throughout the firm. Under fixed budgeting, standard fixed overheads will be over- or under-applied whenever actual output is greater or less than the standard output, giving rise to favourable or unfavourable volume variances.

Firms will need always to plan their financing requirements on the assumption that they will attain the budgeted output level. In this sense, the financial budget will always be a *fixed budget*. The disadvantages of using the fixed budget for control purposes lies in the inability to control costs under fluctuating output conditions.

Flexible budgeting

Flexible budgeting is intended to overcome the difficulties posed by fixed budgeting for controlling overhead costs. Flexible budgeting does not replace fixed budgeting for planning the financing requirement purposes. It only replaces fixed budgeting for control. The particular difficulties that make fixed budgeting redundant for control are:

1 overhead allowances are budgeted in respect of only one output volume, namely, the standard output;
2 fixed overheads will generally be under- or over-applied, but responsibility for volume variances cannot be attributed to cost centre managers, since they are not responsible for output variations.

Flexible budget allowances

Flexible budgeting allows fluctuations in output levels to be taken into account for cost control purposes by means of flexible budget allowances.

Example

Jobin Ltd is a small manufacturing company that has a budgetary planning and control system based on the fixed budgeting principle. The fixed budgeted overhead allowance for assembly cost centre A is £20 000 for a period during which the standard output was represented by 5000 standard hours. The budgeted allowance was calculated as follows:

	£
	£
Indirect material	5 000
Indirect labour	2 500
Repairs and maintenance	5 000
Insurance	1 500
Rates	3 000
Depreciation	3 000
	£20 000

The overhead costs per unit are:

£20 000 ÷ 5000 = £4

The firm has experienced severe fluctuations in demand for its products over several months. As a result, actual costs have diverged significantly from budget allowances. It has now decided to introduce flexible budgeting making it possible to match any given actual output with a corresponding budget allowance. During the month of June, actual activity level of cost centre A was 4000 standard hours, for which the following flexible budget allowance was calculated:

	Total variable costs	Fixed costs	Total budget allowance
	£	£	£
Indirect material	4 000		4 000
Indirect labour	2 000		2 000
Repairs and maintenance	2 400	2 000	4 400
Insurance	800	500	1 300
Rates		3 000	3 000
Depreciation		3 000	3 000
	9 200	8 500	17 700

Flexible budgeting improves the control of overhead costs by establishing a flexible budget allowance for each output level, once that output is known. In effect, cost centres are allowed to incur overhead costs at a predetermined standard rate. Control is applied routinely for each management reporting period, usually monthly, when the flexible overhead allowance for the actual output achieved is calculated.

Example

Jobin Ltd has a fixed financial budget providing for a monthly output of 5000 units. On this basis, each cost centre has been given a monthly budget allowance corresponding to predetermined standard costs per unit. Jobin Ltd uses flexible budgeting for cost control. During the month of June, actual output was 4500 units. Actual overhead costs incurred amounted to £19 150. The following overhead cost control report was prepared.

	(1) Actual cost of production	(2) Total budget allowance	(3) Original budget	(4) Variation from original budget	(5) Variation from budget allowance
Units produced	4 500	4 500	5 000	(1)–(3)	(1)–(2)
Indirect materials	£4 700	£4 500	£5 000	£300F	£200U
Indirect labour	£2 400	2 250	2 500	100F	150U
Repairs and maintenance	4 600	4 700	5 000	400F	100F
Insurance	1 450	1 400	1 500	50F	50U
Rates	3 000	3 000	3 000	—	—
Depreciation	3 000	3 000	3 000	—	—
	£19 150	£18 850	£20 000	£850F	£300U

Variance analysis for overhead costs

The analysis of overhead cost variances fall into two parts:

1 the analysis of variable overhead costs;
2 the analysis of fixed overhead costs.

Variable overhead cost variance

The analysis of the variable overhead cost variance begins by identifying the variable overhead budget variance, which is *the difference between the actual expenditure and budgeted expenditure.* It provides a measure of the overall difference that has to be investigated. It is composed of two elements:

1 expenditure variance, that explains the proportion of the budget variance that is caused by differences in the price paid services charged as overhead costs. It is calculated as follows:

Expenditure variance = Actual overheads – (Actual hours × Standard variable overhead rate)

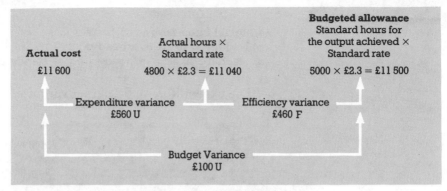

Fig. 5.27 Analysis of variable overhead variances.

2 efficiency variance, that explains the proportion of the budget variance that is due to difference in the usage of services charged as overhead costs. It is calculated as follows:

Efficiency variance = (Actual hours – standard hours) × Standard variable overhead rate).

Example

Scat Ltd has an assembly cost centre that is budgeted for an output of 5000 standard hours. The following information is given with respect to October 19X3:

(a) actual hours worked   4 800
(b) variable costs incurred   £11 600
(c) standard variable overhead rate per standard hour   £2.3

    The expenditure and efficiency variances are calculated as shown in Fig. 5.27.

Fixed overhead cost variances

Fixed overhead cost variances fall into two types:

1 *expenditure variance,* calculated as follows:

    Fixed overhead cost expenditure variance = actual fixed overheads – budgeted fixed overhead costs,

2 *volume variances,* calculated as follows:

    Fixed overhead cost volume variance = budgeted fixed overheads – (Standard fixed overhead rate × Standard hours in the output achieved)

Example

Refer to example above, where the assembly department is budgeted for an output of 5000 standard hours and actual hours worked were 4800. The following fixed overhead cost information is given with respect to October 19X3:

	£
(a) actual fixed overhead costs	6 200
(b) budgeted fixed overhead costs	6 000
(c) standard fixed overhead rate per standard hour	1.7

The expenditure and volume variances are calculated in Fig. 5.28.

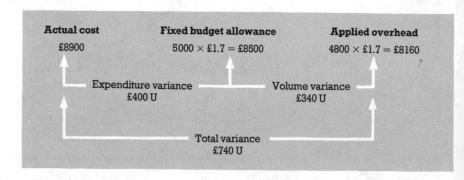

Fig. 5.28 Analysis of fixed overhead variances under fixed budgeting.

The analysis of fixed overhead cost variances will be different under fixed budgeting and flexible budgeting cost control systems with respect to the volume variance. As mentioned earlier, the use of fixed budgeting will lead to the appearance of a fixed overhead cost volume variance, since the fixed overhead rate used for recovering fixed overheads will have been determined on the basis of a fixed output level. Under flexible budgeting, however, the fixed overhead cost volume variance disappears, and there is only an expenditure variance.

Sales variance analysis and the control of revenue

In general terms, the procedures appropriate for the control of revenue are similar to those applied to the control of costs, and may be summarized as follows:

1 The establishment of a sales plan.
2 The prompt determination and reporting of variances between actual and planned performance.
3 The investigation and analysis of variances so as to ascertain their causes and those responsible for them.
4 The implementation of appropriate corrective action.

The determination of the sales plan has both long-range and budgetary aspects. Long-range planning will be concerned with establishing revenue objectives and goals, from which may be derived specific sales targets and prices for the budget planning period. Since the level of demand for most products exhibits a seasonal pattern, the annual sales plan should be divided into smaller periods so as to make possible a system of responsibility accounting based on a meaningful comparison of actual and planned performance.

So far, we have discussed the control of revenue in terms of analysing the difference between actual and planned sales. It should be apparent, however, that management is not really so much concerned about sales themselves as the profit from sales. It is for this reason that sales variance analysis has been developed to measure the effects on profits of variances between actual sales and planned sales, and not the effect of such variances merely on revenue.

Three different variances are commonly applied to the analysis of sales:

1 Sales price variance
2 Sales volume variance
3 Sales mix variance.

Sales price variance

It is quite common for actual selling prices to differ from the planned selling price. Numerous factors may be responsible for sales price variances, such as the need to adjust prices to meet competition, or to provide a new marketing strategy. By far the largest factor is the discretion allowed to individual sales managers to adjust prices to meet particular circumstances, such as price reductions for slightly spoiled goods or to secure the goodwill of a client.

The sales price variance is an ordinary price variance of the type we have already discussed. It may be calculated from the following formula:

sales price variance = units sold
$\quad$ × (actual contribution per unit less the standard contribution)

It indicates, therefore, the total effect on profit of differences between set prices and the prices at which goods were actually sold.

Sales volume variance

This variance discloses the effect on profits of differences between the planned sales volume and the actual volume of sales. It is calculated as follows:

sales volume variance = standard contribution per unit
$\quad$ × (actual number of units sold – budgeted units of sales)

Sales mix variance

A change in the product mix may change the profitability of the total mix if the contribution margin of the different products is different. In these circumstances, changes in the product mix will lead to a variance between planned and actual profits. The dimension of this variance may be computed as follows:

sales mix variance
$\quad$ = standard contribution per unit of each product
$\quad$ × (actual quantities of units sold
$\quad$ – actual total sales of units in budgeted mix proportions)

Example of all 3 variances

The following data relate to products X and Y sold by Biproducts Ltd during the quarter ended 31 December 19X0:

Budgeted sales:

    X 5000 units at £10 (standard contribution margin £4)
    Y 5000 units at   £5 (standard contribution margin £2)

Actual sales:

    X 4000 units for £44 000 (i.e. £11 per unit)
    Y 8000 units for £32 000 (i.e.   £4 per unit)
    These data may be tabulated as follows:

	(a) Actual contribution	(b) Actual quantity	(c) Standard contribution margin	(d) (b)×(c) Value	(e) Actual quantity in standard proportions	(f) Standard contribution margin	(g) (e)×(f) Value	(h) Budgeted margin
	£	Units	£	£	Units	£	£	£
X	20 000	4 000	4	16 000	6 000	4	24 000	20 000
Y	8 000	8 000	2	16 000	6 000	2	12 000	10 000
	28 000	12 000		32 000	12 000		36 000	30 000

Notes

1   Column (a) is derived from the following formula:
actual contribution
    = actual sales less (actual units × standard cost)
    = £44 000 – (4000 × £6)
    = £20 000

2   Column (e) is derived by taking total actual sales of 12 000 units and applying the budgeted mix proportions. According to the budget, 50 per cent of X and 50 per cent of Y should be sold. Total sales were 12 000 units, which expressed in budgeted mix proportions amount to 6000 units of X and 6000 units of Y.

The variances which may be extracted from these data are as follows:

Sales price variance

X = units sold × (actual contribution per unit less standard contribution)
    = column (a) – column (d)
    = £28 000 – £32 000
    = £4000 U

The sales price variance is unfavourable to the extent of £4000 because 3000 units of Y were sold at a price which was £1 lower than the standard, while only 1000 units of X were sold at a price which was £1 higher than the standard price.

Sales volume variance

X = standard contribution per unit × (actual number of units sold less budgeted units of sales)

= column (g) – column (h)

= £36 000 – £30 000

= £6000 F

This variance reflects the fact that 12 000 units were actually sold as against a budgeted volume of only 10 000 units. Its value is the contribution which the extra 2000 units would have brought if they were at standard price and mix.

Sales mix variance

= (standard contribution per unit of each product × the actual quantities of units sold) – standard contribution per unit of each product × actual total sales in budgeted mix proportions)

= column (d) – column (g)

= £32 000 – £36 000

= £4 000 U

This variance discloses the reduction in budgeted profits caused by selling a greater proportion of units having a lower contribution margin than the standard.

Responsibility for variances

Under responsibility accounting only those costs incurred by a responsibility centre over which it can exercise control may be used as a basis for evaluation. In variance analysis it is necessary that the precise cause of a variance be determined and that the cause be traced to the individual responsible. It is the function of the individual in charge of each responsibility centre to act promptly upon reports of variances within his control. Variances are not ends in themselves. Rather, they raise the questions: 'Why did the variance occur? What must be done to eliminate them?' Obviously the importance of these questions depends on the significance of the deviations. We see how the significance of a variance is determined in the next section.

The material usage and labour efficiency variances respectively reveal that the quantities of material and labour used in production are either more or less than planned, depending on whether the variances are unfavourable or favourable. If more material is being used than planned, the cause may lie elsewhere than in the production department, for example in the purchase of inferior materials by the purchasing department. The fault may lie in the production department and may be found to be attributable to careless supervision, or the use of untrained staff, or faulty machines. An unfavourable labour efficiency variance may be due to poor control by the foreman, bad labour relations, health factors, production delays, inferior tools and badly trained staff. Again the responsibility for the variance should be located. For example, if due to badly trained staff, this may be caused by inefficiency on the part of the personnel department; but if, on the other hand, the variance is caused by the economic traditions prevailing at the time which had produced a shortage of specialized labour, the variance is considered to be uncontrollable.

Price and wage rate variances may not be controllable by the firm, and this is particularly true of raw material prices and wages agreed nationally with trade unions. On the other hand variances may occur in the negotiation of contracts for materials which are the responsibility of the purchasing department. Purchasing department controls prices by getting several quotations, taking advantage of economic lots and securing cash discounts. Inefficiency in these areas will reveal unfavourable variances for which that department should be held responsible.

With regard to overhead variances, spending variances are usually the responsibility of the department head, because they are usually controllable by him. The volume variance is not normally controllable by the departmental manager; it is usually the responsibility of the sales department or production control.

The investigation of variances

Managerial time is too valuable to be wasted on the unnecessary checking of performance. When standard costs are properly established, they provide an automatic means of highlighting performance variances upon which management may concentrate its attention. Thus, the investigation of variance is concerned only with exceptional variances and not those which are minor deviations from the established standards.

The investigation of a variance is a three-stage process consisting of:

1 an investigation to determine whether the variance is significant;
2 if it proves to be significant, its causes are investigated;
3 if the variance can be corrected, action is taken to ensure that it will not occur in the future.

The determination of the significance of a variance in itself may be problematic. If its definition is left to managerial judgement and experience, inconsistencies may arise in the treatment of different variances solely by reason of behavioural factors affecting a manager's judgement of a situation. Thus, pressure of work in itself may lead him to perceive the significance of a variance as less important than it really is. Moreover, there is unlikely to be complete agreement between different managers about the investigation of borderline cases.

It is necessary, also, to distinguish 'chance' or 'random' variances from significant variances requiring investigation. By viewing the standard as an arithmetical mean about which fluctuations will occur, it is possible to eliminate random variances from significant variances. Experience of the investigation of variances shows that random variances are inherent in standard costing systems. Such variances assume the shape of a 'normal distribution' about the standard, and they are not controllable. It follows that a statistical control chart may be utilized to enable a manager to determine whether a variance is significant or not. It will define the limits within which random or normal variances occur, so that those variances which fall outside these limits may be assumed to be abnormal and, therefore, significant variances.

Statistical control charts have been used for many years for the purpose of quality control, but it is only recently that this technique has been applied to the control of standard cost variances. Statistical control charts permit the elimination of random variances while providing a high probability that non-random variances will be revealed.

The use of statistical control charts requires that upper and lower limits of random variance tolerance be laid down with precision. Setting these limits requires an analysis of the pattern of sample variances, and the standard deviation of the sample may be used to determine the acceptable limits of tolerance. These limits are illustrated in Fig. 5.29.

Fig. 5.29

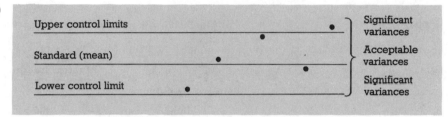

Summary

Standard costing underlies most business activities. The cost of a product must be ascertained prior to production for pricing and control purposes. Standard costing may also lead to cost reductions. Perhaps the most important benefit which results from a standard costing system is the atmosphere of cost consciousness fostered among managers.

Standard cost data are compared with actual cost data for the purpose of ascertaining variances. Such variances are normally broken down into two basic components—quantity variances and price variances. The control of overhead costs as distinct from direct costs requires a method which takes into account the possibility of changes in the level of production during the planning period. Flexible budgeting affords such a method, and provides for each department a series of budget allowance schedules for various volume levels within the normal range of operations.

The ascertainment of variances is only the first stage in assessing results. Variances should be analysed in depth in order to establish whether they are significant, whether they are controllable and if so where responsibility lies. At the same time, the analysis of variances enables established standards to be validated and methods for establishing standards in the future to be improved.

Questions

1 Distinguish standard costs and budgeted costs.
2 State some applications of standard costing.
3 Examine the problems of setting cost standards.

4 Explain what is meant by a budget variance.
5 What is the formula for calculating:

(a) direct material price variance,
(b) direct material usage variance,
(c) wage rate variance,
(d) labour efficiency variance?

6 What problems are involved in setting overhead cost standards?
7 Distinguish between fixed and flexible budgeting.
8 What is the formula for calculating:

(a) variable overhead expenditure variance,
(b) variable overhead efficiency variance,
(c) fixed overhead expenditure variance,
(d) fixed overhead volume variance?

9 State three variances that can be applied to the analysis of sales.
1 0 Comment briefly on the problems that are implied in the investigation of variances.

Problems

1 For March 19X6 the master budget and actual results for Dept A of a firm are as follows:

	Master budget	Actual
Output— Units A	600	500
Units B	400	500
	£	£
Costs: Materials	13 200	13 300
Direct labour	7 000	8 400
Machining	9 600	9 450
Overhead costs	4 400	4 400
	£34 200	£35 550

The master budget was constructed on the following production specifications:

(a) Material required per unit—A, 4 kg; B, 5 kg.
(b) Direct labour hours required per unit—A, 1 hour; B, 2 hours.
(c) Matching costs include a variable element of £4 per machine hour. Machining time required per unit—A, 0.5 hours; B, 0.25 hours.
(d) Overhead costs include a variable element of £1 per direct labour hour worked.

Required:
(a) Construct a flexible budget for the actual output and show any variances.
(b) If it is known that in fact 1400 direct labour hours were worked in March what further information about the direct labour variance can be given?

2 The Vitrox Manufacturing Co. Ltd is a single product company and employs a standard absorption costing system. The standard cost per unit is calculated as follows:

	£
Direct labour 4 hours at £3.00	12.00
Direct materials 10 kg at £1.00	10.00
Overhead	10.00
Total standard cost per unit	32.00

The standard volume of output is 10 000 units per month. The variable overhead cost component is £1.00 per standard direct labour hour.

The following information is available for the month of December 19X1:

	£
Units completed	8 000
Direct materials used 83 000 kg at £1.05	87 150
Direct labour hours recorded 33 000 hours at £3.10	102 300
Variable overhead costs incurred	32 500
Fixed overhead costs incurred	65 000

Required:

(a) Analyse the following variances:
- direct material variances;
- direct labour variances;
- variable overhead variances;
- fixed overhead variances.

(b) Explain possible reasons for the appearance of these variances.

Chapter 37

The control of managed costs

Traditionally, accountants have been concerned with the control of manufacturing costs, where clear-cut input–output relationships may be established. Accordingly, such costs suggest an engineering approach to cost control and they are described as engineered costs. Standard costing typically represents the development of cost control techniques in this regard.

In recent years, the growing significance of non-manufacturing costs has underlined the importance of developing effective methods of cost control for such costs. The major obstacle that has been encountered lies in the absence of clear-cut input–output relationships. In this chapter, we review some of the methods that are applied in the control of managed costs.

The nature of managed costs

Essentially, managed costs are non-manufacturing costs. Their level is determined at the discretion of management, and for this reason, they are often referred to as 'discretionary costs'.

There are three major categories of managed costs:

1   Administrative costs, incurred in providing the administrative structure. Unlike engineered costs, they are not strictly defined in terms of short-term output, and for this reason, they are considered as relatively fixed. Administrative costs include not only management salaries, but also costs associated with the provision of a host of administrative, accounting and secretarial services.

2   Research and development costs, incurred in developing new products and processes. Research and development is in the nature of capital investment, and for this reason is related to long-term planning. There are two reasons why research and development costs are difficult to control:

   (i)   Given the speculative nature of research, and the uncertainty of a return from expenditure invested in research, research spending is no indicator of the effectiveness of a research department or as a means of evaluating a research project.

   (ii)   There is a long lead time between incurring costs and obtaining results, even when research is successful.

3   Marketing costs, incurred in maintaining and increasing market share for the firm's products and services. Marketing costs include a variety of costs, such as advertising, market research, selling, warehousing, distribution, etc. Some of these costs, such as advertising that are concerned with introducing new products or extending market share are in the nature of capital expenditure: others, such as selling costs, are in the nature of operating expenditure. These costs may be difficult to control for the following reasons:

(i)   Some costs, such as advertising, are acknowledged to have an impact on sales, but the relationship between cost and benefit is not easily ascertainable. Furthermore, the long-term and short-term nature of these benefits cannot be measured with accuracy.

(ii) Other costs may be susceptible to input–output analysis, for example, warehousing costs, but most of them, such as salesmen's salaries and sales administration costs lack accurate performance measurement standards.

The control of managed costs

The discretionary nature of managed costs implies that budgeted volume of spending is not analysed in terms of expected output. None the less, despite the difficulties of applying an input–output analysis to discretionary costs, there are implicit assumptions as to the volume and especially to the quality of the activity and services that such costs are expected to provide. In effect, the benefits associated with managed costs are both qualitative and quantitative.

Two main methods that have been developed for controlling managed costs are:

1   Work study measurements, that are in the nature of work engineering studies in which tasks are analysed in terms of workloads, techniques used and number of people required to perform the work efficiently. Work study measurements rely on establishing key control factors to apply to particular activities. Examples of control factors are:

Activity	Control factor
Purchasing	Number of orders placed
Typing	Number of letters typed
Receipting cheques	Number of cheques received

Work study measurements are more suitable for controlling routine costs. They are not useful for controlling non-routine activities that characterize management and specialist functions, in which qualitative factors are critical to success.

2   Budgetary controls, which treat discretionary costs are controlled in terms of departmental spending budgets. This approach to the control of discretionary costs is an application of the methods used to control variable and fixed overhead manufacturing costs discussed in Chapter 36.

Budgetary control

The key to the control of discretionary costs lies in spending budgets relying on the principle of responsibility accounting. The initial problem to be resolved is whether such costs are variable costs or fixed costs for budgeting purposes.

A variable-costing approach to the development of departmental budgets rests on the assumption that there is a cost–volume relationship in which costs rise directly with the volume of activity, and that the relationship is quantifiable.

A fixed-cost approach to the development of departmental budgets treats discretionary costs fixed during the budget period. This approach more correctly reflects the assumptions made by large organizations that existing organizational structures, with which discretionary costs are typically associated, are not changed in the short term, even if they are reviewed from time to time.

Zero-base budgeting

Zero-base budgeting (ZBB) is a method of exposing discretionary centre costs to a critical analysis in the search for an understanding of how activities generate costs. It involves a number of questions that are not normally investigated in traditional budgeting. For example, it involves relating the costs associated with activities to objectives, and critically examining those activities in terms of work performance and possible alternatives.

The control of administrative costs

These costs are relatively fixed in the short run irrespective of short-term changes in the level of business activity. As yet the stricter costing procedures applied to manufacturing activities have not been applied generally to administrative activities. Management would certainly argue that administrative functions are not susceptible to work study methods. Nevertheless, certain tasks such as clerical ones are susceptible to work study, and some organizations have attempted to establish standards of efficiency by which to determine staff requirements. Examples of some of the control factors employed were quoted earlier, namely:

Activity	Control factors
Purchasing	Number of orders placed
Typing	Number of letters typed
Receipting cheques	Number of cheques received

Generally, administrative services are rendered indirectly to many different departments, and it is practically impossible to establish input–output relationships which would enable overall evaluations to be made. Hence, the control of administrative costs is one of the most difficult areas of management control.

To some extent, budgets can assist in exercising control over administrative costs. The budgetary control of such costs requires that accounting responsibility be clearly identified with particular managers.

Financial requirements must be submitted as budget requests by individual managers, and should be scrutinized, modified as necessary and incorporated subsequently into an overall administrative budget. The administrative budget becomes the standard against which expenditure is to be assessed.

The difficulty in using this method of controlling administrative costs lies in determining whether the initial budget is reasonable for the proposed level of activity, for there is no way of establishing an acceptable standard of administrative expenditure in relation to particular activity levels. Hence, decisions regarding administrative cost budgets must be based largely on executive judgement and experience.

The control of research and development costs

There are two main reasons why research and development costs are difficult to control. First, since there is little connection between research costs and their benefits, research spending is no indicator of the effectiveness of a research department, or indeed, of a research project. Second, there is a long lead time between costs incurred and benefits received.

Research and development is an activity directly related to long-range planning. The effectiveness of research and development expenditure may be assessed only in relation to the attainment of goals specified in the long-range plan. These goals should be selected by top management as crucial areas to which major research effort should be directed. In this connection, research expenditure should be concentrated on specific projects which form part of the research effort in a particular area. The control of such expenditure may be exercised by reference to the progress made towards the completion of such projects.

The control of marketing costs

Marketing costs have become significant elements in total costs, owing to the rising burden of such costs as advertising and market development. It follows that attention should be directed towards developing the most efficient cost control methods in this area to provide marketing managers with information which will enable them to make the best decisions from the firm's point of view.

Marketing costs cover a wide range of activities, including obtaining sales orders, warehousing and distribution, handling returns and after-sales service. They may be analysed on three different bases—the nature of the cost, the function performed and the appropriate sector of the firm's business, as follows:

1   *Classification as to costs*
    Salesmen's salaries and commission
    Travelling
    Advertising

2   *Classification as to function*
    Selling
    Advertising
    Transportation
    Credit collection
    Warehousing
    Invoicing
3   *Classification as to business sector*
    Territory
    Product
    Marketing channels
    Operating divisions
    Customers

The analysis of marketing costs is helpful in providing information which is useful for a number of purposes, such as:

- Determining the profitability of sales territories.
- Evaluating the profitability of product lines.
- Setting selling prices.
- Evaluating salesmen's performance.
- Determining the importance of individual customers.
- Analysing order size profitability.

It is evident from the description of the range of decisions for which information is required that the analysis of marketing costs is concerned essentially with profitability, which is a function both of revenue control and cost control.

Determining the profitability of sales territories

Most marketing activities are organized on a territorial basis. As a first stage in the analysis of territorial profitability, it is necessary to distinguish direct and indirect marketing costs. Direct costs are those incurred in respect of a territory: indirect costs are those incurred for all the various sales territories. Direct costs will be controllable by territorial sales managers: indirect costs are beyond their control. Nevertheless, despite difficulties in effecting accurate apportionments of indirect costs, such apportionments serve the useful purpose of providing regional managers with information of the back-up services which support their own activities and should be made, provided that they are distinguished from controllable items on reports.

Table 5.1 shows how the analysis of the profitability of sales territories may be made. Its purpose is to locate territories where weaknesses and problems exist. Once they have been located, prompt and intelligent managerial action is required, which may include such decisions as an increase in the number of salesmen operating in the area, or an improvement of the services provided. It will be recalled that the existence

Table 5.1 Profit analysis by territories

	Territory 1	Territory 2	Territory 3	Total
Sales	£500 000	£300 000	£100 000	900 000
Direct costs by territories:				
Cost of goods sold	250 000	160 000	40 000	450 000
Transport and outside warehousing	30 000	20 000	10 000	60 000
Regional office expenses	50 000	30 000	20 000	100 000
Salesmen's expenses	25 000	15 000	6 000	46 000
Other regional expenses	15 000	10 000	5 000	30 000
Total direct cost by territories	370 000	235 000	81 000	686 000
Contribution to headquarters' overheads and profit	130 000	65 000	19 000	214 000
Indirect costs:				
Central administration	50 000	22 000	8 000	80 000
Central warehousing	20 000	8 000	2 000	30 000
Advertising	30 000	15 000	5 000	50 000
Total indirect costs	100 000	45 000	15 000	160 000
Net profit	30 000	20 000	4 000	54 000
Percentage of net profit	56%	37%	7%	100%
Percentage of sales	56%	33%	11%	100%
Contribution/sales %	26%	22%	19%	23%

of a contribution margin warrants the continuance of operations in the short run even though conventional calculations indicate a loss.

Determining the profitability of products

The analysis of the profitability of different products is useful to management in a number of ways. Not only does it indicate the relative profitability of different products, but also areas of strength and weakness which should be noted in the development of corporate strategy. The application of techniques such as contribution margin analysis may assist in deciding whether or not to drop a product line. Pricing decisions may also be based on profitability analysis.

The selection of appropriate bases for determining profitability is problematical, as it is for other management purposes which require the apportionment of indirect costs.

Table 5.2 below shows how the analysis may be conducted. It indicates that product C is the least profitable product in the product range, for although it makes a contribution of £78 000 to fixed expenses and profit, a net loss of £28 000 is associated with its manufacture. Hence, the analysis implies that action should be taken to improve its profitability in the future.

Table 5.2 Profitability analysis by product

	Products A	B	C	Total
Sales	£350 000	£300 000	£250 000	900 000
Variable costs of goods sold	90 000	85 000	125 000	300 000
Gross contribution	260 000	215 000	125 000	600 000
Variable marketing costs:				
Transport and warehousing	15 000	12 000	13 000	40 000
Office expenses	30 000	30 000	20 000	80 000
Salesmen's salaries	20 000	15 000	10 000	45 000
Other expenses	6 000	5 000	4 000	15 000
Total variable marketing expenses	71 000	62 000	47 000	180 000
Contribution to fixed expenses and profit	189 000	153 000	78 000	420 000
Fixed expenses:				
Manufacturing	55 000	50 000	45 000	150 000
Administration	30 000	25 000	25 000	80 000
Marketing	50 000	50 000	36 000	136 000
Total fixed costs	135 000	125 000	106 000	366 000
Net profit (loss)	£54 000	£28 000	£(28 000)	£54 000
Contribution/Sales %	51%	51%	31%	47%

Controlling marketing costs

Marketing costs may be classified into order-getting and order-filling costs. The former are associated with such activities as advertising, sales promotion and other selling functions: the latter are incurred after the order has been obtained, and cover such costs as packing, delivering, invoicing and warehousing finished products.

Order-getting costs

The effectiveness of such costs may only be satisfactorily assessed by relating them to sales revenue. Many factors which affect sales, however, are outside the control of the sales department, and for this reason it is difficult to establish standards of performance which are relevant to the problem of maintaining and increasing the effectiveness of order-getting activities. Budgetary control may be used to determine the limits of expenditure but it is not possible to use such budgetary control methods as flexible budgeting in respect of some items, particularly advertising. Flexible budgeting is designed to control expenditure through changing levels of activity: advertising is incurred in order to increase the level of activity. It would be nonsense, therefore, to attempt to apply flexible budgeting to the control of advertising expenditure.

The search for suitable methods of controlling order-getting costs continues. Objective measures may be too limited in their scope to be useful. Firms are using such objective measures as selling costs per order, selling costs per call, or calls per day to control selling costs. These measures should be used with care, for they do not necessarily reflect difficulties in selling to different markets at different times.

Advertising costs, in particular, involve such a large financial commitment that it is necessary that the effectiveness of such costs should be assessed. Market research departments are better equipped than accountants to assess the effectiveness of advertising, since its effects go beyond the expansion of immediate sales.

Order-filling costs

It is comparatively easier to control order-filling costs than order-getting costs, since order-filling costs are associated with internal procedures. These procedures are of a standard form and of a repetitive nature making them susceptible to standard control methods: the costs of invoicing, packaging and despatching can be controlled by reference to such objective standards as number of invoices dealt with, number and size of packages, etc. Moreover, unlike order-getting costs, flexible budgeting may be applied to the control of order-filling costs.

Example
Bloxwich Ltd has a sales budget which envisages the sales of 100 000 units of its product in the current year. Budgeted delivery costs are based on standard delivery costs of £1 per unit. If only 80 000 units were sold and delivered by the end of the year at a cost of £90 000, it would be evident that the unfavourable delivery costs variance of £10 000 would require investigation.

Summary

There are two main cost classifications—manufacturing and non-manufacturing costs. Non-manufacturing costs may be subdivided into three categories—administrative, research and development and marketing costs. These costs are frequently referred to as 'managed' or 'discretionary costs' since they are incurred at the discretion of management.

The difficulty of controlling managed costs is created by the absence of a method for determining appropriate cost levels since it is not possible to relate accurately and in financial terms the benefits associated with such costs. Moreover, it is not possible to determine whether a change in managed costs represents an improvement in performance. For example, providing product specifications are maintained, a reduction in manufacturing costs represents an improvement in performance. No such inference may be drawn from a reduction in managed costs.

In view of the rising proportion of managed costs as a percentage of total costs, the analysis and control of such costs is important and means should be found of overcoming the problems caused by the inability to establish rigorous standards.

Questions

1 What do you understand by managed costs?
2 Describe three major categories of managed costs.
3 Explain the problems implied in the control of managed costs.
4 To what extent are work study measurements useful in controlling managed costs?
5 Examine the process of budgetary control as applied to managed costs.
6 What is zero-base budgeting?
7 Discuss the problems associated with the control of administrative costs.
8 Review the problems of controlling research and development costs.
9 Indicate some of the considerations implied in the control of marketing costs.
1 0 Review three bases on which marketing costs may be analysed.

Chapter 38

Behavioural aspects of performance evaluation

Traditionally, accountants have followed economists in assuming the main organizational problem to be the maximization of profits and the optimization of resource allocation to this end. Consequently, accountants have tended to regard organizations in purely technical terms, subjecting human resources to the same analysis as that applied to other economic resources in the search for maximizing productivity and profits.

For more than two decades, social progress, political change and the internationalization of corporate organizations have created a strong awareness of the uniqueness of human resources, and in particular, of the way in which the behaviour of both management and workers affects the realization of organizational objectives. Both management and workers are recognized as having variable performance patterns depending directly on management styles and organizational culture. Much of the early work in this area was concerned with managerial performance evaluation, and the reaction of workers to management style and organizational culture was in the literature of accounting. Recently, the success of Japanese organizations that is seen as a function of organizational culture has prompted more research into the influence of culture on business performance.

In this chapter, we review briefly some of these developments.

Managerial style and organization culture

According to Horngren and Foster (1987) managerial style is 'the set of behaviors exhibited by key managers in an organization.' This is interpreted as a tendency to authoritarian as against participative management styles in relation to decision making and the context in which performance is evaluated.

Again, according to these authors, organization culture is 'the set of beliefs and values shared by members of the organization'. This is interpreted as relating to prevalent interpersonal relationships and other significant constraints on social behaviour.

The considerable success of Japanese industry has underlined the importance of culture as a key success factor, and points to a definition of this concept in an organization setting that arguably is much broader than the definition adopted by Horngren and Foster. In effect, culture may be deemed to determine the manner in which both workers and management interact, and also the manner in which management decisions are made. Accordingly, management style may be viewed as subsumed in the concept of organization culture.

Much of the international comparisons of the relative success of business organisations made currently tends to find substantial cause for disparity precisely in different national cultures as they find their expression in business enterprises. How far this may be substantiated as against the weight of other success factors may be questioned. Nevertheless, the existence of the belief is in itself symptomatic of the importance attached to culture.

There is considerable controversy in the debate regarding the deterministic influence of culture as an organisational success factor. Moreover, culture is not transmissible in the peculiar way in which it is associated with national traits. For these reasons, we shall concern ourselves with the traditional accounting concern of evaluating management performance, as expressed in the literature of the English-speaking nations.

The objectives of performance evaluation

The objectives of performance evaluation may be stated as follows:

1 to assess how effectively the responsibilities assigned to managers have been carried out;
2 to identify areas where corrective actions should be taken;
3 to ensure that managers are motivated towards organizational goals;
4 to enable comparisons to be made between the performance of different sectors of an organization, to discover areas where improvements may be made.

In our analysis of the process of control, we have so far discussed two important prerequisites for performance evaluation:

1 identifying areas of responsibility over which individual managers exercise control (responsibility accounting), and
2 the setting of standards of performance to be used as yardsticks for the evaluation of performance. In this chapter, we address ourselves to some of the behavioural problems of budgets as measures for evaluating performance.

Leadership styles and the problem of control

There is a tendency for firms to expect desired results merely from the use of appropriate techniques, thereby failing to recognize that success in organizational control depends upon the actions of responsible individuals and their appreciation of the importance of sound interpersonal relatonships. The manner in which the budgeting process is viewed depends on the leadership style adopted by management. McGregor has characterized the two extremes of management styles as 'Theory X' and 'Theory Y' (McGregor, 1960). According to McGregor, these extreme views are conditioned by the manager's view of man.

Theory X

The Theory X view of man, as summarized below, is supportive of an authoritarian leadership style:

1   Management is responsible for organizing the elements of productive enterprise—money, materials, equipment and people—in activities directed to economic ends.
2   As regards people, management is concerned with directing their efforts, motivating and controlling their actions, and modifying behaviour to fit the needs of the organization.
3   Without this active intervention by management, people would be passive—and even resistant—to organizational needs. Therefore, they must be persuaded, rewarded, punished, controlled. In short, their activities must be directed, and therein lies the function of management. This view is often summed up by the assertion that management consists of getting things done through other people.

Theory Y

By contrast, Theory Y is supportive of a more democratic and participative leadership style:

1   Management is responsible for organizing the elements of productive enterprise—money, materials, equipment and people—in activities directed to economic ends.
2   People are not by nature passive or resistant to organizational needs. They appear to have become so as a result of negative experiences of organizational needs.
3   The motivation, the potential for development, the capacity for assuming responsibility, the readiness to direct behaviour towards organizational goals are all present in people. Management does not put these qualities in people. It is the responsibility of management to make it possible for people to recognize and develop these human characteristics.
4   The essential task of management is to arrange organizational conditions and methods of operation so that people can achieve their own goals best by directing their efforts towards organizational objectives.

There is evidence that the Theory X leadership style is widely prevalent and is clearly operational. Those who prefer the assumptions of Theory Y claim that the Theory X leadership style has a human cost in the frustration and the lack of personal development which results from its application to people. The trend in behavioural research suggests that benefits may be derived from leadership and organizations based on the assumptions of Theory Y. These assumptions recognize, in particular, that the basic motivating forces affecting people at work include biological, egoistic and social factors.

As a person, the employee at whatever organizational level has certain needs which condition his own objectives. He is seeking *compensation* for his efforts to enable him to provide some desired standard of life for himself and his family. He needs outlets for his physical and intellectual energies which provide both *stimulation* and *satisfaction*. He seeks *self-realization* in a sense of his own worth and usefulness. He is pursuing further *growth* and greater *personal effectiveness*. He seeks the *recognition* of his fellows, whether his organizational equals, superiors or subordinates. He appreciates his *identification* with a worthwhile and successful undertaking.

In order to maximize the employee's contribution to organizational activities, it follows that these personal needs and goals should be capable of realization in the task in which he is employed. An awareness of the nature of personal needs, therefore, is an important aspect of control.

The effects of budgets on people

Research suggests that there is a great deal of mistrust of the entire budgetary process at the supervisory level (Argyris, 1953). There is a tendency for traditional budgets to provide the following responses.

Reactions to pressure

The evaluation of a manager's performance in terms of his departmental budget is one of the few elements in performance appraisal which is based on concrete standards. There is little room for manipulation or escape if results are not going to turn out as expected in the budget. If budget pressure becomes too great, it may lead to mistrust, to hostility and eventually to poorer performance levels as reaction sets in against budgetary control.

The problem of distinguishing between controllable and non-controllable costs is an important cause of tension among managers. The task of the manager of a department or expense centre, for example, is to attain his goals with the minimum cost. One of the initial difficulties which arises in evaluating his performance applies to all levels of management, namely, the treatment of factors beyond his control. This problem is aggravated when the responsibility for an activity is shared by two or more individuals or functions. Labour inefficiency, for example, may be due to excessive machine breakdowns (maintenance function), inferior materials (purchasing function), defective materials (inspection function) or poor-calibre personnel (personnel function). Establishing standards of performance in itself is not an easy task. It demands the clear definition of goals and responsibilities, the delegation of authority, the use of satisfactory surrogates for the activities concerned, effective communication of information and an understanding of the psychology of human motivation.

Overemphasis on the short run

One of the dangers facing organizations which evaluate the effectiveness of managers in profit terms is that too much emphasis is given to achieving short-term profitability, and measures taken to improve short-term profitability may be detrimental to the organization's long-term prospects. Short-term increases in profits gained at the expense of reductions in research and development and the failure to maintain adequate standards of maintenance are two examples of short-term cost savings which are detrimental to the firm in the long term.

Poor-quality decision making by top management

Excessive reliance on the profit performance of divisions may also affect the quality of decisions made by top management. If the managerial competence of divisional managers is assessed solely on the basis of the profit performance of their respective divisions, serious errors of judgement may result. Moreover, if profit results are used as part of an early-warning system, action may be taken by top management which may not be warranted. Therefore, although profit budgets are indispensable for planning purposes, great care should be taken in utilizing them for control purposes. The attainment of profit targets is dependent on many factors, some of which are entirely outside the control of a divisional manager. The uncertainty attached to profit forecasts, in particular, limits the usefulness of profit targets for the evaluation of the performance of a divisional manager. The process of formulating the divisional profit forecast also introduces bias in the evaluation of performance. Divisional profit targets are usually based on the divisional manager's forecast of future events. Therefore, it is his ability to forecast the future successfully rather than his ability to manage successfully, which forms the basis on which his performance is evaluated. This consideration also affects the validity of comparisons between the performance of different divisions. For example, it is easier to determine an attainable profit goal for a division whose major constraint is productive capacity, where sales are limited only by output, than for a division which sells in a highly competitive market.

Another problem arising from the use of profit budgets in evaluating divisional performance stems from the fact that an annual budget covers too short a period in which to obtain a realistic picture of managerial performance. The effects of decisions in some instances may take several years before being reflected in profit performance. Thus, the decision to introduce a new product is one of several decisions whose impacts on divisional profits take some years before they are fully realized. The more complex and innovative the division the longer will be the time period necessary for the evaluation of performance. In the light of these considerations, the use of an annual profit result may give a completely inaccurate view of divisional performance.

Poor communication

Where a Theory X style of management exists, negative attitudes may be generated against organizational goals which may lead to faked budget results and the unwillingness to transmit information. Managers will feel that their own survival justifies these tactics.

The prevalence of negative behaviour in an organization which practices management by domination may be aggravated by the response of top management, when it is realized that information which is needed for decision making is not transmitted. Their immediate reaction may be to impose even tighter controls, which will reinforce the negative attitudes held by subordinate managers leading to the transmission of even less accurate and useful information. The progressive tightening of the managerial reins may well result, therefore, in a progressive deterioration of the information flow.

The communication of information is of central importance to the processes of planning and control, as it provides the link between various levels of management and the various decision points. Any reluctance on the part of subordinate managers to communicate information is a serious impediment to the efficiency with which planning and control decisions are made. It is not a sufficient condition for success that an organization should have accounting control systems and that it should have stipulated standards of performance. These control methods will not operate successfully and standards of performance will not be attained if the style of management adopted fails to secure a high degree of motivation and goal congruence within the organization.

Departmental self-centredness
The budget process which involves defining areas of responsibility, measuring and comparing performance accordingly, concentrates the manager's entire attention on his own department. The tendency to departmental self-centredness which is thus encouraged obscures the important relationships between departments, so that interdepartmental dependencies may be ignored or overlooked in the quest for optimizing departmental results. Consequently, economies which would result from greater interdepartmental collaboration may be lost to the organization.

The stifling of initiative
The planning and control aspects of budgeting may be overemphasized within an organization with the result that opportunities for the exercise of personal initiative may be excluded. Budgets which appear to be strait-jackets discourage managers from deviating from budget stipulations even when circumstances indicate that individual action should be taken.

Bias in budgeting
In the last analysis, the process of setting budget targets may be said to be a matter of making subjective judgements, and, as a result, bias may inevitably be found in the budgeting process in a conscious or unconscious form. Managers may inflate costs and reduce revenue expectations when setting budget targets, thereby ensuring that they are more readily achievable. In this way, the introduction of conscious bias

is a deliberate means of ensuring that their performance as managers will be highly evaluated.

The introduction of bias into estimates that find their way into budget standards typifies the behavioural responses of individuals to organizational pressures. Take the example of a salesman threatened with the possibility of redundancy as a result of falling sales. In such circumstances, he may well find it to his advantage to make optimistic forecasts of sales expectations in his area. By contrast, he may make pessimistic forecasts of achievable sales if his bonus and his performance are evaluated in terms of the extent to which he improves upon the budget target.

The presence of bias in setting budget targets may be met either through the process of counter-biasing, which leads to gamesmanship in budgeting, or by reducing ignorance of fears about the objectives of the firm in relation to personnel. The reduction of conflict between the firm's objectives and the objectives of managers and personnel is discussed later in this chapter, in the context of the system known as management by objectives.

Budget information and performance evaluation

According to Hopwood (1974), budget information may be used in three different ways for the purposes of assessing managerial performance, as follows:

1 Budget-constrained evaluation, where the manager's performance is primarily evaluated on the basis of his ability to continually meet budget targets on the short-term basis.
2 Profit-conscious evaluation, where the manager's performance is evaluated on the basis of his ability to increase the general effectiveness of the operations of his unit in relation to the long-term objectives of the firm. In this case, budget information will be used with a degree of flexibility.
3 Non-accounting evaluation, where budget information plays a relatively small part in the evaluation of the manager's performance.

A summary of the effects of these different styles of managerial evaluation on managerial behaviour is given below:

	Budget-constrained	Profit-conscious	Non-accounting
Involvement with costs	High	High	Low
Job-related tension	High	Medium	Medium
Manipulation of accounting reports	Extensive	Little	Little
Relations with supervisor	Poor	Good	Good
Relations with colleagues	Poor	Good	Good

The need for several measures of performance

While the use of standard costs and variable budgets play an important role in the control of activities and in the evaluation of performance, undue attention to cost control tends to diminish the importance of other goals. For example, a factory manager is expected to maintain a high level of productive efficiency, to maintain the quality of the product, to meet production schedules on time, to minimize expenses and to maintain satisfactory relations with employees.

The evaluation of performance therefore requires both quantitative and qualitative measures of performance. It is evident that some organizational and departmental goals may conflict, such as for example the need to minimize costs and to maintain product quality. Emphasis on specific goals will therefore mean that other goals may not be attained. The objectives of performance evaluation, which we have stipulated, require a balanced view of performance covering the various areas of managerial responsibility. If management uses only conventional measurement of revenues, expenses, profit, cost variances and output, it is possible that short-run economic gains may be achieved at the expense of long-run goals. The failure to appreciate the impact of control techniques on individuals responsible for organizational activities may adversely affect employee morale, loyalty, trust and motivation.

The importance of participation

The active participation by managers in the planning process not only enhances their personal sense of involvement in the organization, but improves the efficiency of the planning process. Moreover, such participation establishes a common understanding of purpose, and promotes the acceptance of organizational objectives and goals at all levels. Likewise, the control process is aided by the active participation of managers in the investigation of variances, the evaluation and selection of appropriate solutions and the development of related policies.

The degree of effort expended by members of an organization in attempting to achieve designated goals is particularly dependent upon their personal aspiration level. The aspiration level may be defined as that level of future performance in a familiar task which an individual explicitly undertakes knowing his past performance level. For example, a manager's aspiration level as regards costs is the spending level which he accepts as realistic and with which he will strive to comply. Hence, we may identify three potential levels of cost performance:

1   the budgeted level
2   the aspiration level
3   the actual level

Since the aspiration level is the real inner goal acceptable to the manager, the purpose of participation is to bring the aspiration level in harmony with the budgeted level (or vice versa). Clearly, a budgeted level significantly at variance with the aspiration level will have a negative effect on managerial behaviour.

It follows that managers should be motivated and not pressurized into achieving their budgetary goals. This may be achieved by recognizing the importance of aspiration levels in the planning stage and the timely communication of results as a basis for improving performance, where necessary. The purpose of participation in the control process is, therefore, to motivate managers and to generate in each participant the desire to accomplish or even improve his level of performance.

Management by objectives

From the foregoing discussion of the problem of controlling the activities of an organization and evaluating managerial performance, it follows that several conditions must be satisfied if the accounting function is to play a useful role.

1 Divisional and departmental goals must be clearly identified and defined, and appropriate measurements selected by which to express them and evaluate managerial performance. Where objectives are too vague or too ambiguous to be susceptible to clear definition in conventional terms, surrogates should be sought which will enable them to be defined and measured.

2 There should be participation by all levels of management in the control process, thereby ensuring good communication between supervisor and subordinate.

3 A style of management is required which pays particular attention to the human element in organizations, and in so doing provides an environment conducive to the employment of all resources.

The aim of management by objectives is to provide a framework for administering a control system which embraces the above-mentioned three conditions. By translating organizational objectives and goals in such a way that they become the personal objectives and goals of all management personnel, whether they be divisional or departmental managers, management by objectives seeks to create a high degree of goal congruence within an organization. The unity of personal and organizational objectives encourages managers to take actions which are in the best interest of the organizations.

Some organizational goals are too remote from individual managers, and therefore, have little significance for them, for example, goals relating to the return on capital employed or overall growth targets envisaged in the long-range plan. Management by objectives seeks to establish personal targets at all levels as a means of overcoming this problem. By relating personal goals to department and divisional goals and thence to organizational goals, an integration is achieved between them which may be depicted as follows:

Personal goals → Divisional goals → Organizational goals

Management by objectives involves the following processes:

1 The review of long-term and short-term organizational objectives and goals.

2 The revision, if necessary, of the organizational structure. An organizational chart is required to illustrate the titles, duties and the relationships between managers.

3 Standards of performance necessary to fulfil key tasks are set by the job holder himself in agreement with his immediate supervisor. Unless the job holder participates in setting performance standards, he will not feel committed to them. The standards of performance which result from systems of management by objectives are not 'ideal', nor are they minimum acceptable levels of performance. They indicate what are agreed to be 'satisfactory' levels of performance. As far as possible, they should be expressed in quantitative terms.

Management controls are operated so that supervisors do not act as watchdogs but rather as sources of help and guidance to their subordinates. A divisional profit goal in this sense is not only a target for the divisional manager, for it may also act as a means whereby top management may help to solve divisional problems should they become apparent through the failure to reach a stipulated figure.

4 Results are measured against goals. An important aspect of this stage is the use of periodic performance appraisal interviews, in which supervisor and subordinate jointly discuss results and consider their implications for the future. The performance appraisal interview is essentially a discussion between manager and subordinate about objectives and their achievement. Performance appraisal should evaluate the manager not merely in terms of current performance as expressed in tangible results; it should also enable his performance as a manager, his personal qualifications and character and his potential for advancement to be assessed. It is an integral part of the process of managing by results by which both parties to the interview assess their efficiency as managers. The manager himself assesses his role as tutor to the subordinate; the subordinate considers his role in supporting the manager.

5 Long- and short-term organizational goals are reviewed in the light of current performance.

These stages in management by objectives are illustrated in Fig. 5.30.

Organization theory

Some of the assumptions upon which we have so far relied have been necessary for the purpose of facilitating the examination of the basic aspects of accounting for planning and control. If an accounting system is to be effective in providing information for planning and control purposes, it should be capable of adapting to organizational and environmental factors peculiar to individual enterprises. Different enterprises may require different methods of control, depending on the internal and external influences affecting their own activities. Hence, some of our assumptions may be more applicable to some organizations

Fig. 5.30

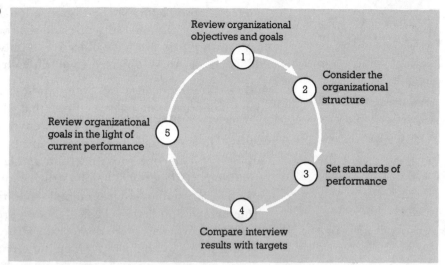

than to others. In this respect, organization theory attempts to provide a framework for understanding the influences which bear upon organizations and is important, therefore, for clarifying issues of importance to the accountant.

Approaches to organization theory

By regarding the organization as a logical and rational process, the classical approach focuses in some detail on the organizing function of management. Hence, the classical theory is concerned with the structure of organizations and the determination of the tasks necessary to attain organizational objectives. By contrast, the human relations approach stresses people rather than structures, their motives and behaviour rather than the activities which need to be harnessed for achieving organizational goals. This approach originated in the Hawthorne experiments of the 1920s, which revealed that social and human factors in work situations were often more important than physical factors in affecting productivity. The human relations theory asserts that since the most important factors are individual needs and wants, the structure of organizations should be geared to individuals rather than the individual being geared to the structure.

Finally, there has developed the contingency approach which starts with the premise that there is no single organizational design that is best in all situations. According to this approach there are four factors or forces of particular significance in the design of an organizational structure, namely: *1* forces in the manager; *2* forces in the environment; *3* forces in the task; *4* forces in the subordinates.

1 Forces in the manager. This refers to factors relating to the personalities of managers and their influence on the design of the organizational structure. Managers tend to perceive organizational problems in a unique way, which is a function of background, knowledge, experience and values. These factors shape organizational decisions in such areas as strategy, organizational structure and style of management. Accordingly, organizations do not have objectives—only people have objectives. In this analysis, these objectives will differ from manager to manager.

2 *Forces in the environment.* Some studies suggest that the most effective pattern of organizational structure is that which enables the organization to adjust to the requirements of its environment (Burns and Stalker, 1961). These studies indicate that organizations with less formal structures are best able to cope with uncertain and heterogeneous environmental conditions. Conversely, highly structured organizations will be more effective in stable environmental conditions. Hence, bureaucratic structures, as implied in classical theory, are more appropriate to stable conditions, whereas more democratic structures are required to enable organizations to adapt to a changing environment.

3 *Forces in the task.* Empirical studies indicate that technology has an important impact on the design of an organizational structure. For example, Woodward (1965) has found that organizational structures varied according to the technology involved. According to Woodward, fewer managers are required under systems of unit production than under systems of mass production. The technology associated with unit production systems may also require relatively higher levels of operative skill, and there is evidence to suggest that skilled workers feel more involved in their jobs and are more anxious for an opportunity to participate in decision making relating to their jobs than unskilled workers. This makes it possible to delegate more authority to lower levels in an organization and has important implications for devising schemes based on 'management by objectives'.

4 *Forces in the subordinates.* This refers to the psychological needs such as the subordinate's desire for a measure of independence, for the acquisition of skills and the motivation for assuming responsibility. The desire to participate in decision making is not uniform among employees, and as implied earlier it is much stronger among skilled workers and employees with a professional background than it is among unskilled workers. Hence, organizations employing relatively more skilled than unskilled employees will be faced with a greater desire for a democratic structure.

Agency theory

According to Antle (1989), agency models are highly stylized logical tools for discovering basic relationships. They extend the traditional intellectual boundaries of accounting by assuming that its problems have psychological, sociological, economic and political dimensions. Heretofore, these problems have been recognized to some extent in articles dealing with the behavioural aspects of performance evaluation, which have been discussed earlier in this chapter.

Specifically, agency theory re-examines extant basic assumptions about human behaviour in organizations, by considering behaviour in terms of a model in which actors are acting out a principal and agent relationship. This relationship grants the agent delegated powers to act on behalf of the principal.

Agency theory is claimed to be particularly relevant when focusing on financial reports generated by agents whose performance is in part evaluated on the basis of those reports. If the choice of accounting method rests with the agents, as is normally the case insofar as management information systems are concerned, agency theory assumes that the information reported through these systems will reflect management preferences over what is reported.

E. O. Williamson's seminal work on the existence of managerial discretion as highly significant in organization decision making brought new light on the manner in which personal interests influenced decisions. Williamson's thesis conflicted with the traditional view assumed in accounting theory that the interests of shareholders and managers are joined in the maximization of shareholders' wealth. Agency theory addresses the problem of information reporting for assessing managerial behaviour where management holds private information and does not communicate it, or communicates only the information that it wants to communicate.

From the foregoing, it is evident that agency theory considerably extends the debate over the assessment of managerial performance. It shifts this debate from one in which performance is seen as a reactive problem to be examined in the light of managerial styles to the much wider issue of the vested interests that exist in organizations and that are not adequately recognized in extant theories of the firm.

Summary

The budget process alone is not sufficient to maintain adequate management control. Too often, organizations tend to expect results from budgetary control and fail to recognize its behavioural implications. As a result, pressures are created leading to mistrust, hostility and actions detrimental to the long-term prospects of an organization. It follows that accountants should work more closely with behavioural scientists and that they should learn more about the behavioural implications of organizational control.

Participation schemes may be introduced into organizations with due consideration for the psychological problems entailed. One such scheme is management by objectives. Management by objectives differs from the conventional budgetary control theory in that it enables the precepts of Theory Y to be put into practice by creating an environment which allows employees to develop as individuals and to exercise responsibility through self-control. Self-control is found to induce stronger work motivation, for by giving individual managers greater freedom of action, it affords them in greater measure the satisfaction and pleasure which a sense of accomplishment confers.

Being concerned with the provision of information for planning and control, the accountant should find a knowledge of organization theory particularly useful in understanding the internal and external influences which affect the nature of organizational activities and the environment in which decisions are made. These influences have implications for the design of control systems, and the significance of contingency theory lies in the identification of their sources.

New considerations in the assessment of managerial behaviour have been inspired by protagonists of agency theory, which looks at the impact of discretionary managerial behaviour on management information.

References

Antle, R. (1989). Commentary on intellectual boundaries in accounting research, *Accounting Horizons*, June 1989, pp. 103–9.

Argyris, C. (1953). Human problems with budgets, *Harvard Business Review*, January–February.

Burns, T. and Stalker, G.M. (1961). *The Management of Innovation*, Tavistock Publications.

Hopwood, A. (1974). *Accounting and Human Behaviour*, Accountancy Age Books.

Horngren, C.T. and Foster, G. (1987). *Cost Accounting: A Managerial Emphasis* (6th edn), Prentice-Hall.

McGregor, D.M. (1960). *The Human Side of the Enterprise*, McGraw-Hill.

Woodward, J. (1965). *Industrial Organization: Theory and Practice*, Oxford University Press.

Questions

1 State what you understand by 'managerial style'.
2 What is meant by 'organization culture'.
3 List the objectives of performance evaluation.
4 Explain 'theory X'.
5 Contrast 'theory X' with 'theory Y'.
6 Comment on possible managerial reactions to budgets.
7 State three different ways in which budget information may be used to assess managerial performance.
8 Describe three possible levels of cost performance.
9 Define 'management by objectives'.
10 What do you understand by 'contingency theory'?
11 What do you understand by 'agency theory'?

Problem

The following extract is taken from a conversation between the chairman of Westway Engineering Company and James Brown, accountant, on the day Brown took up his appointment with the company.

Chairman: 'We apply a system of payment by results to foremen as well as to operatives. For each department, budgeted allowances are set for the expenditure which should be incurred over varying levels of output. The greater the saving on budgeted expenditure for a department, the greater the bonus received by the foreman concerned. For example, this report shows how the bonus the foreman of our assembly department had built up suffered a severe jolt last month'.

He hands the following report to Brown.

Westway Engineering Co.—Assembly Department
Foreman: W. Rodgers

	Budget allowance	Actual	For month (Over) under budget	Year to date (Over) under budget
	£	£	£	£
Direct material	4 000	5 000	(1 000)	(3 000)
Direct labour	10 000	12 000	(2 000)	(3 500)
Indirect labour	5 000	4 500	500	1 000
Indirect material	2 000	1 700	300	(1 000)
Power	6 000	6 500	(500)	(2 000)
Maintenance	7 000	10 000	(3 000)	4 000
Depreciation	5 000	4 000	1 000	2 000
Insurance	100	80	20	500
General expense	10 000	8 500	1 500	4 500
			(3 180)	2 000

Chairman: 'Since the new accounting system was installed a year ago, there appears to have been a general deterioration in morale. The relations between a number of staff certainly need improving. Two months ago an error was made on an order, and the goods were returned for correction, a process which cost £700. None of the departmental foremen were prepared to accept the cost of the error, which was finally charged to general factory loss. Because of the incident two foremen stopped talking to each other.'

Required:

Discuss what improvements should be made in the accounting system in operation at Westway's.

Index

Absorption costing, 541–5, 546, 565
Accountants, 8
  and the management team, 486–7
Accounting, definitions of, 3–4
Accounting bases, 65
Accounting concepts, 30, 40, 320–2
Accounting equation, 85–8
Accounting policies, 66
Accounting profession, management influence on, 376
Accounting rate of return, capital expenditure, 487–8
Accounting responsibility and direct costs, 601
Accounting Standards Board (ASB), 44, 377
Accounting Standards Committee, 28, 44, 58, 64–5, 67, 102, 140, 296, 376, 377, 380, 392,
  Corporate Report, 395, 399, 408, 416, 417, 425
  ED 35, 360
  TR 780, 176
  see also Statements of Standard Accounting Practice (SSAPs)
Accruals concept
  adjustments in profit and loss accounts, 149–50
  of financial accounting, 53–4, 103
  financial statements, 381
  periodic measurement and, 117–23
  in SSAP 2, 66–7
ACT (Advance Corporation Tax), 221, 224
Activity ratios, 255–7
Activity-based costing systems, 460–2, 466
Administrative costs, 513
  control of, 618, 620–1
  forecast, 508
Advertising costs, 625
Advisory Conciliation and Arbitration Service (ACAS) Code of Practice, 415–16
Agency theory, 28, 638–9
AICPA (American Institute of Certified Public Accountants), 3, 131
Alexander, S. S., 316, 322
Altman, E. I., 264, 265
American Accounting Association (AAA), 31
Annual reports, 56
Aquisitions, 293
Argenti, J., 265
Argyris, C., 630
Arnold, J., 392
Arrow, K. J., 35
Arrow's general impossibility theorem, 423
ASB, *see* Accounting Standards Board
Articles of association, 188
Assets
  accounting equation, 84–5

Assets (*contd*)
    accounting for the disposal of, 139–40
    ascertaining useful life of, 132–3
    and capital, 312–13
    characteristics, 29
    definition of, 552
    in financial statements, 383, 384, 385
    identifying costs of, 131
    intangible, 173–6, 209
    leasing, 176–9
    loss in value, 128–9
    monetary, 329
    non-monetary, 333
    operate or lease, 569
    in profit and loss accounts
      loss in value, 151–2
    ratio analysis of, 264–5
    residual value of, 133
    standardized, 111
    valuation of, 48–9, 49–51, 167–78
    see also Current assets; Depreciation of assets; Fixed assets
Assets and Liabilities statements, 406
Associated companies, 272
    consolidated acounts, 291–3
Auditors' reports, 199
Audits, 157
    environmental, 429–30
    of forecasts, 402
    position, 473–4
    reports to employees, 413
Authorized capital, 194

Backer, M., 389
Baker, H. K., 392
Balance sheets, 30, 45–6, 159
    associated companies, 292
    based on accounting equation, 85–8
    budgeted, 503, 522
    Companies Acts requirements, 198, 199, 206–18
    concept of periodicity, 56
    consolidated accounts after merger, 297, 298
    deferred taxation, 222–4
    elements, 383
    formal presentation of, 158
    funds flow statements, 230, 231, 232, 233, 234–7
    groups of companies, 271, 272–4, 274–7
    historical cost and replacement cost, 345
    inflation problems, 302
    leases, 176
    minority interest calculations, 287, 288, 289, 290
    money measurement concept, 47–8
    preparing, 155–8
    shareholders' equity, 181–2
    solvency analysis, 252, 253
    standardized, 109, 110
    and variable costing, 545–6
Bank reconciliation statements, 75, 157–8
Barton, A. D., 134, 179
Barwise, P., 176
Basic accounting model, 104–5
Batch transfer of data, 81

Baxter, W. T., 336
Bearer shares, 189
Beaver, W. H., 264
Behavioural theories
    of the firm, 435
    and performance evaluation, 627–41
Bell, P. W., 326
Benefits balanced with costs, 383–4
Bird, P., 391
Bonbright, J. C., 350
Bookkeeping, 5
    uniformity in, 102–3
    see also Double-entry bookkeeping
Brands, 176
Break-even analysis, 523–4
Budget-constrained evaluation, 633
Budgetary controls, 619–20, 624
Budgetary controls, 619–20, 624
Budgetary planning, 441, 500–20, 550
Budgeted cash flow statements, 241
Budgeted costs
    and standard costs, 598–9
    direct labour, 511
Budgets, effects on people, 630–3
Buildings, valuation of, 167
Business failure, ratios as predictors of, 263–5

Capacity ratio and the standard hour, 605
Capital
    accounting equation, 84–5
    characteristics, 29
    concepts of, 311–13
    in corporate enterprises, 187, 188, 189, 191–8
    cost of, 493–4
    funds flows, 236
    investment decisions, 483–5
    maintenance, 313, 314, 317, 341, 385–6
Capital account, 156
Capital expenditure
    budget, 501, 502, 513
    planning, 483–98
Cash books, 75–6
Cash budgets, 514–15
Cash flow statements, 240–3
    and pay bargaining, 418
    reporting to investors, 398–9
    versus profit reporting, 404–5
Cash flows
    and capital expenditure, 485
    discounted (DCF), 488–9, 493, 496
    forecast, 508
    importance of, 473
Cash payments, accruals concept, 5–4
Cash transactions, 97
Centre for Interfirm Comparisons, 251
Chambers, R. J.,
Charts of accounts, 102, 105–6
Classical approach to organization theory, 637
Closed systems, 12
Closing stocks, 347
    in profit and loss accounts, 150

Collective bargaining, reporting for, 415–19
Communication as management function, 444–5
Community involvement, 427
Companies
    corporate enterprises, 188–90
    small and medium-sized, 219, 220
    Companies Act (1980), 198
    Companies Act (1981), 67, 199–200, 294
Companies Act (1985), 171, 198, 413
Companies Act (1989), 199, 200
    and groups of companies, 271–2
Company secretaries, 190
Computers, 22, 81–2
    financial accounting data, 77
Concepts, accounting, 30, 40
Consistency, concept of, 58, 103, 166
    in SSAP 2, 66
Consolidated accounts, preparation of, 272–81
Construction contracts, valuation of, 171–2
Contingency approach to organization theory, 637
Contingent liabilities, 180, 213
Contract costing, 464
Contracts, long-term valuation of, 171–2
Contribution margin
    in break-even analysis, 525–6
    and changes in fixed costs, 530
    and changes in selling price, 532
    and changes in variable costs, 530
    in cost-profit analysis, 523
    and profitability, 623
    in the sales mix, 534
    and short-run tactical decisions, 564–7
Control
    budgetary, 517
    extended meanings of, 448–9
    and leadership styles, 628
    as management function, 442–4
    organizing for, 581–96
    and planning, 442–4, 581–2
Conversion-cost pricing, 556–7
Corporate objectives in financial statements, 406
Corporate planning, 476
Corporation tax, 198, 219–21
Corporations, 46–7
    financial accounting information for, 187–225
    rules for financial reporting, 158
COSA (cost of sales adjustment), 353–4, 355
Cost allocation, 454
    depreciation as, 130–1
Cost analysis and profit planning, 522–3
Cost apportionment, 454
Cost centres, 584, 608
Cost concept of financial accounting, 49–51
Cost control, 583–4
Cost of goods sold budget, 513
Cost value, 130
Cost-based pricing theories, 552–3
Cost-based transfer pricing, 589
Cost-volume-profit (c-v-p) analysis, 521–37
    applications, 521–2
    use in selecting sales mix, 533–4

Costing systems, 463–7
Costs
    accounting framework, 451–688
    administrative, 508, 513, 620–1
    analysis, 451–2
    appropriation of and ROCE calculations, 594
    balanced with benefits, 383–4
    budgeted, 598
    control of managed, 618–25
    depreciation and total asset costs, 136
    historical, 451, 466; *see also* Historical cost method
    limitations of full cost calculations, 462–3
    manufacturing, 452
    operating, and solvency, 257–8
    opportunity, 494, 567–8, 569
    overhead, 453–63
    relevant, 546
    relevant to short-run tactical decisions, 563–4
    replacement, 451
    research and development, 174–5, 618, 621
    standard, 598–601, 614, 618, 634
    see also Fixed costs; Overhead costs; Variable costs
    CCP (Current purchasing power), 329–30, 334–6
CPU (Central processing unit), 82
Creative accounting, 9
Credit balances, 156
Credit limits, electronic data processing, 78–80
Credit transactions, 96
Credit-worthiness, income as guide to, 317
Creditors
    in balance sheets, 211
    funds flows, 235
    information needs, 17
    sundry creditors balance, 508
Cumulative preference shares, 191
Currency translation and multinational groups, 299–302
Current assets, 156, 167, 173
    in balance sheets, 211
    funds flows, 234, 235
    ratios of cash elasticity of, 255–7
    solvency analysis, 253, 254–5
    valuation of, 168–71
Current cost accounting, 309, 341, 350–60
Current cost method in financial statements, 385
Current cost reserve, 359
Current liabilities, 156, 180
Current purchasing power, 309
    accounting procedures, 329–36
    monetary items, 330–1
    non-monetary items, 331
Current replacement cost, 309
Current value accounting, 340–65
Customers, information needs, 19

Data storage, 81
Data transfer systems, 81
Databases, 78
Day books, 75
DCF, *see* Discounted cash flows
Dearing Report, 376–7, 377, 378
Debentures, 191, 197, 231, 258

Debit balances, 118, 155
Debtors
  cash elasticity of debtor balances, 256
  losses through default, 142–3
Debts
  bad, 143–4
  doubtful, 144–5
    calculation of, 151
Decision making, 8
  behavioural aspects of, 21
  decentralization of, 583–4, 586–8, 591
  and information, 446–8
  limiting factors, 571–3
  and linear programming, 573–7
  short-run tactics, 563–78
  by top management, 631
Decision usefulness theories, 31–2
Deferred liabilities, 180
Deferred shares, 192
Delivery notes, 71
Departmental overheads, 459–60
Departmental self-centredness and budgetary control, 632
Departmentalization, 441–2
Depreciation of assets, 129–31, 140–2
  adjustment in current cost accounting, 352
  calculation of, 151
  selecting method of, 134–7
Derwent, R., 430
Descriptive approach to accounting theory, 27–8
Developing countries and national accounting plans, 113
Development costs, 210
  valuation of, 173, 174
Dewhurst, J., 429
Differential costs, 564
Direct costs
  marketing, 622
  variance analysis for, 601–3
Direct labour costs, 452, 457–8, 466–7
  setting standards for, 600
Direct labour hours, 457, 458, 459
Direct labour variances, 603
Direct material costs, 452
  setting standards for, 600–1
Direct material variances, 601–3
Direct materials purchase budget, 510–11
  Direct materials usage budget, 510
Directors
  calculating expenses, 203
  in corporate enterprises, 189–90
Directors' reports, 199, 219, 428
Discounted cash flows (DCF), 488–9, 493, 496
Discretionary costs, 618
  control of, 619–20
Disposable wealth concept, 313, 315
Distributable profit, 189
Dividend cover ratio (payout ratio), 263
Dividend yield, 263
Dividends
  income as guide to dividend policy, 317
  and long-range profit goals, 478–9
  and ratio analysis, 252

Doherty, J., 429
Double-entry bookkeeping, 5, 45, 88–93
    mathematical implications of, 96–7
    and periodic measurement, 115–26

Earning power, analysis of, 259–61
Economic concepts of valuation, 322–7
Economic forecasting, 474
Economic income, 340
    subjective nature of, 326–7
Economic theories and pricing, 550–1
Economics and accounting practice, 9–10
ED14 'Accounting for Research and Development', 379
Edwards, E. O., 326
Effectiveness, 20
Efficiency, 20
Efficiency ratio and the standard hour, 605
Efficient market hypothesis, 386–8
Electronic data storage and retrieval, 78–80
Empirical research, 32
Empirical theories, 25
Employees
    calculating expenditure, 203
    information needs, 16–17
    and organization theory, 637–8
    participation in management, 189–90
    reporting to, 412–20
Employment Act (1982), 419
Employment Protection Act (1975), 35, 413, 415
Energy and social responsibility, 426
Engineered costs, 618
Entity concept of financial accounting, 45–7, 312
Environment
    and organization theory, 638
    and the planning process, 440
    and social responsibility, 426, 429–30
EPS (Earnings per share), 261–2
Equation method in break-even analysis, 524–5
Equity shareholders, 294
European Community, 7
    accounting rules, 106–7
    Fourth Directive, 103, 109, 199, 299
    national accounting plans, 113
    Seventh Directive, 199, 271, 293, 299
Exchange value, 130
Exit values, limitations of, 349
Expenditure variance, 608, 609
Expense centres, 584–6, 591
Expense transactions, 104
Expenses, 115–16
    accrual, 53–4, 119–22
    characteristics, 29
    elements, 384
    format for calculating, 203
    matching concept, 54
    matching with revenue, 124
Extraordinary cash flows, 399

Factory costs forecast, 506–7
Factory overhead costs, 452, 454–5
Fair business practices, 427, 428

Favourable variances and direct costs, 601

Feedback, information, 443–4

FIFO method (first in, first out) of stock valuation, 169–70, 171, 211, 261, 346, 387–8

Financial accounting, 5–7, 15
concepts, 43–59
definition, 39
generation of data, 69–82
standards, 62–7

Financial capital
concept, 314
maintenance, 385

Financial information, effects on welfare, 32–4

Financial performance, analysis of, 259–63

Financial planning, 467, 480–1

Financial reports, 9, 187–8
concept of periodicity, 56–7
to employees, 413–15
evaluation of current practice, 376–92
income concepts for, 318
interim, 407
interpretation and comparison, 250–66
to investors, 394–410
research findings, 386–92
and user education, 409–10
value-added, 408–9

Financial Reporting Council (FRC), 377, 378

Financial statements, 30–1, 198–200
and accounting standards, 63
consolidated, 287–302
objectives of, 380–1
standardized, 109, 110, 111

Financing cash flows, 242–3

Financing transactions, 103

Fisher, Irving, 315

Fixed assets, 167–8, 172–3
on balance sheets, 208–10
budgeted, 504–5
funds flows, 233–4
losses in value of, 128–9
revaluation of, 168
valuation of, 167–8

Fixed budgeting, 606

Fixed costs, 461, 463, 522–3, 535, 563, 566.
and budgetary control, 620
changes in, 530
and variable costing, 540–1
and volume changes, 554–5

Fixed overheads, 603, 604, 606
cost variances, 609

Flexible budgeting, 606–8, 624, 625

Floppy disks, 81

Forecasts
and the external audit, 474
publishing
advantages of, 399–401
disadvantages of, 401–4

Foster, G., 389, 407, 627

France
National Accounting Plan, 107–9, 109–11
Plan Comptable Révisé, 298

Friedman, Milton, 422

Full-cost pricing, 553–5
Full-cost transfer pricing, 589–90
Funds flow statement, 229, 230–7
Future costs, 563, 564, 567
Future markets and going-rate pricing, 559–60

Gains in value, 52
Gap analysis, 475–6
Gearing of capital structure, 192–4, 258
    adjustment in current cost accounting, 356–8
    and the cost of capital, 494–5
General Electric Company, residual-profit method of performance appraisal, 595
Gibbins, M., 390
Goals
    long-range, 471, 472–3
    long-range profit, 477–80
    and Management by Objectives, 635, 636
Going-concern concept, 103
    of financial accounting, 48–9, 320
    financial statements, 381
    in SSAP 2, 66
Going-rate pricing, 559–60
Goods received notes, 73
Goodwill, 175–6, 210
    and subsidiary companies, 274, 278, 279
Goudeket, A., 314
Government
    and acocunting policy, 35
    information needs, 17
Graph method in break-even analysis, 526–7
Gray, R., 428, 429, 430
Greening of accounting, 429–30
Griffiths, I., 9
Gross profit, calculating, 152–3
Groups of companies, 210
    accounts, 199
    consolidated accounts, 287–302
    financial accounting for, 270–81
    multinational, 298–302
Gynther, R. S., 335

Hagerman, R. L., 390
Hard disks, 81
Health and Safety at Work Act (1974), 428
Hendriksen, E. S., 25–6
Hicks, J. R., 316, 322, 323
Historical cost method, 309, 320–1, 330
    in financial statements, 385
    profit measurement by, 342–5
History of accounting, 5–7
Holding gains, 52, 341–2, 345–6, 349
Hopwood, A., 391, 633
Horngren, C. T., 627
Human relations approach to organization theory, 637
Human resources, 427
    and social responsibility, 427

IASC (International Accounting Standards Committee), 378, 380–6, 392
Ijiri, Y., 26
Imputation system of taxation, 220–2, 262
Income

Income (*contd*)
  accrual, 118–19
  concepts of, 315–18, 340
  economic concept of, 322–7
  estimation of ex-ante, 323–4
  estimation of ex-post, 323, 325–6
  investment, 204
  as a measure of efficiency, 316
  other operating, 204
Income statements, elements, 384
Industrial democracy, White Paper on (1978), 419
Inflation
  and capital expenditure, 495–7
  and the cash budget, 514–15
  and long-range profit goals, 478
  problems, 302
Information, disclosure of financial, 7
Information system, 12–23
  boundaries, 13–14
  output, 14–15
Institute of Chartered Accountants in England and Wales, 27, 63–4
Institute of Chartered Accountants of Scotland (ICAS), 396, 399, 401, 403, 406, 408
Intangible assets, 173–7
Interest in profit and loss accounts, 204
Interest coverage ratio, 258
Interest rates and economic income, 326–7
Internal rate of return (IRR), 490–3
International Accounting Standards Committee (ISAC), 102
Investment centres, 591–5
Investment purchasing power concept, 314
Investment transactions, 104
Investments
  appraisal, 495–7
  on balance sheets, 210–11
  decisions, 261–3, 483–5
  income as guide to future, 316
  methods of appraising capital, 485–95
  net investment outlays, 485
  return on investment pricing, 557–8
  valuation of, 172–3
Investors
  in corporate enterprises, 188, 189
  financial accounting information, 39–40
  and financial information, 7
  information needs, 16–17
  reporting to, 394–410
    and employee reporting, 412–13
  see also Shareholders
Invoices, 71, 72, 73, 75, 79
Issued capital, 189, 194

Job order costing, 464
Joint stock companies, 5–6, 15
Just-in-time accounting, 438
Just-in-time production systems (JIT), 464, 466–7

Koontz, Harold, 435

Labour costs and inflation, 496
Land, valuation of, 167
Leadership styles, 628–30

Leases, 176–8
Ledgers, 75, 76
  basic accounting model, 104
Legislation and social responsibility, 424
Liabilities
  accounting equation, 84–5
  in balance sheets, 211–12
  characteristics, 29
  contingent, 180
  current, 156
  deferred, 180–1
  non-monetary, 331
  ratio analysis of, 265
  standardized, 110
  valuation of, 179–81
Licensing systems, 424
LIFO method (last in, first out), 169
  of stock valuation, 169, 170, 171, 261, 336, 346, 387–8
Limited companies, 198
Limited liability, concept of, 6
Linear programming and decision making, 573–7
Liquid funds, 233, 238
Liquidity
  and cash management, 514–15
  and solvency, 251–2
Littleton, A. C., 3, 27, 312, 540
Loan capital, 191, 192, 197, 225
Local community information needs, 19
Long-range planning, 441, 442–3

Machine hours, overhead rate based on, 458–9
Machinery, valuation of, 168
Management
  and the budgetary process, 630–3
  and cash flows, 473
  information needs, 15
  performance and expense centres, 584–6
  processes, 439–46
  styles of leadership, 628–30
Management accounting, 7, 39
Management by exception, 601
Management by Objectives, 472, 635–6
Management control, 581
  decisions, 446, 447
Management Information Systems (MIS), 70, 446
Management theory, 435–6
Managerial effectiveness, income as indicator of, 316–17
Managerial style and organization culture, 627–8
Manufacturing costs, 452
Margin of safety ratio in break-even analysis, 526
Marginal (variable-cost) pricing, 558–9
Market capitalization, 406
Market-based transfer pricing, 588
Marketing costs, control of, 619, 621–2, 624–5
Marshall, Alfred, 51
Matching concept of financial accounting, 54–6, 57
May, G. O., 59–60
May, R. J., 33
Memorandum of association, 188, 195
Mergers, 293–8
Minority interests, consolidated accounts, 287–91

Mixed costs, 461
Money amount concept, 313–14
Money measurement concept of financial accounting, 47–8
Morley, M. F., 409
Motivation as management function, 445–6
Multinational companies, 270, 302
MWCA (Monetary working capital adjustment), 354–6
Myers, J. H., 349

Naive market hypothesis, 386–7
National accounting plans, 107–9
    advantages and disadvantages, 109–12
Negative payoffs, 35
Negotiated pricing, 590–1
Net cash flows, 485
Net investment outlays, 485
Net present value (NPV), 326–7, 489–90, 491–2
Net profit, 31, 198
    and budgetary planning, 503
    calculating, 153–4
    funds flows, 236–7
    gearing in capital structure, 192–4
    ratio of, on sales, 261
Net realizable value (NRV), 309, 408
Newell, G. E., 430
Non-accounting evaluation, 633
Non-recurrent cash flows, 398–9
Norby, W. C., 374
Norkett, P., 413
Normative theories, 32
    of control, 448–9
    of pay bargaining information, 416–17
    reporting to investors, 395–8

Objectives, long-range, 471–3
Obsolescence, 132–3
Online computer systems, 81
Open systems, 12
Opening stocks in profit and loss accounts, 150
Operating capability, 350
Operating capability concept, 314–15
Operating cash flows, 242–3
Operating gains, 52
Operational control, 581
    decisions, 446, 447–8
Operational research, 22
Operations costing, 465
Opportunity costs, 494, 567–8, 570
Order-filling costs, 625
Order-getting costs, 624–5
Organization culture and managerial style, 627–8
Organization theory, 636–8
Organizing as management function, 441–2
Overhead costs
    budget, 511–12
    setting standards for, 600–1, 603–6
    variance analysis for, 608–10
Overhead variances, 614

Pacioli, Luca, 5
Patents, 173, 210

Paton, W. A., 540
Payback method of investment appraisal, 497
Payback period, capital expenditure, 485–7
Payoffs, 34, 35
Penetration price policies, 560
Performance evaluation
    behavioural aspects of, 627–40
    and Management by Objectives, 635–6
Period costing, 540–1
Periodic measurement and double-entry bookkeeping, 115–26
Periodicity, concept of, 56–7
Petty cash boxes, 76
Physical capital maintenance, 386
Planning
    budgetary, 500–18, 550
    capital expenditure, 483–98
    and control, 442–4, 581–2
    financial, 476, 480–1
    long-range, 471–81, 500, 550, 610, 621
    as management function, 439–41
Plant, valuation of, 168
Point-of-sale terminals, 80
Policy makers, accounting, 35
Pooling method (mergers), 293–5, 298
Portfolio theory, 388–9
Positive payoffs, 35
Posting, 74
Practice, accounting and accounting theory, 26
Preference shares, 191, 192
Present value method, 309, 318
Price changes and capital maintenance, 386
Price discrimination, 559
Price variances, 601–2
Price/earnings ratio, 262
Prices
    adjustments, 329–34
    and CCP accounting, 335
    changes in selling price, 532–3
    depreciation as fall in, 129–30
    variances, 613–14
Pricing, 549–61
    concept of fair price, 552–3, 555
    cost-based and budgeted costs, 553–60
    target, 560
    theories, 550–3
    transfer, 587–91
Private companies, 188
Procedures, accounting, 30
Process costing, 465
Product costing, 584
Production
    constant, 542–3
    fluctuating, 543–5
Production budgets, 502, 509–10
Production cost, fixed assets, 208, 209
Production cost centres, 454–5, 456–8
Production volume ratio and the standard hour, 605
Products
    costing, 464–5, 539–40
    determining profitability of, 623–4
    dropping a product line, 568–9

Products (*contd*)
full product costs, 453
pricing, 549–61
production cost centre costs, 456–7
sales mix, 533–5
Profit and loss accounts, 31, 148–55, 159
associated companies, 291
budgeted, 503, 504, 515–16
cash flow statements, 241–2
Companies Acts requirements, 198, 199, 200–6
concept of periodicity, 57
deferred taxation, 223–4
and depreciation account, 138–9
and depreciation of assets, 138, 139, 140
formal presentation of, 154–5
funds flow statements, 230, 232, 236–7
groups of companies, 271, 272, 273–4, 278, 279, 280–1
inflation problems, 302
leases, 176–7
minority interest calculations, 287, 289
solvency analysis, 252–3
stock adjustments, 124–6
standardized statements, 109, 111
Profit centres, 586–91
Profit sharing, 17
Profit-conscious evaluation, 633
Profit-volume charts, 527–9
Profits
calculating periodic, 151, 152–4
characteristics, 29
components of realizable, 348–9
distributable, 198
distribution of, and current cost accounting, 358
impact of variable and absorption costing, 545
intragroup profit elimination, 290–1
long-range goals, 477–9
margins, 552–3
measurement, 342–5
as objective, 473
planning, and cost analysis, 522–3
planning through change, 530–3
significance of forecasted, 389
and social responsibility, 422–3
targets, 479–80
see also Net profit
Project planning, 441
Promoters, 188
Prudence, concept of, 58–9, 103, 187–8
in SSAP 2, 67
Public companies, 188
Purchase method (acquisitions), 293, 298
Purchase price, 208
fixed assets, 208–9
Purchases, related source documents, 72–3
Purchases day books, 75

Quantitative methods, 8

Ramanathan, K. V., 425
Ratio analysis, 250–66
and business failure predictions, 263–5

Real time computer systems, 81
Realizable value accounting, 341, 347-9
Realization concept of financial accounting, 51-3, 124
Realization convention, effects on valuation, 321-2
Recurrent cash flows, 398
Redeemable preference shares, 191
Replacement cost accounting, 314-15, 341-7
Replacement cost profit (RCP), 341-2, 346
Reports, *see* Financial reports
Research, accounting, 9
Research and development costs
   control of, 618, 621
   valuation of, 174-5
Reserves in balance sheets, 212
Resources, allocation of and accounting information, 20
Responsibility accounting
   and budgetary control, 620
   and control, 582-96
   and variances, 613-14
Responsibility budgets, 584-6
Retail Price Index (RPI), 330
Retained profit, 189
Revenue curves, 536
Revenue transactions, 104
Revenues, 116-17
   accruals concept, 53
   characteristics, 29
   and costs, 539
   matching concept, 54
   matching with expenses, 124
Risk, business and financial, 259
ROCE (return on capital employed), 259-60, 477-9
   investment centres, 591-5

Sales
   budget, 502, 509, 513
   changes in selling price, 532-3
   constant, 543-5
   day books, 75, 79
   electronic order processing, 78-9
   fluctuating, 542-3
   forecasting, 503-4, 506, 509
   mix, 533-5
   mix variance, 611-13
   price variance, 611
   profitability of territories, 622-3
   related source documents, 70-2
   revenues and inflation, 496
   selling costs forecast, 508
   selling or further processing, 569
   selling price, 553, 554
   volume variance, 611
Sandilands Report, 35, 168, 308, 318, 335, 346
   on cash flow forecasting, 403
Scientific method, 25
Segment reporting, 405-6
Service costing, 465
Share capital, 190, 191-2, 194-7, 225
   in balance sheets, 212
Shareholders
   in corporate enterprises, 46, 47, 188, 189, 190, 191

Shareholders (*contd*)
    equity ratio, 258, 259
    financial accounting information, 39–40
    information needs, 15
    liabilities, 179
    limited power of, 473
    and long-range profit goals, 478
    and mergers, 294, 295
    and ratio analysis, 251, 252
    valuation of equity, 181–2
    see also Investors
Shares
    bearer, 189
    merger accounting, 295–8
    of no par value (US and Canada), 197
    ordinary, 192, 193
        issued at a premium, 196–7
        issued at par, 195–6
    preference, 191, 192
    prices, 386–8
    in related companies, 210
Skimming price policies, 560
Smith, Adam, 6
Social responsibility accounting, 4, 8, 10, 421–30
Social science, accounting as, 5–8
Socio-economic decisions, income as guide to, 317
Sole traders, 198
Solvency, 251–9
    long-term, 257–9
Source documents, 69–73
Speculative theories, 25
Spreadsheets, 78
Stakeholder, concept of, 423
Standard costs, 598–600, 614, 618, 634
Standards, 62–8
    bookkeeping, 102–3
    evaluation of current, 376–8
    and national accounting plans, 112
Statement of source and application of funds, 231, 232, 233, 237, 238
Statements of account, 79
Statements of Standard Accounting Practice (SSAPs), 62, 64–7, 199
    SSAP 1: Accounting for Associated Companies, 270, 272, 291, 292
    SSAP 2: Disclosure of Accounting Policies, 65–7, 379, 381, 539
    SSAP 6: Extraordinary Items and Prior Year Adjustments, 205
    SSAP 8: The Treatment of Taxation Under the Imputation System, 224–5
    SSAP 9: Stocks and Long-Term Contracts, 169, 171–2, 211, 379, 541
    SSAP 10: Statements of Source and Application of Funds, 229, 238–9
    SSAP 12: Accounting for Depreciation, 140–1
    SSAP 13: Accounting for Research and Development, 174–5, 210
    SSAP 14: Group Accounts, 270, 271, 288, 293
    SSAP 15: Accounting for Deferred Taxation, 223, 224
    SSAP 16: Current Cost Accounting, 351–2, 355, 357, 358, 359–60
    SSAP 18: Accounting for Contingencies, 180
    SSAP 19: Accounting for Investment Properties, 141–2
    SSAP 20: Accounting for Foreign Currency, 301–2
    SSAP 21: Accounting for Leases and Hire Purchase Contracts, 177, 178
    SSAP 22: Accounting for Goodwill, 175
    SSAP 23: Accounting for Acquisitions and Mergers, 294, 295
Statistical control charts, 615
Staubus, G. J., 34
Sterling, R. R., 347, 410

Stewardship accounting, 5, 166, 308, 311, 321
Stock Exchange, 22, 63, 173, 182
  and corporate enterprises, 188, 189, 191
  market hypotheses, 386–7
Stocks
  adjustments, 124–6
    in profit and loss accounts, 150
  closing stock budget, 512
  forecast, 507
  valuation, 169–71
    and variable costing, 539
Stone, F. G., 374
Strategic planning, 441, 446
Strategy, formulation of, 474–6
Sundem, G. L., 33
Sunder, S., 387, 388
Sundry creditors balance, 508–9
Sunk costs, 563, 565
Systems analysis, 13
Systems approach to accounting, 9, 21–2

Taffler, R. J., 264
Target pricing and target costs, 560
Taxation
  accounts, 235–6
  and capital expenditure, 493
  Companies Acts requirements, 205–6
  company accounts, 220–5
  corporation tax, 198
  deferred, 223–5
  deferred tax liabilities, 181
  income as tax base, 317
  imputation system, 220–2,
  and social responsibility, 424–5
Techological forecasting, 474
Technology and organization theory, 638
Terminals, computer, 82
Theory of accounting, 24–36
Theory X leadership style, 628–9, 631
Theory Y leadership style, 628, 629
Thomas, A. L., 140
Time differences and cost data, 465–6
Tisshaw, H., 264, 265
Tomkins, C., 374, 402
Trading gains, 52
Transactions
  and the accounting equation, 85–7
  accounts, 103–4
  accounts as descriptions of, 95–6
  characteristics, 29
Transfer pricing, 587–91
Trial balances, 97–8, 116–17, 119–22, 148
Trueblood Report, 396, 402, 408
Turnover, 202
  asset/turnover ratios, 260
  average stock turnover ratios, 255–6

Uniform Chart of Accounts, 103
United States
  audit of forecasts, 402
  financial accounting, 6–7

United States (*contd*)
  Financial Accounting Standards Board, 44, 102, 174, 404
    Concepts No. 1, 404
    Statement No. 14, 405–6
Urgent Issues Task Force (UITF), 378
Usage variances, 602–3
Users, external financial accounting information, 40–1

Valuation
  accounting concepts, 308–9, 320–2
  economic concepts, 322–7
Value, depreciation as fall in, 129–30
'Value to the business', concept of, 350–1
Value-added financial reporting, 408–9
Variable costs, 461, 463, 522–3
  and budgetary control, 620
  changes in, 530–2
  and stock evaluation, 539–45
Variable overheads, 604, 605, 606
Variable-cost pricing, 558–9
Variable-cost transfer pricing, 590
Variance analysis
  for direct costs, 601–3
  investigation of variances, 614–15
  for overhead costs, 608–10
  responsibility for, 613–14
  sales, and the control of revenue, 610–13
VDUs (visual display units), 82
Volume variances, 609

Watts, R. L., 28
Watts Report ('Setting Accounting Standards'), 376, 379
Weighted average cost method of stock valuation, 169, 170–1
Welfare approach to accounting, 32–4
Williamson, E. O., 639
Woodward, J., 638
Word processing packages, 78
Work study measurements, 619

Z scores, 265
Zero-base budgeting (ZBB), 620
Zimmerman, J. L., 28
Zimmerman, V. K., 27

Advanced Financial Accounting *3rd edition*

Richard Lewis, Deputy Chief Executive, Council for National Academic Awards & **David Pendrill**, Esmee Fairbairn Professor of Accounting, University of Buckingham

The new edition of this well-established text has been thoroughly revised and updated to incorporate developments in company law and Accounting Standard setting. This includes the provisions of the Companies Act 1989, a review of all current Accounting Standards, Statements of Recommended Practice, Statements of Intent and other professional developments. The book covers the framework for financial reporting, financial reporting in practice, interpretation and valuation, and accounting and price changes. It also includes a wide range of questions for use on professional and degree level courses to test understanding and develop interpretational skills when dealing with financial statements. The answers are provided in a separate Solutions Manual.

It is recommended by ACCA for papers 2.9 Advanced Accounting Practice and 3.1 Advanced Financial Accounting, and is ideal for all advanced level professional accountancy examinations, and for second and final year degree and diploma courses.

672 pp   ISBN 0 273 03142 2

Financial Reporting, Information & Capital Markets

Michael Bromwich, Professor of Accounting at the London School of Economics

This scholarly and controversial book reviews the theory of the economic measurement of income and wealth in financial accounting and presents an informational perspective on accounting information. A major objective is to integrate the relevant aspects of current finance theory, and information economics into accounting theory at a fairly general level.

It is aimed at second and third year accounting undergraduates and first year postgraduates. It can be used as a text for either a financial theory course or for the financial theory component of a more general financial accounting course. The considerable emphasis placed on the treatment of uncertainty and information is necessary to understand recent major contributions to accounting theory. It also allows students to obtain some access to much of the current research literature.

1991   388 pages   ISBN 0 273 03464 2

Accounting Standards *3rd edition*

John Blake, Loughborough University of Technology

This well-known text has been fully up-dated to cover all current Accounting Standards. John Blake's clarity of style and carefully structured approach ensure that the student appreciates the requirements laid down by each Standard, the problems that each addresses and the practical difficulties of compliance with each Standard. Particular emphasis is given to the controversy attached to each Standard, so that an understanding is gained of the way in which rules have developed. Questions are provided, including questions taken from recent professional examination papers, so that practical application of the accounting framework to computation problems can be practised.

It has been written for undergraduate courses in accounting and finance and for professional courses ACCA 2.8, 2.9 & 3.1, ICAEW, AAT, CIMA Stage 2 Financial Accounting and Stage 3 Advanced Financial Accounting.

1991   352 pp   ISBN 0 273 03462 6

A Workbook of Accounting Standards

Alan Sangster, Aberdeen University

This novel textbook is designed to improve understanding of the Standards which regulate the profession. The workbook has a problem-based approach which provides students with a wealth of varied examples and questions on interpreting the Standards for practical application. Chapters are introduced by a brief review of the Standard and common problem areas. Next, detailed flowcharts isolate the content of each Standard and take the student through a systematic analysis of application. This is followed by 40 short questions testing different aspects of interpretation, and one or two examination-standard, case-style questions. All current Standards are included.

Solutions to all of the questions are provided at the end of the book.

It has been written for undergraduate courses in accounting and finance and for professional courses ACCA 2.8, 2.9 & 3.1, ICAEW, AAT, CIMA Stage 2 Financial Accounting and Stage 3 Advanced Financial Accounting.

1991416 pages   ISBN 0 273 03189 9